Short-term Financial Management

Short-term Financial Management

Ned C. Hill

Brigham Young University

William L. Sartoris

Indiana University

Macmillan Publishing Company
NEW YORK

To Claralyn and Karen

Copyright ©1988, Macmillan Publishing Company,
a division of Macmillan, Inc.

Printed in the United States of America

Macmillan Publishing Company
866 Third Avenue, New York, New York 10022

Collier Macmillan Canada, Inc.

Library of Congress Cataloging in Publication Data

Hill, Ned C.
    Short term financial management.

    Includes index.
    1. Working capital. 2. Corporations—Finance.
I. Sartoris, William L.   II. Title.
HG4028.W65H54   1988   658.1'5244   88-1461
ISBN 0-02-354820-7

Printing: 2 3 4 5 6 7 8   Year: 8 9 0 1 2 3 4 5 6 7

PREFACE

Short-term financial management has only recently emerged as a full-fledged discipline within the more general field of corporate finance. Whereas short-term finance (some use the name "working capital management") was usually relegated in the past to conveniently-skipped, last chapters in financial texts, today there is a growing number of universities offering courses devoted exclusively to the topic. In parallel, the number of academic researchers in short-term finance has grown dramatically in recent years. These are providing a conceptual framework from which to view the many interesting problems encountered in short-term finance.

Short-term finance covers essentially the upper half of an organization's balance sheet: cash, short-term investments, receivables, and inventory on the asset side and payables, short-term debt and accruals on the liability side. In magnitude, these accounts represent well over half the assets and liabilities of the average firm. Yet, it is curious to note, nearly all texts in corporate financial management treat almost exclusively the lower half of the balance sheet: capital budgeting, capital structure, dividend policy, etc. We argue that an understanding of short-term financial assets and liabilities is equally vital to a complete understanding of the firm.

This text is an attempt to bring together two important ingredients. First, an understanding of institutional background is essential to appreciate short-term finance problems. We discuss the banking system, the payment system, the regulatory environment, and other needed background. We show that these institutional factors create or at least influence the problems we seek to solve. Second, we bring financial theory to bear on short-term finance problems. The objective of financial management is taken to be shareholder wealth maximization subject to constraints imposed by institutions, resources, etc. In this framework it is possible to cast most short-term finance problems as a timeline with events and costs arrayed along it. The use of this framework conveniently ties problems of short-term finance to present value techniques introduced to most students in beginning finance courses.

An understanding of short-term financial management is essential to anyone preparing for responsibilities in the corporate treasurer's department. In addition, bankers are interested in short-term finance because, besides making loans, they frequently provide service products directly related to short-term finance. Corporate controllers' departments also encounter short-term finance problems on a daily basis. Because many MBA students are interested in these areas, the course Short-term Financial Management became one of the most popular MBA electives at Indiana University and at Brigham Young University.

This text is directed to second-year MBAs or upper division undergraduates who have already had a basic corporate finance course; accounting is also useful in understanding the cash forecasting chapter. The mathematical level assumed is college algebra. After the first five background chapters, the remaining chapters are modular and can be given in almost any order. Hence, the text can be used for a complete semester course or for a part of a semester.

We are indebted to many of our colleagues and students who critiqued this material and made helpful suggestions. MBA students at Indiana University provided vital feedback in a course setting. We have greatly benefited from the tutelage of our friend and colleague Bernell K. Stone (Harold R. Silver Professor of Finance at Brigham Young University) who has done so much to elevate the field of short-term finance. We also received very helpful feedback from Yong M. Kim (University of Cincinnati), Hugh McLaughlin (Bentley College), Jack W. Trifts (University of South Carolina), Venkat Srinivasan (Northern University), and Jarl G. Kallberg (New York University). We also appreciate the patience and support of our wives, Claralyn and Karen, and our children while we labored on this text. We received help and encouragement from the staff at Macmillan including Ken MacLeod, Editor, and John Molyneux, Production Supervisor. Despite all this help, we are sure we still managed to sneak through a number of errors for which we alone are responsible.

N. C. H.
W. L. S.

BRIEF CONTENTS

PART I

Introduction

1 Introduction to Short-term Financial
Management   3

2 A Valuation Framework   23

PART II

Cash Management

3 The U.S. Banking System   61

4 Keeping Score on Bank Balances and Bank Compensation   78

5 Payment Systems   103

6 Collection Systems   139

7 Cash Concentration Systems   171

8 Disbursement Systems   203

PART III

Short-term Investments

9 Money Market Investments   235

10 Managing the Short-term Investments
Portfolio   253

11 Hedging Uncertain Cash Flows   287

_____ PART IV _____
Short-term Borrowing

12 Short-term Borrowing from Commercial Banks   313

13 Non-bank Sources of Short-term Credit   339

_____ PART V _____
Receivables and Payables Management

14 Introduction to Credit and Collections   367

15 Managing Credit Policy and Accounts Receivable   390

16 Management of Accounts Payable and Accruals   428

_____ PART VI _____
Special Topics in Short-term Finance

17 Managing and Financing Inventories   447

18 Forecasting Cash Flows   463

19 International Short-term Finance   498

20 Electronic Data Interchange   522

Index   541

DETAILED CONTENTS

———————————— PART I ————————————

Introduction

1 Introduction to Short-term Financial Management   **3**

Definition of Short-term Finance   4
Operating Cash Flow Focus   4
The Cash System   4
Scope of Short-term Financial Management   5
The Use of a Cash Flow Timeline   6
Balance Sheet Focus   7
Short-term versus Long-term Finance   8
A Closer Examination of the Cash Flow Timeline   9
An Aggregate Timeline for a Retailer   9
Cash Operating Cycle   9
Framework for Financial Management Decisions   10
Basic Objective   10
Pricing of Financial Assets   10
Decision Model Structure   11
Objectives of Short-term Financial Management   11
Importance of Short-term Financial Management   12
Organizational Structure and Short-term Finance   16
Organizational Structure Impediments   16
Organizational Structure and the Cash Flow Timeline   19
Institutional Considerations   20
Summary   20
Discussion Questions   21
Selected Readings   21

2 A Valuation Framework   23

Present Value Concepts: Timing and Risk   23
Time Value of Money   23
Financial Risk   25
Asset Valuation Models and Short-term Finance   29
The Basics of the Capital Asset Pricing Model   29
Role of CAPM in Short-term Finance   34
A Framework for Short-term Financial Decisions   34
Basic Model   34
The Aggregate Cash Flow Timeline and Liquidity   46
The Choice of an Opportunity Cost Rate   47
Summary   48
Discussion Questions   48
Problems   49
Selected Readings   50
Appendix A: Present Value Calculation Approximations   51
Compounded Value Calculation   51
Simple Interest Calculation   51
Discount Interest Calculation   51
Comparison of Procedures   52
Appendix B: A Cash Flow Timeline Present Value Framework   53
The Basic Model   53
Nonconstant Sales   55

––––––––––––––––––––––––––– **PART II** –––––––––––––––––––––––––––

Cash Management

3 The U.S. Banking System   61

U.S. Commercial Banks   61
Functions of Commercial Banks   61
Banking Regulation   65
Federal Reserve System   70
Organization   70
Roles of the Fed   72
Current Issues in the Commercial Banking System   73
Deregulation of Financial Services   73
Foreign Commercial Banks   75
From Paper to Electronic Information and Funds Transfer   76
Summary   76
Discussion Questions   76
Selected Readings   77

4 Keeping Score on Bank Balances and Bank Compensation   78

Working with Bank Balances   78
   Ledger and Available Balances   78
   Business Days versus Calendar Days   80
   Relationship Between Deposits and Presentments   80
   Other Issues   81
   Another Example of Balance Computations   82
   Uses of Available Balances   84
   Company Book Balances   84
Bank Compensation   89
   Account Analysis   90
   Strategies for Bank Compensation   93
Summary   98
Discussion Questions   99
Problems   99
Case: Pica Enterprises   101

5 Payment Systems   103

An Overview of Payment Systems   103
   Components of a Payment System   103
   Payment Systems Compared and Contrasted   104
Coin and Currency   108
   Security   108
   Counting   109
   Timing   110
   Intermediaries   110
Checks   111
   How Checks Transfer Value   111
   The MICR Line   113
   Check-Clearing Mechanisms   115
   Returned Checks   117
   Check-like Payment Instruments   118
   Availability Schedules   120
   Federal Reserve Float   122
   Causes of Fed Float   122
Automated Clearing House (ACH) Transfers   124
   History   124
   Ownership and Administration   125
   Steps in an ACH Debit Transaction   125
   ACH Credit Transactions   127
   Timing of ACH Settlement   128

Other Features of ACH Payments   128
ACH Data Formats   129
Pros and Cons of ACH Payments   129
Future Developments in ACH   131
Wire Transfers   132
Features   132
Mechanics of a FedWire Transfer   133
CHIPS   135
Summary   135
Discussion Questions   136
Selected Readings   137

6 Collection Systems 139

Requirements of a Collection System   139
Cash Mobilization   140
Accurate Cash Flow Information   141
Updating the Central Information System   141
Audit Trails and Controls   141
Design of a Collection System   142
Collection Float   142
Float Measurement   143
Cost of Float   144
Optimizing the Collection System   145
Types of Collection Systems   147
Over-the-Counter Collections   147
Mailed Payments Collection System   150
Other Collection Systems   152
Lockbox Systems   154
Lockbox Operation   154
Lockbox Net Cost Savings   154
Lockbox Networks   155
Collection Location Studies   157
Data Required for a Study   158
Solution Approaches   160
Reevaluating the Current Collection System   164
Summary   164
Discussion Questions   165
Problems   166
Case: The Nationwide Electric Corporation's Collection System
Design   167
Cash Flow Timing   167
Selected Readings   169

7 Cash Concentration Systems

Cash Concentration Tasks   172
  Advantages of Concentration   173
Objective Function of Cash Concentration   173
  Opportunity Cost of Excess Balances   174
  Transfer Costs   176
  Dual Balances   176
  Administrative Costs   179
  Control   179
Cash Concentration Practice   180
  Field versus Lockbox Concentration Systems   180
  Example of a Cash Concentration System   181
  Decentralized Transfer Initiation   181
  Centralized Transfer Initiation   183
Reducing Cash Concentration Costs   186
  Reducing Information, Processing, and Clearing Delays   186
  Reducing Transfer Costs   188
  Increasing Dual Balance Benefits   192
  Reducing Administrative Costs   194
Summary   195
Discussion Questions   196
Problems   197
Case: Fast Burgers, Inc.   199
Selected Readings   201

8 Disbursement Systems

Disbursement Practices   205
Objective Function   206
  Time Value Costs   206
  Excess Balances   209
  Transaction Costs   210
  Dual Balances   211
  Payee Relationships   211
  Administrative Costs   212
  Control Costs   212
Types of Disbursement Decisions   213
  Strategic Decisions   213
  Tactical Decisions   214
  Centralized versus Decentralized Disbursing   215
Disbursement Tools   216
  Zero Balance Accounts   217
  Reconciliation Services   218

Stop Payment Services   219
Automatic Investment Services   219
Payable Through Drafts (PTDs)   219
Controlled Disbursing Accounts   219
Remote Disbursement Services   221
Disbursement Account Funding   222
Wire Funding   222
DTC or ACH Funding   222
Disbursement System Studies   223
Example of a Simple Disbursement Study   224
Summary   226
Discussion Questions   226
Problems   227
Case: Fleener Microcomputers, Inc.   228
Selected Readings   231

---------- **PART III** ----------

Short-term Investments

9 Money Market Investments   235

The Money Market   235
Transactions Agents   236
Market Participants   237
Characteristics of Money Market Securities   238
U.S. Government and Agency Securities   241
U.S. Treasury Securities   241
Federal Agency Securities   242
Bank Securities   244
Negotiable Certificates of Deposit (CDs)   245
Banker's Acceptances (BAs)   245
Commercial Paper   245
Repurchase Agreements   246
Eurodollar Securities   247
Investment Pools   247
Money Market Mutual Funds   247
Pooled Repurchase Agreements   248
Financial Futures   248
Municipal Securities   248
Summary of Security Characteristics   249
Summary   249
Discussion Questions   249
Selected Readings   251

10 Managing the Short-term Investments Portfolio 253

Portfolio Management Process   254
  Information Gathering   254
  Formulating Expectations and Strategies   255
  Constructing and Monitoring the Portfolio   256
Security Characteristics   262
  Calculating Security Returns   262
  Interest Rate Risk   267
Term Structure of Interest Rates   268
  Pure Expectations Theory   269
  Liquidity Preference Theory   270
  Market Segmentation Theory   272
  Implications of Different Theories   272
  Riding the Yield Curve   272
Tax Based Strategies   274
  Tax Exempt Securities   274
  Buying the Dividend   275
Summary   275
Discussion Questions   276
Problems   276
Case: Farmington Auto and Truck Sales Company   279
Selected Readings   280
Appendix: Determining the Size of the Cash Balance   281
  Baumol Model   281
  Miller and Orr Model   283
  Stone Model   284

11 Hedging Uncertain Cash Flows 287

Commodity Forward and Futures Contracts   288
  Price Risk   288
  Alternative Mechanisms for Reducing Price Risk   288
  Forward Contracts   289
  Futures Contracts   289
Financial Forward and Futures Contracts   295
  T-Bill Futures   295
  Example of a T-Bill Futures Contract   296
  Why Hedges Are Imperfect   300
  Uses of Financial Futures   301
Interest Rate Swaps   302
  General Concept of a Swap   303
  Illustration of an Interest Rate Swap   303
  Terminology   305
  Features of an Interest Rate Swap   305

Risks of Interest Rate Swaps   306
Interest Rate Swaps Using Assets   306
Summary   307
Discussion Questions   307
Problems   308
Selected Readings   310

—————————————————— **PART IV** ——————————————————

Short-term Borrowing

12 Short-term Borrowing from Commercial Banks   313

Bank Credit Arrangements   314
Single-Payment Loan   314
Line of Credit   315
Revolving Credit Agreement   318
Term Loan   318
Letter of Credit   319
Banker's Acceptance   319
Master Notes   320
Reverse Repurchase Agreement   320
Unsecured Borrowing   321
Secured Loan   321
Collateralized Loan   321
Asset-Based Loan   323
Comparing the Effective Cost of Funds   325
Single-Payment Loans   325
Line of Credit   326
Revolving Credit Agreement   331
Variable Interest Rate   331
Summary   332
Discussion Questions   333
Problems   333
Case: The McMillen Boat Company   336
Selected Readings   338

13 Non-bank Sources of Short-term Credit   339

Commercial Paper   339
Direct versus Dealer Paper   341
Rating   341
Interest Costs   342
Commercial Finance Companies   345
Interest Rate   345
Asset-Based Loans   345

Factoring   346
Maturity Factoring   346
Conventional Factoring   347
Maturity Factoring with Assignment of Equity   347
Cost of Factoring   347
Captive Finance Companies   348
Separation of Manufacturing and Credit   352
Better Quality of Receivables   352
A More Diversified Receivables Portfolio   352
Legal Separation of Obligations   353
Off-Balance-Sheet Financing   353
Fixed- versus Variable-Rate Financing   354
Cash Flow Characteristics   354
Expectations of Future Interest Rates   354
Interest Rate Swaps   357
Degree of Risk Aversion   357
Summary   358
Discussion Questions   358
Problems   359
Case: Nut House, Inc.   361
Current Operations   361
Financing Needs   361
Financing Alternatives   362
Selected Readings   363

_____ PART V _____

Receivables and Payables Management

14 Introduction to Credit and Collections   367

Importance of Credit in Today's Corporations   367
Credit Policy Decisions   368
Where Credit Decisions Are Made   368
Conceptual Framework: The Cash Flow Timeline   369
Accounts Receivable: Not a Logical Focus for Credit Policy   369
Total Collection Time Focus   370
Should Firms Extend Credit?   370
The Notion of Perfect Markets   370
Market Imperfections and Credit   371
Credit Terms   372
Factors to Consider in Setting Credit Terms   373
Survey of Credit Terms   375
Other Credit Term Issues   379
Determining Credit Terms for Specific Customers   380
Types of Errors in Making Credit Decisions   380

Credit Information Sources 380
Analysis of Credit Information 382
Financing Directly Related to Accounts Receivable 384
Direct Financing 384
Indirect Financing 385
Summary 386
Discussion Questions 387
Problems 387
Selected Readings 388

15 Managing Credit Policy and Accounts Receivable 390

Collection Procedures 391
Objective Function 391
Billing 391
Credit Term Enforcement 392
Monitoring Accounts Receivable 393
Monitoring Individual Accounts 393
Monitoring Overall Accounts Receivable 396
Forecasting Accounts Receivable 408
Percent of Sales Method 408
Receivable Balance Fraction Method 408
Example of an Accounts Receivable Forecast 409
Receivables Monitoring and Forecasting:
Summary and Synthesis 412
Evaluating Credit Policy Alternatives 412
Cash Flows Relevant to Credit Policy Alternatives 412
Timing and Uncertainty Considerations 414
The Cash Flow Timeline and the Present Value Approach 414
Summary 419
Discussion Questions 419
Problems 420
Case: General Moulding, Inc. 423
Selected Readings 426

16 Management of Accounts Payable and Accruals 428

Spontaneous Sources of Financing 429
Accounts Payable Decisions 431
Terms of Purchase 431
Payment Options 431
Accrued Expenses 436
Benefits of Increased Accrued Expenses 436
Cost of Increased Accrued Expenses 437
Effect on Liquidity 437

Information System Requirements   437
Summary   439
Discussion Questions   440
Problems   441
Selected Readings   442

———————————— **PART VI** ————————————

Special Topics in Short-term Finance

17 Managing and Financing Inventories   447

Why Inventories Exist   447
    The Nature of an Inventory   447
    Types of Inventories   448
    Motives for Holding Inventory   448
Traditional Approach to Inventory Policy   449
    Inventory Management Cost Tradeoff   450
    Economic Order Quantity   450
    Safety Stock and Variability of Demand   452
Present Value Timeline Approach to Inventory Decisions   452
    Comparison of Alternative Inventory Policies   453
Comparison of Economic Order Quantity (EOQ) and Present Value
Approaches   455
    Timing of Payments   455
    Financing Provided   456
Just-in-Time Inventory   456
    Setup Costs   456
    Planning Requirements   457
    Supplier Relations   457
    Suppliers and Cost Tradeoffs   458
Summary   458
Discussion Questions   458
Problems   459
Case: Hog Motors   460
Selected Readings   462

18 Forecasting Cash Flows   463

The Need to Focus on Cash   463
Cash Forecasting Horizons   464
    Long-range Forecasts   464
    Medium-range Forecasts   464
    Daily Cash Forecasts   465
    Objectives of Cash Forecasting   465
Medium-range Cash Forecasting   466

Driving Variable   467
Computation of Dependent Variables   467
Example of Medium-term Cash Forecasting   468
Three Approaches to Net Cash Flows   471
Short-term Cash Forecasting   474
Benefits of Daily Cash Forecasting   475
Steps in Making Daily Cash Forecasts   476
Individual Transactions versus Aggregate Input Data   479
Survey of Forecasting Tools   485
Judgment   485
Moving Average   485
Exponential Smoothing   486
Time Series Analysis   487
Regression Analysis   488
Summary   488
Discussion Questions   489
Problems   490
Selected Readings   494
Appendix: Spreadsheet Software for Cash Flow Forecasting   495
Spreadsheet Software   495

19 International Short-term Finance   498

Why International Differs from Domestic Short-term Finance   498
Exchange Rates   499
Time Delays   499
Credit Risks   499
Taxation   500
High Transaction Costs   500
Attitudes Toward Cash Management   500
Information Availability   500
Objective Function of International Short-term Financial
Management   501
Managing Foreign Exchange Risk   501
Measuring Foreign Exchange Risk   502
Vehicles for Converting Currencies   503
Strategies for Hedging Foreign Exchange Exposure   506
The Problem of Timing in International Transactions   508
Value Dating   508
Check Clearing   509
Credit Risks and International Finance   510
Documentary Collections   511
Collections Through Letters of Credit   512
International Cash Management Services   513
Wire Transfers   513

Lockbox Systems   514
Balance Reporting   514
Demand Deposit Practices: Interest and Overdraft Banking   515
GIRO Systems   515
Pooling Services   515
Intracompany Netting Systems   516
Reinvoicing Centers   518
Summary   518
Discussion Questions   519
Problems   520
Selected Readings   520

20 Electronic Data Interchange   522

The Cash Flow Timeline and EDI   522
Definitions   522
Example of a Typical Business Transaction   523
Problems with the Current System   526
Benefits and Costs of EDI   527
Benefits of EDI   527
Magnitude of Cost Savings   529
Costs of EDI   530
EDI Standards   531
The Need for Standard Formats   531
Industry Standards Development   531
Network Communications   532
Need for Networks   532
Credit Terms and EDI Transactions   534
Zero-Sum Games   534
Negotiating Shared Benefits   534
Example of Negotiated Payment Terms   535
Summary   538
Discussion Questions   538
Selected Readings   539

Index   541

PART

I

Introduction

1

Introduction to Short-term Financial Management

A substantial portion of the financial manager's working day is spent dealing with solutions to short-term financial management problems. These may include decisions such as the level of cash balance to maintain, the amount of cash to be invested in securities over the weekend, when particular suppliers are to be paid, whether a credit limit for a customer should be increased, or the amount of borrowing to be done under the line of credit for the month. Frequently the first assignment as a corporate finance analyst for a recent graduate from an undergraduate business or MBA program involves some aspect of short-term finance.

In this book we address the short-term financial problems that are faced by practicing managers and provide a method for addressing them. Often these problems can be cast in the framework of well-established and familiar financial concepts and techniques, such as present value, breakeven analysis, or cost minimization. The approach is the same as that encountered in long-term finance: namely, we identify, estimate, and evaluate the impact of short-term finance decisions on shareholder wealth.

Definition of Short-term
——————————— Finance ———————————

Before we outline the approach to short-term finance decisions, we should define this term. In general, *short-term finance* includes all decisions that have a financial impact on the firm and a short time horizon, usually less than a year. As with any general statement, more specification is needed before we have a working definition.

Operating Cash Flow Focus

In defining short-term finance, we focus on the cash flows connected with the operations of a firm. An elementary function of all firms is that they provide goods and/or services for which they expect to receive cash inflows. They also pay out cash for goods and services provided by other parties.

Because the inflows and outflows are not synchronized, a firm needs a temporary parking place for cash, which we call a *liquidity portfolio*. This liquidity portfolio may consist of a combination of cash and securities. Since cash flows for a firm are uncertain, both in amount and in terms of when they may occur, the amount of cash in temporary storage may not be adequate for all time periods. Thus, it is necessary to provide some *backup liquidity* for periods when the normal store of liquidity is insufficient.

Finally, there is a need to move cash from one point to another within a firm. We have internal cash flows to connect these various inflows, outflows, and sources of liquidity. A schematic diagram of these several elements of short-term finance is presented in Figure 1.1.

The Cash System

The *cash system* of a firm is the mechanism that provides the linkage between cash flows. The financial manager of the firm has the responsibility, at least in part, to develop and maintain the policies and procedures necessary to achieve an efficient flow of cash for the firm's operations. The external elements of the cash system include a *collection system* for getting cash into the firm and a *disbursement system* for paying the suppliers and other receivers of cash. The internal portion of the cash system consists of a *concentration system* to move cash from the entry point in the firm to the concentration bank and a *disbursement funding system* to move funds from the concentration bank to the disbursement banks so that payments can be made. Since banks are the major institutions involved in the payment system, the financial manager is also responsible for maintaining adequate *banking relations* to ensure the smooth flow of cash into, through, and out of the firm. These activities constitute the *cash management system* of the firm. A schematic diagram of a cash system is shown in Figure 1.2.

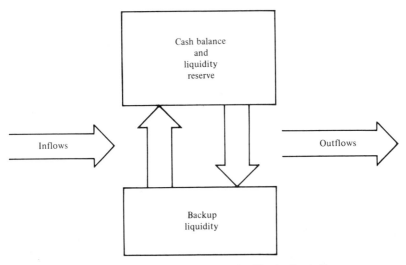

Figure 1.1   Schematic Diagram of a Firm's Cash Flows.

Scope of Short-term Financial Management

Short-term financial management thus encompasses decisions about activities that affect cash inflows, cash outflows, liquidity, backup liquidity, and internal cash flows. Many decisions of a firm have a short-term financial management aspect. For example, the decision to sell a bond issue in order to raise funds to finance an expansion in plant and equipment is clearly a long-term decision. However, the decision on how to invest the proceeds from the bond issue until they are needed to pay for the construction is a short-term financial decision.

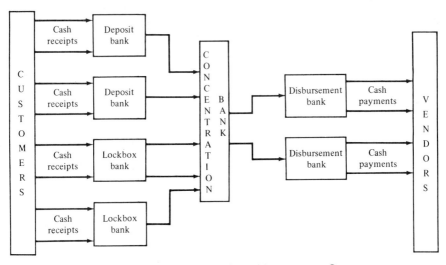

Figure 1.2   Elements of a Cash Management System.

The Use of a Cash Flow Timeline

One of the most effective ways to organize this discussion of short-term financial management is identify the cash flows connected with a decision and to locate these cash flows along a timeline. This approach allows the identification of all of the cash flows that are relevant to a decision and provides a straightforward adjustment for any differences in the timing of the cash flows. This approach bypasses issues such as which of several accounting definitions to use and whether the item is a long-term or a short-term finance issue. If the problem involves cash flows that occur in the near future, it has elements that require short-term financial management decisions. This focus allows the treatment of issues that involve short-term cash flows, even in instances when the decision is not normally considered to be in the realm of financial management.

This use of a cash flow timeline focus is perhaps most easily understood by the use of an illustration. Consider the sequence of events and cash flows involved in the sale of an item, say, a pair of black aerobic exercise shoes by The Ersatz Athlete, a retail sportsware shop, on its own credit card. To be able to support the credit operation, Ersatz had to establish a credit department, make decisions on the credit worthiness and credit limits of customers, and establish collection policies. When the sale is made, an account receivable is created. Ersatz does not get its cash until the account receivable is collected. This delay in the receipt of the cash affects the liquidity requirements and has to be financed. Since the cash is received through the mail, a system is needed to process the check and deposit it in the banking system. The timing of events connected with the cash flow from the sale is illustrated in Figure 1.3.

We could expand the scope of the cash flows considered by extending the analysis backward to the purchase of the shoes on credit from the manufacturer. We would now have both a cash outflow and a cash inflow. If payment to the manufacturer occurs before receipt of cash from the customer, the financial manager may have to arrange to obtain the cash, perhaps through a short-term loan from a bank. If the inflow from the collection on the accounts receivable occurs prior to the payment to the manufacturer, Ersatz has some cash that can be invested temporarily in short-term securities. The cash flow timeline concept allows expansion or contraction of the horizon to include the full range of issues connected with the decision.

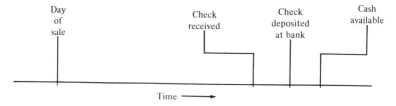

Figure 1.3 Cash Flow Timeline for a Sale by The Ersatz Athlete.

Balance Sheet Focus

An alternative focus for the definition of short-term finance relies on accounting conventions connected with the balance sheet. A balance sheet for Ersatz is shown in Table 1.1. The top, or current, portion of the balance sheet contains those assets and liabilities expected to be converted to cash or paid off within a year. An approach to short-term finance focused on the balance sheet encompasses issues connected with cash, marketable securities, accounts receivable, and inventory on the asset side, and accounts payable, accrued expenses, and short-term loans on the liability side.

There are two problems with a focus on accounting concepts. First, while the balance sheet may adequately categorize some of the activities related to short-term financial management, financial decisions require cash flow information, not accounting numbers. Second, short-term financial decisions involve cash flows connected with many elements that either may not appear on the balance sheet or may appear in its long-term portion.

The focus on an accounting definition of short-term finance results in the classification of certain levels of current assets and liabilities as *permanent current assets* or *permanent current liabilities*, since they are constantly rolled over. However, even though these assets and liabilities may have a degree of permanence, the decisions to alter them are actually short-term because they can be made quickly.

Frequently the term *working capital* is used interchangeably with the term *short-term finance*. To many people the term *working capital* connotes an accounting concept of the excess of current assets over current liabilities. However, even when not defined so specifically, this term tends to have a somewhat narrow, balance sheet focus. To maintain a broader perspective and to emphasize the cash flows required for financial decisions, we shall

Table 1.1 Balance Sheet for The Ersatz Athlete

Assets		Liabilities and Owner's Equity	
Cash	100	Accounts payable	4,750
Marketable securities	4,500	Accrued expenses	130
Accounts receivable	6,000	Short-term borrowing	4,800
Inventory	5,700	Current liabilities	9,680
Current assets	16,300		
		Long-term borrowing	10,000
Plant and equipment	43,700	Capital	6,000
		Retained earnings	34,320
		Total liabilities and	
Total assets	60,000	owner's equity	60,000

generally use the term *short-term financial management* in place of the term *working capital management*. We discard the balance sheet approach for the more encompassing approach focusing on a cash flow timeline applied to short-term financial decisions.

Short-term versus Long-term Finance

The use of a 1-year time horizon to separate short-term and long-term decisions is arbitrary and, in some cases, ambiguous. To refine further the definition of short-term finance, it is helpful to examine the differences and interrelationships between the decisions that are classified as short-term finance and those that are considered long-term finance. If we think about the nature of the decisions rather than the time horizon, the distinction between short-term and long-term becomes a little more clear. Decisions typically classified as long-term concern issues such as products to be produced, the type of equipment used to produce the goods and services, capital structure, mergers and acquisitions policy, or dividend policy. One unifying characteristic of these decisions is that, once made, they are difficult to reverse. Long-term decisions essentially determine the basic nature of the business and how it will be carried out.

Short-term financial problems take the results of these decisions as a starting point and concentrate on how they can be efficiently and economically carried out. We can think of short-term decisions as being more operational. Once implemented, they are easier to change.

In many situations, the short- and long-term natures of the decision are interrelated. An example is the decision by ARCO to eliminate its credit card program in 1982. Was this a short-term or a long-term decision? Clearly, the decision had a major impact on a short-term asset (accounts receivable) and the liquidity requirements of the firm. However, it also had a long-run impact on the way that the company does business.

It is sometimes tempting to try to separate the decisions along strategic versus tactical lines. However, both short-term and long-term decisions have both strategic and tactical aspects. For example, the design of a lockbox system for collection of mailed payments is a strategic decision.[1] The day-to-day management of the lockbox system is a tactical decision.

Whether to treat a particular problem as short-term or long-term should not be a major issue if we have a decision process that allows us to make short- and long-term financial decisions in a consistent manner. There may still be an organizational issue of who has the responsibility for the decision and how far up the organization chart the issue has to progress for final resolution. However, if a consistent decision process is being used, the kind of information required and the concepts being employed will be the same.

---

[1] A lockbox is a collection system operated by a bank for the benefit of a client. The details and decisions involving the use of lockboxes in a collection system are presented in Chapter 6.

A Closer Examination of the
_____ Cash Flow Timeline _____

In Figure 1.3 we illustrated a *transaction timeline*, i.e., a timeline for an individual transaction. Transactions do not usually occur in isolation, but rather are part of a sequence of activities. If we aggregate the individual transactions connected with an event and array them on a timeline, we have an *aggregate timeline*. Through the use of an aggregate timeline, we can illustrate the range of activities included in short-term financial management.

An Aggregate Timeline for a Retailer

Let us now explore the issues in short-term financial management by examining an aggregate timeline for a retailing firm. Consider the sequence of events triggered by the decision of the manager of The Ersatz Athlete to stock the pair of black aerobic exercise shoes. The order for the shoes is placed with the manufacturer. The shoes arrive, are placed on a display, and are carried as *inventory*. The invoice accompanying the shoes is routed to the back office to be processed for payment on the due date, say, 30 days later. During this time, the liability to make the payment is carried on Ersatz's books as an *account payable*. On the payment date a check is cut and mailed to the manufacturer, and after some delay (due to the nature of Ersatz's payment system, the manufacturer's processing, and clearing through the banking system) cash is withdrawn from the checking account at Ersatz's bank.

Meanwhile, back on the sales floor, Kathy Klerk has just talked Sean Smith into buying the shoes, which he purchases with his Ersatz credit card. The sale is recognized immediately, but since no cash changes hands, Sean's purchase is listed as an *account receivable*. The credit for Kathy's commission on the sale, which she will receive at the end of the next pay period, is recognized as an *accrued expense*. At the end of the month Ersatz sends a bill to Sean, which he "promptly" pays by mailing in a check 1 month later. After the check is received, credited to Sean's account, deposited, and processed through the banking system, Ersatz has the cash available for use in its checking account. The *aggregate timeline* for this process is illustrated in Figure 1.4.

Cash Operating Cycle

By focusing on the aggregate timeline, we can understand the set of activities involved in the sale of this pair of shoes. The purchasing department, in discussions with the manufacturer, agrees on the delivery date and the payment terms for the shoes. Ersatz's accounts payable policy and payment system affect the timing of cash outflow for the payment for the goods. The inventory, pricing, promotion, and other policies affect the time between the arrival of

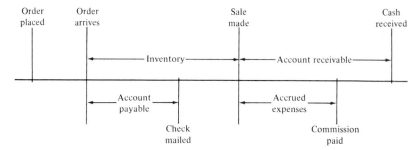

Figure 1.4 Aggregate Cash Flow Timeline for The Ersatz Athlete.

the shoes and the sale. The credit and collections policies and systems used by Ersatz affect the time lag between the sale and the ultimate receipt of cash for the sale. Finally, the time lag between the outflows of cash and the receipt of cash from Sean help determine the liquidity requirements of Ersatz, which may result in borrowing. This whole sequence of cash flows generated by the physical activities of the firm's operations is sometimes known as the *cash operating cycle* or the *short-term operating cycle* of the firm.

The cash flow approach includes all of the elements that would be included with a balance sheet focus. However, the cash flow approach makes it easier to incorporate factors that are not normally considered an integral part of an asset or a liability decision, such as the cash disbursement system, but that may affect the amount of assets or liabilities. In addition, the focus on cash flows provides a good starting point for the incorporation of the short-term financial decisions in a general financial valuation approach.

Framework for Financial
Management Decisions

Basic Objective

The development of financial management over the last two decades has been based on the idea that the management of the firm is hired by the shareholders to act in their best interests. Shareholders are generally *utility maximizers* with a positive utility of wealth—more wealth is preferred to less. Since management has the most direct impact on shareholders' wealth through their investment in the equity of the firm, management acts in the best interests of the shareholders if it attempts to maximize the market value of the equity.

Pricing of Financial Assets

Financial valuation models for pricing assets are based on the concept that investors pay for the present value of a discounted stream of cash flows. While attempts to measure the amount, timing, and risk of a future stream of cash flows being priced in the market are fraught with myriad complexities, as well as fortunes made and lost, the basic principle of price setting using the present value of future cash flows is well established.

Decision Model Structure

Financial decision models must be structured to be consistent, both in approach and in application of concepts, with valuation in financial markets if they are to assist management in achieving its objective. While various policy areas and decision techniques are treated as separate decisions—such as capital budgeting, dividend policy, and credit policy—in part to reduce the complexity to a manageable level, these approaches must fit into an overall framework and have the same objectives if consistent decisions are to be made. The linkage of all of these models is the attempt to maximize the value of the firm to the shareholders, as measured by the present value of cash flows. Models developed without this basic focus are subject to two major problems. First, they may result in decisions that are not optimal for the firm as a whole. Second, they may be ignored because they do not fit into the framework that is used for other decision models.

Objectives of Short-term
_____ Financial Management _____

Short-term financial policies are established to manage efficiently the cash flows of the firm. Consistent with the other financial objectives of the firm, the objective of short-term financial management is to maximize the value of shareholder wealth. Operationally, this can be reduced to the following objective function:

Maximize: Net present value of
(operating cash inflows − operating cash outflows)

The net present value is the sum of all of the cash flows connected with the decision after an adjustment for the opportunity costs associated with the timing of the flows. With this objective function as the focus, we can be assured that short-term finance decisions will be consistent with other finance decisions and with the overall goal of maximization of shareholder wealth.

In attempting to maximize this objective function, the financial manager will try to speed cash inflows, to slow cash outflows, to minimize idle cash, to minimize transactions costs, to minimize administrative costs connected with the cash flows, to minimize the cost of providing backup liquidity, and to maximize the value of information provided to management.

Clearly, there are tradeoffs involved in the objective function. Reduction of idle cash may be possible only through an increase in transactions costs.

The value of information to management may be increased only by incurring higher administrative costs to obtain the information. In addition, management cannot pursue unconstrained maximization. The attempt to maximize the value of the cash flows is constrained by legal and ethical considerations, by system capabilities, by the need to provide adequate liquidity, and by the need to maintain good customer and supplier relationships.

Importance of Short-term
———————— Financial Management ————————

As we have seen, the financial manager's responsibility involves establishing, maintaining, and using the institutional arrangements and systems for operating decisions of the firm. These operating decisions, which have a shorter time horizon than, say, capital budgeting or capital structure decisions, encompass the activities that include most of the short-term assets and liabilities of the firm.

The importance of these short-term assets and liabilities to the firm can be seen by the data presented in Table 1.2 and illustrated graphically in Figure 1.5. We can see that in 1985 over 40% of all of the funds invested by manufacturing firms were in current assets. It is easy to see why a substantial portion of the financial manager's time is devoted to short-term financial decisions. There has been a fairly steady decline in current assets as a percentage of total assets

Table 1.2 Current Assets and Liabilities as a Percentage of Total Assets for All Manufacturing Corporations

	1960 (%)	1970 (%)	1980 (%)	1985 (%)
Current Assets				
Cash	6.0	4.3	2.8	2.5
Marketable securities	4.8	0.7	2.5	2.9
Accounts receivable	15.6	17.3	17.0	15.8
Inventory	23.6	23.0	19.8	17.8
Other cur. assets	2.3	3.5	2.8	3.1
Total cur. assets	52.3	48.8	44.9	42.1
Current Liabilities				
Notes payable	3.9	6.3	5.0	5.5
Accounts payable	7.9	8.5	9.9	8.5
Accruals and other cur. liabilities	9.0	9.9	12.0	12.9
Total cur. liab.	20.8	24.7	26.9	26.9

Source: Quarterly Financial Report for Manufacturing, Mining, and Trade Corporations, U.S. Department of Commerce, various dates.

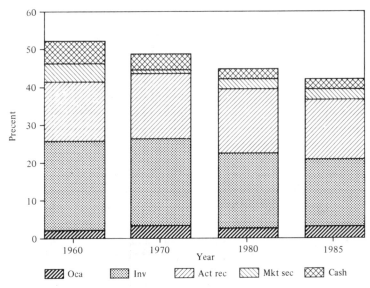

Figure 1.5   Current Assets as a Percentage of Total Assets, All Manufacturing Companies.

from a level of 52.3% in 1960. In part this decline is a result of the attention paid to the amount of the investment in these short-term assets. Examining the details of the composition of the current assets, we can see that most of this decline is due to a reduction in the relative amount of cash and inventory during this time period.

Looking at the other side of the balance sheet, we see that the percentage of short-term liabilities to finance the firm has increased over this period from 20.8% of total assets in 1960 to a high of 26.9% in 1980 and 1985. The most noticeable increase has been in the category of accruals and other current liabilities, which typically carry no explicit interest charge. There may be several reasons for this increase in short-term liabilities, not the least of which was the high level of interest rates during the late 1970s and early 1980s. During this period, managers of firms shortened the maturity structure of debt to take advantage of the somewhat lower rates on short-term debt. In addition, they were understandably reluctant to take on a long-term commitment of debt, say, 20 or 30 years, at interest rates that were felt (at the time) to be abnormally high.

There are two general reasons why current assets and liabilities are maintained by a firm. First, some of the assets and liabilities are a natural consequence of the components of the operating cycle of the firm and the normal institutional arrangements for the industry in which they operate. We expect the importance of the individual assets and liabilities to be, in part, a function of the industry. For example, the materials and work-in-process inventories may be a function of the production process used by the firm, and the relative amount of cash committed to these assets may be dictated by characteristics of the product. Since firms in an industry have similar operations, they would be expected to have a similar reliance on particular short-term assets and liabilities.

The current assets and liabilities as a percentage of total assets are shown for selected industries in Table 1.3 and graphically in Figure 1.6. Looking at the composition of current assets, we see that the inventory of the aircraft industry is proportionately much larger than that of the other industries. Aircraft companies have invested almost twice the proportion of funds in current assets as the industrial chemicals industry or the iron and steel industry. This pattern is understandable when we recognize that the inventory for an aircraft manufacturer consists of the airplanes under construction. Not only do these planes have a very high value, but the construction time is quite lengthy.

In contrast, the printing and publishing industry has a relatively low investment in inventory but a substantial investment in accounts receivable. This is a result of several factors, such as the relatively low cost of the product and the fact that publishers offer credit terms to bookstores to ensure that the stores carry an adequate supply of the product. Essentially, publishers have encouraged bookstores to carry the inventory. The tradeoff is that accounts receivables are high. Thus, attention must be paid to the product, company, and industry characteristics when addressing the question of the appropriate level or composition of current assets and liabilities.

However, industry characteristics do not explain all of the similarities or differences in the composition of the assets and liabilities. Note the similarity

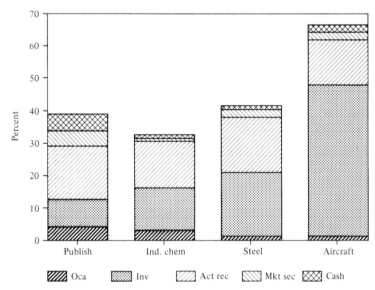

Figure 1.6 Current Assets as a Percentage of Total Assets, Comparison of Selected Industries, 1985.

Table 1.3 Current Assets and Current Liabilities as a Percentage of Total Assets for Selected Industries, 1985

	Printing and Publishing (%)	Industrial Chemicals (%)	Iron and Steel (%)	Aircraft and Missiles (%)
Current Assets				
Cash	5.2	1.1	1.3	2.2
Marketable securities	4.8	0.8	2.4	2.6
Accounts receivable	16.4	14.5	16.9	13.8
Inventory	8.4	13.0	19.8	46.8
Other cur. assets	4.3	3.2	1.3	1.3
Total cur. assets	38.7	32.6	41.7	66.7
Current Liabilities				
Notes payable	2.9	4.3	5.6	4.0
Accounts payable	7.9	6.6	9.5	8.4
Accruals and other cur. liabilities	10.3	11.8	13.6	44.1
Total cur. liab.	21.1	22.7	28.7	56.5

Source: Quarterly Financial Report for Manufacturing, Mining, and Trade Corporations, U.S. Department of Commerce, various dates.

of the various current asset percentages for the industrial chemicals industry and the iron and steel industry, even though their production processes and product characteristics are very different.

Organizational Structure
and
_____ Short-term Finance _____

Almost all business problems are multidimensional and involve a combination of potentially conflicting goals in personnel, marketing, production, and finance. Many problems are addressed in the finance literature by ignoring these other dimensions and approaching the solution with a narrow concentration on the finance factors, concepts, and theories. Many long-term financial problems, such as financial structure or dividend policy, are almost always the province of the financial manager. Addressing them almost exclusively from a financial perspective may not be too far removed from reality.

However, for many short-term financial decisions, it is not possible to ignore the multidimensional aspects of the problem. Take, for example, the credit policy of the firm. The basic reason for selling on credit is to enhance sales, which implies a strong marketing involvement in the decision. The financing of accounts receivable created by selling on credit clearly involves the financial manager. The credit policy adopted by the firm also presents a monitoring and control problem that may be addressed by the credit manager or the controller. Some of the manager's titles and the short-term financial decisions in which the manager is involved are given in Table1.4.

As we saw earlier, the objective function of short-term finance decisions involves various tradeoffs in attempting to maximize the value of the firm. Ideally, the manager examines these tradeoffs to make the optimal value-maximizing decision. However, when different people manage different components of the objective function, it is more likely that decisions will be made that may be optimal from the standpoint of their individual considerations but suboptimal for the entire firm. Each person may take a narrow view, considering only the impact of the decision on his or her component.

Organizational Structure Impediments

In a small firm, management of the elements of the entire cash flow timeline is usually the responsibility of one person who is relatively close to day-to-day management. This permits relatively easy and consistent consideration of the necessary tradeoffs. In a large corporation, however, a high degree of specialization is necessary to allow for a sufficiently manageable span of control and to understand the technical aspects of the area. Marketing, production, controller, and treasury functions are usually performed by separate

Table 1.4 Managers Who Deal with Short-term Financial Problems

Title of Manager	Duties Related to Short-term Financial Management	Assets/Liabilities Influenced
Cash manager	Collection, concentration, disbursement; short-term investments; short-term borrowing; banking relations	Cash, marketable securities, short-term loans
Credit manager	Monitoring and control of accounts receivable; credit policy decisions	Accounts receivable
Marketing manager	Credit policy decisions	Accounts receivable
Purchasing manager	Decisions on purchases, suppliers; may negotiate payment terms	Inventory, accounts payable
Production manager	Setting of production schedules and materials requirements	Inventory, accounts payable
Payables manager	Decisions on payment policies and on whether to take discounts	Accounts payable
Controller	Accounting information on cash flows; reconciliation of accounts payable; application of payments to accounts receivable	Accounts receivable, accounts payable

departments. An abbreviated organization chart for The Ersatz Athlete that highlights some of the individuals with responsibility for managing a portion of the timeline is shown in Figure 1.7.

In a large organization, the lines of communication tend to be vertical and frequently do not cut across functional areas. In addition to this organizational separation, the functions may be fragmented into geographically dispersed divisions or subsidiaries. This separation can make it more difficult to manage the timeline with an overall focus of maximizing the value of the firm.

An example of how organizational structure may impede the solution of a short-term financial problem involves the disbursement decision. Three (or more) people may be involved and may deal with a different—sometimes conflicting—component of the objective function.

1. The purchasing agent can affect the payment terms by the choice of supplier or by negotiation with the supplier. The focus of the purchasing agent is on maintaining good supplier relations in order to ensure a steady flow of supplies.
2. The accounts payable manager decides when the payment to suppliers should be initiated, that is, whether the payment should be made during the cash discount period, made on the net terms, or delayed for some time after the net period. The focus of the accounts payable manager is on control, with attention to a complete audit trail documented by purchase orders, invoices, and so on.
3. The cash manager designs the disbursement system used to route the payment to the supplier. The focus of the cash manager is on delaying the

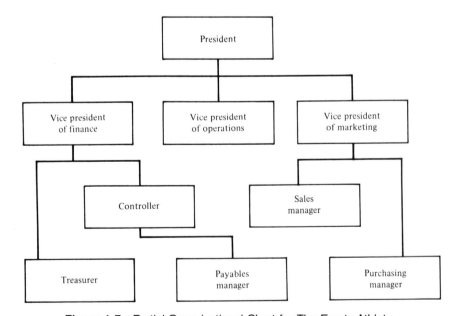

Figure 1.7 Partial Organizational Chart for The Ersatz Athlete.

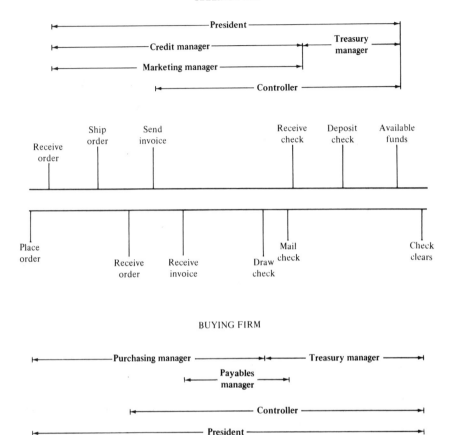

Figure 1.8 Individual Responsibilities on the Cash Flow Timeline

time at which cash for payment actually flows out of the bank account to increase interest income on investments.

Thus, we may have three different managers addressing different parts of the timeline and focusing on different components of the objective function. If they are reporting to different people in the organization, their decisions may be made without coordination with one another.

Organizational Structure and the Cash Flow Timeline

We can further examine these interrelationships with the help of the cash flow timeline shown in Figure 1.8, where the people involved with an order for both the buying and selling organizations and their areas of responsibility are indicated. We can see that, for example, a decision by the credit manager to change credit terms directly affects the marketing manager and the controller of the selling firm. Indirectly, the cash manager is affected because his forecast of when cash flows occur has to be altered. The change in credit terms affects the controller, the payables manager, and the cash manager for the buying firm. To the extent that the purchasing manager is sensitive to the credit terms, this change may also affect her choice of firms from which to purchase materials.

Because of the inescapably multidimensional nature of many of these problems, attention directed to the solution of short-term financial problems has not always been finance oriented. Even when there has been a finance orientation, the decision process has frequently been narrowly concentrated on the specific aspects of the particular problem at hand, with little concern with whether it is consistent with the direction and thrust of the approach to the solution of other finance problems of the firm.

Institutional Considerations

Institutional factors are important in the treatment of the problems and issues in short-term financial management. For example, to address the question of an optimal cash concentration system appropriately, it is necessary to understand the different methods that are available to move cash from one bank to the next, as well as the banking practices related to creating deposits. One of the problems in trying to address short-term financial management issues in a general economic or financial framework is that many of these approaches use general equilibrium models that assume markets with few, if any, imperfections. In the next chapter we argue that the existence of institutional constraints, which are essentially market imperfections, makes the treatment of short-term financial issues in a world in equilibrium very difficult, if not impossible.

The existence of the institutional environment or of market imperfections does not preclude the treatment of short-term finance problems in a general, unifying framework. However, it requires that any models used be sufficiently flexible to capture the institutional constraints and allow for optimal decisions in light of, not in spite of, these institutional issues.

Summary

Short-term financial management is involved with the decisions that have an impact on the operating cash flows of the firm. These cash flows include inflows from customers and other payors, internal flows, and flows out of the firm to suppliers, employees, and so on. The scope of the issues addressed in short-term finance decisions can be identified by examining the cash operating cycle. The objective of short-term financial management is to maximize the net present value of the operating cash inflows minus the operating cash outflows.

This objective can be operationalized by examining the issues surrounding a short-term finance problem in the framework of a cash flow timeline. This approach to a problem ensures that the decision will be consistent with the overall goal of maximizing shareholder wealth, with pricing of financial assets, and with other finance decision models. Many short-term finance problems are multidimensional and involve tradeoffs between components of the objective function. The separation of functional areas in many large companies serves as an impediment to a decision that properly considers the tradeoffs necessary to be consistent with the overall objective of maximization of shareholder wealth.

Discussion Questions

1. Why are cash flow data superior to accounting data in making financial decisions?
2. How do the goals of the financial manager in dealing with a short-term finance problem differ from those in a long-term problem?
3. In what ways does the cash flow cycle for a nonprofit organization, such as a government agency, differ from that for a profit-oriented company?
4. Explain how the interrelationships between accounts payable and inventory are captured by an examination of the cash flow cycle timeline.
5. Contrast the aggregate cash flow timeline for the operations of a steel manufacturer and an international oil producer. How do the relative amounts of assets and liabilities of the two companies differ?
6. What types of companies tend to have a large proportion of current assets? A small proportion?
7. What is a suboptimal decision? How will such a decision hurt the firm's shareholders?
8. Explain how suboptimal decisions can occur when the production department makes inventory policy decisions separately from the credit policy decisions made by the credit department.
9. What emphasis would you expect to find on credit policy decisions for a firm that has the credit function located under the treasurer? Under the controller? Under the marketing vice-president?
10. Choose a large firm for which you can obtain an organization chart. Identify the organizational barriers to an integrative approach to short-term financial problems.

Selected Readings

ALTMAN, EDWARD I. (ed.), *Financial Handbook*, 5th ed., New York: Wiley, 1981.
BEEHLER, PAUL J., *Contemporary Cash Management: Principles, Practices, and Perspectives,* New York: Wiley, 1983.

BEEHLER, PAUL J., "Treasury Management Evolution: Challenge for the 80s," *Journal of Cash Management* (January 1984), pp. 10–18.

HAMILTON, FRANK W. III, "Turning Cash Management Into a 'Line' Function," *Journal of Cash Management* (August 1983), pp. 60–80.

HILL, NED C., and DANIEL M. FERGUSON, "Cash Flow Timeline Management: The Next Frontier of Cash Management," Robert R. Fentress Prize Paper. Bank Administration Institute, Rolling Meadows, IL (July 1984).

KALLBERG, JARL G., and KENNETH PARKINSON, *Current Asset Management: Cash, Credit, and Inventory*, New York: Wiley, 1984.

MEHTA, DILEEP R., *Working Capital Management*, Englewood Cliffs, N.J.: Prentice-Hall, 1974.

NAPOLI, MICHAEL J., "Float Reduction Along the Cashflow Timeline," *Journal of Cash Management* (July 1984), pp. 44–47.

PETERSON, EDWARD D., *Cash Management*, Belmont, CA: Lifetime Learning Publications, 1984.

SMITH, KEITH V., *Guide to Working Capital Management*, New York: McGraw-Hill, 1979.

SMITH, KEITH V., *Readings on the Management of Working Capital*, 2nd ed., St. Paul: West Publishing, 1980.

STONE, BERNELL K., "Cash Management," in *Financial Handbook*, 5th ed, Edward I. Altman (ed.), New York: Wiley, 1981.

STONE, BERNELL K., "The Expanding Scope of Cash Management," *Journal of Cash Management* (November 1982), pp. 6ff.

VANDER WEIDE, JAMES, and STEVEN F. MAIER, *Managing Corporate Liquidity: An Introduction to Working Capital Management*, New York: Wiley, 1985.

A Valuation
Framework

A basic principle of most financial decision models is that the value of an asset is determined by the net present value of the stream of cash flows generated by the asset. A major component of the short-term financial management objective function is the net present value of cash inflows minus cash outflows. In this chapter, we develop a net present value framework for addressing short-term financial problems. The aggregate cash flow timeline for the operating aspects of the firm presented in the last chapter is used to integrate the elements in short-term finance decisions. However, before developing the decision framework, we briefly review the concepts of present value and risk in financial decisions.

Present Value Concepts:
Timing and Risk

Time Value of Money

A basic behavioral trait of people is that, all else equal, they prefer to have things sooner rather than later. This applies to people's preference for money: they prefer having their money today instead of tomorrow. This concept, referred to as the *time value of money*, is the basis for the use of *future value* or *present value* in finance.

Future Value
When using future value, we have an amount today, an interest (investment) rate, and are trying to determine the equivalent value at a future point in time. Sometimes the rate is referred to as an *opportunity cost*: the rate

that would be earned on the opportunity forgone by investing in the proposal under consideration. We find the value at some future time t by multiplying the investment by the quantity 1 plus the interest rate raised to the t power. [1] In symbolic terms this is

$$V_t = PV \times (1 + r)^t, \tag{2.1}$$

where
$r =$ the interest rate
$t =$ the number of time periods in the future
$PV =$ the initial investment
$V_t =$ the value at the end of period t

Present Value

The same concepts are used in the determination of present value. However, in present value, the cash amount in the future and the interest rate are known, and the equivalent value today is the item to be determined. The calculation procedure is the inverse of that for finding the future value: where we multiplied for future value, we divide for present value. A general present value formula using the same notation as previously is

$$PV = \frac{V_n}{(1 + r)^n}. \tag{2.2}$$

The present value for a sequence of cash flows at multiple times in the future is found by adding the present values of the individual cash flows. If we have a series of cash flows occurring at times 1, 2 and 3, the present value of the total series is

$$PV = \frac{V_1}{(1 + r)^1} + \frac{V_2}{(1 + r)^2} + \frac{V_3}{(1 + r)^3}. \tag{2.3}$$

Calculation Simplification

The algebraic formulas just presented are the correct way to calculate future value or present value for discrete cash flows when the interest is compounded each period. In addition to being correct, the compound interest formula is convenient when working with mathematical symbols. For this reason, when using a mathematical representation of a present value, we use the compound interest approach to present value.

There are two simple interest rate approximations to this compound interest formulation that make numerical calculations on a basic calculator much easier. In the first, the interest rate for the period is multiplied by the number of periods. This product is then added to 1, and the quantity is divided into the future cash flow. In symbolic terms this is

---

[1] It is assumed that the reader has a basic understanding of the concepts of present and future value. For a review of these concepts, the reader is referred to a basic financial management text such as J. Fred Weston and Thomas E. Copeland, *Managerial Finance*, Dryden Press, New York (1986).

$$PV = \frac{V_n}{1 + r \times n}. \tag{2.4}$$

In the second approximation, sometimes called a *discount calculation*, the interest rate is multiplied by the number of periods and subtracted from 1. The quantity is then multiplied by the future value. In symbolic terms this is

$$PV = V_n(1 - r \times n). \tag{2.5}$$

When working with small interest rates and short time periods, as is usually the case in short-term finance decisions, both simple interest approximations are very close to the compound interest calculation. (See Appendix A for a comparison of the accuracy of these approximations.) To simplify the number crunching, we adopt the convention of using one of the simple interest calculations for numerical examples and problems throughout the remainder of this book.

Net Present Value

Financial decisions usually involve both benefits and costs. To make a correct decision, we examine the *net present value*, that is, the present value of the benefits minus the present value of the costs. A positive net present value means that, after adjusting for the timing of the cash flows and the opportunity cost, the value of the benefits is greater than the costs; shareholder wealth will increase if the proposal is accepted. For a negative net present value, the value of the benefits is outweighed by the costs, and shareholder wealth is decreased by adopting the proposal. It should be obvious that we want to adopt proposals with positive net present values and to reject those with negative net present values.

Financial Risk

In general, *risk* can be defined as the chance of incurring injury, damage, or loss. In a financial context, risk is due to uncertainty either about the amount or the timing of the cash flow. An example of uncertainty about the amount involves the manager of Jalapeno Julio's Taco Restaurant, who knows he will receive cash for Saturday's sales, but not how much. An example of timing uncertainty involves the cash manager of the Allrisk Insurance Company, who knows that Zeener Manufacturing will submit a check in the amount of $1,562 for group insurance for March, but not when during the month the check will arrive.

Financial risk is the uncertainty of an outcome, not just the occurrence of a loss. We could play a game of flipping a coin for $1 a toss, with the payoff being "heads I win, tails you lose." There would be no risk in this opportunity. You might consider it foolish for you to play, but there is no uncertainty about the outcome.

Table 2.1 A Choice Between Two Gambles

Both gambles involve a flip of the coin. The outcomes, the payoffs, and the probabilities are as follows:

	COIN LANDS HEADS		COIN LANDS TAILS	
Gamble	Payoff	Probability	Payoff	Probability
A	$3,000	0.50	$ 7,000	0.50
B	$ 0	0.50	$10,000	0.50

Reaction to Risk

We address the question of how people react to risk and of the adjustments necessary in a present value formulation to account for risk through the use of an example. Assume that Paul must choose between entering into either gamble A or gamble B in Table 2.1. Although we don't know which outcome will occur, we can measure the average outcome of each gamble by the *expected value*. The expected value is the payoff times the probability of the outcome summed across all outcomes. The expected value is ($3,000 × .5) + ($7,000 × .5) = $5,000 for gamble A and ($0 × .5) + ($10,000 × .5) = $5,000 for gamble B. Even though the individual outcomes are different, the expected value is the same for both gambles. If people are indifferent to risk, they would be indifferent to two choices that offer the same expected value. However, most individuals are not indifferent to the two gambles even though they have the same expected value.[2] In fact, most people would prefer gamble A.

Utility of Wealth

Economists use the concept of *utility of wealth* to explain this and other similar choice situations. People make choices based on the utility of the payoff, or the value that it has for them, not just on the dollar amount of the payoff. It has been shown that most individuals have a *diminishing marginal utility* of wealth. This means that a given addition to wealth is less valuable the wealthier you are.

In terms of the two gambles, if a head occurs, the player receives $3,000 more from gamble A than from gamble B. If a tail occurs, the player receives $3,000 more from B than from A. However, because of diminishing marginal utility, the additional $3,000 is worth more at $0 than it is at $7,000. Thus, if gamble A is chosen, the additional utility of having the "extra" $3,000 if a head occurs outweighs the "extra" $3,000 that is given up if a tail occurs.

---

[2] If you are indifferent to the two gambles presented in Exhibit 2.1, try adding three zeros to each payoff and see if you are still indifferent.

Risk Aversion

Persons with a diminishing marginal utility of wealth exhibit *risk-averse* behavior, that is, they dislike risk. They are willing to accept risk, but only if they *expect* to be rewarded by a higher payoff. For example, people accept a higher risk by investing in equities instead of government bonds, but they do so with the expectation of receiving a greater return from the equities. Of course, this greater return is not guaranteed. If there was no additional risk in equities, the price of equities would be bid up (and the future return driven down) until they offered the same return available on the government securities.

Sources of Risk

BUSINESS RISK. There are several sources of risk for a financial asset, say, a share of common stock in Floppi, Inc., a manufacturer of computer storage systems. One element is the basic risk that comes with the vagaries of the demand for a product or service. A second element is the risk associated with the production process and the production costs. A third element of risk is the ability of management to adapt to changing conditions. These elements affect the degree of risk in the profits, or cash flow from operations, of the firm. The term *business risk* is frequently used to refer to this source of risk.

FINANCIAL RISK. A second source of risk in our share of common stock is due to the way the company is financed. Elements such as the proportion of capital provided by the common stockholders, the maturity structure of the debt, and whether the interest rate is fixed or variable affect the nature and amount of the financing costs. This source of risk to the holders of the common stock is known as *financial risk*.

There is also an element of *interest rate risk* that contributes to the risk of the firm. Interest rate risk is due to a combination of uncertainty about future interest rates and the maturity structure of the assets and liabilities of the firm. The firm is subject to *primary interest rate risk* if it faces the risk directly, such as a manufacturer of heavy equipment using a large amount of short-term financing and suffering uncertainty regarding future financing costs.[3] A firm is subject to *secondary interest rate risk* if the level of interest rates affects its customers and, therefore, its demand. A home builder, for example, faces a great degree of variability in demand depending upon the interest rate of home mortgages. This secondary interest rate risk, while due to variation in interest rates in the financial market, is frequently included as an element of business risk.

TOTAL RISK. The total risk of a financial asset, our share of common stock, is the sum of these sources of risk. This is represented schematically in Figure 2.1. As previously discussed, most investors are risk averse with respect to their financial investments and expect to be compensated for taking on a higher level of risk by receiving a higher return.

---

[3] More will be said about this type of interest rate risk when we discuss short-term investments in Chapters 9 and 10 and short-term financing in Chapters 12 and 13.

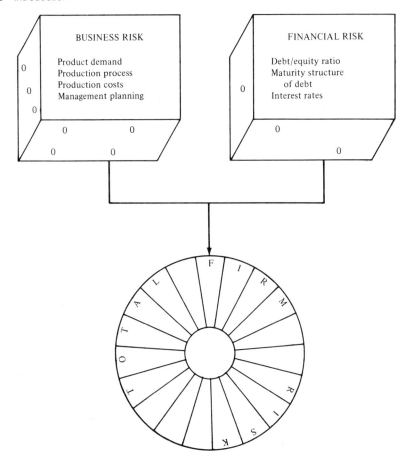

Figure 2.1 Components of Total Risk for a Firm.

Adjustments for Risk

In pricing an asset, an adjustment is made for the degree of risk that the asset is perceived to have. As previously described, assets are priced by finding the present value of the future cash flows. Two procedures are used to adjust the present value to incorporate risk. (1) Adjust the cash flows for the degree of risk. This is an adjustment downward for cash inflows (to make them less valuable) and an adjustment upward for cash outflows (to make them more costly). This adjustment is shown in Equation (2.6), where A_1 is the dollar value of the adjustment:

$$PV = \frac{V_n - A_1}{1 + rn}. \tag{2.6}$$

(2) Adjust the rate that is used in the present value calculation, using a higher rate for riskier cash flows. This is shown in Equation (2.7), where A_2 is an adjustment to the interest rate:

$$PV = \frac{V_n}{1 + (r + A_2)n}.$$
(2.7)

Either of these approaches reduces the present value of a risky asset and makes it less valuable. The adjustment of the discount rate is easier to apply in practice and is the method that has gained greater acceptance.

When we adjust the interest rate for the degree of risk, we are actually saying that the interest rate consists of two components: a *risk-free rate* and a *risk premium*.

Expected return on a risky asset = risk-free return
+ risk premium.
(2.8)

The risk-free rate is simply the time value of money, that is, the cost of deferring the cash flow, with no uncertainty about either the timing or the amount. The risk premium is the additional return that is necessary to compensate investors for bearing risk. If the expected return on a risky asset is not large enough in comparison to the risk-free return to compensate for the risk, the asset will not be purchased at its current price.

Although the nature of the risk adjustment is straightforward, the measurement of the amount of adjustment for risk is difficult. We now examine a model that addresses the question of how to measure this risk premium for financial assets and investigate its applicability to short-term finance problems.

Asset Valuation Models and Short-term Finance

The Basics of the Capital Asset Pricing Model

Capital Market Assumptions
Over the past two decades, much of the theoretical development in finance has been based on equilibrium models of asset valuation in markets that are *perfectly competitive*. Much as the physicist assumes the absence of friction to develop the underlying laws of physics, the finance theorist assumes the absence of financial frictions to develop the basic underlying relationships in asset valuation. The characteristics of perfect markets are as follows:

1. There are no transactions costs of any type.
2. There are no taxes.
3. There are no costs for bankruptcy.
4. Information is costless and is instantaneously distributed to all participants in the market.
5. Assets are infinitely divisible.
6. Borrowing and lending at a risk-free rate are possible for both firms and individuals.

The Basic Model

The general financial model that has gained the widest acceptance and use is the *capital asset pricing model (CAPM)*. This model was developed by Sharpe and refined by Lintner and Mossin in the mid-1960s.[4] It filled a major gap in finance theory at the time by providing a normative model that could be used for pricing and valuation of all types of financial assets. The contributions of the CAPM in this area are two: (1) focusing attention on the measurement of risk and (2) providing a mechanism for determining the amount of the risk premium necessary to compensate for the degree of risk.

MEASURING AND PRICING RISK. There are two questions that are raised by a discussion of the pricing of risk: (1) For what risk can an investor expect to be compensated? (2) How is the risk adjustment factor to be measured? Let us address the first question by examining the concept of systematic and unsystematic risk as treated in the CAPM.

ASSET VERSUS PORTFOLIO RISK. An investor holding a portfolio of investments is concerned with the risk of the entire portfolio, not just a single asset. The risk of a portfolio of assets may be less than the sum of the risks of the individual assets, since the risk of the assets may partially offset each other. Thus, by appropriately combining assets into a portfolio, an investor can diversify away (reduce) some of the risk. If an investor holds a portfolio of assets—and evidence indicates that most investors do—it is not the total risk of an asset that matters, but rather the contribution that the asset makes to the risk of the entire portfolio.

SYSTEMATIC VERSUS UNSYSTEMATIC RISK. Using the terminology of the CAPM, the risk of the asset can be broken down into two components: (1) *systematic* (undiversifiable) risk and (2) *unsystematic* (diversifiable) risk. Systematic risk is defined as that portion of the risk that cannot be eliminated by diversification. In the CAPM, systematic risk is shown to be due to the correlation with the overall market or economy. Unsystematic risk is defined as that portion of risk that is specific to the individual asset and that can be diversified away. In the CAPM, unsystematic risk is shown to be that portion of risk that is not correlated with the market. Since this latter component of risk can and is diversified away by investors, no additional return should be required to compensate for unsystematic risk. The only risk that should be priced in the market is systematic risk.

MEASUREMENT OF SYSTEMATIC RISK. If only systematic risk is priced in the market, the question of how to measure this risk remains. As shown in the CAPM, systematic risk is measured by the *beta* of a security. Beta is the covariance of the return on a security with the return on the market divided

---

[4] See W. F. Sharpe, "Capital Asset Prices: A Theory of Market Equilibrium Under Conditions of Risk," *Journal of Finance*, (September 1964), pp. 425–442; J. Lintner, "The Valuation of Risk Assets and the Selection of Risky Investments in Stock Portfolios and Capital Budgets," *Review of Economics and Statistics* (February 1965), pp. 13–37; or Jan Mossin, "Equilibrium in a Capital Asset Market," *Econometrica*, (October 1966), pp. 768–783, for the development of this model.

by the variance of the market return.[5] This beta, or standardized covariance, measures the riskiness of the return on a security relative to that of the market. The risk premium for any security is found by multiplying its beta by the market risk premium.

Using these CAPM concepts, the expected return on an individual asset is expressed as follows:

Expected return on an individual asset = return on a risk-free asset
+ systematic risk measure × market risk premium. **(2.9)**

This model is represented mathematically as follows:

$$R_i = R_f + B_i(R_m - R_f),$$ **(2.10)**

where R_i = the expected return on asset i
R_f = the risk-free return
R_m = the expected return of the market portfolio
B_i = beta, the relationship of security i with the market, also defined as $\text{cov}(R_i, R_m)/\text{var}(R_m)$

The risk–return tradeoff implied by the CAPM is shown graphically in Figure 2.2. The intercept on the vertical axis is the risk-free rate of return. The slope of the line is the risk premium for the market. The market has a beta of 1. A security lying to the right of M has a beta greater than 1. This means that its return is more volatile than that of the market. For example, if the return

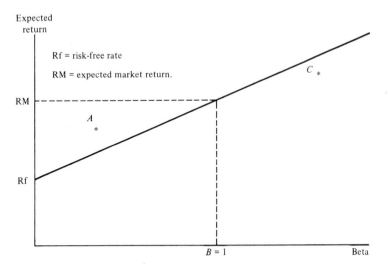

Figure 2.2 Relationship of Risk and Return Under the CAPM.

---

[5] The covariance of x and y is defined as $(x_i - \bar{x})(y_i - \bar{y})(P_i)$ summed over all observations, where x_i is the individual observation, $\bar{x}$ is the mean, and P_i is the probability of the observation. See investments text, such as W. F. Sharpe, *Investments*, Prentice-Hall, Englewood Cliffs, N.J. (1981), for details on the calculation of beta.

on the market increases by 5%, the return on a security with a beta of 1.5 increases by 7.5%. A security lying to the left of *M* has a beta less than 1, and its return is less volatile than that of the market.

In equilibrium, the risk–return tradeoff for all assets should lie on the line. During a temporary disequilibrium an asset, such as A, might lie above this risk–return line. Since asset A offers a return in excess of that needed to compensate for its risk, the price (return) is bid up (down) until the risk–return coordinates fall on the line. The converse is true for an asset, such as C, that is selling at a return that places it below the line.

EXAMPLE. Floppi, Inc., our manufacturer of computer storage systems, has a beta of 1.7. In a study encompassing more than 50 years of historical data, Ibbotson and Sinquefield determined that common stocks have offered an average return that is 8.3% greater than the return on T-bills, which were defined as offering a risk-free return.[6] If we accept this estimate as valid for current conditions, and if the current T-bill rate is 6%, we calculate that the expected return on common stock of Floppi, Inc., should be

$$R_i = R_f + B_i(R_m - R_f) = 6\% + 1.7(8.3\%) = 20.11\%.$$

Application of the CAPM

The CAPM has had a widespread influence on the field of finance. In addition to being included in most finance textbooks, the term *beta* is well established in the lexicon of Wall Street. Investment advisory services report the beta of a security along with more traditional measures such as the dividend yield. Several *index funds* whose goal is to duplicate the market portfolio, with a beta of 1.0, have been created.

The application of CAPM has been extended to the valuation of real assets in financial management, particularly in the assessment of the discount rate in capital budgeting under uncertainty.[7] The fact that product markets meet fewer of the conditions of perfect capital markets than financial markets is not thought to invalidate the use of CAPM for long-term finance decisions; rather, it provides more opportunities for managers to exploit, temporarily, a greater number of profitable disequilibrium situations. For example, a firm may develop a new technology that reduces production costs and temporarily allows it to achieve higher than normal profits. Eventually competitors develop a similar technology, and competition forces prices down and reduces the profits to a more normal level.

Market Imperfections and Short-term Finance

We have mentioned six conditions of perfect capital markets assumed in the derivation of the CAPM. The markets for financial securities appear to come

---

[6] See R. G. Ibbotson and R. A. Sinquefield, *Stocks, Bonds, Bills and Inflation: The Past and Future*, Financial Analysts Foundation, Charlottesville, Va. (1982).

[7] See Donald L. Tuttle and Robert H. Litzenberger, "Leverage, Diversification, and Capital Market Effects on a Risk-Adjusted Capital Budgeting Framework," *Journal of Finance* (June 1968), pp. 427–444, for an early application of the ideas of the CAPM to capital budgeting.

close to meeting these conditions. However, the existence of some market imperfections, which can be represented as deviations from these conditions, is more critical for short-term financial decisions. We now examine three of these conditions that are critical in addressing short-term financial problems.

NO TRANSACTIONS COSTS EXIST. If there were no transactions costs involved in obtaining loans, there would be no need to maintain cash balances or marketable securities to cover any potential cash shortages. Instead, any cash shortfalls would immediately be covered by borrowing from a bank. Similarly, if there were no transactions costs for the purchase or sale of securities, cash balances would not be held; any cash needs would be covered by the sale of securities, and any cash available at the end of the day would be invested.

Since brokerage and other costs for security transactions are fairly small as a percentage of the value of the securities, they may not cause much distortion in the return on long-term assets. However, because of the small absolute amount of return on short-term investments, these costs may be substantial. For example, an annual rate of 10% translates into an overnight return of only 0.027%. A brokerage commission of only 0.1% on an investment returning 10% for a year might not be significant, whereas a short-term investment would have to be held for at least 4 days to cover the transactions costs.

INFORMATION IS COSTLESS AND IS INSTANTANEOUSLY DISTRIBUTED. If information truly had no cost and was instantly disseminated, the decision on whether to sell to a particular applicant on credit would not only be easy, but all potential sellers would have the same information. The granting of credit is a complex process, with substantial search costs required to obtain the information necessary to decide if an applicant represents an acceptable credit risk. A company that has granted credit to an applicant in the past has access to more data and at a lower cost than a company that has not dealt with the applicant previously. Consequently, the search costs to obtain comparable information differ between potential sellers. Because of the relatively small amounts of money raised and the frequency of short-term transactions, these costs are a much larger proportion of the financing than is true for long-term financing.

BORROWING AND LENDING CAN BE DONE AT A RISK-FREE RATE. The ability to borrow at a risk-free rate would eliminate the need to obtain prearranged credit for which there is a fee, such as a credit line. Any firm would simply borrow the money as needed. The firm would be indifferent to selling short-term securities or to borrowing, since the rate would be the same. Credit policy would again be a nonissue, because if a firm failed to grant credit to an applicant, the applicant could easily obtain a loan elsewhere at the same (risk-free) rate.[8]

Comparable arguments can be made for other short-term finance issues under conditions of perfect markets. Thus, the conditions required for perfect

---

[8] See Wilbur G. Lewellen, John McConnell, and Johnathon Scott, "Capital Market Influences on Trade Credit," *Journal of Financial Research* (Fall 1980), pp. 105–113 for a discussion of the uselessness of trade credit if there are perfect markets for short-term finance issues.

markets may not hold for many areas in short-term finance. While this does not necessarily invalidate the use of the concepts of the CAPM, it does present some complications in its application.

Role of CAPM in Short-term Finance

In studying the issues and problems in short-term finance, we accept the basic concept of the CAPM that investors have to be compensated for higher risk with higher returns. However, market imperfections cannot be assumed away. Indeed, in many cases, market imperfections and institutional practices are at the center of many of the problems in short-term finance. The goal is to be able to investigate the problems and to develop rules or models that correctly use financial concepts and can be cast in a framework consistent with the objective of maximization of shareholders' value. We can't develop appropriate quantitative decision approaches without understanding the institutional framework. By the same token, we don't want to focus only on the institutional framework, without an underlying foundation of economic and finance principles.

The CAPM yields a consistent way to measure the risk premium in expected returns. It provides a useful framework in which to measure the required return for any financial decision that involves risky cash flows.

A Framework for Short-term _____ Financial Decisions _____

Basic Model

Let us return to the idea of arraying the elements of short-term finance decisions on a timeline, discussed in Chapter 1. It is the impact that the decisions have on the firm's cash flows that is of most interest to the financial management of the firm. The financial manager is concerned with the amount, timing, and degree of uncertainty of the cash flow. The basis for evaluation of financial alternatives is the present value of cash flows, where cash inflows are positive and cash outflows are negative. The decision criterion is to accept the proposal if it has a positive net present value.

The Cash Flow Timeline Revisited

The financial manager for Floppi, Inc., is evaluating a proposal to replace a piece of production equipment. The new equipment will have an installed cost of $50,000 and will generate net after-tax cash flow savings of $15,000 per year for 5 years. The time pattern of the cash flows is given in Figure 2.3.

The cost of capital, or opportunity cost, for Floppi has been determined to be 10%, and the financial manager feels that this is the appropriate risk-

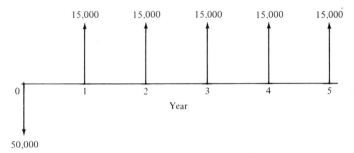

Figure 2.3 Cash Flow Timeline for Equipment Replacement.

adjusted rate to use in discounting the future cash flows. The present value of the project is[9]

$$PV = -50,000 + \frac{15,000}{(1 + .1)^1} + \frac{15,000}{(1 + .1)^2} + \frac{15,000}{(1 + .1)^3}$$

$$+ \frac{15,000}{(1 + .1)^4} + \frac{15,000}{(1 + .1)^5}$$

$$= -50,000 + 56,865 = +6,865.$$

Since the present value is positive, the new equipment should be purchased and shareholder value will increase.

This is a simple example of the familiar capital budgeting problem. We can now see how we can apply the same techniques to short-term financial problems, where cash flows occur over several days rather than over several years.

A Single Cash Flow

Sue Bannif, the financial manager for Floppi, Inc., received a request from one of its customers, Droste Stores, to allow taking a 2% discount for payment within 10 days on a $100,000 purchase. Current terms of sale are net 30 days, and Droste typically pays on the 30th day. Sue feels that if the funds are received earlier, they will be invested in money market securities at a 9% return. She sketches the cash flow timelines under the two alternatives, as shown in Figure 2.4. She decides to evaluate the decision, using present value concepts, by converting the cash flow on day 30 to an equivalent amount on day 10, that is, the day the earlier payment would be received. Since day 10 is 20 days earlier than day 30, she calculates the present (day 10) value of the day 30 payment by discounting for 20 days as follows:

$$PV = \frac{\$100,000}{(1 + .09 \times 20/365)} = \$99,509.27.$$

---

[9] We use the compound formula here because we are dealing with cash flows over multiple time periods on a long time horizon.

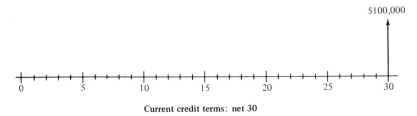

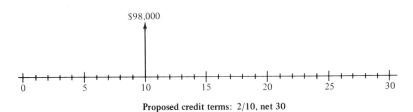

Figure 2.4 Cash Flow Timelines for Single Cash Flow.

She then compares this amount to the $98,000 that would be received if the payment is made on day 10 with the 2% discount.

Clearly, the equivalent day 10 value of the day 30 payment is larger than the discounted payment received on day 10. Sue concludes that the granting of the discount credit terms would cost Floppi $1,509.27 in day 10 funds and should not be done.

CHOICE OF DAY FOR EQUIVALENT VALUE. Although Sue evaluated the decision in terms of day 10 funds, she could have also evaluated the decision in terms of day 0 (today's) funds. If she had chosen day 0 as the evaluation date, she would have had to find the equivalent day 0 value of each of the cash flows before making the comparison. The present value of the day 30 payment would be

$$PV30 = \frac{\$100,000}{(1 + .09 \times 30/365)} = \$99,265.71.$$

The present value equivalent of the payment on day 10 would be

$$PV10 = \frac{\$98,000}{(1 + .09 \times 10/365)} = \$97,758.95.$$

Comparison of the two alternatives shows that granting the discount would cost Floppi $1,506.76 in day 0 funds. Floppi would be better off staying with the current credit terms.

We note that the resulting decision is the same—the discount credit terms would cost Floppi money—whether the proposal is evaluated in terms of day 0 or day 10 funds. However, when evaluated in terms of day 10 funds, the cost was $1,509.27, compared to only $1,506.76 in day 0 funds. Why does this difference exist? Simply because we are evaluating the decision at two different times.

The $1,506.76 is approximately the present value (at time 0) of the $1,509.27 in day 10 funds.[10] The specific day on which the cash flows are evaluated is not of critical importance as long as all cash flows are brought back and/or forward to a *common* day. Since the decision does not depend upon the evaluation date, a day can be chosen that is convenient for calculation purposes. This is usually the day on which the first cash flow occurs, since it eliminates one calculation.

Multiple Cash Flows

During lunch in the executive dining room, Sue mentions the issue of offering a cash discount to the company attorney. He points out, using some eloquent Latin phraseology, that Floppi cannot offer different credit terms to different customers without substantial justification. He suggests that she consider the impact of offering the discount credit terms to all of the customers.

After lunch, Sue starts thinking about the longer-range consequences of offering this discount. First, Droste is a repeat customer who will undoubtedly order again. Second, if other customers who are offered the same terms take the discount, the impact will be similar to that calculated for Droste. Sue decides that the best way to approach this issue is to assume that the sale to Droste of $100,000 represents an average day's sales. Sue modifies the cash flow timelines as shown in Figure 2.5.

The cash flow from sales on day 0 (today) will be received either on day 30 (under the current terms) or on day 10 (with the discount terms). The cash flow from sales on day 1 will be received either on day 31 or day 11, depending upon the credit terms offered. The cash flow from day 2 sales will be received on day 12 or day 32, and so on. Sue recognizes that this situation raises two major questions: (1) How should these cash flows be expressed in equivalent amounts from a present value standpoint? (2) How far out in the future should she go before terminating the sequence of events?

EQUIVALENT PRESENT VALUES. The question of how to handle the calculation of equivalent present values is easy to answer. The value on day 0 of the cash flow from day 0 sales is the same as the value on day 1 of the cash flow from day 1 sales. To express these flows in equivalent present value terms, it is only necessary to discount the day 1 value for one additional day in order to obtain the day 0 value. Similarly, the day 2 value has to be discounted for 2 days, the day 3 value for 3 days, and so on. We saw that the day 0 value had a cost to Floppi of $1,506.76. This is the day 1 value of the cost for sales from day 1, the day 2 value of the cost for sales from day 2, and so on.

---

[10] This is only approximately equal because we are using a simple interest formulation as an approximation of the true compounded value formula. If we were using the compounded formulation, it would be exact.

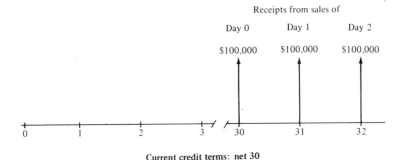

Figure 2.5 Cash Flow Timelines for Multiple Cash Flows.

We now convert this sequence of future values to day 0 values. The day 0 value of the day 1 sales cost to Floppi is

$$\text{Day 0 value of day 1 sales} = \frac{\$1,506.76}{(1 + .09 \times 1/365)}.$$

The day 0 value for day 2 is

$$\text{Day 0 value of day 2 sales} = \frac{\$1,506.76}{(1 + .09 \times 2/365)}.$$

The total present value of the decision is found by adding these individual present value terms for as many days into the future as the analysis is carried.

TIME HORIZON. Before performing any of the calculations, Sue realizes that the second question—how far into the future to continue the analysis—is easily answered. She rearranges the sum of all of the terms as follows:

Total present value =

$$-\$1,506.76 \times \left[\frac{1}{(1 + .09 \times 1/365)} + \frac{1}{(1 + .09 \times 2/365)} + \dots \right].$$

Since the terms in brackets are all positive, the sign of the total present value—and, therefore, the acceptability of the proposal—depends only upon the sign of the present value for 1 day's activity. While the distance into the future that the analysis is carried certainly has an impact on the total present value of the decision, it does not affect the sign of the calculation. If the present value of 1 day's sales is positive, the proposal will enhance the present value of the firm, regardless of how far into the future it will continue. If the present value of the proposal is negative, the firm will be hurt by adopting the proposal, regardless of how short or how long a time span is involved. Thus, Sue can consider the cash flows from only 1 day's sales and be confident that she will make the correct decision.

Stopping to check our bearings at this point, we have seen that a short-term finance problem, such as whether to change credit terms, can be analyzed using a present value cash flow approach similar to that used in capital budgeting. The cash flows connected with the different alternatives are arrayed on a timeline. Cash flows occurring in different time periods are adjusted with present value techniques to a common point in time. A comparison between the alternatives is made by subtracting the present value of the proposed alternative from that of the current arrangement. The proposed alternative is accepted if the difference in present values is positive. Finally, we saw that a repetitive sequence of events can be analyzed by simply examining the present value of the first element in the sequence, since the sum of the indefinite sequence of present value adjustment factors will not alter the sign of the difference.

Cash Inflows and Outflows

Before Sue decides to reject the request for the discount credit terms, she recognizes that the new terms are essentially a price reduction. Recalling the concept of price elasticity from basic economics, she thinks that a price reduction might lead to a larger amount of sales. She calls the sales manager to ask his opinion. The sales manager's best guess is that sales will increase by 5% with the new credit terms. Sue now realizes that she cannot make the decision based only on an examination of the change in the timing of the cash inflows; she must also consider any changes in the amount of the cash outflows.

Sue checks the items ordered by Droste and finds that the $100,000 has variable costs of $60,000.[11] The remaining $40,000 represents a contribution to fixed costs and profits. Thus, for every $1.00 increase in sales, variable costs will increase by only $.60. Sue decides that she needs to consider a full array of the cash inflows and outflows under the two alternative conditions before she can make a decision. Upon checking with the accounts payable department, she determines that, on average, the cash flows for payments to suppliers and employees connected with the variable costs occur on the day the sale is made. She sketches the cash flows involved in the decision as shown in Figure 2.6.

---

[11] We assume that the $60,000 variable costs are all paid out on the day of the sale—day 0 for the single day being considered.

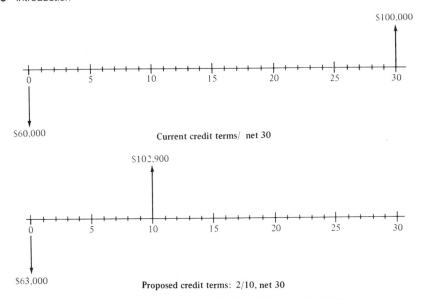

Figure 2.6 Cash Flow Timeline for Decision on Credit Terms.

We can represent the present value of the cash flow from 1 day's sales under the current system as follows:

PV of current cash flows =
    present value of cash inflows − present value of cash outflows. **(2.11)**

Using the simple interest approximation, we can represent this mathematically as follows:

$$PV \text{ of current cash flows } = \frac{\text{cash receipts}}{(1 + rC_t)} - \frac{\text{cash payments}}{(1 + rP_t)}, \quad \textbf{(2.12)}$$

where r = the daily interest rate
    C_t = the number of days from the evaluation date that the collections are received
    P_t = the number of days from the evaluation date that the payments are made

For the cash flows with which Sue is dealing, the present value of 1 day's sales under current credit terms is

$$PV \text{ of current cash flows} = \frac{100,000}{1 + .09 \times 30/365} - 60,000 = +39,265.71.$$

Under the current credit terms, each day's sales of $100,000 results in an increment in the present value of the firm of $39,265.71. Note that the $60,000 did not have to be adjusted with the present value techniques because we assumed that the cash flow occurs on the day of the sale, which is our evaluation date.

If the early payment discount terms are offered, the present value will be as follows:

$$PV \text{ of proposed cash flows} = \frac{105,000 \times .98}{1 + .09 \times 10/365} - 63,000 = -39,646.90.$$

We can see that the firm will be better off by a present value of $381.19 from 1 day's sales under the proposed credit terms than it is under the current credit terms. This increase in present value is the net effect of the several items connected with the decision: the larger cash outflow for the purchase, the larger amount of sales, the change in the timing of the receipt of cash for the sale, and the receipt of only 98% of the sales price because of the discount. Thus, when considering the net present value of the full set of cash flows connected with this issue, the decision is to offer the discount credit terms to achieve the increase in sales.

Again stopping to get our bearings, we have seen that the capital budgeting framework can be expanded to include the full set of cash flows in a short-term finance problem. The method is to identify all of the cash inflows and outflows for each alternative being considered. Once the timing of the cash flows is identified, the net present value for each alternative can be determined on a common evaluation date. The present value of the current alternative is subtracted from that of the proposed alternative, and the proposed alternative is adopted if the difference is positive.

A More Complete Model

Some assumptions were made to keep the preceding presentation of the decision framework in its simplest form. Several of these assumptions can readily be incorporated into the framework, with only minor modifications. First, the cash outflows connected with the sale may not all occur on the day of sale. A more realistic situation would have multiple cash outflows occurring at different times. Present value techniques would be used to adjust all of the inflows and outflows to a common evaluation date.

Second, not all of the customers would pay within the discount period if discount terms were offered. In general, some proportion of the customers would pay in the discount period, while others would pay in the net period (or later). The proportion of the sales collected on the discount date would have to be estimated. This amount, less the discount, would then be converted to an equivalent present value amount on the evaluation date. There would also be a second inflow from those customers who would not pay in the discount period for which a present value would be calculated.

Third, it is likely that some of the sales will be bad debts and will never be collected. The existence of bad debts is most easily handled by reducing the collection in the net period by the estimated amount of the uncollected items.

Sales Growth

The preceding framework assumed that the sales for the firm are level, with no growth or seasonality. Under current conditions, sales are expected to be $100,000 per day. To be sure, the adoption of new credit terms changes the amount of the sales to $105,000 per day. However, this is an instantaneous change in the level of the sales. Still, no growth in future sales is recognized. Clearly, this is an unrealistic assumption. The question is, how will growth, or even seasonality, in sales affect the applicability of the framework? In Appendix B we show that the existence of sales growth (seasonality) presents no problem as long as the pattern of the growth is not affected by the decision.

As long as the pattern is not affected, the decision can be made, using the preceding framework, by analyzing all of the cash flows connected with the sales for 1 day (or another convenient time period). Under these conditions, the time horizon does not affect the decision and need not be considered. If, however, the decision alters the time pattern of the cash flows, such as a change in seasonality or in the rate of growth, the decision cannot be made correctly using the framework of the cash flows connected with only one period's sales. Rather, the decision will have to be analyzed over the entire time horizon connected with the problem.

APPLICABILITY OF THE FRAMEWORK. What kinds of decisions result in changing the level of sales but not the time pattern, and, consequently, can be evaluated with this type of framework? To address this question, it is useful to divide the decisions affecting the firm's cash flows into three categories: (1) those affecting neither the market share nor the total market demand, (2) those affecting the company's market share but not the total market demand, and (3) those affecting the total market demand.

NEITHER MARKET SHARE NOR MARKET DEMAND AFFECTED. Items that fall into the first category primarily affect the timing of the cash flows of the firm. An example is a change in the collection or disbursement system to improve the float. Such a change does not affect the growth pattern of a firm's cash flows. Thus, decisions in category 1 can be analyzed using the simplified decision framework.

ONLY MARKET SHARE AFFECTED. Decisions that affect the market share without having an impact on market demand do influence the *amount* of the cash flows in addition to the *timing* of those flows. For example, a decision for a hardware store to inventory a full range of sizes of screws would likely result in an increase in sales. However, any such increase would be at the expense of competing hardware stores' sales rather than due to an increase in the total number of screws purchased by consumers. Once the hardware store had achieved its new, higher market share, the pattern of growth in the sale of screws would not change because of this decision. Thus, the decision could be analyzed using the simple framework of the present value of the cash flow connected with one period's sales.

MARKET DEMAND AFFECTED. Decisions that affect the total market demand are likely to influence the growth pattern of sales. Take, for example, the credit decision of automobile manufacturers in the 1980s to offer below-market rates on loans for selected models. Although it may be argued that the first company to offer the low rates did so in an attempt to garner market share, the continued use of these programs, with the knowledge that competition would follow, had to be motivated by the idea of increasing total sales. This type of decision cannot be made using a simplified framework by analyzing the cash flow connected with one period's sales. This is a long-term, as well as a strategic, decision. It must include careful consideration of the time horizon, the impact on capital equipment, and other factors. This decision cannot be made by examining the cash flows over a very short time horizon.

The relevant question at this point is, into which of the three categories do short-term financial decisions fit? Most short-term financial decisions fit into category 1 or 2 and can be evaluated using the framework previously presented. Decisions concerning cash management (such as collection, concentration, or disbursement systems), marketable securities, short-term loans, or accounts payable generally fit into category 1: the predominant effect is on the timing of the cash flows.

Inventory decisions would likely be either in category 1 or category 2. If these decisions affect the sales of the firm at all, they do so by attracting customers from, or driving them to, competitors, that is, by affecting market share. It is unlikely that inventory decisions would have an impact on total demand unless the firm is in a monopoly position.

Credit decisions, to the extent that they have an impact on sales, may affect either market share or total market demand. Many credit decisions are largely marketing tools used to differentiate the service offered from that of competitors. In these cases, the decision could be evaluated using the preceding framework on the cash flow from one period's sales. However, in some instances, the credit decision may have an impact on total market demand. This is actually a strategic decision involving the growth path of the firm, and must be evaluated as such.

Integrated Short-term Financial Decisions

INTERRELATIONSHIP OF SHORT-TERM FINANCIAL DECISIONS. The policies affecting short-term assets and liabilities result in a mixture of separate and interrelated decisions. Some of the decisions affect only the timing of the cash flows for one part of the overall operating cycle. For example, a decision to change from paying sales commissions at the end of a biweekly payroll period to paying them at the end of the month only affects the timing of the cash flow connected with the payment to the salespeople. There is unlikely to be any impact on any other part of the operating cash flows.

Other decisions affect the amount and timing of the cash flows of several elements on the timeline. For example, a liberalization in credit terms to increase sales would increase the collection period, the amount of accounts receivable, and the amount of cash flow from sales. However, an increase in the volume of sales necessitates stocking a larger amount of inventory.

The greater volume of sales causes an increase in the *amount* of the cash flow payment for the inventory, although the *timing* of the cash flows for the inventory may not change (unless there is a simultaneous change in inventory policy). To assess correctly the impact of the credit policy decision on the value of the firm, the interrelationships of the timing, amount, and uncertainty of all of the cash flows connected with the decision have to be considered.

INTERRELATIONSHIPS IN THE MODEL. Let us return to the case of Floppi and incorporate the inventory elements in the timeline. Assume that the inventory policies of Floppi are such that the goods are produced an average of 30 days prior to sale and that payment for the materials and labor occurs 30 days after production. Thus, the payment is made on the day of the sale (see Figure 2.7). We know that the firm has an average of $100,000 per day in sales and that the cost of goods sold is 60% of the selling price. The firm has a total of 30 days × $60,000 = $1,800,000 in inventory for sales under current credit terms. If the

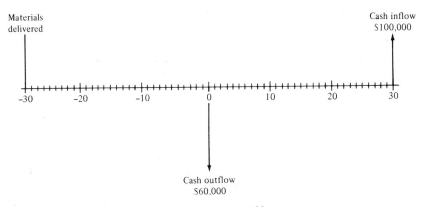

Current credit terms: net 30

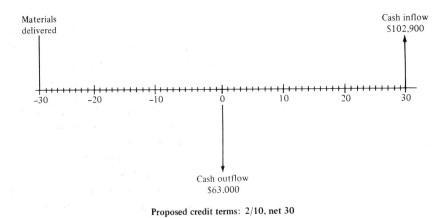

Proposed credit terms: 2/10, net 30

Figure 2.7 Cash Flow Timeline Including Inventory Policy.

firm adopts the proposed terms of 2/10, net 30, it will now carry an inventory value of $63,000 for each day's sales. If the inventory policy is not changed (the firm continues to carry an average inventory to cover 30 days' worth of sales), the inventory will be $1,890,000. Also, as the amount of the production increases, the amount of supplier credit in the form of accounts payable and deferred wage payments in the form of accrued expenses increases. Clearly, the impact of the increase in inventory and accounts payable must be included in the analysis if the correct decision is to be made.

Fortunately, these interrelated activities are directly incorporated by the use of the cash flow timeline approach. The increase in inventory is captured by an increase in the cash outflow to $63,000 from $60,000 under the current credit terms. The impact of the accounts payable and accrued expenses is captured by deferral of the cash outflow for 30 days from the date of the order.

The interrelationships are easily and properly considered by using the cash flow timeline approach to short-term financial decisions. The only requirement is that all of the cash flows connected with the problem being addressed are arrayed on the timeline. If this is done, full consideration is given to the amount and timing of all of the cash flows connected with the decision. This integrated treatment of the interrelationships between the various areas of the firm reduces the possibility that a suboptimal decision will be made.

Data Requirements to Use the Decision Framework

TYPES OF DATA REQUIRED. In order to apply the decision framework presented in this chapter, management must be able to identify all of the cash flows connected with the alternative policies being considered and to estimate their amount and timing. Although these data requirements may seem severe, they are the same as those needed if management attempts to approach each of the elements in the various policy decisions in a separate rather than an integrated manner.

FORM OF THE DATA. All of the data needed for the application of the decision framework are in the form of cash flows. The form of the data requirements is the same for all types of decisions in all areas of the firm. A major problem encountered in many piecemeal approaches to short-term financial management problems is the differences in the form of the data required for the analysis. Accounting data are often used to try to identify the costs and/or benefits from a change in policy. Frequently there is a question of whether full or incremental costs should be used to determine the "investment" required by the change in the policy. These approaches raise unnecessary questions concerning the nature of the accounting data, such as these: Should the accounting system provide full costs or direct costs? Are costs symmetrical for both increases and decreases in assets?

An example of this latter problem can be encountered when examining a policy change that causes a change in the level of accounts receivable. For an increase in accounts receivable, it is easy to see that the incremental investment is the variable cost of producing, selling, and delivering the product. However, since a decrease in the level of accounts receivable frees up funds equal to the amount of the decrease, is the decrease in investment only the variable costs, or is it the full amount of the accounts receivable? Problems such as these can be avoided by concentrating on the actual timing and amount of the cash flows that are connected with the policy changes.

SOURCE OF THE DATA. The source of the data for application of this decision framework is the cash management information system of the firm. This includes historical records of actual cash receipts and disbursements, as well as information from the cash forecasting system. Institutional arrangements are considered in estimating cash flows connected with the short-term financial policies being analyzed.

For example, the process for estimating the cash flows connected with the payment of suppliers for materials purchased is a function of the purchasing process, the accounts payable policies and processing system, and the cash disbursement system. Estimation of the cash flows connected with a change in the credit policies is a function of estimates of the credit elasticity of the customers, the payment mechanism used, the collection effort, and the adequacy of the cash forecasting system.

There are differing degrees of uncertainty and of synchronization connected with the cash flows in short-term financial decisions. This causes the financial manager to focus also on the liquidity of the firm.

The Aggregate Cash Flow Timeline
and Liquidity

In our discussions so far, we have ignored the impact of the policies on the liquidity of the firm. Our focus has been on the impact of the policies on the timing and/or amount of the cash flows on the timeline. We have not addressed the question of how gaps in these cash flows are financed. The need for liquidity in the firm can be thought of as the bridge over the gap between cash outflows and inflows.

For the sequence of cash flows illustrated in Figure 2.7, the gap in financing occurs because payment for the goods is made approximately at the time of the sale, while the firm has to wait 30 days to collect the payment from its customers. This gap in the timing of the cash flows requires the firm to find alternative ways of financing its operations until the cash inflows are received. This can be done either by maintaining a liquidity reserve in the form of marketable securities or by maintaining a credit rating sufficient to allow the firm to borrow the necessary funds from a bank or other financial institution.

Changes in policies that affect the timing, amount, or predictability of the cash flows have an impact on the liquidity of the firm. The magnitude of the impact depends upon the cash collection and disbursement systems, the balance reporting services available to the firm, the information system for cash flow monitoring, and the forecasting system. Management may react to these cash flow impacts in different ways. It may adjust the marketable securities portfolio of the firm. It may try to adjust the timing of the cash flows. It may try to improve the forecasting system to reduce the uncertainty in the cash flow estimates. It may strive to improve its banking relationships to make credit readily available. All of these approaches have an impact on the liquidity needs of the firm. The issues of the measurement and management of liquidity are covered in Chapter 13.

The Choice of an Opportunity
_____ Cost Rate _____

In our discussion of the decision framework, we have simply specified a rate to be used in the present value calculations without paying much attention to why the particular rate was chosen. There are two factors to consider in choosing the appropriate opportunity cost rate: (1) the riskiness of the cash flows and (2) the maturity of the alternative use of the funds.

RISK. We have seen that most financial decisions involve an element of risk. The riskiness of the cash flows involved in the particular decision should be estimated, and a rate that adequately reflects the risk should be used in the analysis. For some decisions, such as a change in the credit terms across all of the products of the firm, the cash flows of the entire firm are altered. In this case, the appropriate risk-adjusted rate is the overall, or average, cost of capital for the firm. In other decisions, such as a decision to alter the disbursement process of the firm, which affects only the disbursement float, the degree of risk in the decision is considerably less than that of the average project in the firm. In this case, a rate lower than the overall cost of capital is appropriate because of the lower degree of risk. A similar line of reasoning applies to proposals that have a greater degree of risk than the average project in the firm. Essentially, the risk adjustment process is the same as that employed for capital budgeting decisions and, unfortunately, is fraught with the same difficult measurement problems.

MATURITY. The second factor by which the appropriate opportunity cost rate should be judged is the maturity of the alternative use of the funds. The opportunity cost should be based on the cost of funds for a maturity that most closely matches the maturity of the alternative use for the funds. If the decision being considered affects only the short-term funds, such as marketable securities or the amount of the line of credit used, a short-term risk-adjusted rate is appropriate. However, suppose a firm changes its collection system, which allows it permanently to free up funds through faster collection. Would these funds be invested in short-term securities or would they likely be invested in plant and equipment, new products, or higher levels of inventory to support expanded sales? If the investment of funds would be permanent, an opportunity cost rate determined from the cost of long-term funds is appropriate.

Summary

In this chapter, we reviewed the basic approach to financial asset valuation: a risk-adjusted present value of cash flows. We examined risk adjustment through the use of the CAPM, in which only undiversifiable risk affects the risk premium on a risky asset. We also investigated the market imperfections that raise some questions about the direct application of the CAPM to short-term finance problems. The net present value capital budgeting decision process was expanded to provide a decision framework for short-term finance problems that is consistent with our objective of maximizing shareholders' value. The basic framework consists of estimating cash flows for a relatively short time period, such as a day or a month, and determining the net present value of the alternatives over this time period. This simple framework can be used to find the correct answer to many short-term finance problems. In the remaining chapters, we address the market imperfections, the institutional considerations, and the estimation of the cash flow necessary to use this decision framework to solve specific short-term finance problems.

Discussion Questions

1. Why does money have a time value? What impact does this time value have on financial valuation?
2. Contrast the use of future and present values to compensate for the time value of money.
3. Why is the issue of whether we use a simple interest calculation or a compound value calculation less important for short-term financial decisions than for long-term decisions, such as capital budgeting?
4. Why should a decision that increases the net present value of a firm increase shareholder wealth?
5. If people are supposed to be risk averse, how do you explain the major success that states have had in raising money through lotteries?
6. Would it be inconsistent for a person to engage in parimutual betting and also buy insurance?
7. Contrast the difference in the systematic and unsystematic risk for New England Airlines, which operates only in the New England area, and Trans National Airlines, which has extensive transcontinental and international flights.
8. Would prearranged lines of credit not be observed if perfect capital markets really existed? Why or why not?

9. How would the use of a cash flow timeline allow you to incorporate the impact on accounts receivable of a decision to alter inventory policy?

10. What cash flows would be affected by a decision to accept a riskier class of customer for credit sales, which are expected to increase sales by about 10–15%, by a firm that has 35% excess capacity?

11. How would your response to Question 10 differ if the firm had only 5% excess capacity?

12. Could either or both of the decisions in Questions 10 and 11 be analyzed using the cash flow timeline approach? What differences might there be in the analysis?

—————————————— **Problems** ——————————————

1. Calculate the value at the end of 5 years of $10,000 deposited into an IRA account that pays 9% compounded annually.

2. How would the answer to Question 1 differ if the interest was compounded semiannually?

3. What is the present value of $15,000 received 2 years from now if the opportunity cost is 12%?

4. Graph the present value of the amount in Problem 3 as the interest rate changes from 5% to 30%.

5. A firm expected to receive $100,000 ninety days from now. If the opportunity cost is 9%, how much of a difference is there in the calculated present value if the manager uses the compounded value formulation instead of the simple interest formulation?

6. Security A has a beta of 1.2, while security B has a beta of 0.65. How much of a return should be expected on each security if the risk-free rate of return is 8% and the expected return on the market portfolio is 14%?

7. **a.** Assume that the betas of the securities in Problem 6 are the same, but now the risk-free rate is 10% and the expected market return is 16%. What are the expected rates of return on each security?

   b. What are the expected rates of return if the risk free rate is 10% and the expected market return is now 18%?

   c. What is the reason for the differences in your answers to parts (a) and (b)?

   d. For what reasons might the different conditions in parts (a) and (b) occur?

8. Your electric bill contains a gross amount of $76.24 and a net amount of of $75.34. You are to pay the net amount if the bill is paid by the 10th of the month. Sketch the cash flows connected with the alternatives of paying by the 10th or waiting until you get your paycheck on the 15th of the month. If the opportunity cost to you is 14%, which is preferred? Would your answer change if you waited until you received your paycheck on the 30th before paying the bill?

9. Johnson Supply is a food distribution company. Its current policy is to maintain, on average, a 14-day supply of a particular commodity in inventory. Under the current purchase terms, payment is due 10 days after the invoice date. Johnson currently purchases $150,000 every 2 weeks and sells it with a markup of 33% on 10-day terms. The supplier has offered 30 days' credit to customers who purchase only once per month. Sketch the cash flow timelines for the alternative decisions.

10. Quick Collect and We'll Wait are two firms operating in the same industry. Both sell on credit terms of net 30 days, but they have different collection experiences. Quick Collect customers pay, on average, on the 28th day. We'll Wait customers, on the other hand, pay, on average, on the 65th day. Both firms have an opportunity cost of 12% and are thinking of instituting new credit terms of 2/10, net 30. Sketch the cash flow timelines for the two firms and decide which, if either, should offer the new credit terms.

11. The Rand Printing Company does custom printing. They currently maintain an inventory of 20 days of paper, which they purchase on terms of net 30 days. They invoice their customers when the job is finished on terms of net 15 days. The customers pay, on average, on the 20th day. The manager is considering reducing the inventory to half of its current level and changing the billing terms to net 30 days. He anticipates that there will be no effect on the level of sales. Sketch the cash flow timelines associated with these two alternatives.

Selected Readings

COHN, RICHARD A., and JOHN J. PRINGLE, "Steps Toward an Integration of Corporate Financial Theory" in *Readings on the Management of Working Capital*, 2nd ed., Keith V. Smith (ed.)., St. Paul, Minn.: West, 1980, pp. 35–42.

COPELAND, T. E., and J. F. WESTON, *Financial Theory and Corporate Policy*, 2nd ed., Reading, Mass.: Addison-Wesley, 1983.

IBBOTSON, R. G., and R. A. SINQUEFIELD, *Stocks, Bonds, Bills and Inflation: The Past and Future*, Charlottesville, Va.: Financial Analysts Foundation, 1982.

LEWELLEN, WILBUR G., JOHN MCCONNELL, and JOHNATHON SCOTT, "Capital Market Influences on Trade Credit," *Journal of Financial Research*, (Fall 1980), pp. 105–113.

LINTNER, J., "The Valuation of Risk Assets and the Selection of Risky Investments in Stock Portfolios and Capital Budgets," *Review of Economics and Statistics* (February 1965), pp. 13–37.

MOSSIN, JAN, "Equilibrium in a Capital Asset Market," *Econometrica* (October 1966), pp. 768–783.

MOSSIN, JAN, "Security Pricing and Investment Criteria in Competitive Markets," *American Economic Review* (December 1969), pp. 749–756.

SARTORIS, WILLIAM L., and NED C. HILL, "Evaluating Credit Policy Alternatives: A Present Value Framework," *Journal of Financial Research* (Spring 1981), pp. 81–89.

SARTORIS, WILLIAM L., and NED C. HILL, "A Generalized Cash Flow Approach to Short-Term Financial Decisions," *Journal of Finance* (May 1983), pp. 349–360.

SHARPE, W. F., "Capital Asset Prices: A Theory of Market Equilibrium Under Conditions of Risk," *Journal of Finance* (September 1964), pp. 425–442.

SHARPE, W. F., *Investments*, Englewood Cliffs, N.J.: Prentice-Hall, 1981.

TUTTLE, DONALD L., and ROBERT H. LITZENBERGER, "Leverage, Diversification, and Capital Market Effects on a Risk-Adjusted Capital Budgeting Framework," *Journal of Finance* (June 1968), pp. 427–444.

Appendix A:
Present Value Calculation
Approximations

Compounded Value Calculation

The present value formulation used in financial valuation models relies on the concept of compound value, that is, interest earned during one time period is assumed to earn interest during succeeding time periods. To find the present value of any future amount using this compound value approach, we divide by 1 plus the interest rate raised to the power representing the number of periods in the future during which the cash flow occurs. This is represented symbolically as follows:

$$PV = \frac{FV_t}{(1 + r)^t}.$$

Simple Interest Calculation

Present value can also be calculated using simple interest, where compounding is ignored. In a simple interest calculation it is assumed that the interest is earned for the entire time horizon with no compounding for interim time periods. Simple interest present value is calculated by dividing the future cash flow by 1 plus the product of the interest rate and the number of periods. This is represented symbolically as follows:

$$PV = \frac{FV_t}{(1 + r \times t)}.$$

Discount Interest Calculation

There is one other approximation that is sometimes used in present value calculations: a discount interest approach. In this approach, the interest for the entire time horizon is calculated on a simple interest basis, and this interest is subtracted from the future amount to determine the present value. This is represented symbolically as follows:

$$PV = FV_t(1 - r \times t).$$

Theoretically, the correct procedure is to use the calculation approach that most accurately represents the situation. If the present value is desired for a cash flow occurring 1 year in the future when the interest is actually compounded quarterly, the correct calculation is to set r equal to the quarterly interest rate and compound for four quarters—divide by 1 plus r raised to the fourth power. However, if interest is paid at the end of the year and is not compounded, the simple interest calculation is appropriate. Finally, if the item is a discount financial instrument, such as a T-bill, where the face value is paid at maturity and the price is a discount from the maturity value, the discount approach is appropriate to find the present value. To determine the correct calculation procedure, the decision maker needs to know which of the present value calculation approaches most closely represents the situation. However, this may present a problem in comparing alternatives that may involve different interest assumptions.

For many of the issues in short-term finance, there is a practical solution to this problem. Because of the short time periods and the relatively small interest rate per period, say, a day or a month, all three of these calculation procedures give similar results. A numerical example will help illustrate the closeness of the approximations.

The treasurer of Slo-Pay is comparing the present value of paying a bill today, the 10th day after the invoice date, and taking the 2% discount offered with the alternative of paying the net price 20 days from now. The invoice amount is for $2,500 and the current interest rate is 9% per year, which is 0.02466% per day.

For the calculation with the compounded value approach we have

$$PV = \frac{2,500}{(1 + .0002466)^{50}} = \frac{2,500}{(1.012404)} = 2,469.37.$$

If the calculation is made using the simple interest approach, we have

$$PV = \frac{2,500}{(1 + .0002466 \times 50)} = \frac{2,500}{(1.012329)} = 2,469.55.$$

Finally, if we use the discount approach, we have

$$PV = 2,500(1 - .0002466 \times 50) = 2,469.18.$$

Comparison of Procedures

Each of the calculation procedures has its own virtues and drawbacks. The compounded value formulation is conceptually the correct approach. In most short-term finance decisions the option of overnight investment, and thus daily compounding, is almost always available. However, the compounded value approach almost always necessitates the use of a calculator with an exponential or power function key to keep the calculation from becoming onerous. The other two procedures can readily be performed using a four-function calculator. The simple interest formulation retains the form of dividing by 1 plus the interest rate that is familiar to present value calculations.

The remaining question is, how much of a difference does it make if one of the simpler procedures is used instead of the compounded value formulation? If we assume that the compounded value formulation is correct for the preceding example, using either the simple interest or discount approach yields an error of approximately 0.0073%. While the amount of the error varies with the interest rate and the number of time periods, it is doubtful that the cash flow estimates being discounted have an accuracy greater than 99.9927%. For short-term finance issues, we can adopt the calculation procedure that is easiest to use with the assurance that any errors introduced are minimal. We prefer to use the simple interest calculation procedure because of its simplicity of calculation and its retention of the normal present value form.

Appendix B:
A Cash Flow Timeline Present Value
Framework

The Basic Model

Assume that we have a one-product firm with a production function containing only variable costs C_p, expressed as a percentage of the sales, S_t per day. The payment for production is a cash flow of C_pS_t on day t_p. The firm collects $(1 - d)qS_t$ on day t_d from customers who take the cash discount, where d is the discount and q is the fraction of the sales paid with a discount. The final cash flow received on day t_c is $(1 - q)S_t$.

Assume further that the cash flows are certain, so that we can discount the cash flows at the risk-free rate of r. We arbitrarily choose a day as the unit of analysis and anchor the time line with zero on the day that the order for materials is placed. The firm has a planning horizon of N days.

The Net Present Value for Current Policies
The net present value on day t for that day's sales is

$$NPV_t = \frac{-C_pS_t}{(1 + r)^{t_p}} + \frac{(1 - d)qS_t}{(1 + r)^{t_d}} + \frac{(1 - q)S_t}{(1 + r)^{t_c}}.$$

The net present value of the operations over the entire planning horizon is the present value sum of the series of each day's present values from $t = 0$ to $t = N$.

$$NPV_N = \left[\frac{-C_pS_t}{(1 + r)^{t_p}} + \frac{(1 - d)qS_t}{(1 + r)^{t_d}} + \frac{(1 - q)S_t}{(1 + r)^{t_c}} \right] \frac{1}{(1 + r)^t}.$$

The Net Present Value of Proposed Policies

The firm is considering an alternative policy. With a "prime" indicating an element under the proposed policy, the day t value of the cash flows under the proposed policy is

$$NPV_t' = \left[\frac{-C_p'S_t'}{(1 + r)^{tp'}} + \frac{(1 - d')q'S_t'}{(1 + r)^{td'}} + \frac{(1 - q')S_t'}{(1 + r)^{tc'}} \right].$$

The net present value of the cash flows under the new policy over the entire planning horizon is

$$NPV_N' = \left[\frac{-C_p'S_t'}{(1 + r)^{tp'}} + \frac{(1 - d')q'S_t'}{(1 + r)^{td'}} + \frac{(1 - q')S_t'}{(1 + r)^{tc'}} \right] \frac{1}{(1 + r)^t}.$$

The Decision Criterion

The decision criterion for the manager of the firm to choose in deciding between the alternative policies must be consistent with the objective of maximizing the value of the firm for the shareholders. The new policy should be adopted only if it increases the present value of the firm. Our decision criterion is then to adopt the new policy if $NPV_N' - NPV_N \geq 0$.

This difference in net present values can be found by subtracting the net present value of the old policy from the net present value of the new policy as follows:

$$NPV_N' - NPV_N = \left[\frac{-C_p'S_t'}{(1 + r)^{tp'}} + \frac{(1 - d')q'S_t'}{(1 + r)^{td'}} + \frac{(1 - q')S_t'}{(1 + r)^{tc'}} \right] \frac{1}{(1 + r)^t}$$

$$- \left[\frac{-C_pS_t}{(1 + r)^{tp}} + \frac{(1 - d)qS_t}{(1 + r)^{td}} + \frac{(1 - q)S_t}{(1 + r)^{tc}} \right] \frac{1}{(1 + r)^t}.$$

Assume that sales are constant over the planning horizon under each policy, that is, $S_t = S$ and $S_t' = S'$. Since none of the terms in brackets vary with t, the expression can be simplified by factoring those terms outside of the summation sign:

$$NPV_N' - NPV_N = \left(\left[\frac{-C_p'S_t'}{(1 + r)^{tp'}} + \frac{(1 - d')q'S_t'}{(1 + r)^{td'}} + \frac{(1 - q')S_t'}{(1 + r)^{tc'}} \right] \right.$$

$$\left. - \left[\frac{-C_pS_t}{(1 + r)^{tp}} + \frac{(1 - d)qS_t}{(1 + r)^{td}} + \frac{(1 - q)S_t}{(1 + r)^{tc}} \right] \right) \frac{1}{(1 + r)^t}.$$

Effect of Planning Horizon

In the preceding expression, the summation term is not affected by the proposed policy and is positive for all policies. Thus, the sign of the present value difference between the policies is independent of the planning horizon.

The length of the time period over which the summation is performed is a function of the planning horizon, but this only affects the total amount of the difference in present values and not the sign. Thus, the decision can be made without concern about the length of the planning horizon.

The sign of the terms in parentheses is what determines whether the difference in net present values is positive or negative and, therefore, which policy is preferred. The net sum of the terms in parentheses is the difference in the present value of 1 day's sales under the two policies. The correct decision can be made unambiguously by examining the net present value of the cash flows from only 1 day's production–sales cycle.

Nonconstant Sales

In the previous section, we made the restrictive assumptions that sales were level over the planning horizon and that the change in policies simply altered the amount of the sales. We now examine the changes that are necessary in the model when we apply it to an environment with nonconstant sales. For simplicity we refer to sales growth, while recognizing that this growth necessarily causes changes in other cash flows connected with those sales. If we have carefully constructed the cash flow timeline, we can be confident that all of the relevant cash flows are incorporated.

Consider the case where sales are expected to grow along some generalized growth path, $F(t)$, over time. The sales in any time period t would be $S_0F(t)$, where S_0 represents the sales at $t = 0$. If sales grow at a constant rate per period (exponential growth), $F(t) = (1 + g)^t$, where g represents the percentage growth per period. If sales grow by a constant dollar amount each period, $F(t) = t(K)$, where K is the constant dollar increase per period. A product life cycle growth pattern can be incorporated by having a different growth rate for each period, with some of the growth rates possibly being negative, that is, $F(t) = (1 + g_1)(1 + g_2)\ldots(1 + g_N)$. It should be apparent that this formulation is quite general and could be used to represent virtually any growing or declining pattern of sales, and consequently, of overall operations of the firm.

Present Value of 1 Day's Sales

We can now express the present value of the cash flows from 1 day's sales using our generalized sales pattern and the symbols of our earlier model. To simplify the presentation, we assume that all payments are made on the net payment day and we anchor the model on the day the cash flow payment is made for the cost of the materials. The present value of 1 day's sales is

$$NPV_t = \left(-C_p + \frac{1}{(1 + r)^{tc}}\right)S_0F(t).$$

The net present value over the total planning horizon is the present value sum of the present values of the individual day's activities, or

$$NPV_N = \left[\left(-C_p + \frac{1}{(1 + r)^{tc}}\right)S_0 F(t)\right]\frac{1}{(1 + r)^t}.$$

We again use the prime to signify the terms that change under the proposed policy. The net present value for the proposed policy over the entire planning horizon is

$$NPV_N' = \left[\left(-C_p' + \frac{1}{(1 + r)^{tc'}}\right)S_0' F'(t)\right]\frac{1}{(1 + r)^t}.$$

Decision Criterion

The decision criterion is to accept the new policies if the change in net present value is greater than zero. This is expressed as accept the new policies if

$$NPV_N' - NPV_N = \left[\left(-C_p' + \frac{1}{(1 + r)^{tc'}}\right)S_0' F'(t)\right]\frac{1}{(1 + r)^t}$$
$$-\left[\left(-C_p + \frac{1}{(1 + r)^{tc}}\right)S_0 F(t)\right]\frac{1}{(1 + r)^t} > 0.$$

We can see that if $F'(t) = F(t)$, this can be further simplified as follows:

$$NPV_N' - NPV_N = \left(\left[\left(-C_p' + \frac{1}{(1 + r)^{tc'}}\right)S_0'\right]\right.$$
$$\left.-\left[\left(-C_p + \frac{1}{(1 + r)^{tc}}\right)S_0\right]\right)F(t)\frac{1}{(1 + r)^t} > 0.$$

The terms in parentheses represent the difference in present value for the cash flows connected with day 0's sales under the two policies. The sign of this term generally controls the sign of the entire present value difference. Thus we are back in the same position we were in with an assumption of level sales; we only need to examine the present value of the cash flows connected with one period's sales to make the correct decision. Even if sales are expected to grow over time along some general time path, the correct decision is made by evaluating only the present value of one period's cash flows, as long as the change in short-term financial policies does not affect the pattern of growth.

If the change in short-term financal policies does have an impact on the pattern of growth, that is, $F(t)'$ does not equal $F(t)$, the terms in parentheses cannot be separated from the respective growth term. Now the difference in present values is a function of the ways that the patterns of growth are altered and in general are a function of the planning horizon. Under these conditions, the decision is a strategic one and must be made by considering the long-run effects on the operations and the cash flows of the firm if suboptimal decisions are to be avoided.

Fixed Costs

If we allow for a more general cost structure that has both fixed and variable costs, certain changes in the decision model are necessary. We must now restrict the minimum time period for evaluation to the periodic cycle for the fixed costs; that is, if the fixed costs are paid on a monthly cycle, the minimum time period that must be examined is a month. Similar to the situation with growth, if the fixed costs are not changed by the change in policy, we unambiguously make the correct decision by examining the present value over one fixed cost cycle. If, however, the fixed costs are changed by the decision, we have a strategic decision and in general cannot be assured of making the correct decision unless we examine the cash flows over the life (planning horizon) of the decision.

Cash Management

3

The U.S. Banking System

Knowledge of the banking system is crucial to an understanding of short-term finance—especially cash management. Except for a relatively small amount of coin and currency, cash isn't found in firms; it exists only in banks. Banks store cash for firms. Banks also help firms collect, disburse, borrow, invest, and provide information about what to do with cash. In this chapter, we outline some of the important features of the U.S. banking system that pertain to short-term finance. We examine the Federal Reserve System as well as commercial banks.

U.S. Commercial Banks

A *commercial bank* is defined by law as a depository institution that takes deposits and makes business loans. There are other depository institutions besides commercial banks. Savings and loan associations and mutual savings banks also take deposits, but they are limited—more so than commercial banks—in the volume of commercial loans they can make. They were organized primarily to fund the residential housing market. Credit unions take deposits and make loans but are limited to doing business with credit union members. Because of such limitations, corporations deal chiefly with commercial banks for their business needs. In the remainder of this book, the term *bank* will refer to a commercial bank.

Functions of Commercial Banks

Banks provide short-term financial services to firms in several areas: (1) they serve as a depository for the firm's cash; (2) they help firms collect,

61

concentrate, and disburse cash; (3) they provide short-term credit; (4) they offer several kinds of short-term investments; (5) they serve as a fiduciary; and (6) they provide consulting services in cash management and other fields. The following sections discuss these functions in more detail.

Depository Function

Banks offer several types of depository accounts. There are two basic types of depository accounts: time and demand. For *time deposits*, the cash in the account receives interest and must be held in a bank for a specified time period. *Demand deposits* may be withdrawn at any time by the account holder or other party on presentation of a valid draft or check drawn on the account.

TIME DEPOSITS. The length of time a time deposit must be held to receive a given interest rate is specified by the policies of each depository institution. If cash is withdrawn before the period of time ends, an interest penalty is usually charged. There are several types of time deposits. The most commonly known type is a savings deposit (or passbook savings). Although banks do not enforce it, there is a provision that deposit holders must notify the bank 30 days in advance of a pending withdrawal. Corporations do not, of course, generally keep cash in savings accounts because the rate paid is significantly lower than the rate for other alternatives.

Retail certificates of deposit (CDs) are bought primarily by individuals or smaller corporations. There is no secondary market for them—that is, the holder cannot sell the CD to another party. Jumbo CDs are retail CDs of $100,000 or more.

Negotiable certificates of deposit (NCDs or just CDs) are generally sold in million dollar blocks (some are available in smaller blocks) to corporations, money market funds, and other large investors. NCDs from large banks are actively bought and sold in the secondary market after they are issued. Because of their higher interest and greater marketability, negotiable CDs are a popular form of deposit for firms. Chapter 10 discusses CDs further.

DEMAND DEPOSITS. Demand deposits are transaction (checking) accounts. Cash may be removed from the account and paid to a third party "on demand" by presenting a check (electronic or paper) or by requesting a wire transfer. Current law prohibits banks from paying corporations interest on demand deposits. Hence, one of the primary objectives of cash management is to reduce the amount of cash kept in demand deposits and move it as quickly as possible into accounts or investments that earn interest.

If these accounts do not earn interest, why do firms keep cash in demand deposits at all? Balances in demand deposits arise from two possible sources.

1. Transaction Balances. Cash flows in firms are usually not easy to predict. For example, a large, unexpected deposit may be made into a collection bank account at the end of the day—too late for the cash manager to invest the amount in an interest-bearing security or time deposit. Similarly, on the disbursement side, the cash manager may deposit in the payroll account

enough cash to cover the week's payroll (not very good cash management practice, we might add). Yet employees may not all cash their checks on the first day. Demand deposit balances exist until all checks are cashed.

2. **Compensating Balances.** Banks frequently specify that credit lines and other services to the firm are to be compensated by holding demand deposit balances. Though by law (Banking Act of 1933) demand deposits may not pay interest, banks may give "earnings credits" based on the level of balances held. Chapter 4 discusses bank compensation in more detail.

MIXED ACCOUNTS. Within the past decade, changes in banking regulations have created accounts that provide the transaction features of demand deposits and the interest rate features of time deposits. The introduction of these accounts may portend the eventual lifting of interest rate prohibition on corporate demand deposits. For the time being, however, the accounts are aimed almost exclusively at consumers rather than corporations.

Negotiable orders of withdrawal (NOW accounts) were permitted at all depository institutions by the Banking Act of 1980 (although New England states experimented with them in the 1970s). These accounts are equivalent to checking accounts that pay interest. Only individuals, government entities, and nonprofit organizations may have them. With the passage of the 1982 Garn-St. Germain Act, the interest rate is unregulated and required minimum balances are left to each bank to decide. An unlimited number of withdrawals may be made. Corporations, however, may not hold such accounts.

Money market deposit accounts (MMDAs) were also created with the Garn-St. Germain Act. They are similar to NOW accounts, but only six withdrawals are permitted per month and only three of those may be checks. Although corporations are allowed to have these accounts, they have not become popular because of the restrictions on transactions.

Some observers think that Congress, in the spirit of continued deregulation, will eventually permit corporate interest-bearing demand deposit accounts. When that happens, many of the cash manager's tasks will change. We discuss the implications of this possibility later in the text.

EURODOLLAR DEPOSITS. U.S. dollars held offshore are called *Eurodollars* (even though they may not all be controlled in Europe). Banks offer various types of Eurodollar deposits through their offshore subsidiaries or affiliates. Internationally, there is a large demand for dollars to purchase oil and perform other transactions. As discussed further in Chapter 10, cash managers can loan money to participants in this market through either Eurodollar time deposits or Eurodollar CDs.

Collection, Concentration, and Disbursement Functions
Banks serve as clearing houses for checks. When a firm receives a check in payment for some good or service, the firm deposits the check in a bank. The bank gives the firm credit for the check and returns the check to the bank on which it was drawn. Banks also serve as initiating and receiving points for wires and automated clearing house transfers.

After cash has been collected in one bank, the cash balance generated is usually concentrated or pooled into a larger account at a centralized bank. Banks offer a number of services to assist firms in concentrating their cash.

On the outflow side, disbursement checks sent to vendors are drawn on banks. These processes are important enough to merit separate discussions (Chapters 6, 7, and 8).

Short-term Credit

Banks provide financing to corporations to help meet short-term cash needs. Since banks take in cash in the form of short-term deposits, they in turn lend cash primarily in the form of short-term loans.

A common vehicle for lending short-term cash is a credit line. A *credit line* is an agreement by the bank to provide up to a specified amount of cash to the firm over a specified period of time. Usually an agreement to provide a credit line lasts for 1 year and is renegotiated each year. Revolving credit lines, in contrast, last for more than 1 year. The firm often borrows, repays, and borrows again up to the credit limit. Chapter 12 discusses short-term borrowing in more detail.

Besides short-term lending, banks make longer-term loans. *Term loans* are loans that extend for several years and often require a regular repayment schedule. Mortgages are long-term loans secured by physical assets such as real property. Since this book deals primarily with short-term assets and liabilities, we will not treat credit that extends for more than a few years.

While credit lines often require no collateral, *acceptance financing* is a short-term loan (for example, 90 days) backed by accounts receivable. It is commonly found in financing foreign trade.

Banks often provide *letters of credit* in which they agree to give cash to a third party on behalf of the firm once certain conditions have been met. Such letters are used in import and export as well as some domestic transactions. We will treat letters of credit further in Chapter 19.

Investment

In addition to the interest-bearing deposits previously mentioned, commercial banks provide other opportunities for cash managers to invest short-term funds. They are major brokers for U.S. T-bills, notes, and bonds, government agency securities, and municipal notes and bonds. They also sell bank commercial paper and deal extensively in repurchase agreements (all of which are discussed in some detail in Chapter 10).

Fiduciary

Many banks are empowered to operate a trust department. We said previously that banks could not own stock. Actually, they can—but only on behalf of someone else through a trust department. A fiduciary acts on behalf of another party. Banks that provide trust services invest, manage, and distribute monies as requested in wills, trusts, estates, and retirement plans. Starting in 1984, banks were permitted to purchase brokerage firms to help them buy and sell stock and bonds more efficiently. The law states, however, that a bank can only own a discount brokerage firm—one that only performs transactions and does *not* give investment advice.

A trust department may be appointed to serve as a corporate trustee or overseer for a corporate bond or preferred stock issue. The bank monitors compliance with the indenture agreements, ensures that the corporation pays interest to the bondholders, and redeems bonds as required by the agreement. In addition, a bank may serve as a transfer agent to keep records of the sale and purchase of a corporation's stocks and bonds, or as a registrar to maintain lists of current stockholders and bondholders for the purpose of remitting dividend and interest payments.

Consulting Services

Large banks generally offer consulting services, especially in the area of cash management. Such services are used in designing optimal collection, disbursement, and concentration systems. In several later chapters, we discuss the specific role of banks in providing these services.

Customer Base

Commercial banks may be placed in three categories, depending on the kinds of customers they serve. Wholesale banks focus their attention primarily on serving corporate customers. Retail banks are directed more to consumer deposits and loans. Wholesale/retail banks have a more balanced mix of corporate and consumer customer bases. Very large wholesale banks that have a national customer base are often called *money center banks*—though exactly how large and how national has never been explicitly determined. Large wholesale banks that have a more regional focus are called—not surprisingly—*major regional banks*.

Banking Regulation

Since banks deal with the one commodity upon which so much of our society is based—money—governments have found it necessary to establish extensive regulations for the industry. In this section we outline the bank regulatory environment, touching primarily on those regulations that have an impact on short-term finance. Table 3.1 summarizes major banking regulations that directly or indirectly affect short-term finance.

DUAL BANKING. In a system unique to the United States, there are two governmental units that may issue commercial bank charters: the state governments and the federal government. The distinctions between the two types of banks used to be numerous. But in the current environment, these differences are generally immaterial to the corporate banking customer. The agencies that regulate the two types are essentially the same.

OFFICE OF THE COMPTROLLER OF THE CURRENCY (OCC). The OCC issues charters to national banks and examines federally chartered banks on a regular

Table 3.1 Major Commercial Bank Regulations

Regulation	Major Provisions	Implications for Cash Management
McFadden Act (1927)	Prohibits banks from accepting deposits across state lines. Establishes the state as the foremost party in determining geographical restrictions.	Creates problems in designing collection and concentration systems.
Glass-Steagall Act (1933)	Prohibits banks from entering the securities market and other businesses. Prohibits securities firms from engaging in banklike activities, such as deposit gathering. Requires the Fed to impose interest rate ceilings on all types of accounts and prohibits the payment of interest on demand deposits.	May prevent banks from offering services that would help solve short-term finance problems. Examples are investment and security services, computer information packages, etc. Securities firms have been able to get around this restriction by offering money market mutual funds. A big problem for cash managers who must move cash from non- (or low) interest-bearing accounts to investments or accounts that earn interest at market rates.
Douglas Amendment (1956)	Permits banks to merge across state lines if both states agree. Prohibits bank holding companies from acquiring banks across state lines.	Led to regional banking pacts starting in 1985. Simplifies collection systems. Restricts bank growth and, hence, potential services.

Depository Institutions Deregulation and Monetary Control Act (DIDMCA) (1980)	Permits all depository institutions to offer NOW accounts.	Opens the door to possible interest on demand deposits.
	Requires the Fed to price previously free services.	Raises banking costs.
	Requires the Fed to eliminate or price the Fed float (see Chapter 7).	Increases banking costs and makes disbursement services more complex and costly
	Calls for the elimination of interest rate ceilings (Regulation Q) that banks pay on various depository accounts. The phaseout period ended in 1986.	Gives better yield on some deposits but raises banking costs.
	Requires all depository institutions to keep reserve deposits at the Fed. Formerly, only Fed member institutions had to maintain reserves. Now state banks, thrift institutions, and credit unions must do the same.	Makes banking more uniform across state and federally chartered banks (as well as credit unions and thrift institutions.
	Opens Fed services to all financial institutions.	Makes cash movement simpler since more institutions are involved. May have increased banking costs.
Garn-St. Germain Act (1982)	Creates money market deposit and Super NOW accounts; both accounts lack interest rate ceilings.	Gives added interest on limited number of accounts. Increases banking costs.
	Permits banks to lend up to 15% of their capital and surplus (net equity) to any one customer (the former limit was 10%).	Adds flexibility to short-term lending decisions. May increase bank risk, however.

basis. Nationally chartered banks have the words *national* or *national associ-ation (N.A.)* associated with the name of the bank.

FEDERAL RESERVE SYSTEM (THE FED). The Fed carries out policies of the OCC and Congress through a series of bank regulations. Most of these reg-ulations apply to all banks, whether state or federally chartered. As we dis-cuss later in this chapter, the Fed also sets policies that attempt to influence the nation's money supply and plays a key role in the payment system. Fed employees regularly examine state chartered banks that hold Fed membership.

FEDERAL DEPOSIT INSURANCE CORPORATION (FDIC). Created in response to the failure of nearly 10,000 banks in the depression of the 1930s, the FDIC is primarily concerned with protecting depositors from loss. It operates an insur-ance fund supported by premiums charged to participating banks. Depositors are insured up to $100,000 per depositor (*not* per account) per institution in all commercial banks having FDIC insurance. All federally chartered banks must carry FDIC insurance, and most states require state chartered banks to do so as well.

A similar federal insurance program insures other depository institutions. The Federal Savings and Loan Insurance Corporation (FSLIC) insures savings and loan associations. The savings and loan panics in Ohio and Maryland in 1985 occurred in state chartered savings and loan associations that lacked federal insurance. Both states subsequently required state banks to obtain such insurance.

FDIC examiners regularly examine state banks that have FDIC insurance but are not Fed members. The FDIC also plays an important role in determining the course of action in the event of a bank failure. It is usually appointed the receiver and is charged with finding a merger partner or liquidating the bank's remaining assets.

STATE BANKING REGULATION. Each state is independent in determining bank chartering criteria. Besides regulating state chartered banks, each state deter-mines how all banks (state or national) may branch within state boundaries. Non-Fed, uninsured banks (of which there are only some 600 nationwide) are examined by state banking commissions.

SECURITIES AND EXCHANGE COMMISSION (SEC). The SEC is charged with ensuring that investors receive adequate investment information. The SEC pri-marily regulates bank holding companies that have more than 500 shareholders and issue securities to the public.

JUSTICE DEPARTMENT. The Justice Department enters the banking arena when antitrust issues arise. It is also involved in violations of a wide variety of federal government statutes.

With all of these agencies regulating commercial banks, it is not surpris-ing that change in industry practices is slow and constraints on innovation numerous. It is doubtful that any other industry in the United States has a larger regulatory burden than the banking industry. As the reader will observe throughout this book, many of the cash management problems we discuss result either directly or indirectly from this regulatory burden.

NUMBERS OF BANKS. Laws restricting bank expansion across state lines and, in many states, outside counties have resulted in the formation of a very large number of commercial banks. Currently there are some 14,500 commercial banks in the United States—and this number does not include the thousands of branch locations. At the end of 1983 there were 4,751 national banks, 1,051 state member banks, 8,648 state nonmember, insured banks, and some 600 uninsured state banks in the United States.[1] In comparison, there are 10 banks in Canada (only 5 of which are large clearing banks with extensive branch networks) and like numbers in virtually all other countries. This large number of banks itself creates cash management problems, since it is difficult for a corporation to keep track of cash in so many locations and move it into a larger pool. Large information systems and many more cash transfers are required.

Geographical Restrictions

Regardless of whether the state or federal government charters a bank, the McFadden Act of 1927 requires all banks to adhere to branching restrictions imposed by the state. Each state determines its own laws restricting the geographical activities of banks in the state.

UNIT BANKING. Some states have *unit banking*. Strict unit banking means that a bank is allowed only one facility in the state. No branches are permitted. While no state currently practices strict unit banking, Illinois, for example, has restrictions that approach it. Texas has unit banking but permits bank holding companies to own multiple banks. This somewhat mitigates the extreme restrictions of unit banking.

STATEWIDE BRANCHING. At the opposite extreme is *statewide branching*, by which a bank may branch anywhere within the state. California, for example, permits statewide branching.

LIMITED BRANCHING. Most states are between these two extremes. Some states, like Indiana before 1986, permit branching within a home county but no branches outside it. Others permit branching within a radius of so many miles, while still others permit branching in counties contiguous to the county of the home office of the bank. Geographical restrictions place limitations on bank services and dictate the kind of collection and concentration system a firm must design. For example, in a unit banking state, a firm would have to deal with multiple banks if it needed a collection bank in different parts of the state. In a state that permits statewide branching, the firm need deal with only one bank for services in all parts of the state.

Most laws restricting geographical access are defined in terms of deposit gathering and ownership. A bank, for example, may be prohibited from having a full-service branch in another area of the state, but it may have an office there to generate new loan business or other services. Similarly, national laws may forbid deposit gathering across state lines, but they permit loan production offices (LPOs) that funnel credit and other financial services.

---

[1] *Bank Operating Statistics*, FDIC (1983).

EDGE ACT BANKS. Another way banks can partially overcome tight geographical restrictions is to establish an Edge Act bank. The Edge Act of 1919 permitted U.S. banks to invest in corporations that engage in international banking and finance. Some large banks have developed domestic networks of Edge Act corporations. For example, several major West Coast banks have established Edge Act banks in New York City and Chicago. While Edge Act corporations may not take domestic deposits and may engage in only those activities that service foreign trade, this avenue for expansion has provided a useful base for serving multinational customers and gaining access to world money markets.

Line of Business Restrictions
The Glass-Steagall Act of 1933 was passed in the midst of the Great Depression. People generally blamed the banking and securities industries for precipitating the dire economic conditions of the time and called for stringent new regulations. The resulting law separated banking from the securities industry. Banks were not permitted to hold or deal in stocks and bonds or engage in any way in brokerage functions. Securities firms were likewise prevented from performing banking functions. Banks were also prohibited from engaging in any businesses that do not relate directly to the practice of banking. Though the line separating banks and brokerage firms has blurred somewhat lately, the Glass-Steagall Act still prevents banks from offering some services that would simplify short-term financial management (Table 3.1).

_____ Federal Reserve System _____

In 1913 Congress created the Federal Reserve System (Fed) to improve supervision of banks and to provide a nationwide collection and clearing center for checks of members banks. In addition, the Fed was to provide a lending facility for commercial banks and to attempt to manage the money supply more effectively.

Organization

District Banks
The country is divided into 12 Federal Reserve Districts, with a semiautonomous district bank in each. They are located in the following "Fed cities":

1. Boston	7. Chicago
2. New York	8. St. Louis
3. Philadelphia	9. Minneapolis
4. Cleveland	10. Kansas City
5. Richmond	11. Dallas
6. Atlanta	12. San Francisco

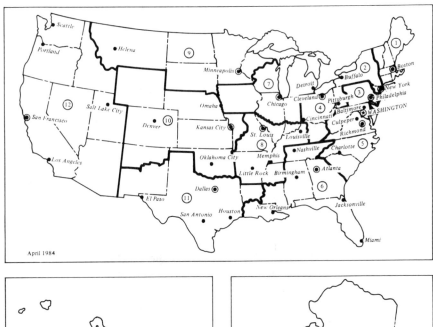

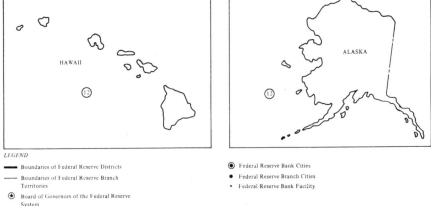

Figure 3.1 Map of Federal Reserve Districts.

In addition to the district banks, there are 25 branch banks located in other major cities. Each branch provides most of the services available at the district offices. Figure 3.1 shows the Fed district banks and their branches.

Regional Check Processing Centers (RCPCs)

In addition to district banks, the Fed operates 30 check processing centers. These centers do not offer all the services of district banks or their branches. Their primary function is to clear checks for banks in the immediate area.

Management

The Fed is directed by a seven-person board of governors. Each governor is appointed by the president of the United States to a 14-year term. The lengthy term is designed to insulate the governors as much as possible from political manipulation. The chairman and vice chairman of the board are appointed to 4-year terms by the president. They are chosen from among the seven. The board of governors is supported in its policymaking decisions by a large staff of research economists and three advisory committees. (1) The Federal Advisory Council consists of one member from each of the 12 districts, and meets with the board to review business and financial conditions and to make recommendations. (2) The Consumer Advisory Council advises the board on consumer-related matters. (3) The Thrift Institution Advisory Council consists of representatives from mutual savings banks, savings and loan associations, and credit unions.

Roles of the Fed

Payment System

The Fed is the center of cash movement for the United States. It receives deposits of checks from commercial banks and other depository institutions and then routes them back to the bank on which they are drawn. In the process, the Fed keeps track of the accounts to be debited and credited. Through the Fed's wire transfer network, cash can be moved quickly from a depository account at one bank to an account at another bank. The Fed is also the main operator of the automated clearing house system that clears payments among banks electronically rather than using paper instruments. Chapter 5 discusses the Fed's role in the payment system in much more detail.

Control of the Money Supply

Controlling the money supply is considered to be the Fed's most powerful role. The money supply is thought by many to be linked to economic factors such as inflation, interest rates, and employment. The Fed attempts to control the money supply through several mechanisms.

RESERVE REQUIREMENTS. First, the Fed sets *reserve requirements*. That is, the Fed requires that all depository institutions maintain a specified percentage of their deposits with the Fed. Currently, these deposits earn no interest. The Fed has the authority to change the reserve requirement as it sees fit. By increasing the reserve requirement, it takes money out of the economy. By decreasing the requirement, it increases the money supply. As of 1987, there are reserve requirements of 3% on time deposits under 18 months and of 12% on demand deposits (and other transaction accounts, even if they receive interest). In practice, the Fed rarely changes these percentages more than once every several years.

DISCOUNT RATE. Second, the Fed sets a *discount rate*, the rate at which it lends to member institutions. Although very few banks borrow at the *Fed discount window* at any given time, the discount rate is often viewed as an indicator of Fed policy. When the rate is lowered, the Fed is assumed to want to increase the money supply. When the rate is increased, the opposite is assumed.

MONEY MARKET PURCHASES AND SALES. Third, perhaps the most powerful activity of the Fed is exercised through its *Fed Open Market Committee (FOMC)*. The committee is made up of the seven board members, the president of the New York District Bank, and four other district bank presidents in rotation. This committee is charged with promoting economic growth, full employment, stable prices, and a balance in international trade and payments. Its primary activities involve the sale and purchase of government securities. The sale of securities from its portfolio reduces the money supply by taking cash out of the economy. The purchase of securities in the open market increases the money supply, since the Fed makes purchases simply by crediting the seller's account with additional reserves. When a bank has additional reserves, it can lend more money, further expanding the money supply.

Regulation of Banking Policies

The Fed regulates depository institutions through a series of regulations coded (currently) from *A* through *BB*. Some of the more important regulations that pertain to short-term finance are as follows:

Regulation D specifies the percentage of each class of deposit that must be held in reserve balances.

Regulation E operationalizes the Electronic Fund Transfer (EFT) Act of 1978, which details the rights and responsibilities of parties to EFT transactions.

Regulation J spells out Fed policies on check collection and funds transfer.

Regulation Y regulates the activities of bank holding companies.

Current Issues in the Commercial Banking System

In recent years the financial industry has seen dramatic changes. Many of the changes we discuss have resulted from the prevailing deregulatory mood in the United States. Deregulation has opened the door to intense competition between various types of institutions that provide financial services. Still other changes have come from technological developments, particularly in the area of electronics. As the financial industry changes, the problems (and solutions) encountered by the cash manager also change.

Deregulation of Financial Services

Over the past decade or so, a growing number of industries have been deregulated, such as airlines, natural gas, and trucking. It is not surprising that steps have been taken to reduce governmental restrictions on the banking industry as well.

Lifting Interest Rate Ceilings

With the passage of the Depository Institution Deregulation and Monetary Control Act of 1980, Congress mandated that Regulation Q be phased out by 1986. Banks and other depository institutions are now free to offer whatever rates they choose. The single glaring exception to this rule is perhaps the most important deposit account from the corporate standpoint. Banks are still precluded from paying interest on corporate demand deposits.

While regulations formally lifted interest rate ceilings, in reality ceilings were removed in some areas several years ago. Entities such as brokerage firms started offering deposit-type accounts in the form of money market mutual funds. These accounts earned interest at an unregulated rate and had check-writing privileges. As these firms are not members of the Fed, no reserves were required by the Fed and rates could be offered that could not be matched by commercial banks. In addition, there were no branching restrictions imposed by states, so deposit gathering could be nationwide. Until the 1970s, banks were not permitted to compete with such accounts (in the form of money market CDs), so billions of dollars flowed from the banking system into money market mutual funds. While large corporations could afford their own money market investment portfolios, small businesses for the first time had access to market rates.

Geographical Restrictions

As noted previously, geographical restrictions on bank branching create many cash management problems. However, these restrictions have been easing along several fronts: the merging of troubled institutions, a relaxation of state restrictions, the creation of regional banking pacts, the introduction of national collection networks, the formation of automated teller machine networks, and the invention of a legal entity called a *nonbank bank.*

The Fed has often permitted a bank in one state to acquire a troubled bank or other institution in another state if no in-state partner could be found. The Bank of America in California, for example, acquired the Seattle First National Bank in 1984 when the latter encountered serious financial difficulties. No bank in the state of Washington was large enough to come to the troubled bank's aid. Similarly, Citicorp in New York City acquired the First Federal Savings and Loan Association, a $4 billion Chicago institution.

States are relaxing geographical restrictions formerly imposed on branching. For example, in 1983, Pennsylvania legislated a program that will eventually lead in phases to statewide branching. Banks were permitted to acquire other banks in neighboring counties, then in bicontiguous counties, and finally in an additional distant part of the state. Indiana passed a limited multibank holding company law in 1985. Where banking was formerly restricted to in-county branching, banks can now own other banks throughout the state.

In 1985 the Supreme Court upheld the right of states to form regional banking pacts permitting banks in selected neighboring states to branch within the region. At the same time, the Court ruled, these pacts may be selective in terms of which states they admit. This has led to fairly extensive merging of institutions across state lines. Many large banks in the Southeast, for example, now own or are owned by banks in neighboring states.

In 1983 several banks announced nationwide check collection services (national operating banks). As discussed in Chapter 6, such banks effectively gather deposits across the country as if they had a nationwide branching system. If this is done cleverly, these banks circumvent the McFadden Act, which prohibits taking deposits across state lines. Now most major banks offer some form of nationwide collection.

Technology has also widened a bank's geographical reach. Many banks now belong to one or more automated teller machine (ATM) networks. These networks allow customers in one state to withdraw cash from (or transact other business related to) an account in another state.

In addition, the Fed has permitted some banks to operate nonbank banks across state lines. A commercial bank, says the fine print, accepts deposits *and* makes commercial loans. Hence, if an institution does only one of these and not the other, it is really not a commercial bank and does not come under the McFadden Act restrictions. Several New York City banks have won approval from many states to operate consumer-oriented banks that take deposits but do not make commercial loans.

Industry Restrictions

The regulatory boundaries that have traditionally separated various financial institutions have been gradually melting away. Thrift institutions may now offer checking accounts and make commercial loans. Credit unions also have check-like accounts and offer mortgages. Brokers advertise money market rate savings plans with check-writing privileges, and banks are beginning to provide discount brokerage services. Even a package delivery firm entered the banking business by offering a check-clearing service. If current trends continue, the differences between financial institutions will be of more interest to financial historians than to financial service users. Cash managers will find that commercial banks are not the only corporate financial service providers.

Foreign Commercial Banks

Over the past two decades, there has been a dramatic growth in foreign banks either operating in the United States or purchasing U.S. banks. Although most do not offer all of the services of domestic commercial banks, they compete very aggressively in the commercial loan market. They frequently offer credit lines and term loans at very competitive rates. These banks are at least partially responsible for the narrowing of profit margins on commercial bank loan portfolios. Non-U.S. headquartered banks offer a wide variety of international services that compete with international departments of domestic banks. However, these offshore banks generally do not compete in offering most cash management services.

From Paper to Electronic Information and Funds Transfer

For centuries, the banking system has functioned primarily as a paper-based, mail-oriented system. Though accepted by tradition, such a system is labor intensive, costly, and slow. With current technology, the computer may be used not only for internal bookkeeping functions but also for electronic data interchange and funds transfer. One of commercial banking's next great challenges is to implement such electronic systems and help cash managers do likewise.

Today over 12,000 commercial banks are members of an automated clearing house (ACH). An ACH permits low-cost, batch-processed cash transfers to be electronically settled on an overnight basis. Banks serve as entry points into the ACH system. The availability of such a system is changing the kinds of services cash managers use. Chapter 5 explains the ACH system in more detail.

Summary

An understanding of the banking system is crucial to those who manage the short-term assets and liabilities of the firm. The banking system plays a vital role in so many activities related to short-term financial management—especially cash management. Banks store cash value and assist in the transfer of value from one party to another. Banks (and the Fed) influence the volume of cash in the market place and, therefore, interest rates. Banks assist in gathering, concentrating, and disbursing cash and provide avenues for the investment of cash for short periods of time.

Nevertheless, useful as banks are, they are highly regulated—and the regulations vary from state to state. Banking regulations limit the kinds of services banks can provide to corporate users. Therefore, an understanding of bank regulations is important if corporate managers are to deal effectively with banks.

Discussion Questions

1. What are the primary functions of a commercial bank that pertain to short-term financial management?
2. Explain the differences between time and demand deposits.
3. Compare and contrast the problems posed for the cash manager in a unit banking versus a branch banking state.
4. Who are the main competitors of commercial banks in providing corporate financial services?
5. Explain the role of the Federal Reserve System in the banking industry.
6. How does the Federal Reserve System, either directly or indirectly, affect the cash manager of a corporation?

7. Explain how the following laws influence cash management:
   a. McFadden Act (1927)
   b. Glass-Steagall Act (1933)
   c. Douglas Amendment (1956)
   d. Depository Institution Deregulation and Monetary Control Act (1980)
   e. Garn-St. Germain Act (1982)
8. Explain how removing geographical restrictions would change the job of the cash manager.
9. Explain how interest rate deregulation may help or hurt the cash manager.
10. If the Fed were to pay banks interest on reserve balances, what would be the impact on bank service costs?

--------------- **Selected Readings** ---------------

FORD, WILLIAM F., "The Changing Role of the Federal Reserve in the Payment System," *Journal of Cash Management* (April–May 1983), pp. 12ff.

GARN, JAKE, "Legislation and Financial Service Deregulation: The Level Playing Field," *Journal of Cash Management* (April 1983), pp. 20–26.

HEMPLE, G. H., A. B. COLEMAN, AND D. G. SIMONSON, *Bank Management: Text and Cases*, New York: Wiley, 1983.

HUMPHREY, DAVID B., "Reducing Interbank Risk on Large Dollar Payment Networks," *Journal of Cash Management* (September–October 1984), pp. 20–27.

JESSUP, PAUL F., *Modern Bank Management*, St. Paul, Minn.: West, 1980.

LONGBRAKE, WILLIAM A., "Commercial Bank Capacity to Pay Interest on Demand Deposits," *Journal of Bank Research* (Spring 1976), pp. 8–21.

McCLINTOCK, RAY M., "Impact of the Monetary Control Act," *Journal of Cash Management* (March–April 1984), pp. 34–42.

MURPHY, NEAL B., "Commercial Banking," in *Financial Handbook*, 5th ed., Edward I. Altman (ed.), New York: Wiley, 1981, chapter 6.

STORRS, THOMAS I., "Forces Affecting the Structure of the Banking Industry," *Journal of Cash Management* (December 1981), pp. 28–31.

WOLKOWITZ, BENJAMIN, "The Case for the Federal Reserve Actively Participating in Electronic Funds Transfer," *Journal of Bank Research* (Spring 1978), pp. 15–25.

Keeping Score on Bank Balances and Bank Compensation

In 1984 E. F. Hutton was accused of defrauding many of its small deposit banks by intentionally undercompensating them. It was widespread practice in the firm to overdraft deposit accounts, but not in a way that would be noticed by most small banks. The result was a large fine imposed by the government and adverse publicity that caused severe harm to Hutton's otherwise fine reputation. The entire affair was caused by taking advantage of how some banks count deposit balances. It shows that a financial manager's understanding of the technical mechanics of bank balances may be important for the health of the entire organization.

Much of cash management involves moving cash into and out of demand deposit balances in banks. This chapter introduces some of the fundamentals of cash movement without talking specifically about wires, checks, and ACH transfers. Those subjects are covered in Chapter 5. We begin by discussing different kinds of bank balances. We show that all cash balances are not created equal; some kinds are better than others. We then discuss how balances are used to compensate banks for their services and contrast balances to payment by fees.

Working with Bank Balances

Ledger and Available Balances

Cash kept in a checking account is called a *demand deposit*. Banks—especially larger ones—keep track of at least two kinds of demand deposit

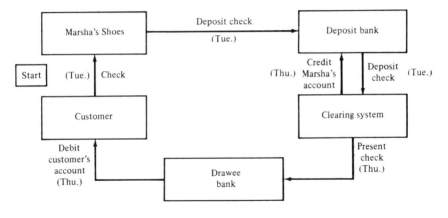

Day	Ledger balance	Available balance	Activity/comment
Mon.	$0	$0	Initial balances
Tues.	$100	$0	Marsha deposits check Deposit bank: a. gives Marsha ledger credit b. assigns two-day availability c. deposits check in clearing system
Wed.	$100	$0	Check in process of clearing
Thu.	$100	$100	Bank receives credit for the check Bank gives Marsha available credit Customer's account at drawee bank is debited

Figure 4.1 Timing of Ledger and Available Balances.

balances: ledger and available. To understand the difference, we present a simple example illustrated in Figure 4.1. Suppose that on Tuesday morning a customer pays for a purchase at Marsha's Shoe Store with a $100 check. Tuesday at noon, Marsha endorses the check, takes it to the deposit bank, and deposits it into her corporate checking account. At the close of its business day, the bank gives Marsha's account a ledger credit of $100—that is, her ledger balance increases by $100. The term *ledger* is used because it implies an *accounting* transaction but not necessarily a value change. The deposit bank now holds a check—but a check is not cash. It only represents a demand to move cash from one account to another. Since the deposit bank does not receive value for the check without some time delay and since banks generally attempt to be profitable businesses, the bank generally won't give Marsha value for the deposit either.

To receive value for the check, the deposit bank must return it to the bank on which the customer drew the check. This bank is called the *drawee bank*. In Chapter 5 we define check clearing in more detail and discuss several avenues open to the deposit bank for clearing the check. For now, assume that it takes 2 business days for the deposit bank to move the check back to the drawee bank and receive value for it. The deposit bank would likely give Marsha 2-day availability as well. We call this process *assigning availability*. On Thursday— 2 business days later—the deposit bank receives value for $100 and the drawee bank loses value for the same amount. Correspondingly, the deposit bank gives Marsha's account available credit for the check on Thursday; this means that her available balance increases by $100 on that day. She receives value on that day. Also on Thursday, the drawee bank debits the customer's account for $100 and everyone is even.

Business Days versus Calendar Days

It is important to recognize the distinction between business and calendar days. Most banks assign availability based on *business days*—Monday through Friday, except legal holidays. This means that if Marsha had deposited her check on Friday, she would have received available credit on Tuesday—not Sunday or Monday. Current practice generally does not include presenting checks to drawee banks on weekends or holidays, though that practice could change. As we will see later, many check processing services are beginning to be available on weekends.

When banks compute average balances, they use *calendar days*—365 days per year. Hence, balances in an account on weekends and holidays are just as important in computing averages as balances on Tuesday or Friday. For example, any available balance in an account on Friday will be counted for Saturday and Sunday, too.

Relationship Between Deposits and Presentments

Returning to Marsha's Shoe Store, assume that Marsha had written a $50 check several days ago to pay her telephone bill for the month. The check was sent by mail. After being processed by the postal service, by the telephone company, and finally by the telephone company's bank, the check is returned for payment to Marsha's bank on Wednesday morning. The bank loses value for the $50 and at the close of business on Wednesday subtracts $50 (transfers value) from the ledger balance *and* the available balance. Both accounts are reduced by $50 on the same business day.

To see how this practice influences the relationship between ledger and available balances, consider a firm that deposits checks and has checks presented against a demand deposit account according to the schedule given in Table 4.1. Assume that all checks deposited are available in 1 business day. Also assume that on Monday morning the opening ledger and available balances are both $50,000. Table 4.1 shows the ending balances by day. Monday's deposit is a ledger deposit on Monday but not an available deposit until Tuesday. The presentments of checks drawn against the account are subtracted from both ledger and available balance on the same day.

Table 4.1 Example of Ledger and Available Balances of Marsha's Shoes

DEPOSIT AND PRESENTATION SCHEDULE

Day	Checks Deposited	Checks Presented
Mon	$50,000	$70,000
Tue	$40,000	$20,000
Wed	$10,000	$30,000

LEDGER BALANCE

Day	Opening Balance		Deposit		Checks Presented		Closing Balance
Mon	$50,000	+	$50,000	−	$70,000	=	$30,000
Tue	30,000	+	40,000	−	20,000	=	50,000
Wed	50,000	+	10,000	−	30,000	=	30,000

AVAILABLE BALANCE

Day	Opening Balance		Deposit		Checks Presented		Closing Balance
Mon	$50,000	+	0	−	$70,000	=	$−20,000
Tue	−20,000	+	50,000	−	20,000	=	10,000
Wed	10,000	+	40,000	−	30,000	=	20,000

Note that because available deposits lag behind ledger deposits, the ledger balance is always at least as large as the available balance. Since this will always be the case, barring some unusual circumstances, it is possible for the available balance to dip below zero (as it does on Monday in the example) while the ledger balance is still positive. Therefore, it is possible to have an overdraft or negative balance on either a ledger or available basis. Of course, a ledger overdraft implies an available overdraft. We discuss later how banks handle overdrafts.

Other Issues

Banks have a cutoff time during the day before which deposits must be made in order to receive ledger credit for the deposit at the close of the day. For example, a typical cutoff time is 4 P.M. A check deposited before this time would be given ledger credit on that business day. Checks deposited after this time would be given ledger credit the following business day. Even cash deposits—which are generally immediately available—must be deposited before the cutoff time to receive credit on the day of deposit.

In addition to ledger cutoff times, most larger banks also have cutoff times for determining availability assignments for checks. For example, a check deposited at 3 P.M. may be given immediate ledger credit but 2-day availability. If the same check had been deposited by the bank's 9 A.M. availability cutoff, it would have been given 1-day availability. Unfortunately, there is almost never *one* cutoff time for availability. As we will see later, cutoff times for checks vary greatly and depend on where the check is drawn and other factors. For example, for a check drawn on a bank down the street, the cutoff time may be 4 P.M. For a check drawn on a bank in a distant city, the cutoff time may be 6 A.M. Less sophisticated banks, presumably because they lack the computer systems to assign and track availability, often treat all deposits— even checks drawn on distant banks—as cash deposits. They do not make any distinction between ledger and available balances. Both are one and the same. To these banks, a check drawn on an out-of-state bank is given the same credit as a deposit of coin and currency. Unfortunately, some large firms have taken advantage of such banks to enrich themselves at the expense of the banks. This was the issue in case of the large brokerage firm we discussed at the beginning of this chapter.

Another Example of Balance Computations

Table 4.2 provides a slightly more complex illustration of how banks account for ledger and available balances. Assume that we have just opened an account at a deposit bank. The pattern of the first week's deposits and clearings are shown in the table. Assume that 20% of the amount deposited on a given day will be given immediate availability, 70% 1-day availability, and 10% 2-day availability. This is often the case when a mixture of checks is deposited into an account. Some checks may be local and receive immediate available credit. Most checks are granted 1-day availability, while a few are drawn on distant banks and are delayed by an additional day.

On Monday, for example, the ledger balance increases by the total Monday deposit. On the other hand, the available balance on Monday increases by only 20% of that day's deposit. The remainder of the Monday deposit is carried over to Tuesday (70%) and Wednesday (10%). The closing balance at the end of each day is determined by the following formulas:

Closing ledger balance = Opening ledger balance

$$+ \text{ ledger deposits} - \text{clearings}$$

and

Closing available balance = opening available balance

$$+ \text{ available deposits} - \text{clearings.}$$

The available deposit is made up of 20% of today's deposit plus 70% of yesterday's deposit plus 10% of the deposit 2 days ago. For example, on Wednesday, the available deposit is computed as follows on page 84:

Table 4.2 Ledger and Available Balances: More Complex Case*

	Weekly Deposits	Average Clearings
Mon	$200,000	$ 0
Tue	$100,000	$ 0
Wed	$100,000	$200,000
Thu	$140,000	$100,000
Fri	$160,000	$100,000
Total	$700,000	$400,000

LEDGER BALANCE

Day	Opening	+	Deposits	−	Clearing	=	Closing
Mon	$ 0		$200,000		$ 0		$200,000
Tue	$200,000		$100,000		$ 0		$300,000
Wed	$300,000		$100,000		$200,000		$200,000
Thu	$200,000		$140,000		$100,000		$240,000
Fri	$240,000		$160,000		$100,000		$300,000
Sat	$300,000		$ 0		$ 0		$300,000
Sun	$300,000		$ 0		$ 0		$300,000
Average Closing Balance (Ledger)							$262,857

AVAILABLE BALANCE

Day	Opening	+	Deposits	−	Clearing	=	Closing
Mon	$ 0		$ 40,000		$ 0		$ 40,000
Tue	$ 40,000		$ 20,000 $140,000		$ 0		$200,000
Wed	$200,000		$ 20,000 $ 70,000 $ 20,000		$200,000		$110,000
Thu	$110,000		$ 28,000 $ 70,000 $ 10,000		$100,000		$118,000
Fri	$118,000		$ 32,000 $ 98,000 $ 10,000		$100,000		$158,000
Sat	$158,000		$ 0		$ 0		$158,000
Sun	$158,000		$ 0		$ 0		$158,000
Average Closing Balance (Available)							$134,571
Bank Float (Ledger Minus Available)							$128,286

* Note: Checks receive availability as follows:
  20% immediate
  70% 1-day
  10% 2-day

Wednesday's available deposit

$$
\begin{aligned}
&\quad\quad\quad\;\;(\text{Wed})\quad\quad\quad\;\;(\text{Tue})\quad\quad\quad\;\;(\text{Mon})\\
&= .20(100{,}000) + .70(100{,}000) + .10(200{,}000)\\
&= 20{,}000 + 70{,}000 + 20{,}000\\
&= 110{,}000.
\end{aligned}
$$

Other days' available deposits are computed in a similar fashion.

Note that when the presentments begin to come in on Wednesday, both ledger and available balances are reduced on the same day by the full amount of the clearing. There are no availability delays for clearings.

The result of all of this activity is that the ledger balance, as we saw before, is larger than the available balance each day. The average balance is computed by summing up the closing balances for each day of the week and dividing by 7. Saturday and Sunday closing balances are included in the weekly average. In this example, the average difference between ledger and available balances is $128,286.

The difference between the bank ledger balance and the bank available balance is often called *bank float*. We will see later how this number plays a role in determining bank compensation.

Uses of Available Balances

To summarize, a ledger balance keeps track of cash movements into and out of a demand deposit account but does not reflect actual value transfers affecting the account. In contrast, an available balance, as the name implies, is available for use by the firm. It reflects transfers of value into and out of the account. There are two basic ways firms use available balances. First, available balances may be transferred to other banks. The firm, for example, may want to pay other firms or to buy short-term investment securities. Most banks allow only available balances to be transferred out of the account. Second, only available balances count as compensating balances that pay for services the firm receives from the bank. We discuss this topic later in this chapter.

Company Book Balances

So far, the cash balances we have discussed relate to cash residing in a bank. The kind of cash balance we now consider is the one reported by accountants on the firm's cash ledger. It is called the *company book balance*. The reason we discuss this balance is that it is readily available and often reported by accountants to management and shareholders—not because it has any economic value.

The company book balance is equivalent to the balance you record in your checkbook. When you write a check, the amount is subtracted from the checkbook balance. When you make a deposit, the amount is added to the balance.

Company Book Balance Is Not Cash

The problem with a company book balance is that it doesn't reflect how much cash the company has available in its demand deposits—now or perhaps ever. It is purely an accounting record. The reason is obvious: when a check is written and subtracted from the company ledger balance, it generally takes several days before the amount is subtracted from the bank balance. As illustrated in Figure 4.2, this delay is due to payor processing after recording, mail time, processing delays by the payee, and delays caused by the clearing system. Therefore, the company book balance shows an immediate subtraction of an amount that will not actually clear the company's account for several days.

The reverse is true for deposits. When the company makes a deposit, it adds the amount to the company book balance. However, several days may elapse before the deposit results in an available balance at the bank. First, the deposit may not be taken to the bank immediately or may arrive after the bank's cutoff time. Second, once the deposit is made, it may not become available without some availability delay. Therefore, the company book balance shows an immediate addition of an amount that will not become available until sometime in the future.

The result is that the company book balance is generally an inaccurate representation of the cash that the firm actually has available in its bank accounts at any point in time. The difference between the bank available balance and the company book balance is sometimes called *net float*.

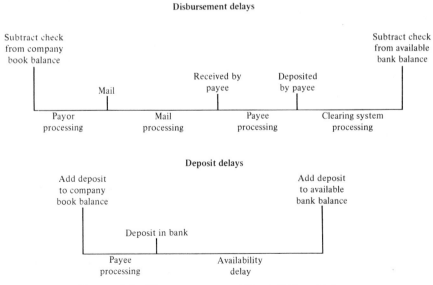

Figure 4.2 Disbursement and Deposit Time Delays.

Example of Net Float Computation

Table 4.3 gives a numerical example that shows how net float is computed. Assume that the ABC Company makes deposits averaging $2,000,000 each business day. The deposits are made on the day they are recorded on the company books and are given on average 1-business-day availability. ABC also writes checks of $2,000,000 per business day. After entering the checks

Table 4.3 Illustration of Company Book Balance versus Bank Available Balance

A. COMPANY BOOK BALANCE

Day	Opening Balance	+	Deposits Made	−	Checks Written	=	Closing Balance
Mon	0		2		2		0
Tue	0		2		2		0
Wed	0		2		2		0
Thu	0		2		2		0
Fri	0		2		2		0
Sat	0		0		0		0
Sun	0		0		0		0
Mon	0		2		2		0
Tue	0		2		2		0
Wed	0		2		2		0
Thu	0		2		2		0
Fri	0		2		2		0
Sat	0		0		0		0
Sun	0		0		0		0

B. BANK AVAILABLE BALANCE

Day	Opening Balance	+	Deposits Available	−	Checks Cleared	=	Closing Balance
Mon	0		0		0		0
Tue	0		2		0		2
Wed	2		2		0		4
Thu	4		2		0		6
Fri	6		2		0		8
Sat	8		0		0		8
Sun	8		0		0		8
Mon	8		2		2		8
Tue	8		2		2		8
Wed	8		2		2		8
Thu	8		2		2		8
Fri	8		2		2		8
Sat	8		0		0		8
Sun	8		0		0		8

on the ledger, ABC immediately mails them out. Mail time, payee processing time, and clearing time back to the bank average 5 business days.

As far as the company book balance is concerned, the firm has zero cash at the end of each day. Deposits exactly match disbursements—at least on an accounting basis. However, from the standpoint of available balances, ABC has $8,000,000 on average during the second week. The Monday deposit becomes available on Tuesday. The Monday checks, however, take 5 business days—to the following Monday—to clear. The balance builds up for the first week until the checks begin to clear. At that time, a steady state is reached at the $8,000,000 level.

In this case, the net float is bank available balance minus company book balance or $8,000,000 − $0 = $8,000,000. This means that, on average, the company has $8,000,000 more in available funds in the bank than the amount reflected on the company cash ledger.

There is actually an easier way to compute net float without constructing a table. Net float may also be also defined as follows:

$$\text{Net float} = \text{disbursement float} - \text{deposit float.}$$

Disbursement float is defined as the time delay between recording a disbursement on company books and presentment against the disbursing account times the average dollar amount disbursed per day. In other words, it is the disbursement delay (in Figure 4.2) times dollars per day. Similarly, *deposit float* is defined as the time delay between recording a deposit on company books and availability in the deposit account times the average dollar amount deposited per day. In other words, it is the deposit delay (in Figure 4.2) times dollars per day.

Because disbursement delay includes more time elements (mail time being the largest), disbursement float is generally significantly larger than deposit float for most firms. This means that net float is generally positive and firms have more cash available to them than indicated in their annual reports.

Red Book Balances

If net float is positive, it is possible for a firm to show a negative amount for the company book balance while still maintaining positive available balances.

To illustrate, the average daily cash flows of $2,000,000 per business day for both deposits and disbursements translate into $2(5/7) (million) per calendar day. Disbursements require 7 calendar days, while deposit delays are 1 calendar day for Monday through Thursday and 3 calendar days for Friday. The average deposit float is therefore 1.4. Thus the net float for ABC is as follows:

$$\text{Net float} = \text{disbursement float} - \text{deposit float}$$
$$= \$2,000,000(5/7)7 \text{ days} - \$2,000,000(5/7)1.4$$
$$= \$8,000,000.$$

This is the same number we saw in the table. This means that if the company showed $5,000,000 cash on the company books, there would actually be $13,000,000 in available balances in the banking system.

What if the firm showed negative $6,000,000 on the company books? There would be in reality $-6,000,000 + 8,000,000 = \$2,000,000$ in available balances. When the company book balance is negative, it is sometimes called a *red book balance*.

While most firms maintain red book balances, few are brave enough to report them to the public in annual reports. Managers are afraid that investors would misunderstand and assume that the firm had run out of cash. Hence, firms sometimes go through unusual contortions to avoid having to report negative balances. There are at least three options available. In Table 4.4, we illustrate them by continuing with the ABC Company example. The partial balance sheet with a negative company book balance is seen in Table 4.4A.

1. *Borrow short-term cash.* The most expensive way of handling the problem is borrowing short-term funds just before the close of the accounting period. The amount borrowed must be sufficient to increase the company book balance to a comfortable level. Once the balance is reported, the loan is paid off and the cash returns to a negative position again. In Table 4.4B, ABC borrows $8,000,000 on, say, December 30 in order to "dress up" the year-end annual report. Then on January 2 the amount is repaid—with interest, of course. This may seem a bit foolish to many readers, but a number of firms do it. Unfortunately, not only does this method hide information by not reporting the usual cash balance, it is expensive.

2. *Combine cash and marketable securities.* As long as marketable securities exceed the amount of the negative cash balance, the two can be added

Table 4.4 Handling Negative Cash Balances on Accounting Reports: ABC Company's Balance Sheet (Partial)

A. Reporting Actual Company Book Balances			
Cash (book balance)	–$ 6	Trade payables	$10
Marketable securities	8	Short-term debt	20
. . .		. . .	
B. Borrow Short-term Debt			
Cash $-6 + 8 =$	$ 2	Trade payables	$10
Marketable securities	8	Short-term debt $20 + 8 =$	28
. . .		. . .	
C. Combine Cash and Marketable Securities			
Cash plus mkt sec $-6 + 8 =$	$ 2	Trade payables	$10
		Short-term debt	20
. . .		. . .	
D. Create Net Drafts Payable			
Cash $-6 + 8 =$	$ 2	Trade payables	$10
Marketable securities	10	Short-term debt	20
. . .		Net drafts payable	8
		. . .	

together to obtain a positive number. Many annual reports show "Cash plus marketable securities" rather than reporting each separately. For ABC, the balance sheet would look like Table 4.4C. This method hides information but is less expensive than borrowing short-term cash. Unfortunately, this method does not work for firms that have a large amount of net float but small amounts of marketable securities.

3. *Create a drafts payable account.* By far the easiest and most informative method of reporting negative balances is to report in the "Cash" account the true *bank available balance.* Then another account is created on the liability side of the balance sheet to reflect the net float. In Table 4.4D, this account is called *net drafts payable.* It is computed as the dollar amount of checks that have yet to clear minus the dollar amount of deposits that have not become available. (This is, of course, net float.) It represents a true liability of the firm, since if the firm were to cease operations immediately, this amount would eventually clear against the firm's bank accounts.

PROBLEMS WITH NEGATIVE BALANCES. Not too many years ago, some managers thought that if a firm permitted its company book balance to drop below zero, the company was in danger of being charged with check kiting, or at least with being unethical or immoral. Most managers now recognize that negative company book balances are simply an artifact of the timing of additions to and subtractions from account balances. The firm usually subtracts and adds to its account before the bank does. Provided that the available bank balance remains where it should for fair compensation, no one can complain of being harmed. *Check kiting* refers to state laws that are intended to prevent banks from being harmed. To qualify as kiting, checks must be written on accounts that initially have insufficient funds *and* still have insufficient funds when the check is presented. However, that a firm has red book balances does not necessarily imply that it is drawing checks on accounts that have insufficient funds. Most firms can operate with negative company book balances for long periods and never create an overdraft condition. This is because anticipated cash inflows usually materialize and the firm stands ready to sell short-term securities or borrow on credit lines to cover any potential overdrafts. Using red book balances is now widely accepted as standard cash management practice.

Volatility of Net Float

If cash flows were the same every day, net float would be constant. Unfortunately, inflows and outflows vary considerably on a daily basis for most firms. Therefore net float also varies.

Bank Compensation

Bank charges arise from services the bank provides to the firm. Such services include deposit processing, credit voucher handling (generated by credit card sales), checks paid, account maintenance, wire transfers, return item processing, and so on.

Account Analysis

Many banks provide a summary of bank charges to a customer on a regular basis. This summary of charges, together with an analysis of the balances that the firm has maintained during the reporting period, is called an *account analysis*. While the format for account analysis varies greatly from bank to bank, all analyses have common elements. Table 4.5 illustrates a simplified account analysis. The balances come from Table 4.2 by assuming that the 1 week presented represents the entire month.

Table 4.5 Account Analysis Example

A. Service Charges for November

Item	Number	Each	Total
Deposits	286	$ 0.14	$ 40
Wire transfers	20	$ 7.50	$150
Coin and currency	10	$ 5.00	$ 50
Account maintenance	10	$30.00	$300
Checks presented	2,000	$ 0.08	$160
Total Charges			$700

B. Balance Analysis

Average ledger balance	$262,857
Bank float	− $128,286
Average available balance	$134,571
Reserve requirement: 12.00%	− $ 16,149
Free balances	$118,423
Earnings credits: 8.11%/12	$800
Excess Earnings Credits	$100

Service Charges

Historically, banks did not provide an analysis of service charges. Until two or three decades ago, banks had sufficient corporate balances to allow them to provide "free" services. Of course, the customer, in effect, compensated the bank by providing interest-free balances. Now, however, all large banks and even some small ones specify charges for all services from check processing to bank-sponsored seminars. Service charges are usually broken down by type of service provided. A per unit or penny charge is reported together with the volume used for the reporting period. For example, in Table 4.5, the deposit volume for the month was 286 and the penny charge was $0.14 per item, giving total deposit charges of $40 for the month. Usually the reporting period is 1 month. Penny charges vary widely from bank to bank and are sometimes negotiable. Frequently there are discounts for high-volume usage.

In addition to bank service charges, a firm may be charged for FDIC insurance in proportion to its average balances. Banks must pay the FDIC a percentage of their total available balances—whether any given account exceeds the $100,000 FDIC deposit limit or not. This charge is sometimes passed on explicitly to corporate customers. Usually the charge is hidden in the profit margins of other charges. While some argue that the fee should not be assessed on amounts over the FDIC insurance limit, the bank is charged by the FDIC for all balances. The argument is that banks and corporate customers alike benefit from the economic stability provided by such insurance.

Since the passage of the Banking Act of 1980, the Fed has started charging banks for a portion of the Federal Reserve float. Some banks pass these charges on to customers as a percentage of demand deposit balances. Other banks bury the cost in other charges.

Compensating Balances

Up to the past few years, a great majority of corporations paid for service charges by leaving compensating balances in the bank. The *compensating balance* is usually understood to be the average available balance in a demand deposit account. If the bank keeps track of ledger balances, bank float must be subtracted to compute available balances.

There are several ways of keeping track of bank float for a particular corporate customer. First, for banks that assign availability to each check, the available balance is computed on a daily basis. This is the most accurate method, but it requires expensive information systems that are not available to all banks. A second method involves computing an average bank float across all checks deposited at that bank. This average is applied to each customer. This approach may be used when a small bank deposits most of its checks in a larger regional or money center bank. The larger bank keeps track of the smaller bank's float numbers, and the resulting percentage is passed on to the smaller bank's customer. A given firm could be either better or worse off, depending on whether its mix of check deposits had more or less float than the average. A third method involves taking a sample of check deposits for a specific firm and tracking the associated bank float for a period of time. The average percentage is then applied to that firm for the entire year. In Table 4.5 the average available balance is $262,857 (from Table 4.2), while the bank float is $128,286. This leaves an average ledger balance of $134,571.

Reserve Requirements

Once the available balance is computed, an adjustment is usually made for the reserve requirement imposed by the Fed. A certain percentage (currently 12% at the margin) of the available balance is subtracted. This amount represents the reserves the bank must hold with the Fed, earning no interest. Since the bank earns no interest on reserve balances, it generally does not give earnings credits for that portion of the firm's balances. When reserves are subtracted from the average available balance, the remainder is termed the *free balance*. In Table 4.5, 12% of the available balance is $16,149. Subtracting this number from the average available balance leaves a free balance of $118,423.

Earnings Credits

Because of regulatory restrictions, a bank cannot explicitly pay interest on corporate demand deposits. For example, it can never write a firm a check or credit the firm's account for the interest earned in a demand deposit. It may, however, pay interest in the form of earnings credits, provided that such credits are only used at that particular bank for compensation purposes. To compute earnings credits, the free balance is multiplied by the earnings credit rate (ECR). In Table 4.5, the free balance is multiplied by .0811/12. We must divide by 12 to get the monthly ECR, since charges are computed monthly. This results in an earnings credit of $800.

Each bank decides on its ECR and often changes the rate as market conditions change. Some banks tie the rate to the rate on T-bills. Others use some other market rate. Some banks just use a policy rate that may not follow market movements closely.

We can develop a formula summarizing the ingredients discussed so far. We use the following notation:

$$LB = \text{ledger balance}$$
$$AB = \text{available balance}$$
$$SC = \text{service charges (monthly}$$
$$EC = \text{earnings credits (dollar amount)}$$
$$ecr = \text{earnings credit rate (monthly)}$$
$$bf = \text{bank float as a percentage of LB}$$
$$rr = \text{reserve requirement}$$

The relationship between ledger and available balances is

$$AB = (1 - bf)LB. \tag{4.1}$$

Earnings credits are computed from available balances after subtracting reserve requirements:

$$EC = AB(1 - rr)ecr. \tag{4.2}$$

Assuming that the account earns enough credits to cover service charges exactly ($SC = EC$), the available balance needed is given by replacing EC with SC and solving Equation (4.2) for AB:

$$AB = SC/[(1 - rr)ecr]. \tag{4.3}$$

In the example we are using from Table 4.5, the available balance needed to pay exactly the $700 service charges is

$$AB = 700/[(1 - .12)(.0811/12)] = \$117,700.$$

Since the actual available balance is \$134,571, there is an excess balance of \$134,571 − \$117,700 = \$16,871. At the current ECR, this excess would pay for \$16,871 × (1 − .12) × .0811/12 = \$100 worth of service charges. Some banks report the excess in terms of credits (the \$100), while others report the excess available balance (the \$16,871).

CARRYING OVER EXCESSES AND DEFICIENCIES. What happens when the service charges are more or less than the earnings credits? In Table 4.5 the excess amounted to \$100 in earnings credits or \$16,871 in available balances. Banks treat such amounts in different ways.

The most common policy is to allow a firm to carry over any excess or deficiency for a specific period of time—usually a year. The firm can be deficient for several months as long as the deficiency is averaged out against other months of excesses. Some banks permit only a limited carryover, say, for 1 quarter. Any accumulation of excess balances will be appreciated by the bank but not compensated—at least, not directly. Any accumulated deficits must be paid for in cash at the end of the quarter. Some banks go further and require deficits to be paid for in cash at the end of each month. Excesses are absorbed by the bank.

Alternative Compensation by Fees

Instead of paying for the service charges through compensating balances, a firm may write a check to the bank. Banks handle fee-based compensation by either sending out invoices or by directly debiting the customer's account.

Mixed Compensation

A bank may allow mixed compensation. This means it will give earnings credits for any balances in the account for the month. If these balances are not sufficient, the firm is invoiced for the difference. This practice is becoming more common.

Strategies for Bank Compensation

Recently, corporations have begun to move away from balance compensation toward fee compensation. We now explore some of the factors that should be considered in deciding between the two alternatives.

Fee Compensation

There are several important reasons why corporations may prefer fee-based compensation.

RESERVE REQUIREMENT. Because of the reserve requirement, firms can always earn more than the earnings credit rate by investing balances themselves. In Table 4.5, 12% of the available balance, or \$16,149 of the available balance, earned no credit toward payment for bank services. Hence, the effective rate the bank is paying the corporation is not really the ECR, but ECR × (1 − reserve requirement rate). If the firm removed the balances and invested them in a short-term security, it would be ahead as long as it could earn a rate, i, such that

$$i > ecr(1 - rr). \tag{4.4}$$

INTEREST OPPORTUNITY COST. Even if the reserve requirement is zero, it may be possible for the firm to earn more than the ECR offered by a particular bank. Of course, care must be taken to ensure that the risk of the alternative investment is similar to the risk of holding balances in a bank. For deposits under the FDIC insurance limit (currently $100,000), the risk is essentially zero. Even for larger amounts, bank deposits are generally considered quite safe investment instruments.

TAX DEDUCTIBILITY OF FEES. So far, we have neglected the influence of taxes on bank compensation. There is a good reason for this neglect: it doesn't influence the decision on fees versus balances. It is sometimes argued that since bank fees are a direct expense, they can be deducted from income, while balances cannot. While this reasoning is plausible at first glance, closer inspection shows that it is flawed. If a firm decides to change to fee compensation from balance compensation, balances would be removed from the bank and invested in interest-bearing securities. Suppose that just enough in balances were being kept to cover the service charges. According to Equation (4.3), the amount needed is $AB = SC/[(1 - rr)ecr]$. This amount, AB, is now invested in securities earning interest rate i. The amount left after taxes that can be used to cover service charges is $(1 - t)iAB$, where t is the corporate tax rate. The after-tax service charges amount to $(1 - t)SC$. To determine if the corporation is better off by switching to fee compensation, we ask if the after-tax income from short-term investments is larger than the after-tax payments for service charges:

$$(1 - t)iAB > (1 - t)SC. \tag{4.5}$$

We divide both sides of the inequality by $(1 - t)$ and the issue becomes $iAB > SC$. Substituting for AB from Equation (4.3) and canceling the SC that will appear on both sides, we can rewrite this expression as $i > ecr(1 - rr)$, which is Equation (4.4). This tells us that the move to fee compensation depends on the effective interest rates of the two investment opportunities—bank balances versus securities—and *not* on the tax deductibility of fees. In other words, the taxes paid on income from short-term investments exactly offset the tax savings from the deductibility of fees. Hence, taxes alone do not affect the net cost of bank compensation.

CONTROL OF BANKING COSTS. Fees can be put in a budget and compared with other services the corporation receives. It is thought to be easier for senior management to control costs if they are in the form of fees rather than balances. Balances can sometimes hide the true cost of banking services.

PREVENTING OVERCOMPENSATION. As noted previously, excess balances may end up being absorbed by the bank. In contrast, it is difficult to overpay an invoice from a bank. This factor may become more important as banks move to shorter and shorter carryover periods.

Compensation by Balances

While it seems that fees should always dominate balance compensation, there are strong reasons to favor balances in some cases.

TRANSACTION BALANCES. Moving from balances to fees assumes that the balances can indeed be removed. In many demand deposit accounts, however, there is a constant inflow and outflow that makes it impossible to remove all balances completely each day. Information and clearing delays coupled with other problems to be discussed later may leave what we call *transaction balances* in an account. If balances will appear in an account anyway, they might as well be used for compensation. Paying by fees would, in this case, result in overcompensation.

BANK NEGOTIATIONS. In the past, banks seemed to prefer balances to fees. Some bankers may view the firm's relationship with the bank more favorably if balances are used for compensation. This may lead to lower negotiated interest costs. While many larger banks have taken a more profit-oriented approach in recent years, balances may still be a critical factor for firms that depend on medium-sized or small banks for cash management–related services such as credit and financial advice.

LIQUIDITY. Compared to short-term investments, bank balances are more readily accessible when the firm needs cash quickly. Short-term securities would have to be sold and may be sold at a loss, depending on the maturity date and movement in interest rates. Hence, a firm may see bank balances as a more flexible storage vehicle for cash than short-term securities.

DOUBLE COUNTING. Some banks still allow balances kept to compensate for credit provided to the firm to count toward the payment for service charges as well. Balances so counted are essentially a free good, and replacing them with fees would not be advantageous.

HIGHER SERVICE CHARGES FOR FEE-BASED COMPENSATION. Some banks levy a surcharge if they are paid in fees. For example, deposit charges might be $.10 per item if compensated by balances but $.12 if paid in fees. This cost differential must be taken into account when comparing compensation alternatives.

SOFT-DOLLAR BUDGETING. We have pointed out that some firms favor fees because that alternative clearly states bank costs and permits cash management costs to be included in the firm's standard budgeting procedures. For exactly this reason, some cash managers favor balance compensation. Balances can conveniently hide certain costs and give the cash manager a means of obtaining services without being subjected to normal budgeting constraints.

DUAL BALANCES. When a firm moves cash from one of its corporate accounts to another, it is sometimes given credit for the same balance in both banks for a short period. One bank may count the balances for compensation purposes, while, at the same time, the firm may be investing the cash moved into the other bank. If dual balances are present to any significant extent in a firm's banking system, compensation by fees may result in unnecessary expense. Since dual balances have been greatly reduced in recent years, this factor is much less important than other factors in most accounts. We will say more on this topic in Chapter 7.

Compensation Model for Evaluating Alternatives

There is no correct answer to the question "What is the least expensive way to pay for banking services?". The answer depends on the characteristics of a particular account and on how important the previously discussed factors are in each situation. In general, if an account can be closely managed at low cost so that the average balance is zero, fee compensation is probably the best alternative. This is primarily because of the reserve requirement. Most firms can invest in safe, short-term securities that yield a higher effective rate than most ECRs offered by banks after accounting for the reserve requirement. On the other hand, if an account has a significant transaction balance that would be difficult to remove, compensation by balances may be the least expensive alternative.

We can quantify some of these factors and develop a model for determining the cost of compensation alternatives. We will not include taxes because they are not a factor in the preference of one form over the other. Taxes do, however, affect the magnitude of the difference in costs. We use the same notation developed earlier in this chapter. In addition, let TCF be the total cost of paying by fees, TCB the total cost of paying by balances, and TCM the total cost of paying by a mixture of fees and balances.

COST OF FEE ALTERNATIVE. The cost of paying by fees is

$$TCF = SC. \tag{4.6}$$

COST OF BALANCE ALTERNATIVE. From Equation (4.3) we compute the balances that must be maintained in an account to cover service charges. The opportunity cost of leaving these balances is i times the required balance. Hence, the total cost of compensating by balances is

$$TCB = i\,\frac{SC}{ecr(1 - rr)}. \tag{4.7}$$

If an account has available transaction balances (TRB) that cannot be removed, these represent a sunk cost and should not be included in the opportunity cost. Therefore we modify Equation (4.7) to remove them:

$$TCB = i\left(\frac{SC}{ecr(1 - rr)} - TRB\right). \tag{4.8}$$

COST OF MIXED COMPENSATION. If transaction balances are allowed to earn credits, fees would be reduced. The amount of reduction is $ecrTRB(1 - rr)$. Therefore, removing all but the transaction balances would result in fee payments of

$$TCM = [SC - ecrTRB(1 - rr)]. \qquad (4.9)$$

In using all of these formulas, care must be taken to state the interest rates in terms of the same time period as the service charges. If service charges are levied monthly, interest rates should be given monthly as well.

Sample Computations of Bank Compensation Alternatives

Table 4.6 illustrates the concepts just developed. In Case 1 we assume that there are no transaction balances; this means if we pay by fees, all balances can be removed. In this case, by applying Equation (4.6), the annual cost of paying by fees is $10,000. Using Equation (4.7), the opportunity cost of tying up balances is $11,910. This difference is primarily due to the reserve requirement and to the differential between the firm's opportunity cost of 8.5% and the bank's ECR of 8.11%.

In Case 2, we assume that the account has $30,000 in transaction balances that cannot be removed. This lowers the cost of the balance alternative to $9,360 because the $30,000 cannot be invested to earn 8.5%. Now balance compensation is lower than fee compensation.

In Case 3, we again assume the existence of $30,000 in transaction balances and now add the assumption that the bank permits a mixture of fees and

Table 4.6 Bank Compensation Alternatives

Assumptions

1. Service charges, annual	$10,000
2. Bank's ECR (annualized)	8.11%
3. Reserve requirement	12.00%
4. Alternative short-term security	8.50%

Case 1: Assume That All Balances Can Be Removed
Cost of fee alternative = $10,000
Cost of balance alternative =

$$.085\frac{10,000}{.0811(1 - .12)} = \$11,910$$

Case 2: Assume a Transaction Balance of $30,000
Cost of fee alternative = $10,000
Cost of balance alternative =

$$.085\left(\frac{10,000}{.0811(1 - .12)} - 30,000\right) = \$9,360$$

Case 3: Assume a Transaction Balance of $30,000 and Assume That the Bank Permits Mixed Compensation
Cost of mixed compensation =

$$[10,000 - .0811(30,000)(1 - .12)] = \$7,859$$

balances. Now the $30,000 earns credits toward service charges. The compensation is $7,859. This is lower than either pure balance or fee compensation, as shown in Case 2. This illustrates the general principle that mixed compensation is usually superior to either balance or fee compensation.

Summary

In this chapter we learned that there are several different kinds of cash balances. Figure 4.3 summarizes the relationship between the four main balances we discussed. Ledger balances are used primarily for accounting purposes and provide a record of deposits. After allowing for availability delays associated with check and ACH deposits (bank float), an available balance is computed. Available balances represent real value to the firm. They are used for bank compensation and can also be used by the firm for other forms of investment. After subtracting reserve requirements, banks may compute still another balance. This balance is sometimes called the *free balance*—presumably because it is now free of all other corrections. An earnings credit rate is often applied to the free balance to determine the credits a depositor earns toward payment for bank charges.

We then illustrated the relationship between these balances that exist in an account analysis. An account analysis simply translates service charges into balance equivalents at some specified interest rate, the earnings credit rate.

Finally, we discussed alternatives for bank compensation: fees only, balances only, or a mixture of the two. We found that in choosing between fees

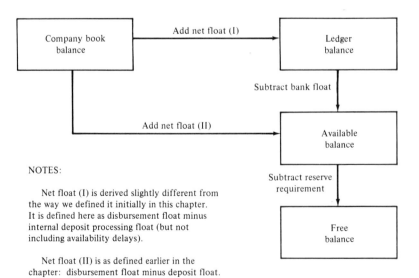

NOTES:

Net float (I) is derived slightly different from the way we defined it initially in this chapter. It is defined here as disbursement float minus internal deposit processing float (but not including availability delays).

Net float (II) is as defined earlier in the chapter: disbursement float minus deposit float.

Figure 4.3 Relationship Between Various Cash Balances.

and balances, there is no general answer: it depends on the characteristics of a particular account. When balances can be easily and inexpensively held close to zero, compensation by fees is economically advantageous. The reason is primarily the reserve requirement. If firms keep cash invested in short-term investments instead of in bank demand deposits, they do not donate a fraction of their investment to the Fed, as the banks do. If balances cannot be easily removed or if dual balances or double accounting are present, balance-based compensation may be preferred. If a bank permits mixed compensation, that alternative generally dominates the other two.

Discussion Questions

1. Describe the differences between bank ledger, bank available, and company book balances. What is the economic significance of each?
2. Why is it important to convert business days into calendar days when dealing with bank balances and investments?
3. Why are ledger balances always greater than available balances?
4. If coin and currency are deposited in a bank, will the amount always be available immediately? Explain.
5. Explain what is meant by net float and state two ways in which it can be computed.
6. Define red book balances and explain three ways of handling them in accounting reports. Comment on the ethics of maintaining such balances.
7. Explain how banks pay "interest" on demand deposit balances in spite of regulations stating that they cannot do so.
8. What is meant by a free balance?
9. What are some alternative methods banks use in computing bank float for a corporate account?
10. Compare and contrast the three methods of bank compensation: fees, balances, and mixed.
11. How do taxes influence the fees versus balances debate?

Problems

1. Mary's Millinery Shop receives a check for $1,000 for a very fancy hat. Mary prepares a deposit ticket, records the deposit on her cash ledger, and takes the deposit to the local bank at about 6 P.M. on a Thursday evening. She puts the deposit into the night depository. The check receives 1-day availability from the bank. Show the impact of this deposit on Mary's book balance, the bank ledger balance, and the bank available balance by creating a balance table showing how each balance changes over time.

2. A firm has $20,000 in ledger balances and the same available balances at its deposit bank on Monday morning. Ledger deposits and disbursement clearings for this week follow the following schedule. Each deposit consists of a mixture of checks and cash receiving availability according to these ratios:

20%	Immediate availability
50%	1-day availability
30%	2-day availability

Day	Deposit Schedule	Clearing Schedule
Mon	$100,000	$ 20,000
Tue	$ 50,000	$ 0
Wed	$ 80,000	$100,000
Thu	$200,000	$ 50,000
Fri	$100,000	$ 80,000
Mon	$120,000	$200,000

a. Construct two balance tables: one for ledger balances and one for available balances. Each should show the opening balance, deposits, transfers, and closing balance.

b. Compute the average ledger and average available balance for the 8-day period based on the closing balance. Be sure to include weekends. What is the average bank float for this time period?

c. Explain why the ledger balance, in general, is always at least as great as the available balance.

3. Cash flow into and out of the Longhorn Leaf Company averages about $25,000,000 per month. Disbursements take, on average, 7 days from check preparation to check clearing. Deposits are processed the same day they are received and deposited for an average availability of 1 calendar day. Longhorn Leaf tries to maintain about $2,000,000 in average available balances to compensate its bankers.

a. Compute Longhorn Leaf's average disbursement and deposit float volume (dollar amount).

b. Compute the average net float.

c. On average, how much should Longhorn Leaf keep in its company book balance when fairly compensating its banks?

d. At an opportunity cost of 10% per year, how much would the company lose if it assumed that it should keep the required $2,000,000 in the company book balance instead of the bank available balance?

e. Explain how Longhorn Leaf could maintain a negative company book balance while dealing with the potentially adverse reactions of unsophisticated investors.

4. Big City Bank is producing a monthly account analysis for the Hill Pickling Company. Service charges for the month of July are as follows:

Service	Per Item	Number
Deposits	$ .10	500
Checks cleared	$ .15	2,000
Wire transfers	$ 14.00	5
Account maint.	$ 25.00	7
ACH deposit	$ 5.00	4
ACH transactions	$ .03	1,500
Consulting fee	$300.00	1

Big City grants an earnings credit rate of 5.7% on free balances held during the month. The reserve requirement on demand deposits is 12%. Bank float averages about 40% of ledger balances.

a. What are the total service charges for July?

b. What available balances should be maintained to cover these charges? What if Hill keeps more than this amount? What if they keep less?

c. What should the average ledger balance be for July?

5. Suppose that service charges for a particular account amount to $400 for a given month. The earnings credit rate is 6% and the reserve requirement is 12%. Assume that the firm can earn 7.2% if it removes balances and invests in an equivalent liquid, low-risk investment. Assume a corporate tax rate of 40%.

a. How much would the firm have to keep in available balances to compensate the bank?

b. If the firm removes its balances and invests them in the alternative investment, how much better or worse off would it be after taking taxes into account?

c. Explain why the tax deductibility of fees should not be a persuasive argument against balances.

══════════ **Case: *Pica Enterprises*** ══════════

Tom Taylor, the assistant treasurer for Pica Enterprises, is reviewing the banking arrangements for the Pennsohio Division. He has received an account analysis from the Mideast Commercial Bank (MCB) for the activities of the division for November 1987 and wonders if they could do the banking at a lower cost. In addition to the following account analysis, Tom has gathered the following information: the current rate on T-bills is 7.75%, the Pennsohio Division maintains available balances of $75,000 for transactions purposes, MCB applies the average float for the entire bank to all accounts, and MCB allows a mixture of fees and balances as compensation for the account.

For several months, a representative of the Hutton National Bank (HNB) has been calling on Tom, attempting to get the banking business of the Pennsohio Division. Since Tom is in the process of reviewing the account, he wants to see how much it would cost to do business with HNB. HNB's per unit charge data are shown in the following table, and they pay an earnings credit rate of 6.75% on free balances. HNB uses actual float instead of an average for the bank. Tom thinks that this practice might be a factor, since his calculations indicate that the average float for the division is approximately $45,000.

Mideast Commercial Bank: Account Analysis for Pica Enterprises

Activities and Charges for November 1987

Item	Number	Unit Cost	Total
Account maintenance	1	$25.00	$ 25.00
Deposit items	2,589	$ 0.07	$181.23
Checks encoded	2,569	$ 0.02	$ 51.38
Coin and Currency	10	$ 5.00	$ 50.00
Wire transfers	20	$10.00	$200.00
Checks presented	1,567	$ 0.09	$141.03
Total			$648.64

Balance Analysis for the Month

Average ledger balance		$195,670.90
Less: bank float		$ 52,831.14
Average available balance		$142,839.76
Less: reserve requirement	0.12	$ 17,140.77
Free balances		$125,698.99
Earnings credits	0.075	$ 785.62
Fees Owed (Excess Earnings Credits)	($	136.98)

Hutton National Bank: List of Charges

Item	Unit Cost
Account maintenance	$30.00
Deposit items	$ 0.08
Coin and currency	$10.00
Wire transfers	$ 7.50
Checks presented	$ 0.08

5

Payment Systems

A large midwestern firm adopted a new system for collecting payments from its network of distributors. The former system was a paper check system, with billing, mail, processing, and clearing delays sometimes taking 3 weeks or more. The new system enabled headquarters to debit distributor accounts directly and collect some $8,000,000 in daily cash flows in only 2 days. The cost was less than $.50 for each transaction, and control of payment moved from the distributor to the treasurer's office. What kind of payment system did this firm employ? What alternatives are available? What are the pros and cons of different types of payments?

Chapter 4 discussed different types of bank balances. This chapter presents alternative methods of moving cash from one bank balance to another. Payment systems are primarily differentiated by the timing effect that they have on different kinds of bank balances, on costs, and on control of transfer initiation. We focus in this chapter on payment systems in the United States: coin and currency, paper check, wire, and automated clearing house (ACH) transfer. Chapter 19 deals with the basic concepts of payment systems available in other countries.

An Overview of Payment Systems

Components of a Payment System

A *payment system* is the means whereby cash value is transferred between a payor and a payee. It includes (1) policies and procedures, including rules for crediting and debiting balances; (2) a medium for storing and transmitting payment information; and (3) financial intermediaries for organizing information flow, carrying out value transfer instructions, and generally administering payment activities.

The four basic types of value transfer (coin and currency, check, wire, and automated clearing house) are designated as *primary payment systems* because each one alone is sufficient to transfer value from one party to another. There are also different types of *secondary payment systems* that convey payment information but ultimately require one of the primary payment systems to transfer value. An example of a secondary payment system is a charge card system. Value transfer information is collected when a consumer uses a charge card for a purchase. Ultimate payment, however, is usually made by paper check.

Table 5.1 illustrates the stocks and flows of cash in the U.S. economy. Table A shows that currency represents about 25% of the money supply (measured by M1). The percentage has been shrinking over the past few years. There are no statistics on the volume of transactions represented by coin and currency. Check transactions account for over 99% of non-coin and non-currency transactions. Wires represent a small (0.11%) percentage of the transactions but the relative proportion is increasing. ACH transactions are growing at the fastest rate and now account for nearly 1% of total transactions.

Dollar volume reverses the relative importance of checks and wires. While wires present only a tenth of a percent of transaction volume, they account for nearly 80% of the dollar volume. Check dollar volume—at least a crude estimate of it—represents a shrinking percentage, now below 20%. Data is scarce on ACH dollar volume but the percentage is growing.

Payment Systems Compared and Contrasted

We first give an overview of the four primary payment systems and then go into detail in four separate sections. Table 5.2 highlights some of the differences between these systems.

Coin and Currency
For coin and currency, cash value information is stored on a metal or paper medium. Value is transferred by simply moving the medium itself from payor to payee. No bank or other intermediary is needed, since the bearer holds the value. Usually coin and currency transactions are relatively small (barring Las Vegas jackpots) and have a very low cost per transaction.

Checks
For checks, value information is contained on a piece of paper; the cash value itself is stored in a bank account. A transaction intermediary, often a commercial bank, is needed to process the check and make the value transfer from one account to another. The Fed may or may not be involved as an intermediary, as we will see later. Checks may be written for any amount and are relatively inexpensive to process. The check itself is limited in terms of the amount of supporting information it may contain (information such as invoice number, payment terms, etc. is often essential to process a payment).

Table 5.1   Relative Measures of the Stock and Flow of Cash in the U.S. Economy

A. MONEY SUPPLY VOLUME (BILLIONS)

Year	Currency	Percentage	Checks	Percentage	Total M1	Percentage
1980	$117	28	$298	72	$415	100
1981	$124	28	$318	72	$442	100
1982	$134	28	$346	72	$480	100
1983	$148	28	$379	72	$527	100
1984	$159	28	$399	72	$558	100
1985	$171	27	$456	73	$627	100
1986	$184	25	$547	75	$731	100

Source: Federal Reserve Bulletin, August, 1987

B. TRANSACTION VOLUME (MILLIONS)

Year	Checks	Percentage	Wires	Percentage	ACH Trans	Percentage	Total	Percentage
1980	34,800	99.74	27.7	0.08	64.4	0.18	34,892	100
1981	36,900	99.69	31.1	0.08	83.3	0.23	37,014	100
1982	39,100	99.64	35.4	0.09	105.2	0.27	39,241	100
1983	40,600	99.52	38.0	0.09	156.5	0.38	40,795	100
1984	42,300	99.40	41.6	0.10	214.4	0.50	42,556	100
1985	43,900	99.26	45.1	0.10	282.9	0.64	44,228	100
1986	45,000	99.09	49.8	0.11	362.6	0.80	45,412	100

Source: Discussion with Federal Reserve information office, Sept. 1987

Table 5.1 (*continued*)

C. DOLLAR VOLUME (TRILLIONS)

Year	Checks[a]	Percentage	Wires	Percentage	ACH Trans	Percentage	Total	Percentage
1980	$23.8	33.04	$ 48.3	66.96	N/A	N/A	$ 72.1	100
1981	$25.3	30.46	$ 57.7	69.54	N/A	N/A	$ 83.0	100
1982	$26.8	26.58	$ 74.0	73.42	N/A	N/A	$100.8	100
1983	$27.8	24.06	$ 87.8	75.94	N/A	N/A	$115.6	100
1984	$29.0	22.82	$ 98.0	77.18	N/A	N/A	$127.0	100
1985	$30.1	21.33	$109.1	77.39	1.8	1.28	$141.0	100
1986	$30.8	19.51	$125.0	79.10	2.2	1.39	$158.0	100

[a] Federal Reserve does not keep track of dollar volumes of checks since it only clears 35–36% of all checks. The number reported is a very rough estimate obtained by multiplying the number of checks cleared by the Fed's average dollar check size for 1985.

Source: Discussion with Federal Reserve information office, Sept. 1987

Table 5.2 Payment System Features

Feature	Coin and Currency	Check	Wire	ACH
Medium for storing or transmitting value information	Paper or metal	Paper	Electronic	Electronic
Where value is stored	Federal Reserve	Bank balance	Bank balance	Bank balance
Time delay for value transfer	0 days (0–3 days)*	0–3 days (0–5 days)†	0 days	1–2 days (1–4 days)†
Relative dollar amount per transaction	Small	Any size	Large	Any size
Intermediaries involved	None needed	Bank (Fed optional)	Bank and Fed	Bank and Fed
Expense per transaction	Very low	Low	High	Low
Notification	No	No	Yes	No
Confirmation	No	No	Yes	No
Messages	No	No (except for attached documents)	Limited	Limited Extensive (CTP) Extensive (CTX)

* Days are calendar days. Deposits made into a bank after the bank's cutoff time on a Friday afternoon may not be given ledger credit until the following Monday. For a cash deposit, that would mean a 3-calendar-day delay in receiving available funds.

† A check with 2-day availability deposited after the bank's cutoff time on Friday would not become available until the following Wednesday, 5 calendar days later. Holidays extend the time even further.
Source: Bernell K. Stone, "Electronic Payment Basics," *Economic Review*, March 1986, pp. 9–18.

Therefore, most check transactions are accompanied by additional documentation containing information required for the transaction.

Wire Transfers

In making a wire transfer, a payor gives instructions to a bank in which the payor has an available balance. The bank passes instructions on to the Fed to move value from the bank's reserve balance account to the reserve balance account of another bank in which the payee has an account. Though initially generated by voice, paper instructions, or electronic means, the actual transfer of value is merely a bookkeeping entry at the Fed. The Fed credits the reserve account of the payee's bank and debits the reserve account of the payor's bank. Wires also provide *confirmation* to the payor that value was actually transferred to the payee. This is important for some types of contract payments where exact timing is specified. When a bank receives an incoming wire, the receiving firm is given *notification* that value has been received. This is also an important feature for many types of transactions. No other mechanism provides essentially immediate confirmation and notification to the parties in a payment transaction. Unfortunately, wires do not permit additional information to be carried along with the wire information. It is not uncommon for a firm to receive a wire payment and to be in the dark concerning the purpose of the payment (what invoices were covered, whether a discount was taken, which subsidiary sent the payment, etc.).

Automated Clearing House (ACH) Transfers

An ACH transfer is very similar to a paper check transfer. The major difference between the two is that for an ACH, value information is stored on a computer tape or disk rather than on a piece of paper. As we show later, clearing a paper check and an ACH transfer involves essentially the same processes. The advantage of moving information via computer rather than paper is that the sorting and transmitting processes are much faster and potentially less expensive. Data for an ACH transfer may be formatted in several ways. Most formats permit only limited associated information to be transmitted to the payee. Two other possible formats permit extensive documentation to accompany a payment.

Coin and Currency

Coin and currency are used by firms that sell products and services directly to consumers over the counter. Fast food, some financial institutions, public transportation, retail petroleum, and vending are examples of industries in which a large percentage of transactions are in the form of coin and currency. On the other hand, many firms have virtually no coin and currency, since all payments are in the form of check, wire, or ACH transfers. Of the total money supply (M^1) 25% is represented by coin and currency. The remainder is represented by tiny magnetic fields contained on computer tapes and disks at banks.

Security

Since coin and currency represent immediate value to any bearer, there are security problems associated with this type of payment. First, there is a risk that the cash will be lost or stolen at the collection point. Second, there is a risk that the firm's representative at the collection point may abscond with the cash rather than deposit it in the firm's deposit bank. Third, there is a risk that unethical employees at the deposit bank may skim off a portion of the cash deposit.

The primary reason for these risks is that the value and the information storage are one and the same. In contrast, a paper check represents only the instructions to transfer value; it does not store the value itself. Hence, to solve the security problems posed by cash, two approaches are used: (1) *physical security,* which makes the coin and currency more difficult for unauthorized individuals to obtain, and (2) *independent information flow,* which creates a reliable, independent information stream to verify the cash amounts. We illustrate both of these points.

Physical Security

Transit companies obtain the bulk of their cash flow from fare boxes. To ensure the physical security of the cash, fare boxes are made difficult for potential thieves (including passengers and bus drivers) to remove or enter. Removing cash from fare boxes is a process independent of the driver. Cash removed is stored in a secure area until it can be counted, deposited, and checked against fare box records.

Firms that collect or disburse large amounts of coin and currency often use armored car services to protect cash physically from the point of receipt to the point of deposit. Such services offer protection from theft and reduce the management time required to make deposits physically. In some areas, employee safety is also a need filled by armored car services. Of course, the cost for such services may be relatively high.

Independent Information Flow

Most firms use some form of cash register when receiving cash from customers. Not only does such a device enable the salesperson to tally up the bill, it gives the company an additional source of information about how much cash should have been received and deposited at the end of the day. For example, when a customer pays cash to an airport parking lot attendant, the amount paid is often displayed on a screen. There may be a small sign in view of the customer saying, in effect, "If the amount you are charged differs from the amount shown here, please report the discrepancy to — — —." This technique ensures that the attendant doesn't charge a customer $10, pocket $4, and put the remaining $6 in the till. At the end of the day, if the amount totaled on the cash register differs from the amount deposited, an inquiry is made.

As another example, when a firm's representative deposits cash in a night depository, he or she generally reports the amount of the deposit to firm headquarters—perhaps by using a copy of the deposit ticket. As an independent confirmation, the firm may also ask the bank to report the amount of the deposit. If the two numbers differ, an investigation is initiated.

Counting

Firms that collect large amounts of money in coin and currency have the task of counting and verifying their deposits. *Verification* means making sure that the reported cash agrees with the actual amount. Though automated optical scanning equipment is available, most currency is manually counted. Coins, however, are most often counted by mechanical devices. These machines sift the coins by size into appropriate slots and count each coin. Most banks and some firms have such machines. A less expensive process is to separate coins into denominations (pennies, dimes, etc.) and weigh them. Though this method is less accurate, the cost saved may be more than the value of the added accuracy.

Separating coin and currency into denominations is sometimes not an easy task. One transit authority complains that cash received in the fare box is often a mixture of crumpled bills with embedded coins and other objects like bubble gum. This company had a difficult time finding a bank that would sort through the conglomeration at any reasonable price.

Timing

Generally, a deposit of coin and currency is credited by a bank as an available deposit at the same time it is counted as a ledger deposit. The Fed allows banks to count all coin and currency as part of their Federal Reserve balance requirement. Hence, there is usually no bank float with coin and currency. Nevertheless, there are sometimes delays in coin and currency deposits because of the need to count and verify the deposit. A deposit made after the bank's cutoff time for cash deposits is carried over to the following day. A Wednesday deposit into a night depository, for example, is usually counted the following morning and credited as a ledger and available deposit on Thursday. A Friday night deposit is credited on Monday.

In other cases, the counting process may be further delayed. For the transit company previously mentioned, the deposit bank counted the company's deposit bags only once every week or so when time was available. Some banks may hold coin and currency deposits until a representative from the firm can be present when the deposit is opened and counted. The bank, in this case, is trying to protect itself from deposit discrepancies. The person who made the night deposit may claim to have deposited $5,000 but the bank may find only $4,000 in the deposit pouch. Who is in error? If the bank opens a locked deposit pouch in the presence of a representative of the firm and requires the representative to sign a document certifying the amount, then the bank reduces its liability. The result may be a delayed deposit—and an administrative cost to send a representative of the firm.

Intermediaries

The banking system receives deposits of coin and currency from parties that receive cash payments from their customers. The coin and currency are then recirculated to consumers and other businesses that use coin and currency. In this way, the bank is acting as an intermediary in the flow of coin and currency.

The Fed also acts as an intermediary by removing coin and currency from net generating banks and funneling it into banks that are net users of coin and currency. Banks schedule deliveries of coin and currency to and from the Fed to coincide with projected needs of their customers. Although banks generally have a reserve of coin and currency in bank vaults, they may require advance notice if a firm intends to remove a significant amount at any one time.

Banks monitor the currency flowing through their operations and sort out defective bills for return to the Fed. Large banks have optical scanners that flag worn bills and send them to the Fed for shredding. Government mints print new bills continually and enter them into the system through the Fed.

Checks

A check itself is not value but an order—in banking parlance, a *draft*—to move value from one account balance to another. One of several types of drafts, a check is characterized by being complete in and of itself; it requires no supporting documentation, which may be required by other types of drafts. It is a demand instrument that requires the bank on which it is drawn to provide value to the payee on demand. This means that value transfer is not delayed, as it is in a time draft.

How Checks Transfer Value

Figure 5.1 illustrates how a $5,000 check is used to transfer value from a payor to a payee. The following steps are included in the process.

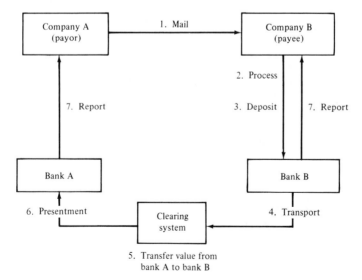

Figure 5.1   The Check System.

Check Preparation
The payor prepares a check by drawing it to the order of the payee. The amount is indicated by numbers ("$5,000") and also, to lessen the chance of error, by words ("Five thousand dollars and 00/100 cents"). Though most checks are signed by hand or stamped by a signature facsimile plate, some companies now send signatureless checks. These checks have only a computer-printed signature in ordinary characters. Usually, however, to guard against misuse, the signature line will contain a few special print characters that can be printed only with a special printer. The purpose of a signatureless check is to reduce the expense and administrative time required by duplicate processing — once to print the numerical amount and the name of the payee and again to affix a signature.

Check Delivery
The check is mailed to the payee. A great majority of checks processed by firms are sent through the mail. Alternatives to regular mail are hand delivery and courier service.

Payee Processing
The payee processes the check by recording the amount on its cash ledger and crediting the payor's account receivable with a $5,000 payment.

Deposit
The payee deposits the check in its demand deposit account at bank B. If the check is deposited before the bank's cutoff time, the payee receives a $5,000 ledger credit in its account at the end of that business day. If the deposit is received after the cutoff time, the payee receives a $5,000 credit at the end of the following business day.

Payee Bank Processing
Bank B processes the check by, among other things, recording a ledger credit for the payee, by scheduling when the check will become available to the payee's account, and by physically transporting the check to the clearing system. We discuss alternatives for clearing checks later in this chapter.

Check Clearing
According to processing schedules, the clearing system gives $5,000 in value to bank B. The value transfer is generally nothing more than a computer entry. Sometimes the Federal Reserve System is the clearing agent, while at other times a correspondent bank performs this task. We discuss how the value transfer takes place later in this chapter.

Check Presentment
The check is physically delivered (presented) by the clearing system (such as the Federal Reserve, clearing house, or another bank) to bank A and $5,000 in

value is subtracted from bank A's account. Bank A then deducts $5,000 from the payor's demand deposit account.

Reporting

The banks provide reports to their respective parties in the form of periodic bank statements and sometimes daily deposit reports.

The MICR Line

To ensure that the check is returned efficiently to the account on which it was drawn, the amount of the check and information about the payor's bank and account number are stored on the check. To lessen the need for manual check processing, this information is stored in the form of characters that can be quickly read by computers. The characters are printed at the bottom of the check in what is called the *MICR line*. *MICR* stands for *magnetic ink character recognition*. The characters may be read by optical scanning equipment or, more quickly and inexpensively, by magnetic read heads.

Elements of the MICR Line

Figure 5.2 illustrates a typical check. The MICR line contains the following information.

FEDERAL RESERVE DISTRICT. The first two digits (numbers 01 to 12) identify the Federal Reserve district in which the drawee bank is located. For example, "07" in the first two places indicates the seventh Fed district or the Chicago Fed. See Table 5.3 for a listing of Fed district banks, branches, and other

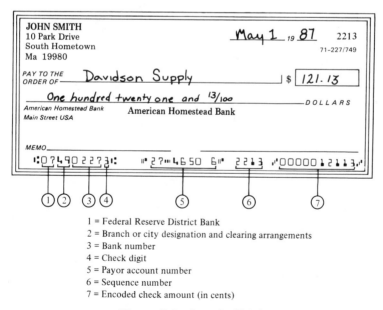

1 = Federal Reserve District Bank
2 = Branch or city designation and clearing arrangements
3 = Bank number
4 = Check digit
5 = Payor account number
6 = Sequence number
7 = Encoded check amount (in cents)

Figure 5.2 Sample Check.

Table 5.3 Locations of Federal Reserve District Banks, Branches, and Offices

Fed No.	District Bank	Branches	Other Offices
1	Boston		Lewiston, Me. Windsor Locks, Conn.
2	New York	Buffalo	Cranford, N.J. Jericho, N.Y. Oriskany, N.Y.
3	Philadelphia		
4	Cleveland	Cincinnati Pittsburgh	Columbus, Ohio
5	Richmond, Va.	Baltimore Charlotte, W. Va.	Columbia, S.C. Chesterton, W. Va. Culpeper, Va. (Communications and records center)
6	Atlanta	Birmingham, Ala. Jacksonville, Tenn. Miami Nashville, Tenn. New Orleans	
7	Chicago	Detroit	Des Moines Indianapolis Milwaukee
8	St. Louis	Little Rock, Ark. Louisville Memphis	
9	Minneapolis		
10	Kansas City	Denver Oklahoma City Omaha	
11	Dallas	El Paso Houston San Antonio	
12	San Francisco	Los Angeles Portland Salt Lake City Seattle	

Source: Federal Reserve Bulletin (Vol. 72, 1986).

offices. Numbers greater than 12 indicate that the drawee is a nonbank entity such as a savings and loan institution or a credit union.

FEDERAL RESERVE OFFICE. The next two digits give further information about how the check is to clear. The third digit identifies the Fed district office or branch. The fourth digit indicates any special clearing arrangements.

BANK IDENTIFICATION NUMBER. Digits five through eight make up the American Bankers Association four-digit identification number. Each bank (or other depository institution) has a unique number within a particular Fed district.

CHECK DIGIT. The last digit is only for computer purposes. It enables the computer to determine if a mistake was made in reading the other eight digits. A tear in the paper or smeared ink may cause a machine to misread a number. In that case, the check would be flagged and handled manually.

PAYOR'S ACCOUNT NUMBER. Within a depository institution, each account is assigned a unique number. This enables the bank to debit (or credit) the appropriate account after the check is presented.

SEQUENCE NUMBER (OPTIONAL). This field enables the bank to sort checks to a particular account in numerical order. It is also called the *auxiliary on-us field* and can be used by the bank for any other purposes.

ENCODED AMOUNT. At the deposit bank, the amount for which the check is drawn is read (by people) and then printed (*encoded,* to use the bank term) on the right-hand side of the MICR line. Unless an error has been made, this number (in cents) will agree with the amount written or typed in the body of the check. Once a check is encoded, it is completely computer readable from that time on. The bank of deposit is usually the party that encodes the check. Some firms, if they have a large number of checks to process, find it cheaper and faster to do their own encoding.

Check-Clearing Mechanisms

When we refer to the *check clearing process,* we mean the procedure by which the payee receives value, the payor loses value, and the check is returned to the payor. There are several possible ways in which a check is transferred from the payee's deposit bank back to the payor's disbursement account. Each implies a variation in the way value is transferred.

On-Us Checks

If the payee deposits the check in the same bank on which it is drawn, the check is termed an *on-us* check. Clearing the check involves just one bank. The payor's account is debited, the payee's account is credited, and the check is returned to the payor. If the check is deposited by the bank's cutoff time, the payee receives value and the payor loses value at the end of the business day.

Local Clearing Houses

Banks in the same geographical area usually find that a large volume of their checks are drawn on other banks in the same area. Such banks may form a local clearing house owned and operated by them. Each bank has an account with every other bank in the clearing house group. To clear checks through a clearing house, representatives from each bank meet daily to present checks to each other. The checks are bundled together to form a *cash letter*, or set of one or more checks accompanied by a listing of each check and the dollar amounts. A cash letter is essentially the same as a corporate deposit, which includes a list of checks on a deposit ticket.

If bank A presents $4,000,000 worth of checks drawn against bank B and bank B presents $5,000,000 worth of checks drawn against bank A, only the net value of $1,000,000 has to be transferred. This amount can be transferred by bank A crediting bank B's correspondent balance at bank A. Alternatively, bank B can debit bank A's correspondent balance at bank B. A third possibility is for the clearing house to report net transfers to the Federal Reserve Bank in the area where the $1,000,000 would be credited to bank B's account and debited against bank A's account.

Local Correspondent Banks

Banks often use larger banks to collect their checks. For example, a small bank in the suburbs may open an account with a larger bank that is a member of a large clearing house in the city. The smaller bank deposits into its account with the large bank all checks drawn on clearing house member banks. That way the small bank has the advantages of the clearing house without meeting the volume criteria often imposed on members.

Local Federal Reserve Banks

As we discussed in Chapter 3, a major role of the Fed is to act as a check-clearing agent. Each depository institution has a reserve account with the Fed. Cash letters presented to the Fed are given credit in the reserve account. Figure 5.3 shows how a check deposited by bank A drawn on bank B for $5,000 is cleared through the Fed. Let's suppose that the Fed decides that the check is to receive 1-day availability and that the check is deposited on a Tuesday morning. In a process identical to the availability delays discussed in chapter 4, the Fed gives bank A ledger credit on Tuesday. Ledger credit doesn't count toward bank A's reserve requirement. On Wednesday, bank A receives available credit in its reserve account. Meanwhile, the Fed sorts all deposited checks and transports the $5,000 check to bank B, along with all other checks drawn on that bank. On the day of presentment, value is subtracted from bank B's reserve account. Usually the amount is also subtracted from the payor's account on the same business day.

Direct Send to a Correspondent Bank

A bank may choose to bypass the Fed and send a cash letter directly to a correspondent bank in a distant city. This is called a *direct send*. It may result in faster availability for the bank and the customer. For example, suppose customers deposit checks drawn on Florida banks into accounts in a San

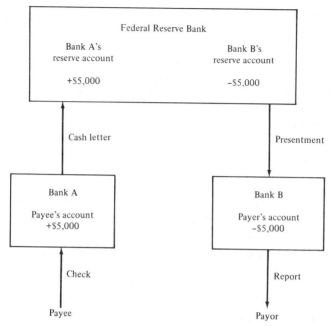

Figure 5.3   Check Clearing Using the Federal Reserve System.

Francisco bank. If the checks were cleared through the Fed, the San Francisco bank might receive 2-day availability. However, if the San Francisco bank were to send the checks via courier directly to a large Miami bank, availability could be reduced to 1 day or less. As in the local correspondent bank example, value is transferred between banks through correspondent balances.

Direct Send Through the Fed

Another way for the bank to receive faster availability is to bypass the local Fed and send checks directly to a Fed in another city. A bank can do this by sorting the checks the way the Fed would sort them and by delivering cash letters to join the Fed's cash letters being sent to that particular distant Fed. Since a bank in one Fed district will not have an account with a distant Fed, the Fed that the bank normally uses will credit the bank's deposit even though it doesn't physically handle the check. This is sometimes called a *commingled shipment*.

Returned Checks

When a check is presented to the drawee bank, it may be returned for several reasons. The account numbers may represent a closed or nonexistent account, there may be insufficient funds (ledger balance smaller than the amount of the check), or there may be an uncollected funds condition in the account (ledger balance is sufficient but available balance is smaller than the amount of the check). Any of these conditions will cause the check to become a return item. The check must then be returned via the channels through which it came. To trace how a check reached the drawee bank, one examines the many rubber stamped blocks on the back of the check. The check must be sent by each institution back to the one from which it came. Since the ink easily smears and the stamps often overlap, routing a check backward is often a tedious task. On average, it takes 7 business days to return a check to the point of deposit, but some checks require a much longer period.

For this reason, banks often impose a *hold period* on accounts. This means that the account holder may not remove the deposited amount from the account until sufficient time has elapsed to allow the bank to make sure that the check doesn't come back as a return item before the value of the deposit is released.

More efficient return item processing is an important objective of the Fed and the banks. One reason is that the Fed has been giving the deposit bank credit for the check according to the Fed's availability schedule. When the check is returned, the Fed usually "backs out" the credit the day the check comes back. This results in the Fed giving an interest-free loan to a bank for several days. One computer company has developed a bar coding system for electronically scanning the route of a check. Each processor adds a small bar code to the back of the check. Thus, instead of manual handling, the return process can be automated.

Check-like Payment Instruments

Other payment mechanisms may also be considered drafts with check-like attributes. Table 5.4 compares and contrasts a number of check-like instruments. All are processed through the same clearing channels but differ from checks in a few features.

Payable Through Draft (PTD)

While a check is drawn against a bank, a PTD is drawn against the payor. After a PTD is presented to a bank, the payor has 24 hours in which to honor or to refuse payment. PTDs are used primarily in situation where (1) payment is initiated by a representative of the firm (such as a salesperson or branch office manager) and (2) there is some chance that the payment should not be authorized. For example, insurance firms sometimes have field agents issue PTDs for claim settlements. Before the draft clears, headquarters can make sure that the claimant has a valid insurance policy and that everything else is in order.

Preauthorized Check (PAC)

Regular checks are drawn by the payor. A PAC, however, is a check drawn by the *payee* against the account of the *payor*. The MICR line of the check is the same as the one that would appear if the payor had produced the check

Table 5.4 Comparison of Check-like Payment Instruments

Instrument	Drawn On	Initiated By	Accompanying Documents	Time Delay[*]	Intrafirm Only
Regular check	Payor's bank	Payor	No	No	No
Payable through draft (PTD)	Payor	Payor	No	24 hours	No
Preauthorized check (PAC)	Payor's bank	Payee	No	No	No
Money order	Third party	Payor	No	No	No
Depository transfer check (DTC)	Payor's bank	Payor	No	No	Yes
Traveler's check	Third party	Payor	No (second signing)	No	No
Sight draft	Payor's bank	Payor	Yes	No	No
Time draft	Payor's bank	Payor	Yes	Yes	No

[*] By *time delay* we mean the specified delay inherent in the payment instrument, not availability or clearing. There will be, of course, availability and clearing delays for all of the instruments.

and mailed it to the payee. The payor must, of course, authorize the payee to draw such a check. PACs are most commonly used when the payor makes regular payments of the same amount. They are, therefore, useful for mortgage, insurance, budget utility, and other similar repeat payments.

Money Order

A payee that accepts a regular check for payment is running a risk that the payor may not have sufficient cash in the disbursement account to cover the check when presented. A money order greatly reduces this risk. The payor simply has a more creditworthy third party (such as the post office, bank, drug chain, etc.) write the check. The third party avoids this risk by requiring the payor to pay in coin and currency before writing the money order.

Depository Transfer Check (DTC)

When a firm wants to move money from its account at one bank to its account at another bank, a depository transfer check may be used. Such checks are valid only for intrafirm payments and may not be drawn in favor of other parties. DTCs need not be signed. One of the most popular uses for DTCs is in the area of cash concentration, or moving cash from distant depository banks to the firm's concentration bank. This application is discussed in depth in Chapter 7.

Traveler's Check

Traveler's checks are prepaid drafts similar to money orders. The risk of insufficient funds is transferred to the bank that issues the traveler's check. Traveler's checks differ from money orders in that an additional signature is required at the time of use.

Sight Draft

While a check is payable when presented and requires no supporting documents, a sight draft must generally be accompanied by other documents showing that the terms of a transaction have been met. Sight drafts are generally used in foreign trade transactions.

Time Draft

Similar to a sight draft, a time draft is payable subject to documentation but, in addition, is subject to specified time delays. Time drafts are also used in foreign trade transactions that contractually specify delayed payments.

Availability Schedules

As we discussed in Chapter 4, when a payee deposits a check in a bank account, availability may be delayed by 0 to 5 days. Having discussed check clearing in some detail here, we are prepared to understand how availability is assigned.

Banks and the Fed generally specify the time delay through what is called an *availability schedule*. This schedule is usually in the form of a long table organized by transit routing number. Table 5.5 shows a portion of a simplified and abbreviated availability schedule. An actual schedule may contain 20–40 pages.

Line 1 of the availability schedule indicates that a check drawn on the bank itself receives same-day availability if deposited by 5:00 P.M. Line 2 shows that checks drawn on any bank that is a member of the Chicago clearing house (they have transit routing numbers starting with 0701) must be deposited by 7:00 A.M. to receive same-day availability. Deposits made after 7:00 A.M. are given 1-day availability. Line 3 shows that checks drawn on any bank in the Chicago Regional Check Processing Center (RCPC) receive same-day availability if deposited by 6:00 A.M., while (line 4) those drawn on Detroit

Table 5.5 Sample Availability Schedule

Drawee Point	TR Number	Cutoff Time	Availability
1. On-us	07000001	5:00 P.M.	0
2. Chicago clearing house	0701	7:00 A.M.	0
3. Chicago RCPC	0702–0709	6:00 A.M.	0
4. Detroit RCPC	0801–0809	2:00 A.M.	0
5. First San Francisco	12089333	5:30 A.M.	1

RCPC banks must be deposited by 2:00 A.M. Sometimes a single bank is listed, as on line 5. The bank has a direct send to the First San Francisco Bank, giving 1-day availability on checks deposited by 5:30 A.M.

Determinants of Availability

A number of factors determine how a bank assigns availability to a specific check. If a bank uses the Fed primarily to clear its checks, the bank's schedule will look very much like the Fed schedule (with a few hours added to permit the bank to sort checks and deliver them to the Fed). If a bank uses direct sends, bank availability can be faster than Fed availability.

Transportation distance is a major factor in determining Fed and bank availability. Generally checks drawn on distant banks or harder-to-reach banks are assigned longer availability times than those drawn on nearby, easy-to-reach banks. A check drawn on an Oregon bank deposited in a New York City bank will likely receive longer availability than a check drawn on a New Jersey bank.

There are, however, many exceptions to this rule. The New York City bank may have a direct send to the Oregon bank. Thus, instead of going through normal Fed clearing channels and receiving 2-day availability, the bank may deliver cash letters to the Oregon bank directly, thereby reducing availability to 1 day.

Availability is generally tied to a cutoff time. Checks must be deposited in the bank and reach the processing center by a specified time to be assigned that day's availability schedule. Checks processed after the cutoff time are treated as if they came into the bank the following business day. This adds 1 calendar day for deposits made during the week and 2 extra days for Friday deposits.

If a depositor sorts its checks by transit routing number, the bank may grant faster availability. Alternatively, the bank may reduce its processing fees or grant a later deposit cutoff for sorted checks. Similarly, if a customer MICR-encodes the dollar amount on the checks it deposits, the bank may grant faster availability, a later cutoff time, or reduced service charges.

Availability is sometimes *negotiated* between the firm and the bank. Instead of using the bank's normal availability schedule, a firm may negotiate a blanket availability on all checks deposited, regardless of other considerations. For example, the firm may receive 1-day availability on *all* checks, even if some would have received immediate and some 2-day availability.

Some banks offer multiple availability schedules. For a higher deposit fee, a firm may receive an *accelerated availability schedule*. The higher price pays for the bank's cost of direct sends and otherwise faster processing.

Availability Is a Contract

Most banks view availability as a contractual obligation. Once a check is deposited into an account and assigned an availability, the bank considers itself obligated to credit the firm's available balance as scheduled even if the bank is subsequently unable to process and clear the check in the time allotted. For example, the bank may assign 1-day availability and then be unable to process the check in time to meet the direct send schedule. The bank may therefore not receive value for the check for 2 business days. In most cases, the bank will "eat the float" and will not charge back the lost interest to the depositor's account.

Federal Reserve Float

Definition

When the Federal Reserve acts as the clearing agent for a check, it sometimes grants availability to the payee's bank before (or after) it presents the check and debits the payor's bank's Federal Reserve account. The difference between the dollar amount credited to payees but not yet debited to payors is called *Federal Reserve float* or *Fed float*. For each check, Fed float may be positive, negative, or zero. In aggregate, Fed float is positive, meaning that the Fed has, on average, added extra money to the money supply.

For example, suppose bank A deposits a $5,000 check drawn on bank B at the Fed on Monday morning. Fed availability for the check is 1 day. This means that on Tuesday, bank A's reserve account increases by $5,000. Suppose that the Fed cannot present the check to bank B until Wednesday. On Wednesday, bank B's reserve account is reduced by $5,000 and the check clears. For 1 day, Tuesday, the money supply was $5,000 higher than it was the day before or the day after. Both banks had the same $5,000 in their reserve accounts.

Fed float has diminished over the past decade. In 1987, average Fed float was under $500,000,000 and dropping. It has run as high as $60,000,000,000 for a few days during bad weather. Before the DIDMCA of 1980 was enacted (see Chapter 3), average Fed float was over $6,000,000,000. The DIDMCA "declared war" on Fed float and created a number of procedures to ensure a reduction in its level.

Causes of Fed Float

Federal Reserve accounts of drawee banks are not debited until checks are physically presented to the bank. As banks do for their customers, the Fed grants availability to banks on a contractual basis. The Fed agrees to credit a bank with an available deposit based on the Fed availability schedule, which assumes that planes and trucks run on schedule. Any delays due to bad weather or other transportation problems may create Fed float.

Sometimes Fed check processing centers cannot process the entire volume of checks on particularly heavy days. This creates holdover from one business day to the next.

Costs of Fed Float

Why is Fed float a problem? Primarily because it represents interest-free loans to banks and, indirectly, to corporations. Through Fed float, taxpayers essentially subsidize inefficiencies in the check-clearing system. As an example, suppose a firm has $1,000,000 on deposit in a Waco, Texas, bank. The firm writes a check drawn on that bank and deposits it into an account in Chicago. The check receives 1-day availability. The next business day, the firm has $1,000,000 in its Chicago bank account. Now suppose the Fed has difficulty delivering the check to Waco because a dust storm has cancelled flights into the Waco airport. The Fed cannot present the check to the Waco bank for 2 days. The firm therefore has $1,000,000 in both the Waco and Chicago banks for 1 day—the same $1,000,000. This "dual balance" effect is discussed more fully in Chapter 7. The firm can earn credits for the deposit at the Waco bank at the same time it is investing the $1,000,000 that has come into the Chicago bank. The extra interest the firm earns is interest the Fed loses. It could have been investing the $1,000,000 in T-bills or other securities.

Reducing Fed Float

When Fed float came to the attention of Congress, the issue was included in the 1980 Monetary Control Act. The DIDMCA mandated that the Fed either eliminate Fed float or price it so that those who benefit from float pay for it. Over the past several years, the Fed has created programs that have resulted in drastic reductions in Fed float.

INTERDISTRICT TRANSPORTATION SYSTEM. The Fed now has an efficient check transportation system that minimizes delays and maximizes the number of checks cleared quickly. This Interdistrict Transportation System (ITS) is based on a hub–spoke concept. Several major transportation center cities are designated as hubs. All other cities are designated as spokes connected to one of the hubs. Check processing flows from spokes to hubs, then between hubs, then out to spokes. This new design has resulted in significant improvements in the number of checks processed in a timely manner.

NOON PRESENTMENT. It used to be common practice for the Fed to present all checks to small banks early in the morning. The Fed now makes a second presentment of checks later in the morning (*noon presentment*). This policy leaves fewer checks on hold until the next day. Furthermore, it began expediting the processing of large checks through the system. (Chapter 8 provides a more detailed discussion of noon presentment and the impact it has had on corporate disbursement systems.)

ACTUAL AVAILABILITY. Instead of granting availability on the basis of a fixed schedule, the Fed adjusts availability schedules every few months to reflect its actual clearing experience. If the Fed expresses the actual clearing experience in terms of average clearing time (which could be, for example, 1.3 days), it is called *fractional availability*.

CHECK TRUNCATION. Rather than transporting paper checks back to the drawee bank, the bank of first deposit captures electronically the essential information contained on a conventional paper check. This electronic information, in the form of an ACH transfer, is sent through the clearing system. Transmitting electronic data is much cheaper and faster than physically moving paper checks from city to city. The paper check may or may not be sent afterward as a verification of the transfer. Check truncation is only in the pilot stage at this time. Existing proposals call for the Fed to truncate checks above a specified dollar amount. Smaller checks would continue to be processed as paper items.

Check truncation is not to be confused with *warehousing*, in which the *drawee bank* (not the bank of first deposit) stores or warehouses the checks. Firms may prefer to have the bank store cancelled checks rather than try to keep track of them themselves. The bank provides either electronic, microfilm, or microfiche listings of checks to the firm. If the firm needs to examine a cancelled check, the bank's retrieval service provides photocopies or the actual check.

CHARGING FOR FED FLOAT. The Fed charges banks for Fed float. Many banks pass these charges along to their corporate customers through account analysis. Generally, however, the charges reflect averages for the entire bank rather than for specific Fed float generated by a particular firm. Hence, some firms attempt to generate Fed float to their own benefit.

Automated Clearing House (ACH) Transfers

The ACH system is the newest primary payment system in the United States. ACH transfers are large-volume, batch-processed transfers. Along the route of an ACH transfer, payment information is stored, sorted, and forwarded in batches to the next processor. Hence, it is called a *store-and-forward* or *store-process-forward* system. The ACH system is like a special-purpose electronic mail system that includes financial institutions to facilitate value transfer. An ACH system has high fixed costs (for computers, transmission links, etc.) but very low variable costs. Hence, pricing of ACH services is very sensitive to volume. As volume increases across the system, the price will eventually drop accordingly.

History

The ACH system was conceived in California in 1968 when the San Francisco and Los Angeles clearing houses formed a joint committee to study methods banks could use to exchange paperless entries. In 1970 10 California banks formed the Special Committee on Paperless Entries (SCOPE) and initiated a pilot project that resulted in software and operating policies for an ACH. The first ACH services were offered in 1972 for transfers between banks served by the California region. A second group in Atlanta under the direction of the Federal Reserve Bank of Atlanta formed the Committee on Paperless

Entry (COPE), which implemented a Federal Reserve–managed ACH system using SCOPE software in 1973. Involvement by the Fed enabled interregional transfers to take place between regional clearing house centers. There are currently (1987) 29 regional ACH associations that each serve hundreds of financial institutions in their areas. In addition, there are 13 private ACH networks operated by individual banks or small groups of banks. The Fed operates most of the regional associations.

The ACH system was initially designed to handle government transfer payments, such as Social Security, military retirement, and railroad pension checks. Table 5.6 shows the growth in volume of ACH transactions over the past 5 years. Government-initiated transactions, which made up the vast majority of all transactions in the early years of the ACH, now account for only 46% of the total volume. Corporate ACH transactions have been growing at a rate of 34% per year, while government transactions have been growing at 18%, about half that rate.

Ownership and Administration

While the Fed is the primary operator, regional ACHs are owned by member financial institutions. Of the approximately 14,000 commercial banks in the country, about 12,000 are members of an ACH. Other depository institutions may also be ACH members. The National Automated Clearing House Association (NACHA) is the member-run organization that sets policies for the ACHs and performs other functions such as research, pilot programs, and marketing.

Steps in an ACH Debit Transaction

Instead of using paper as the medium for carrying payment information, as a paper check does, an ACH transaction carries the information electronically on computer tapes. Figure 5.4 shows the steps in a simplified ACH debit transaction in which company A moves cash from a number of deposit banks

Table 5.6 Growth of ACH Transfers (in Millions of Transactions per Year)

	1982	1983	1984	1985	1986	Compound Ann. Growth
Goverment sector	209	241	269	298	398	
annual rate	—	15%	12%	11%	34%	18%
Corporate sector	106	159	218	289	345	
annual rate	—	49%	22%	32%	20%	34%
Total ACH activity	315	399	487	586	743	
	—	27%	22%	20%	27%	24%

Source: Index, Automated Clearing House, Indianapolis (1987).

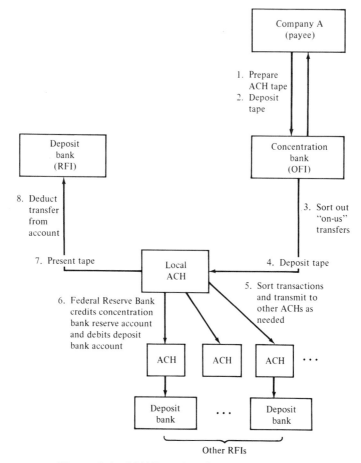

Figure 5.4 ACH Transfer. Cash Concentration.

in distant cities into its lead or concentration bank. This is one of the more popular applications of the ACH system for corporations.

1. Company A prepares a computer tape containing payment instructions for the firm's deposit banks. Information on the tape includes each deposit bank's transit routing and bank numbers, account number, transfer amount, and the bank and account numbers for company A's concentration bank.
2. Company A deposits the transactions by either transmitting the data or taking a tape or disk to the concentration bank, the *originating financial institution (OFI)*. Let's say this takes place on a Tuesday evening.
3. The concentration bank sorts out any on-us transactions (transactions involving the concentration bank or its branches) and debits these accounts by the close of Wednesday's business. Company A's concentration account is

credited on Wednesday for all transactions (both on-us and other transactions).

4. The concentration bank merges company A's transactions with transactions it has received from other firms. A combined tape containing transactions affecting other banks is transported (usually physically) to the local ACH on Tuesday night.

5. The local ACH sorts out intraregional transactions and sends the remaining interregional transactions to other ACHs. This process takes place Tuesday night and early Wednesday morning. Intraregional transactions are combined into a tape or disk for each financial institution in the region for presentment on Wednesday. Interregional transactions are generally sent electronically over the Fed communication network that handles wire transfers during the day.

6. The ACH transfers value to the concentration bank's account by instructing the Fed to credit that bank's reserve account. Similarly, the ACH instructs the Fed to debit reserve accounts for each deposit bank (these banks are called *receiving financial institutions*, or *RFIs*). Both debiting and crediting take place on Wednesday.

7. The ACH to which a particular deposit bank belongs presents a tape or data transmission to that bank. The electronic presentment contains all the transactions pertaining to that bank. RFIs that do not have computer equipment to handle ACH tapes or transmissions are given printouts listing the transactions.

8. The deposit bank debits company A's deposit account on Wednesday.

Uses for Debit Transactions

ACH debit transactions are primarily used for cash concentration (see Chapter 7). In addition, many corporations use ACH debits to collect payments from distributors (as in the example cited in the first paragraph of this chapter), from dealer networks, and from customers. Some public utilities debit users accounts on a monthly basis for the amount of the utility bill. Insurance companies use debits to collect premium payments from customers. Mortgage companies collect monthly mortgage payments using debits. In practice, ACH debits work best when the payment amount is standard each month. Consumers are wary of giving a vendor open access to checking accounts.

ACH Credit Transactions

The largest corporate application of the ACH system is in the area of direct deposit of payroll. In a similar transaction, the government uses the ACH to make Social Security payments and other transfer payments. The steps for an ACH credit are identical to those of the debit transaction previously outlined except that the tape contains a code indicating that in the Federal Reserve accounts the OFI is to be debited and the RFI is to be credited.

Uses of ACH Credit Transactions

Besides payroll, ACH credits are sometimes used for moving cash from a concentration bank to a disbursement bank. Dividend and coupon payments sometimes make use of credits. A few corporations have attempted to use ACH credits to make invoice payments to each other. This application has, however, not met with much success. One drawback to ACH credits is that, while corporations would be happy to be paid by ACH transactions (especially if they control payment, as in the case of the ACH debit), corporations are not excited about paying others using ACH credits. The ACH moves cash out of corporate accounts fast, and opportunity losses could be high. We will come back to this point again in Chapter 20 when we discuss how electronics affects credit policy.

Timing of ACH Settlement

In the concentration example, the ACH debits are initiated on Tuesday evening, while value transfer or *settlement* occurs on Wednesday. We speak of ACH transactions as having a *settlement* date rather than an availability time — although the concept is the same. ACH transactions are initiated on 1 day and settled sometime in the future. Banks often give both ledger and available credit on the settlement date. Settlement time is 1 or 2 days, depending on how the ACH transaction is used. In the example of a cash concentration transaction (the first preceding example), settlement requires 1 business day. There is a higher charge for 1-day settlement. Most consumer transactions (like direct deposit of payroll or telephone bill paying) usually settle in 2 business days. Some banks have the ability to *value date* ACH transactions so that they may be initiated on one day and settled several days in the future. In general, on the settlement date the account at the RFI is debited (credited) and the account at the OFI is credited (debited). Thus, Fed float is usually not created.

For certain consumer transactions such as direct deposit of payroll, the payor may want to allow an additional day for processing. The extra day allows the OFI to send a *memo posting* — an electronic report that informs the RFI that an ACH transaction is about to come. This is useful because an ACH payment that settles on Wednesday means that, for most financial institutions, the amount is added to the employee's account on Wednesday *evening* when posting is commonly performed. This means that the employee will not be able to use the funds during the day on Wednesday even though they are technically in the employee's account by the close of the day. To solve the problem, banks send the memo posting 1 day in advance of actual value transfer. Another reason for allowing an extra day is that 2-day settlement is charged at a lower rate.

Other Features of ACH Payments

1. *Prenotification.* Before any account may be used for ACH transactions, a prenotification transaction (a *prenote*) must be sent. This is a zero-dollar

transaction that is sent to ensure that the OFI has correct account information and that the RFI can process ACH transactions.

2. *Weekend processing.* Some OFIs have instituted weekend processing. Firms can make deposits on Sunday for Monday settlement. While most associations can process such tapes, few banks provide this service.

3. *Reconciliation.* Because payments are computerized, check reconciliation is eliminated and cash application can be more fully automated than in manual systems that deal with paper checks.

4. *Return items.* What happens when an account to be debited by an ACH has insufficient or uncollected funds? As in paper check processing, a return item is generated by the RFI. The RFI has the option of sending back an electronic return message through the ACH or a paper return document through the paper check clearing house channel. The latter is more expensive and slower, but some banks lack the software to prepare electronic return items.

ACH Data Formats

To achieve the economies of scale necessary to keep the per item costs of an ACH transaction low, they must be processed in large batches by computers without human intervention. This calls for highly standardized formats to contain and transmit the information. By *format* we mean the way the information is organized on the computer tape or disk. There are currently seven different formats for various ACH applications (Table 5.7). Banks must have special computer software (programs) to read these formats.

The most commonly used format is probably the PPD format, which is used for direct deposit of payroll and government transfer payments. CCD is also widely used for cash concentration. The CTP format was designed to help corporations use the ACH to pay each other electronically. It has achieved little application, however. The new CCDX and CTX formats are designed to overcome one of the main drawbacks of the CTP format by making the information associated with the payment conform to a widely accepted standard (see Chapter 20). CCDX incorporates a short ANSI message while CTX incorporates a longer ANSI payment advice. If it is successful in capturing any significant portion of the 10 billion corporate-to-corporate payments per year, CTX could revolutionize the cash flow timeline.

Pros and Cons of ACH Payments

Advantages

The primary advantages of using the ACH to transfer funds are controlled settlement dates, price, and automated processing. Checks may take several days to clear, and the clearing time is often uncertain. On the other hand, ACH payments can settle overnight, and the time delay is certain regardless of the physical distance between the two banks involved in the transfer.

Table 5.7   ACH Formats

Format	Name	Use	Notes
Consumer Transactions			
PPD	Prearranged payment or deposit	Payroll, Social Security payments	94 characters
POS	Point of sale	Transactions from point-of-sale terminals	94 characters
MTE	Machine transaction entry	Transaction in an automated teller machine network	94 characters
CIE	Customer-initiated entry	Payments initiated via a telephone bill paying service or home computer	94 characters
Corporate Transactions			
CCD	Cash concentration and disbursement	Used for cash concentration and disbursement account funding and some other corporate payments	94 characters
CCDX		Used for corporate-to-corporate payments. Initially used by U.S. Treasury.	Same as CCD but addenda record is in ANSI X12 format (See Chapter 20)
CTP	Corporate trade payment	Used for corporate-to-corporate payments	94 characters (plus up to 4,990 addenda records)
CTX	Corporate trade exchange	Planned corporate-to-corporate payments	94 characters plus addenda records to incorporate ANSI X-12 standards in a variable format

Source: Index, Automated Clearing House, Indianapolis (1987).

While pricing of ACH transfers varies with the bank, typical charges are $.10–$.50 per item. These costs are usually slightly below regular check prices. In contrast, wire transfers currently cost about $10–$15 per bank (the sending and receiving banks both charge this price). In addition, there is a fixed fee for depositing an ACH tape. The price for CTP-formatted ACH items varies, depending on the number of addenda records used. Since the ACH system is largely a fixed-charge operation, it is likely that, as volume increases, ACH costs will decline further relative to paper transactions. A complicating factor, however, is that the government has been subsidizing the ACH system since its inception. As the subsidy runs out, there may be some short-term price rises for ACH transfers.

Because ACH transfers are electronic, they can be produced directly by the firm's data processing system and then reconciled electronically. This reduces keying errors and permits faster, more automated reporting to management than is possible with corresponding check systems.

Disadvantages

A major expense in using ACH transfers is the loss of float from the payor's perspective. Payors lose the disbursement float benefits accruing from mail, customer processing and clearing delays. Second, since some banks are not members of any ACH, they cannot process ACH payments or disbursements. Therefore, a firm may have to maintain both a paper system and an ACH system. Third, since ACH transactions involve negligible dual balances (see Chapter 7), using the ACH for concentration may be more costly than using paper DTCs. Fourth, in forms of ACH where the payee directly debits the payor's account, the payor loses the use of accounts payable as a discretionary source of short-term funds. Lastly, running an ACH system may require an investment in hardware, software, and administrative time for adequate development and integration.

Future Developments in ACH

As a new payment system, the ACH continues to evolve as user needs mesh with technological capabilities. New services are being developed each year, and the evolution of the system shows no sign of halting. Among the new services envisioned are the following:

Same-day Availability

There is no reason why future ACH transactions initiated early in the morning could not clear by the end of the same business day. Such a feature would make low-cost ACH transfers a substitute for much more expensive wire transfers under some circumstances.

Conditional Transactions

To assist in the public acceptance of variable-amount ACH debits (for example, a public utility bill that varies each month), the ACH could send the payor notification that the deposit account would be debited by so many dollars unless steps were taken to object.

Value Dating

Value dating means specifying not only the amount of the transaction but also its future effective date. This feature would allow transactions for the coming month, for example, to be stored by the OFI or ACH system until the designated transfer day. Though some banks now allow such storage, most do so for only a few days.

Faster Electronic Return Items

It should be possible for ACH return items to be processed in 1 business day. This would make the ACH more valuable for concentration and consumer debit transactions.

Wire Transfers

There is currently one major wire transfer system in the United States: the FedWire system operated by the Federal Reserve. FedWire is a real-time method of transferring cash value from one bank to another using Federal Reserve account balances. With a FedWire transaction, the payor's account is debited and the payee's account is credited the same day. Transaction information flows through a computer network residing in the Fed's 12 district banks.

Features

Communications and Transfer System

FedWire is both a communications and a transfer system. Besides transferring value, FedWire can be used to send messages throughout the banking system. Such messages might include instructions for a distant bank to send a wire transaction or inquiries about the status of a previous wire transfer. The wire system is also used to record the ownership of Treasury securities and transfer such securities from one owner to another.

Confirmation and Notification

After a FedWire transaction is completed, a confirming message is sent to the payor stating that the payee's bank has received the payment. This is an important feature of a wire system for certain types of transactions such as contract payments, real estate closings, and other time-sensitive transactions. When a wire transfer is received at the payee's bank, the payee is notified on a real-time basis—at least theoretically. Such notification is not usual for other types of payments, and yet it is important for some transactions involving the release of shipments or titles to property.

Messages

Wire transfers do not allow for extensive ancillary information to accompany payment. For example, if one firm pays another with a FedWire and takes a discount for early payment of an invoice, the firm would have to notify the payee of the discount taken by means other than the wire itself. This feature of wires causes extensive confusion at times because incoming wires cannot be matched to specific transactions.

Settlement by Reserve Balances

Value is transferred in a FedWire transaction by debiting the reserve account of the sending institution and crediting reserve account of the receiving institution. All depository institutions must maintain reserve balances with the Fed.

Wire Costs

The price charged to corporate wire customers by a bank range from $5 to $20. Since both the sending and the receiving institution may impose a charge, the total cost of a wire is $10 to $40.

Mechanics of a FedWire Transfer

Credit Transaction

As an example of a FedWire credit transfer, suppose firm A wants to wire $40,000 to firm B. Figure 5.5 illustrates the steps that occur.

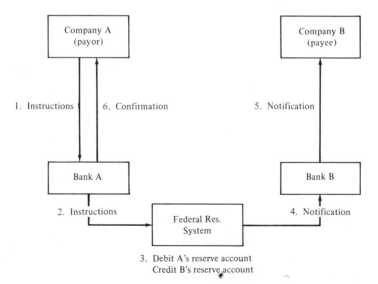

Figure 5.5 Wire Transfer.

1. Firm A instructs bank A to make the transfer of $40,000 and gives the bank number and account number of the payee. The instructions could come in the form of a written request, telephone message, or computer transmission. If the request is by telephone, the caller must verify that the request is authentic by providing prearranged code words. Careful banks will call back to double check. Sometimes telephone requests must be confirmed later by written requests. Preformatted wires, such as those that always go to the same party, require less security. Computer-initiated wire requests are becoming very popular. Many banks offer balance reporting systems that include software modules for sending wire instructions to the bank.

2. Bank A deducts $40,000 from firm A's available balance. If firm A has an overdraft in the account, bank A will check with the account officer to make sure that prearranged overdraft limits will not be exceeded. Many firms experience *daylight overdrafts*, meaning that during the day the available balance in the account falls below zero but the closing balance is nevertheless positive. Before sending wire instructions to the Fed, the bank must also make sure that its own overdraft position in its Fed reserve account does not exceed Fed-imposed levels. In early 1986, the Fed implemented policies to reduce its risk regarding such overdrafts. Banks are permitted some degree of daylight overdrafts, but these are limited by the size of the bank equity and other factors.

3. Bank A sends instructions to the Fed to transfer $40,000 to bank B in favor of firm B. Bank A has two means of sending instructions to the Fed: telephone calls (for banks that use few FedWires) and computer-to-computer transmissions (for banks that have a large number of wires). The former case is called *off-line* and the latter is *on-line*.

4. Value is transferred by the Fed, which subtracts $40,000 from bank A's reserve balance and adds $40,000 to bank B's reserve balance.

5. The Fed notifies bank B of the transfer (again, either on-line or off-line). Bank B credits firm B's available balance with $40,000 and notifies firm B via a phone call, balance report, and/or written communication.

6. The Fed confirms the transfer with a message back to bank A, which then confirms it back to firm A. This transaction assumes that both banks are members of the same Federal Reserve District. If they are located in different Fed districts, the information is routed through the Fed's communication network to the appropriate receiving Fed.

Debit Transaction

Besides sending value from a payor to a payee in a crediting transaction, FedWires can be used to debit accounts. Such transactions are called *wire drawdowns*. In the debit case, the bank being debited is sent instructions via the FedWire message system to initiate a credit transaction to the bank to be paid. Of course, for such a transaction to take place, the bank to be debited would have to have instructions from the account holder to release wires to the bank to be credited. Wire drawdowns are frequently used in concentration systems and disbursement account funding.

CHIPS

In New York City, a pseudo-wire system handles an enormous volume of cash flow between local financial institutions. *CHIPS* stands for *Clearing House Interbank Payment System*. It is a settlement system involving primarily about 135 New York City financial institutions and is operated by the New York Clearing House Association. Many other institutions have access to CHIPS through offices or correspondents in New York City.

CHIPS works as a netting system. This means that only information, and not value, is transferred during a specified time period (see Chapter 19 for a more detailed description of netting systems). At the end of the time period (for CHIPS the period is 1 business day) only the net amount is actually transferred from one party to the other. If bank A sends $10,000,000 in transfers to bank B and bank B sends $8,000,000 in transfers to bank A, only the net amount of $2,000,000 is transferred at the end of the day.

As outlined in Figure 5.6, during the day, member banks send instructions to CHIPS regarding transfers they wish to make to other banks in New York City. Only information flows during the day. In the evening, value transfer occurs. There are two classes of banks in CHIPS. Settlement banks are the largest New York City banks. At the end of the day, CHIPS reports to the Federal Reserve Bank of New York the net amounts to debit and credit at each of the settlement banks. Nonsettlement banks use the larger settlement banks as correspondents to settle their accounts with CHIPS.

Over $400,000,000,000 passes through CHIPS daily. This represents about 90% of all international interbank dollar denominated transactions. Most international dollar-based transactions flow through New York correspondent banks that clear transactions through CHIPS.

Summary

This chapter discussed the methods used to move cash from place to place. This knowledge is essential in order to understand how to design systems to collect, concentrate, and disburse cash more efficiently. There are four primary mechanisms for moving value from one place to another; two depend on physical means (currency and check), and two depend on electronic means (ACH and wire). Each mechanism has unique characteristics and, therefore, a special role to play in almost all corporations. In later chapters we will build on this information to help determine which payment mechanism may be appropriate for different parts of a short-term financial management system.

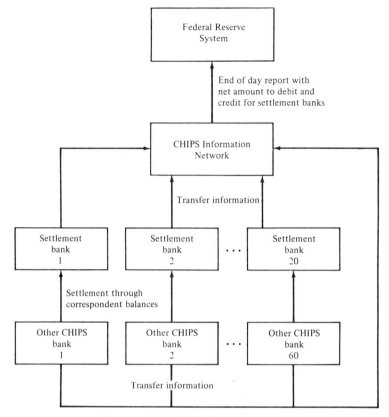

Figure 5.6 CHIPS Netting System.

_____ **Discussion Questions** _____

1. Under what circumstances would a deposit of coin and currency *not* receive immediately availability on the date of deposit?
2. Explain how a check clears through each of the following channels, and which accounts are debited and credited along the way.
   a. On us
   b. Local clearing house
   c. Local correspondent bank
   d. Local Federal Reserve bank
   e. Distant Federal Reserve bank
   f. Distant correspondent bank
3. What is the difference between a primary and a secondary payment system?
4. Compare and contrast the following check-like drafts:
   a. Check
   b. PTD

   c. Money order
   d. PAC
   e. DTC
   f. Sight draft
   g. Time draft
   h. Traveler's check
5. Under what circumstances should a firm consider encoding its own checks prior to deposit?
6. Explain what is contained in the MICR line of a check.
7. Explain how a check is returned for insufficient funds. Why does it generally take much longer to return a check than it does to clear a check?
8. What steps has the Fed taken to reduce Fed float and improve check-clearing efficiency?
9. What factors determine the availability a firm receives for a check?
10. How may restriction on daylight overdrafts hinder banks from providing prompt wire transfers at times?
11. Explain why wire transfers may cause a daylight overdraft at a commercial while checks and ACH payments do not.
12. Explain what is meant by noon presentment. How does this program reduce Fed float? What impact does it have on cash management?
13. Outline the steps in an ACH credit transfer and in an ACH debit transfer. How is the Fed involved in the transfer of value?
14. What kinds of payments would be best handled by the PPD format? By CCD? By CTX?
15. Why hasn't the ACH caught on for corporate-to-corporate payments?
16. What improvements in the ACH system are being proposed? Which ones are most important to corporations?
17. Outline the steps in a FedWire transfer. Explain alternative ways in which a wire transfer can be initiated.
18. What is the advantage of using CHIPS compared to sending transfer instructions through FedWire?

Selected Readings

CAREY, KRISTEN E., and KEVIN CARR, "ACH Transaction Processing: An Overview of Information Flows and Controls," *Journal of Cash Management* (September 1982), pp. 32–39.

"Changes at the Fed: ACH Pricing," *Journal of Cash Management* (May–June 1984), pp. 34–38.

DRISCOLL, MARY C., "Electronic Check Collection: Issues and Problems Posed by a Hybrid Technology," *Journal of Cash Management* (June 1982), pp. 20–27.

FRISBEE, PAMELA S., "The ACH: An Elusive Dream," *Economic Review,* (March 1986), pp. 4–8.

HILL, NED C., and DANIEL M. FERGUSON, "Negotiating Payment Terms in an Electronic Environment," in *Advances in Working Capital Management,* ed. Yong Kim, Greenwich, Conn.: J.A.I. Press, 1987 (forthcoming).

KEENAN, GERALD L., "ACH Return Items," *Economic Review,* (March 1986), pp. 19.

LISS, RONALD E., "The ANSI X12 Committee: A Status Report on Standards for Cash Cycle Management," *Journal of Cash Management* (August-September 1983), pp. 39–48.

MILLER, DONALD G., "How Secure Are Electronic Funds Transfers?", *Cashflow* (March 1981), pp. 30–37.

MITCHELL, GEORGE W., "From Paper to Electronics," *Journal of Cash Management* (December 1981), pp. 32–35.

MOYER, JERRY M., "Implementing a Pre-authorized ACH Payment System," *Journal of Cash Management* (October 1981), pp. 55–57.

STONE, BERNELL K., "Cash Cycle Management and the ANSI X12 Committee," *Journal of Cash Management* (August–September 1983), pp. 37–38.

STONE, BERNELL K., "Desiderata for a Viable ACH," *Economic Review*, (March 1986), pp. 34–43.

STONE, BERNELL K., "Electronic Payment Basics," *Economic Review*, (March 1986), pp. 9–18.

STONE, BERNELL K., "Corporate Trade Payments: Hard Lessons in Product Design," *Economic Review*, (April 1986), pp. 9–21.

STONE, BERNELL K., and GEORGE C. WHITE, "Scenarios for the Future of the ACH," *Economic Review* (April 1986), pp. 29–49.

TOMICK, DAVID P., and ESTHER A. LORD, "Resourcefulness in Funds Transfer: New Alternatives to Wires Lower Costs and Improve Information Flow," *Journal of Cash Management* (October–November 1983), pp. 24ff.

WHITE, GEORGE C., "EFT Opportunities for the Innovative Corporation," *Journal of Cash Management* (June 1982), pp. 42–48.

WHITE, GEORGE C., "Electronic Payments Commentary: CCDs—Corporate to Corporate Electronic Payments 'Secret' Format," *Journal of Cash Management* (March–April 1984), pp. 50–52.

WHITE, GEORGE C., "EDTs: Later Processing and Better Service," *Journal of Cash Management* (May–June 1984), pp. 46–48.

Collection Systems

The Bureau of Government Financial Operations in the Department of the Treasury, the government's "money manager," recently conducted a study to determine how it should change the cash management system. The first part of the study concentrated on the collections system. The following were among the key recommendations: (1) establish a preauthorized debit system as a key method for collecting recurring payments, (2) put tax withholding by corporations on the corporate-to-corporate ACH system, (3) use automated lockboxes for collecting small to medium-sized recurring payments, (4) expand the use of wire transfers for large government collections, and (5) prepare for long-term government collection through video banking.

A *collection system* is a set of institutional arrangements and management procedures used to receive cash, move cash into the banking system, and obtain accurate and timely information on cash availability. In this chapter we build on the payments mechanisms described in Chapter 5, examining the characteristics of a collection system and a procedure to evaluate collection system efficiency. The process of moving the cash obtained from a collection system into a concentration bank is described in Chapter 7.

—————— Requirements of a Collection System ——————

The collection system of a company consists of the set of institutional arrangements and procedures used to collect and to channel incoming cash into its banking system. In Chapters 1 and 2 we discussed the role of maximization of present values as the primary objective of the financial policies of the firm. We know that present value is a function of both the timing and the amount of cash flows. A collection system affects the timing of cash inflows. A speedup in the availability of cash to the firm results in increased present value. The objective function in designing a collection system is as follows:

Maximize   – Cost of collection float
          – Collection system operating costs
          – Administrative costs
          + Value of reports to management

Since most of the items in a collection system are costs, the objective function is likely to have a negative value. In trying to maximize the present value of costs, we are trying to make them larger in an algebraic sense by making them as close to zero as possible.

Cash Mobilization

Cash mobilization means moving cash from the payor, frequently the customer, to the available funds account in the firm's bank.[1] This includes receiving the payment, processing it, depositing it in the banking system, and the final crediting of available balances. Cash mobilization is the primary function of any collection system. In Exhibit 6.1 we illustrate how Small Computers, Inc., can increase its present value by speeding up the receipt of the cash flow from a customer. Under the current procedure, Small Computers is paying a

Exhibit 6.1   Present Value Benefits from Speeding Up a Collection

A check for $2,000,000 for the purchase of computer equipment is mailed from the purchaser in San Francisco to the headquarters of Small Computers, Inc., in Silicon Valley, California, on Friday. The check arrives on Monday. It is processed, and a deposit ticket is made out for Small Computers' bank in San Francisco. The deposit ticket and check are mailed to the bank on Tuesday afternoon. The deposit arrives at the San Francisco bank in the Friday afternoon mail and is credited to the account of Small Computers as of Monday morning. On Monday the treasurer of Small Computers buys $2,000,000 worth of marketable securities that earn an annual interest rate of 10%. Although the funds were technically Small Computers' on the Friday that they were mailed, they were not available until 10 days later. The present value (on Friday) of the delayed receipt of the cash is as follows:

$$PV(\text{Friday}) = \frac{\$2,000,000}{(1 + .10/365 \times 10)} = \$1,994,535.50.$$

If, as an alternative, the treasurer of Small Computers could have arranged to have the check picked up from the customer on Friday morning and deposited at the San Francisco bank, it would have been credited to the account on that same day. This would then have a present value of $2,000,000 on Friday. The increase in present value would be

Increase in PV = $2,000,000 − $1,994,535.5 = $5,464.50.

---

[1] The concept of available funds, that is, funds that count for bank compensation or can be used for disbursement, was developed in Chapter 4.

present value cost of $5,464.50 on a $2,000,000 collection because of the delay in the system. A revision of the collection system will save Small Computers this $5,464.50 in opportunity costs, less any additional costs for the courier's service.

Accurate Cash Flow Information

More rapid collection of cash is worthwhile only if the manager knows that the cash is there. Obtaining accurate and timely information on cash flows and the level of bank balances is an important part of any efficient collection system. Desired information includes the arrival pattern of the payments (at least daily and, in some cases, more frequently), the firm's processing time, the pattern of deposits into the banking system, and the availability delay of the deposits. To be useful, the information should be in a form that is easily integrated with other information systems of the company. With computer storage in virtually all information systems, this has become a critical element for smooth functioning of a collection system. This is true whether the information system is internal or provided and monitored by outside vendors such as banks or service companies. Considerations in the choice between internal and external control include compatibility with other information in the firm, the cost, the type and form of information available, and the ability to make changes in the system.

Updating the Central Information System

In addition to providing information on cash flows, the capability of updating the other parts of the firm's information system in an accurate and timely manner is important. An example is updating the accounts receivables files of customers. Failure to reflect payments quickly could result in a deterioration of customer relations, extra time and expense to correct misinformation, and a loss of potential sales due to incorrect application of credit limits. This is an area in which close coordination is needed between the treasurer, the controller, and the credit department.

Audit Trails and Controls

The collection system must be designed to ensure proper control of cash coming into the firm. This is particularly critical when payments are received over the counter in currency, such as in a retail establishment, rather than through the mail in the form of checks. While this is usually the concern of the internal auditor or the controller, it should also receive the attention of the financial manager because the mishandling of even a very small percentage of the incoming payments might eliminate the planned present value advantages of a very speedy collection system.

Design of a Collection System

As previously mentioned, a collection system is designed to move payments from payors to available deposits in the banking system as efficiently as possible. There are four major elements in this system: (1) the number of collection points, (2) location of the collection points, (3) internal or external operation of the collection points, and (4) assignment of individual payors to collection points. A model for an optimal collection system must incorporate interactions of these design elements in an attempt to increase the present value of the firm.

The value of the firm is affected by the collection system by the increase in present value created by speeding the conversion of payments into available cash, the operating costs for the system, and the administrative costs to manage the system. The elements that affect the timing of the cash flows are illustrated by the timeline for a generalized collection system shown in Figure 6.1.

Most payments in the United States today are made by paper documents, usually checks. In a general collection system, there are three elements that may delay the process of receiving value for payments at the bank: (1) mail delay, (2) processing delay, and (3) availability delay. While certain specialized collection systems (to be discussed later) may not be subject to all of these delays, we will design our general system with all of them in mind.

Collection Float

The term *collection float* refers to the total time lag between the mailing of the payment by the payor and the availability of cash in the bank. The components of collection float are due to the sources of delay in the collection process. *Mail float* results from the time that elapses from the mailing of the check until its receipt. *Processing float* is due to the processing time before the check is deposited in the banking system. The last component of collection float

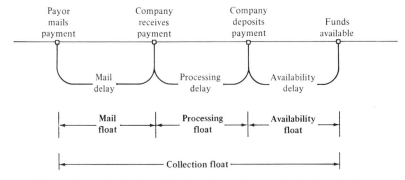

Figure 6.1 Cash Flow Timeline for a General Collection System.

is *availability float*, which is a result of the firm's not being granted immediate availability on all deposit items. These last two elements of collection float were referred to as *deposit float* in Chapter 4. They represent the difference between the cash that is recorded as a deposit on the company's books and the increase in the available balance at the bank.

Float Measurement

As we saw in Chapter 4, the measurement of float is a function both of the time lag and of the dollar amount involved. Float is usually measured in dollar-days, which are calculated by multiplying the time lag in days by the dollar amount being delayed. Float can be measured either on each item that is processed or on an average daily basis. As we will see later, each measurement of float has unique characteristics that make it valuable in different applications.

Individual Item Float
The float on each item is found by multiplying the amount of the payment by the number of days of delay for that payment. It is the product of these two quantities, and not either one individually, that is important in measuring float. We can see from the calculation of collection float in Exhibit 6.2 that the float on a $10,000 item that is delayed for 6 days is identical to the float on a $20,000 item that is delayed for 3 days.

Average Daily Float
The analysis of many situations requires the use of a measure of *average daily float* for a set of collection items over some time period, say a month. There are two ways that this measure can be calculated. While they both result in the same average daily float calculation in the end, different insights can be gained from each calculation.

1. The average daily float is determined by calculating the float for each item, summing the dollar-days of float for the set of items during the period, and dividing this total by the number of days in the period (see Exhibit 6.3A).

Exhibit 6.2 Calculation of Float for an Individual Item

A check for $10,000 is mailed from customer A on July 6, a Friday; because of mail, processing, and availability delays, it is not credited as available funds in the bank of Small Computers, Inc., until the following Thursday, 6 days later. The float for this check is

$$\text{Float} = \$10,000 \times 6 \text{ days} = 60,000 \text{ \$-days.}$$

A check for $20,000 is mailed from customer B on July 6, but it is available on Monday, 3 days later. The float for this check is

$$\text{Float} = \$20,000 \times 3 \text{ days} = 60,000 \text{ \$-days.}$$

Exhibit 6.3 Calculation of Average Daily Float

A firm receives three items each month, as shown in the following table. The float for each item is calculated using the procedure given in Exhibit 6.2.

Item	Dollar Amount		No. of Days Delay	Dollar-Days
1	$ 4,500,000	×	3	13,500,000
2	$ 3,000,000	×	4	12,000,000
3	$ 2,500,000	×	7	17,500,000
Total	$10,000,000			43,000,000

A. Following the calculation procedure given in (1), we have

$$\text{Average daily float} = \frac{\text{total float}}{\text{total days}} = \frac{43,000,000}{30 \text{ days}} = 1,433,333.$$

B. Following the calculation procedure laid out in (2), we have

$$\text{Average daily receipts} = \frac{\text{total receipts}}{\text{total days}} = \frac{10,000,000}{30} = 333,333.$$

$$\text{Weighted average delay} = \left[\frac{4.5}{10} \times 3\right] + \left[\frac{3}{10} \times 4\right] + \left[\frac{2.5}{10} \times 7\right] = 4.3 \text{ days.}$$

$$\begin{aligned}\text{Average daily float} &= \text{average daily receipts} \times \text{weighted average delay} \\ &= 333,333 \times 4.3 = 1,433,333.\end{aligned}$$

2. The average daily float is calculated as follows: determine the average daily receipts by dividing the total receipts by the number of days in the period. Calculate the weighted average delay by multiplying the delay for each item by that item's proportion of the total receipts during the period. Finally, find the average daily float by multiplying the average daily receipts by the weighted average delay (see Exhibit 6.3B).

Cost of Float

The cost of float represents the opportunity cost because the cash is unavailable for use during the time the payments are tied up in collection. The cost of float is determined by multiplying the average daily float by the opportunity cost. In the previous example, assume that the data represent a typical month for Small Computer and that it has an annual opportunity cost of 10%. The monthly cost of the collection float is $1,433,333 × 0.10/12 = $11,944, while the annual cost is $1,433,333 × 0.10 = $143,333.

Present Value Float Costs

At this point, the reader who is a present value purist may be thinking, "Wait a minute! I thought we were going to deal in present values, not monthly or annual opportunity costs." To reduce your confusion, let's look at a present value calculation of the cost of float. In the previous example, we have a cash flow of $333,333 per day. The float results in this being delayed by a total of 4.3 days. The present value of this delayed cash flow is[2]

$$PV = \frac{\$333,333}{(1 + 0.1 \times 4.3/360)} = \$332,935.33.$$

Thus, we lose in present value $333,333 − $332,935.33 or $397.67 for each day's collections. For a 30-day month, this is a loss of value of $11,930.10. When we compare this figure to the previous result of a cost of $11,944, we see that the error is only $14 or 0.1%. Although we adhere to our present value concepts, we will use the opportunity cost approach for the calculations in the remainder of this and the next two chapters for three reasons: (1) the magnitude of the error is small, (2) most of the other literature on the cost of float uses the simple opportunity cost calculation, and (3) the opportunity cost calculation frequently makes it easier to see the source of the benefits.

Optimizing the Collection System

Potential for Increased Present Value

Three areas of collection system design can potentially increase present value, as was seen in the objective function. (1) Reduce float costs by increasing the availability of cash in the banking system. This can be done by reducing mail, processing, or availability delay. (2) Reduce the operating costs of the collection system. This may involve a tradeoff between fixed and variable costs and may include the use of outside contractors to perform some of the functions of the collection system. (3) Reduce the administrative costs of managing the system. While these costs may be hard to identify in many cases, at least the direction is clear; the more complex the system, the more difficult it is to manage and the higher are the administrative costs. The attempt to optimize a system usually involves a tradeoff between these three cost elements; a reduction in one type of cost is available only with an increase in another.

REDUCE MAIL FLOAT. Mail float can be reduced by careful location of the collection points. In general, the closer the collection points are to the payors, the shorter is the time needed for the item to arrive at the collection point. The geographical dispersion of payors affects the number and location of the collection points. A large number of collection points reduces mail float but increases administrative costs and possibly operating costs associated with the collection points. We consider this tradeoff between float costs and operating costs further when we discuss the collection point and lockbox location procedure later in this chapter.

REDUCE PROCESSING FLOAT. Payments must be processed and conveyed to the bank before the cash is available in the banking system. The three issues to

---

[2] Note that we are using 360 days to calculate the daily interest rate here in order to be consistent with our previous use of 12 30-day months.

be considered are speed, accuracy, and security. For reasons of both security and availability, the payments should be processed and deposited at least once per day. The timing of this processing is a function of the pattern of the receipts during the day, the cutoff times at the bank, whether the processing is done by the firm or by an outside agent, and the schedules of courier services, if used, to transport the deposit to the bank. The number of items received, the form of payment, the average size of an item, and the pattern of arrival are all factors in determining who does the processing and how much automation is used. There is frequently a tradeoff between reducing the float cost by processing the items more rapidly and increasing the cost of processing. An example of a reduction in processing float by altering the timing of deposits is given in Exhibit 6.4.

REDUCE AVAILABILITY FLOAT. The form of payment, the location of the bank on which it is drawn, and negotiation with the deposit bank affect the availability float. Currency is immediately available upon deposit into the bank, assuming that the cutoff time for the day is met. The availability granted checks depends upon the location of the institution on which they are drawn relative to the deposit bank and the size of the item. The factors affecting the availability schedule offered by a bank were discussed in Chapter 4. Reduction of availability delay can be achieved by locating the deposit points close to the bank on which the check is drawn and, in some cases, by better negotiation with the deposit bank on availability schedules.

We have seen that the design of a good collection system can enhance the present value of the firm by reducing the opportunity cost of the different types of delay in receiving the funds. An optimal system is one that makes the maximum contribution to the present value of the firm. The nature of the business and the way the receipts arrive affect the type of collection system used.

Exhibit 6.4 Illustration of a Reduction in Processing Float

The Milan office of the County Farm Insurance Company collects an average of $24,000 per day in payments, mostly by personal checks. The receipt of the checks is spread relatively evenly throughout the day, from 8:30 A.M. when the office opens until 4:30 P.M. when it closes. The current procedure is to deposit the receipts once per day at the end of the day, using the night deposit box at the First National Bank of Milan. The First National Bank has a cutoff time of 2:00 P.M., after which deposits are registered as being received the next day. The manager of the office estimates that they could process the payments received by 1:30 P.M. and make the 2:00 P.M. cutoff. This would result in receiving available funds 1 day sooner for five-eighths of the day's receipts, or $15,000. This occurs for each day's deposits and 1-day earlier availability is achieved on all types of deposits. If the funds could earn 10% interest, this would be additional profits for the office of $1,500 per year. If the company has 50 local offices, this would represent an increment to profits of $75,000 per year.

Types of Collection Systems

Over-the-Counter Collections

The first specialized collection system that we describe is an *over-the-counter* collection system, where the payment is received in a face-to-face meeting with the customer. Most retail or consumer businesses receive at least some of their payments on an over-the-counter basis. Since payments are not mailed, an over-the-counter system does not contain mail float. The cash flow timeline for an over-the-counter system is shown in Figure 6.2.

Basic Components
The basic components of an over-the-counter collection system include the *field unit* at which the payment is received, a *local deposit bank* that serves as the entry point for the firm's banking system, and an input into the firm's central information system. A schematic diagram of the components of an over-the-counter collection system is given in Figure 6.3.

System Design
In designing an over-the-counter collection system, the issues addressed are the location of the field units, the type of payment accepted, location and compensation of deposit banks, and the reporting system. Some of these elements are solely the function of management decisions, while others may be influenced by competition and the institutional arrangements that are available.

FIELD OFFICE LOCATION. Field units are generally locations where the firm delivers goods or services to the customer and collects payments. In many retail establishments (such as a restaurant) the payments are received when the merchandise or service is delivered to the customer. In most cases, the location of field units is dictated by marketing concerns (an attractive location, good traffic patterns, proximity to competitors, availability of adequate facilities, etc.) and is not an element in collection system design.

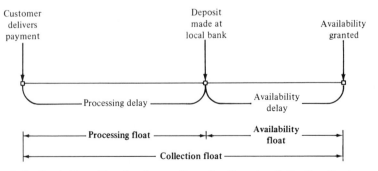

Figure 6.2 Cash Flow Timeline for an Over-the-Counter Collection System.

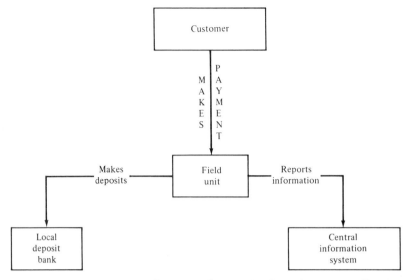

Figure 6.3 Components of a Collection System for Over-the-counter Receipts.

TYPE OF PAYMENT ACCEPTED. Over-the-counter payments can be made by currency, check, or third-party credit (debit) card.[3] Each form of payment has unique advantages and disadvantages. Currency is immediately available for use, is convenient for small purchase amounts, has small handling costs for small quantities, and involves little risk that the payment is invalid. The disadvantages are that it is inconvenient for large payments, requires tight controls in processing, and requires security in handling because it is easy to divert and difficult to trace. A check is convenient for large purchases, and security problems are minor. The disadvantages are that there is a processing delay (checks must be deposited before the cash is usable), there may be availability delay before value is received, and there is a risk that the check will not be honored when presented for payment. Third-party credit (debit) cards are convenient, have low security risks, and have a certainty of payment if proper procedures are followed.[4] The disadvantages are the cost, in the form of a discount from the face value, and a possible delay in receipt of value for the payment.

SELECTION OF DEPOSIT BANKS. For convenience and safety in handling currency, geographical proximity is a major factor in the choice of banks for deposit of over-the-counter payments. Where regional or statewide branch

---

[3] We treat only the use of third-party credit cards here because their handling is similar to that of checks in an over-the-counter collection system. The use of a firm's own credit cards is not an over-the-counter type of payment; rather, the actual payment is usually received after the customer is billed at a later date. The collection system aspects of this own-credit-card system is handled as part of the mailed payment, which is treated in the next section.

[4] There may be an additional marketing advantage of enhanced sales through the use of credit cards, but this topic will be delayed until the discussion of credit issues in Chapter 13.

banking is available, there may be a tradeoff between geographical proximity of a particular branch and administrative and concentration costs of dealing with fewer banks.

BANK COMPENSATION. In addition to acting as an input for deposits into the banking system, local banks may provide services such as currency replenishment, coin counting, or payroll check cashing for local employees. They must be fairly compensated for these services. Prices charged for services, flexibility to pay in balances or in fees, availability on deferred items, and compatibility with the concentration system affect the contribution of the collection system to the net present value of the firm.

INFORMATION GATHERING. The treasurer must know the amount of deposits and their availability before she can put the money to use. It is desirable to have dual reporting of the information for control purposes. One report usually comes from the field manager, containing the amount of receipts and the deposit. Another comes from the deposit bank, containing deposit and availability information. While these bank reports are useful as part of the accounting control system, they may not be timely for the treasurer's needs. A simple reporting system for timely deposit information is for the manager of the field unit to call headquarters and report the deposit information prior to going to the bank to make the deposit.

In a more sophisticated reporting system, the field manager enters the amount of the deposit into an on-site computer that records sales, inventory, and other information. Periodically, perhaps after hours, these data are transmitted directly to the information system at headquarters or to a service bureau for further processing.[5] If the system is set up to gather and transmit information overnight, the treasurer knows exactly how much is available in each bank at the start of the day and the identity of any nonreporting field units.

System Optimization

Since the number and location of collection points in an over-the-counter collection system are chosen for reasons other than collection system design, the primary areas for enhancing present value are processing float, availability float, and processing and administrative costs. The nature of the payments virtually requires that the firm does its own processing of the payments for deposit. Efficient standardized company procedures are important, with deposits made as soon as possible after receipt of payment and with careful consideration of bank cutoff times. Since availability delay is a function of the nature of the items being deposited, restriction of payment to currency or to local checks can eliminate or at least reduce availability float. However, the monster's other head of potentially reduced sales has to be considered. The other major area of potential savings is compensation to local banks for services provided.

---

[5] See Chapter 7 for additional details on how the automated reporting of deposit information can be used in the concentration system.

This calls for careful negotiation with the banks and may represent a potential tradeoff with geographical proximity to the field units.

Mailed Payments Collection System

For many companies, payments, almost always paper checks, are mailed by the customer in response to a billing notice or an invoice. A mailed payments system contains all three components of collection float: mail float, processing float, and availability float.

Basic Components

The mailed payments collection system consists of collection centers, deposit banks, and an information system. A schematic diagram of the components is given in Figure 6.4. Payments are mailed by customers to a designated collection center operated either by the company or by an outside agent. Payments are processed at the collection center: checks are encoded, the deposit is prepared and made, and data are transmitted to the company's central

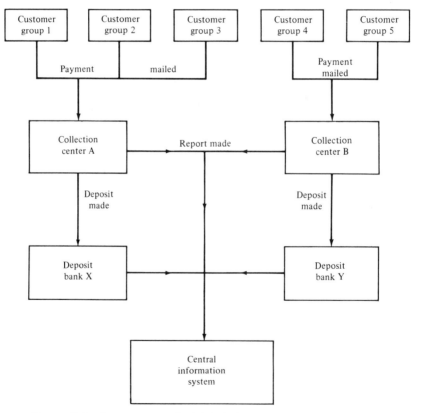

Figure 6.4 Components of a Mailed Payments Collection System.

information system. The cash flow timeline for a mailed payments collection system has all of the elements shown in the generalized timeline in Figure 6.1.

System Design

NUMBER OF COLLECTION POINTS. The number of collection points needed is a function of the number of payments, the average size of payments, and the geographical dispersion of the customers. For a firm with many small payments, processing costs may be more important than float costs. Such a firm will likely use an automated processing system at one or two sites. For a firm with a few large payments, float costs represent a large portion of the total costs of the collection system. Some manual processing is tolerable; however, locating collection sites close to the customers to reduce mail and availability float costs becomes important. Such a firm will likely use a relatively larger number of collection points.

COLLECTION POINT LOCATION. The optimal location of the collection points is a function of the geographical distribution of the payors' mail and disbursement points, the mail and availability times for different locations, the number and average size of the items, the number of collection points used, and the costs of collection at different sites. The factors to consider and the method of determining the best collection point locations are discussed later, when we focus on lockbox location.

IN-HOUSE VERSUS EXTERNAL OPERATION. The firm has the choice of operating its own collection points or contracting for outside operation. A typical procedure for a company-operated collection center is to have mail delivered to the processing center, where employees open the envelopes, remove the checks, process the deposit, and take it to the bank. After the deposit is made, administrative processing continues, with updates to the information system. When an in-house process is used, the company maintains total control over the operation, it is easier to make changes in the system, and the information is geared to the company's needs. If an outside contractor (usually a bank operating a lockbox) is used, the agent intercepts the mail, removes and makes a record of the check, processes the deposit, captures the information accompanying the remittance, and sends or transmits the data to the company. The advantages of contracting out may include lower processing costs because of the greater efficiency of a specialized operation, a larger window for using the deposit cutoff times, or availability of facilities in a good location for collection where the company does not have operations. More will be said about company versus outside operation in the discussion of lockboxes.

PAYOR ASSIGNMENT. In Figure 6.4 the company's payor base is divided into five groups, but there are only two collection points. As part of the determination of an efficient collection system, each customer group is assigned to a collection point, which results in the lowest total cost for that payment group. A company can increase the probability of having the payments sent to the correct collection location by including addressed return envelopes.

The assignment to collection points is not restricted to the geographical location of payors; it may also be a function of size. For example, Small Computers may have the option of directing a customer to send payment either to its internal collection point in Silicon Valley or to a lockbox it has established in Chicago. If Small Computers has a customer in Detroit send its remittance to the company, it will have a total float time of, say, 8 days. If the customer sends the remittance to Chicago the delay will only be 3 days, but there will be an additional $1.10 processing cost. If the company has a 10% opportunity cost, we can determine how large the remittance has to be before it is worth the extra processing costs:

$$\text{Float savings} \; = \; \text{extra processing costs}$$

$$(5 \text{ days saved})(0.1/365)(\$ \text{ amount of payment}) \; = \; 1.10$$

$$\$ \text{ amount of payment} \; = \; \$803.$$

Thus, if Small Computers *size sorts,* or directs remittances to different locations based upon size, it should direct any customers in Detroit with remittances of less than $803 to send the payment to Silicon Valley, while those with larger payments should be directed to Chicago. The opportunity cost savings on the float for payments smaller than $803 do not justify the larger processing costs of sending the payment to Chicago. A similar analysis of the tradeoff of variable float and processing costs would be conducted for other customer locations.

TYPE OF PAYOR. The characteristics of the payors that remit payments to a firm influence the type of collection system that is established. *Corporate payors* generally make payments in response to specific invoices, but the payments are frequently for an amount different from the invoice amount because of adjustments made for discounts, returns, or allowances. Manual processing may be required to handle these alterations. In addition, the checks tend to be for large dollar amounts. The primary emphasis of the collection system is on float reduction and timely handling of information related to the invoice being paid. On the other hand, *retail payors,* consumers or small businesses, generally make payments for a small dollar amount, frequently use installment or recurring payments for an ongoing credit or service, generally pay the amount on the bill, and include a machine-readable standard document that is returned with the remittance. The emphasis is on automation to hold down processing costs.

Other Collection Systems

Several other types of collection systems are used. Many of them use electronics and advanced communication systems. Although not widely used at present, they are expected to grow in importance as electronic communications and transactions gain greater acceptance.

Preauthorized Payments

Preauthorized checks (PACs), preauthorized drafts (PADs), or *preauthorized ACH debits* are sometimes used when the payment amount (or range) and the payment date are specified in advance. On the agreed date, the payee initiates the value transfer from the payor through the banking system, with no need for further action on the part of the payor. Preauthorized payments eliminate mail float, reduce processing and availability float, and improve both parties' forecasting ability. If they are handled by ACH, paperwork costs are reduced and availability can be controlled. The widest acceptance has occurred where regular, equal payments like insurance payments, mortgage payments, or budget utility payments are involved.

Electronic Trade Payables

Electronic transmissions of corporate-to-corporate payments and related invoice data are made through the banking system and the ACH. This type of payment offers the potential benefit of moving payment information, as well as many of the advantages and disadvantages of preauthorized payments for moving cash. A suggested enhancement of the process is to incorporate electronic order placement in the same system. Several pilot projects have met with mixed success. The application of this type of system has been very limited but is expected to grow in the future. More information on electronic information flow is presented in Chapter 20.

Net Settlements

In several industries, such as airlines and oil, with a large number of reciprocal payments, payments are netted out between companies at a set time and only the differences are actually transferred. The transfers are usually done by wire. This process eliminates all float and reduces the administrative costs; however, the specific timing is subject to negotiation between the parties.

Automated Teller Machine (ATM) Networks

Through the use of ATM networks and point-of-sale (POS) terminals, cash is transferred electronically from the customer's account to the company's account at the time of the sale. To date, these systems have been developed on a limited basis for supermarkets and other retail chains. Potentially, they represent an alternative to present over-the-counter systems.

We have seen that although the goal of any collection system is to speed inflows, the type of collection system that a firm uses is a function of the characteristics of the customer base and the method of the delivery of the product or service. The closer the payment is tied to the delivery of the product or service, the less flexibility there is in the design of the collection system. We next take a look at the use and design of the collection alternatives for a mailed collection system.

Lockbox Systems

Lockbox Operation

A *lockbox* is a collection point operated for a company by a bank, where the bank picks up the mail, processes the deposit, and transfers information to the company. The bank maintains post office boxes for receipt of payments at a central post office. Many banks have a unique zip code and do the final (box number) sort on the mail to avoid one step in post office processing. The bank picks up the mail several times (perhaps as many as 20) per day. The checks are removed, photocopied or microfilmed, and entered into the clearing process. Because the bank can enter checks into the clearing system even when the bank is not open, processing and availability delay can be reduced. Check and deposit information, along with other remittance data and any return documents, are transmitted to the firm after the deposit has been processed and the checks are entered into the clearing system.

Two major types of lockboxes are offered by banks. *Wholesale lockboxes* are used for processing a moderate number of large-dollar remittances, usually from business payors. Since many business payors do not return a standard document with the payment, manual processing, designed to meet specific needs of the company, is used. Detailed deposit information, often including a breakdown of the total deposit by days of availability, is transmitted daily to the company or to its concentration bank, either by phone or electronically. Remittance data, either on paper, tape, or microfilm, are usually sent to the company by courier. If image processing equipment is used, the data are captured and electronically transmitted to the company.

Retail lockboxes are characterized by a large number of relatively small-dollar remittances, usually from consumers. A standard return document, often machine readable, accompanies the payment. The data captured are frequently transmitted electronically to the firm, and if information system linkages are appropriate, there can be automatic updating of accounts receivable information.

Lockbox Net Cost Savings

The economic benefit of using a lockbox typically involves a tradeoff between the freeing of funds by faster collection (lower collection float) and the cost of dealing with a bank or third party.

Float Savings

A lockbox can reduce float in the following ways: Mail time is reduced by locating the lockbox close to the customer's mailing point. Processing time is reduced because the bank is a more efficient processor and because deposits are entered even though the teller windows are closed. Availability is reduced because fewer items are deposited after the cutoff time and because checks clear faster when the deposit point is closer to the bank on which they are drawn. The value of float savings is calculated by multiplying the dollar-days of float saved by the opportunity cost.

Operating Costs

The bank's price for the service may have both a fixed and a variable component. The bank assesses a fixed charge to cover the costs of deposit ticket preparation, post office box rental, funds transfer, transmission of remittance data, and balance reporting. The bank assesses a per item charge to cover processing costs such as labor, supplies, copying, and microfilming. In analyzing the use of a lockbox instead of a company collection point, any operating cost savings due to a reduction or elimination of company collection efforts are deducted from bank operating costs. Additional administrative costs for monitoring the relationship should be added to the operating costs charged by the bank, even though these may be hard to estimate. The analysis of the use of a lockbox in Miami to service customers in the Southeast for Small Computers, Inc., is given in Exhibit 6.5.

For this example, the use of the lockbox will save Small Computers a net of $2,514.40 per month. These calculations do not include any allowance for increased administrative costs. The treasurer of Small Computers should weigh these savings against an estimate of the extra administrative burden of dealing with an additional bank.

Lockbox Networks

Several types of lockbox networks have been developed to offer a company additional collection locations without having to expand the size of its system. As mentioned in Chapter 3, banks are generally prohibited from operating full-service commercial branches outside their headquarter state, although many large banks do operate loan production or other types of offices across state lines. The development of lockbox networks, through one of the systems to be described, has allowed some banks to take on the appearance of a national operating bank and to circumvent some of the obstacles posed by interstate banking prohibitions.

From the company's standpoint, the advantages of using a lockbox network are (1) lower administrative costs of a small number of banking relationships; (2) lower internal processing costs due to the use of standardized information formats; and (3) lower concentration costs. The disadvantages are that (1) the "bundled" nature of network pricing makes cost comparisons difficult; (2) dual balances are eliminated from some types of transfer systems (see Chapter 7); (3) there is an increased risk in having all of the collection, concentration, and reporting functions performed by one bank; and (4) loss of flexibility results from standardized processing by one bank. Following are some options that banks have developed to offer these collection services.

Exhibit 6.5 Calculating the Savings from Using a Lockbox

Small Computers, Inc., has a group of retail customers in the southeastern portion of the country that mail about 500 payments with an average size of $5,500 per month. The collection delay from these customers is currently 7 days: 4 days mail time, 1 day processing, and 2 days availability. The Eighteenth National Bank of Miami has offered to operate a lockbox service for Small Computers that would save 2 days mail time, eliminate the processing delay, and speed availability by 1 day. The bank's charges are $1.10 per item processed and a service charge of $100 per month. Small Computers has a short-term investment portfolio earning a return of 10.5%.

The cash flow timeline for the current collections is

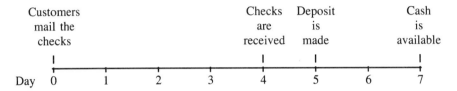

The cash flow timeline for the lockbox operation will be

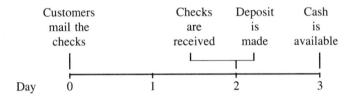

Value of float savings $= \$5{,}500 \times (.105 \times 4/365) \times 500 = \$3{,}164.40$.

Operating costs $=$ monthly service charge $+$ charge per item
$$\times \text{ number of items per month}$$
$$= \$100 + (\$1.1 \times 500) = \$650.$$

Net value $=$ float savings $-$ operating costs $= \$2{,}514.40$ per month.

Multistate Bank Holding Company
Some banks have taken advantage of changes in banking legislation that allow multistate bank holding companies. With a multistate operation, a bank can offer collection sites in more than one state through the affiliated banks in its holding company.[6]

Consortium
A group of independent banks may operate under a contractual agreement to provide lockbox services for each other's customers. A company using a

---

[6] An interesting, although somewhat less extensive, system was created when Pennsylvania allowed statewide bank holding companies. Mellon National Bank merged with Girrard National Bank and offered collection facilities in Philadelphia as well as in Pittsburgh. The advantage is that these two Pennsylvania cities are in different Federal Reserve Districts.

consortium chooses one bank as the lead bank or concentration bank but may have to establish relationships with each bank in the group that it uses.

Joint Venture

A bank establishes a joint venture with a nonbank firm that has multiple collection centers, such as an insurance company, and uses its processing capabilities. The firm processes remittances and deposits, while the bank handles concentration of funds and reporting.

Multiple Processing Centers

A bank establishes processing centers at multiple locations across the country where mail is picked up and processed. Deposits are made in accounts at correspondent banks in the company's name. Cash is then concentrated in the company's account at the lockbox bank's headquarters.

Mail Intercept

The bank contracts with couriers to pick up remittances at multiple locations across the country and transport them to its processing center. There is a reduction in mail and processing times but probably no change in availability. This system appears to be beneficial for a regional company with a substantial concentration of customers in one other area of the country who wants to maintain only one banking relationship.

_____ Collection Location Studies _____

We have seen that the use of multiple collection locations can generate float savings by decreasing the total collection float; however, the multiple locations can also increase costs. As stated earlier, the financial manager seeks to design a collection system to maximize the contribution to the net present value of the firm. In the context of the opportunity cost approximation that we are using in this chapter, the collection system that makes the greatest contribution to the net present value is the one that minimizes the total cost (float, operating, and administrative costs). The system design includes the number, location, and operation of collection points and the assignment of payors to these points.

Many studies have approached this decision strictly in terms of lockbox location, and are therefore called _lockbox location models_. However, the possibility of company-operated collection centers should also be considered in the analysis. The approach that we consider here uses the same solution procedures as lockbox location models but is broadened to include the possibility of company collection centers.

The objective function of a collection location study is to minimize the total cost of the collection system. However, many solution models start with a single collection point as a base system and add additional collection points if the incremental float savings resulting from the addition of one more collection point are larger than the incremental costs of adding it. Operationally, these models attempt to maximize a net savings objective function.

In practice, few financial managers actually do collection cost studies themselves. Decisions on collection system design are not made frequently enough to justify the development of the computer models necessary for an efficient solution. The financial manager usually hires a consultant, frequently a consulting group in the corporate services area of a large bank, to conduct a collection study. However, an understanding of the design of the study, the data used, and the method of analysis is necessary to judge the correctness and quality of the study.

Data Required for a Study

A collection study requires the following data, whether the study is done by management or by a consultant.

Customer Remittance Data

Customer remittance data include the number and average size of remittances from customers for some representative time period. Usually, the data are organized by the zip code of the mailing location. Each zip code can be treated as a separate receivables class or group. A further refinement is to divide each receivables class into subclasses based on size or on whether the drawee bank is located in the same Federal Reserve district as the mailing location. If sampling is necessary because of the magnitude of the data, care must taken to ensure that the sample is representative.

Potential Collection Sites

Potential collection sites to be considered in the solution are identified. They include potential (or existing) company locations and potential lockbox locations. Potential lockbox locations may be identified by specific banks or only by city locations, with the bank to be chosen later. In making a list of potential locations, attention is given to airline schedules (for mail delivery), the location of Federal Reserve banks, customer concentrations, and existing banking relationships.

Timing Data

Mail, processing, and availability times are obtained for each combination of customer classes and potential collection sites. There are different ways of obtaining each of these data elements.

MAIL TIMES. Mail times can be obtained either by taking a sample of actual mail times experienced by the firm or by using data from a survey such as "Phoenix-Hect Surveyed Mail Times." To use observed mail times, it is necessary to have a history of customers remitting to the potential location. Measurement errors may occur because of incorrectly stamped dates or adverse weather at the time of the sample. The Phoenix-Hect–type data represent standardized conditions, with mailings from one central post office to another. However, if customers do not mail their remittances from central post offices, actual mail times experienced may be different from the survey times.

PROCESSING TIMES. Processing times are site specific and should be the same for all receivables collected at that site. The company can estimate the processing delay for its own operations. Potential lockbox processors provide an estimate of their processing times. These should be confirmed with several of the processor's current customers.

AVAILABILITY TIMES. Three types of availability schedules are commonly used in the studies. (1) *Federal Reserve schedules*: although these are easily obtained, they may not reflect the actual availability that is granted by banks. Banks participating in direct sends should be able to beat the Federal Reserve schedule. (2) *City averages*: these data represent the average availability granted by major clearing banks in a city, which takes into account the actual clearing systems used. The accuracy of the study using these data is generally greater than that of studies using Fed availability but worse than that of studies using individual bank availability. (3) *Individual bank availability*: these data, supplied by individual banks, most accurately reflect unique bank availability characteristics. Most major banks will make their availability schedules available for use in lockbox studies.

Fixed and Variable Costs

The variable costs of processing the remittances from each customer group through each collection site and any fixed costs of operating the site are included in the objective function. The financial manager should be able to obtain internal estimates of these costs for company-operated collection points. Cost data for individual lockboxes must be obtained from the banks. These data are costly to obtain and may vary from quoted prices if a good customer relationship is developed. Because float costs are generally considered to be more critical than fixed and variable cost differences between banks, many studies either use representative costs or do not include individual bank costs. One potential result of the failure to include these costs is that the system will contain more collection sites than is economically justified.

Opportunity Cost

The opportunity cost that the firm incurs in the delay of receiving the cash is identified. This opportunity cost includes an adjustment for the degree of risk in the cash flows, as well as for the time value of money.

Administrative Costs

Administrative costs associated with managing a collection system increase with the number of collection sites. Although these costs are difficult to quantify, they are an important factor in correctly estimating the economical size of a lockbox system.

These data for Small Computers, Inc., are presented in Table 6.1A. For Small Computers the customers have been grouped into four receivables classes and four potential collection points are being considered. The delay listed in the matrix is total collection delay, consisting of mail, processing, and availability delays.

Solution Approaches

The objective of a collection study is to determine the most cost-effective collection system for a company's receipts. Three approaches are used to consider the quantifiable factors: (1) *complete enumeration,* (2) *mathematical programming,* and (3) *a heuristic algorithm.* Qualitative factors such as current banking relationships, other service requirements, and management preferences must also be considered before a lockbox system is implemented, but these are usually not part of the quantitative study.

Complete Enumeration

In complete enumeration, every combination of collection locations is considered separately. A total of $2(n - 1)$ combinations are possible with n potential collection sites. While complete enumeration is easy for a small number of sites, say, three or four, it is clearly time-consuming for a large number of potential sites; 10 sites would present 1,023 combinations. This approach, however, does guarantee an optimal solution.

Mathematical Programming Solutions

The problem can be formulated as a mathematical programming problem and solved for an exact, optimal solution. However, because the problem contains a mix of integer requirements (we cannot use half of a lockbox) with fixed and variable costs and a large number of alternatives, a solution can be obtained only at a very substantial computing cost, if at all, for other than a very small problem. Consequently, not many studies have actually attempted to use mathematical programming to obtain an optimal solution.

Heuristic Solution Algorithms

Several *heuristic algorithms,* systematic applications of a rule of thumb, are used to identify the best system from the standpoint of both size and site location. Two common search algorithms used are the *greedy algorithm* and the *interchange algorithm.*[7]

GREEDY ALGORITHM. The greedy algorithm approaches a solution by systematically adding collection points to the system. A collection point is added only if it reduces the cost of the overall system. At each level the "best"

---

[7] The greedy algorithm was first proposed by Ferdinand K. Levy in "An Application of Heuristic Problem Solving to Accounts Receivable Management," *Management Science* (February 1966), pp. B236–B244. The terms *greedy* and *interchange* were first used by Gerard Cornuejols et al. in "Location of Bank Accounts to Optimize Float: An Analytical Study of Exact and Approximate Algorithms," *Management Science,* (April 1977), pp. 789–810.

Table 6.1 Greedy Algorithm for Collection System Design

A. Input Data

			POTENTIAL COLLECTION POINTS			
			A	B	C	D
Receivables Classes	$ Size	Number	Collection Delay (in Days)			
1	$ 5,500	500	4	6	3	3
2	$10,000	350	3	5	5	2
3	$ 8,500	760	3	4	4	5
4	$15,500	945	3	7	5	4
Variable costs (per item)			$1.10	$1.25	$0.85	$1.05
Fixed costs			$200	$250	$150	$200

Opportunity cost = 10.00%

B. Total Cost Matrix

Receivables Classes	TOTAL VARIABLE COSTS			
	A	B	C	D
1	$ 3,564	$ 5,146	$ 2,685	$ 2,785
2	$ 3,262	$ 5,232	$ 5,092	$ 2,285
3	$ 6,146	$ 8,029	$ 7,725	$ 9,647
4	$13,079	$29,272	$20,868	$17,044
Fixed cost	$ 200	$ 250	$ 150	$ 200
Total cost	$26,250	$47,929	$36,521	$31,962

C. Savings from Reassignment—First Iteration

Receivables Classes	SAVINGS FROM REASSIGNMENT			
	A	B	C	D
1	—	$ 0	$878	$ 778
2	—	$ 0	$ 0	$ 976
3	—	$ 0	$ 0	$ 0
4	—	$ 0	$ 0	$ 0
Less fixed costs		($250)	($150)	($ 200)
Net savings		($250)	$728	$1,555

(Continued on next page)

Table 6.1 (cont.)

D. *Savings from Reassignment—Second Iteration*

Receivables Classes	SAVINGS FROM REASSIGNMENT			
	A	B	C	D
1	—	—	$100	—
2	—	—	$ 0	—
3	—	—	$ 0	—
4	—	—	$ 0	—
Less fixed costs			($150)	
Net savings			($ 50)	
Cost of collection system = $24,695				

Sum of columns may not equal totals due to rounding errors.

collection point of those not included in the system is added. This process continues until the inclusion of an additional collection point fails to reduce the costs. For small numbers of locations, it is possible to use this algorithm on a personal computer. The following is a description of one application of this approach.

The cost function is defined as[8]

$$TC = \sum F_k Y_k + \sum \sum N_c(i A_c T_{ck} + h_k) X_{ck},$$

where: i = the daily opportunity costs
   F_k = the fixed cost of collection point k
   Y_k = 1 if collection point k is in the system, 0 otherwise
   N_c = the number of items from collection group c
   A_c = the average size of an item in group c
   T_c = the average total time for an item in group c to be sent through collection site k
   h_k = the variable cost per item at collection point k
   X_k = 1 if group c is assigned to collection point k, 0 otherwise

The first step in the solution procedure is to generate a matrix of total variable costs for each collection alternative for each receivables class. This variable cost per item sent to a particular collection point consists of the opportunity cost of the delay for the average payment in the receivables class plus the processing cost per item. This per item variable cost is multiplied by the number of items in the class to obtain the total variable cost for each receivables class at each collection point. This variable cost matrix is shown in Table 6.1B. The next

---

[8] This formulation of the problem closely follows that presented by Bernell K. Stone in "Design of a Receivable Collection System: Sequential Building Heuristics," *Management Science* (August 1981), pp. 866–880.

step is to add the variable costs for all receivables classes and the fixed cost to obtain the total cost of each collection system.

Collection point A in Table 6.1, with a cost of $26,250 per month, is the least expensive collection alternative and is chosen as the best single-point collection system. Since there is only one collection point in the system, all receivables groups are assigned to this collection point.

The next step is to calculate the change in the cost function that occurs if an additional collection point is brought into the system. For each collection point not in the system, the variable cost savings are determined for any receivables groups that would be assigned to the new collection point if it is part of the system. The reassignment takes place only if the variable cost of assigning a receivables class to a new collection point is lower than its current assignment. The cost reduction is calculated by determining the variable cost savings that occur for the reassignments and subtracting the fixed costs of adding the collection point. The collection point that generates the greatest reduction in the cost function is brought into the system. From Table 6.1C we can see that Small Computers would save $1,555 per month on the cost of the collection system by bringing collection point D into the system along with collection point A. Receivables classes 1 and 2 would be reassigned to be collected at D instead of at A. This would result in a variable cost savings of $1,755. After subtracting the fixed cost of $200 for operating D, the net savings is $1,555.

As long as costs are reduced by bringing an additional collection point into the system, the process is repeated. If no cost reduction is achieved, the process stops. Table 6.1D shows the results of the second iteration of this reassignment process. Since the variable costs of all of the receivables classes at point B are higher than the current assignment, point B no longer needs to be considered. There are still some variable cost savings to be generated by reassignment to point C. We could switch class 1 from its current assignment at D and save $100 by reducing variable costs from $2,785 to $2,685. However, to achieve this we would incur additional fixed costs of $150. Thus, C would not be brought into the system.

Since there are no additional net savings to be generated from reassignment, the process stops. The collection system for Small Computers now consists of collection point A, at which classes 3 and 4 are collected, and collection point D, at which classes 1 and 2 are collected. The cost of the system is $24,695 per month.

While this process is relatively straightforward and can readily be programmed, it does not guarantee an optimal solution. In many cases, the collection point that is the best single-point system might not be in the best two-point system. For example, perhaps a lockbox located in Chicago is the best single-point system. The algorithm would proceed by trying to add additional collection points to the one in Chicago. Perhaps the best two-point system consists of a lockbox in Atlanta and one in Dallas. This option is never considered by the greedy algorithm.

INTERCHANGE ALGORITHM. An interchange algorithm attempts to get around the problem of not being able to remove a collection point once it is in the system. There are several different procedures for considering the removal of a collection point currently in the system. One approach is to take out the worst collection point in the current system, stepping back to a collection system with one less collection point. Then one considers expanding the system by adding the best two collection points not in the system. If the collection point removed is still viable, it will come back into the solution. If it does not, it is not an economically feasible alternative to the current size collection system. Additional modifications might use a two-out–two-in or a two-out–three-in process instead of one-out–two-in.

STOPPING POINT. The heuristics just described continue to add collection points to the system as long as the larger system results in lower costs. If all costs, including administrative costs, are properly considered in the cost function, this is acceptable. However, it is very difficult to model and include all costs. Frequently, the financial manager will have a subjective stopping point, beyond which she knows that the system will become unmanageable at a reasonable cost. The model is then altered to stop at a maximum size collection system.

Reevaluating the Current Collection System

It may be necessary to change a collection system due to changes in the distribution or disbursement practices of payors—they may be using remote disbursing (see Chapter 8)—or changes in bank pricing, interest rates, or sales volumes. Often this leads to fine-tuning a system by reassigning payors to collection sites. Occasionally, these changes may be so substantial that the system must be altered by dropping and/or adding sites.

Summary

An efficient collection system performs the functions of mobilizing cash, providing accurate cash flow information, providing timely information on sales and customers' accounts, and providing an audit trail for good control. Collection systems are designed to minimize the total opportunity cost from the float delay due to mail, processing, and availability and operating costs. Collection system design is largely influenced by the delivery of the product or service and by whether payment is made by cash, check, or credit card. An organization has the greatest design flexibility for a mailed payment system with payments by check. To design an efficient collection system, the customer base is divided into classes and information is obtained on potential collection sites. A solution procedure is used to move systematically through alternative systems in order to find the best system in terms of both size and specific locations. Because of the difficulty in quantifying administrative costs, many solution procedures ignore them. A subjective inclusion of these costs will usually reduce the number of collection points in the collection system.

_____ **Discussion Questions** _____

1. Contrast the differences in the information that you would want a collection system to provide if you were operating a chain of pizza restaurants versus an office supply store that deals primarily with repeat business customers.
2. Define collection float and identify the role of each type of float.
3. How can a collection system affect the amount of collection float?
4. What influences the location of the collection points in an over-the-counter system versus a mailed payments system?
5. Contrast the design of a collection system for a regional fast food restaurant chain with that for a supplier of machine tools to a national clientele of manufacturers.
6. Explain how a lockbox works and how the use of a lockbox can increase the present value of a company.
7. Discuss the differences between a wholesale and a retail lockbox and the types of companies that would use each.
8. Why might a company want to maintain a company collection center even if it is using a lockbox system?
9. How does the McFadden Act affect the ability of a bank to operate a nationwide collection system? What steps can banks take to get around these restrictions?
10. How is the process of assigning payors to lockboxes complicated by those who mail from one location but draw the checks on a bank in a different location?
11. Why is it desirable to fine-tune a collection system from time to time?
12. Contrast the data sources, the options considered, and the type of model you would use to do a lockbox study for a company with a current lockbox system versus one with a single-point, company-operated collection center.
13. What are the characteristics of a city in which you would consider locating a lockbox?
14. What alternatives exist to using Federal Reserve availability schedules, and what are the advantages and disadvantages of each?
15. Evaluate the following statement: "The only reason lockboxes are used is high interest rates. If rates fall, there will be no need for lockboxes."

_____ **Problems** _____

1. A firm currently receives, on average, $2,000,000 per day. Assume that the firm shortens the cash flow timeline by 3 days by implementing a new cash management system. Assume interest rates are 12%.
   a. Sketch the series of cash inflows under the old system and under the new system.
   b. Subtract the old series from the new one. (What assumptions must you make about the length of the series?)
   c. What is the lump sum savings in the new system?
   d. If the new system costs $100,000 per year to implement, should it be adopted?

The following information applies to Problems 2–5.
   The Ace Aviation Company currently has all incoming checks mailed directly to its headquarters in Chicago. An examination of postmarks shows that the average mail time is 4 days. Checks are credited to the proper accounts by a manual process taking, on average, 2 days. Checks are entered into the company's cash ledger after the first day of this process. Average availability time is 1.5 days, since many checks are drawn on distant banks. Average cash inflow per calendar day is $2,000,000.

2. Calculate the average collection float.
3. On average, how much does the company have recorded on its ledger balance that is not available at the bank? (Ignore any outgoing checks that may not have cleared.)
4. By installing two lockboxes, Ace estimates that mail time will be cut to 2 days and availability to 1 day. The lockbox banks will forward the remittance information to Ace on the same day that the checks are received, and Ace will show the increase in its cash accounts. What is the expected collection float if the lockboxes are used?
5. If Ace can invest any excess funds at an annual rate of 10% and the lockbox system will cost $350,000 per year to operate, how much will Ace save over the first year by operating the lockboxes?
6. A company earns 9% interest per year on short-term investments. A lockbox would save 2 days of mail time and 1 day of availability time for checks mailed from a particular area. Variable processing costs are $0.50 per check if the company processes the collection and $0.75 if it is processed through the lockbox. The bank charges $250 per month for fixed charges, including the rental of the post office box. What is the breakeven size for a remittance to be routed through the lockbox?
7. Given the following, find the best collection system and specify the assignment of the receivables classes to the appropriate collection points.

POTENTIAL COLLECTION POINTS

Receivables Classes	Dollar Size	Number	A	B	C	D	E	F
1	450	2,000	5	6	2	3	4	4
2	250	1,500	3	4	4	5	2	3
3	175	450	4	5	5	3	3	2
4	370	900	4	3	3	5	5	3
5	500	350	3	7	5	2	4	6
Variable costs (per item)			.75	.90	.85	.95	.60	.80
Fixed costs (per month)			200	150	250	225	350	400

Opportunity cost is 10%.

Case: *The Nationwide Electric Corporation's Collection System Design*

The Nationwide Electric Corporation is an electrical components manufacturer with five different major geographical divisions in the United States. Revenues for 1986 totaled $1,200,000,000. Nationwide produces electrical components that are purchased by other manufacturers for inclusion in household appliances, automobiles, machinery, computers, and so on. Product sales are headed by divisional marketing vice presidents and, in turn, by regional and district sales managers who manage the sales effort in local market areas.

Nationwide is headquartered in Dallas, Texas, where the treasury staff is located. Trevor Edwards is the cash manager. He reports to Lois Murphy, Assistant Treasurer, Banking Relations. Mr. Edwards has been asked to review the company's collection efforts to see if improvements can be made. He is to produce a report that critiques current practice and suggests needed policy changes, if any.

Mr. Edwards visits several regional and district sales offices and divisional accounting offices to observe firsthand the process required to convert purchase orders into eventual cash flows. He traces through several different sales transactions and makes the following notes.

Cash Flow Timing

Ordering and Billing. Each month, Nationwide customers place orders (via telephone and/or written purchase orders) through the district sales representatives, who, in turn, report to district sales offices. Purchase orders are forwarded, sometimes by mail and at other times by company courier, to regional warehouses. In the regional warehouse, orders are adjusted for out-of-stock items and goods are shipped to the customer by an appropriate common carrier. The regional warehouse mails a copy of the shipping documents back to the regional sales office where shipping documents and copies of original orders are manually matched up. Regional sales offices then adjust the original orders for out-of-stock items, price changes, and substitutions and mail copies of adjusted purchase orders to the divisional accounting office. Each division has an accounting office that is responsible for billing. The divisional accounting office prepares invoices based on adjusted purchase orders and shipping documents and mails invoices to Nationwide's customers. Mr. Edwards notes that the typical time delay between order filling and invoicing is about 10–14 calendar days.

Credit Terms. Credit terms for most product lines are stated on the invoice as net 30 days. Many product lines, however, offer a 2% discount for payments received by the 10th day following the invoice date. In practice, the divisional accounting office allows a 30-day grace period following the net 30-day time period before taking any follow-up action. Each divisional office maintains an aging schedule giving a breakdown of credit purchases by customer and showing amounts that are current (0–30 days), 31–60 days, 61–90 days, and over 90 days. Action against late customers (defined as those who have not paid in 61 days) includes sending a duplicate invoice. If no response is received in a reasonable time, a phone call is sometimes made to the customer. Regional sales offices are notified if payments extend over 90 days. In this case, orders are held up until differences can be resolved.

If a discount is taken for payment postmarked 15 days (10 days plus a 5-day grace period) after the invoice date, the amount of the unauthorized discount is included in the next bill. Customers do not, however, often pay the back-billed discounts.

Company Processing Centers. Payments are received in several different ways. About 60% come through the mails and are processed by company processing centers in each of the five divisional accounting offices. The processing centers manually prepare a voucher for each check received and forward the voucher, check, and accompanying documents to the Divisional Manager of Corporate Accounts. Here payments are checked against original invoices and shipping documents and then applied to customer accounts. After application, checks are endorsed and deposit tickets prepared. Deposits are typically made in local banks each day at approximately 5 P.M. From the time a check is received in the mail, processing procedures take an average of 3 to 4 days until the check is deposited. If the payment amount does not match the invoiced amount, an exception report is produced. A special office handles such discrepancies. Most differences are resolved in 3 to 5 days. A check is not deposited until all uncertainties have been resolved. At the conclusion of the processing cycle, reports from divisional accounting offices are mailed to regional offices and to company headquarters on a weekly basis.

Hand-Delivered Payments. About 15% of the payments are hand delivered by customers to district sales representatives. Almost all of these are payments in which the 2% discount is taken. Customers submit them just in time to make the 10-day deadline. Sales representatives are required to mail such checks to the divisional accounting office on the 15th and the 30th of each month. Company policy permits discounts to be taken if a check is received anywhere in the company by the 15th day following the invoice date. It is up to the district sales manager to decide which payments qualify for the discount.

Lockbox. Another 15% of customer payments are mailed to a lockbox in Boston operated by the company's original lead bank. These checks are all from the northeastern division. That division was persuaded by its Boston bank to experiment with lockbox services. Collections seem to have improved for that division. Photocopies of checks, together with the invoice copy and other documents mailed with the check, are returned by an express courier to the divisional accounting office for account application. The credit manager has vigorously complained that the bank sometimes takes 2–3 days to send check copies, while the promise was for overnight delivery. The company insists on rigid controls for lockbox processing. For example, the lockbox bank may not process any checks that say "paid in full" or any checks that do not exactly agree with the invoice amount. Rejected items are mailed to the divisional accounting office for problem resolution.

Problem Customers. The final 10% of incoming payments are from delinquent customers. Their checks are mailed directly to district sales managers. Deposits are made into local bank accounts. Depository transfer checks are prepared by managers on a weekly basis and mailed to the divisional account office for concentration.

_____ **Selected Readings** _____

BATLIN, C. A., and SUSAN HINKO, "Lockbox Management and Value Maximization," *Financial Management* (Winter 1981), pp. 39–44.

CORNUEJOLS, GERARD, MARSHALL L. FISHER, and GEORGE L. NEHMAUSER, "Location of Bank Accounts to Optimize Float: An Analytical Study of Exact and Approximate Algorithms," *Management Science* (April 1977), pp. 789–810.

FERGUSON, DANIEL M., "Optimize Your Firm's Lockbox Selection System," *Financial Executive* (April 1983), pp. 8ff.

FERGUSON, DANIEL M., and STEVEN F. MAIER, "Finding the Real Float: A New Standard for Lockbox Studies," *Cashflow* (September 1980), pp. 55–59.

FIELITZ, BRUCE D., and DANIEL L. WHITE, "A Two-stage Procedure for the Lockbox Location Problem," *Management Science* (August 1981), pp. 881–886.

FIELITZ, BRUCE D., and DANIEL L. WHITE, "An Evaluation and Linking of Alternative Solution Procedures for the Lockbox Location Problem," *Journal of Bank Research* (Spring 1982), pp. 17–27.

JOHNSON, THEODORE O., "Credit Terms Policy and Corporate Payment Practices," *Journal of Cash Management* (September 1982), pp. 14ff.

LEVY, FERDINAND K., "An Application of Heuristic Problem Solving to Accounts Receivable Management," *Management Science* (February 1966), pp. B236–B244.

MAIER, STEVEN F., and LARRY H. FORMAN, "Collection System Design," *Journal of Cash Management* (January 1984), pp. 20ff.

MAIER, STEVEN F., and JAMES H. VANDER WEIDE, "What Lockbox and Disbursement Models Really Do," *Journal of Finance* (March 1983), pp. 361–371.

MAIER, STEVEN F., and JAMES H. VANDER WEIDE, *Managing Corporate Liquidity;* New York: Wiley, 1985, chapter 3.

MATHUR, IKE, and DAVID LOY, "Corporate Banking Cash–Management Relationships: Survey Results," *Journal of Cash Management* (October 1983), pp. 35–46.

NAUSS, ROBERT M., and ROBERT E. MARKLAND, "Theory and Application of an Optimizing Procedure for Lock Box Location Analysis," *Management Science* (August 1981), pp. 855–865.

ROLLINS, CATHY L., and ANTHONY J. CARFANG, "Lockbox Networks," *Journal of Cash Management* (May 1984), pp. 56–58.

STONE, BERNELL K., "Design of a Receivable Collection System: Sequential Building Heuristics," *Management Science* (August 1981), pp. 866–880.

7

Cash Concentration Systems

A large retail convenience store chain owns over 7,000 stores throughout the country. Each store makes a nightly deposit of some $4,000 into one of over 5,000 deposit banks. Even after the day's receipts are collected, accounted for, and safely deposited at the deposit bank, the firm's collection problems are not quite over. Cash deposited in a far-flung network of small local banks is essentially useless. It cannot yet be invested or used to pay for goods and services. It may earn credits to pay for local banking services, but any extra balance beyond a nominal compensating balance is essentially useless until it can be moved into a central cash pool. The cash manager of this firm is charged with efficiently moving the cash from deposit banks into one or more concentration banks so that the cash can be invested, used to cover disbursements, or pay loans. One day's delay in transferring the cash means that $28,000,000 is left in the deposit bank system. Two days' delay would result in $56,000,000 in balances. How can the cash manager of this firm gather cash from this network of deposit banks at low cost without leaving large amounts of wasted balances?

Chapter 6 discussed how firms collect cash from customers and transfer it to deposit banks. This chapter describes how firms perform the next step: the task of *cash concentration*, or moving cash from deposit banks (lockbox or field banks) into the firm's central cash pool residing in one or more concentration banks. It is not sufficient simply to collect cash and have it deposited into one of the firm's deposit accounts. Cash must be usable by the firm. It must be moved into an account where it can be actively put to work. This is the role of cash concentration.

_____ Cash Concentration Tasks _____

As illustrated in Figure 7.1, a concentration system consists of deposit banks that feed cash into a concentration bank and disbursement banks that draw cash from a concentration bank. In addition, the concentration bank is tied to a portfolio of short-term investments and borrowings. This portfolio is used to balance out any excesses or deficiencies in the concentration account. A concentration bank is simply a bank designated by the firm to perform three main tasks: (1) receive deposits from banks in the firm's collection system, (2) transfer funds to the firm's disbursement banks, and (3) serve as the focal point for short-term credit and investment transactions. To perform the last function, cash in the concentration bank is monitored. When the level becomes too high, extra cash is moved into short-term investments or used to pay off credit lines. When the level dips too low, needed cash is pumped in from the sale of short-term investments or a draw on short-term borrowing sources. This process is called *aggregate cash position management*. In this chapter, we focus primarily on tasks 1 and 2.

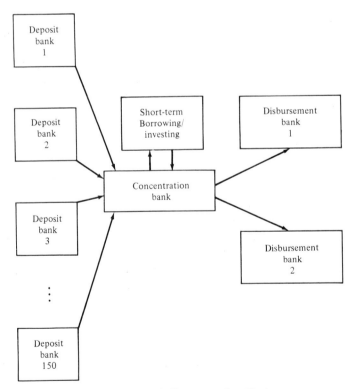

Figure 7.1 Cash Concentration System.

Though any bank can theoretically serve as a concentration bank, most firms use the larger commercial banks for this purpose. The reason is that concentration banks often serve additional functions besides the three mentioned. First, they may provide a balance reporting function. Such reporting services gather information from the firm's banking system and provide a daily report of the firm's deposits, disbursements, and balances. Second, concentration banks often serve as a source of short-term security investments such as repurchase agreements, commercial paper, T-bills, and certificates of deposit (all of which are discussed in Chapter 9) and provide short-term liquidity in the form of credit lines. Third, they provide assistance in preparing concentrating transfers. Smaller banks generally cannot perform all of these functions. While it is possible to receive these services from parties other than the concentration bank, administration is simplified, it is argued, if the concentration bank provides them all as a package.

Advantages of Concentration

Cash concentration simplifies short-term borrowing and investing decisions. If deposits are more or less routinely transferred to the concentration bank, the cash manager need only make decisions about what to do with one (or a few) cash balances. If investment and borrowing decisions had to be made about the accounts at each separate deposit bank, cash managers—especially those having 5,000 banks—would have long days indeed.

Concentrating cash into a central cash pool also facilitates investment in short-term securities. Money market securities that give the highest rates are sold in large dollar blocks (e.g., $1,000,000). Accumulating cash in a concentration account provides the quantities needed to purchase such securities.

Short-term forecasting is usually simpler for a concentration account than for individual deposit and disbursement accounts. This is because forecast errors in smaller accounts often offset each other when summed over the firm's banking system. This is important in forecasting credit line needs. It is much easier to have one large credit line tied to a concentration account than many small credit lines tied to each bank in the firm's system.

Objective Function of Cash
Concentration

In evaluating the costs of collection systems in Chapter 6, we examined primarily time value, processing, and administrative costs. In cash concentration, we analyze these same costs plus some additional ones. Unfortunately, the costs are more complex and difficult to measure because we are dealing with cash that is already in the firm's accounts but that is being valued differently in different banks. In designing and managing a cash concentration system, these various cost components must be traded off to achieve an overall minimum cost.

Cash concentration costs arise from several sources: (1) opportunity costs of holding excess balances in deposit banks, (2) transaction costs of moving cash into the concentration bank, (3) the value of dual balances (in which the same cash is counted in both the deposit bank and the concentration bank at the same time), (4) administrative costs of managing the concentration system, and (5) control costs associated with the risks of cash losses encountered in some concentration systems. Each of these cost factors will be discussed in detail. We can express them qualitatively in an objective function as follows:

> Minimize: opportunity costs of excess balances
> + transaction costs
> − interest on dual balances
> + administrative costs
> + control costs

The dual balance factor has a negative sign because as dual balances increase, costs are reduced.

Opportunity Cost of Excess Balances

Demand deposit balances become *excess balances* when the average available balance in an account is above that required for compensation of the account. Most larger banks—which include virtually all lockbox banks— provide a monthly account analysis showing the required available balance compared to actual balances. However, many smaller field banks do not have the computer capability to provide such analyses. In these cases, excess balances must be computed by estimating a fair level of compensating balance and comparing that figure to the estimated average available balance.

Estimating Excess Balances

Suppose we want to know if we are compensating a particular field bank fairly or if we have excess balances there. The bank provides no account analysis. First, we determine the services they provide for us. Suppose they receive seven deposits per week from our field office. Each deposit consists of coin, currency, and a few checks and would cost $1 per deposit at similar banks. The bank processes five DTCs per week in transferring out our deposits (typical charge is $.20 per DTC) and provides rolled coin and currency services that we estimate to be worth $5 weekly. Earnings credit rates from other banks that we use average roughly 7% per year, and we know that the reserve requirement is 12%. The bank's estimated charges would be as follows:

Deposits	7 × 1.00	=	7.00
DTC transfers	5 × 0.20	=	1.00
Coin and currency			5.00
Estimated total weekly charges			$13.00

Second, we translate these weekly charges into a required available balance. As discussed in Chapter 4, we do this by dividing the weekly charges by the weekly earnings credit rate times 1 minus the reserve requirement:

$$\text{Required available balance} = \frac{13.00}{(.07/52)(1 - .12)} = 11,000.$$

To compensate the bank fairly, we would need to keep $11,000 (we rounded slightly) in average available balances.

Third, we compute the actual average available balance from the monthly bank statement. Since usually only the daily ledger balance is given in the monthly report, a bank float factor must be estimated to convert the ledger to the available balance. To estimate the bank float factor for fairly even deposits with no strong weekly cycles, the following is computed:

$$\text{Float factor} = ADLD \times P,$$

where $ADLD$ is the average daily ledger deposit and P is the percentage of the deposit that has delayed availability of 1 day. This is only an approximation and must be computed by other means if deposits follow a strongly cyclical pattern and if availability delays are longer. [1]

For example, assume that the average daily deposit is $7,000 and the fraction of the deposit that receives 1-day availability is 10%. The remaining is coin and currency or local checks that receive immediate availability. The float factor in this example is therefore

$$\text{Estimated bank float} = \$7,000 \times .10 = \$700.$$

If the average ledger balance is $16,700, the average available balance is $16,000. Since the target or required compensating balance was computed to be $11,000, we have an excess balance of $5,000 for the week.

Cost of Excess Balances

Excess balances represent an opportunity cost. Since these balances are primarily corporate demand deposits, they do not earn interest. If such balances could be removed, the firm could invest the cash in expanded operations, pay off debt, take trade discounts, and so on.

Sources of Excess Balances

Excess balances are caused primarily by information-gathering, processing, and clearing delays in the concentration system. Deposit reports from field units may be delayed by field managers or persons in the deposit information-gathering system. For example, some multidivisional firms channel deposit reports through several levels of management before they are processed by

---

[1] There is no simple formula for computing a general float factor. The easiest way to determine average bank float is to construct a ledger balance table and an available balance table. Starting with an opening balance of zero and an assumed deposit pattern, simply work through a few weeks and compute the average difference between the two balances.

the cash manager. The information flow may take several days. Depository transfer checks may be deposited after the concentration bank's cutoff time and may therefore miss 1 day's availability. The clearing process for DTCs and ACH transfers requires one or more days between transfer initiation and clearing. Any of these time delays may cause a buildup of excess balances at the deposit bank. Some delays are unavoidable, while others may be eliminated by managerial policy changes. We discuss specific techniques for dealing with excess balances in a later section.

Transfer Costs

A further expense in managing a concentration system consists of the transfer costs associated with the banking system and reporting services. Such charges include deposit bank charges for outgoing wires, ACHs, or DTCs, as well as for overdrafts if the account has insufficient funds when a transfer is presented. Banking charges have been increasing at a rapid rate in recent years as a result of Fed pricing and the general unbundling of bank service charges. The concentration bank charges for preparing wires, ACHs, or DTCs, for receiving transfers from deposit banks, and for reporting to the firm. In addition, the bank generally charges for receiving deposit information from the third-party vendor or other source. Vendors charge for collecting deposit information from field units and transmitting data to the concentration bank. For mailed DTC systems, postage and paper costs are incurred.

In addition to bank and vendor charges, which tend to be direct and measurable, managerial costs of concentration must be considered in evaluating concentration system costs. Transfer preparation may require the time of the field manager and the headquarters staff. These costs are more difficult to measure but may be substantial for some systems.

Dual Balances

The dual balance cost does not exist for the collection portion of the cash flow timeline, but it may be present in certain concentration systems. Dual balances arise in concentration systems because of inefficiencies in the transfer clearing mechanism. Such balances generally occur only for DTCs but may occasionally be found in some instances when ACHs are used. They occur when a deposit into the concentration bank receives availability at the concentration bank *before* the transfer clears the field bank. During the time of the overlap, the firm "owns" the same cash at two different banks.

Example

As illustrated in Table 7.1, a DTC drawn on the field deposit bank for $10,000 is deposited in the concentration bank on Wednesday and is given 1-day availability. The DTC becomes an available balance on Thursday. Now suppose that the DTC, for some reason, is not presented to the deposit bank

Table 7.1 Example of Dual Balances: Weekday Transfer

DTC clearing time back to deposit bank = 2 days
DTC availability time at concentration bank = 1 day

Day	Available Balance in Deposit Bank	Available Balance in Concentration Bank
Tue	10,000	0 (initial balance)
Wed	10,000	0 (DTC deposited)
Thu	10,000	10,000 (DTC available)
Fri	0 (DTC clears)	

for 2 business days. The deposit bank will not subtract the $10,000 from the firm's available balance until Friday. Hence, on Thursday the firm has the same $10,000 in both banks. On Thursday, the firm may remove the available cash from the concentration bank and invest it. At the deposit bank on Thursday, the cash is earning credits to pay for bank services. The $10,000 balance is therefore a dual balance.

Weekend Effect

Suppose the preceding example is repeated, but the transfer is on Thursday instead of Wednesday. As shown in Table 7.2, the concentration bank gives availability on Friday but the check does not clear the deposit bank until Monday (2 *business* days later). In this case, the firm has 3 days' worth of dual balances: Friday, Saturday, and Sunday. The transfer day that results in a dual balance over the weekend is called a *critical day*. When the clearing time is 2 days and availability time is 1 day, the critical day is Thursday. If clearing time were 3 and availability time 2 days, the critical day would be Wednesday.

Table 7.2 Example of Dual Balances: Weekend Transfer

DTC clearing time back to deposit bank = 2 days
DTC availability time at concentration bank = 1 day

Day	Available Balance at Deposit Bank	Available Balance at Concentration Bank
Wed	10,000	0 (initial balances)
Thu	10,000	0 (deposit DTC)
Fri	10,000	10,000 (DTC becomes available)
Sat	10,000	10,000
Sun	10,000	10,000
Mon	0 (DTC clears)	10,000

Causes of Dual Balances

Since dual balances arise from inefficiencies in the check-clearing system, the causes are to be found in the parties involved in the clearing process. The Fed, for example, may promise the concentration bank faster availability than it can deliver. When this happens, Fed float is created, as explained in Chapter 4. Transportation delays, bad weather, equipment failures, labor problems, and other factors are all potential causes of dual balances. Fed float has been reduced dramatically over the past few years, with a corresponding drop in dual balances.

The concentration bank's availability schedule may grant faster availability than it can realize because of transportation problems. For example, it may promise 1-day availability on a check that is usually sent directly to the drawee bank. Because of a traffic jam, the courier cannot get the cash letter to the airport in time to make the scheduled flight. Some banks grant fast availability for competitive reasons. They may know that they will not be able to provide the promised availability, but they make up the loss by charging higher prices for bank services or by doing a larger volume of lockbox business.

Rarely is the deposit bank the source of dual balances. But occasionally a deposit bank will receive a presentment of checks that it cannot sort to drawee accounts until the following day. This phenomenon was observed in the earlier days of ACH usage. Many banks could not automatically handle incoming ACH transactions and relegated them to manual posting. The result was sometimes delays of 1 or more *weeks* before a debit was posted to a field deposit account. The authors have not heard such stories for several years, however.

Negative Dual Balances

Now that positive dual balances have been largely eliminated, the pendulum has seemingly swung back in the other direction. Many firms now report *negative dual balances*. These occur when the clearing time is *shorter* than the availability time. Table 7.3 shows the result of a Thursday transfer when

Table 7.3 Example of Negative Dual Balances: Weekend Transfer

DTC clearing time back to deposit bank = 1 day
DTC availability time at concentration bank = 2 days

Day	Available Balance in Deposit Bank	Available Balance in Concentration Bank
Wed	10,000	0 (initial balances)
Thu	10,000	0 (deposit DTC)
Fri	0 (DTC clears)	0
Sat	0	0
Sun	0	0
Mon	0	10,000 (DTC becomes available)

clearing time is 1 day and availability time is 2 days. In this case, cash completely disappears on Friday, Saturday, and Sunday. As the Fed and concentration banks try to become more realistic in their availability schedules, it is likely that negative dual balances will appear more frequently.

Dual Balances and Transfer Mechanisms

Wire transfers rarely, if ever, generate dual balances. ACH transfers also seldom generate dual balances; however, as noted previously, some banks may not post ACH transactions on a regular or timely basis. A DTC may occasionally result in a dual balance. DTCs are also the main source of negative dual balances.

The existence of dual balances for DTCs means that DTC concentration systems are sometimes cheaper to operate than systems built on ACH or wire mechanisms. This is because some of the compensating balances are being provided "free" by the banking system when DTCs are used.

Administrative Costs

Receiving and monitoring daily deposit reports from field managers or lockbox banks and deciding on the timing and amount of cash transfers can be a major cost in a concentration system. Concentration systems have occasional overdrafts or lost transfers with which managers must be concerned. Systems that concentrate check deposits must also deal with checks deposited at a field or lockbox bank that must be returned for insufficient funds after the amount has been included in a concentrating transfer.

Managers must also determine and monitor bank compensation at all banks in the system. This task can be very difficult in a field system where bank deposit, balance, and cost data are untimely or unavailable.

Also included in managerial costs are the costs of adverse banking relationships and public image. Some concentration systems may potentially lead to strained banking relationships and an adverse media image if concentration practices are seen as taking advantage of the banking system. Measuring administrative costs is difficult, but consideration must be given to such costs since they may be quite important.

Control

The fifth and final cost factor in the objective function is control. Control costs are encountered almost exclusively in field concentration systems. These costs include possible theft or fraud losses and the costs of minimizing them. Concentration systems may influence fraud losses. For example, a loosely organized system with plenty of excess balances in field banks and lengthy deposit reporting delays may invite a field manager to divert deposits to the trunk of a car rather than the deposit bank—knowing that it will be weeks before the theft is discovered. Some concentration systems may require incentive programs to induce field managers to cooperate with concentration policies. Like administrative costs, control costs are very difficult to quantify, but should nevertheless be considered in evaluating concentration system costs.

Cash Concentration Practice

We now discuss current practices in cash concentration and then return to using the objective function concept in designing more efficient concentration systems.

Field versus Lockbox Concentration Systems

There are two basic types of concentration systems, each associated with a potentially different set of problems and practices. In Chapter 1 we discussed in general the two types of banking systems used for gathering cash. The first is a field banking system that collects cash and other over-the-counter deposits. The second is a lockbox banking system that collects mailed deposits. The characteristics of the two are contrasted in Table 7.4.

Field Concentration Systems

A *field bank* is defined as a deposit bank that receives cash or checks over the counter from a sales office or another cash collection point. The task of cash concentration here is to move the cash from potentially hundreds of field banks over a wide geographical area to the concentration bank.

Table 7.4 Contrasting Field and Lockbox Concentration Systems

Feature	Field System	Lockbox System
Number of banks	Usually many	Fewer than 10
Bank size	Usually small	Usually large
Source of deposit	Over the counter	Mailed in
Geographical constraints	Bank must be near a cash collection point	Bank can be anywhere
Deposit size	Relatively small	Often large
Type of deposit	Cash and checks	Checks only
Availability	Usually immediate	Often delayed by availability schedule
Information from bank	Monthly statement	Monthly statement Daily balance and deposit report
Account analysis	Generally none	Customary
Services	Coin and currency deposit and transfer	Wide variety; sometimes credit

Most field banking systems typically have the following features. They may have a large number of banks. Firms like Sears or Southland (Seven-Eleven) may deal with thousands of field banks. Most of the banks in a field system are small and lack the information capabilities of larger banks. For example, a monthly statement may be the only deposit information available from a field bank. Daily deposits in field banks are generally quite small compared to lockbox deposits. Field banks frequently provide coin and currency, deposit, and transfer services, but rarely credit lines or other services. Deposits into a field bank often consist of cash or locally drawn checks. Both are usually treated as if they were immediately available. (Remember, as we discussed in Chapter 4, small banks sometimes don't make a distinction between ledger and available balances.)

Lockbox Banking Systems

In contrast to field systems, few corporations have lockbox systems consisting of more than five or six banks. As discussed in Chapter 6, *lockbox banks* are generally large banks with advanced information-gathering and reporting capabilities. Daily balance- and deposit-reporting systems and regular account analyses are standard. Deposits into a lockbox tend to be much larger than typical field bank deposits. Lockbox banks are sometimes used for credit lines and other specialized services and, hence, may require large balances (or a combination of fees and balances—see Chapter 4). Since lockbox banks receive only check deposits, a significant portion of the daily deposit may have delayed availability.

Example of a Cash Concentration System

To illustrate current concentration practice, we take the example of Sudden Shrimp, a hypothetical fast food restaurant chain with a concentration bank in Chicago. Sudden Shrimp has 1,000 company-owned restaurants throughout the country. On Monday evening, the manager of the Bedford, Indiana, restaurant takes the day's receipts of $5,000 down to the local field bank. A deposit ticket is made out and, together with the coin and currency, is placed in the night depository. On Tuesday morning the bank counts the deposit and credits the Bedford restaurant account with $5,000.

Two basic methods are used to move the deposit from Bedford to Chicago. Each is characterized by whether the transfer initiation to Chicago is decentralized or centralized. There are also several possible payment mechanisms that can transfer value between banks: depository transfer check, wire transfer, and ACH transfer. Transfer initiation and payment mechanism are, however, virtually independent decisions.

Decentralized Transfer Initiation

When transfer initiation is left to the field manager or field bank, we define the concentration system as decentralized. Table 7.5 shows the various

Table 7.5 Parameters for Decentralized Concentration Systems

Mode of Deposit Report from Field Manager	Deposit Information-Gathering Party	Transfer Size Decision Maker	Transfer Preparer	Form of Transfer
Mailed DTC is the deposit report Written report	None needed (DTC is the information)	Field manager Field bank	Field manager	Mailed DTC Wire ACH credit (rare)

Note: In designing a decentralized concentration system, one selection from each column is made. This gives a variety of possible design features.

options available in designing a decentralized system. These systems require no centralized deposit information gathering; the transfer itself is the information. Transfer control is left in the field. The two most common transfer mechanisms used in decentralized systems are mailed depository transfer checks and wires, although it would be possible—though not practical—to use ACH for this purpose.

Mailed DTCs

For many years, mailed DTCs were popular; they are still used by some firms. Recall that DTCs are used to transfer cash between two accounts for the same firm. No signature is required, and field employees cannot misdirect DTCs into their own accounts. To concentrate cash with a mailed DTC, Sudden Shrimp's restaurant manager writes a DTC for $5,000 drawn on the Bedford bank and mails it with a deposit ticket for $5,000 to Sudden Shrimp's concentration bank in Chicago. The concentration bank receives the DTC, deposits it in Sudden Shrimp's concentration account, grants availability according to its schedule, and clears the check back to the deposit bank. Mailed DTCs are simple and require no deposit information-gathering facility. The DTC is essentially the manager's deposit report to headquarters. Administrative and transfer costs are low compared to those of alternative methods.

Wire Transfers

Wires are another way to leave control in the field. The field bank is given daily instructions by the field manager or is given standing instructions regarding the amount to transfer to the concentration bank. This is a fast method of concentration since availability is immediate, but it is also very expensive (currently $10–$30 combined charges). In terms of our objective function, wire transfers remove excess balances because of their speed but add transaction costs. The value of removing excess balances must be weighed against the increased cost. In Sudden Shrimp's case, management probably would not want to transfer $5,000 by a wire transfer. We will come back to this analysis in a later section.

ACH Credits

ACH credits are not used often for field-initiated transfers because ACHs are currently not economical except for larger batches. It is possible for the field manager to instruct the field bank to send an ACH credit to the concentration bank.

Pros and Cons of Decentralized Initiation

The advantages of decentralized initiation are two. (1) Decentralization requires no information-gathering system at firm headquarters. This lowers administrative costs. The transfer itself is the information system. (2) Decentralization may also be consistent with corporate decentralization policies that permit field managers autonomy in controlling their own cash flows.

The disadvantages are also two. (1) Headquarters lacks control over deposit discipline and transfer decisions. To minimize overall concentration costs, it may be necessary (as we will see later) to make centralized transfer decisions. (2) Decentralized systems—especially those relying on mailed DTCs—usually lead to longer mail, processing, and availability time delays, resulting in excess balances. In practice, few firms still use mailed DTCs because of these disadvantages.

Centralized Transfer Initiation

Starting in about 1972, it became possible for transfers to be initiated centrally at relatively low cost. In this process, deposit information must flow to headquarters or the concentration bank independently of the actual transfer. National Data Corporation was the first commercial vendor to offer a deposit report-gathering service specifically designed for cash concentration. Table 7.6 shows all of the variations in centrally initiated transfers. To illustrate how

Table 7.6 Parameters for Centrally Initiated Transfers

Mode of Deposit Report from Field-Manager	Decision Information-Gathering Party	Transfer Size Decision Maker	Transfer Preparer	Form of Transfer
Telephone	Third-party	Field	Headquarters	Automated
Point-of-sale	vendor	manager	Concentration	DTC
terminal	Headquarters	Third-party	bank	ACH debit
Written	Concetration	vendor		Wire
report	bank	Headquarters		drawdown
		Concentration		
		bank		

Note: In designing a centralized concentration system, one selection from each column is made. This gives a variety of possible design features.

centralizing transfer initiation can shorten the cash flow timeline relative to that of a mailed DTC, we change our example slightly. Sudden Shrimp's manager in Bedford makes the deposit, as before, on Monday night. The manager telephones a third-party service provider and reports the $5,000 deposit for the Bedford restaurant number. The third-party provider receives phone calls late Monday night from the Bedford manager and all other Sudden Shrimp managers. The deposit information is then merged and electronically transmitted or physically delivered to the concentration bank early on Tuesday morning. Compared to mailed DTCs, gathering deposit information by telephone saves the mail time component and may therefore reduce excess balances.

Third-Party Providers

The reason firms use a third-party service provider is that most field deposits are made in the evening hours. Banks and headquarters offices are often closed. A third-party vendor can achieve economies of scale that make affordable the necessary computer systems, high-volume long-distance telephone lines, and round-the-clock teams of operators. Few firms can justify the expense of such a system unless they have a very large field collection system.

Variations

In addition to this basic scheme for a centrally initiated concentration system, there are many possible variations, as outlined in Table 7.6. Some firms prefer to have third-party vendors transmit deposit information to headquarters rather than directly to the concentration bank. This enables them to decide on transfer amounts themselves and initiate transfer instructions personally if they so desire. Other firms send deposit information directly to headquarters and bypass the third-party vendor. For example, one firm collects inventory, labor, and marketing data on a daily basis from point-of-sale cash register terminals in each field unit. Each evening, the day's data—including the deposit data—are transmitted directly to headquarters' computers. Deposit data are sorted out and taken to the concentration bank. A few banks offer a service that enables field managers to phone the bank directly rather than go through a third-party service. Transfer amounts, though usually simply the amount deposited, may be decided by the field manager, third-party vendor, concentration bank, or headquarters. Some service providers permit firms to use an algorithm that transfers an amount not equal to the reported deposit. We will discuss why a firm would want to do this later in this chapter.

Once the deposit information is received by the concentration bank, that bank can initiate transfers from the field bank by DTC, ACH, or wire.

Automated DTC

To use a DTC for centralized transfer initiation (sometimes called an *automated DTC*), it is important to remember that printing a check only requires that the appropriate MICR-encoded characters be printed along the bottom of a check. The field bank's printing company does not have to be the one to do the printing. Anyone can. A centrally initiated DTC recognizes this and uses the idea as illustrated in Figure 7.2. Within a few hours, the concentration bank prints DTCs for each field bank in the amount of the reported deposits. From that point on, the DTC clears just like any check. Availability is granted according to the concentration bank's availability schedule, and the DTC clears back to the deposit bank through normal check-clearing channels by Wednesday or Thursday, in our example.

ACH Debit

Rather than preparing a DTC, the concentration bank can create an ACH debit drawn against the field bank. If the customer pays a surcharge, ACH debits can be submitted late in the evening for settlement the next business day. Some banks will even accept ACH tapes on Sunday, thereby permitting the concentration of weekend deposits by Monday. Using ACH transfers for concentration is now very widely practiced. Surveys show that this use has been accepted by more firms than any other corporate application of ACH.

A problem encountered by some firms in using the ACH is that not all commercial banks are members of an ACH. Therefore DTCs must still be used for some subset of field banks.

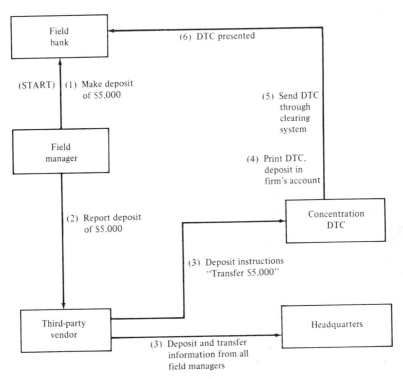

Figure 7.2 Centrally Initiated DTCs.

Wire Drawdown

Headquarters either gives daily instructions to the concentration bank or leaves standing instructions to wire down to a certain level or to wire the amount of the reported deposit. This procedure is called a *wire drawdown*; the concentration bank instructs the field bank to initiate a wire transfer. Wires result in same-day availability. This causes generally reduced excess balances in the deposit bank but does so at a relatively high cost. In practice, wire drawdowns are used mainly for concentrating large deposits from lockbox banks.

—————— Reducing Cash Concentration Costs ——————

We now discuss techniques for reducing cash concentration costs. While each technique seeks to reduce one or more cost factors, we must keep in mind that other factors may be adversely affected at the same time. The goal is to realize an overall reduction in the objective function.

Reducing Information, Processing, and Clearing Delays

Excess balances are caused primarily by delays in gathering and processing deposit information and by clearing transfers back to the deposit bank.

Information and Processing Delays

Delays often occur in receiving deposit information from field managers. One firm, for example, requires deposit information to be gathered along with sales and inventory information and processed through several administrative levels. The result is a delay of several days before the cash manager receives deposit information to pass along to the concentration bank. By removing deposit information at an early stage and routing it directly to the cash manager, a significant reduction in excess balances is realized.

Another firm finds frequent delays caused by field managers' irregular reporting habits. This firm begins including reporting promptness as part of its field manager review. Again, excess balances are significantly reduced. Generally, no complex mathematical algorithms are required to trace through information and processing pathways in order to determine ways to shorten the timeline.

Anticipation—Moving Transfer Initiation Forward

Anticipation means initiating a transfer at the concentration bank before cash becomes available at the deposit bank. Thus, by the time the transfer clears the deposit bank, available cash will be there to cover the transfer. This is essentially a method for counteracting information and processing delays. There are two types of anticipation, one less risky than the other.

Ledger anticipation means to initiate a transfer on the basis of ledger deposit information from the deposit bank. Ledger deposits become available deposits according to an availability schedule. Thus it is known with virtual certainty that a ledger deposit will be converted into an available deposit on a known date and will be able to cover a transfer on that date. For example, suppose a field manager reports a Monday deposit of $100,000 in checks with availability of 1 day. A $100,000 DTC can also be deposited in the concentration bank on Monday. The DTC clears on Tuesday when the deposit becomes available. There is little risk of overdraft with this form of anticipation. Ledger anticipation presupposes that management has access to ledger deposit information before the ledger deposit becomes available. Many lockbox banks, however, report on a next-day basis—that is, they post deposits to accounts late in the evening and let the firm know the next morning about the amount of the ledger deposit. By then, of course, much of the deposit has already become available.

Deposit anticipation means to initiate a concentrating transfer before expected deposits in a deposit bank have been reported. For example, a recreation firm expects to have a deposit of $20,000 from weekend sales at one of its field locations. Rather than wait until Monday to transfer the deposit out, an ACH for $20,000 is initiated by the concentration bank on Friday evening. The ACH transfer clears the field bank account on Monday when the field deposit is made.

Deposit anticipation is clearly more risky than ledger anticipation, since there is no guarantee that the full $20,000 will be deposited. Furthermore, deposit anticipation may require some form of forecast of daily receipts and may entail more complex reconcilement of transfers and deposits.

The practice of *one-time-transfer-out* may not appear to be deposit anticipation, but in reality it is. It occurs when, after a period of time, the average available balance in a deposit account is observed to be consistently above the target compensating balances.

For example, if the actual balance at one of Sudden Shrimp's field banks is $17,000 and the target is only $10,000, on average, the cash manager would transfer out the extra $7,000 with a one-time transfer. This recognizes that various delays in the concentration pipeline have caused a more or less permanent buildup of balances. This practice is a form of anticipation because deposits must continue to come into the account at about the same level as before or overdrafts will result.

A one-time-transfer-out is limited by the variability of the account. The more variable the balance in the deposit account, the less can be transferred out on a one-time basis. This is because a one-time transfer simply lowers the balance on each day by a constant amount. One particular day's balance may be less than the amount transferred out, even though the average for the period is above the target. This would cause an overdraft.

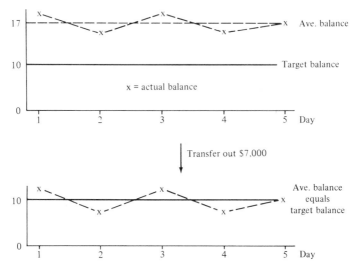

Figure 7.3 One-Time-Transfer-Out Illustration. Relatively Level Balances.

EXAMPLE. Figure 7.3 shows that for relatively constant balance levels, removal of $7,000 from an account averaging $17,000 causes no overdraft. On the other hand, Figure 7.4 illustrates what happens when there is high variability in the account. Day 3 is in an overdraft condition because its original balance was less than $7,000. The average balance in the second case is fine, but the overdraft condition would result in either a charge by the deposit bank or some strong words of warning to the firm.

Faster Transfer Mechanisms

Another way to reduce excess balances is to employ a faster transfer mechanism. Where excess balances are high, mailed or automated DTCs might be replaced with wire or ACH transfers. ACH transfers may be replaced with wires. Of course, wires are more expensive than either DTC or ACH transfers.

Reducing Transfer Costs

There are two primary ways to reduce transfer costs: choose a less expensive transfer mechanism and transfer less often than daily. If the less expensive transfer mechanism is slower, we must trade off speed with cost. One approach is to use breakeven analysis.

Breakeven Analysis

The tradeoff between excess balance and cost makes it tempting to formulate the mechanism choice problem as a breakeven analysis. Assume that a deposit of D dollars in the deposit bank is an excess balance earning no interest. If we use mechanism A (for example, a wire) to transfer it to the concentration

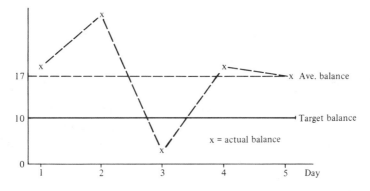

Transfer out $7,000

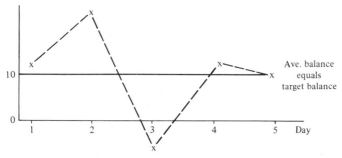

Figure 7.4 One-Time-Transfer-Out Illustration. Highly Variable Balances.

bank, the cost is C_a dollars per transfer and takes T_a days. As an alternative, the D dollars could be transferred using mechanism B (a DTC), which costs C_b per transfer and takes T_b days. The opportunity cost of leaving the deposit in the deposit bank is i per day. We would be indifferent if the opportunity cost over the time lag of the slower mechanism is just equal to the difference in the transaction costs of the two mechanisms. We can express this breakeven point as follows:

$$S \times i \times (T_b - T_a) = C_a - C_b.$$

To determine the transfer size at the breakeven point, we solve for S:

$$S = \frac{C_a - C_b}{i(T_b - T_a)}.$$

As an example, assume that a wire costs $20 and a DTC costs $1, considering all costs at both banks. Assume that the wire clears immediately but the DTC takes 2 days. If the deposit can be invested at 9.125% per year (.025% per day), the breakeven size is

$$S = \frac{20 - 1}{.00025(2 - 0)} = \$38,000.$$

This means that interest on $38,000 for 2 days at .025% per day earns just enough ($19) to make up for the cost of the faster mechanism. In other words, for deposits over $38,000, a wire is justified. For deposits under $38,000, the extra $19 is not worth it.

BREAKEVEN IS GENERALLY INVALID. Unfortunately, transfer decisions are not really this easy. First, we had to assume that the deposit would earn no interest at the deposit bank. Deposit banks—implicitly or explicitly—give earnings credits for balances unless there is an excess over a longer period. Recall that most banks allow excess balances to carry over to subsequent periods. Hence, it is difficult to determine for any particular transfer what portion, if any, is really in excess. For the portion of the deposit that does earn interest, the interest is probably less than the opportunity cost. Hence, the real opportunity cost is a complex blend of the interest opportunity cost and the differential between the opportunity cost and the earnings credit rate.

Second, we have assumed that the DTC takes 2 days longer than the wire. With anticipation, however, a DTC may be effectively just as fast as a wire.

Third, we have considered only two cost factors: excess balances and transfer costs. By taking the dual balances into account, the DTC may prove much less expensive than the wire. With DTCs it is possible to generate occasional dual balances that are essentially free to the firm. As we mentioned before, however, this factor is becoming much less important than it once was.

RULES OF THUMB. Since breakeven analysis greatly oversimplifies mechanism selection, what other choices are left? The problem may be formulated as a fixed-charge programming problem—but that is beyond the scope of this book. Fortunately, there are rules of thumb that can be developed from the framework of our objective function without actually doing the mathematics. Table 7.7 summarizes the findings. Where dual balances are significant, a DTC is usually the preferred mechanism. If negative dual balances exist, ACH or wire transfers are preferred. Where there are few or no dual balances, an ACH is usually the mechanism of choice unless the deposit is very large compared to the target compensating balance. If accounts often receive large, unanticipated

Table 7.7 Mechanism Selection Rules of Thumb

	Deposit Size Relative to Target Balance	
	Small	**Large**
Conditions	**Preferred Mechanism**	
Dual balances present	DTC	DTC
No or negative dual balances present	ACH	Wire
Forecasting relatively easy	DTC, ACH	DTC, ACH
Forecasting relatively difficult	ACH	Wire

Note: Mechanisms are assumed to be centrally initiated.

deposits, wire transfers may be the only way to remove excess balances. On the other hand, if cash flows into a deposit are regular and can be forecast, wires are not needed; anticipatory DTCs or ACH transfers are less costly.

Balance Averaging

Another way to reduce transfer costs is to transfer less often. Because firms receive deposit information daily, most firms assume that transfers should also occur daily. This may be unnecessary for some deposit banks. The key is to recognize that compensation is measured by averaging daily balances over some time period. The target compensating balance need not be met daily but may be met on an average basis. The technique of allowing the balance in a bank to fluctuate above and below the target level is sometimes called *managing about a target* or, as we prefer, *balance averaging.*

RELATIONSHIP BETWEEN DEPOSIT AND TARGET. The ability to balance average depends on the relationship of the target balance level to the daily deposit size. For example, if the target balance is $10,000 and the average daily deposit is $1,000, daily transfers are not necessary. Transfers once a week (or less often) are sufficient. The balance can be below $10,000 on some days and above $10,000 on others. On the other hand, if the target is $10,000 and the daily deposit is $100,000, balance averaging is not possible (unless the bank permits the balance to dip far below zero). Daily transfers from the account are mandatory to avoid a buildup of excess balances.

EXAMPLE. Table 7.8 illustrates the way balance averaging reduces transaction costs. Assume that the firm must maintain an average of $200,000 in the deposit bank. Wire transfers are used to move cash into the concentration bank. Each day a deposit of $70,000 comes into the account. In scenario 1, showing daily transfers, the firm begins with $200,000 in the account. Each day's deposit is wired out. At the close of each day, the balance in the account is $200,000. Scenario 2 shows an alternative approach in which the account begins with $100,000 and deposits accumulate until the end of the week, when all $350,000 is wired out of the account. The average balance in the account is exactly $200,000 in both examples.

Which is best for the firm? In scenario 2 the firm saves 80% of its wire transfer costs. Are there any offsetting costs? One might be tempted to argue that the firm does not get the use of the $70,000 until the end of the week, so there must be some opportunity costs involved. This is not true. Scenario 2 ties up, on average, exactly the same amount of cash as scenario 1. It begins with $100,000 less invested in the account and then expands to $380,000 on Thursday, but the average in both is identical.

Does the second scenario lead to problems in banking relationships? No. In general, banks do not care how the account fluctuates on a daily basis as long as the average balance is acceptable and there are no overdrafts. Overall, therefore, the second scenario involving balance averaging is an effective way to reduce transaction costs in cases where deposits are less than the target balance.

Table 7.8 Balance-Averaging Example

1. Daily wire of amount deposited

Day	Opening Balance	+	Deposit	−	Transfer Out	=	Closing Balance
Mon	$200,000	+	$70,000	−	$70,000	=	$200,000
Tue	$200,000	+	$70,000	−	$70,000	=.	$200,000
Wed	$200,000	+	$70,000	−	$70,000	=	$200,000
Thu	$200,000	+	$70,000	−	$70,000	=	$200,000
Fri	$200,000	+	$70,000	−	$70,000	=	$200,000
Sat	$200,000	+	0	−	0	=	$200,000
Sun	$200,000	+	0	−	0	=	$200,000
Average balance						=	$200,000

2. Balance averaging (nondaily wire transfers)

Day	Opening Balance	+	Deposit	−	Transfer Out	=	Closing Balance
Mon	$100,000	+	$70,000			=	$170,000
Tue	$170,000	+	$70,000			=	$240,000
Wed	$240,000	+	$70,000			=	$310,000
Thu	$310,000	+	$70,000			=	$380,000
Fri	$380,000	+	$70,000	−	$350,000	=	$100,000
Sat	$100,000	+	0			=	$100,000
Sun	$100,000	+	0			=	$100,000
Average balance						=	$200,000

There are other reasons for not making the transfer amount the day's deposit or balance averaging. Anticipation of deposits usually involves transferring an amount that is in excess of the day's deposit. Maximizing dual balances also requires that transfer amounts be larger on critical days in order to take advantage of weekend balances.

Increasing Dual Balance Benefits

While dual balances have been diminishing in recent years, they may still be a significant factor in some firms' concentration cost functions. For example, some firms, having tried concentrating with ACH transfers, have moved back to DTCs because they have found that larger dual balances were present with DTCs.

Weekend Timing

Dual balance benefits may sometimes be increased by using DTCs rather than other mechanisms and may be further increased by initiating DTCs primarily on critical days, as previously mentioned (to achieve balances in both banks over weekends).

COMPARING TRANSFER MECHANISMS. To see how this works, Table 7.9 compares four scenarios for transferring one $700 deposit from a deposit bank to a concentration bank. The deposit is presumed to have come into the deposit bank on Tuesday. For the ACH, the transfer is initiated on Tuesday and becomes available and clears the following day. The average in both accounts, combined, is $700. For a wire transfer initiated on Wednesday, the result is precisely the same. For a DTC, we assume that the clearing time is 2 days but the availability is 1 day. If the DTC is initiated on Tuesday, it becomes available on Wednesday and clears on Thursday. The average combined balance is $800 because of the extra day. When the DTC is initiated

Table 7.9 Comparison of Dual Balances Using Different Transfer Mechanisms

ACH Transfer
CT = 1   AT = 1

Day	Deposit Bank	Conc. Bank	
Tue	700	0	← deposit
Wed	0	700	ACH
Thu	0	700	
Fri	0	700	
Sat	0	700	
Sun	0	700	
Mon	0	700	

$$\text{Ave.} = \frac{700}{7} + \frac{4,200}{7} = 700$$

Wire Transfer
CT = 0   AT = 0

Day	Deposit Bank	Conc. Bank	
Tue	700	0	
Wed	0	700	← wire
Thu	0	700	
Fri	0	700	
Sat	0	700	
Sun	0	700	
Mon	0	700	

$$\text{Ave.} = \frac{700}{7} + \frac{4,200}{7} = 700$$

Tuesday DTC
CT = 2   AT = 1

Day	Deposit Bank	Conc. Bank	
Tue	700	0	← deposit
Wed	700	700	DTC
Thu	0	700	
Fri	0	700	
Sat	0	700	
Sun	0	700	
Mon	0	700	

$$\text{Ave.} = \frac{1,400}{7} + \frac{4,200}{7} = 800$$

Thursday DTC
CT = 2   AT = 1

Day	Deposit Bank	Conc. Bank	
Tue	700	0	
Wed	700	0	
Thu	700	0	← deposit
Fri	700	700	DTC
Sat	700	700	
Sun	700	700	
Mon	0	700	

$$\text{Ave.} = \frac{4,200}{7} + \frac{2,800}{7} = 1,000$$

CT = clearing time; AT = availability time.

on Thursday, the combined balance is $1,000 because of the 3 days' dual balances. Therefore, balances in the firm's banking system increase by 14% for a weekday DTC but by 43% for a weekend DTC.

Estimating Dual Balances

In general, to estimate the amount of dual balances generated by transfers on various days of the week, we can use the following formula:

$$\text{Average dual balance} = \sum_{i=1}^{5} \frac{D_i}{7} T_i,$$

where D_i is the number of calendar days between the day a transfer on day i becomes available and the day it clears and T_i is the dollar amount transferred on day i. In the preceding example, the average dual balance for a Tuesday transfer is $(1/7) \times 700 = 100$. For a Thursday transfer the average balance is $(3/7) \times 700 = 300$. If we had transfers on other days, we would add them to the summation. This formula can be used for negative dual balances as well. In that case, the values for D_i would be negative.

In our computations, we are assuming that the firm can benefit from the dual balance. If there are excess balances already at the deposit bank, increasing dual balances will not benefit the firm.

Variability of Dual Balances

As we have stressed, dual balances are diminishing and cannot be generally relied upon. They usually occur only occasionally. However, even if their presence is only sporadic, they might benefit some firms. For example, suppose that, in the preceding example, a Thursday DTC clears on Monday only 10% of the time. This would mean that instead of a 43% increase in balances in the banking system, there would be only a 4.3% increase. A firm may decide that this amount is sufficient to warrant using DTCs.

Reducing Administrative Costs

Administrative costs arise from the management of the concentration system. Several tools are available to assist in concentration management. As discussed earlier, third-party information services can assist in gathering deposit information from the field. Besides providing a pure data collection function, such vendors may assist in making concentration decisions, for example, deciding how much to transfer on which days. Some banks already provide relatively simple decision support systems that permit firms to specify which days should be transfer days. This enables firms to depart from the customary—perhaps suboptimal—practice of making transfers equal deposits and allows them to balance average and perhaps use anticipation.

Administrative Control Systems

Other firms have developed their own concentration administrative control systems that incorporate cash flow forecasts into anticipatory transfers. One firm, for example, develops a daily cash forecast of next week's deposits for each store in its chain. The forecast is based on previous weeks' sales reports. Anticipatory DTCs are then initiated based on the forecast deposit for the following day. The amount of each transfer is

$$T_i = F_i + \text{(error from yesterday)},$$

where T_i is the transfer amount and F_i is the forecast amount. The additional term is used to make up for the fact that yesterday's transfer contained an error and was off by the difference between yesterday's actual deposit and yesterday's forecast, which is computed as follows:

$$\text{Error from yesterday } = D_{i-1} - F_{i-1}.$$

This control system enables the firm to combine forecast information with cash concentration procedures in a way that reduces the balance in the firm's banking system.

Improving Concentration Control

Recall that a major component of control in field systems is theft and fraud control. The concentration system should provide safeguards that minimize the possibility of cash being taken from field points before entering the firm's banking system. When complete control is left in the hands of the field manager, this can be a serious problem. One way to reduce the risk of loss is to obtain verifying deposit reports from the deposit bank. Most field banks are not part of balance reporting networks, so a source of information common in lockbox systems is lacking in field systems. To overcome this problem, one firm requires its field banks to phone in to a third-party information gatherer with a report of the day's deposits. This provides a confirming source of deposit information to substantiate the report from the field manager.

Unfortunately, most firms rely on insufficient-funds notices from the field bank to alert them to potential problems. If the field manager has not been depositing cash as reported, the only way some firms find out is by eventually overdrafting the account when attempts are made to concentrate the cash. Systems that have large excess balances are likely to take longer to overdraft than systems that exercise more control.

Summary

Concentration is sometimes a neglected part of cash management because firms tend to think that when the cash is in their banking system, the battle is over. Nevertheless, there are significant managerial decisions that must still be made to insure that cash is moved efficiently to accounts where it can benefit the firm. The major cost components of the objective function are (1) the opportunity cost of excess balances, (2) transfer costs, (3) dual balance benefits, (4) administrative costs, and (5) fraud and theft control. Intelligently designing a concentration system and establishing concentration policies must deal with all of these five cost factors simultaneously.

Discussion Questions

1. Why do some firms neglect the importance of cash concentration systems in designing a cash management system?
2. Explain how concentrating cash into a central cash pool is superior to managing funds in many smaller balances at various banks.
3. Explain the differences between field and lockbox concentration systems.
4. Compare and contrast centralized and decentralized concentration systems. Can a decentralized firm have a centralized concentration system?
5. Explain the various methods for moving deposit information from the field to the concentration bank in a centralized concentration system.
6. What are the components of an objective function for a cash concentration system?
7. Explain how excess balances arise even in systems that transfer daily all balances that are deposited in the field bank.
8. Define anticipation as it is used in cash concentration. Contrast ledger and deposit anticipation.
9. Explain why a one-time-transfer-out is really anticipation.
10. What is meant by balance averaging and why is it important in managing efficient concentration systems?
11. What is meant by dual balances? If they benefit the firm, who pays for the benefit? Are all dual balances useful to a firm?
12. Suppose banks were permitted to pay interest on corporate demand deposits. How would concentration practices likely change?
13. What is meant by control in concentration systems? Which types of systems would have more problems with control issues?
14. Explain how weekend-initiated ACH transfers may affect cash concentration.
15. Why have dual balances diminished in importance over the past several years?
16. What factors determine how frequently transfers should be made from a deposit account to a concentration account?

Problems

1. Assume that a field bank receives a deposit of available cash for $10,000 on Monday morning. The cash is to be transferred to a concentration bank. There are no other deposits during the week, and there is no balance in the firm's concentration bank account on Monday morning. Produce a table showing the available balance in the deposit bank and the available balance in the concentration bank on Monday through Sunday for each of the following transfer mechanisms. Assume that the transfer is initiated on Monday during the business day.

> Wire transfer
> DTC (1 day avail./1 day clearing)
> DTC (1 day avail./2 day clearing)
> DTC (1 day avail./3 day clearing)
> DTC (2 day avail./2 day clearing)
> DTC (2 day avail./1 day clearing)
> ACH
> Mailed DTC (3 day mail + 1 day avail./1 day clearing)

2. Repeat Problem 1 but start with the $10,000 on Thursday. Assume that mail, availability, and clearing times refer to business days. Compute the average balances for Thursday through the following Wednesday.

3. For each case in Problems 1 and 2, compute interest earned, assuming an effective rate of 6% per year in the deposit bank and 9% per year in the concentration bank.

4. Super Car Wash operates a chain of car wash centers across the country. One center is located in Waco, Texas. At the end of each day, the store manager takes the cash receipts to the local bank, makes a daily deposit, and phones the deposit amount into the Center Data Company. CDC then transmits the deposit data to Big City Bank in Chicago, where DTCs are prepared and deposited into Super's account. The DTC drawn on the Waco bank is given 2-day availability. The *sales* pattern for a typical week is as follows:

Day	Sales
Mon	$2,500
Tue	1,000
Wed	3,000
Thu	3,500
Fri	4,000
Sat	9,000
Sun	6,000

Start with no money in the deposit bank on a Monday morning and assume that this pattern is representative of each week's sales.

a. Produce a balance table showing the opening balance, deposits, transfers, and closing balance for each day for the first 2 weeks.

b. Compute the average closing available balance for the second week (Monday through Sunday).

c. Assuming an earnings credit rate of 6%, reserve requirements of 12%, and service charges of $20 per month, compute the required compensating balance and the excess balance.

d. If Super attempted to remove the excess balance computed in (c) by a one-time transfer, what would happen?

e. Repeat parts (a), (b), and (c), assuming that an overnight ACH transfer is used for concentration.

f. Repeat parts (a), (b), and (c), assuming that Super can use a Sunday ACH in the amount of the Friday and Saturday sales and that this ACH will settle on Monday.

g. Would a wire transfer be helpful in removing excess balances for Super? What are the costs and benefits of using wires in this circumstance?

h. Repeat parts (a), (b), and (c), assuming that Super deposits only checks in the field bank and that all checks deposited have 1-day availability. Assume that an ACH is the transfer mechanism but do *not* transfer on Sunday afternoon. How does delayed availability of the deposit affect excess balances?

5. Current practice for most firms is to transfer on a daily basis. Suppose a firm currently uses a wire transfer mechanism to concentrate funds daily from a lockbox bank. The lockbox receives deposits averaging $60,000 per business day, Monday through Friday. At this level of activity, the firm is required to keep $200,000 in available funds as a compensating balance for transfers and other services. Wires cost $8.80 each.

a. Draw a graph showing the cash flows and daily transfers at the deposit bank. Label all items on the graph, including the initial balance and actual average balance. Include Saturday and Sunday. What are the transfer costs for the week?

b. Now show how to apply balance averaging (or managing about a target). Draw a graph of cash flows that will have the same average balance but require four fewer transfers. Include the weekend in your computations. You will need to solve for the opening balance on Monday morning. Initially, neglect the savings in transfer costs and the effect it will have on the required balance.

c. If the firm is compensating by balances, the earnings credit rate is 5.2%, and reserve requirement is 12%, what is the new target available balance? (Assume a 52 week year.) Can the firm free up the difference in required balances without overdrafting?

6. The following data characterize four possible transfer mechanisms between a field bank and a concentration bank:

Mechanism	Time Delay (Calendar Days)	Total Cost
Mailed DTC	5.0	$ 0.35
DTC	2.1	0.90
ACH	1.4	0.50
Wire	0.0	15.00

a. Compute the breakeven sizes for each of the following pairs of transfer alternatives. Assume an opportunity cost of 11% per year on balances left in field banks.

Mailed DTC vs. DTC	DTC vs. ACH
Mailed DTC vs. ACH	DTC vs. wire
Mailed DTC vs. wire	ACH vs. wire

b. Explain why the breakeven size for DTC versus ACH is negative. How is this fact to be interpreted?

c. What assumptions are implicit in using this type of analysis to determine the least expensive transfer mechanism?

d. Repeat (a) but now assume that balances in field banks can earn 6% per year, while balances in the concentration account can be invested at 11% per year.

=========== **Case: *Fast Burgers, Inc.*** ===========

Fast Burgers, Inc., owns and operates 600 fast food restaurants, primarily in the eastern half of the United States and Canada. Revenues in 1986 totaled $500,000,000 from restaurant operations. Elsie Taylor, manager of Cash and Banking Relations, is currently studying the firm's procedures for collecting and concentrating cash. Although the firm is divided into geographical divisions for marketing and administrative purposes, the cash management function is highly centralized. Disbursements are made at the central office in Cleveland, Ohio. Collection policies and cash concentration are also directed by the firm's cash manager at the central office.

Current System
Restaurants permit only cash transactions. Checks and credit card purchases are extremely rare. Each restaurant shift manager is responsible for preparing a deposit ticket at the end of the shift and taking it personally to the local deposit bank. Shifts end at approximately 4 P.M. and 12 midnight. Shift managers are also instructed to phone in the amount of each deposit to a data-gathering

service using a toll-free number. The data service collects deposit information from each restaurant and transmits it to Fast Burgers' concentration bank in Cleveland. A deposit report is also transmitted to the central office the following morning, showing the deposit amount by each restaurant by shift. The report flags nonreporting managers, and appropriate follow-up is taken by district operations managers.

Early in the morning, after both shifts have reported in for the day and data have been transmitted to the concentration bank, that bank combines both deposit amounts for each restaurant into one transfer amount. Using this transfer amount, depository transfer checks are prepared and deposited into Fast Burgers' concentration account. This usually occurs before 5 A.M. each business day. Availability is assigned by the concentration bank's computers according to the applicable availability schedules. The DTCs clear through regular clearing channels and are finally presented to local deposit banks.

Compensation. A detailed field bank compensation study has not been completed. Most of the field deposit banks that Fast Burgers uses produce only a monthly statement showing ledger deposits and transfers. Very few of the banks produce an account analysis. Bank compensation is performed almost completely by balances. Elsie Taylor suspects that most of the banks in Fast Burgers' system are being overcompensated. She estimates that field balances average approximately $4,500,000. In addition, she has heard at a recent seminar that compensation by fees may be less expensive than balance compensation. In the current study, she would like to consider the pros and cons of fee compensation for the concentration system.

Since account analyses are not available, Fast Burgers has determined that fair compensation for most banks in its collection system should be, on average, 1 day's worth of deposits. This amounts to $2,000 for the average deposit account. Some banks, however, handle more than one restaurant, and some high-volume restaurants deposit much more than the average amount. Adjustments could be made for such high service banks. If all banks were compensated at the appropriate level, Elsie estimates that the average balance would be about $1,300,000 across the entire field banking system.

Weekend Deposits. Analysis of a sample of bank statements from representative field bank accounts shows Fast Burgers' excess balance problems might be caused by weekend deposits. Approximately 70% of a week's revenues can be accounted for by Monday morning deposits from sales on Friday through Sunday evening. Yet, the DTC used to transfer out such deposits does not clear the deposit bank until Tuesday, and in some cases Wednesday.

Table 1 shows two field banks with the pattern of deposits and clearings for a 2-week period. These banks are typical of most banks in Fast Burgers' system.

The firm's current concentration system was designed in 1978 but has not been refined since then. Elsie is considering alternative approaches for attempting to remove excess balances. Wire transfers would be effective but would probably cost $10–$20 per transfer. She is also considering the use of the ACH

Table 1 Representative Deposit Banks Showing Deposit and Cash Concentration Patterns

Deposit Bank 1			Deposit Bank 2		
Opening Balance Mon = $4,300			Opening Balance Mon = $7,800		
Day	**Deposit**	**Clearing**	**Day**	**Deposit**	**Clearing**
Mon	$8,400	$1,800	Mon	$15,300	$ 4,300
Tue	900	0	Tue	1,500	15,300
Wed	1,300	9,300	Wed	2,300	0
Thu	1,600	1,300	Thu	1,700	3,800
Fri	1,900	1,600	Fri	3,600	0
Mon	$7,400	$1,900	Mon	$16,200	$ 5,300
Tue	700	7,400	Tue	1,300	16,200
Wed	1,600	700	Wed	2,500	1,300
Thu	1,500	0	Thu	2,100	2,500
Fri	2,400	3,100	Fri	3,900	2,100

system to replace the current DTCs. ACH transfers would cost about $.20 less than DTCS. The Cleveland concentration bank can accept a Sunday afternoon ACH tape for Monday settlement. Elsie wonders about the effect that ACH transfers would have on dual balances, if any are present in the firm's system.

In addition, Elsie is exploring the possibility of basing transfer (ACH or DTC) amounts on forecasts of expected cash flows into each field bank. A relatively simple forecasting model that requires only the past 4 weeks of deposit data could be used. Installing such a system would cost approximately $70,000 and require another $25,000 per year to use and maintain.

The treasurer of Fast Burgers has been attempting for the past few years to move from balance compensation to fee compensation for all bank accounts. He has asked Elsie to consider fee compensation for all field banks. Since Fast Burgers can invest at approximately 9.5% in virtually risk-free securities, he feels that the company would be far ahead of the earnings credit rate (about 6.5%, currently), especially when reserve requirements are considered.

Selected Readings

Journal of Cash Management. "E. F. Hutton: Reactions and Commentary" (July–August 1985), pp. 24–27.

RINNE, HEIKKI, ROBERT A. WOOD, and NED C. HILL, "Reducing Cash Concentration Costs by Anticipatory Forecasting," *Journal of Cash Management* (March–April 1986), pp. 44–50.

STONE, BERNELL K., and NED C. HILL, "Cash Concentration Design," *Journal of Financial and Quantitative Analysis* (June 1979), pp. 301–322.

STONE, BERNELL K., and NED C. HILL, "Cash Transfer Scheduling for Efficient Cash Concentration," *Financial Management* (Autumn 1980), pp. 35–43.

STONE, BERNELL K., and NED C. HILL, "Alternative Cash Transfer Mechanisms and Methods: Evaluation Frameworks," *Journal of Bank Research* (Spring 1982), pp. 7–16.

STONE, BERNELL K., DANIEL M. FERGUSON, and NED C. HILL, "Cash Transfers Scheduling: an Overview," *The Cash Manager* (March 1980), pp. 3–8.

Disbursement Systems

On February 3, 1977, Senator William Proxmire read a disturbing article in the *New York Times*. The reporter described how large brokerage firms such as Merrill Lynch disbursed checks from banks located in remote areas of the country. A customer in New York City, for example, might be paid with a check drawn on a bank located in Helena, Montana, while a customer in Seattle might receive a check drawn on a bank in Midland, Texas. The brokerage firms were evidently attempting to gain float benefits by delaying check clearing. Senator Proxmire, then chairman of the Senate Banking Committee, dispatched Arthur Burns, chairman of the Federal Reserve Board, to look into the matter. The senator was concerned that consumers were being hurt (since many banks place holds on checks drawn on out-of-state banks) and that large firms were taking advantage of the Federal Reserve and the banking system to enrich themselves. This initial inquiry focused a managerial and legislative spotlight on the formerly mechanical and unglamorous practice of corporate payment systems. The investigation by the Fed led to informal efforts to curb the practice of *remote disbursing* and eventually influenced parts of the Depository Institution Deregulation and Monetary Control Act of 1980 (see Chapter 3).

This chapter discusses the problems of designing and managing a disbursement system. Disbursement systems include the banks and the delivery mechanisms and procedures firms use to facilitate the movement of cash from the firm's centralized cash pool to disbursement banks and then on to suppliers and other payees. Figure 8.1 gives an overview of a typical disbursement system. The concentration bank serves as the valve between the firm's collection system, liquidity portfolio, and disbursement banks. Disbursement banks are the banks on which disbursement checks are drawn. A disbursement system may be more complex than a collection system in one sense: management must choose not only the disbursement banks but also the check-issuing points. In contrast, a lockbox bank is the check-receiving point, and management has no control over the drawee bank. In the example shown in Figure 8.1, the firm has three check-issuing points and two disbursement banks. Issuing points 2 and 3

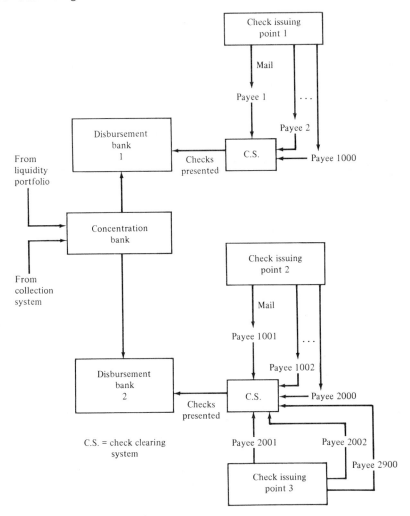

Figure 8.1 Example of a Check Disbursement System.

both draw checks on disbursement bank 2, while issuing point 1 draws checks on disbursement bank 1. Of course, we could imagine an even more complex system in which one issuing point draws some checks on disbursement bank 1 and some on disbursement bank 2. We will see later why that arrangement may be attractive in some cases.

In other ways, disbursement systems are simpler than collection and concentration because disbursement generally falls under more direct control of headquarters and involves generally fewer banks. With this control, however, comes the possibility of ethical problems because disbursement practices can lead to intentionally delayed payments and strained vendor relations, as in the case observed by Senator Proxmire.

Disbursement Practices

While policies differ widely from firm to firm, we illustrate a typical disbursement system by returning to the example of Sudden Shrimp, mentioned at the outset of Chapter 7. Sudden Shrimp's 1,000 company-owned restaurants order supplies partly from headquarters but also from local bakeries. Figure 8.2 illustrates the steps followed. An invoice from the local bakery in Bedford, Indiana, is sent to the Bedford restaurant for $10,000 worth of goods purchased during the past month. The invoice is dated September 1, with terms of net 30. This means that the $10,000 is due on October 1.

The Bedford manager for Sudden Shrimp inspects the invoice to make sure that the items purchased were in fact delivered, and that the $10,000 is actually owed by the firm. The manager approves payment and mails the invoice to the

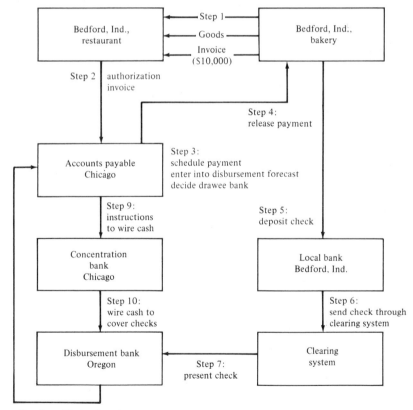

Figure 8.2 Example of a Typical Disbursement System: the Sudden Shrimp Company.

accounts payable section of the home office in Chicago. An accounts payable clerk processes the invoice and schedules the release of the check according to company policy on the due date, October 1.

Sudden Shrimp uses a disbursement bank in rural Oregon. On September 30, a check is drawn on this bank and mailed from Chicago to Bedford. At that time, an estimate is made of how long the check will take to clear back to the Oregon bank. This estimate becomes part of Sudden Shrimp's short-term cash forecast.

The check arrives in Bedford 5 days later, is processed by the bakery, and is deposited in a Bedford bank. The check is sent through the clearing system and, several days later, is presented to the North Carolina bank. The bank notifies the cash manager at Sudden Shrimp in Chicago, and cash is wired from the concentration account in Chicago to the North Carolina bank to cover that day's presentments.

Sudden Shrimp receives a daily report from the disbursement bank by computer-to-computer transmission, listing all checks that have been presented for payment. This information enables accounts payable to reconcile the checks mailed with those paid. Clearing times are recorded and become part of future disbursement forecasts.

Why did Sudden Shrimp choose to disburse checks on a bank in Oregon? Is a wire transfer the best way to move cash into the disbursement account? How could Sudden Shrimp evaluate their disbursement system and measure its costs? We will spend the rest of the chapter answering these and other questions.

Objective Function

In designing and managing a disbursement system, it is helpful to keep an objective function in mind. The cost components appropriate for a disbursement system include the following:

1. Time value costs (including the value of missed cash discounts).
2. Excess balances in disbursement accounts.
3. Transaction costs (transferring cash from the concentration bank and making disbursements).
4. Dual balance benefits.
5. Payee relations.
6. Administrative and information.
7. Control.

Time Value Costs

All other things equal, a firm would rather pay later than sooner. There is value in delayed payments because the firm can either invest cash for a longer

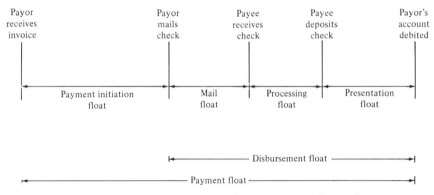

Figure 8.3 Cash Flow Timeline for Disbursements: Paper Checks.

time or put off the cost of obtaining cash from lenders or investors. Figure 8.3 shows elements of the cash outflow timeline, including payment initiation, mail, vendor processing, and clearing times. Lengthening one or more of these segments may be beneficial to the firm. Usually, the disbursement problem is concerned primarily with the latter three elements of this timeline. Nevertheless, as we show later, it is useful to consider the payment initiation time as part of the decision process.

For wire payments, of course, there are no segments for mail, processing, and presentation float. For ACH payments, there is likewise no segment for mail and processing float.

The dollar value of this component of the objective function is computed by multiplying the dollar flow per calendar day by the length of the timeline by an interest rate.

Components of Payment Float

The entire outflow timeline is defined as *payment float*, while *disbursement float* is measured from the point of mail to the time of presentment. Disbursement float consists of (1) mail float, measured as the time between the payor's mailing of the check and the payee's receipt of it; (2) processing float, the time required by the payee to deposit the check after it has been received; and (3) presentation or clearing float, the time required by the banking system to return the check and present it against the payor's disbursement account. There is an additional time segment that is not associated with the transfer of value, and so we do not show it as part of the timeline. That segment has to do with reconciling checks that have cleared and otherwise processing the information associated with value transfer. Most of these activities take place after the value transfer has been affected.

EXAMPLE. Valley-Hi Foods pays suppliers with paper checks. Invoices are net 30 (meaning that payment is due 30 days from the invoice date), and Valley-Hi usually mails checks an average of 30 days from the invoice date. Mail time from Valley-Hi to suppliers averages 4 calendar days. Most checks are received by lockboxes and are processed, on average, .5 day after receipt.

Clearing time back to Valley-Hi's disbursement bank averages 1.5 days. An average of $36,500,000 is disbursed to suppliers each year. The interest rate is considered to be 10%.

The payment float associated with this disbursement system is computed as follows. First, compute the average number of days.

Payment initiation time	=	30.0 days
Mail time	=	4.0
Processing time	=	0.5
Presentation time	=	1.5
		36.0 days

Second, the value of payment float is computed by multiplying the daily cash flow by the interest by the number of days.

$$\text{Float value} = \frac{\$36,500,000}{365} \times .10 \times 36 \text{ days} = \$360,000/\text{year}.$$

If Valley-Hi were to change its disbursement system policies by increasing the payment initiation float to 34 days and its presentation float to 3.5 days, then the total timeline would be lengthened as follows:

Payment initiation time	=	34.0 days
Mail time	=	4.0
Processing time	=	0.5
Presentation time	=	3.5
		42.0 days

The new float value would be computed as follows:

$$\text{Float value} = \frac{\$36,500,000}{365} \times .10 \times 42 \text{ days} = \$420,000/\text{year}.$$

We must be careful not to stop here and conclude that Valley-Hi is now $60,000 better off per year. They would be *if* no other costs had to be considered. In this case, payments are made 4 days after the due date. That may have an adverse effect on supplier relationships or it may not. In addition, lengthening the clearing time may also adversely affect the supplier, who may not receive available funds for the extra 2 days. Therefore, time value differences must be viewed in conjunction with all other costs in the disbursement system.

MAIL FLOAT ISSUE. One must be cautious regarding decisions to increase disbursement float by lengthening the mail float component. In part, the decision depends on whether the postmark date or the receipt date is the valid payment date. If the *postmark date* is used by the payee to determine whether an invoice has been paid on time, the mail time is considered a part of disbursement float. Lengthening the mail time will increase the time value benefit to the firm. On the other hand, if the *receipt* date is considered the valid payment date, lengthening the mail time may have to be accompanied by an offsetting decrease in payment initiation time. There would then be no economic benefit to the firm.

MISSED DISCOUNTS. Many credit terms permit discounts to be taken if payment is made before a given time period. Disbursement systems must consider the possible costs of missing discounts if payment cannot be made in time.

Present value concepts are useful in computing the cost of missing discounts. Suppose Valley-Hi, in the first preceding example, were offered terms of 2/10 net 30 instead of net 30. This means that Valley-Hi receives a 2% discount from the invoice amount if payment is sent on day 10 instead of day 30. What would it cost them if their disbursement system were unable to process payments by the 10th and, instead, continued to make all payments on the 30th?

We compute the present value of both alternatives. The present value of not taking discounts is the annual payment amount brought back to the present by dividing by the present value factor at 10% annual interest. We use 36 for the number of days because the 6 extra days represent disbursement float after payment is mailed.

$$PV(\text{no discount}) = \frac{36,500,000}{\left(1 + \frac{36 \times .10}{365}\right)} = \$36,140,000.$$

The present value of the discount alternative is computed similarly, but including the 2% and using 16 days (including the extra 6 of disbursement float) instead of 36.

$$PV(\text{discount}) = \frac{36,500,000(1 - .02)}{1 + \left(\frac{16 \times .10}{365}\right)} = \$35,610,000.$$

The difference in net present value terms is $530,000 per year. This means that if Valley-Hi misses all discounts and pays on the net day, it loses that amount each year. The issue of missed discounts is discussed further in Chapter 13.

Excess Balances

Excess balances are defined as available balances above the level necessary to compensate the disbursement bank(s) for its services. Excess balances may be determined from the bank's daily balance report or monthly account analysis if these are provided. Otherwise, they must be estimated by methods illustrated in Chapter 7.

Excess balances arise in disbursement banks primarily because transfers of available funds into the disbursement account may not synchronize with amounts presented against the account. For example, suppose the firm estimates that $200,000 will clear the disbursement account by the end of the day but is uncertain of the exact amount. It wires $250,000 into the account to cover possible forecast errors. At the end of the day, only $210,000 was presented against the account, causing an excess balance of $40,000.

One cause of excess balances is a timing problem. Banks usually post checks to accounts late in the day—too late for even wire transfers to cover presentments against the account. To solve this problem, several alternatives are available.

1. The disbursement bank can sort out checks drawn on the firm's account and report the totals to the firm in advance of posting. This enables the firm to transfer in enough cash to offset clearings.
2. At the end of the day, the bank can automatically transfer cash into the account from another account at the same bank. This is discussed further in the section "Zero Balance Accounts." This assumes, of course, that the firm has another account at the disbursement bank with sufficient balances to cover presentments.
3. The bank can arrange to sweep any balances left at the end of the day automatically into an interest-bearing account.

Transaction Costs

Transaction costs refer to the costs of transferring cash from the concentration account to the disbursement account and to the costs of disbursements to vendors. Included in this category are bank charges, third-party vendor information charges, and in-house expenses associated with payments. We also include in transaction costs the costs of overdrafting the disbursement account and any borrowing costs incurred as a result of the overdraft. Some banks permit available overdrafts but consider it a loan and charge daily interest. Other banks do not charge interest on available overdrafts.

Funding disbursement accounts can be expensive over time. For many firms, wires are used to fund these accounts on a daily basis. At $20 per transfer (the sum of the wire charges at both concentration and disbursement banks) with four disbursement accounts, the yearly transfer costs amount to $20 × 4 × 52 weeks × 5 days per week = $20,800 per year, exclusive of information-gathering costs. In comparison, the cost is about $1,000 per year if depository transfer checks are used. Of course, the decision on the transfer mechanism must include other factors besides the cost of the transfer. We return to this point later in the chapter.

The cost of making disbursements includes the costs of payment preparation, delivery costs, and bank charges. For paper checks, these can total several dollars per payment when personnel costs are allocated to the costs of check preparation. ACH payments are cheaper but clear faster. Hence, transaction costs must be traded off against time value costs.

For example, suppose the total cost of disbursing by paper is $5 per check, while that of disbursing by ACH payment is $2 per payment. The average payment is $400, and paper checks take 4 calendar days longer to clear the disbursing account than ACH payments. Which payment mechanism is preferable when the opportunity cost of cash is 10.0%?

The value of keeping the $400 4 extra days is

$$\text{Interest/day} \times \text{amount} \times \text{time} = \text{value}$$

$$(.10/365) \times 400 \times 4 = \$0.44.$$

Since the firm saves $3 when using the faster mechanism and loses only $.44 in interest, ACH payments are preferred in this case.

Dual Balances

As in concentration systems, dual balances are also possible in disbursement systems. As discussed in Chapter 7, they arise when the disbursement account is funded by a depository transfer check that becomes available at the disbursing account on one day but does not clear the concentration account until a later time. For the time of overlap, available balances exist in both banks at the same time.

Though dual balances are much less common than they were several years ago, they are believed to be more prevalent in some kinds of disbursement systems than in concentration systems. Most concentration banks are large banks with aggressive availability schedules and many direct sends. On the other hand, if disbursement banks are small, out-of-the-way banks, they may not be efficient check processors and may grant availability before the DTC clears the concentration bank.

For example, suppose that on Tuesday a firm instructs a disbursement bank to deposit a DTC for $2,000,000 in its disbursement account. Assume that the DTC is given 1-day availability but clears in 2 days. On Wednesday, the firm would therefore have $2,000,000 in its concentration account *and* the same $2,000,000 in its disbursement account. Presumably, the firm earns credits or invests the cash at both banks. If the interest rate is 7%, this means an extra $384 in interest income.

The lingering existence of dual balances influences the selection of a funding mechanism. Wires give no dual balances. DTCs give some, but ACH transfers generally do not. As discussed in the previous chapter, however, dual balances have been diminishing over time. They occur only sporadically. Therefore, most firms do not take them into account when designing disbursement systems.

Payee Relationships

While they are less important in collection and concentration systems, relationships with other parties are a primary concern in managing a disbursement system. For the collection problem, the seller has provided a good or service to the buyer. Therefore, almost any effort to speed cash inflows is generally considered ethically sound. With disbursement systems, however, the shoe is on the other foot. Now a good or service has already been provided, and payment is due. Efforts by the buyer to delay payment may be considered unfavorably by the seller. Designing disbursement systems that intentionally delay payments are considered by many to be tantamount to stretching payments. The payor benefits at the expense of the payee. The payor, in turn, may find further business dealings with the payee strained or even more expensive as the payee tries to recover some of its costs caused by delayed payments.

Measuring the costs of good supplier relationships is very difficult. Some payment delays may seem virtually costless. But beyond a certain point, consequences may be felt in the form of general ill will, higher prices, delivery holdups, damaged image, and so on. Further delays may even bring legal action and harmed credit ratings.

One buyer for a manufacturing firm tells the story of the benefits of timely payments. For years the company policy was to pay bills on time—never to stretch payments. Competitors seemed to pay much later than this firm and yet suffered no apparent consequences. Then war broke out and raw materials needed for manufacturing processes had to be rationed by suppliers. The buyer claims that because of their prompt payment practices in the past, his company always had its orders filled first, while its slow-paying competitors had to wait in line.

Administrative Costs

Administrative costs include the management of the disbursement information system and the provision of information support for funding decisions. The objectives of management are to obtain timely information about the disbursed amounts so that disbursements can be covered. In this way, good banking relations can be maintained. Another perhaps greater motivation is to preserve the firm's central cash pool and keep it invested as long as possible in securities.

Another administrative cost relates to reconciliation. Disbursements must be reconciled to payables to ensure that payments have actually cleared against the firm's disbursement account. If not, the check may have been lost in the mail, misdirected to another party, or lost by the supplier. In any case, inquiries should be made to ensure that valid obligations are honored.

Control Costs

Costs of control relate to the problem of unauthorized disbursements. Most firms have careful controls to minimize this likelihood. Such controls include limiting signature authorization to only two or three individuals at one site, requiring two signatures per check, performing frequent audits, and even removing disbursement control from field personnel.

In addition, it is sometimes necessary to stop a payment after it has been initiated. For a check payment, this is done by having the bank issue a stop payment instruction that will flag the check when it is presented against the disbursement account. This enables the firm to stop erroneous payments.

With this objective function in mind, we now discuss the decisions related to the design of the disbursement system.

Types of Disbursement Decisions

It is convenient to think of disbursement decisions in two categories: strategic and tactical. Strategic decisions are those that have longer-range consequences and are generally more difficult to change on short notice. Tactical decisions are the day-to-day operating decisions.

Strategic Decisions

Selection of Disbursement Bank Set

A major strategic decision involves the selection of one or more disbursement banks. Decisions in this area include the following: How many disbursement banks should be used? Where should they be located? What should be the firm's policy toward intentionally taking advantage of availability and clearing delays?

Selection of Concentration Bank

A second strategic decision is the selection of the concentration bank to fund disbursement banks. This decision, rarely made by field managers, is often not considered an active decision variable. The concentration bank has usually already been selected on the basis of other criteria, and the decision becomes moot.

Disbursement Payment and Account Funding Mechanisms

A third strategic decision involves selection of the mechanisms used for making payments and moving cash from the concentration bank to the disbursement banks. Checks are by far the most common payment mechanism, although the use of the ACH system is growing. It is common for firms to use wire transfers from the concentration account, but other mechanisms such as DTC and ACH are possible.

Level of Authority for Authorizing Disbursements

Firms must decide who can authorize the release of the firm's cash. Some firms retain close control at headquarters and do not permit disbursements to be authorized in the field. Other firms leave all authority with field managers. Some set limits: large disbursements can be authorized only by certain officers of the firm.

Policies for Determining When and How Much to Pay

Some firms have a simple policy: "take all discounts and pay on the discount date." Other policies are possible, such as "Take only those discounts that are economically justified" or "Make all payments on the 10th of the month." We discuss such decisions in Chapter 13.

Tactical Decisions

Disbursement Authorization

The first tactical decision is whether to authorize a particular disbursement. Within the authority guidelines already established, someone in the firm must determine if a particular disbursement should be made. Is the invoice valid? Has it already been paid? Have the goods or services actually been received in the amount and quality specified? To assist in making this decision, purchase orders and receiving reports are matched with invoices to ensure that the firm actually owes the amount stated on the invoice.

Funding Amount and Timing

Within strategic policy guidelines, decisions must be made about the amount and timing of transfers from the concentration bank into the disbursement account. Should cash be transferred daily or nondaily? Can forecasts be used? Will the bank permit available overdrafts? This decision is analogous to the cash transfer scheduling problem discussed in Chapter 7. Later in this chapter we discuss several alternative funding strategies in more detail.

Payment Preparation and Release

A third tactical decision involves the preparation of the payment and release of the check. This includes deciding on the vehicle for making payment and the payment amount. Should payment be in the form of a paper check, wire, or ACH transfer? Should any amount be subtracted for discounts, spoilage during shipments, and so on? From some firms these decisions are made in the field, while for others they are made at company headquarters.

Drawee Bank Selection

A fourth tactical decision is closely related to the third. This decision involves the selection of a particular drawee bank from the existing set of disbursement banks. It is possible, either at headquarters or in the field, to draw a check on one of several banks, depending on the firm's disbursement policies.

Mail Point

For mailed checks, a fifth tactical decision is required: from which point to mail the check. The mail point and the drawee bank are independent decisions. For example, a check drawn on a Texas bank may be mailed by a Seattle firm from a West Virginia mail point. For most firms, the matter is decided by default and checks are mailed from the point of the check preparation.

However, some firms want to extend mail time by mailing checks from distant locations. To receive any benefits from mail time extension, one must assume that the postmark date is the valid payment date. Studies show that this is true only half of the time. It also assumes that costs of mail time extension (such as ill will, missed discounts, and transportation) do not exceed any benefits provided.

Centralized versus Decentralized Disbursing

More often than not, disbursement control lies between completely centralized and completely decentralized decision making. Strategic decisions tend to be made on a centralized basis, while tactical decisions may be made in the field. Although some speak of centralized or decentralized systems as if a system must be one or the other, it is generally clearer to characterize systems by their degree of centralization or decentralization for various disbursement decisions. As illustrated in Table 8.1, most disbursement decisions may be made at either level, depending on the policies of the organization. Rarely are all decisions made either at headquarters or in the field.

Primarily Decentralized Systems

In a disbursement system in which most tactical decisions are left to the field manager, payment authorization, preparation, and release are performed at the field level and checks are drawn on a local bank. This system has some advantages. The field manager retains more autonomy and therefore may be more highly motivated to perform. In addition, relationships with payees may be enhanced because payees receive faster availability of checks and can resolve disputes more readily.

On the other hand, maintaining many local disbursement accounts may require much larger bank balances than a comparable system in which only two or three disbursement banks serve the entire firm. Field managers may not always follow prudent practices in taking cash discounts or making payments in accordance with company policies. In addition, disbursement float is usually lower if local banks are geographically close to payees. Leaving authorization completely in the hands of field managers may increase the risk of unauthorized disbursements.

Primarily Centralized Systems

In a largely centralized disbursement system, payment authorization, preparation, release, and drawee bank selection are preformed by headquarters. The advantages and disadvantages are, of course, the opposite of those in a decentralized system. The advantages are several. The disbursement function may become large enough to warrant the systematic attention of a cash manager who can employ more sophisticated techniques. Excess cash balances at local banks can be moved into centralized cash pools where they can be more profitably employed. The payment of invoices can be timed and discount policies imple-

Table 8.1 Disbursement Decisions

Decision	Problems to Be Solved
Strategic	
Determine set of drawee banks	How many drawee banks should be used? Where should they be located? What is the firm's policy toward taking advantage of clearing delays?
Determine concentration bank	Which concentration bank should be used? If there is more than one concentration bank, which should fund which disbursement banks?
Select funding mechanism and method	Which payment mechanism should be used to fund the disbursement account? When should disbursement account be funded and on what basis? Should forecasts be used? Overdrafts?
Determine level of authorization	Who is responsible for authorizing payment, and what criteria are used for determing a valid payment?
Determine policies for timing and amounts	When should payments be made? Under what circumstances should discounts be taken?
Tactical	
Payment authorization	Is invoice valid? Should payment be made?
Fund disbursement account	How much should be transferred into the disbursement account, and when should the transfer take place?
Prepare and release payment	What amount should be paid? (Consider discounts, adjustments, etc.) When should payment be released? What payment mechanism should be used?
Select drawee bank	On which bank should the payment be drawn?
Determine mail point (mailed check only)	From which point should the check be drawn?
Reconcile payments	Do payments initiated match payments cleared against the disbursing account?

mented in the best interest of the firm. Disbursement float can be managed more systematically and unauthorized disbursements can be reduced.

On the other hand, local autonomy is reduced and relationships with payees may be adversely affected. Additional timing delays caused by moving invoice and other data from field units to headquarters may result in missed discounts and delays in resolving payment disputes.

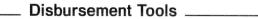

Disbursement Tools

Commercial banks and other providers offer a number of tools that assist managers in designing efficient disbursement systems.

Zero Balance Accounts

To appreciate how a zero balance account works, consider the case in which there is no zero balance account. As shown in Figure 8.4, suppose a firm has three disbursement accounts in the same bank. Why would a firm keep three separate accounts? The answer is: primarily for accounting and control reasons. One account may be for vendor payments, another for customer refunds, and a third for payroll. In order to place accountability with the appropriate manager, the firm would likely choose to have separate accounts and let the bank sort out the checks for each one. In this way, each area of responsibility receives its own bank statement and paid checks.

Reduced Excess Balances
The problem is to keep enough money in each account to cover checks presented against it. If a buffer of cash must be kept in each account, excess balances would result. Zero balance accounts are designed to help remove the excess balances while retaining the advantages of separate accounts.

A zero balance account has a balance of zero in it at the start of the day. When checks are cleared against the account at the end of the day, the bank moves just enough cash back into the account to zero it out. Where does the money come from? As illustrated in Figure 8.4, it is usually moved in from a master account at the same bank. How does this benefit the firm?

A. Three regular accounts

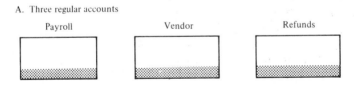

B. Three zero balance accounts tied to a master account

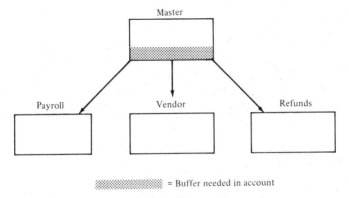

= Buffer needed in account

Figure 8.4 Zero Balance Account.

The master account buffer needed to ensure that presented checks are covered is less than the sum of the buffers in each of the individual accounts.

Example

To understand how a zero balance account works, consider that the size of the buffer needed in an account is proportional to the probability of an overdraft in the account. For example, suppose that the probability of overdraft on any given day in each of the three accounts is 5% with a $4,000 balance in each one (above the expected clearings). If the three are zero balance accounts, we would be concerned with the probability of master account overdraft. If the accounts are independent with respect to checks presented against them, the probability of overdraft of the master account is the joint probability of overdraft of the three individual accounts. That would be $.05 \times .05 \times .05 = .000125$—very small indeed. Hence, we would not need to keep much of a buffer to protect against overdrafts—certainly less than the $12,000 tied up in the three separate accounts.

Master Accounts in a Different Bank

Some banks offer a service in which a zero balance account in one bank is funded through another bank. Instead of debiting the firm's master account in the same bank, the zero balance account is funded by a wire transfer from the second bank or by a direct transfer from a correspondent account. Firms often use their concentration banks for this purpose. The reasons for this separation will become clear in the next section.

Another variation is to have the zero balance account bank notify the firm about the amount presented. If this occurs early enough in the day, the cash manager can initiate a transfer to fund the account. This is sometimes called a *pseudo-zero balance account* since transfer into the account is not automatic, but the result is the same.

The Value of Zero Balance Accounts

Zero balance accounts result in several cost savings. Excess balances are generally reduced. In addition, presentation time may be lengthened if the account is in a bank that provides longer clearing times. Zero balance accounts lower information costs by furnishing separate accounting for each account and by (except in the last case mentioned) providing automatic funding of disbursing accounts. In addition, the use of zero balance accounts can facilitate decentralization by providing local check-writing authority while maintaining funding control at headquarters.

Reconciliation Services

Check reconciliation involves assembling a list of checks presented against a disbursement account and comparing that list to the checks written. Banks can perform more or less of this task, depending on how much the firm wants to pay. The simplest service is simply a return of paid checks. The firm does all of the matching in house. At the other extreme, the firm provides the bank with a list of checks sent with dates. The bank produces reports of checks paid and those still outstanding, together with disbursement float information.

Stop Payment Services

When the firm issues a check that it wishes to recall, it issues a stop payment order to the disbursement bank. The bank then intercepts the check before it is posted to the firm's account and returns it to the payee's bank. Some banks offer an on-line service so that the firm's computer can send stop payment information directly to bank computers.

Automatic Investment Services

Some banks provide an automatic investment service for disbursement accounts. The bank must have the ability to post checks to the firm's disbursement account early in the day. The firm funds the account periodically based on expected clearings. After posting, remaining balances above some specified target amount are automatically invested in overnight investments such as repurchase agreements or bank holding company commercial paper. These types of accounts are sometimes called *sweep accounts*.

The effect of sweep accounts is to reduce excess balances and lower administrative costs.

Payable Through Drafts (PTDs)

As discussed in Chapter 5, PTDs are drafts that appear as checks but are drawn on the issuing firm, not the disbursing bank. When PTDs are received, the bank notifies the firm. The firm has 1 business day to approve or deny payment. This gives the firm a short time to verify that the payment was authorized and that other conditions have been met. The effect is to decrease excess balances, since cash need not be kept in the disbursing account.

Controlled Disbursing Accounts

Controlled disbursing means using a disbursing account in a certain way. The idea is to use a bank that is small enough to receive only one presentment of checks early in the morning. The bank then sorts through the checks, posts them against the firm's account, and notifies the firm of the amount presented. The firm then transfers the appropriate amount of cash from a concentration bank. Why must this process take place early in the morning? Because often the best rates on investment securities are available early in the day. The money markets begin to close at about 11 A.M., Eastern Standard Time. The firm must know how much is available in its concentration bank to invest before this time.

If the bank cannot perform these tasks until later in the day, the firm has to guess how much it can invest and leave a buffer in the concentration account to cover wrong guesses, and excess balances would result.

Large versus Small Banks

Large banks usually receive multiple presentments from the Fed each day. They may also receive direct sends late in the day. Hence, they do not make good controlled disbursing banks. Because of their relatively small volume of checks, small banks often warrant only one presentment a day from the Fed and have no direct sends. Hence, smaller banks are almost always selected as candidates for controlled disbursing accounts.

Noon Presentment

Since the enactment of the Banking Act of 1980, the Fed has significantly improved check processing. Many of the changes made have important implications for disbursement systems. To permit them to reduce the number of checks that were held over from one day to the next (*holdover float*), the Fed extended the final check presentment of the day to 12 noon. The result is that banks that formerly received presentments by 8 A.M. began to receive them later in the morning. A later presentment does not allow the bank to post accounts and notify firms in time for investing activities to occur.

The extended presentation deadline applies to Federal Reserve city banks and RCPC banks. Under a *high dollar group sort* program, any country bank (smaller banks not near Fed cities or RCPCs) that receives a high volume of check presentments from other Fed districts is also targeted for later presentments. In 1986, the amount necessary to trigger noon presentment at a country bank was $10,000,000 per day. Furthermore, the Fed reserves the right to present later cash letters to any bank thought to be giving too much float.

MICR Line Information

The effect of noon presentment is somewhat mitigated, however, by a Fed program to provide an early morning electronic message to a disbursement bank. The message contains MICR line information from checks that will clear later in the day. Unfortunately, not all checks to clear on a given day arrive early enough at the Fed to be included in the electronic report. Hence, this service provides an incomplete estimate of actual presentments, leaving the bank and the firm to negotiate over how to handle "surprises."

Coping with Noon Presentment

Although concern was widespread when noon presentment was announced, most firms have found ways to preserve the practice without problems. Many larger banks offer controlled disbursing services by forming correspondent relationships with small country banks or by using their own branch banks that have separate transit routing numbers. The larger banks ensure corporate customers that the volume of disbursements through the smaller bank will not exceed the Fed's targets for noon presentment. If the smaller bank becomes "filled up," the larger bank adds another small bank to the network. The larger bank provides services to fund presentments, thereby removing the administrative burden from the firm.

One large company approached the problem differently. They found a small bank that was willing to become the exclusive disbursing bank for the company. Hence, the customer determines whether or not the dollar volume exceeds Fed guidelines for high dollar group sort.

Remote Disbursement Services

Remote disbursing is actually controlled disbursing with one added feature: the disbursement bank is selected largely because it extends the clearing time of checks. The line between remote and controlled disbursing is very fuzzy. A Philadelphia firm disbursing off a Yakima, Washington, bank may be considered to be practicing remote disbursing. What about a Chicago firm disbursing off a bank in Baghdad, Kentucky, just two states away?

Presentation Float Components
The intent of remote disbursing is not only to reduce excess balances but also to extend disbursement float. The primary component of disbursement float targeted by remote disbursing is *presentation float*, or the delay between the time the payee deposits the check and the time it is presented to the disbursement bank for payment. As seen in Figure 8.5, presentation float consists of *availability float*, or the delay between the time a check is deposited and the time the payee receives availability, and *clearing slippage*, the additional delay between the time the payee receives availability and the payor gives up availability.

Costs of Remote Disbursing
Extending the disbursement timeline may benefit the firm in a present value sense, but there are opposing costs that may outweigh the benefits. To the

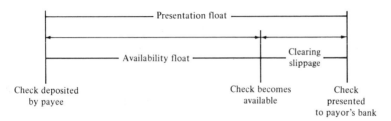

Figure 8.5 Presentation Float Components.

degree that float extension is the result of increasing availability float, the payee is harmed. The delay in availability may have adverse consequences in future price negotiations and in general ill will. To overcome disbursement float problems, a few firms require payment in good funds by a specific date to qualify for cash discounts, and more firms are considering that option.

Clearly, an alternative to availability time extension is simply to release checks at a later date (*stretching*). This may be less expensive than remote disbursing and is considered by some to be more forthright. Stretching payables involves lengthening the payment initiation section of the outflow timeline rather than the clearing section. Lengthening either segment produces the same time value effect on the firm.

To the degree that float extension is the result primarily of clearing slippage, the payee is not harmed. The party creating the slippage is footing the bill (the Fed or the banking system). Some consider this to be a free good.

The problem with designing a system that focuses on clearing slippage to achieve benefits is that the system may have to be changed. In recent years, as we have discussed several times, clearing slippage has been largely removed from check processing. The free good is no longer quite as free. First, there is less of it to spread around; second, what remains is being priced. The net result is that remote disbursing may be much less valuable than it was in years past and threatens to become even less valuable in the future.

Disbursement Account Funding

In the past, disbursement accounts were primarily funded by wire transfers. This practice continues to dominate, but other methods have become increasingly popular.

Wire Funding

Funding by wire transfer permits an immediate movement of cash from a concentration bank to the disbursement bank. Because funds are immediately available, there is little risk to the disbursement bank. Wires are more expensive and result in no dual balances.

DTC or ACH Funding

DTCs or ACH transfers move cash to the disbursement account with a 1-day availability delay. These methods are cheaper, of course, than a wire and can lead to extended clearing times. However, neither represents good funds on the day of deposit. DTC or ACH funding may therefore periodically produce negative available balances—even though the ledger balance remains positive. Table 8.2 illustrates this problem. Note that although the ledger

Table 8.2 Disbursement Account Funding: ACH or DTC

	Mon	Tue	Wed	Thu	Fri
Opening ledger balance	$1,000	$1,000	$1,000	$1,000	$1,000
Presentment	(500)	(1,600)	(800)	(1,500)	(600)
ACH/DTC deposit	500	1,600	800	1,500	600
Closing ledger balance	1,000	1,000	1,000	1,000	1,000
Available bal.	500	−600	200	−500	400

Note: The available balance equals the beginning available balance ($1,000) minus the presentment plus the previous day's deposit.

balance remains constant throughout the week, the available balance dips below zero twice.

The risk to the disbursement bank is that the DTC or ACH transfer will not be honored when it is presented at the concentration bank. The bank would then be in the position of extending a bad loan to the company. The disbursement bank may therefore charge interest and require that the firm meet its credit standards.

Another problem the disbursement bank faces is that a large disbursing firm—relative to the size of the bank—could cause the firm to exceed its legal lending limit. This would cause action by the Fed.

To make sure that accounts are not overdrafted, the firm could leave higher balances in the disbursement bank. This, of course, would partially defeat the purposes of a controlled/remote disbursing bank. Alternatively, the firm could use a mixture of DTC/ACH transfers plus a wire transfer whenever the available balance dips below zero.

Disbursement System Studies

Disbursement studies are quite similar to lockbox studies. Some of the same data bases and computer algorithms are used. The objective of disbursement studies, however, is to maximize (within limits) the total collection time rather than minimize it.

Disbursement studies are actually more difficult because of the desire of most firms to maintain good relationships with their vendors and other payees. Some of the constraints may be the following:

Subject to maintaining availability time of 1 day.
Subject to not increasing mail float.
Subject to clearing slippage of no more than 1 day.

Within these guidelines, computer models can be used to maximize the value of float in a firm's disbursement system. The dollar volume disbursed to various vendor groups is obtained from the firm's current disbursement files. Mail time and clearing times are available from commercial data bases.

Example of a Simple Disbursement Study

Table 8.3 illustrates the data needed for a relatively simple disbursement study that assists the firm in selecting appropriate disbursement banks and determines which vendor groups should be paid by a given bank. We assume that the initial set of possible disbursement banks chosen already fulfills any requirements the firm may have regarding mail time and slippage extension. (Disbursement computer models can take some of these requirements into account.)

The algorithm we use in this example is exhaustive search, with float maximization as the objective function. This type of model neglects several other cost factors in our objective function, but these may be considered outside the algorithm.

For this example, the firm's vendors have been grouped into four areas of the country. In actual studies, the division may be by two-digit zip codes, giving 99 possible areas. The total disbursement time between vendors of an area and a specific disbursement bank represents a weighted average taken from a sample of checks written over some time period. Disbursement time includes mail, processing, and clearing delays. Mail and clearing times come from data bases and are based on standard samples taken several times per year.

Table 8.3 Disbursement Bank Selection Study

Area of Country	Disbursements per Day (000's)	Total Disbursement Time Between Area and Disbursement Bank:		
		1	2	3
1	$300	2.5 days	2.7 days	3.3 days
2	$250	3.2	2.3	2.5
3	$100	3.9	3.4	2.0
4	$200	1.8	1.9	1.3

DOLLAR-DAYS DISBURSEMENT FLOAT

Area	1	2	3
1	750	810	990
2	800	575	625
3	390	340	200
4	360	380	260
	2,300	2,105	2,075

Once the weighted average disbursement times and average daily cash outflow are computed, the next step is to compute the dollars per day. This is done by multiplying disbursements per day by disbursement time, as illustrated in the second part of Table 8.3.

In this example, it is not difficult to compute the float (dollars per day) that would result from all permutations and combinations of one, two, or three disbursement bank systems. For larger problems, computers would have to be employed for this task.

The best one-disbursement bank system is disbursement bank 1, which gives a total float value of $2,300,000. Disbursement bank 2 is the next best, and disbursement bank 3 has the lowest float value.

We next compute the combinations 1–2, 1–3, and 2–3. This is done by taking, for each area, the largest dollar per day float amount of the two banks in the combination. Lastly, we compute the float value of having all three disbursement banks.

Combination	Dollars per day (000's)
1–2	810 + 800 + 390 + 380 = 2,380
1–3	990 + 800 + 390 + 360 = 2,540
2–3	990 + 625 + 340 + 380 = 2,335
1–2–3	990 + 800 + 390 + 380 = 2.560

From these computations, it appears that the combination 1–2–3 results in the highest float time. But note that this represents only a $20,000 float savings over the next best combination, 1–3. At 10% interest, this is only $2,000 per year. Recall that this model does not include all of the cost factors, such as transaction costs (including the costs of funding the disbursement account) and administrative costs. In practical terms, most firms would not choose a three-bank system over a two-bank system for a savings of only $2,000. The hidden administrative and other costs would outweigh the value of this level of savings. Besides, the error in measuring mail and clearing times would obliterate such a small difference.

The best one-bank system, however, is $240,000 dollars per day worse. This represents an annual dollar amount of about $24,000 (at 10%). Hence, the firm may pick the 1–3 combination rather than just disbursement bank 1 alone. With this combination of Bank 1 and Bank 3, vendor assignments are made to maximize float values:

Area	Assigned to Disbursement Bank
1	3
2	1
3	1
4	1

_____ Summary _____

While disbursement systems are, in some ways, the mirror image of collection systems, management must be very careful not to allow aggressive disbursement arrangements to lead them into unethical and otherwise questionable business practices. Lengthening the cash outflow timeline must be traded off against the possible costs of strained vendor relations and a poor public image. Rather than just seeking to maximize disbursement float, a more fruitful basis for structuring a disbursement system may involve other factors in the disbursement objective function. For example, controlled disbursing results in lower excess balances and gives better management control of disbursement funding without (usually) lengthening availability time for payees. As another example, using the ACH system for payments may result in lower administrative and transaction costs that outweigh float losses.

_____ Discussion Questions _____

1. How do excess balances arise in a disbursement system?
2. Why are ethical problems a greater issue in disbursement than in collection?
3. What are some of the costs that involve payee relationships?
4. What are the potential conflicts among the objectives of a disbursement system?
5. Discuss the pros and cons of a disbursement system with local check writing and centralized disbursement bank selection.
6. Define a zero balance account and describe how it is used in disbursement accounts. What is a pseudo-zero balance account?
7. How do PTDs differ from checks in disbursement systems? Could their use harm the firm's relationships with payees?
8. Why is a controlled disbursement system attractive to cash managers even though it may not increase disbursement float?
9. Explain how a money center bank can offer controlled disbursing services.
10. Contrast remote and controlled disbursing.
11. Explain the conditions needed for controlled disbursing to work. How has noon presentment affected those conditions?
12. What are banks and firms doing to counter the impact of noon presentment?
13. Explain the pros and cons of using a DTC or an ACH transfer to move cash into a disbursement account.
14. What is the objective function of a typical disbursement study? How are other cost factors taken into account?

_____ **Problems** _____

1. A firm has measured the various segments of the cash outflow time line in its disbursement system. The average calendar day delays are as follows:

Time Segment	Calendar Days
Invoice processing	35 days
Mail to vendor	5
Clearing to disb. bank	3
Total	43 days

Disbursements average $25,000,000 per month. If the firm were to extend invoice processing by 3 days and clearing time by 1 day, how much would the firm save per year? Assume an opportunity cost of 10%. What must your answer assume about the cost of ill will?

2. Disbursements for one firm are processed on a daily basis, Monday through Friday. A typical pattern for disbursements is as follows:

Day	Checks Mailed
Mon	$100,000
Tue	$200,000
Wed	$200,000
Thu	$300,000
Fri	$400,000

Under a new automated system, disbursements would be batch processed once a week. The firm has decided to move all payments in 1 week to the *following* Monday. In other words, the $100,000 payment in the preceding table would be delayed 1 full week. The Tuesday disbursements would also be delayed until the following Monday (6 days), and so on. Considering only the time value costs, compute the gain (loss) to the firm by adopting the new system.

3. Under its current disbursement system at a large regional bank, Mid-Sized Company has had to keep an average balance of about $100,000 in its disbursement account to protect against possible overdrafts. This is necessary because checks are frequently presented over the counter by local vendors late in the afternoon. Management does not want to endanger the firm's banking relations by frequent overdrafts. The balances earn no credits, since Mid-Sized has excess credits in other accounts. The treasurer of Mid-Sized has been studying the possibility of using a controlled disbursing bank that is affiliated with the large regional bank. The controlled point would extend the clearing time by about .5 calendar days but would cost an extra $500 per

month. Cash flow through the disbursing account averages $250,000 per calendar day. Mid-Sized considers its cost of funds to be 11%. Compute the savings (or loss) that the controlled disbursing system would provide.

4. The K&G Company is considering a new type of disbursement service. A disbursement bank offers a controlled disbursing service that is funded with ACH transfers or DTC rather than wires. This is a benefit to the firm because forecasting is not required and late presentments do not create problems. The bank, however, assumes some risk because an ACH transfer or DTC could bounce. The bank charges extra for this account and permits firms to compensate the bank in two alternative ways. K&G has average clearings of $100,000 per calendar day.

Under the first alternative, the firm keeps 150% of average daily clearings in the account as an average available balance. The bank gives an earnings credit rate of 7% (minus the reserve requirement of 12%). Service charges for K&G would be $500 per month with this service. K&G could earn 9% on the balances if they could invest in short-term securities.

Under the second alternative, K&G could keep an average available balance of zero. This exposes the bank to more risk, and the service charges would increase to $700 per month. While a zero average balance is maintained, K&G has computed that half of the time the available balance would be −$50,000 and the other half of the time it would be +$50,000. When the available balance is negative, the disbursement bank will book a loan and charge 8.5% interest per year on a daily basis.

Given only these costs and neglecting taxes, compute the monthly cost of each alternative for K&G.

Case: *Fleener Microcomputers, Inc.*

Fleener Microcomputers, Inc., provides custom computer services to small businesses. In addition to its consulting and training services, Fleener assembles hardware and software packages and installs turnkey systems. Haywood Morgan is the corporate controller and is in charge of the firm's accounts payable system. He has recently undertaken a consulting study of the system with the help of a bank consulting group. Disbursement data for the past several months have been collected, and adjustments have been made to compensate for seasonality and reporting errors.

Current System. Fleener's current payables system is highly decentralized. Each of its 15 divisions uses a local bank for disbursements. A good example is the Boston division, which services the New England states. Invoices are processed in its accounts payable section in Boston, where they are validated by matching them to purchase orders and receiving reports. Checks are then prepared and mailed to vendors. Vendor inquiries and complaints are handled locally by the accounts payable section. The Boston office draws checks on a large regional bank in Boston.

Fleener's headquarters, located in Palo Alto, California, receives weekly reports from division controllers showing actual bank balances and requesting cash be wire transferred to divisional disbursement accounts. The request is based on the divisional controller's estimate of expected clearings for the coming week. To prevent overdrafts, division controllers frequently request amounts higher than actual disbursements. The requests are processed by Haywood's office in Palo Alto, which wires cash from a large bank in San Francisco each week. Extra wires to cover misestimates are sometimes done, but division controllers are told such wires should be rare.

Payment Practices. The accounts payable study has determined that the divisions are inconsistent in their payment practices. As shown in Table 1, some divisions pay relatively early, while others pay quite late. Common credit terms from vendors are net 30. Discounts for early payment are not a significant issue with Fleener's vendors. Haywood is concerned that certain Fleener divisions may sometimes be stretching payments and may eventually damage Fleener's relations with suppliers. In addition, Haywood is concerned that some divisions are not carefully controlling the release of checks and may be paying too early.

Disbursement Bank Balances. Since each divisional disbursement bank receives a weekly wire to cover presentments for the coming week, idle balances are left in the disbursement account for several days until all presentments are covered. These balances have been considered bank compensation by Fleener. No fees are paid to any of the disbursement banks. If balances remain at the end of the week, they are usually adjusted for by division controllers in their request for the following week's wire. This practice has resulted in

Table 1 Fleener Microcomputers, Inc.: Report of Payables Delays by Division

Division	Average Disbursements per Calendar Day	Average Delay Between Invoice Date and Mail Date (Days)
San Francisco	$107,000	24
Seattle	93,000	26
Phoenix	67,000	37
Denver	41,000	19
St. Louis	34,000	21
Minneapolis	52,000	31
Chicago	66,000	36
Dallas	39,000	34
Atlanta	27,000	22
Miami	37,000	21
New York	75,000	41
Boston	83,000	44
Philadelphia	28,000	24
Washington, D.C.	35,000	22
Cleveland	28,000	31

balances, as shown in Table 2. The consultants also computed the compensating balance on the basis of a reasonable estimate of bank service charges, earnings credit rates, and reserve requirements or by the disbursement bank's account analysis if this was available.

Alternative Proposal. The consultants have suggested that Haywood consider the use of a controlled disbursing bank. Rather than disburse checks drawn on local accounts close to division headquarters, the consultants suggest disbursing checks centrally in Palo Alto but drawing them on a controlled disbursement bank located in Texas. Each day the disbursement bank would notify Fleener, through a balance-reporting service, of the total presentments for the day. Fleener would then wire cash into the account in Texas from its concentration bank. The deposit information would be available to Fleener at approximately 9 A.M. Since the bank is small, no over-the-counter checks or direct send cash letters are received later in the day.

Haywood is concerned about keeping track of disbursements on a divisional basis. The consultants assure him, however, that divisional accounting would be maintained. The controlled disbursing bank could keep separate accounts for all 15 divisions by using zero balance accounts.

Nevertheless, this plan would entail a significant redesign of Fleener's decentralized system. Division controllers have enjoyed considerable control over payment authorization and have been able to resolve any vendor payment disputes locally. Haywood is concerned that this function would now be complicated by moving check writing to headquarters. The consultants point out that

Table 2 Fleener Microcomputers, Inc.: Actual versus Target Balances

Division	Average Available Disb. Bank Balance	Required Balance for Bank Compensation
San Francisco	$230,000	$60,000
Seattle	45,000	22,000
Phoenix	39,000	20,000
Denver	40,000	15,000
St. Louis	55,000	15,000
Minneapolis	28,000	20,000
Chicago	94,000	25,000
Dallas	68,000	20,000
Atlanta	42,000	18,000
Miami	56,000	25,000
New York	184,000	55,000
Boston	145,000	51,000
Philadelphia	49,000	17,000
Washington, D.C.	67,000	14,000
Cleveland	45,000	15,000

Data are from a sample of a typical month adjusted for seasonality and errors.

authorization would still come through divisional personnel, but procedures for handling payment problems would have to be designed.

The consultants also point out that by using a bank in Texas, the clearing time should be significantly longer than that under the current system of using local disbursement banks. On average, according to the consultants' report, the controlled disbursement site would add approximately 1.6 calendar days to the clearing segment of the timeline.

Corporate Image. Haywood and his manager are concerned about Fleener's relations with its vendors. How would they respond to receiving checks drawn on a small, unknown bank in Texas after previous checks have been drawn on large, well-known banks? Would vendors have difficulty cashing out-of-state checks or would their banks give them longer availability delays?

Cost Considerations. Haywood decides to quantify the possible costs of the new system. He estimates that overall staff costs should net out to zero, since any savings in divisional offices would be compensated for by cost increases at headquarters. New payables software would have to be purchased to manage the centralized check writing. This should cost about $15,000 in customization, testing, and training expenses. The controlled disbursement bank estimates that its cost will be $2,500 per month to handle the volume of disbursements that Fleener expects. Fleener would be able to close all disbursement accounts in the divisions. Haywood estimates that Fleener's cost of funds at this time is about 11.5%.

Selected Readings

BRANDON, MARGARET B., "Contemporary Disbursing Practices and Products: A Survey," *Journal of Cash Management* (March 1982), pp. 26–39.

FERGUSON, DANIEL M., and STEVEN F. MAIER, "By Any Other Name. . .Controlled Disbursing in the New Environment," *Cashflow* (May 1981) pp. 30–35.

FERGUSON, DANIEL M., and STEVEN F. MAIER, "Disbursement System Design for the 1980s," *Journal of Cash Management* (November 1982), pp. 56–69.

FERGUSON, DANIEL M., and STEVEN F. MAIER, "Reducing the Risk in Corporate Disbursing Systems," Fentress Prize Paper, Bank Administration Institute (1983).

GITMAN, LAWRENCE J., D. KEITH FORRESTER, and JOHN R. FORRESTER Jr., "Maximizing Cash Disbursement Float," *Financial Management* (Summer 1976), pp. 15–23.

HAAG, LEONARD H., "Using Money Funds for Business Disbursing," *Journal of Cash Management* (October 1981), pp. 51–54.

HAMILTON, FRANK W., III, "Insulated Controlled Disbursing: A Way to Win the War on Fed Float," *Cashflow* (January–February 1984), pp. 25–27.

MAIER, STEVEN F., DAVID W. ROBINSON, and JAMES H. VANDER WEIDE, "A Short-term Disbursement Forecasting Model," *Financial Management* (Spring 1981), pp. 9–20.

MAIER, STEVEN F., "Insulated Controlled Disbursing: A Technique for Coping with Noon Presentment and Other Possible Check System Changes," *Journal of Cash Management* (November 1982), pp. 32–36.

PREDMORE, LESLEY, "Using EFT for Controlled Disbursing," *Cashflow* (November 1982), pp. 45–46.

ROSS, IRWIN, "The Race is to the Slow Payer," *Fortune* (April 18, 1983), pp. 75–80.

STONE, BERNELL K., and TOM W. MILLER, "Forecasting Disbursement Funding Requirements: The Clearing Pattern Approach," *Journal of Cash Management* (October 1983), p. 67ff.

Short-term Investments

Money Market Investments

Short-term marketable securities are traded in what is known as the *money market*. This market does not exist in a definitive place; it is a market conducted over the telephone by a collection of dealers and traders who stand ready to buy and sell securities. Money market investments serve two roles in the corporation: (1) they represent a liquidity reserve that can be quickly called upon in times of need, and (2) they represent a temporary parking place for excess funds that can earn a return. In this chapter, we discuss the characteristics of money market investments that are used by financial managers. In the next two chapters, we discuss strategies and techniques for managing the money market portfolio.

The Money Market

The term *money market* usually refers to the markets for short-term securities such as Treasury bills, federal agency issues, commercial paper, negotiable certificates of deposit, banker's acceptances, repurchase agreements, and federal funds. While the maturity of the securities traded in these money markets can be anywhere from 1 day to 1 year, the usual maturity is 90 days or less. The market for these short-term credit instruments is decentralized, although a significant amount of the activity takes place in New York City. Buyers and sellers from around the world communicate by telephone with the brokers and dealers who trade the securities.

The money market is very large and efficient. Its numerous participants are very well informed. The normal trading denomination, usually called a *round lot*, is $1,000,000 for several of the securities. However, the market is so large that no one participant is large enough to have an impact on market prices.

Transactions Agents

The purchase and sale of money market instruments are conducted or assisted by three participants in the market: brokers, dealers, and the Federal Reserve.

Brokers

Brokers are agents who bring together buyers and sellers in the market. Their function is to provide a communication network that links the large number of buyers and sellers, who may be geographically separated. They also provide an important link between the banks that handle the transfer of funds in a money market transaction. The brokers' only source of income is the fee or commission charged for arranging transactions. Because of their specialized and constant activity in the market, they can maintain this network at a lower cost than could individual buyers and sellers. This lower cost helps keep transactions costs low and improves market efficiency. By definition, brokers never take a position in a security for their own account.

Dealers

Dealers make markets in securities by quoting prices at which they stand ready to buy, the *bid price*, or sell, the *ask price*, for their own account. A dealer can buy and hold an inventory of a security, that is, maintain a *long* position in the security. A dealer can also sell a security that she does not own, that is, have a *short* position in the security. Because the dealer has funds invested in a position in the securities, she is subject to risk from a potential change in price. In some instances where there is a ready buyer and a seller for the same security, the dealer may act more like a broker in arranging the transaction, even though she may appear to be buying and selling for her own account. Frequently, dealers work through brokers in carrying out their transactions in order to remain anonymous.

Dealers trade with several different types of clients. They trade with other dealers in what is sometimes called the *inside market*. Dealers frequently use brokers for trading in this market. They trade with their customers in what is called the *retail market*. They underwrite new securities issued by federal, state, and municipal governments, buying a substantial portion of the initial offering in hopes of reselling it later at a higher price. It is their auction bids on T-bills that set the price and the interest rate on the securities sold by the federal government.

DEALER INCOME. Dealers receive their income from several different sources. First, since they take a position in the security, they stand to profit if the price changes (in the proper direction, of course) before they close out their position. Second, they earn a commission when they act as brokers. Third, they may be able to maintain a positive spread between the rate they earn on the security and their financing costs. This spread is sometimes called the dealer *carry*. Finally, they may generate income by their arbitrage activities, buying and selling securities at the same time (or very nearly so) at slightly different prices. This arbitrage activity helps to maintain efficiency in the market.

Dealers must obtain funds to finance their position. They can borrow the necessary funds from commercial banks. These loans may be convenient for small amounts, but they tend to be expensive relative to the other method used. Dealers can obtain funds directly from their customers, including commercial banks, by engaging in *repurchase agreements* or *repos*. The dealer sells the security to the customer with an agreement to repurchase it at a stated price. Essentially, this is a loan made to the dealer with the security as collateral. Most repos have a term of 1 day. Repos are discussed in greater length later in the chapter.

The Federal Reserve

The Federal Reserve, through its Open Market Committee operations, buys and sells federal securities to control the amount of bank reserves and the money supply. It is the largest participant in the money market, particularly in the market for T-bills. The Federal Reserve carries out its transactions through a select set of dealers, called *primary dealers*. To be listed as a primary dealer, a firm must have an adequate capital base relative to the position it assumes; have a significant volume (at least 1% of the market activity); be willing to make a market at all times, and have high-quality top management that understands the government securities market and is making a long-term commitment to stay in the market.

While the Federal Reserve generally works through dealers for its transactions, it also acts as an agent for foreign banks that desire to buy or sell money market securities in the United States. This has become an increasingly important activity in recent years as the volume of foreign investment in U.S. securities has grown.

Market Participants

Two of the most important participants in the money market, dealers and the Federal Reserve, have been discussed. The other participants are those who desire to either borrow or lend money for short periods of time. Lenders tend to be portfolio managers who have excess funds and desire to earn a return on them without accepting much risk. Borrowers tend to be large organizations with high credit ratings that find it less expensive to borrow directly from the lenders than to deal through an intermediary.

Lenders

A list of lenders, or suppliers of funds, in the money market includes commercial banks, nonbank financial institutions (such as sales or commercial finance companies), state and local governments, and nonfinancial corporations. In recent years, individuals have also become active in supplying funds to the money market either through direct purchase of T-bills and bank Certificates of Deposit (CDs) or through indirect purchase via mutual funds. The U.S. Treasury is almost never a participant in the money markets as a lender.

Borrowers

A list of borrowers of funds in the money market includes many of the same economic entities that appear in a list of lenders. The primary participants on this side of the market are the U.S. Treasury, which issues T-bills to finance the federal deficit; commercial banks, which issue CDs to fund their loans and other activities; nonbank financial institutions and nonfinancial corporations, which issue commercial paper; and state and local governments, which issue short-term notes in advance of receipt of funds from taxes or other sources. Because of the large denomination of the transactions and the high credit standards, small businesses and individuals generally are not participants on the borrowing side of the market.

Given the short-term nature of the instruments and the frequency of the transactions, the market can operate efficiently only if costs and risks are small. Two significant components of the costs are *transactions costs* and *information costs*. Since many of the actual transactions costs are fixed, these costs as a percentage of the transaction can be kept low by keeping the transactions large. The information costs can be held down by lending only to borrowers who are well known in the market. This has traditionally meant that only large, high-credit-rated borrowers could raise funds in the money markets. With advances in communications, computerization, and data bases, both the information and the transactions costs have been reduced. The result has been a dramatic reduction in the size of the economic unit that can directly utilize the money market to raise funds. This trend has been most noticeable in the reduction in the size of the issue and the companies raising short-term funds by selling commercial paper.

Characteristics of Money Market Securities

The suppliers of funds are those economic units that have excess cash and are willing to invest temporarily in money market instruments rather than having them remain in non-interest-bearing demand deposits. In choosing between alternative securities, lenders make a major tradeoff between liquidity and yield.

Liquidity

Securities purchased for a short-term portfolio must be ones that can be converted easily and quickly into cash at a known price. That is, they must be *liquid*. There are three factors that have a major effect on the perception of the liquidity of a security.

SAFETY OF PRINCIPAL. In most cases, the portfolio manager is purchasing marketable securities because temporarily he has some excess funds and desires to earn a return on them. However, he anticipates that at some time in the future the funds will be needed. A primary consideration is that the funds placed in the security will be available at the maturity date, that is, that the principal is not in jeopardy. The borrower must have a high likelihood of redeeming the security according to the specified terms.

MARKETABILITY. The future cash flow needs of a firm can be predicted only imperfectly. Unless a firm places all of its money market investments in overnight securities purchased late in the day, it may have to sell a security prior to maturity to generate cash to cover an unexpected need. A security that is marketable can be sold in large volume very quickly without a substantial price concession. The existence of a large, active secondary market is necessary for a security to have high marketability.

PRICE STABILITY. The price of a security varies inversely with interest rates. The longer the term to maturity, the greater will be the change in price for a given change in interest rates. Since investors in money market securities want the liquidity to withdraw funds if necessary, they must be able to do so at close to a known price. To avoid the price instability that comes with longer-term securities, portfolio managers generally confine their investments to securities with a relatively short term, generally less than 1 year.

Yield

Yield, or the return that is earned on the security, is a second major dimension considered when making a money market investment. While yield is important, for most portfolio managers it is secondary to liquidity. There are four factors that have a major influence on the yield on a security.

MATURITY. The relationship between the yield of a security and the maturity is described by the yield curve. We briefly describe the tradeoff between yield and maturity here, and defer discussion of the determinants of the shape of the yield curve to Chapter 10. In general, the yield curve has been upward sloping, meaning an investor can expect to receive a higher yield on a security with a longer maturity than on a short-term security. The relationship between yield and maturity at a time when expectations, at least those published by various advisory and forecasting services, were for rates in the future to remain at about the same level is given in Table 9.1. We can see that although the curve is not uniform, in general higher rates correspond to longer maturities. We can

Table 9.1 Yield versus Maturity for
T-Bills, May 30, 1986

Days to Maturity	Annualized Yield (%)
7	5.39
14	6.26
21	6.25
28	5.75
35	6.14
42	6.26
49	6.27
56	6.33
63	6.31
70	6.42

Source: The Wall Street Journal, June 2, 1986, p. 27.

also see that the sharpest jump in the rates for an additional week's maturity occurs in moving from 7 to 14 days.

MARKETABILITY. If a portfolio manager attempts to sell a security for which there is no active secondary market, he will incur greater transactions costs in terms of higher search costs to find a buyer, a higher fee to a broker, or a lower price. A less marketable security has to offer a higher yield to compensate for these transactions costs.

RISK. Investors are primarily interested in security of principal and will refuse to purchase any security in which they perceive a substantial probability of default. However, within the subset of securities that are felt to have acceptable default risk, there will be an increase in yield for securities that are felt to have a higher risk of default. U.S. government securities are considered to be the safest in terms of default, at least for investors in the United States, and have no premium for default risk. Other securities are evaluated in comparison to them and offer a premium yield for a perceived increase in default risk.

TAXABILITY. When it comes to taxability of income from securities, not all securities are created equal. There exists a mutual agreement on nontaxability of securities between the federal government and state and local governments. Interest on U.S. Treasury securities is generally not taxable by states or local municipalities, and interest on most securities issued by state and local governments, called *municipals* or *munis*, is not subject to federal taxes. Since the federal tax rate for most taxable investors is higher than state and local tax rates, federal nontaxability of munis receives the most attention. There have been numerous attempts to change this relationship by making income on state and local securities taxable by the federal government. While there has been some encroachment by the federal tax code on special issues, general-purpose security issues of state and local governments still remain nontaxable. Clearly, the yield on a nontaxable security is lower than that on a taxable security of similar maturity and default risk. To compare the purchase of taxable and nontaxable securities properly, the analysis must be conducted on an after-tax basis.

Another taxability feature is the way that foreign securities are taxed. Depending upon the countries involved, both countries may tax the income from the securities, or credits may be granted by one country for taxes paid to another country. Since the tax codes change frequently, investors must check the tax code before committing their funds.

The Tradeoff Between Risk and Return

Money market securities illustrate the second law of finance: there is a tradeoff between risk and return. This can be thought of in two different ways. (1) An investor must be offered a higher return (yield) to bear additional risk. (2) To obtain a higher return, an investor will have to accept greater risk. Securities that offer higher yields are seen, sometimes only after careful investigation, to possess less liquidity, less marketability, a higher default risk, or a higher effective tax rate than securities offering lower yields. In choosing securities to purchase for a marketable securities portfolio, the manager considers the role they play in providing liquidity to the firm, the timeframe and accuracy of the forecasting system, and the acceptability of the risk.

U.S. Government and Agency ─────────── Securities ───────────

There are two broad classifications of securities that are frequently called *government securities: U.S. Treasury securities* and *federal agency securities*, or *agencies*.

U.S. Treasury Securities

Treasury securities are direct obligations of the U.S. Treasury. As such, they are backed by the full faith and credit of the United States government. Congress could, and would, use its extensive tax-raising ability, if necessary, to provide the funds to pay off the securities. Thus, these securities are considered to be free of default risk. The rate on a short-term security, frequently a 30 day T-bill, is considered by many to be the definition of a risk-free rate. Treasury securities are also considered low risk because they have excellent marketability. They are very actively traded in secondary markets in large volumes with very narrow spreads.

Treasury securities have entered the electronic age. All new issues of these securities are issued in *book entry* form. That is, they are delivered and cleared electronically. They no longer exist as paper certificates, or *physical securities*. This change has increased their safety: it is now necessary to carry out a very sophisticated computer crime to steal a Treasury security instead of mugging a courier. The use of electronic clearing has also increased the speed with which the transactions can be made.[1]

Treasury Bills

Treasury bills, also known as *T-bills*, have a maturity at issue of 1 year of less, usually either 13, 26, or 52 weeks. These securities are sold at a *discount*. They do not bear interest. The investor earns a return because they are sold for less than the face value and redeemed at face value at maturity. The Treasury does not set the rate on T-bills; rather, they are auctioned periodically, with the securities going to the bidders with the lowest discount (highest price). This way the Treasury does not have to guess at the appropriate rate; it always gets the market rate. The quotes on T-bills are discount quotes on a 360-day year, not the effective yield to maturity. In Chapter 10 we will consider how

---

[1] Additional information on how the book-entry system is operated can be found in Chapter 13 of Marcia Stigum, *The Money Market: Myth, Reality and Practice*, 2nd ed., Homewood, Ill, Dow Jones-Irwin (1983).

this difference affects the yield to maturity. The denominations in which T-bills are available are $10,000, $15,000, $50,000, $100,000, $500,000 and $1,000,000. However, a round lot for trading is $5,000,000.

Treasury Notes

The Treasury periodically issues interest-bearing notes. The interest is paid semiannually and is based on a 365-day year. The original maturity of the notes can be between 1 and 10 years, with 2- and 4-year notes being issued on a regular cycle. Notes with other maturities are issued on an irregular basis, depending upon the financing needs of the Treasury. These notes are usually sold at auction, with the coupon rate being set by low-rate bidders. Thus, the Treasury is able to get the market rate on these issues as well. These notes are available in denominations of $1,000, $5,000, $10,000, $100,000, and $1,000,000, with a round-lot trade of $1,000,000. While these notes have an *original maturity* that may be too long for most marketable securities portfolios, the large volume and regular issue cycle result in many securities with a *remaining maturity* that fits the time horizon of many portfolios.

Treasury Bonds

The Treasury also issues interest-bearing bonds that have an original maturity of more than 10 years. As with the notes, the interest is stated on a 365-day year and paid semiannually. They are issued by an auction similar to that for notes. They are issued in the same denominations as notes, but a round-lot trade is $500,000. Several times in the past, the volume of bonds issued was very low because Congress established a ceiling on the rate that could be paid on bonds that was below the prevailing market rate. The place for bonds in the marketable securities portfolio is similar to that for notes; the manager is interested only in those with a short remaining maturity.

Federal Agency Securities

At various times, Congress has become concerned about the amount or terms on which credit is supplied to particular sectors of the economy. One possible solution to the problem is to set up a federal agency to provide credit to that sector. The agency is empowered to issue securities to the public to raise funds. Initially, almost all government agencies issued securities directly to the public, but now many of them obtain funds by borrowing from the Treasury through an institution known as the *Federal Financing Bank*. The agencies that continue to market securities directly to the public will be discussed. Their interest-bearing securities are generally issued and redeemed at face value. Unlike government securities, they are not sold at auction. These securities are generally not backed by the full faith and credit of the U.S. government, although many consider it inconceivable that the government would let one of these agencies default on its obligations. Agency issues are usually smaller and less marketable than government securities. They usually have a higher yield than governments.

Federal Home Loan Bank

The Federal Home Loan Bank (FHLB) System was created to provide funds for savings and loan associations, particularly at times of tight money and/or high interest rates. The FHLB also regulates the activities of the savings and loan industry and operates the savings and loan insurance fund, the Federal Savings and Loan Insurance Corporation (FSLIC). The FHLB issues consolidated bonds, which are the joint obligation of all 12 FHLBs and have an initial maturity of 1 year or more. These bonds pay interest semiannually and are issued in denominations of $10,000, $25,000, $100,000, and $1,000,000. The FHLB also issues short-term discount notes in denominations of $100,000.

Federal National Mortgage Association

The Federal National Mortgage Association (FNMA), known as *Fannie Mae*, was established to create a secondary market in home mortgages. It maintains this market by purchasing and selling government-insured mortgages. It finances its purchases by issuing discount notes, with a maturity of from 30 to 270 days with a minimum denomination of $50,000, and debentures, which pay interest semiannually. Originally, Fannie Mae was a government agency. In a series of steps the agency was privatized, and it is now owned by its stockholders. Although it is no longer a government agency, it is still under some government control, and it is considered unlikely that the government would let it default on its obligations. The interest on the securities is subject to federal, state, and local taxes.

Government National Mortgage Association

The Government National Mortgage Association (GNMA), known as *Ginnie Mae*, is a wholly owned government corporation that operates within the Department of Housing and Urban Development. Its function is to supply special-assistance funds to particular segments of the real estate market. It carries out its activities either by buying and reselling mortgages or by purchasing pools of mortgages and selling *pass-through securities*. With the latter securities, Ginnie Mae passes the payment of interest and principal from the mortgages through to the holder of the security on a monthly basis. Both interest and principal are guaranteed and are backed by the full faith and credit of the U.S. government. However, because of the long-term nature of the instrument and the uncertain monthly cash flow, these securities may not be suitable for many marketable securities portfolios.

Federal Home Loan Mortgage Corporation

The Federal Home Loan Mortgage Corporation buys residential mortgages from federally insured financial institutions and resells them through mortgage-related instruments. It issues *mortgage participation certificates*, which are very similar to the pass-through securities of Ginnie Mae, and *guaranteed mortgage certificates*. The latter certificates pay interest semiannually and return principal annually in specified amounts. Both types of securities are issued only in registered form and have denominations of $100,000, $500,000, and $1,000,000. The securities are fully taxable for both state and federal purposes. Like Ginnie Mae securities, they may not be suitable for many marketable securities portfolios.

Banks for Cooperatives

The Banks for Cooperatives make seasonal and term loans to cooperatives owned by farmers to provide working capital or to finance investments in buildings and equipment. Originally the Banks for Cooperatives were owned by the government, but they are now privately owned. They issue Consolidated Collateral Trust Debentures, usually on a monthly schedule. The maturity of these debentures is usually 6 months, with interest paid at maturity; however, occasionally longer-term securities (from 2 to 5 years) are issued. The obligations of the banks are not guaranteed by the U.S. government. The interest on these securities is exempt from state and local taxes.

Federal Land Banks

The 12 Federal Land Banks make first-mortgage loans on farm properties and other loans through local Federal Land Bank Associations. Originally government owned, the Federal Land Banks are now owned by the local associations, which, in turn, are owned by farmers. The Federal Land Banks issue Consolidated Federal Farm Loan Bonds with an original maturity of 1 to 15 years, with interest paid semiannually. The securities are not guaranteed by the government. The income is exempt from state and local taxes.

Federal Intermediate Credit Banks

The 12 Federal Intermediate Credit Banks make loans and issue discount paper for financial institutions that make loans to farmers for the production and marketing of livestock and crops. These banks issue consolidated collateral trust debentures on a monthly basis. Many issues have a 9-month maturity with interest payable at maturity, although the banks are authorized to issue securities with up to a 5-year maturity. The securities are not guaranteed by the U.S. government. They are exempt from state and local taxes.

Bank Securities

Commercial banks and other financial institutions issue short-term instruments to finance their loan and securities portfolios. Many of these time deposits or certificates are not negotiable, that is, they cannot be sold to a third party. They can be redeemed prior to maturity only by turning them in to the bank, usually with a substantial penalty. There are two major types of negotiable instruments that banks issue: negotiable certificates of deposit, and bankers acceptances.

Negotiable Certificates of Deposit (CDs)

The lack of liquidity of normal time deposits and CDs led the banks to create negotiable CDs. These CDs can have any maturity longer than 30 days, and some have had a maturity as long as 5 to 7 years. Most CDs have a maturity between 1 and 3 months. Their interest is usually stated on a 360-day year; it is paid at maturity for a certificate with an original maturity of less than a year and semiannually on a longer-term CD. They are generally sold at face value and have a denomination of $1,000,000. The interest on a CD can be either at a *fixed rate* or a *variable rate*. The interest is usually paid and the rate adjusted quarterly on variable rate CDs, and the original maturity is usually 1 year. Since the number of variable rate CDs is quite small, there is no active secondary market for them.

The yields on negotiable CDs are higher than those on government and agency securities. The yield varies with the perceived riskiness of the bank and the marketability of the CD, which is a function of the volume of CDs that the bank issues.

Banker's Acceptances (BAs)

BAs are essentially time drafts that arise out of the financing of commercial trade, frequently on international transactions, involving a letter of credit that has been accepted by a bank. The process by which a banker's acceptance is created is discussed in Chapter 19. Our interest here is limited to the features that make it useful in a marketable securities portfolio. BAs are discount instruments that are redeemed at face value at maturity. The interest is usually stated on a 360-day year. Because they originate from the credit needs of commercial trade, they come in a wide variety of maturities and denominations. Liquidity of BAs is provided by dealers who make an active secondary market in these securities.

Commercial Paper

Commercial paper is an unsecured short-term promissory discount note issued for a specific amount and maturing on a specific day. The interest is usually stated on a 360-day year. Industrial firms, bank holding companies, finance companies, utilities, and municipalities are frequent users of commercial paper. Finance companies, such as Ford Credit, GMAC, and Household Finance, usually sell their paper directly to investors. Most other users sell commercial paper through dealers. The dealers charge a fee, usually about 1/8th of 1%, for handling the paper for the issuer. Although commercial paper is negotiable, there is no active secondary market for most paper, so it is held until maturity. Because of the weak secondary market, the yield on commercial paper is higher than that of securities of comparable risk with greater marketability.

The maturity on commercial paper can be anywhere from 1 day to 1 year. However, in practice, there is a limit on the maturity of 270 days. If paper with a longer maturity is sold, it has to be registered with the Securities and Exchange Commission, a costly and time-consuming process. Most paper sold has 30 days or less to maturity.

With such a maturity, which is generally shorter than the need for funds, most issuers plan to roll the paper over at maturity. A sudden change in market conditions or in the condition of the firm might make it difficult, if not impossible, for the issuer to replace the paper. To guard against this possibility, almost all commercial paper issuers maintain a bank line of credit to back up the paper.

The rate paid on commercial paper varies with the maturity, the market conditions, and the quality rating of the issuer. Almost all paper issued is rated by Moody's Investors Service, Standard and Poor's Corporation, or the Fitch Investor Service. Although their rating procedures are somewhat different, they all use basically the same criteria: liquidity, ability to borrow from other sources, quality of management, trend in earnings, and strength in the industry. Very little paper is sold that doesn't receive a prime rating from one or more of these rating services. Any paper that is sold without a prime rating must pay a significantly higher yield.

Repurchase Agreements

A *repurchase agreement*, often called a *repo* or an *RP*, is the purchase of a security from another party, frequently a bank or a securities dealer, who agrees to buy it back at a specified time and price. The repurchase might work as follows. Late in the day a government bond dealer finds that she has more securities, say, $10,000,000, than she has funds to carry the securities overnight. She finds a corporation that has excess funds. She sells the $10,000,000 worth of securities for almost that price. The payment is made in federal funds (immediately available) from the corporation's bank to her bank. At the same time, she agrees to buy the securities back the next day at a slightly higher price. Effectively, the buyer of the securities is making the dealer an overnight loan for which the securities serve as collateral. The difference between the purchase and the sale price represents the interest that the corporation is receiving on the loan to the dealer.

The rate on repos tends to be slightly less than that on federal funds for several reasons. First, there are many nonbank investors who have overnight funds to invest and who do not have direct access to federal funds. The repo may be the only alternative available. Second, because the prices of both sides of the transaction are included in the agreement, the investor takes no price risk. Third, the loan is essentially collateralized by the security, whereas a sale of federal funds is an unsecured loan to a bank.

While overnight repos are most common, longer-maturity repos are also available. A repo for longer than overnight is known as a *term repo*. Because there is a loss of liquidity on a term repo, as well as increased risk of nonperformance on the other side of the transaction, the yield increases with the maturity.

Eurodollar Securities

Eurodollar deposits are dollar-denominated deposits that are held in banks outside the United States, although not necessarily in Europe. Most Eurodollar deposits are time deposits and suffer from the same illiquidity as a domestic time deposit. *Eurodollar CDs* are dollar-denominated CDs that are issued by London banks or branches of other foreign banks in London. The original maturity can range from overnight to several years. However, most Eurodollar CDs have original maturities of 6 months or less. An active secondary market is maintained. The yield is higher than on domestic CDs because of the added risk associated with deposits outside of the United States.

Investment Pools

Money Market Mutual Funds

A *mutual fund* is a professionally managed portfolio of securities that pools funds from a number of investors. Most mutual funds invest in equity securities. However, when the interest rates soared above the rates that financial institutions were allowed to pay on deposits, a new type of mutual fund was born. A *money market mutual fund* is a mutual fund that invests in high-yield, short-term securities. These funds calculate earnings on the investor's account daily and usually credit it monthly. For tax purposes, the income is treated as interest rather than dividends. These funds provide liquidity by allowing withdrawal without a penalty on demand by check or wire, or by allowing the investor to write a check on the fund through a bank that has arranged to provide this service. There is frequently a minimum amount allowed for withdrawal, perhaps $250 or $500. Some money market mutual funds invest in municipal notes. The interest from these funds is exempt from federal taxes, and possibly from some state taxes.

Because these funds pool the money of a large number of investors, they can deal in larger-denomination securities than the individual investor can purchase. Even after paying the management fee, many investors earn more than they could on their own. In addition, with an average portfolio maturity of 20 to 100 days, there is not much price risk. The investor is provided liquidity through on-demand withdrawal privileges.

Money market mutual funds were first created to attract individual investors; however, they can also be useful to the portfolio manager. For a small firm with little expertise in investments and a tightly stretched staff, they can serve as the portfolio manager. For a slightly larger firm, they can provide a way of investing small amounts of excess funds that perhaps cannot be invested in larger-denomination securities. For all firms, they can provide a benchmark against which to measure the performance of the portfolio manager. If the portfolio manager cannot exceed the performance of the money market mutual fund, what is the justification for keeping the portfolio manager?

Pooled Repurchase Agreements

Some commercial banks will arrange a *pooled repurchase agreement*. They combine the excess funds from several of their commercial customers who are each too small or who don't have enough excess funds to deal in a repo. Suppose a bank has a $1,000,000 security that it would like to use in an overnight repo. The bank has one customer with $500,000 in excess funds and two customers with $250,000 in excess funds. By combining the funds from these three customers, the bank has enough funds to make it worthwhile to conduct a repo. As would be expected, the rate on these pooled repos is somewhat less than that on a straight repo. However, this may still be an attractive option for an overnight investment.

Financial Futures

A recent development in the financial markets has been the creation of financial futures contracts. These contracts give the portfolio manager an opportunity to control the risk in the portfolio by hedging his position in certain securities. However, for the portfolio manager who does not understand all of the complexities of these contracts and the way that they are traded, their use may increase the risk rather than reduce it. Financial futures are treated extensively in Chapter 11.

Municipal Securities

Debt instruments, both short-term notes and bonds, issued by state and local governments are referred to as *municipal securities* or *munis*. However, because of the maturity and the weaker secondary market for municipal bonds, they are not usually considered for a marketable securities portfolio.

Most muni notes are general obligation notes, that is, payment is backed by the full faith and credit, and of course the taxing authority, of the municipality.

However, recent near defaults by both New York City and Cleveland empha-
sized that the investor is bearing some credit risk. The maturity of the notes
varies from 1 month to 1 year, and denominations range from $5,000 to
$5,000,000. Most are interest-bearing securities. The yields are below those
on T-bills because munis are not subject to federal taxes, and in most states
they are not subject to state tax in the state of the issuer. The yields vary with
the perceived credit risk. Moody's Investor Service rates muni notes, similar
to its rating on commercial paper.

Summary of Security Characteristics

The securities previously discussed include most of the securities that can be
used for a marketable securities portfolio. The most important characteristics of
the securities that are most commonly found in marketable securities portfolios
are summarized in Table 9.2.

Summary

In this chapter we discussed some of the characteristics of the securities that
qualify for investment in a money market portfolio. These money market
securities are traded in a loosely organized market of dealers and brokers.
The major participants in the market consist of the federal government, the
Federal Reserve, financial institutions, nonfinancial corporations, individuals,
and other governmental units. These participants can be on either side of the
market, with the exception of the federal government, which is almost always
a borrower, and individuals, who are always lenders.

Investment in money market securities involves a tradeoff between liquidity,
the ability to sell a security quickly without suffering a price decline at a small
transactions cost, and the yield. The yield is a function of the maturity, the
marketability, the default risk, and the taxability of the security. In making
the tradeoff between liquidity and yield, most marketable security portfolio
managers prefer liquidity over yield.

Discussion Questions

1. Where would you go if you wanted to visit the money market?
2. What factors cause the money market to approximate the definition of an
   efficient market?
3. What role do brokers play in the money market?
4. Describe the activities of money market dealers. Which of these activities
   represent a source of risk to the dealers?

Table 9.2 Characteristics of Common Money Market Securities

Security	Type	Original Maturity	Taxability	Interest Year
U.S. T-bills	Discount	< 1 year	Federal	360 days
U.S. notes	Coupon	1–10 years	Federal	365 days
U.S. bonds	Coupon	> 10 years	Federal	365 days
FHLB notes	Discount	< 1 year	All	365 days
Bank CDs	Coupon	> 30 days	All	360 days
Banker's acceptances	Discount	Varied	All	360 days
Commercial paper	Discount	< 270 days	All	360 days
Eurodollar CDs	Coupon	Varied	All	365 days
Repurchase agreements	Discount	1+ days	All	?
Municipal notes	Discount	< 1 year	Some state	360 days(?)

5. Contrast the income sources and financing requirements of dealers and brokers.
6. What role does the Federal Reserve play in the money market?
7. Who are the primary borrowers in the money market? Who are the primary lenders?
8. What factors contribute to the liquidity of a security?
9. List the factors that make the liquidity of a security important to the marketable securities portfolio manager.
10. In the tradeoff between risk and return, why do most marketable securities portfolio managers prefer to avoid risk?
11. What factors affect the yield on a money market instrument?
12. What is considered to be the most liquid of the money market securities? Why?
13. How are T-bill yields quoted?
14. Agency securities are not backed by the full faith and credit of the U.S. Treasury, yet they are considered default free by a number of investors. Why? What risks are there in making this assumption?
15. If agencies are considered to be default free, why do they usually sell at a premium above a U.S. Treasury security with a comparable maturity and coupon?
16. Describe the characteristics of CDs.
17. Contrast the use of a CD from Chase Manhattan Bank and from the First National Bank of Bloomington, Indiana, for the marketable securities portfolio.
18. What is a banker's acceptance (BA)?
19. What influence would the credit rating of the company behind the BA have on the yield on the BA?
20. What is a Eurodollar deposit?
21. How do Eurodollar deposits differ from domestic deposits?
22. How do Eurodollar CDs compare with domestic CDs in terms of the various factors that affect liquidity and yield?
23. Describe how a repurchase agreement is created and the relative positions of the two parties to the agreement.
24. What are the risks to the two parties of a repurchase agreement?

Selected Readings

BENCH, JOSEPH, "Money and Capital Markets: Institutional Framework and Federal Reserve Control," in *Financial Handbook*, 5th ed., Edward I. Altman (ed.), New York: Wiley 1981, Chapter 1.

BENCH, JOSEPH, "Government Obligations: U.S. Treasury and Federal Agency Securities," in *Financial Handbook*, 5th ed., Edward I. Altman (ed.), New York: Wiley 1981, Chapter 2.

COOK, TIMOTHY Q. and BRUCE J. SUMMERS, (eds.), *Instruments of the Money Market*, 5th ed., Richmond, Va.: The Federal Reserve Bank of Richmond, 1981.

Handbook of Securities of the United States Government and Federal Agencies, and Related Money Market Instruments, 31st ed., New York: First Boston Corporation, 1984.

SMITH, TILDON W., "Short-Term Money Markets and Instruments," in *Financial Handbook*, 5th ed., Edward I. Altman (ed.), New York: Wiley, 1981, Chapter 25.

STIGUM, MARCIA, *The Money Market: Myth, Reality, and Practice*, 2nd ed., Homewood, Ill.: Dow Jones-Irwin, 1983.

VAN HORNE, JAMES C., *Financial Market Rates and Flows*, 2nd ed., Englewood Cliffs, N.J.: Prentice-Hall, 1984.

10

Managing the Short-term Investments Portfolio

Traditionally, companies have invested spare cash in a safe temporary parking place such as jumbo CDs, commercial paper, or repurchase agreements. With recent changes in yields, some companies have become more aggressive with their investments. The MDU Resources Group, Inc., is able to earn twice the after-tax yield on T-bills through the use of more aggressive cash investments. The Trans World Manufacturing Corporation uses money market preferred stock to take advantage of the tax exclusion on dividend income. The Enron Corporation takes advantage of this tax exclusion by purchasing common stock to capture the dividend. Foote, Cone and Belding Communications, Inc., pursues a strategy of purchasing common stock and writing options on it.[1] However, while these strategies generate higher returns, they have less liquidity and more risk than traditional investment strategies.

Managing the short-term investment portfolio requires an accumulation of information about the firm, the markets and instruments, the economic environment, and a selection of investment options—all in a very short period of time. In Chapter 9 we discussed the securities and the markets in which they are traded. In this chapter we examine the management of the investment process. This includes measuring the liquidity of the firm, deciding on the size of the cash balance and the securities portfolio, calculating the effective yield of a security, and identifying the relationship between yield and maturity.

---

[1] Farrell, Christopher and Jeffrey M. Laderman, "More Profits from Idle Corporate Cash," *Business Week*, (May 12, 1986), pp. 85–86.

Portfolio Management Process

The existence of a specific, well-defined process for managing a marketable securities portfolio increases the probability that short-term investments will effectively contribute to the goal of maximization of shareholder value. The completeness and complexity of the process depend on the resources devoted to managing the portfolio. A large firm with extensive marketable securities holdings may have several people whose primary, if not sole, function is managing the portfolio. A firm with a small amount of funds invested may have the controller spending 10 minutes after his morning coffee break managing the portfolio, along with many other responsibilities.

Regardless of the resources available or the size of the portfolio, there are several steps that facilitate effective portfolio management. The steps in the portfolio management process are shown in Figure 10.1.

Information Gathering

Portfolio management starts with an assessment of the objectives of the marketable securities portfolio. These objectives include the purpose for holding

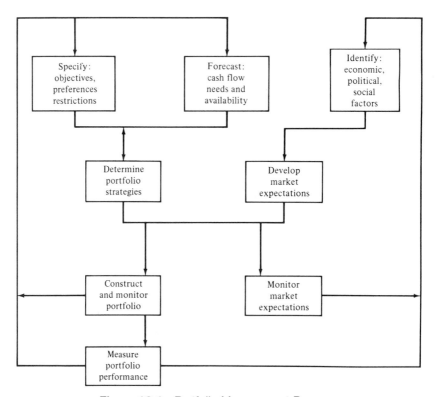

Figure 10.1 Portfolio Management Process.

marketable securities, the return expected, the acceptable risk level, permissible financial instruments, and the time frame for the investment. It is also important to identify any preferences and restrictions, either managerial or legal, that shape investment strategies.

A second type of information needed for the design of a marketable securities portfolio is a forecast of future cash flows.[2] The accuracy and frequency of the update of the cash flow forecast available to the portfolio manager determine, in part, the strategy used to manage the portfolio. For example, an accurate and up-to-date forecast of daily cash flows for, say, the next 2 weeks allows the manager to fine tune the investment portfolio and purchase securities whose maturities will help smooth the cash flow pattern.

A third input is an assessment of information on external factors expected to prevail over the planning horizon. These include the present and likely future course of the economy, the political climate, and the social conditions. These factors have an impact on the estimates of the risk and return of investment alternatives, which, in turn, affect the choice of securities.

The first and second pieces of these data are internally generated. The third is frequently obtained from outside sources, such as investment advisory firms, investment bankers, or brokerage firms.

Formulating Expectations and Strategies

Investment Strategies

After determining the investment objectives, the cash flow forecast, and the available resources, the portfolio manager formulates strategies for investment in marketable securities. Some portfolio managers adopt a *passive strategy*, such as placing any excess cash at the end of the day in a sweep account, which earns interest on a daily basis. Such a strategy might be appropriate for a firm with a small portfolio, a high degree of uncertainty regarding cash flows, or a paucity of resources for managing the portfolio. Other managers adopt a more *active strategy*. A portfolio manager for a firm with an accurate daily cash flow forecast might purchase or sell securities with specific maturities to smooth daily cash flows. A manager for a firm with a forecast of rates and a willingness to take a moderate degree of risk might try to take advantage of a perceived temporary disequilibrium in returns of securities with different maturities or different degrees of risk. A manager with sufficient resources might actively use swaps or financial futures to modify the portfolio risk–return characteristics.[3]

Market Expectations

Information on the external environment is used by the portfolio manager to form expectations about the risk and return of investment alternatives. The size

---

[2] See Chapter 18 for a discussion of the techniques that can be used for cash flow forecasting.

[3] The use of swaps and financial futures to hedge the risk of the portfolio is covered in Chapter 11.

of the staff and the commitment of resources determine whether this assessment can be done internally. A part-time portfolio manager with no staff has to rely on externally prepared, and likely publicly available, risk assessments and forecasts of future returns from alternative investments.

Investment Policy Statement

The development of the investment strategy should culminate in a written statement of the firm's investment policies and procedures. The policy should spell out the objectives of the investment, the types of securities and maturities considered, the dealers or brokers used, and the dollar amount or relative concentration allowed by security type or maturity. In addition to providing a portfolio manager with a clear guide, a written policy serves as a means of communicating policy to top management and to subordinates, to whom some of the investment decisions may be delegated. This is particularly important in a large, multi-division firm with more than one portfolio investment activity or with several outside brokers and money managers.

Constructing and Monitoring the Portfolio

Size of the Portfolio

One of the critical decisions of a portfolio manager is the amount of securities held. This decision is inextricably linked to the decision on how much cash to hold for liquidity purposes and the accuracy of the cash flow forecast.

Liquidity

An asset is said to be *liquid* if it can be easily and quickly converted into cash without substantial transactions costs or loss in value. Since a firm is a collection of assets, it is tempting to define the liquidity of a firm as the sum of the liquidities of its assets. However, a manager who views the liquidity of a firm in the context of quickly selling assets is not likely to see a long future for the company or for his job. Viewed as a going concern, a firm is liquid if it is able to meet its cash obligations when they are due.

MEASURES OF LIQUIDITY. A traditional approach to measuring and managing liquidity is to use an asset-liability ratio, such as the current ratio (current assets divided by current liabilities) or the quick ratio (current assets less inventory and prepaid expenses divided by current liabilities). Occasionally, creditors even specify certain levels of these ratios to be maintained to keep the credit arrangement in force.

However, if a going concern approach is used to define liquidity, it should also be used to measure liquidity. There are several problems with balance sheet ratio measures that are not consistent with a going concern approach. (1) They do not take into account the true liquidity of the assets. A firm that has trouble meeting its liabilities is unlikely to be able to convert accounts receivable or inventory into cash quickly without loss of value. (2) They do not consider the cash flow–generating capability of the operations. Most firms generate cash to pay bills from their ongoing operations. (3) They are not adaptable to a time horizon other than 1 year. (4) They ignore the existence of any unused credit capacity, such as stretching accounts payable, or an additional take-down on a line of credit.

An illustration of the inefficiency of the use of the current or quick ratio to measure liquidity is given in Exhibit 10.1. We can see that the action taken to pay off 25 accounts payable increases both the current ratio and the quick ratio but does not really enhance the liquidity.

An efficient measure of liquidity should do the following: (1) capture all of the liquid resources of the firm, (2) exclude all items that are not liquid resources, (3) incorporate any cash flow from operations, (4) relate the preceding to the probability of meeting liabilities, and (5) be adaptable to different time horizons. Inventory and accounts receivable are not immediately available

Exhibit 10.1 One Problem with Traditional Liquidity Meaures

Indy Glass Works has a bank loan with a requirement that a current ratio of 2.0 and a quick ratio of 1.25 be maintained at the close of each quarter. It is 4:30 P.M. on September 30 and the manager has just received the preliminary statement of the ending balance sheet, a portion of which is as follows (all figures are in millions):

Current Assets		**Current Liabilities**	
Cash	30	Accounts payable	50
Marketable securities	20	Bank loan	75
Accounts receivable	100	Accrued expenses	10
Inventory	75		125
Total	225		

$$\text{Current ratio} = \frac{225}{125} = 1.8 \qquad \text{Quick ratio} = \frac{150}{125} = 1.2$$

The manager realizes that the company will be in default on the loan covenants if he doesn't do something in the next half hour. He quickly gets out the checkbook, and writes and mails checks to suppliers for 25. The final closing balance sheet for September 30 now shows the following:

Current Assets		**Current Liabilities**	
Cash	5	Accounts payable	25
Marketable securities	20	Bank loan	75
Accounts receivable	100	Accrued expenses	10
Inventory	75		100
Total	200		

$$\text{Current ratio} = \frac{200}{100} = 2.0 \qquad \text{Quick ratio} = \frac{125}{100} = 1.25$$

Although the ratio measures of liquidity have been improved, one can hardly argue that the liquidity of the firm has been increased. Certainly, the bank is not in a better position than it would have been if the "window dressing" had not occurred.

(readily converted into cash) to the firm, except as part of the operating cycle; consequently, they should not be included as liquid resources. Only cash and marketable securities are truly liquid. Any unused credit capacity represents an almost immediately available source of cash to meet obligations and should be counted as liquid resources. Added to (subtracted from) these resources should be the anticipated net cash inflow (outflow) during the time horizon of the analysis. The final element in the measure of liquidity is uncertainty about the net cash flow during the time horizon. Emery and Cogger have incorporated these elements in a measure they call *lambda*.[4] Lambda is expressed as follows:

$$\text{Lambda} = \frac{LR + NCF}{UNCF}, \tag{10.1}$$

where LR = liquid resources
            NCF = net cash flow anticipated during the horizon of the analysis
            $UNCF$ = uncertainty of the net cash flow

Lambda can be thought of as the expected liquid resource position at the end of the horizon divided by the uncertainty of the cash flow during the period. If the distribution of cash flows approximates a normal distribution and the standard deviation is used as the measure of uncertainty, lambda is the number of standard deviations that the expected liquid resource position is above zero.

Indy Glass Works has liquid asset resources of 50. Assume that there is available an unused bank credit line of 150. This gives total liquid resources of 200. Assume that the horizon is 1 month, the expected cash flow during the next month is a positive 75, and the standard deviation of the monthly cash flow is 50. Thus,

$$\text{Lambda} = \frac{(50 + 150) + 75}{140} = \frac{275}{140} = 1.96.$$

If we assume that the cash flow distribution for Indy Glass Works is approximately normal, the lambda value corresponds to the z value common to statistical hypothesis testing. A z value for a one-tailed statistical test of 1.96 means that the probability that the net cash position will be less than zero at the end of the period is approximately 2.5%.[5]

While there are difficulties in estimating some of these components, particularly for someone outside a firm, this approach to measuring liquidity is superior to a ratio of balance sheet items. Empirical tests have found a statistically significant relationship between lambda and commercial paper ratings,

---

[4] For the development of this measure of liquidity, see Emery, Gary W. and Kenneth O. Cogger, "The Measurement of Liquidity," *Journal of Accounting Research,*, (Autumn 1982), pp. 290-303

[5] See, for example, Johnston, J. *Econometric Methods*, 2nd ed., New York: McGraw-Hill, 1972.

while no such relationship has been found between the ratings and liquidity ratios such as the current ratio or the quick ratio.[6]

Lambda can be used as a management tool to determine the amount of liquid resources to be maintained as follows. First, determine the probability of not being able to meet cash requirements (represented by lambda) that the firm is willing to accept during a specified time horizon. Next, estimate the expected net cash flow and the uncertainty of the cash flow for the horizon. Finally, adjust the amount of liquid resources (cash, marketable securities, or unused credit facility) to give the desired lambda value.

For example, assume that the treasurer of Indy Glass Works wants to reduce the probability of not having enough liquid resources to .5%. This can be accomplished by having a lambda value of 3. (Recall that the probability of being outside in either direction of a range of plus or minus three standard deviations is approximately 1%.) To have a lambda value of 3, the numerator would have to be increased to 420 by some combination of additional marketable securities or unused credit line in the amount of 145.

SIZE OF THE CASH BALANCE. As we have seen, both cash and marketable securities represent liquidity reserves for a firm. After establishing the total amount of reserves necessary for the desired level of liquidity, attention is focused on how to determine the split between cash and securities. Since the securities portfolio generates an explicit return, whereas the cash balance does not, the choice generally becomes one of establishing the minimum size of the cash balance and holding the remainder in marketable securities.

The question of why firms hold non-interest-bearing cash balances instead of interest-bearing securities has long been addressed by economists. Three classical reasons have been identified for holding cash: a transactions motive—to pay bills; a precautionary motive—to meet unforeseen cash needs; and a speculative motive—to take advantage of temporary opportunities, such as buying materials at an attractive price. Because short-term securities can be sold quickly and easily, and because most transactions between businesses are conducted on credit, the precautionary and speculative motives are not thought to have much of an impact on a firm's cash balance. Instead, the focus is on determining the size of the transactions cash balance.

CASH BALANCE MODELS. Two approaches to finding the optimal transactions balance have viewed cash as an inventory problem. The inventory of cash is replenished by inflows, either from operations or from the sale of securities, while the inventory is depleted by outflows, either to pay obligations or to purchase securities. The optimal cash balance is determined by a trade-off between the opportunity costs of holding cash and the transactions costs of buying or selling securities. A model proposed by Baumol and extended by

---

[6] Results of these tests can be found in Emery, Gary W. and Kenneth O. Cogger, "An Empirical Test of Alternative Liquidity Measures," Indiana University School of Business Working Paper (1983).

Beranek assumes a certain and continuous cash flow.[7] The solution is obtained by using an economic order quantity model to specify the size and frequency of the purchase or sale of securities. Miller and Orr also take an inventory approach but assume that the cash flows are completely random.[8] They use a control limit model to determine the upper and lower bounds on the cash balance and the amount of purchase or sale of securities.

A different approach to the determination of the level of the cash balance is taken by Stone.[9] As we saw in Chapter 4, firms hold cash balances to compensate commercial banks for services. For many large corporations, the balances needed to compensate banks determine the level of cash maintained. Stone shows that under this condition the objective becomes one of minimizing the transactions costs of buying and selling securities while maintaining the required balance. The model developed incorporates the cash forecast to maintain the balance between the upper and lower limits. The development of these three cash balance models is discussed in the appendix to this chapter.

The amount of funds to be invested in the short-term securities portfolio is a derivative of two other decisions: the amount of liquid assets required to achieve the desired level of liquidity and the size of the cash balance. Of course, the actual amount of securities may temporarily be above or below the desired level. Cash flows may differ from the forecast, or the firm may temporarily deviate from the desired level while awaiting the purchase of long-term assets or the completion of long-term financing.

Constructing the Portfolio

The portfolio manager is now ready to construct a portfolio that is consistent with the investment policy. Individual securities are chosen that contribute to the risk, return, and liquidity characteristics desired for the portfolio. Although a risk assessment is made for each security in the portfolio, it is also important to examine the overall risk–return characteristics of the portfolio in order to take advantage of any correlations among securities that can be used to reduce the overall portfolio risk.

Monitoring the Portfolio

Monitoring the portfolio requires an accurate, up-to-date data base that includes information on all securities in the portfolio. Confirmation letters, which may consist of a prepared form, are completed and filed for each transaction. These provide the basic record of the security purchased, the amount, the maturity, the date and time of the transaction, the name of the authorizing person, the dealer, and the delivery instructions. These data should

---

[7] Baumol, William J., "The Transactions Demand for Cash: An Inventory Theoretic Approach," *Quarterly Journal of Economics*, (November 1952) pp. 545–556, and Beranek, William *Analysis for Financial Decisions*, R.D. Irwin, Homewood, Ill.: (1963).

[8] Miller, Merton H. and Daniel Orr, "A Model for the Demand for Money by Firms." *Quarterly Journal of Economics* (August 1966) pp. 413–435.

[9] Stone, Bernell K., "The Use of Forecasts and Smoothing in Control-Limit Models for Cash Management," *Financial Management*, (Spring 1972) pp. 72–84.

be maintained in a form that facilitates the generation of regular summary reports that can be organized by type of security, maturity of security, dealer, and date of investment. Periodic reports on the portfolio profile allow monitoring of the characteristics of the portfolio, such as the maturity, the income generated, and the performance of particular brokers or advisors. A schedule of portfolio cash flows—from interest receipts, maturing securities, and planned purchases or sales—is prepared and communicated to the cash manager as an input to the cash flow forecasting process.

Reports of portfolio performance, including the cost of portfolio administration as well as the return on the portfolio, should be prepared periodically, at least quarterly and probably monthly for many firms. These reports provide a basis for assessing the performance of the portfolio manager. An evaluation of the manager's performance includes the types of securities, the average maturity, the risk of the portfolio, and current market conditions, in addition to the return generated. A useful benchmark for performance evaluation is the return available from an institutionally managed portfolio. The return generated by a money market mutual fund with a maturity similar to that of the portfolio can be a good benchmark and is readily found in financial publications.

Portfolio Revisions

From time to time, perhaps daily, it is necessary to revise the portfolio, usually because actual cash flows deviate from the forecast. Actual cash flow information is obtained from the daily cash position data compiled by the cash manager from daily balance reports from banks. The cash manager uses this cash position and any new information on future cash flows to revise the cash forecast. The more quickly the portfolio manager receives this information, the more effective he or she is in making portfolio revisions to best achieve the investment objectives. The time of day when information is received is critical, since the money markets are inactive by late morning. The portfolio manager forced to buy or sell securities in the afternoon is likely to find limited options and an absence of price shopping for the best deal.

An important factor in portfolio revision is the transactions costs for buying or selling securities to meet cash flow needs or to reinvest funds from maturing securities. Portfolio revisions frequently involve a tradeoff between yield and transactions costs. The following process considers the impact of transactions costs on portfolio revision with a strategy of maturities timed to smooth cash flows.

If it is necessary to sell a security currently in the portfolio to meet cash flow needs, tentatively select for sale the security with the lowest yield. Check to see if another security matures on a day that has a positive cash flow forecast, and whose sale would eliminate an additional transactions cost. If the combined effect of the loss of income and reduced transactions costs on the portfolio income is less than from the first security, sell the second security; otherwise, sell the first security. Similarly, when a purchase is contemplated, a security whose maturity date coincides with a large cash outflow may reduce transactions costs by eliminating the need to sell a security from the portfolio and may give better results than a security with a different maturity but a higher yield.

An example for Indy Glass Works may help illustrate this process. It is April 1, a forecasted receipt did not arrive, and the treasurer has determined that the bank account will be overdrawn by approximately $100,000 if no action is taken. The treasurer has two securities that could be sold to generate the needed cash: a T-bill maturing on April 7 with a yield of 6.75% to maturity and a CD maturing on April 14 with a yield of 7.25% to maturity. Without considering transactions costs or cash flow patterns, the temptation is to sell the T-bill since it is yielding 50 basis points less than the CD. However, the T-bill was purchased with a maturity of April 7 because of a payroll disbursement on that day. If it is sold on April 1, the CD will have to be sold on April 7 to cover this disbursement.

Thus, the alternatives are (1) to sell the T-bill on April 1, which requires selling the CD on April 7, or (2) to sell the CD on April 1 and leave the maturing T-bill on April 7 to fund the payroll disbursement. By selling the T-bill, the company picks up an additional 50 basis points for the week but incurs a second transactions cost from selling the CD on April 7. With either alternative, the company has a reduced investment from April 7 to April 14. The extra return of 50 basis points for 7 days on a $100,000 security is approximately $9.60. Since this is certainly less than the extra transactions cost on a $100,000 security, the CD should be sold, not the T-bill.

Security Characteristics

Many of the security characteristics of the short-term portfolio, such as liquidity, marketability, maturity, yield, risk, and taxability, were discussed in Chapter 9. We now take a more in-depth look at two of these characteristics: effective yield from holding a security and interest rate risk.

Calculating Security Returns

Effective Yield
There are several ways to calculate the yield, or return, on a security. To make a proper comparison of alternative investments, it is necessary to calculate the yield on a consistent basis. Factors affecting the yield calculation include the time period for which the interest is stated, the length of the compounding period, and whether the security is a coupon or a discount instrument.

TIME PERIOD. As we saw in Chapter 9, interest for some securities is stated on a 360-day year and for others on a 365-day year (366 days in leap year). A common question is, "Why do some securities state interest on a 360-day year and others on a 365-day year?". There is undoubtedly some good historical reason for the use of 360 days in the stated rates and the calculation of prices, such as the fact that in the days before the use of portable electronic calculators it was much easier to perform monthly and quarterly calculations with a number that was evenly divisible by 12. However it is more satisfying to respond, in the words of Tevia in *Fiddler on the Roof*, "Its tradition!" Regardless of the historical reason, a standard has to be adopted and an adjustment made in comparing the yields for different securities.

Holding Period Yield

The *holding period yield (HPY)*, or return, for a security is calculated by dividing the difference between the cash flow received at the end of the holding period and the initial investment, by the initial investment.

$$HPY = \frac{ECF - Invest.}{Invest.} = \frac{ECF}{Invest.} - 1, \qquad (10.2)$$

where HPY = holding period yield
ECF = total end-of-period cash flow
$Invest.$ = the initial cash investment in the security

Suppose the treasurer of Indy Glass Works has a security with a face value of $1,000,000 that pays $15,000 in interest plus the face value at the end of 60 days. If she purchases this security for $1,002,000 and holds it for the full 60 days, she will have the following holding period yield:

$$HPY = \frac{\$1,015,000}{\$1,002,000} - 1 = 0.012974 = 1.2974\%.$$

COMPOUNDING PERIOD. Although the holding period yield is good for identifying the benefits from investing in an individual security, holding periods vary by the type of security held, the purpose for holding the security, and economic conditions at the time. Comparisons of the holding period yields for alternative securities with different maturities or situations may not be meaningful.

One of the factors for which an adjustment should be made is the compounding period. Since the security held by Indy Glass has no cash flow prior to maturity, it is not possible to reinvest any cash before the 60 days are up. It is, therefore, tempting to say that the compounding period is 60 days. However, if the treasurer invested in a sequence of two 30-day securities, would the appropriate compounding period be 30 days? Again, consistency is required so that valid comparisons can be made across securities. The usual convention adopted in dealing with short-term investments is to use simple interest (no compounding at all) for any investments of less than 1 year and to use annual compounding for those with more than 1 year to maturity.

Bond Equivalent Yield

A frequently used yield calculation that adopts this compounding convention is the *bond equivalent yield (BEY)*. It is a simple interest yield calculation expressed on a 365-day year. To convert from a holding period yield to a bond equivalent yield, multiply the holding period return by the number of holding periods in a 365-day year:

$$BEY = HPY \times \frac{365}{n}, \tag{10.3}$$

where BEY = the bond equivalent yield
           n = the number of days in the holding period.

In our previous example, the bond equivalent yield would be

$$BEY = HPY \times \frac{365}{60} = 1.2974\% \times \frac{365}{60} = 7.893\%.$$

This yield can be compared with the bond equivalent yield from other securities with different terms.

Yield on Discount Securities

PRICING OF DISCOUNT SECURITIES. A discount security is sold at a price below face value and pays the face value at maturity. The return is earned from price appreciation. The dollar amount of the discount is calculated by multiplying the *discount quote* or *discount yield* by the fraction of the year remaining until maturity by the face value. The rate quote on a discount instrument is the discount rate that is used in calculating the dollar discount, and not the yield earned from holding the security. Since most discount securities quote the interest on a 360-day year, the dollar discount (D) is calculated as follows:

$$D = \frac{F(d \times t)}{360}, \tag{10.4}$$

where F = the face value,
           d = the discount rate
           t = the days remaining until maturity

The price (P) is calculated as follows:

$$P = F - D = F\left[\frac{1 - (d \times t)}{360}\right]. \tag{10.5}$$

The treasurer of Indy Glass Works is considering purchasing a T-bill with a $1,000,000 face value, a remaining maturity of 45 days, and a discount rate quote of 7.25%. The dollar discount and price are

$$D = \frac{F(d \times t)}{360} = \frac{\$1,000,000(0.725 \times 45)}{360}$$
$$= \$9,062.5$$

and

$$P = \$1,000,000 - \$9,062.5 = \$990,937.5.$$

YIELD OF A DISCOUNT SECURITY. The investment in a discount security is less than the face value of the security. It should be apparent that the effective yield, the dollar discount divided by the investment, is higher than the discount quote, the dollar discount divided by the face value.

For the T-bill being considered by the treasurer of Indy Glass Works, the bond equivalent yield is

$$BEY = \left(\frac{\$1,000,000}{\$990,037.5} - 1 \right) \times \frac{365}{45} = .07418 \qquad \text{or} \qquad 7.418\%.$$

A potential point of confusion about when to use 360 or 365 days can be avoided by remembering the following. The interest is stated on a 360-day year; therefore, use a 360-day year to calculate the amount of the discount and the purchase price. The bond equivalent yield is defined on a 365-day year; therefore, use 365 when calculating this yield. Although we used a T-bill in this example, the calculation of the bond equivalent yield for any other discount instrument (commercial paper, banker's acceptance, etc.) with interest stated on a 360-day year is done the same way. If the interest is stated on a 365-day year for a discount instrument, the only change is to use 365 in the calculation of the dollar discount. Since there is no coupon interest payment, the original date of issue or maturity does not matter for a discount security; only the remaining time to maturity is important.

Yield on Coupon Bearing Securities

PRICING OF COUPON SECURITIES. A coupon-bearing security pays interest, either at maturity or periodically over the life of the security, plus the face value at maturity. For most securities with an original maturity of less than 1 year, the interest is paid only at maturity.[10] Since the dollar interest payment depends upon the original maturity, both the original maturity and the remaining term to maturity must be known before the effective yield can be calculated.

The price of a coupon-bearing security may be stated in two ways: a *yield quote* or a *price quote*. The yield quote represents the rate that is used in determining the total purchase price. This total purchase price is the present

---

[10] The calculation of the yield on a security with multiple coupon payments becomes quite complex because of the implications of compounding. We restrict our yield calculations to those with a single-coupon payment at maturity. The interested reader is referred to the treatment of the calculation of the effective yield for multiple-coupon instruments in Stigum, Marcia, *The Money Market: Myth, Reality, and Practice*, 2nd ed., Dow-Jones Irwin, New York, (1983).

value of the future cash flows calculated at the quoted rate. The formula for this price is

$$P = F\left[\frac{1 + (c \times m)/360}{1 + (i \times t)/360}\right] \qquad (10.6)$$

where $c =$ the coupon rate
$m =$ the original maturity
$i =$ the rate quote

The treasurer of Indy Glass Works is considering buying a $500,000 face value CD issued by the National Bank of Detroit (NBD). The CD was originally issued 30 days ago, with a maturity of 90 days and a coupon rate of 9%. The current yield quote on the CD is 8.25%. The total purchase price for the CD is

$$P = \frac{\$500,000[1 + (.09 \times 90/360)]}{1 + (.0825 \times 60/360)}$$

$$= \frac{\$511,250}{1.01375} = \$504,315.66.$$

The numerator represents both the principal, $500,000, and the interest, $11,250, received at maturity. Since interest on CDs is quoted on a 360-day year, the interest to be received is calculated by multiplying the face value by the interest rate times the original maturity divided by 360. It is the original maturity that determines the amount of interest paid at maturity, not the remaining time to maturity. The present value calculation takes into account both the current rate quote, 8.25%, and the remaining time to maturity. This calculation is based on an actual number of days left to maturity, but on a 360-day year.[11] As with discount securities, if the interest was stated on a 365-day year rather than a 360-day year, the calculation would be modified by using 365 rather then 360 in the formula.

YIELD TO MATURITY. The yield to maturity on the security is calculated by finding the bond equivalent yield on the CD.

$$BEY = \left(\frac{\$511,250}{\$504,315.66} - 1\right) \times \frac{365}{60} = .08365 \qquad or \qquad 8.365\%.$$

This is larger than the 8.25% rate quote because the rate quote is stated on a 360-day year, whereas the bond equivalent yield is stated on a 365-day year. The clever reader has already noted that we can obtain the bond equivalent yield on a coupon-bearing security by simply multiplying the yield quote by the ratio of 365/360 for differences in the length of year being used.

---

[11] The rate is multiplied by the fraction of the year in the denominator rather than being raised to a power because we are using simple interest. Refer to Chapter 2 for a discussion of the practical differences between the use of simple interest and compound interest for present value calculations in short-term finance.

Yield on a Security Not Held to Maturity. What yield is realized by the original investor, the one who bought the CD when it was issued and sold it after 30 days? CDs are usually sold at face value at issue, so the original investor paid $500,000 for the security. He sold it for $504,315.66. The annualized bond equivalent yield for the original investor is

$$BEY = \left(\frac{504,315,66}{500,000} - 1 \right) \times \frac{365}{30} = .1050 = 10.50\%.$$

Price Quote. Sometimes the offer for a security is made by quoting the price instead of the yield. For a coupon-bearing security, the price quote does not include any interest that has accrued to previous owners of the security. This quote is comparable to that of most long-term bonds.

Assume that the treasurer for Indy Glass Works obtains a price quote for the CD of $500,565.66. To this she has to add the accrued interest to determine the total purchase price, that is, the amount of cash that changes hands at the purchase. The accrued interest (AI) is found as follows:

$$AI = \left[\frac{F(c \times m)}{360} \right] \left[\frac{(m - t)}{m} \right] = F \frac{[c(m - t)]}{360}. \tag{10.7}$$

For the CD in question the accrued interest is

$$AI = \frac{\$500,000(.09 \times 30)}{360} = \$3,750.$$

The total amount of cash required to purchase the security (the total purchase price) is

$$P = AI + \text{price quote} \tag{10.8}$$
$$= \$3,750 + \$500,565.66 = \$504,315.66.$$

Thus, the sum of the price quote and the accrued interest is equal to the present value of the cash flow at maturity. To determine the price quote for a coupon-bearing security, the preceding process is reversed—accrued interest is subtracted from the present value of the cash flow.

Interest Rate Risk

Interest rate risk arises from the possibility that returns over some time horizon will be different than anticipated because of a change in interest rates during the period. Interest rate risk can affect a security portfolio under two circumstances. (1) The maturity of a security is less than the time horizon. In this case, proceeds from the maturing security have to be reinvested for the remainder of the period at a rate that is currently unknown. A numerical example of this dimension of interest rate risk is given in Table 10.1A. (2) The maturity of the security is longer than the time horizon. In this case, the security has to be sold at the end of the period at an unknown price, which will

Table 10.1 Numerical Examples of Interest Rate Risk

A. Maturity Shorter Than the Time Horizon

Time horizon	90 days	
Type of security	Discount	
Maturity	45 days	
Current rate	8%	
Initial price	.99 times face value	
Rate on day 45	7%	9%
Value on day 90	1.00875	1.01125
BEY	7.68%	8.71%

B. Maturity Longer Than the Time Horizon

Time horizon	90 days	
Type of security	Discount	
Maturity	180 days	
Current rate	8%	
Initial price	.96 times the face value	
Rate on day 90	7%	9%
Value on day 90	.9825	.9775
BEY	9.50%	7.39%

depend upon the interest rates prevailing at that time. A numerical example of this component of interest rate risk is given in Table 10.1B.

Interest rate risk can be avoided by matching investment maturity with the investment time horizon. Then the cash flow from the security at the end of the desired time period, and therefore the realized yield, are known when the investment is made.[12] It should be apparent that interest rate risk cannot be eliminated if the security is a coupon-bearing bond that pays interest prior to maturity. In this case, the interest payments would have to be reinvested at a rate that is unknown when the original investment is made.

_____ Term Structure of Interest Rates _____

In Chapter 9 we briefly discussed the *term structure of interest rates*—the relationship between the maturity of a security and its yield. This relationship embodies several factors that are important in establishing an investment strategy and is particularly relevant for active portfolio management. Economists have devoted considerable attention to the topic and have developed three theories related to this concept: pure expectations theory, liquidity preference theory, and market segmentations theory. Each of these theories has unique strengths and weaknesses in trying to explain the relationship between rates and maturities.

---

[12] This assumes that there is no default risk, that is, no uncertainty about the contract terms being met.

Pure Expectations Theory

Pure expectations theory (PET) can be thought of as the perfect markets version of the relationship between interest rates and maturities. Assume that the rates shown in Table 10.2 are observed for discount government securities. [13] Proponents of PET argue that the expected yield for a given time period should be the same regardless of the sequence of securities held. An investment in a 2-year security generates a yield of 8% per year, compounded annually. If an investment is made in a sequence of two 1-year securities, the expected yield for the 2-year period is calculated by taking 1 plus 7% for the first year times 1 plus the expected return on a 1-year security for the second year.

If the yield on a 2-year security is greater than expected on a sequence of two 1-year securities, the 2-year security is preferred to the two 1-year securities. The cumulative effect of all investment decisions drives the price up and the yield down on the 2-year security. This preference for the 2-year security continues until the yield is expected to be the same for both investments. The same logic is applied to a situation where the expected yield is greater on the sequence of two 1-year securities.

The requirement that the expected return be the same regardless of the sequence of the investments imposes a particular pattern on the *term structure of interest rates*. If PET applies, we have

$$(1 + {}_1r_1)(1 + {}_2r_1) = (1 + {}_1R_2)^2, \tag{10.9}$$

where ${}_1r_1$ = the known return on the 1-year security in period 1
${}_2r_1$ = the expected return on the 1-year security in period 2
${}_1R_2$ = the two-period, annually compounded, known return on the 2-year security.

For the securities in Table 10.2, we have

$$(1.07)(1 + {}_2r_1) = (1.08)^2$$
$${}_2r_1 = 9.009\%.$$

Table 10.2 Interest Rates
on Different Maturity Securities

Maturity (Years)	Rate (%)
1	7.0
2	8.0
3	8.5

[13] There are two important factors implicit in the choice of the types of securities usually used in term structure models. The use of government securities eliminates the need to consider any differences in default risk. The use of discount securities allows all of the funds from a security in a particular time period to be reinvested at the rate for the next period, without the complications arising from a difference in the timing of coupon and principal payments. The development of a term structure without these assumptions would follow along the same lines, although the discussion would be more complex.

This logic can be extended to more than two periods. We can find the expected return on a 1-year security in year 3 to be

$$(1.07)(1.09009)(1 +_3 r_1) = (1.085)^3$$
$$_3r_1 = 9.507\%.$$

We can also find the expected return on a 2-year security for an investment in year 2 as follows:

$$(1 +_1 r_1)(1 +_2 R_2)^2 = (1 +_1 R_3)^3 \qquad\qquad \textbf{(10.10)}$$
$$(1.07)(1 +_2 R_2)^2 = (1.085)^3$$
$$_2R_2 = 9.258\%.$$

If interest rates on 1-year securities are expected to increase, the yield curve is upward sloping. If rates are expected to decline, the curve is downward sloping. The yield curve is flat if there is no expected change in interest rates. These yield curve shapes are illustrated in Figure 10.2. Given the yield curve and any two expected rates, the expected rate for any other time period can be derived.

PET has implications for the investment decisions of portfolio managers. Since the expected return is the same for a given time period regardless of the specific investments made, the maturity of the securities in which the cash is invested is irrelevant. If the treasurer has a cash flow commitment of $100,000 in 2 years and she wants to invest today, she would need $100,000/(1.07)(1.09009) = $85,734 if she invested in two 1-year securities and $100,000/(1.08)^2 = $85,734 if she invested in the 2-year security. Alternatively, she could invest in a 3-year security with a face value of $109,507, which will sell for $109,507/(1.085)^3 = $85,734 today and can be sold for $109,507/(1.09507) = $100,000 at the end of year 2. Of course, this assumes that transactions costs are the same for the two strategies.

Liquidity Preference Theory

Proponents of the *liquidity preference theory (LPT)* argue that investors are not indifferent to the maturity of securities; portfolio managers are interested in liquidity as well as yield. Because a 2-year security is less liquid than a sequence of 1-year securities, portfolio managers invest in 2-year securities only if the expected return is higher than in a sequence of 1-year securities.

Using our previous notation, the relationship between rates under the LPT is

$$(1 +_1 r_1)(1 +_2 r_1 + l_1) = (1 +_1 R_2)^2, \qquad\qquad \textbf{(10.11)}$$

where l_1 is the premium (extra expected return) required for an investor to purchase a 2-year security and forego liquidity instead of purchasing a sequence of two 1-year securities. While there may be a premium for each additional

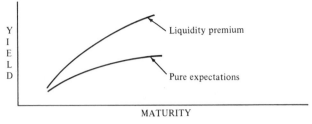

A. Rates expected to increase

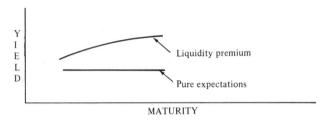

B. Rates not expected to change

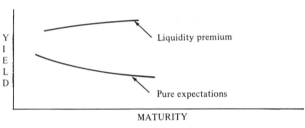

C. Rates expected to decrease

Figure 10.2 Yield Curve Shape Under Different Expectations. (Continued on next page.)

year of maturity, the premium is expected to decline with increases in maturity. The loss of liquidity from investing in a 10-year security instead of a 9-year security is small compared to the loss of liquidity from investing in a 2-year security instead of a 1-year security, so the liquidity premium for year 10 is small compared to that for year 2.

The existence of a liquidity premium creates an upward bias in the slope of the yield curve. Even if rates are expected to fall in the future, the slope of the yield curve could still be upward if the expected decline in rates is less than the liquidity premiums. Only if rates are expected to decline sharply in the future will the yield curve have a downward slope. The yield curves under these different expectations are shown in Figure 10.2.

Market Segmentation Theory

Both PET and LPT require portfolio managers to shift between different maturities, depending upon relative returns and expectations of future rates. The *market segmentation theory (MST)* assumes that both suppliers and purchasers of securities have a range of preferred maturity habitats. A portfolio manager of a manufacturing firm prefers to invest in short-term securities because of the uncertainty of the firm's short-term cash flow fluctuations. A portfolio manager of a life insurance company, on the other hand, prefers to invest in long-term securities based on the actuarial expectations of the distribution of benefits. On the supply side, some issuers, such as consumer finance companies, prefer to issue short-term securities, while other issuers prefer long-term securities.

Under MST, purchasers and issuers of securities are not tempted by attractive yields of securities with other maturities to leave their preferred habitats. The shape of the yield curve thus depends upon the relative supply of and demand for securities in each of the maturity segments, and not on expectations of future rates.

Implications of Different Theories

Under either PET or LPT, the shape of the yield curve provides some information about the expected direction of interest rates. This can be used by a portfolio manager in assessing future market conditions and deciding on the maturity of the securities to be purchased. An upward-sloping yield curve (depending upon the existence and amount of any liquidity premium) may be a signal that rates are expected to rise in the future. Since the purchase of long-term securities results in acceptance of both interest rate and liquidity risks, the portfolio manager is willing to invest long only if the rate is high enough to compensate for the extra risk.

Riding the Yield Curve

The question of which yield curve theory is correct is also important to a portfolio manager because several active strategies are derived from the yield curve. One such strategy is to *ride the yield curve*. The basis for this strategy is that there is an upward bias to the shape of the yield curve, that is, LPT holds. To ride the yield curve, a portfolio manager invests in a security with a maturity longer than the investment horizon and "rides it down the yield curve" as the maturity approaches.

This strategy can be illustrated by a numerical example. Assume that the treasurer of Indy Glass Works has funds available for 90 days. She is considering investing in a 90-day T-bill at a rate quote of 7.0% or in a 180-day T-bill at a rate quote of 7.25%, which she will sell at the end of 90 days. The 180-day T-bill will be a 90-day T-bill at the end of 90 days. If the shape and level of the yield curve do not change, it will then sell at a rate quote of 7.0%.

From the data presented in Table 10.3.A, the investment in a 90-day T-bill results in an effective yield of 7.22%, whereas riding the yield curve results in a yield of 7.89%. The manager has increased her yield by 67 basis points by riding the yield curve. Of course, we know that she has accepted some interest rate risk by investing in a 180-day instead of a 90-day security, and it is up to her to decide if the increased yield is enough to compensate for the increased risk.

Although the idea of riding the yield curve sounds like a sure thing, there are a couple of potential problems. First, the example presented ignores transactions costs. A transactions cost is incurred in the purchase of either the 90-day or the 180-day security. A second transactions cost is incurred in selling the 180-day security at the end of 90 days, which is avoided if the 90-day security is purchased.[14] Second, the example assumes that the yield curve does not change over the 90 days. Suppose the yield curve shifts upward so that at the end of the period the 90-day rate is 7.75% instead of 7.0%. As shown in Table

Table 10.3 Example of Riding the Yield Curve

A. Yield Curve Does Not Change

	Alternative A: 90 Day T-bill	**Alternative B: 180 Day T-bill**
Rate quote:	7.0%	7.25%
Face value:	$1,000,000	$1,000,000
Purchase price:	$982,500	$963,750
Price in 90 days: (Yield quote 7.0%)	$1,000,000	$982,500
Bond equivalent yield:	7.22%	7.89%

B. Yield Curve Shifts Upward

For Alternative B if 90 day quote is 7.75%

Price in 90 days:	$90,625
Bond equivalent yield:	7.10%

[14] Osteryoung, Jerome S., Gordon S. Roberts, and Daniel E. McCarty, "Riding the Yield Curve—A Useful Technique for Short-Term Investment of Idle Funds in Treasury Bills?", Reading 15 in *Readings on the Management of Working Capital*, 2nd ed., Keith V. Smith, (ed.), West, St Paul, Minn. (1980), have investigated the benefits of using real data and including transactions costs. They conclude that transactions costs are more than the extra yield generated by riding the yield curve in all except the longest maturity category considered. However, their empirical analysis was conducted at a time of generally rising interest rates, so they probably captured both the effect of transactions costs and an increase in interest rates.

10.3.B, the security is sold at a price of $980,625 and the yield for the 90-day period is only 7.10%. Thus, the preferred alternative in this case is to purchase the 90-day security. Since the selling price at the end of the holding period cannot be known for a security with a maturity greater than the holding period, riding the yield curve is a riskier strategy. Simply earning a higher return from this strategy is not sufficient; the return must be sufficient to compensate for the greater risk.

Tax Based Strategies

Tax Exempt Securities

As mentioned in Chapter 9, some money market securities are exempt from federal taxes. A correct comparison of returns from taxable and tax-exempt securities is made on an after-tax basis. The treasurer of Indy Glass Works is considering the purchase of either $1,000,000 worth of commercial paper issued by the Midwest Motor Corporation at a rate of 7.25% or a $1,000,000 5.75% coupon note to be issued at par by Metropolis County, which is exempt from federal taxes. Both securities have a maturity of 60 days. Indy Glass Works has a marginal tax rate of 40%.

The purchase price for the commercial paper is

$$\text{Purchase price} = \$1,000,000\left[1 - .0725\left(\frac{60}{360}\right)\right] = \$987,917.$$

The before-tax bond equivalent yield from the commercial paper is as follows:

$$\text{Before-tax } BEY = \left(\frac{1,000,000}{987,917} - 1\right)\left(\frac{365}{60}\right) = 7.44\%.$$

The after-tax yield is found by multiplying the before-tax yield by (1 − tax rate), or

$$\text{After-tax } BEY = 7.44\%(1 - .4) = 4.46\%.$$

The yield from investment in the Metropolis County note does not have to be adjusted for taxes, since the interest is tax exempt. The after-tax bond equivalent yield is as follows:

$$\text{After-tax } BEY = \left[.0575\left(\frac{60}{360}\right)\right]\left(\frac{365}{60}\right) = 5.83\%.$$

If the risk of the two securities is comparable, the preferred investment is the Metropolis County note.

Buying the Dividend

Under specified conditions, dividends received on stock by corporations have an 80% tax exclusion; only 20% of the dividend is considered taxable income. One of the conditions is that the security must be held for a minimum of 46 days. The partially tax-exempt dividend is earned only by absorbing the price risk on the common stock for the 46 days.[15]

On March 10, the Midwest Motor Corporation announces that it will pay a common stock dividend of $1.25 per share on March 30 to holders of record of March 20. On March 19 the treasurer of Indy Glass Works buys 2,000 shares at a price of $95 per share, or a total of $190,000. On March 30 she receives a dividend payment of $2,500. Since taxes are incurred on only 20%, or $500 of the dividend, the after-tax receipt is $2,500 $-$ (.4)($500) $=$ $2,300. On May 4 she sells the stock at a price of $94.25 per share. Assuming that the capital loss of $.75 per share can be written off against ordinary income, the after-tax loss on the drop in share price is (.75)(2,000)(1 $-$ .4) $=$ $900. The net after-tax cash flow from the transaction is $2,300 $-$ $900 $=$ $1,400. The BEY for this 46 day investment is (1,400/190,000)(365/46) $=$ 5.85%.

This is an after-tax yield and is compared with the after-tax yield from investments with comparable risk.[16] A risk involved in this transaction is the unknown selling price of the stock at the end of the holding period. Part of this risk can be hedged through the use of interest rate futures and options, which are discussed in the next chapter.

Summary

The portfolio management process starts with gathering information about the objectives for investment, forecasted cash flows, and the external environment affecting security yields. These data are used to develop policies on the type, maturity, and riskiness of the securities that are to be considered. An important aspect of investment policies is determining the size and composition of the liquidity reserve to be maintained.

Money market securities are both discount and coupon-bearing, and interest is quoted on a either a 360-day or a 365-day year. The yield must be calculated in a consistent manner in order to compare the yield across securities properly. The bond equivalent yield, which is a simple interest yield on a 365-day year, is a commonly used yield measure.

---

[15] The conditions stated here were in effect for 1987. Check the current tax code for the current conditions.

[16] The difference in the timing of the cash flows can be treated on a present value basis. However, the timing of the tax cash flows complicates the present value treatment. We have chosen to ignore the timing issue here, in order to keep the calculations simple, and to focus on the before- and after-tax comparisons.

In addition to the return of the portfolio, the manager must be concerned with risk. The types of risks in marketable securities are: default risk, liquidity risk, and interest rate risk. Interest rate risk is influenced by the maturity of the security and the investment time horizon. The relationship between maturity and return is governed by the reaction of the market to securities of differing maturity. We discussed three theories of the relationship between the yield and maturity: pure expectations theory, liquidity preference theory, and market segmentation theory. Different portfolio strategies are appropriate, depending upon the relationship that holds and management's attitude toward risk.

Finally, we saw that due to differences in the tax treatment of different securities, it is necessary to compare investment alternatives on an after-tax basis.

Discussion Questions

1. Contrast the differences in the steps in the investment management process for a company operating a single department store with that for a multinational machine tool company.
2. Discuss how the approach to managing the short-term investment portfolio is affected by a shift from using a weekly cash forecast that is updated on a monthly basis to using a daily cash forecast that is updated on a weekly basis.
3. Why is it necessary to have a written investment policy? Is this more important for a large or a small firm?
4. Contrast the definition and measurement of liquidity of an asset with that of a firm.
5. What are the problems with trying to compare the liquidity of companies in different industries? How can you compensate for these problems?
6. What factors are important in deciding how much liquidity is necessary?
7. Contrast the way interest is earned on discount and coupon-bearing securities.
8. What is meant by the term structure of interest rates?
9. Of what value is the concept of term structure of interest rates in formulating expectations of future interest rates under the three different theories about this concept?
10. Why is the general movement in the level of interest rates important for a strategy of trying to ride the yield curve?
11. What risks are present in buying the dividend?

Problems

1. The treasurer of the Sais company is trying to determine the appropriate level of liquidity to maintain. The treasurer uses a time horizon of 1

month. He has determined that the average cash flow for a month is a positive (net inflow) $1,250,000. However, the company has a highly seasonal pattern of cash flows and the standard deviation of the cash flow is $3,500,000. The treasurer wants to provide a liquidity level that reduces the probability of being out of cash to less than 5%. Currently Sais has a total of $3,000,000 in cash and marketable securities. How much of an unused credit line should Sais carry?

2. Calculate the bond equivalent yield for a T-bill with 30 days to maturity that is quoted at 7.25%.

3. A 91-day T-bill with a face value of $1,000,000 was originally issued on June 15 at a quote of 6.67%. It is now August 15 and the quote is 7.45%.
   a. Calculate the price on June 15 and on August 15.
   b. Calculate the effective yield for an investor who bought the security on June 15 and sold it on August 15. Why is this different from the yield quote?
   c. Calculate the effective yield for an investor who purchases the security on August 15 and holds it until maturity.

4. First Chicago National Bank issued a $100,000 CD with a maturity of 180 days on September 1, with a coupon rate of 8%. You have held the security since issue, and it is now December 14. You have decided to sell the CD to buy your family some Christmas presents. You receive a quote of 9% from your broker.
   a. What is the total amount of money you expect to receive when you sell the CD (ignore transactions costs)?
   b. How much of the money in (a) represents accrued interest?
   c. What is the bond equivalent yield that you have received?
   d. What is the bond equivalent yield for the purchaser if she holds the security until maturity?
   e. Why are these yields different from the 8% and the 9% on the CD?

5. You have approximately, $1,000,000 to invest for 30 days and are considering (a) a T-bill with 30 days to maturity and a rate quote of 7.5% and (b) a CD from Wells Fargo Bank with a remaining maturity of 30 days, an original maturity of 60 days, a coupon of 7.75%, and current rate of 8%.
   a. If you are only interested in the effective yield, which security would you prefer?
   b. What other factors would affect your decision?

6. You have a CD issued by Bank One that has a coupon of 8.5%, a face value of $1,000,000, an original maturity of 180 days, and a remaining maturity of 90 days. You receive a rate quote of 8%.
   a. Calculate the price quote, the sale price less the accrued interest.
   b. You new assistant treasurer is confused about why the price quote is now less than $1,000,000 (the original price quote) when interest rates have dropped. Explain why this change does not violate the basic present value concepts of finance.

7. A banker's acceptance is offered at a quoted interest rate of 6%. The maturity is 180 days and the principal amount is $60,000.
   a. What is the purchase price?
   b. What is the yield to the purchaser?
   c. Plot the difference between the quoted rate on the acceptance and the yield versus maturity for maturities of 30, 60, 90, 120, 180, and 360 days.

8. You have some excess funds for the next 60 days. You are considering investing in a sequence of two 30-day T-bills or one 60-day T-bill. The current quote on a 30-day T-bill is 8.2%, while the quote on the 60-day T-bill is 8.85%. What would the effective rate have to be on the second 30-day T-bill to make you indifferent to the choice?

9. You have funds for 30 days. The quote on a 30-day T-bill is 7.35% and the quote on a 60-day T-bill is 7.65%. What is the minimum rate quote that you would have to receive in 30 days to make you favor the 60-day T-bill?

10. You are considering riding the yield curve as an investment strategy. The options you are considering are 90-day and 180-day T-bills. The 90-day bill is quoted at 6.5% and the 180-day bill is quoted at 7.25%. Evaluate the strategy if one-way transactions costs (to buy or to sell) average 0.25% and you expect the yield curve to maintain its current level and shape.

11. You have a marginal tax rate of 28% and are considering purchasing a T-bill with a face value of $100,000, a rate quote of 6.45%, and a maturity of 91 days. Calculate your before- and after-tax bond equivalent yields from holding this security.

12. Notes of the Crawford County Sanitation District, with a maturity of 180 days, have a 4.5% coupon and are exempt from federal taxes. A 180-day CD issued by the First Crawford National Bank has a 6.5% coupon. What marginal tax rate would make an investor indifferent to the two securities, assuming that they have the same risk?

13. The treasurer of JIT Inventory Consultants bought the dividend in Thompson Industries. The stock was purchased at a price of $25 per share, a dividend of $.42 per share was received, and the stock was sold after 46 days at a price of $24.75 per share. If JIT has a tax rate of 40%, what is the after-tax bond equivalent yield from this investment strategy?

14. The money manager of Lotus Blossom Restaurants is considering buying the dividend as an investment strategy. She is investigating the purchase of stock in the Dark Night Lighting Company, which has announced payment of a dividend of $.65 per share on June 15 to stockholders of record on June 5. On June 4 the stock is selling at a price of $43.25. Assume that Lotus Blossom has a marginal tax rate of 33% for both regular income and capital gains, losses can be fully written off against income, and the stock must be held for 46 days to receive an 80% dividend exclusion.
   a. Determine the minimum selling price of the Dark Night stock for Lotus Blossom to just break even.

b. What is the answer to (a) if transactions costs are $.50 per share?

c. If the money manager of Lotus Blossom has the alternative of investing in T-bills to earn an annualized bond equivalent return of 7%, what is the minimum price at which the stock must be sold? (Assume there are no transactions costs and no premium for risk.)

d. Assume that the money manager feels that a risk premium for buying the dividend of 200 basis points is appropriate and that transactions costs are as specified in (b). What is the minimum stock price at which the strategy is worthwhile?

Case: *Farmington Auto and Truck Sales Company*

Jim Waller is the treasurer of the Farmington Auto and Truck Sales Company (FATS). It is 8:30 A.M. on Monday, March 30, and Waller has just received the bank balance report, which shows a cash balance of $550,000. Waller wants to maintain a cash balance of $50,000 as a cushion against errors in cash flow estimates. He therefore feels that it is imperative to make an investment quickly in order to move the excess cash into marketable securities to earn a return.

He types CASHFORE on his computer terminal and the daily cash forecast for the next 4 weeks appears as follows (all figures are in thousands of dollars):

Month	March					April				
Day	M	T	W	R	F	M	T	W	R	F
Date	30	31	1	2	3	6	7	8	9	10
Cash flow	150	−20	15	−35	65	120	−45	−70	−250	60
Cum. CF	150	130	145	110	175	295	250	180	−70	−10

Month	April									
Day	M	T	W	R	F	M	T	W	R	F
Date	13	14	15	16	17	20	21	22	23	24
Cash flow	30	−75	45	−100	55	155	−30	10	−250	25
Cum. CF	20	−55	−10	−110	−55	100	70	80	−170	−145

Being conservative, the FATS top management has a policy of investing only in T-bills. Waller received the following ask quotes (the rate at which the broker will sell) on T-bills from the broker with whom he normally deals.

T-Bill Ask Quotes

Maturity Date	Discount Quote (%)
4–2	4.89
4–9	4.06
4–16	5.01
4–23	5.12
4–30	5.10
5–7	5.18
5–14	5.19
5–21	5.19
5–28	5.20

Waller is uncertain whether he should purchase securities with longer maturities to try to capture their higher yields. He recognizes that if he has to sell, he must pay an additional transactions cost. There are two types of transactions costs: (1) a fixed cost, which amounts to about $25 per transaction, regardless of its size, to cover paper work and a minimum charge from the broker, and (2) a variable cost, in which the broker receives compensation from the bid–ask spread. The broker quotes a different rate for purchase than for sale. Waller estimates that the average spread is about 4 basis points, with the bid quote being higher than the ask quote.

Waller assumes that he will buy or sell T-bills in increments of $10,000. There has been little movement in interest rates lately, so Waller is willing to assume that the yield curve will not shift over the next 4 weeks.

Determine the security transactions that FATS' Waller should plan to make over the next 4 weeks.

———————— Selected Readings ————————

EMERY, GARY W., and KENNETH O. COGGER, "The Measurement of Liquidity," *Journal of Accounting Research* (Autumn 1982), pp. 290–303.

EMERY, GARY W., and KENNETH O. COGGER, "An Empirical Test of Alternative Liquidity Measures," Indiana University School of Business Working Paper (1983).

FARRELL, CHRISTOPHER, and JEFFREY M. LADERMAN, "More Profits from Idle Corporate Cash," *Business Week* (May 12, 1986), pp. 85–86.

HICKS, J. R., *Value and Capital*, London: Oxford University Press, 1946.

JOHNSTON, J., *Econometric Methods*, 2nd ed., New York: McGraw-Hill, 1972.

MAIER, STEVEN F., and JAMES H. VANDER WEIDE, "A Decision Support System for Managing a Short-term Financial Instrument Portfolio," *Journal of Cash Management*, (March 1982), pp. 20–25.

MALKIEL, BURTON G., *The Term Structure of Interest Rates*, Princeton, N.J.: Princeton University Press, 1966.

OSTERYOUNG, JEROME S., GORDON S. ROBERTS, and DANIEL E. MCCARTY, "Riding the Yield Curve—A Useful Technique for Short-Term Investment of Idle Funds in Treasury Bills?", Reading 15 in *Readings on the Management of Working Capital*, 2nd ed., Keith V. Smith (ed.), St. Paul, Minn.: West, 1980.

STIGUM, MARCIA, *The Money Market: Myth, Reality, and Practice*, 2nd ed., New York: Dow-Jones Irwin, 1983.

VAN HORNE, JAMES C., *Financial Market Rates and Flows*, Englewood Cliffs, N.J.: Prentice-Hall, 1978.

Appendix: Determining the Size
of the Cash Balance

Baumol Model

In 1952 Baumol developed a model to determine the optimal level of transactions cash balances.[1] His model contains two assets: cash and marketable securities earning a rate of i per period. The marketable securities portfolio consists of uniform, infinitely divisible securities. The easiest way to visualize this portfolio is to assume that it is a money market mutual fund in which deposits or withdrawals can be made in $1 increments. There is both a fixed charge, b, and a variable charge, k times the amount of the transaction, for each transfer into or out of the securities portfolio.

The firm receives a known inflow of cash, T, at periodic intervals, t_n. Between cash inflows the firm has a continuous outflow of cash of T/t_n per day (see Figure 10.3). The firm invests an amount I at the beginning of each period, while retaining the remainder, R, as a cash balance. At fixed intervals the firm sells securities in the amount of C to replenish the cash balance.

The average cash balance will be $(T - I)/2$ during the initial subperiod and $C/2$ during each subsequent subperiod. The total opportunity cost for holding cash balances is

$$\left[\frac{T-I}{2}\right] i \left[\frac{(T-I)}{T}\right] + \left(\frac{C}{2}\right) i \left(\frac{I}{T}\right).$$

The firm has transactions costs of $(b + kI)$ for the initial investment in securities and $(b + kC)$ for each sale of securities. The total transactions costs are

$$(b + kI) + (b + kC)(I/C).$$

---

[1] The initial development of the model can be found in Baumol, William J., "The Transactions Demand for Cash: An Inventory Theoretic Approach," *Quarterly Journal of Economics* (November 1952), pp. 545–556.

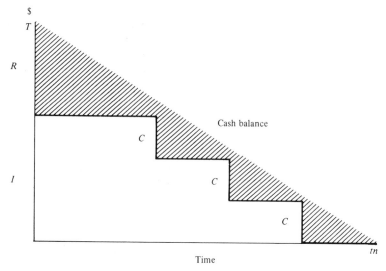

Figure 10.3 Cash Flow Pattern for the Baumol Model.

The optimal cash balance and the level of securities are found by taking the derivative of the sum of the costs, setting the derivative equal to zero, and solving the equation. The optimal amount of securities sold at each interval is

$$C = \sqrt{\frac{2bT}{i}}.$$

The optimal amount of the initial cash balance is

$$R = C + I\left[\frac{2k}{i}\right].$$

Rent-A-Pad is a rental management firm that manages a large number of rental apartments. They receive rent money at the beginning of each month in the amount of $500,000 and disburse the full amount in a continuous stream of cash flow payments for repairs, maintenance, utilities, and exorbitant salaries to the owners. Rent-A-Pad has funds invested in a money market account that pays interest at a rate of 8% per year. There are no variable costs associated with the transactions into or out of this account, but there are fixed costs for paper work, personnel time, and other factors, of $16.67 per transaction. The optimal amount of each transaction is

$$C = \sqrt{\frac{2(16.67)(500,000)}{.08/12}} = \$50,000.$$

Thus, Rent-A-Pad should invest $450,000 in the account at the beginning of the month and withdraw $50,000 every 3 days.

The cash flow assumptions of the Baumol model are rather simplistic and far from realistic for most firms. Adjustments could be made to include uncertainty in the flows. The cash flow sequence could be reversed, providing a fairly steady inflow with periodic outflows, which would represent a more typical pattern for most firms.

Miller and Orr Model

Miller and Orr use the same objective function as Baumol but have a different representation of the cash flows.[2] They assume that the cash flows are completely uncertain and follow a random walk. This means that the cash flow for any day is completely unknown, both in direction and in magnitude. It may follow a pattern similar to that shown in Figure 10.4. Miller and Orr assume that the variance of the cash flows is s^2, that there is a single security (or portfolio) that earns a return of i per period, and that there is only a fixed component to the transactions cost, b.

They use a control-limit model to decide when to purchase or sell securities. They establish an upper limit, h, and a lower limit, r. As long as the cash balance remains within these limits, there are no security transactions. When the upper (lower) limit is reached, securities are purchased (sold) in an amount sufficient to bring the cash balance to the return level, z. The cash balance and security transactions in this model are also shown in Figure 10.4.

For a zero-drift random walk (an equal probability of an increase or decrease), the optimal results occur when

$$z = [(3bs^2)/(4i)]^{1/3}$$

and when

$$h = 3z.$$

Assume that the Varicash Company is considering the use of the Miler and Orr model for managing their cash balance. They estimate that their cash flows follow a random walk distribution, with a variance of $25,000,000. The cash manager estimates that it costs $40 to buy or sell securities, regardless of the amount of the transaction. The current return on the marketable securities portfolio is 10%. Using this information, the manager estimates a return point of

$$z = [3(40)(25,000,000)/(4)(.1/365)]^{1/3} = \$13,989.$$

The upper limit is

$$h = 3(\$13,989) = \$41,967.$$

[2] Miller, Merton H. and Orr, Daniel, "A Model for the Demand for Money by Firms," *Quarterly Journal of Economics* (August 1966), pp. 413–435.

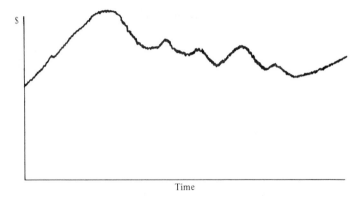

A. Cash balance with no security transactions

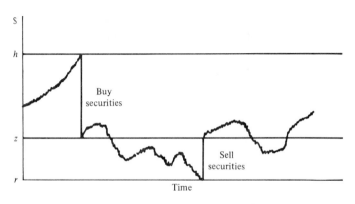

B. Cash balance with security transactions

Figure 10.4   Cash Flow Patterns for the Miller and Orr Model.

Stone Model

Stone approaches the determination of the cash balance with a different objective function.[3] He argues that the average cash balance is determined by the amount needed to compensate the bank for its services. The objective of managing the cash balance is to maintain the agreed-upon average balances while minimizing transactions costs. He represents the cash flows as consisting of a portion that can be forecast and a portion that is random. He uses a control-limit model, similar in spirit to that of Miller and Orr, but with two

[3] Sonte, Bernell K., "The Use of Forecasts and Smoothing in Control-Limit Models for Cash Management," *Financial Management* (Spring 1972), pp. 72–84.

Day	1	2	3	4	5	6	7	8	9	10	11	12	13	14
Begin cash	20	26	29	25	22	31	32	25	26	26	16	22	18	18
Cash flows:														
forecast	+7	+3	−5	−4	+8	−1	−5	0	+1	−14	+5	−3	+1	−4
Actual	+6	+3	−4	−3	+9	+1	−7	+1	0	−16	+6	−4	0	+2
End cash W/O trans.	26	29	25	22	31	32	25	26	26	10	22	18	18	16
Forecast end cash in 3 days	–	–	–	–	27	–	–	–	–	14	–	–	–	–
Trans.	–	–	–	–	–	–	–	–	–	+6	–	–	–	–
End cash	29	29	25	22	31	32	25	26	26	16	22	18	18	16

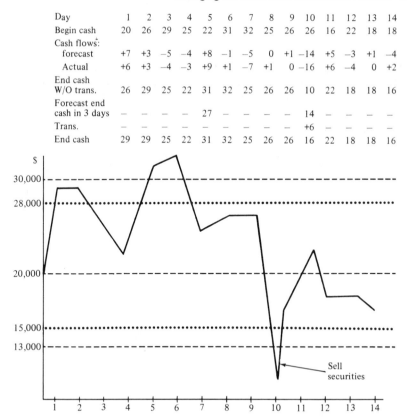

Figure 10.5 The Stone Model for Cash Balance Determination.

sets of control limits. The cash balance is allowed to fluctuate without security transactions as long as the outer control limits, h_1 and h_0 in Figure 10.5, are not reached.

When the outer limits are reached, the manager checks the forecast for the next k days before any security transactions are carried out. If the forecasted cash flow is expected to move inside the inner limits, $h_1 - d_1$ or $h_0 - d_0$, the balance is close enough to the desired target balance, TB, and there is no need to incur any transactions costs.

If, however, the forecasted ending balance is outside these inner limits, the ending balance is too far from the target balance. Securities are bought or sold in an amount that will result in the expected (forecasted) balance at the end of k days being equal to the target balance.

The Look-Ahead Telescope Company has forecasted cash flows for the next 2 weeks as shown in Figure 10.5. The manager has established outer limits of $30,000 and $13,000 and inner limits $2,000 from the outer limits, and starts the period with a cash balance equal to the target balance of $20,000. For the first 5 days the balance is within the outer limits, so no action is taken with regard to any securities transactions.

On day 6 the cash balance is $31,000, which exceeds the upper outer limit. The manager looks at the forecast for the next 3 days. He sees that the cash balance is expected to be $27,000 on day 9, which is inside the inner limits, so no action is taken. On day 10 the lower outer limit is exceeded by a balance of $10,000. From the forecast for the next 3 days, the cash balance is expected to be $14,000 on day 13. This is below the inner limit of $15,000. The manager sells $6,000 in securities to bring the forecasted cash balance up to the target of $20,000 on day 13.

11

Hedging Uncertain Cash Flows

On October 4, 1979, $1,000,000,000 worth of IBM bonds was offered to the public by a group of underwriters. This represented the largest amount of debt ever sold by a U.S. corporation. The underwriters essentially purchased the bonds from IBM at a fixed price and were in the process of selling them to investors when the unexpected happened. On October 6, the Federal Reserve announced that it would no longer attempt to keep interest rates constant in the face of high inflation. It would henceforth focus its energies on controlling the supply of money and let rates seek their own levels.

The effect was like that of a major earthquake. Interest rates skyrocketed. Near-term Treasury bonds, which in early October were yielding 9.5%, rose to 10.5% by the middle of the month. As we discussed in the last chapter, when interest rates rise, the price of fixed-rate securities—like IBM bonds—drops. Investment bankers holding IBM bonds that they had purchased for a fixed price the week before suddenly had to sell them at a loss. Many of the underwriters lost hundreds of thousands of dollars. A few did not. Salomon Brothers, one of the leading underwriters, had agreed to sell $124,000,000 worth of bonds. It is estimated that because of the sudden increase in rates, Salomon lost $3,500,000 between October 4 and October 10 on their IBM position. Fortunately, they also made an offsetting $3,500,000 by selling interest rate futures contracts. What could have been a disaster for the firm turned into a profitable transaction.

As illustrated in this example, future cash flows—even those only a few days away—are often uncertain. We have discussed the uncertainties caused by potential timing delays related to mail and processing steps. In later chapters we discuss uncertainties resulting from credit risks. In this chapter, we discuss the uncertainties caused by potential price and interest rate fluctuations and methods for protecting the firm against them.

We first discuss commodity futures contracts to illustrate how firms can, in some circumstances, protect themselves against adverse price fluctuations. Commodity futures are somewhat simpler to understand than other futures contracts. We then turn to financial futures, which can be used to hedge against interest rate risks and general movements in market prices. Futures contracts can be used to hedge against risks as long as 2 years into the future. In the final section, we treat interest rate swaps, which provide a means of protecting against interest rate shifts for a longer period of time.

Commodity Forward and Futures
Contracts

Price Risk

To understand what futures contracts can accomplish, it is helpful to consider price risk from the perspective of the cash flow timeline. To make the example more concrete, we look at the price risk facing a corn farmer. As illustrated in Figure 11.1, at the beginning of the timeline in May or June, the farmer experiences a cash outflow for fertilizer, seed, labor, and other expenses necessary to plant his crop. Suppose these expenses result in a cash outflow of $1.50 per bushel for 50,000 bushels of corn. (There will be some other expenses during the summer, but we assume that the $1.50 represents the present value of all of these outflows.) At the beginning of the timeline, we don't know the eventual cash inflow when the corn is harvested in September. Suppose corn is selling in the *cash market* (that means exchanging cash for corn *today*) at $1.75 per bushel. At this price, the farmer would make an acceptable profit. However, we don't know the cash price for corn when it is harvested and sold in September.

Alternative Mechanisms for Reducing Price Risk

How can the farmer handle this risk? There are several alternatives available. First, the farmer could do nothing and take the chance that the price for corn

Figure 11.1 Cash Flows Associated with Corn Production Without Hedging.

will be favorable in the future. If the price is over $1.75, the farmer will be pleased. If it is below $1.70, the farmer's profits will not be acceptable. In addition, the farmer has probably borrowed to finance the spring planting and needs to reassure the lender that an acceptable price for the corn will be obtained.

Forward Contracts

The farmer may hedge this price risk by selling a *forward contract*. This is simply an agreement between a buyer and a seller to buy specified goods at an agreed price on a specified day in the future. For example, the farmer may agree to sell to a grain processor 50,000 bushels of corn at $1.71 per bushel on September 10. The terms of the contract are worked out between the buyer and the seller. They may specify whatever the buyer and seller agree upon; they are not standardized but are customized to meet the needs of both parties. A forward contract is not typically sold to other parties without the consent of both the buyer and the seller. Figure 11.2 illustrates the cash flows in this contract. The risk to the farmer is reduced as long as the buyer can be depended upon to follow through on the purchase. The price is fixed and not subject to later negotiation. In May the farmer can confidently plant his crop, knowing that the price in September will be $1.71—not as much as hoped for but marginally acceptable.

Futures Contracts

A second alternative is to sell a *futures contract*. The effect of this contract is exactly the same as that of a forward contract. The route taken to arrive at that end is a bit more circuitous, but the outcome is the same.

While a forward contract is between two parties, a futures contract is between a buyer and an organized exchange or a seller and an organized exchange. (See Figure 11.3) There are a number of commodity exchanges in the United States, such as the Chicago Board of Trade, the Chicago Mercantile Exchange, and the Coffee, Sugar, and Cocoa Exchange. Table 11.1 gives a list of exchanges and the primary commodities traded there.

When a party enters into a formal agreement to *deliver* a commodity at a specified price on a specified delivery date, we say that the party *sells* a

Figure 11.2 Hedging With a Forward Contract.

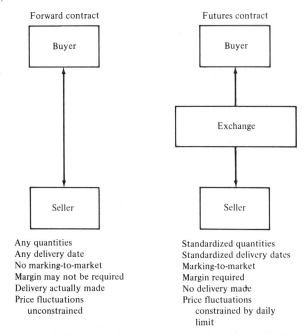

Figure 11.3 Differences Between Forward and Futures Contracts.

Table 11.1 Major Exchanges and Primary Contracts Traded

Exchange	Primary Contracts
Chicago Board of Trade (CBT)	Corn, oats, soybeans, soybean meal, soybean oil, wheat, silver, gold, Treasury bonds, Treasury notes, Municipal Bond Index, Major Market Index, GNMA pass-throughs
Chicago Mercantile Exchange (CME)	Feeder cattle, live cattle, hogs, pork bellies, lumber, S&P 500 Index
International Monetary Market (IMM) (part of CME)	British pound, Canadian dollar, Japanese yen, Swiss franc, West German mark, Eurodollar, T-bills
Commodity Exchange (New York) (CMX)	Copper, gold, silver, aluminum
Coffee, Sugar and Cocoa Exchange (CSCE)	Cocoa, coffee, world sugar, domestic sugar
New York Mercantile Exchange (NYM)	Platinum, palladium, heating oil, gasoline, potatoes
New York Cotton Exchange (CTN)	Cotton, U.S. Dollar Index, propane

futures contract. This is sometimes called a *short position* or a *short hedge*. On the other hand, when a party enters into an agreement to *take delivery* of a commodity at a specified price on a specified delivery date, it is termed *buying a futures contract*. This is called a *long position* or a *long hedge*. The farmer needs to *sell* a futures contract. No cash is exchanged for the corn at this time; the futures contract is a promise that the exchange will occur in the future. In fact, the farmer must pay something for the privilege of selling corn in the futures market.

To see how a futures contract works, assume that a September contract for corn is quoted at $1.75. This means *in effect* that the exchange is willing to buy the farmer's corn at $1.75 per bushel in September—but it is a bit more complex than that.

Standard Quantity

First, the quantity to be delivered is standardized. One corn contract is for 5,000 bushels. Since the farmer needs to sell 50,000 bushels, 10 contracts are needed.

Margin Account

Second, the farmer must place cash in a *margin account* with the broker or investment firm that does the trading for him. The margin account ensures good-faith performance of contract obligations. That is, the farmer must put a specified amount into an account with a broker (who, in turn, has a margin account with the exchange). If the margin per corn contract is $1,000 (this changes from time to time), the farmer must put up $10,000 for the 10 contracts. In addition, a commission is paid to the broker, part of which goes to the exchange.

Marking to Market

Third, the margin account is *marked to market* on a daily basis. This means that if the price changes from the initial $1.75, the amount of the change is put into or taken out of the margin account. For example, suppose that the day after the contract is sold, the quote for September corn drops to $1.73, or $.02 below the initial price. Since the farmer has agreed to sell corn for $1.75 and could buy it in September at $1.73, he would make a profit of $.02 if he purchased September corn at the new price. To reflect this change, the exchange adds $.02 × 5,000 bushels/contract × 10 contracts = $1,000 to the $10,000 already in the margin account, bringing the total to $11,000.

By the same token, if the price quoted for the futures contract increases, money is taken out of the margin account. Suppose that on the second day after the contract is sold, the price increases to $1.77 from $1.73. The exchange subtracts $.04 × 5,000 × 10 = $2,000 from the margin account, leaving it at $11,000 − $2,000 = $9,000. You can see that a large price increase could completely swallow up the margin account. If the margin account dips below a specified *maintenance level*, say $2,500, the farmer will receive a *margin call*

Table 11.2 Relationship between Commodity Price Movements and Margin Account Changes

Position Held	IF	Quoted Commodity Futures Price	THEN	Margin Account
SELL a contract		Increases		Decreases
		Decreases		Increases
BUY a contract		Increases		Increases
		Decreases		Decreases

requiring him to put sufficient money into the margin account to bring it up to the required $2,500. On the other hand, if cash accumulates in the margin account, the farmer may withdraw it as long as the margin requirement is met. See Table 11.2 for a summary of how the margin account moves up or down with changes in the price of the underlying commodity.

Daily Limit

Fourth, to protect the farmer—and the exchange—from large commodity price fluctuations that could absorb the entire margin account, the exchange establishes a *daily limit* for each contract. This is the maximum amount that the contract can move up or down in any 1 business day. If the price rises or falls by this limit, trading must cease until the next business day. This limit gives the owner of a contract a chance to get out of it before losses mount to an unacceptable level. There is usually a close relationship between the margin requirement and the daily limit. The margin is generally set such that if the price moves by the maximum amount on 1 day, no more than the margin amount is lost.

Closing Out a Futures Contract

Fifth, the farmer usually does not actually deliver corn to the exchange. In practice, fewer than 2% of all futures contracts result in the actual delivery of the commodity. Instead, when the farmer decides to close out his position (because he can't handle the mounting losses in his margin account, because he is ready to deliver his corn, or because he wants to void his position for any other reason), he takes a position in an opposite contract. In the example we are using, the farmer would issue an order to *buy* 10 September contracts. The commission he paid when he sold the initial 10 contracts also covers this second transaction. When he buys an opposing contract, the exchange closes out the farmer's position and remits to him whatever is left in the margin account. How much is in the margin account? That depends on the price of September corn on the date he closes out his position.

EXAMPLE: A PRICE DECREASE. For example, suppose it is now September, the farmer still has his contract position, and the cash price for corn is $1.55

per bushel. The price for September corn futures should also be very close to $1.55 per bushel. The cash price and the futures price converge when the contract is ready to expire. The farmer does two things. First, he sells his 50,000 bushels on the open market, giving him $1.75 − $1.55 = $.20 per bushel below what he could have received had he sold the corn for $1.75. In other words, he receives $77,500 (50,000 × $1.55) instead of $87,500 (50,000 × $1.75).

Second, he receives the money in his margin account. Since he sold 10 futures contracts, he will find (if he hasn't taken some money out of the account already) an *additional* $10,000 in the account (50,000 × $.20). Figure 11.4 illustrates the timeline of such a hedging transaction. This timeline is only approximate, since cash is actually flowing into and out of the margin account throughout the timeline.

The transactions at the time the account is closed out can be somewhat confusing. We can think of them as three distinct transactions. (1) The farmer sells corn on the open market for $1.55 per bushel. (2) The farmer buys corn from the exchange for $1.55 per bushel. (3) The farmer sells corn to the exchange for $1.75 per bushel. The last two steps really don't happen. The exchange doesn't enjoy receiving corn delivered to its posh trading floor. Since the net effect of buying and selling 50,000 bushels of corn is a

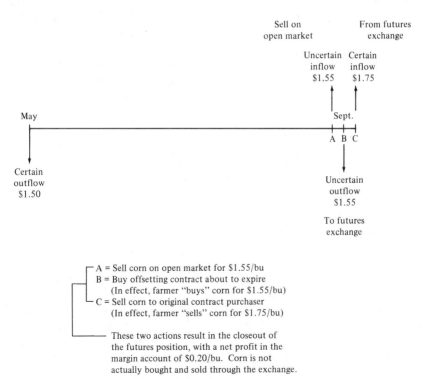

Figure 11.4 Hedging With a Futures Contract.

wash, the exchange just places the difference in price in the farmer's margin account and lets the farmer handle the corn.

The overall result of these somewhat roundabout transactions has the effect of simply selling corn at a guaranteed price of $1.75. The farmer has *hedged* against possibly adverse price movements by selling a futures contract. His profits/losses on these transactions, compared to what would have happened if he had not hedged, may be summarized as follows:

Unhedged Position
    Loss on sale of corn: $(1.55 - 1.75) \times 50,000$ = -$10,000

Hedged Position
    Loss on sale of corn: $(1.55 - 1.75) \times 50,000$ = -$10,000
    Gain on futures contract: $+\$.20 \times 5,000 \times 10$ = +$10,000
    Net gain/loss (relative to $1.75/bu.)   = $0

In this case, the futures position prevented the farmer from suffering a $10,000 loss on the sale of the corn.

EXAMPLE: A PRICE INCREASE. A futures contract is a two-edged sword. Just as it protects a seller against downward price movements, it also prevents the hedger from receiving windfall gains when prices increase. For example, suppose that in September the price has risen to $1.95 from the expected $1.75 in the preceding example. Now when the farmer sells his corn on the open market, he will receive $.20 *more* than he expected. Unfortunately, his margin account will be down by $10,000 ($.20 × 5,000 × 10 contracts). In this case— at least after we know the result—the farmer would have been better off not to have hedged.

Unhedged Position:
    Gain on sale of corn: $(1.95 - 1.75) \times 50,000$ = +$10,000

Hedged Position:
    Gain on sale of corn: $(1.95 - 1.75) \times 50,000$ = +$10,000
    Loss on futures contract: $-\$.20 \times 5,000 \times 10$ = -$10,000
    Net gain/loss   = $0

The farmer's gains and losses offset each other and result in a cash flow identical to the cash flow he realized when the price went down. Both create the effect of selling corn for the agreed price of $1.75. Unfortunately for the farmer in the latter case, he cannot escape the requirements of the contract, and must close out his position and take the loss on the contract. A futures contract—we stress again—insulates the seller from both price increases and decreases.

We have, of course, left out commissions and the opportunity cost of tying up the margin requirement for the duration of the hedge. We discuss how to include these factors in a later example.

Hedgers and Speculators

In the preceding examples, the farmer is a *hedger*. A hedger may either have a commodity to deliver or may want to purchase a commodity. Another hedger may be on the other side of the transaction; in other words, he may *buy* a futures contract. A food processing firm that purchases corn for its production uses may wish to lock in a guaranteed price in order to plan production schedules, set prices, and negotiate contracts.

Individuals or firms that sell or buy futures contracts without any commodity to deliver or to buy are termed *speculators*. Their interest is simply in speculating on the price movement of commodities. For example, a speculator may expect corn prices to rise because of anticipated adverse weather conditions. A speculator would then buy contracts. If prices do rise, cash accumulates in the margin account over time and the speculator makes a profit. If prices fall, however, cash has to be placed in the margin account and the speculator loses money. Speculators have no product to sell or buy to offset fluctuations in the margin account. However, they do provide liquidity to the futures market and permit investors to act on their views regarding future conditions.

Financial Forward and Futures Contracts

Financial contracts are very similar to commodity contracts. In some sense, some financial securities are very similar to commodities. One T-bill, for example, is very much like another, just as bushels of corn are alike. Like commodity markets, financial markets have developed the facility to engage in forward and futures contracts. The principles are much the same, but the computations are slightly more complex for financial contracts.

T-Bill Futures

The market for T-bill futures contracts is perhaps the most frequently used market in short-term finance. Hence, we will use this contract to illustrate how financial futures work. Other financial futures contracts are very similar to those of T-bills but are used to hedge longer-term maturities. The deliverable commodity is a 90-day $1,000,000 T-bill. Although newly issued T-bills actually have a 91-day maturity, 90 is used because it simplifies the computations. Since over 99% of T-bill contracts are closed out before delivery, this timing discrepancy is of little consequence.

As in corn futures, the exchange specifies delivery dates for T-bills. They are currently available for delivery in the months of March, June, September, and December. It is possible to buy and sell contracts with delivery dates up to 2 years into the future. Margin requirements, commissions, marking to market, and closing out positions are very similar to those in the corn futures example.

One complexity immediately noted in interest rate futures contracts is the way the price is specified. For corn, it is enough to simply state the price per bushel. For T-bill futures, the quoted price actually means something different from the price. T-bill futures are quoted as 100 minus the discount rate. For example, suppose the discount rate on a T-bill is 6%. Its price would be quoted as $100 - 6 = 94$. The real price of a 6% discount T-bill (see Chapter 10) is found to be

$$\$1,000,000\left[1 - \frac{90(.0600)}{360}\right] = \$985,000.$$

Rather than quote this price, or the interest rate, it was thought more consistent with other commodities to quote "100 − the discount rate." When the price moves up, a T-bill futures contract buyer will find more money in the margin account because delivery will be taken of a more valuable commodity—as in the corn example. Besides, it is simple to subtract the quote from 100 in order to obtain the implied interest rate.

Nevertheless, because of this convention, care must be taken to relate changes in interest rate to changes in the margin account. What happens to the price of the T-bill in the example just cited when the interest rate changes to 6.01%? We compute the price to be

$$\$1,000,000\left[1 - \frac{90(.0601)}{360}\right] = \$984,975,$$

which is just $25 less than the initial computation. Thus, for T-bill futures contracts, the change of 1 basis point in the interest rate results in a $25 change in the margin account. That is why it is convenient to use 90 days in the numerator and 360 days in the denominator. Otherwise, people would have a harder time keeping track of changes in the margin account.

Example of a T-Bill Futures Contract

Suppose it is now April and a treasurer plans to issue $10,000,000 worth of 90-day commercial paper in September. The rate now is 7.40%. The treasurer is concerned that by September the rate may be higher, and she would like to lock in the current low rate. She decides to use a 90-day T-bill future for the hedge. It would be better to use a 90-day commercial paper contract deliverable in September, but there is currently no exchange that deals with commercial paper futures contracts. As long as changes in T-bill rates are highly correlated with the firm's commercial paper rates, the treasurer should be able to create an effective hedge.

Buy or Sell Contracts?

The treasurer must first determine whether T-bill contracts should be bought or sold. To decide, the treasurer asks, "What kind of interest rate movement will hurt me?" In this case, the answer is: upward movements in rates — commercial paper would be more expensive to issue. What position would she like to be in if rates move up? She wants to have to *deliver* a security. When rates go up, the price on T-bills goes down. If she sells a contract now, she will, in effect, be receiving a fixed amount for the T-bills she delivers in September and yet be able to buy them in the marketplace for a lower amount.

A simple rule of thumb to use for financial futures is based on a mnemonic device. If you would be hurt by rates going *U*P, then *S*ELL futures. *U* and *S* are close together in the alphabet. If you would be hurt by rates going *D*OWN, then *B*UY futures contracts. *B* and *D* are close together in the alphabet.

Number of Contracts Needed

We saw that when rates change by 1 basis point, the price of the T-bill changes by $25. Hence, the margin account changes by $25. What happens to the price of 90-day commercial paper when the rate changes by 1 basis point? The answer is also $25:

$$\$1,000,000 \times .0001 \times \frac{90}{360} = \$25.$$

Thus, for each $1,000,000 of commercial paper we want to hedge, we would need one T-bill futures contract. Then when both rates change by 1 basis point, the price of each will change by $25.

What if the commercial paper to be sold had an 180-day maturity? Then a 1 basis point change would mean a change of

$$\$1,000,000 \times .0001 \times \frac{180}{360} = \$50.$$

This is because the maturity is twice as long. If we wanted to hedge $1,000,000 of 180-day commercial paper, we would need *two* T-bill futures contracts. Then a 1 basis point change will change the commercial paper price by $50 and the T-bill price by two times $25.

In general, the number of T-bill contracts we need to purchase to hedge other financial security is determined by the following formula:

$$\text{Contracts needed} = \frac{\$ \text{ amt. of security}}{\$ \text{ amt. of contract}} \times \frac{\text{maturity of hedged security}}{\text{maturity of contract security}}.$$

For example, to hedge $5,500,000 of a 180-day security with a 90-day $1,000,000 T-bill contract, we need

$$\frac{\$5,500,000}{\$1,000,000} \times \frac{180 \text{ days}}{90 \text{ days}} = 11 \text{ contracts.}$$

This will hedge a position in that security as long as the T-bill rate is highly correlated with the security we want to hedge. If this equation yields a nonintegral number, the decision maker must determine whether to round up or round down, since fractional contracts are not available.

An additional adjustment may have to be made in the number of contracts if changes in T-bill rates do not correspond in magnitude to changes in the security being hedged. Hence, depending on the sensitivity of the security being hedged to movements in the underlying deliverable security, the treasurer may want to use more or fewer T-bills. For example, if the security being hedged moves 300 basis points when the T-bill moves 200 basis points, the treasurer would want to buy (or sell) 300/200 = 1.5 as many T-bill contracts as indicated by the preceding formula.

Selecting the Delivery Date

The next decision the treasurer must make is the delivery date of the contract. Each contract has standard delivery dates. As mentioned previously, the only delivery dates available for T-bills are March, June, September, and December. In the preceding example, there is a T-bill delivery date corresponding to the issue date of commercial paper. The treasurer selects a September contract date. If the dates do not coincide, a later or earlier contract date must be selected. If an earlier date is selected, the futures position must be closed out before delivery. This leads to an exposed position for some period of time. If a later date is selected, the futures position can always be closed out early, creating the effect of an earlier delivery date. The only drawback is that the futures price and the cash price may not converge by the time the position is closed, and an imperfect hedge could result. In practice, the nearest delivery date is usually chosen, with some preference given to a later delivery date rather than an earlier one.

Margin Account and Commissions

As in the corn example, T-bill futures contracts specify the payment of a commission and the posting of a margin account. Assume, for this example, that the commission is $60 and the margin is $1,200 for each contract.

If Rates Move Up

Suppose that when the hedge is entered, the futures prices on T-bills are as follows:

Delivery Date	Price
Jun	94.30
Sep	94.28
Dec	94.25
Mar	94.10

This set of prices implies that the market expects short-term rates to increase gradually. This is evidenced by the increase in the implied discount rate found by taking the price from 100. The implied discount rate is 5.70% for June and 5.9% for March. When the treasurer *sells* 10 T-bill contracts in April, a commission of $10 \times \$60 = \$600$ is paid to the broker and $12,000 is placed in a margin account.

Suppose that the day after the contract is sold, the rate for September T-bills changes from 94.28 to 94.25. What happens to the margin account? This drop of 3 basis points (indicating an expected increase in the discount rate for September T-bills) means that the margin account increases by

$$3 \text{ bp} \times \$25 \times 10 \text{ contracts} = \$750.$$

Thus the margin account now has a balance of $12,750. Each day, any change in the quoted price of T-bills is posted to the margin account.

Suppose September arrives and the rate on the firm's commercial paper has risen to 8.60% and the price on the September T-bill contract is 93.25. Rates, as feared, have increased, and the firm must pay more for its commercial paper. The added cost to the firm from the loss on commercial paper is

$$\$10,000,000 \times (.086 - .074) \times \frac{90}{360} = \$30,000.$$

On the other hand, the firm finds itself with more money in its margin account from a gain on the futures position of

$$10 \text{ contracts} \times (9,428\text{bp} - 9,325\text{bp}) \times \frac{\$25}{\text{bp}} = \$25,750.$$

We also include commissions and margins in the analysis. Commissions amount to $10 \times \$60 = 600$. The opportunity cost on the margin account is determined by multiplying $12,000 by some opportunity cost for 5 months (from April to September). Assume that the firm could have invested the cash at 6% over the time period. The opportunity cost is

$$\$12,000 \times .06 \times \frac{5}{12} = \$300.$$

The firm would have lost $30,000 (relative to the initial commercial paper rate of 7.40%) if it had not hedged. The hedge provided some protection from the adverse interest rate movements. With the hedge, the firm's loss is only $5,200:

Loss on CP issuance	$(30,000)
Gain on futures	25,700
Commissions	(600)
Opportunity cost on margin	(300)
Net gain (loss) on hedge	$ (5,200)

If Rates Move Down

To illustrate what happens when rates move in the opposite direction, suppose that by September the rate on the firm's commercial paper has fallen to 6.40% and the price on the September T-bill contract is 95.15. The firm now pays less for its commercial paper. The reduced cost to the firm from the gain on commercial paper is

$$\$10,000,000 \times (.074 - .64) \times \frac{90}{360} = \$25,000.$$

The firm finds itself with a loss on its futures position of

$$10 \text{ contracts} \times (9,515\text{bp} - 9,428\text{bp}) \times \frac{\$25}{\text{bp}} = \$21,750.$$

The firm would have *gained* $25,000 (relative to the initial commercial paper rate of 7.40%) if it had not hedged. The hedge prevented the firm from benefiting from this windfall. With the hedge, the firm gains only $2,350:

Gain on CP issuance	$ 25,000
Loss on futures	(21,750)
Commissions	(600)
Opportunity cost on margin	(300)
Net gain (loss) on hedge	$ 2,350

If rates fall, as in this example, the treasurer will wish that she had not hedged. Hedging with futures contracts locks in a given price or interest rate. The firm neither benefits nor loses (at least not very much) when rates deviate from the initial locked-in rate.

Why Hedges Are Imperfect

In both of the preceding examples, the firm did not have a perfect hedge. A perfect hedge would have resulted in no gain or loss. There are several reasons why hedges are not often perfect.

1. *Less than perfect correlation.* When price movements on the futures contract and the hedged security are not perfectly correlated, an imperfect hedge results. In this example, we attempted to hedge commercial paper with a T-bill. Although the two securities move up and down roughly in synchro-

nization with each other, they are not perfectly correlated. When rates went up, the T-bill discount rate changed by 103 (9,428 − 9,325) basis points, while the commercial paper rate changed by 120 basis points (8.60% − 7.40%). Had both changed by the same amount, the hedge would have been better. Treasurers attempt to find the futures contract that is as closely correlated as possible with the security they are trying to hedge.

2. *Amount.* In our example, we needed to hedge exactly $10,000,000. Since T-bill contracts are for $1,000,000, it was easy to match 10 contracts with the security we wanted to hedge. If we had been issuing $9,500,000 in commercial paper, we would have had to choose between 10 and 9 contracts and would have had a mismatch either way.

3. *Delivery date.* In our example, we conveniently picked September as the date for issuing commercial paper. There happens to be a September delivery date for T-bills. What if the date had been October or November? We would have had to pick a December T-bill and close it out early or a September T-bill and be unhedged for 1 month or so.

4. *Maturity of contract security.* We conveniently chose 90-day commercial paper to hedge. What if we had wanted to hedge 60-day or 30-day commercial paper? We have two problems with those maturities. First, 90-day T-bills may not be as highly correlated with 30- or 60-day commercial paper as they are with 90-day paper. Second, the price change is not the same for an equal basis point change in rates if maturities differ. We can address this problem by buying or selling fewer than 10 contracts. According to the formula previously developed, we could hedge $6,000,000 of 60-day commercial paper by selling

$$\frac{\$6,000,000}{1,000,000} \times \frac{60 \text{ days}}{90 \text{ days}} = 4 \text{ contracts.}$$

Uses of Financial Futures

Financial futures contracts have many applications in corporate finance. They are also widely used in financial institutions, but we will focus primarily on corporate uses. These examples are only illustrative; there are many others that could be cited.

Creating Fixed Rate Loans

Most short-term borrowing is at a variable rate based on a prime or reference rate (see Chapter 12). A treasurer can create the effect of a fixed rate loan by borrowing at a variable rate and selling futures contracts for delivery at various times of the year corresponding to the amount of borrowing outstanding. If rates increase, the treasurer pays more for loans but recoups the loss on the futures contract.

Creating Variable-Rate Loans

Sometimes firms borrow fixed-rate, intermediate-term money from European markets. To create the effect of variable-rate financing, the treasurer can buy futures contracts. If rates drop, the firm benefits from its future position. If rates increase, the firm suffers a loss in its margin account. In other words, the effect is equivalent to that of a variable-rate loan. Under some circumstances, the combination might prove more attractive than a conventional variable-rate loan.

Hedging Money Market Investment Positions

If a firm holds fixed-rate securities, there is a risk that interest rate increases will result in a loss if the securities need to be sold early. To lock in the current rate, futures contracts could be sold. This is the position the investment bankers found themselves in when they tried to place the IBM bonds discussed at the beginning of the chapter. The wise bankers hedged their positions by selling government bond contracts. When rates suddenly rose, they lost money on their IBM position but had an offsetting gain from their futures position.

Conversely, when a firm holds short-term securities and intends to roll them over for a period of time, interest rate decreases will cut the return. This situation occurs when a firm issues bonds or stock and does not immediately invest all of the proceeds. The firm can buy futures contracts. If rates fall, the firm is hedged against significant opportunity losses.

Hedging Stock Positions

Sometimes firms buy stock in other firms for their investment portfolio or for control purposes. To protect against a general downturn in the stock market—which in turn would adversely affect the price of the stock—the firm may choose to sell an *index future* like the S&P 500 Index or Value Line Index contract. This is another variation on the kinds of futures we have been discussing. Instead of basing fluctuations in the margin account on the price of a T-bill or a bushel of corn, an index future bases its changes on the value of a stock index. A stock index depends on the prices of a large number of individual stocks. When an index contract is sold, the margin account increases when the value of the index drops. Conversely, when an index contract is bought, the margin account increases when the index rises.

Obtaining a perfect hedge with an index future is very difficult because the degree of correlation of a stock index with a specific stock may not be high. Nevertheless, an index futures contract does offer some protection from general stock market movements.

Interest Rate Swaps

Interest rate futures contracts hedge against interest rate movements over a limited period. Most contracts have delivery dates of only 2 years at most.

What can a firm do when it wants to protect itself against interest rate changes in later years? One possible strategy is an interest rate swap.

General Concept of a Swap

An *interest rate swap* occurs when two parties agree to exchange cash flow streams for a specified period of time. The parties may agree to make each others' debt payments or receive payments from each others' securities. The essential ingredient is that they agree to exchange payments. Thus, interest rate swaps are equivalent to saying, "You pay my bills and I'll pay yours."

Swaps exist because of differences in financial markets faced by the two parties. These differences are sometimes caused by geographical separation of financial markets. Swaps often occur between U.S. firms and European or Asian firms. The financial markets have developed differently in different parts of the world. Swaps create a vehicle for taking advantage of possible market inefficiencies existing in a global marketplace.

It is important to realize that swaps do not have to be tied to an underlying security. It is sufficient for the two parties to agree to pay (or receive payments) for each others' cash flow stream.

Illustration of an Interest Rate Swap

Suppose a U.S. financial company is interested in obtaining $50,000,000 in variable-rate financing. It has a strong balance sheet and is highly rated by the rating agencies. It could sell fixed-rate bonds at a rate of 9%. It can borrow variable-rate money in the Euromarket at LIBOR plus 0.5%. *LIBOR* stands for *London Interbank Offered Rate*—the market rate for Eurodollar deposits. It is commonly used as a base rate for European loans. In Germany, a chemical company is planning to expand its facilities and needs the equivalent of $50,000,000 in fixed-rate loans. It could sell bonds, but at a rate of 11%. It could borrow the money in the variable-rate market for LIBOR plus .5% but would rather receive fixed-rate financing.

Through a financial intermediary (usually a large money center bank), the two parties are brought together. As illustrated in Figure 11.5, the U.S. firm agrees to borrow $50,000,000 at 9% and the German firm agrees to borrow $50,000,000 at LIBOR plus .5%. The two firms agree to swap interest payments for the next 10 years. That is, the German firm agrees to make fixed-rate interest payments to the U.S. firm at a rate of 9.50% for the next 10 years. The U.S. firm will pay the German firm a variable rate of LIBOR. The agreement calls for an exchange of payments to occur every 6 months in U.S. dollars.

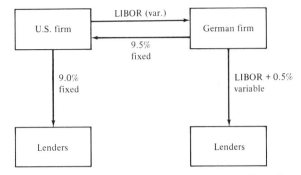

Figure 11.5 Interest Payments in an Interest Rate Swap.

This agreement benefits both parties. To see this, compare the U.S. firm's annual cash outflow now to what it would have been without the agreement:

Without the swap agreement:

Pay Euro banks	$-\$50$ million $\times$ (LIBOR + .50%)

With the swap agreement:

Pay German firm	$-\$50$ million $\times$ LIBOR
Receive from German firm	$\$50$ million $\times$ 9.50%
Pay bondholders	$-\$50$ million $\times$ 9.00%
Net annual benefit:	$\$50$ million $\times$ (.0100) = $\$500{,}000$

In other words, the U.S. firm saves .50% on its variable-rate borrowing in addition to the .50% it makes from the difference between the bond rate paid and the rate the German firm pays. It receives variable-rate financing at LIBOR − .50%.

For the German firm, there are also benefits:

Without the swap agreement

Pay bondholders	$-\$50$ million $\times$ .11

With the swap agreement

Pay U.S. firm	$-\$50$ million $\times$ .095
Receive from U.S. firm	$\$50$ million $\times$ LIBOR
Pay variable rate holders	$-\$50$ million $\times$ (LIBOR + .50%)
Net annual benefit:	$\$50$ million $\times$ 1.00% = $\$500{,}000$

The German firm receives fixed-rate financing at an effective cost of 10%. Both buyer and seller save $500,000 each year relative to what they would have paid without the swap agreement.

Terminology

The $50,000,000 amount in our example is termed the *notional amount*. This is the base on which all interest payments are computed. It may represent the actual level of securities or may just be any specific level to which the parties agree.

The date on which payments are exchanged is called the *payment exchange date*. On that date, the applicable interest payments are computed (using the past average of some specified reference rate). Generally, only the *net amount* is transferred from one party to the other. For example, suppose the LIBOR rate had averaged 6% during the past six months. The U.S. firm would owe the German firm

$$.0600 \times \$50,000,000 \times .5 \text{ year} = \$1,500,000.$$

The German firm owes the U.S. firm

$$.0950 \times \$50,000,000 \times .5 \text{ year} = \$2,375,000.$$

Hence, the net amount transferred between the firms is the difference: $2,375,000 − $1,500,000 = $875,000. This amount is sent from the German firm to the U.S. firm.

Features of an Interest Rate Swap

Interest rate swaps may be made on new or existing debt (or other securities). Sometimes firms will decide to enter the swap market using old bonds or preferred stock. They are said to *swap out* their securities in exchange for variable-rate obligations. Swaps can also be made when there is no underlying security at all, since a swap is simply an agreement to pay a defined cash flow stream for a specified period.

Because of transactions and legal costs, the amounts swapped tend to be quite large—generally $25,000,000 or more. That number may decrease as interest in this market increases.

Swaps need generally not be disclosed on the balance sheet or income statement. (Banks are now required to report significant swap positions.) This has implications for financial analysis. A firm that appears to be heavily burdened by fixed-rate debt may have swapped out that debt for variable-rate debt.

Swaps may be attractive to firms that do not want to sell the underlying assets or eliminate underlying debt. The underlying assets or liabilities remain with the company, but the interest rate effects of the swap replace unwanted assets or liabilities with wanted ones—at least as far as interest rates go.

Swaps are also attractive to firms that need protection from interest rate changes for a longer period of time than the 2 years provided by T-bills. Swaps can be arranged for many years in advance.

Risks of Interest Rate Swaps

There are risks associated with creating a swap. Suppose the firm in the preceding example issues $50,000,000 in debt, assuming that it can swap it out to save—as we saw—$500,000 per year. If the German firm defaults on its swap agreement, the U.S. firm is obligated to make fixed-rate payments for at least the next 10 years. It is not, however, obligated to pay the German firm for the variable-rate loan. Nevertheless, the U.S. firm wanted variable-rate financing and is now stuck with fixed-rate loans. Similarly, if the U.S. firm defaults, the German firm is left with a variable-rate loan when it wanted a fixed-rate one. While this may not be considered to be default risk, since no principal is lost, the firm is exposing itself to a significant level of interest rate risk.

Interest Rate Swaps Using Assets

The previous interest rate swap example tied the swap to debt securities and took place across international borders. While this is a common type of swap transaction, it is also possible to create swaps without using liabilities or international partners. For example, suppose a savings and loan association has a large portfolio of fixed-rate mortgages. It would like to keep them but to create the effects of a variable-rate portfolio in the event that interest rates increase in the future. It is possible to swap out these mortgages for variable-rate cash flow streams. Fixed-rate loans might be desirable for a bank that wants to increase its mortgage portfolio without going to the trouble of setting up a mortgage facility. Such a bank may have a significant number of variable-rate loans on its books.

These two firms would swap the cash inflow streams pertaining to these two types of assets. The parties would agree on a notional amount and on the specific interest rates each would pay the other on the payment exchange date. The cash flows are illustrated in Figure 11.6.

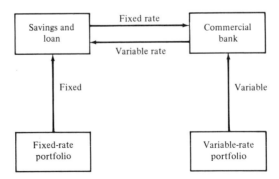

Figure 11.6 Interest Rate Swap Using Assets.

Summary

Dealing with uncertain cash flows is a major problem for the short-term financial manager. In this chapter, we introduced two potential tools for removing some of this risk. Forward and futures contracts offer some degree of hedging against adverse changes in the prices of cereal grains, oil, and other commodities. Financial futures provide the ability to hedge against interest rate movements and stock market swings. However, most futures contracts exist only up to 2 years in the future. If a firm wants to hedge against interest rate changes beyond that time period, it may be able to enter the interest rate swap market. Here firms agree to exchange their cash flow streams for either assets or liabilities. Swaps have the potential of turning variable rates into fixed rates and vice versa. These tools provide—at some cost, of course—the capability of at least partially controlling some of the more important uncertainties faced by a firm.

Discussion Questions

1. Explain the significant differences between the following: forward contract, futures contract, put, call.
2. Define the following terms related to futures contracts: commission, margin account, maturity of hedging security, delivery date, maturity of hedged security, short position, long position.
3. What does it mean to sell a futures contract? What are you selling and to whom? What money changes hands on the date you sell?
4. Very few contracts actually result in the delivery of the commodity. What happens to all of the others?
5. Differentiate between hedgers and speculators. Which party stands to lose more in the futures market?
6. How would you determine whether to buy or sell a commodity futures contract? An interest rate futures contract?
7. Explain how a T-bill futures contract can be used to hedge a firm that has agreed to supply a subsidiary with a fixed-rate, short-term loan 5 months from now.
8. Why don't futures contracts generally result in a perfect hedge?
9. What factors determine how many futures contracts you need to hedge a specific security?
10. What is a stock index futures contract? Under what circumstances might a firm be interested in one?
11. What is an interest rate swap?
12. Define the following terms: notional amount, payment exchange date, LIBOR.

13. Why is it possible for both firms to save money in interest rate swaps? What does that say about market efficiency?
14. How can firms swap the income stream from assets? Give an example.
15. What risks do firms face when they makes interest rate swap agreements?

_____ **Problems** _____

1. For each situation given, indicate whether a futures contract should be bought or sold and specify the type of contract that should be used.
   a. A farmer expects to harvest barley in September.
   b. A grain exporter has negotiated a long-term contract to supply wheat at a fixed price.
   c. A bank has issued a fixed rate, long-term loan for delivery next month.
   d. A treasurer has invested in a high-yielding Treasury bond and expects to have to sell it in 6 months.
   e. A firm would like a fixed-rate, short-term loan but can only get a prime rate–based credit line.
   f. A financial institution has made a number of fixed-rate home mortgages.
   g. An investor believes that the stock market is going to rise over the next few weeks.
   h. An American firm has billed a German firm 300,000 marks payable in 90 days.

2. A farmer expects to harvest 20,000 bushels of corn in September. It is now March, and corn futures are quoted at the following prices:

May	165	(5,000-bushel contracts,
Jul	168	in cents per bushel)
Sep	171	
Dec	174	

   a. How many contracts of which delivery date should be bought or sold? What money changes hands in March?
   b. When September arrives, the actual price of corn is $1.50. What steps does the farmer take to close out the futures position with the exchange and sell the corn to a cooperative?
   c. Overall, how much did the farmer make or lose? (Neglect commissions and margin opportunity costs.)

3. A treasurer plans to issue $10,000,000 in 6-month commercial paper 4 months from now. The current rate for such paper is 7.5%. The treasurer would like to lock in this rate if possible. A 90-day T-bill futures contract for delivery 6 months from now (the closest date available) is quoted at 94.8. Commissions are $50 per contract and the margin requirement is $1,500 per contract.

   a. How many futures contracts should be bought or sold?

   b. Suppose that when the commercial paper is issued, the actual rate is 8.5% and the price on the T-bill futures contract closes at 94.1. Compute the gains and losses on the firm's position.

4. A treasurer has negotiated a credit line with the firm's lead bank. The rate charged will be the prime rate plus 1.5%. Today's prime rate is 7.5%. The total amount outstanding against the line is planned to be $5,000,000 for the first 6 months and $10,000,000 for the next 6 months. T-bill futures contracts are available with the following prices: March (today), 94.8; June, 94.9; September, 94.9; December, 94.7; March (next year), 94.6.

   a. What does this set of prices imply—qualitatively—about market perceptions of future interest movements?

   b. Assume that if this set of interest rates actually occurred, the bank's prime rate would not change from 7.5%. How many contracts of which delivery date should the treasurer buy/sell to lock in a fixed borrowing rate?

   c. Suppose that the following scenario actually occurs in each quarter. (For simplicity of computation, assume that interest rates are constant throughout the quarter.)

Quarter Ending	Prime Rate	Price of the Maturing Contract
Jun	7.5%	94.7
Sep	8.0%	94.5
Dec	9.0%	93.6
Mar	10.0%	92.4

   Compute the firm's interest payments if it had borrowed at a fixed rate (7.5% plus 1.5%) for the entire year. Then compute the firm's interest payments plus the futures contract position if the preceding scenario occurs. Next, compute the interest payments if the firm had not hedged but had just paid the prime rate plus 1.5%.

5. A U.S. firm has a very good bond rating and can borrow at a fixed rate of 9%. It would rather have a variable-rate loan, however, and can borrow in the Eurodollar market at a rate of LIBOR + .5%. A French manufacturer is seeking fixed-rate funds to finance plant expansion. It can borrow at 11% in France. If the French firm were to borrow in the Eurodollar market, it would pay LIBOR + .5%. The two firms are brought together by an intermediary. The deal worked out is as follows: The U.S. firm agrees to pay the French firm LIBOR − 1/8%, while the French firm agrees to pay the U.S. firm 9.75%. The notional amount is set at $50,000,000, and net payments are exchanged every 6 months based on the previous 6 months' LIBOR rate. Neglect commissions paid to the intermediary.

   a. Assuming the LIBOR rate for the first 6 months is 6%, compute the net payment exchanged between the two firms.

b. For this 6 months, compute how much better (or worse) off the U.S. firm is compared to its position without the swap.

c. For this 6 months, compute how much better (or worse) off the French firm is compared to its position without the swap.

d. Over a 5-year period, what savings are realized by each firm relative to its position without the swap? (Does this number depend on the LIBOR rate?)

6. A savings and loan association has a significant number of fixed-rate mortgages on its books. It has been "burned" in the past when interest rates rose significantly above the rates on existing mortgages. The association wants to continue to service the loans and does not want to sell them (or it would have to write off a significant loss). Starting a small business loan division—which would be a source of variable-rate loan business— could be costly. On the other hand, a commercial bank has an oversupply of variable-rate loans and would like to lock in the fixed rates provided by fixed-rate mortgages. It doesn't have the expertise to start a mortgage department and does not want to incur that expense at this time. Explain how these two institutions could use the concept of an interest rate swap to provide a solution to both of their problems.

Selected Readings

A Guide to Financial Futures at the Chicago Board of Trade, Chicago: Chicago Board of Trade (1983).

GUZZARDI, WALTER, JR., "The Bomb I.B.M. Dropped on Wall Street," *Fortune* (November 19, 1979), pp. 52–56.

"How Salomon Bros. Hedged the IBM Deal," *Business Week* (October 29, 1979), p. 50.

Interest Rate Futures for Institutional Investors, Chicago: Chicago Board of Trade (1985).

KAWALLER, IRA G., "How and Why to Hedge a Short-Term Portfolio," *Journal of Cash Management* (January–February 1985), pp. 26–30.

KAWALLER, IRA G., "Hedging with Futures Contracts: Going the Extra Mile," *Journal of Cash Management* (July–August 1986), pp. 34–36.

KOLB, ROBERT W., *Interest Rate Futures: A Comprehensive Introduction*, Richmond, Va.: Robert F. Dame, Inc., 1982.

LOOSIGIAN, ALLAN M., *Interest Rate Futures*, Homewood, Ill.: Dow Jones-Irwin 1980.

SMITH, DEREK, "Consider an Interest Rate Swap," *Journal of Cash Management* (October–November 1983), pp. 29–34.

VANDER WEIDE, JAMES M. AND STEVEN F. MAIER, *Managing Corporate Liquidity*, New York: Wiley, 1985, Chapters 11, 12.

Short-term Borrowing

12

Short-term Borrowing from Commercial Banks

Many companies experiencing a short-term need for funds borrow to cover these needs. These borrowings may involve a Fortune 500 company using its credit rating to borrow funds for a tender offer for an acquisition, a toy company borrowing for a seasonal buildup in inventory, or a printing shop borrowing against its accounts receivable to take quantity and early payment discounts on its paper stock.

In the previous part of this book, we examined the short-term investment portfolio as a source of liquidity. In this part, we examine its counterpart on the liability side of the balance sheet: a short-term borrowing portfolio. Traditionally, anything with a maturity of up to 1 year qualifies as short-term borrowing, although most short-term liabilities have a maturity of substantially less than 1 year. Short-term borrowing may be paid off by a cash inflow but is often rolled over by obtaining additional short-term funds. The short maturity and flexibility to increase or decrease many of these liabilities allow adjustment of the short-term loan portfolio to meet a cash shortfall or surplus. It is the ability to draw upon any unused borrowing capacity quickly that allows potential short-term liabilities to be considered a source of liquidity to the firm.

From the data presented in Table 12.1, we see that, historically, commercial banks have supplied the majority of the short-term credit needs of businesses. However, on a relative basis, commercial banks have declined from providing 66% of the funds in 1970 to providing 52% in 1985. In this chapter, we concentrate on the credit arrangements available from commercial banks. Specifically arranged sources of short-term funds that are not from commerc-

Table 12.1 Sources of Business Loans (All Numbers in Billions of Dollars)

	1970	1975	1980	1985
Commercial banks				
All loans	292.0	516.9	912.7	11,469.3
Commercial and				
industrial	110.0	189.9	325.0	502.1
Commercial finance				
companies				
Business loans	21.8	39.3	72.3	152.8
Commercial paper	33.4	48.4	123.7	300.9

Source: Board of Governors of the Federal Reserve System, *Annual Statistical Digest*, Washington, D.C., various years.

ial banks, such as the use of commercial paper, commercial finance company credit, and captive finance companies are discussed in the next chapter.

Some short-term financing is spontaneously generated by the operating activities of the firm. This includes trade credit, accrued expenses, and other payables. Once the initial arrangements are made, this type of funding automatically increases (decreases) with increases (decreases) in the activities of the firm. Further coverage of spontaneous funding sources is deferred until the discussion of payables in Chapter 16.

Bank Credit Arrangements

Bank borrowing consists of several different types of credit arrangements including lines of credit, term loans, letters of credit, banker's acceptances, and master notes. Each has a unique combination of maturity, interest rate, fees, indentures (such as the collateral required), and the conditions under which the credit can be called or revoked.

Single-Payment Loan

The simplest credit arrangement is a single–payment loan, or note. It is frequently granted for a specific financial purpose, with a definite beginning and ending time. The note can be either a discount note or an add-on note. On a *discount note* the amount of cash advanced under the loan agreement is the face value of the loan less the amount of interest for the period covered. The calculation of the amount of cash advanced is the same as the determination of the purchase price of a T-bill, discussed in Chapter 10. On a discount note the interest rate is fixed at the time the note is originated, since it is necessary to deduct the full interest rate amount at the beginning of the loan period.

On an *add-on note* the full principal amount is received when the note is initiated. The interest is added to the principal to determine the cash flow at maturity. For an add-on note the interest rate can either be fixed or can vary over the life of the loan.

Even though the single–payment note is the simplest type of loan, it is frequently used in conjunction with another type of credit arrangement: a line of credit or a letter of credit.

Line of Credit

A *line of credit* is an agreement for a firm to borrow up to a specified limit during a particular time period. Once the line of credit is approved, actual loans taken out against the line are usually approved by the loan officer (perhaps called an *account executive* or a *relationship officer* in modern banks), with a minimum of delay or additional investigation. The agreement specifies the terms and conditions of the loans to be made under the line of credit. Although technically in force for a set time period, usually a year, most credit lines represent an ongoing relationship with the bank and are renewed at maturity. At renewal the rate, credit limit, or other conditions of the line of credit are altered, depending upon the financial performance, condition, and needs of the borrower. The line of credit provides a very flexible source of short-term financing. The borrower has access to a large amount of credit but pays interest only on the actual borrowing.

Purpose

The primary purpose of a credit line is to supply funds to meet the short-term, frequently seasonal, cash flow needs of the borrower. To ensure that the line is used for short-term purposes, a credit line sometimes includes a requirement of a *cleanup period,* perhaps 30 or 60 days, during which there is no borrowing against the line. While typical at one time, the cleanup period is a feature that has practically been eliminated. Many small borrowers can't clear the line, while large borrowers use the competition to negotiate away the cleanup period.

Much of the borrowing under a credit line takes place through specific short-term notes ranging from overnight to as long as 90 days or more. At maturity the interest on the note is paid along with the principal. If funds are needed when, or perhaps before, the note is due, another note is taken down against the line. Thus, actual borrowing is usually through a sequence of short-term notes made under the terms and conditions of the credit line. Many borrowers roll over the notes at maturity and keep the credit line in force for several years thus effectively using the credit line as a longer–term source of funding.

A second purpose of a line of credit is to provide a backup source of cash to pay off maturing commercial paper. Subsequent to the disruption of the commercial paper market in the early 1970s, triggered by Penn Central Railroad's inability to roll over its commercial paper, most organizations issuing commercial paper maintained an unused credit line in an amount sufficient to back up their commercial paper. Of course, the intention is never to have to borrow under this credit line.

A third purpose of a credit line is to provide a liquidity cushion or financial insurance. A financial manager provides for liquidity by obtaining a credit line that, although not intended to be used, is available if needed.

Committed versus Uncommitted Credit Lines

An *uncommitted credit line* is simply a verbal statement from the banker that as long as conditions don't change, the bank is prepared to lend the potential borrower up to the stated amount. Although an uncommitted credit line can be canceled or the terms or conditions changed at any time, it is unusual for a request for borrowing under the credit line not to be honored. Competitive pressures and the desire for continuing customer relationships ensure that banks do not treat these verbal agreements lightly. Some banks may try to initiate a relationship with a potential client by offering an uncommitted line of credit for a relatively short period, say 6 months. At the end of this period, the bank reevaluates the prospects of developing an ongoing relationship before deciding whether to renew the line.

A *committed credit line* is a written agreement covering the terms and conditions of the credit line. Usually a bank requires some compensation, either in the form of service credits from balances or cash fees, to make a committed credit line. The bank is legally bound to lend money under the line as long as the terms and conditions are met by the borrower.

Pricing of Credit Lines

COMMITMENT FEE. One element in the price of a credit line is the *commitment fee*, which is the price for the bank's commitment to keep the line available. On an uncommitted line there is usually no charge for keeping the line available. The bank does not want to raise the legal issue of whether it can decline to honor a request if a fee is charged. If the bank is using the uncommitted line as a way to initiate a relationship, it does not really think that the line will be used. In addition, few borrowers are willing to pay a fee if the bank is not willing to make a commitment that the funds will be available if needed.

A fee is charged for a committed credit line. The amount of the fee may be based on the total credit line or only on the unused portion of the line. The bank may assess the fee in the form of a direct cash charge, usually in the range of 1/4% to 1/2% but sometimes as low as 1/8%. The amount of the fee depends upon the quality of the borrower, other products and services being purchased from the bank, and other borrowing opportunities available to the client. A bank may also charge for maintaining the line by requiring a certain level of demand deposit balances to be held at the bank. The bank may specify the amount of the balances that must be held, either in dollars or as a percentage of the line, or the balance credits that must be generated by the balances held. Similar to a cash fee assessment, required balances may be based either on the total line or on the unused portion of the line. Occasionally a bank offers several options and allows the borrower to choose. At one time, the use of balances was the most common commitment for a credit line. Due to competitive pressures and attention to cash management procedures by financial managers, the most common compensation for a credit line today is through payment of cash commitment fees.

An example will illustrate the calculation of the commitment fee. The Atlas Paving Company is a road construction company whose motto is "The World Moves Between the Shoulders of Atlas." The treasurer has approached the Metropolis National Bank for a line of credit of $20,000,000 to meet seasonal cash flow needs. Metropolis has offered Atlas the option of paying a cash fee of 3/8% of the line or maintaining a compensating balance of 5% of the amount of the line. Atlas normally averages a balance of $200,000 in its accounts with Metropolis, and none of these balances are used to generate credits to pay for tangible services. The balances would have to be increased by $800,000 to compensate for the line with the balances. The treasurer estimates that she can earn 8% on funds invested in marketable securities, so the additional $800,000 would cost Atlas $64,000 per year. The cash commitment fee would be $75,000. In this case, the treasurer opts for maintaining the higher balances.

INTEREST RATE. The second element in the price is the interest rate paid on borrowings against the line. Virtually all credit lines carry a variable interest rate. The base for the rate depends, at least in part, upon the size and financial soundness of the borrower. A small to middle-market borrower is usually charged an interest rate that is based on the prime rate at the bank.[1] The prime rate is an administered price set by the bank. It usually lags and fluctuates less than market rates. The rate on the credit line may range from prime to prime plus 2% or 3%, depending largely on the financial strength of the borrower. The middle-market to large borrower may be charged an interest rate based on money market rates. The base for the rate may be the bank's cost of funds, the CD rate for a specified maturity, or LIBOR. The borrower is charged the base money market rate plus a risk premium, usually from 1/4% to 1%. The spreads are much narrower on money market–based rates, both because the borrowers tend to be of better quality and because there is greater competition for their business. Foreign banks have been very aggressive in offering very small spreads above the LIBOR rate.

Covenants

The line of credit may carry a set of *covenants*, or conditions, that limit the borrower's actions. These covenants may be positive, such as specifying the amount of working capital that must be maintained or certain financial ratios that must be achieved, or they may be negative, such as limiting the amount of

---

[1] The classification of a middle-market company varies across banks. The basic characteristic of such companies is that they are large enough to use a fairly wide range of banking services, but probably not so large that they have multiple banking relationships.

capital expenditures, management salaries, or payment of dividends without the bank's prior approval. A frequent covenant on loans has the borrower provide the bank with financial statements on a timely, periodic basis. Covenants are more likely to appear on a line of credit to a small, less financially sound borrower for whose business the bank has little competition.

Revolving Credit Agreement

A *revolving credit agreement* is similar to a line of credit but is usually established for more than 1 year. Common maturities extend for 2 or 3 years, during which time the customer may borrow and repay loans several times. Many revolving credit agreements contain a clause that allows the borrower to convert to a term loan. Frequently, the revolving credit agreement is renegotiated prior to its maturity; therefore, it may represent a continuous source of credit. This is sometimes referred to as an *evergreen* loan. The pricing on a revolving credit agreement is similar to that of a credit line. There is a commitment fee, met either by balances or by cash fees. The commitment fee is usually charged only on the unused portion of the credit agreement. The interest rate is usually variable, based either on the prime rate or on money market rates.

Term Loan

A *term loan* is a more specific loan agreement than either a line of credit or a revolving credit agreement. It has a fixed maturity, usually of 2 to 7 years. The total amount of the loan is forwarded to the borrower on origination, and is repaid in periodic installments over the life of the loan.[2] The repayment schedule may provide for equal payments (a combination of principal and interest), equal payments of principal, or some other schedule that matches the expected cash flow–generating capability of the borrower. Repayments can be made monthly, quarterly, or semiannually.

A term loan is frequently obtained to cover a specific financial need that is expected to generate cash for the firm in the future, such as the purchase of a piece of capital equipment. When a tangible asset is financed, it may be pledged as collateral against the loan. The use of collateral for a loan is discussed later in this chapter. An increasingly common use of term loans in the mid-1980s has been for leveraged buyouts or, as they are sometimes called, *financial restructuring*.

Pricing

Most term loans carry variable interest rates. The base for these rates can be the same as those for credit lines, although the prime rate tends to be the

---

[2] It is possible to arrange for a deferred draw-down, or a draw-down in steps, to meet a specific funding requirement such as the delivery of production equipment.

base more frequently used to price term loans than is true for lines of credit. There is seldom a requirement for a compensating balance, since there is no outstanding commitment by the bank to provide future financing.[3] Because of the documentation frequently required for a term loan, there may be higher transaction costs, which are charged to the borrower in the form of an origination fee.

Letter of Credit

A *letter of credit* is a letter from a bank stating that a loan will be made to the client if the specified conditions are met. It is commonly used to finance international trade. Because an exporter does not know an importer or because information, language, and cultural differences make it difficult to perform an adequate credit analysis, the exporter is not willing to sell to the importer on credit. The importer presents a letter of credit from its bank, stating that a loan in the amount necessary for payment of the shipment will be made upon arrival of the goods. This allows the importer to substitute the bank's credit rating for its own credit rating, thereby reducing the risk to the exporter.

The use of a letter of credit for domestic financing has increased in recent years. It is used when the buyer is not known to the seller and the amount of the transaction is large. The letter of credit has also been used by some companies as a form of financial insurance when a performance bond is needed or a potential legal judgment may be assessed.

Revocability

A letter of credit can be either *revocable,* where the bank has the right to cancel the letter, or *irrevocable,* where the bank is bound to honor the terms if the specified conditions are met.

Pricing and Maturity

The maturity of the letter of credit is dictated by the event that evoked the need for the letter. In most instances, it is of relatively short duration. The letter usually has a fixed rate based on the prevailing rate at the time the loan is issued. A commitment fee is usually charged for issuing an irrevocable letter of credit, whether the loan is issued or not.

Banker's Acceptance

A *banker's acceptance* is generated by a time draft for which a bank is committed to making the payment to the holder at maturity if the issuer does not pay. Banker's acceptances most frequently arise from international transactions

---

[3] In the case of a deferred draw-down, there may be a commitment fee for the time period until the draw-down occurs.

when the conditions for a letter of credit have been met.[4] Financing is provided when the bank makes an advance on the time draft issued. Some banks use the term *banker's acceptance* to refer to a loan issued to finance the purchase of specific goods, whether an international or a domestic transaction.

Pricing

The loan made under a banker's acceptance is usually a discount loan. The discount from face value advanced to the borrower includes an amount for the interest at prevailing money market rates plus a fee, or a commission, of approximately 1.5%. Because of the commission, the cost to the borrower is usually above the commercial paper rate, but because it is based on money market rates, it is usually below the prime rate.

Master Notes

Two different kinds of bank credit arrangements are referred to as *master notes*. In the first type, a company signs a master promissory note under which borrowings can take place. This is very similar to a line of credit arrangement. Any loans made under the terms of the note are simply recorded on the note, instead of a separate note being issued for each borrowing. This simplifies the paperwork connected with the loan and speeds the processing. In the second type of note, a large customer of the bank with a good credit rating borrows directly from the trust department instead of through the loan department. This transaction is essentially the sale of commercial paper directly to the bank trust department.

Reverse Repurchase Agreement

We discussed the use of a repurchase agreement as an investment vehicle in Chapter 9. A *reverse repurchase agreement,* or *reverse repo,* is simply the other side of the transaction in a repurchase agreement. The owner of a security needs funds for a shorter period than the maturity on a security held in its marketable securities portfolio. Rather than sell the security and have an investment decision to make when the funds are no longer needed, the firm sells the security with an agreement to repurchase it. This transaction is very similar to a loan with the security used as collateral. Since this is a very secure loan, the rate is usually below that on other types of loans. The sale and repurchase prices are usually sufficiently below the face value of the security used to ensure that the market value will not drop below the repurchase price during the term of the agreement.

We illustrate the use of a reverse repo by returning to the example of the Atlas Paving Company. The treasurer determines that she needs approximately

---

[4] See Chapter 19 for a more complete discussion of how a banker's acceptance is created and how it is used in international trade.

$950,000 for 5 days. She can borrow against her credit line at the Metropolitan National Bank at an interest rate of the bank CD rate plus .5%. Currently the CD rate is 8.25%, so her borrowing costs would be 8.75%. The interest cost would be $1,154.51 for the 5-day loan. She has a T-bill with a $1,000,000 face value and a 24-day maturity in her marketable securities portfolio. With a current rate quote of 7.25%, she could sell the T-bill at a price of $995,166.67. If instead she sells the T-bill at $950,000 with an agreement to repurchase it at $951,000, the purchaser of the security earns, and the treasurer pays, $(1,000/950,000)(365/5) = 7.68\%$. This is cheaper than borrowing under the line of credit. In addition, by doing a reverse repo, the treasurer avoids the transactions costs and investment rate risk involved in selling the security now and reinvesting the funds after 5 days.

Unsecured Borrowing

Many of the lending agreements with commercial banks are unsecured. Lines of credit and revolving credit agreements are usually unsecured, made on the basis of the general financial strength of the borrower. This type of lending is sometimes referred to as *financial statement lending* because the loan is based on the strength of the income statement and the balance sheet of the organization. The bank looks both at the cash flow–generating capability of the organization and at the liquid resources as the repayment source. If the borrower defaults, the bank is a general creditor and has no specific claim on any assets of the firm. Although every company desires a loan with the fewest number of restrictions, banks make unsecured loans only to those customers for which they perceive little, if any, repayment problem. Unsecured loans are usually granted only to firms that have a long, stable history of solid financial performance.

Secured Loan

A *secured loan* is any loan that, as part of the loan agreement, gives the lender a claim on a specific set of assets in case of default. There are two different approaches to secured lending: a collateralized loan and an asset-based loan.

Collateralized Loan

Under a *collateralized loan* the bank still views the credit from a financial statement perspective. However, the customer presents too much risk for the bank to grant credit on an unsecured basis. Just as fire regulations require that there be two exits to any building, the bank wants a second way out of a loan in case the primary "exit" is unavailable. Collateral pledged as security for the loan provides this second exit.

If the borrower defaults on one of the conditions of the loan and the loan cannot be paid when it is called, the collateral can be seized, after the appropriate legal steps are taken, and disposed of to generate (hopefully) the funds to retire the loan. Although the collateral is sometimes called a *secondary repayment source,* the bank does not view it as a means of repaying the loan, but rather as a way of minimizing any potential loss if the loan is not repaid.

The assets most commonly taken as collateral for a short-term loan are accounts receivable and inventory. The bank wants to ensure that the collateral is adequate to cover the loan if the second way out must be used. There are some costs in attempting to use collateral as a means of repayment. If accounts receivable are taken as collateral, it may be difficult for the bank to collect from some accounts because of the lack of a future supplier relationship influencing the willingness to pay, or because of disputes over returned or defective merchandise. The bank may sell the accounts receivable to a collection agent, but this might be at a substantial discount from the full face value.

If inventory is used as collateral, it is necessary to find someone interested in purchasing it. Clearly, work-in-process inventory has virtually no value and raw material has only a commodity value. Only the finished goods inventory can be converted to cash at a reasonable value. Frequently, the reason the borrower has difficulty in generating cash flows to pay off the loan is that sales were below projections. Under these conditions, the salability of the inventory at anything approaching full value must be questioned.

Because of potential difficulties, costs of disposal, and loss of value of the collateral, a bank is not willing to accept collateral at full face value. A bank may be willing to loan up to 80% or 90% of the accounts that are less than 90 days past due. Since costs and potential problems in disposing of inventory are much greater than those of accounts receivable, the percentage of inventory accepted as collateral is much lower. A loan of 40% to 75% of the finished goods inventory value as collateral is common.

Psychological Value of Collateral

There is also a psychological reason for a bank to insist on collateral for a loan. Most borrowers have many different creditors with various degrees of importance. If one of these creditors, the bank, has the ability to lay claim to the accounts receivable or inventory, the borrower may pay more attention to ensuring that the terms of that particular credit arrangement are satisfied first.

Me-First Value of Collateral

Sometimes a bank will insist on collateral for a loan that appears to be of sufficient risk to justify an unsecured loan. The pledging of assets as collateral keeps the borrower from pledging those assets to another creditor, thereby causing a deterioration in the bank's position.

Collateral Management Costs

The use of collateral as security for a loan usually generates additional paperwork and additional costs. If the collateral either is not present or is not in the anticipated condition when acquired by the bank, it is of little value in satisfying the claim from the loan. To ensure that the accounts receivable are of the desired quality, the borrower has to supply a periodic detailed list of accounts receivable.[5] Physical evidence, and possibly physical segregation, of the inventory pledged as collateral is required. Appropriate legal filings are made to "perfect" the bank's position. These costs are usually passed on to the borrower through a higher rate or specific fees. Any such fees and any added costs by the borrower of maintaining or documenting the collateral should be included in the calculation of the effective cost of the loan.

Asset-Based Loan

An *asset-based loan* is a secured loan. However, the approval procedure and the role that the assets play are sufficiently different that it is frequently considered a separate type of loan. As described previously, unsecured and collateralized loans are based on the general financial strength of the company. The cash flow–generating potential of the operations represents the primary repayment source for the loan. The primary source of repayment for an asset-based loan is the value of the asset that represents the security for the loan. Asset-based loans are usually made to companies that do not have a financial history strong enough to receive a financial statement loan. This may be due to poor financial performance or to a lack of history for a new company. In either case, the probability of failure to repay is high. The primary consideration in an asset-based loan is whether the assets secured by the loan have the liquidation value necessary to support the loan.

Ensuring that the supporting assets maintain their value over the life of the loan is essential for an asset-based loan. Establishing safeguards and moving quickly to protect the value of the collateral are more important to the lender than the future well-being of the borrower. If it is necessary to seize the collateral to ensure that the scheduled payment on the loan is made, action is quickly taken. If such action causes the borrower financial difficulties, and perhaps results in bankruptcy, it is unfortunate, but this is not a sufficient reason for delay. For example, it is not unknown for a retailer with inventory financed by an asset-based loan who has missed a payment on Friday to arrive at work on Monday morning and find that the lender has obtained a court order, the locks on the building have been changed, and the lender is in the process of cleaning out the shelves to start liquidating the inventory.

---

[5] In some cases, the customer may have to supply copies of invoices and records of payment for each account.

Security Arrangements

To ensure that the collateral is present to provide for liquidation of the debt, the lender establishes a very stringent set of controls. For an accounts receivable loan, the lender may require that the borrower's customers be instructed to send payments directly to the lender. This can be done by directing them to a post office box that is managed by the lender so that the customers are unaware of the arrangement. The lender applies the funds directly to the repayment of the loan. As additional sales are made, evidence of the receivables generated is forwarded to the lender, who gives the borrower an additional cash advance based on the new receivables.

Security for the inventory presents a different set of problems. The lender insists that the inventory that is the basis for the loan be identified and segregated from any other inventory. The control mechanism depends on the characteristics of the inventory. When the units are of high value and individually identifiable, such as automobiles at a car dealership, the serial numbers and/or other unique descriptions of the items financed is included on the paperwork. This type of loan is sometimes called *floor planning*.

In the case of an inventory consisting of many small, not individually identifiable units, such as the back-room extra inventory for a hardware store, it is necessary to make sure that the financed inventory is segregated. Frequently, the inventory is kept in an enclosed area, and a bonded employee is in charge of the keys and designated as the only one who can enter the area. This arrangement is known as a *field warehouse*. Inventory is moved out of the secured area only after the designated employee receives the approval of the lender.

In some instances, the lender may require that a *public warehouse* be used for the storage of inventory. The lender holds the warehouse receipt as evidence of its claim. The inventory is not released from the public warehouse until this is authorized by the lender and the warehouse bill has been paid. A grocery store financing the advance purchase of frozen turkeys in anticipation of a brisk Thanksgiving business might find this type of arrangement specified by the lender. Cash must be generated from other sources to pay off the loan for the inventory before the turkeys can be brought into the store for sale.

The costs of maintaining this type of security can be quite high; the public warehouse is the most expensive arrangement. All of these costs, from fees to the lender to the costs of maintaining the warehouse arrangements, should be included in the calculation of the effective cost of the financing.

At this point, let us pause and review the types of lending arrangements we have discussed. The simplest loan is unsecured and is based on the general credit standing of the company. Both borrower and lender prefer this type of loan. For a firm with too much risk for an unsecured loan, the lender may insist on collateral. Liquidation of this collateral is not viewed as a repayment source, but rather as a means of minimizing any losses if the loan is not repaid. Least desirable, and most costly, is the true asset-based loan, in which the liquidation value of the asset is the basis for the loan. The lender institutes a control mechanism to ensure that the asset's value is maintained and that it is quickly available to liquidate the loan.

Comparing the Effective Cost
of Funds

In choosing between different loan alternatives, the financial manager compares features such as terms, maturity, security required, and covenants on the loans. One of the most important features is the effective interest rate of the loan. This effective rate must be calculated consistently across loans so that a valid comparison can be made.

An effective interest cost on a loan is calculated using the same measure as that described in Chapter 10 for the effective yield on money market investments: the simple interest bond equivalent yield. We now discuss how the effective rate is affected by the type of loan, the way the charges are assessed, and the use of the loan. For most of the discussion, we assume that the interest rate to be assessed on the loan is fixed and known in advance. Later we examine the complications caused by the existence of a variable rate on the loan.

Single-Payment Loans

Add-On Interest

A single-payment add-on interest loan involves the simplest effective interest rate calculation. To calculate the effective rate, first determine the total payment to be made at maturity, MP. This consists of principal plus interest plus any loan fees paid at maturity. Second, determine the net proceeds of the loan, PR. These proceeds are the amount of cash the borrower receives from the lender. This is the principal amount of the loan less any fees paid at origination. The effective rate, i, is determined as follows:

$$i = \frac{MP - PR}{PR} \times \frac{365}{t} \tag{12.1}$$

Returning to our example of the Atlas Paving Company, we find that the treasurer has a 60-day single-payment add-on loan for $500,000 from the Metropolitan Bank. The loan has an interest rate of 12% per year (assume that Metropolitan uses a 360-day year) and a loan origination fee of $500, which is paid in advance. The effective annual rate is

$$i = \frac{510,000 - 499,500}{499,500} \times \frac{365}{60} = 12.79\%.$$

In some instances, a slightly simplified calculation might be used. Instead of subtracting any advance fees from the principal to get the proceeds, the fee is simply included in the numerator and the principal is used in the denominator. In this example, an effective rate of 12.78% results from the modified calculation. The difference is small in this example because the fee is small relative to the amount of the loan. Since the first calculation is the correct one, and since it is no more difficult than the incorrect one, we will use the first one.

Discount Loan

The procedure for calculating the effective rate on a discount loan is the same as on the add-on loan: determine the cash flow paid at maturity, subtract the cash flow proceeds received at origination, divide by the proceeds, and adjust to an annualized basis. The factor that makes this only slightly more difficult is the calculation of the proceeds, since the interest is subtracted in advance.

The treasurer for Atlas receives a quote from the Second National Bank of a rate of 11.5% with no origination fee on a discount loan of $500,000 for 60 days. Again, assuming the bank is using a 360-day year in specifying the interest, the effective rate is

$$i = \frac{500,000 - 490,416.67}{490,416.67} \times \frac{365}{60} = 11.89\%.$$

The formula given in Equation (12.1) can be used to calculate the effective interest rate for any single-payment loan. Whether the loan is part of a letter of credit arrangement or a stand-alone arrangement does not affect the way in which the calculation is done. Of course, the fees are different for different types of loans, so the effective rates may well be different.

Line of Credit

Determining an effective annual rate for a credit line arrangement is more difficult. First, the financial manager may obtain a credit line larger than anticipated needs to provide a buffer—some built-in excess borrowing capacity or financial insurance. Second, borrowing against the line is not constant for the entire year; rather, it varies with cash flow needs. Third, commitment fees or compensating balances can be based either on the total amount of the line or on the unused portion of the line. These costs must all be assessed and included in the calculation for the effective rate on the credit line to be comparable with that calculated for other borrowing alternatives. Perhaps the easiest way to illustrate the correct inclusion of these costs is through a numerical example.

Cash Flow Needs

The starting point for determining the effective cost of a credit line is to identify the cash flow needs over the year. In most firms, this is an output of the cash flow forecasting or financial planning and budgeting process. The cash flow needs for the Atlas Paving Company are given in Table 12.2. The

Table 12.2 Cash Flow
Needs for the Atlas
Paving Company

Quarter	Cash Needs
1	$1,000,000
2	$2,500,000
3	$5,000,000
4	$ 0

maximum cash flow needs during the year are seen to be $5,000,000 in the third quarter.[6]

Size of the Credit Line

The credit line must be large enough to provide the maximum anticipated cash flow needs, a desired liquidity buffer, and any required compensating balances. As an offset against compensating balances, the firm can use any cash balances normally held and not used to compensate the bank for other services provided.[7]

For the Atlas Paving Company, the maximum cash need is $5,000,000. The treasurer desires to keep a buffer for unexpected cash needs of 20% above the planned maximum, or $1,000,000, and the compensating balance in the credit line agreement is 5% of the amount of the credit line. Atlas is currently using all of its transactions balances as compensation for tangible services, such as lockboxes, and therefore has none available to serve as compensating balances for the loan. Thus, 95% of the credit line, which is the maximum useful funds that can be borrowed under the line, has to equal $6,000,000. This results in a total credit line of $6,315,789. The treasurer rounds this off to a credit line request of $6,300,000. The calculations used in determining the size of the credit line are given in Table 12.3.

A credit line of $6,300,000 does not provide the full buffer that the treasurer desires. Since $315,000 has to be maintained in a compensating balance, only $985,000, or 19.7% of the maximum cash need, is available for unexpected events. The treasurer feels that this is close enough to qualify as approximately 20%.

Calculating the Effective Rate

The next step in determining the effective rate on the credit line is to calculate the amount of the loan borrowed against the line and the interest due for

---

[6] Most companies have a monthly forecast of cash flows. We are using a quarterly forecast in the example to simplify the illustration and the calculations.

[7] In some instances, it is possible for a firm to count the same balances both for compensation for tangible services and for compensation for credit lines. The practice, known as *double counting of balances,* was once fairly common but has all but disappeared today.

Table 12.3 Determining the Size of the Credit Line Required

Credit line	=	maximum cash need + compensating balance + buffer − available cash
Compensating balance	=	5% of the credit line
Buffer	=	20% of the maximum cash need
Credit line (CL)	=	$5,000,000 + .05CL + $1,000,000
	=	$6,315,789

Credit line obtained = $6,300,000

each period. The loan is the total of the cash need for the quarter plus the compensating balance requirements, which for Atlas have to be borrowed. For simplicity in calculating the interest on the loans, we assume that each quarter has an equal number of days. The effective rate is determined by dividing the total interest paid during the year by the average usable loan provided during the year. We can see from Table 12.4 that the effective rate on the planned usage on this line of credit is 13.78%.

A natural question at this point is, why is the denominator the average usable loan? First, the *average usable* loan represents the average amount of cash that the firm receives from the loan during the year. The *total* loan also

Table 12.4 Determining the Effective Cost of Credit Line Borrowing

Credit Line Obtained = $6,300,000
Compensating Balance Required = $315,000
Interest Rate = 12%

AMOUNT OF LOAN AND INTEREST BY QUARTERS

Quarter	Cash Needs	Loan Amount	Interest
1	$1,000,000	$1,315,000	$ 39,450
2	$2,500,000	$2,815,000	$ 84,450
3	$5,000,000	$5,315,000	$159,450
4	$ 0	$ 315,000	$ 9,450

$$\text{Average cash needs} = \frac{1,000,000 + 2,500,000 + 5,000,000 + 0}{4}$$

$$= \$2,125,000$$

Total interest paid = $292,800

EFFECTIVE INTEREST RATE

Effective rate	=	total interest/average cash needs
	=	$292,800/$2,125,000
	=	13.78%

includes the borrowing to provide the compensating balance. This increases the amount of the loan, and consequently the amount of interest paid, but it does not benefit the firm because it cannot be used to cover cash flow needs. Second, because the compensating balance is based on the total line of credit, which is largely a function of the maximum cash need during the year, it is not meaningful to look at an effective rate for a period of less than a year. For example, examining the cost of the loan in the first period, when $315,000 of the $1,315,000 loan provides the compensating balance against the line, does not give a meaningful number. It is the cost of the credit line arrangement and borrowing under that agreement for the entire year that is relevant.

Components of the Effective Rate

The stated rate on the line of credit is 12%, but the effective rate is 13.78%. There are several factors that raise the effective rate over the stated rate. It is useful for the financial manager to be able to break down this effective rate into its components, both to understand and to attempt to lower the borrowing costs. The breakdown of the effective rate into the components of the nominal (stated) rate, the compensating balance, the seasonality of cash needs, and the buffer is shown in Table 12.5.

If there was no compensating balance requirement on the credit line, the firm would only borrow enough to cover the cash flow needs for the period at the time.[8] The effective rate would then be just equal to the nominal rate on the loan of 12%.

The existence of the compensating balance increases the effective cost of the loan because the firm must borrow and pay interest on an amount greater than it is able to use. Since the compensating balance is assessed on the total line, which is a function of the maximum cash needs and the desired buffer, these effects must be separated to identify the increment in cost due to the compensating balance. We separate these effects by assuming that the loan needs are flat at the average need for the year (no seasonality) and that no buffer is included in the credit line. Under these conditions, a credit line of $2,236,842 is required to provide a usable loan of $2,125,000 and the compensating balance of $111,842. The effective rate on this loan would be 12.63%. Thus, the existence of the compensating balance alone increases the effective cost of the loan by .63% above the stated rate.

The next step in determining the component costs of the credit line is to identify the cost of the credit line with seasonal cash flow needs but no buffer for unexpected cash flow. This requires a credit line of $5,263,158, just large enough to cover the maximum cash need of $5,000,000 and provide the compensating balance of $263,158. Under these conditions, the credit line has an effective rate of 13.49%. Thus, the increment in the effective rate due to the seasonality of cash flows is 13.49% − 12.63% or .86%.

---

[8] Recall that we are using a compensating balance as the compensation for keeping the credit line available. A similar approach would be used if a commitment fee were substituted for the compensating balance.

Table 12.5 Determining Components of the Effective Interest Rate

RATE WITHOUT BALANCES, SEASONAL CASH FLOW OR BUFFER

Effective Rate = Nominal Rate = 12%

RATE WITHOUT SEASONAL CASH FLOW OR BUFFER

Average Cash Need = \$2,125,000
Credit Line = 2,125,000 + .05(credit line) − beginning cash
Credit Line = \$2,236,842
Compensating Balance = \$111,842
Effective Rate = \$268,421/\$2,125,000 = 12.63%

RATE WITHOUT BUFFER

Credit Line = \$5,000,000 + .05(credit line)
 = \$5,263,158

Quarter	Cash Needs	Loan Amount	Interest
1	\$1,000,000	\$1,263,158	\$ 37,895
2	\$2,500,000	\$2,763,158	\$ 82,895
3	\$5,000,000	\$5,263,158	\$157,895
4	\$ 0	\$ 263,158	\$ 7,895

Average cash needs = \$2,125,000
Total interest = \$286,579
Effective rate = \$286,579/\$2,125,000 = 13.49%

The last component of the effective rate, the difference between 13.78% and 13.49%, is due to inclusion of the buffer in determining the size of the credit line. These component costs of the effective rate are summarized in Table 12.6.

Use of Component Cost Breakdown

The financial manager can use this breakdown of the component costs of the credit line borrowing in managing the cost of short-term financing. The ease with which the manager can adjust the borrowing costs is inversely related to the order of the cost components investigated. The manager has the most control over the last item, the buffer. Although the specification of the buffer

Table 12.6 Summary of the Components of Borrowing Costs

Nominal rate	=	12.00%
Increment due to compensating balance	=	.63%
Increment due to seasonal cash flow needs	=	.86%
Increment due to buffer	=	.29%
Total effective rate	=	13.78%

can be based on a probabilistic analysis of the forecasting error, it may be a relatively arbitrary number. The treasurer of Atlas has to decide whether the buffer is worth the increase in effective cost of .29%. As with any insurance, the question is whether the coverage is worth the premium. This is a fairly simple decision that can be made independently by the management of the firm.

The next element in controlling the cost of the credit line is the seasonality of cash flows. If cash flow needs can be altered to flatten the peaks and valleys, perhaps by shifting some inflows or outflows into adjacent periods, the maximum loan needs can be reduced, with a corresponding reduction in the size of the credit line and compensating balances. While this might be difficult to achieve, it is an action that can be taken by the management of the firm without any need for negotiation with the bank.

The third element is a reduction in the amount of the compensating balance or the commitment fee. Any reduction here reduces the cost of having a larger credit line. If there are competing banks attempting to lend to the firm, this is a negotiating point. Note that the effect of the compensating balance requirement is to increase the effective rate by .63%, which is probably more than the difference in the nominal rates quoted by competing banks.

The final item is the nominal rate charged on the line. While this is open to negotiation with the bank, the treasurer is likely to have much less success in reducing the stated rate than in negotiating a lower balance requirement. Reduction in the nominal rate probably requires an improved financial picture for the company, as well as access to nonbank financing sources.

Revolving Credit Agreement

The procedure for determining the effective rate for a revolving credit agreement is the same as that for a credit line. The major difference is that the determination of cash flow needs and the likely use of loans over the extended life of the agreement may be more difficult to calculate. However, since many revolving credit agreements are revised annually, the calculation of the effective rate for the first year of the agreement is satisfactory in many instances.

Variable Interest Rate

In calculating the effective interest rate on short-term borrowing, we assumed that the interest rate was fixed for the life of the loan. While this is an acceptable assumption for some loans, such as a single-payment loan issued under a letter of credit, it is not realistic for many types of loans. With a variable-rate loan, it is necessary to estimate the interest rates that will be in force during the time of the loan. This is a task that is likely to be filled with forecasting errors. There is, however, no other alternative if the manager wants to estimate the effective cost of a lending arrangement. Since the estimate can be expected to have a large error, a sensitivity analysis should be performed to estimate the effective rate under different interest rate conditions. A more advanced version of this procedure is to use different economic scenarios and incorporate the effect on the variation in cash flows and the variation in interest rates.

While the forecasting of interest rates in the future appears to be an onerous task, it is not as critical as it may first seem. One of the primary purposes of attempting to determine the effective interest rate on a loan is to be able to compare financing alternatives. The financing alternatives available are likely to use approximately the same base, whether this is the prime rate or a money market rate, from which to determine the rate on the loan. Although there are a few exceptions, most banks change their prime rate within a few days of changes in money center banks and have the same prime rate. A money market–based rate, by its very nature, will be approximately the same at different banks. Thus, errors in estimating the interest rate may result in inaccurate estimates of the effective cost of a particular loan, but there should be little bias in making comparisons across financing alternatives.

Summary

Commercial banks are the single most important source of short-term financing for corporations. Bank financing arrangements include single-payment loans, lines of credit, revolving credit agreements, letters of credit, banker's acceptances, and master notes. Banks prefer to make unsecured loans if the creditworthiness of the customer is adequate. If it is necessary to protect their position in dealing with a less creditworthy borrower, banks may collateralize the loan with assets pledged as security. Whether the loan is unsecured or collateralized, the primary source of repayment is expected to be the cash flow–generating capability of the firm. A true asset-based loan is one that is based primarily on the value of the assets being financed. These loans are characterized by the existence of strong controls to maintain the value of the asset and a willingness to move quickly to seize the asset for liquidation in case of default.

The interest rate on loans can be either fixed or variable. Short, single-payment loans may have a fixed rate that is established at the rate prevailing when the loan is issued. Variable-rate loans are based on a reference rate such as the prime rate of the bank or an externally determined money market rate. In addition to the interest rate on borrowings outstanding, banks may require payment in the form of a commitment fee or compensating balances to lend under a line of credit, a revolving credit agreement, or a letter of credit.

The costs of various financing alternatives are compared by calculating the effective rate expressed in the same manner for each alternative. The effective rate on a single-payment loan is determined by finding the difference between the cash received and the cash paid back, dividing this difference by the cash received, and annualizing the rate. A line of credit presents a more difficult problem because the commitment fee or the compensating balance is based on the total amount of the line, whereas the interest is assessed on the loan actually outstanding, which varies over the year. The effective rate is found by determining the average useful loan outstanding and relating the interest and fee payments to this average.

———————— Discussion Questions ————————

1. What are the characteristics of a single-payment loan?
2. What sources of competition have reduced banks' loans prices?
3. What are the characteristics of a line of credit?
4. What is a letter of credit, and how does its use shift the risk from the borrower to the bank?
5. Why are some firms charged a variable rate based on the bank's prime rate, while others are charged a rate based on money market rates?
6. Why are most bank loans priced with variable rates instead of fixed rates?
7. What are the implications for risk bearing in the shift from fixed-rate to variable-rate pricing on loans?
8. Why is a buffer necessary in setting the size of a line of credit, and how might the amount of the buffer be determined?
9. Outline and contrast the different ways that a bank can receive compensation for a credit line.
10. Why does a bank require compensation based either on the total amount of the credit agreement or on the unused portion of the credit?
11. What factors cause the useful loan to be different from the loan outstanding?
12. Why does a secured, or asset-based, loan usually carry a higher interest rate even though collateral exists to back up the loan?
13. Why are banks primarily short-term lenders?
14. Comment on the statement "A credit line is a good source of off-balance-sheet liquidity."

———————————— Problems ————————————

1. The Davis Company is planning to borrow $150,000 for 90 days on a single-payment, add-on loan at a stated interest rate of 11.5%.
   a. How many dollars of interest will they pay (assume that the bank charges interest on a 360-day year)?
   b. What is the effective annualized rate for this loan?
   c. How would your answer to (b) change if the loan term was 180 days? 360 days?

2. Narrow Tie, Inc., is borrowing to purchase materials for seasonal production. The treasurer has determined that he needs $750,000 for 90 days. Big Green Bank has offered to lend the money on a single-payment discount note with an interest rate of 11%. Determine the amount of the loan that the treasurer must request and the effective interest rate on the loan.

3. The treasurer of the Willow Brook Development Company needs to borrow $500,000 for 60 days. The Western Bank has offered a discount loan at a rate of 10%.

   a. What is the total loan that Willow Brook must obtain to receive the full $500,000?
   b. What is the effective annualized rate on the loan?
   c. Repeat (a) and (b) for a loan maturity of 90, 180, 270, and 360 days.
   d. Graph the spread between the stated rate and the effective rate as a function of maturity.

4. Red, Inc., is borrowing under a secured loan, with its inventory as collateral. The bank charges 13% interest and a 1% origination fee. The maximum loan is 75% of the value of the inventory pledged. The inventory is to be stored in a public warehouse. The warehouse charges a flat fee of $200 per month and a space charge that averages .25% per month of the value of the goods stored. Red has $750,000 in inventory that can be pledged for 90 days. What is the effective rate of this borrowing arrangement if Red obtains the maximum allowed loan?

5. The Hammer and Sickle Company has a loan from the Birch National Bank that is secured by accounts receivable. The terms of the loan are as follows: the maximum loan is 90% of the accounts less than 90 days old and the interest rate is 14%. Although the bank charges no fees for handling the security, the treasurer figures that it costs about $1 per account to keep the bank notified of which accounts are eligible to serve as collateral. Hammer and Sickle's accounts receivable have averaged $2,500,000 over the past year, with about 10% being more than 90 days old. The accounts have an average size of $15,000 each. If the company borrows the maximum allowed under the agreement, what is the amount of financing provided and what is the effective cost?

6. The Pine Wood Company has a credit line of $1,000,000 with its bank, for which it agrees to keep a 5% balance on the line. The loan interest charges are 1% a month for the average loan outstanding during the month. Assume that all needed balances are borrowed from the bank.

   a. During March, Pine Wood had cash needs averaging $500,000. What is the amount borrowed, the compensating balance, and the amount of interest paid?
   b. During July, Pine Wood's operating cash needs were zero, but it borrowed to provide the compensating balance. How much did it borrow and how much interest did it pay?

7. The Exacto National Bank has decided to be completely flexible with the terms for credit line compensation. Exacto's reserve requirement at the Fed is 12%, and it has a target rate of return on available balances of 10% per year. A credit line of $1,000,000 would generally require a 10% compensating balance. What monthly commitment fees should Exacto charge a firm with such a line that wants to pay in fees rather than in balances?

8. The Roget Company has a bank credit line of $2,000,000. The company estimates the cash needs by quarters, as shown in the following table. If the bank requires a 10% compensating balance on the total line and a 10% compensating balance on the loan against the line, what is the maximum loan that is used (assume that the firm has to borrow any compensating balances)?

Quarter	Cash Needs
1	$ 200,000
2	$ 400,000
3	$1,200,000
4	$ 0

9. The Peachy Fruit Company has negotiated a line of credit, with a compensating balance requirement of 10% of the total line. The line is for $12,000,000 and the borrowing against the line averaged $10,000,000 during the year. If the stated interest rate is 13%, what is the effective annual rate that Peachy is paying on the loan?

10. The Fortune Oil Company has projected cash needs over the coming year and plans to use a bank line of credit to provide the funds. The cash needed is as follows:

Jan–Apr	$1,200,000
May–Jun	$ 800,000
Jul–Sep	$ 200,000
Oct–Dec	$1,000,000

Assume that the cash needs occur on the first day of the period and remain until the last day. The cash needs are exclusive of any compensating balance requirements. Two banks have offered to supply a credit line to Fortune under the following terms:

	Big Dallas Bank	Big Houston Bank
Nominal rate	12.5%	14%
Compensating balance on line	10%	0%
Commitment fee	0%	0.5%

a. Assume a credit line of $1,600,000 at the Houston Bank and compute the effective cost of borrowing from it if this is the only bank used.

b. How large a credit line would be needed from the Big Dallas Bank to obtain the same useful borrowing capacity?

c. Compute the effective cost of borrowing from the Big Dallas Bank.

d. Factor the effective interest rate for each bank into four components.

11. A bank is offering terms on a $500,000 credit line of 12% interest, with 5% required balances on the amount of the line and 5% required balances on any usage of the line.

a. If a firm needed a $100,000 useful loan and wanted to borrow all compensating balances from the bank, what would the *total* loan have to be?

b. What is the effective interest rate on the borrowing?

12. The Sears National Bank in Sears, Indiana, is willing to allow the customer to choose its own combination of balance requirements against the line and rates from the following matrix:

Balance requirement	0%	2.5%	5%
Rate: prime plus	1.5%	1%	0.75%

The bank has a commitment fee of 3/8%, which is charged on the total amount of the line. You anticipate having cash flow needs of $800,000 during the first 6 months of the year and $400,000 during the second 6 months. You want a total credit line of $1,000,000 and would have to borrow any compensating balances.

a. If you expect a prime rate of 10% which option would you choose?

b. How would your answer differ at an expected prime rate of 13%?

13. Look Back, Inc., a genealogical survey company, needs to borrow $450,000 for 7 days. It is considering a repo on a $500,000 treasury note that it holds in its marketable securities portfolio. The treasurer has determined that the bank will do a reverse repo (the bank will buy the security) for $450,000, with an agreement to resell it to Look Back at a price of $450,918.75 in 7 days. What is the effective annual interest rate on the repo?

━━━━━━━━━ **Case: *The McMillen Boat Company*** ━━━━━━━━━

Mary Alston, the treasurer of the McMillen Boat Company, is planning her short-term financing needs for the next year. She has estimated the cumulative operating cash flow needs to be as follows (all figures are in $1,000s):

Jan	100	Feb	1,750	Mar	5,500	Apr	7,500
May	8,000	Jun	8,000	Jul	6,000	Aug	4,500
Sep	1,500	Oct	500	Nov	0	Dec	0

Ms. Alston feels fairly confident of most of the items in the forecast, with one exception: sales. Both the seasonality of the business and the state of the economy have invalidated the forecast in the past. A study done by an intern from the state university last summer compared the forecasted cash flow with the actual flow on a monthly basis for a 5-year period. The intern's report showed that the forecast error had a distribution with an expected value of 0% and a standard deviation of about 10%. Ms. Alston knew that this factor should somehow be incorporated in the planning for the credit arrangements, but she wasn't sure how to do so. It had been a long time since her MBA statistics course, which was the last time she worked with probability distributions.

She has made preliminary contact with the company's two banks concerning the terms and the amount of credit line they might be willing to consider for McMillen. The 7th Avenue National Bank has quoted terms of the prime rate plus 3/4% for a maximum credit line of $12,000,000, which would require a compensating balance of 5% of the amount of the line, regardless of the usage on the line. Bank de Boulevard has quoted the prime rate plus 1% on a line of up to $10,000,000, with a commitment fee of 1/4% of the amount of the line unused during a month.

The McMillen Boat Company currently maintains its general disbursement account and the company's lockbox at the 7th Avenue Bank. The bank allows compensation for services by a mixture of fees and balances but insists that at least half of the charges must be covered by balances. McMillen carries an average balance of $500,000 at the 7th Avenue Bank to compensate for services. Service charges are estimated to be $2,300 per month and will just be covered by the average balance.

Bank de Boulevard is used for payroll and other specialized disbursing accounts. McMillen carries an average balance of $150,000 at this bank, which just covers the service charges for the accounts. Bank de Boulevard requires that service charges be covered by balances and not cash fees.

As the new assistant treasurer who will be working with the banks in the future, you have been asked by Ms. Alston to prepare a recommendation on the size of the credit line that McMillen should obtain, and which bank should get the company's loan business this year. As she left your office she said, half to herself, "Now I can go and work on the marketing manager about changing our credit terms to speed our collections. I'll bet we could advance about $1 million from March and April by getting rid of that stupid seasonal dating plan on our Century line of boats."

Although banking relations are important in the decision, you know that Ms. Alston is highly influenced by the lowest-cost alternatives. Furthermore, since both banks want McMillen's business, there may be some room for negotiation on the terms of the credit line.

As you start on your assignment, you realize that you will have to make an assumption about the prime rate for the next year. Both banks currently have the prime set at 9%, and tend to raise and lower the rate within a few days of one another. After glancing at several business periodicals you conclude that the estimates of the "experts" range from a drop of 100 basis points to a rise of the same magnitude.

--- **Selected Readings** ---

BUCK, W. H., "Risk Management Approach to Pricing Loans and Leases," *Journal of Commercial Bank Lending* (April 1979), pp. 2–15.

CARTER, J.N., "Bank Evaluation," *Journal of Cash Management* (October 1983), pp. 10–20.

CRAMER, R. H., and W. E. STERK, "Present Value Approach to Commercial Loan Pricing," *Journal of Bank Research* (Winter 1982), pp. 207–217.

HAYES, D. A., *Bank Lending Policies, Domestic and International,* Bureau of Business Research, University of Michigan (1971).

HEMPLE, D. A., A. B. COLEMAN, and D. G. SIMONSON, *Bank Management, Text and Cases,* New York: Wiley, 1983.

HILL, NED C., WILLIAM L. SARTORIS, and SUE L. VISSCHER, "The Components of Credit Line Borrowing Costs," *Journal of Cash Management* (October 1983), pp. 47ff.

JAMES, C., "Pricing Alternatives for Loan Commitments," *Journal of Bank Research* (Winter 1983), pp. 300–303.

SEVERSON, GARY R., "Determining Pricing Alternatives," *Journal of Commercial Bank Lending* (November 1974), pp. 2–8.

SHERWOOD, HUGH C., *How Corporate and Municipal Debt Is Rated.* New York: Wiley, 1976.

STEVENS, H. B., "Legal Aspects of Bank Loans," *Banker's Magazine* (November 1981), pp. 51–60.

STOCK, K. L., "Asset-Based Financing: Borrower and Lender Perspectives," *Journal of Commercial Bank Lending* (December 1980), pp. 31–46.

STONE, BERNELL K., "Allocating Credit Lines, Planned Borrowing, and Tangible Services Over a Company's Banking System," *Financial Management* (Summer 1975), pp. 65–78.

ULRICH, T. A., "Financial Planning Implications of Bank Loan Pricing," *Journal of Commercial Bank Lending* (September 1980), pp. 64–70.

13

Non-bank Sources of Short-term Credit

When CB Sports, Inc., was turned down in 1980 by a bank on a $4,000,000 loan request to buy out a dissident shareholder and to finance seasonal business needs, they obtained a secured line of credit from Commercial Credit Business Loans, Inc. The General Electric Credit Corporation financed $544,000,000 out of a total of $870,000,000 leveraged buyout of Metromedia, Inc., in September 1986. Merrill Lynch has established a Working Capital Management Account, and for an annual fee of $100 invests incoming revenues in a money market fund, transfers funds to and from banks, and offers a line of credit to qualified customers of up to $2,000,000. In December 1986 the Federal Reserve Board, following an appeal court's ruling, gave Bankers Trust authority to distribute commercial paper through a commercial lending subsidiary.

In Chapter 12 we examined the borrowing arrangements available from commercial banks. As the preceding examples indicate, nonbank funding options are also available to businesses. Common nonbank sources of funding are commercial paper, commercial finance companies, factors, captive finance companies, and off-balance-sheet financing arrangements. In this chapter, we examine these alternative sources of funds, as well as the choice between fixed- and variable-rate financing.

Commercial Paper

Commercial paper is an unsecured promissory note of an organization issued for a specific amount with a fixed maturity. It is issued to the supplier of funds, which allows the borrower to bypass financial intermediaries. [1] Although commercial paper may be a publicly issued security, it does not have to be registered with the Securities and Exchange Commission as long as the maturity is less than 270 days and one of the following three conditions are met: (1) the proceeds are used to finance current transactions; (2) the notes are guaranteed by a bank, either through a backup line of credit or a letter of credit; and (3) the transactions do not involve a public offering. Commercial paper issued under the third condition has been used for interim financing for plant construction and for temporary financing of acquisitions.

Most commercial paper issued in the United States has a maturity of 30 days or less. With such a short maturity, many issuers do not have the cash flow to pay off the paper at maturity and instead roll it over—sell additional paper to generate the funds to pay off the maturing paper. However, unlike rolling over a short-term bank loan, where the replacement loan is usually at the same bank, the replacement commercial paper is frequently sold to different purchasers.

Commercial paper can be issued in any denomination, in some cases as little as $25,000, although the majority is issued in denominations of $100,000 or more. Issuing commercial paper is a wholesale financial transaction dominated by the largest 1,500 or so firms in the United States. The growth in the use of commercial paper from 1965 to 1985 is shown in Figure 13.1.

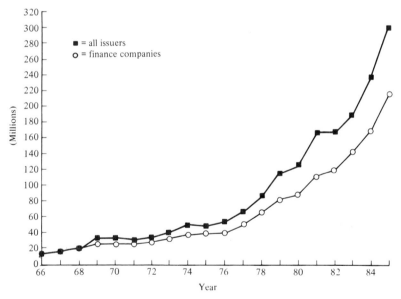

Figure 13.1 Volume of Commercial Paper, 1966-1985.

---

[1] Banks are also involved in commercial paper transactions, since they are typically named as the agent to handle the cash flow connected with issuing and redeeming the note.

Originally, the primary issuers of commercial paper were nonfinancial firms. However, as the role of consumer credit in the purchase of durables increased, finance companies became important issuers. Currently, finance companies account for almost two thirds of the paper issued. The volume of of finance company paper is also shown in Figure 13.1. Bank holding companies have become active in issuing commercial paper to fund their activities in leasing, real estate, and other nonbank lines of business. For example, in 1987 Citicorp issued almost $50,000,000 in commercial paper each week. Recently, a market for commercial paper issued in Eurodollars or other Eurocurrencies has developed. Because of transactions costs and the need for an international reputation, only the largest, most well-known U.S. companies have participated in this market.

Commercial paper is generally a discount note, although a small amount of the paper issued is interest-bearing. Interest-bearing paper has the advantage of presenting a less confusing set of calculations and transactions costs to determine the price at issue. However, when interest-bearing paper is issued, the interest rate and fees are set to be the same as those of an equivalent discount issue. The interest rate is quoted on a 360-day year and is usually fixed for the maturity of the paper, although some longer-term issues have an interest rate that varies at set time periods based upon an index rate.

Direct versus Dealer Paper

The largest finance companies generally issue commercial paper directly to the purchaser. They are in the market on a regular basis and have developed either their own sales force or a network of contacts with investors interested in buying their paper. Their frequent, almost daily, sale of paper and extensive contact with purchasers allow them to assess market conditions. The quantity of directly placed finance company paper is shown in Figure 13.2.

Industrial companies, bank holding companies, and small finance companies generally sell their paper through commercial paper dealers. These dealers have an active sales network through which the paper is sold. The issuer informs the dealer of the amount, maturity, and desired timing of the sale. The dealer advises the issuer on the rate at which the paper is likely to sell. Some issuers give the dealer the right to determine the rate at which the paper is sold. The dealer frequently underwrites the paper, that is, has the obligation to purchase any paper that is not sold on the day of issue. Dealers typically earn 5 to 15 basis points in the form of a spread for selling the paper. In a recent development in this market, large commercial banks have begun to act as agents in selling paper through a capital markets subsidiary.

Rating

Prior to the disruption in the commercial paper market in the early 1970s caused by Penn Central Railroad's default on $82,000,000 in commercial

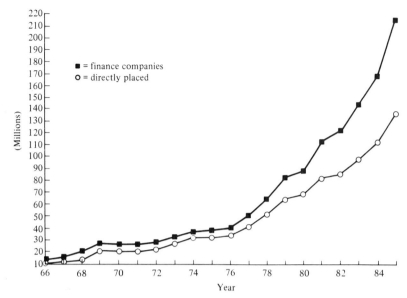

Figure 13.2 Direct and Dealer Commercial Paper.

paper, not many commercial paper issuers had their paper rated. Since that time, it has become almost a necessity to receive a high rating in order to be able to sell commercial paper, particularly in times of tight money. Four companies rate commercial paper: Standard & Poor's, Moody's, Fitch, and Duff and Phelps. Standard & Poor's rates companies A-1 to A-3, B, C, and D, with A-1 being the highest rating. Moody's uses P-1 to P-3, with P-1 being the highest. Fitch uses F-1 through F-4, with F-1 being the highest and F-4 not recommended. Duff and Phelps offers three rating categories, D-1 through D-3, with D-1 being the best.

Although each rating company has its own process and standards, the results are similar. The rating depends upon an evaluation of the management and the financial strength of the company being rated. The issuer is expected to have a strong position in a well-established industry. Strong liquidity ratios, a high long-term debt rating, and steady or growing earnings and cash flows are important. Access to unused borrowing capacity as a source of liquidity, either through a bank line of credit or an irrevocable letter of credit, is imperative. As mentioned in Chapter 12, a bank line of credit is frequently used as backing for commercial paper.

Interest Costs

The interest rate is a function of the prevailing level of interest rates, the size and maturity of the issue, and the creditworthiness and backup credit of the borrower. Commercial paper rates are generally below bank loan rates but

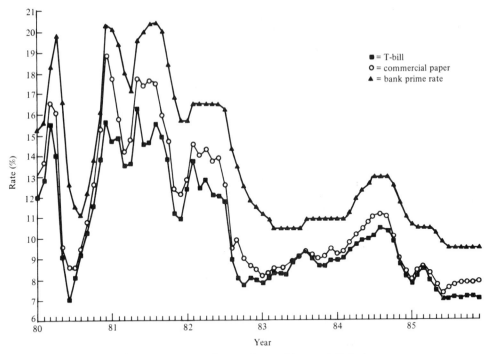

Figure 13.3 A Comparison of Interest Rates.

above T-bill rates. The historical pattern of these three rates is given in Figure 13.3.

Effective Interest Rate

The effective interest rate on commercial paper is affected by the method of distribution (direct paper or dealer paper), by the source of backup credit, and by the interest rate on the paper. The rate is calculated by determining the total charges, dividing this amount by the net cash proceeds, and annualizing the rate. In symbolic form this is

$$\text{Effective interest rate} = \frac{\text{total financing costs}}{\text{net cash proceeds}} \times \frac{365}{\text{maturity}}. \qquad (13.1)$$

The effective rate for commercial paper is illustrated by the calculation for Bloominghills, a large regional chain of department stores, given in Table 13.1. The company issues $5,000,000 in commercial paper for 30 days at a rate of 8%. The plan is to continue to roll over the paper so that approximately $5,000,000 is outstanding at all times. The dealer placing the paper earns a spread of 12 basis points. Bloominghills has a $6,000,000 backup credit line at the Continental Pennsylvania Bank, for which it pays a commitment fee of 1/4%.

Table 13.1 Calculation of the Effective Interest
Rate on Commercial Paper

A. Paper Issued for 30 Days and Rolled Over

Cash Received

Face value of paper issued	$5,000,000
Discount at 8%	33,333
Dealer spread (12 basis points)	500
Cash proceeds	$4,966,167

Financing Costs

Difference between proceeds and face value	$33,833
1-month commitment fee on $6,000,000 line of credit	1,250
Total financing costs	$35,083

Effective annual interest rate:

$$i = \frac{35,083}{4,966,167} \times \frac{365}{30} = 8.60\%$$

B. Paper Issued One Time for 30 Days

Financing Costs

Difference between proceeds and face value	$33,833
Full-year commitment fee	15,000
Total financing costs	$48,833

Effective annual interest rate:

$$i = \frac{48,833}{4,966,167} \times \frac{365}{30} = 11.96\%$$

As seen in Part A of Table 13.1, the total financing charge for the 30 days is $35,083. This financing charge includes the dealer spread, the discount from face value for the purchaser, and 1/12th of the commitment fee for the backup credit line. Since we are assuming that the paper continues to be rolled over at maturity, the commitment fee is allocated across all issues of the paper. The proceeds from the paper, or the useful amount of financing, is $4,966,167. This results in an effective annual interest rate of 8.60%.

If we drop the assumption that Bloominghills plans to roll the paper over at maturity, and instead assume that the issuance of paper is a one-shot deal, we must include the total cost of the commitment fee for the backup credit line for this one issue. This raises the effective cost to 11.96%. If a firm does not plan to roll over its commercial paper, it may be more efficient to use a letter of credit to cover the specific maturity of the paper rather than a backup credit line or to use another source of financing.

The information requirements, the need for a rating, and the issuance costs limit the use of commercial paper to larger firms, although the minimum feasible denomination has fallen in recent years. Commercial paper presents an attractive alternative to bank financing for many firms. In addition to the possibility of a lower effective rate on commercial paper, the competition may result in a bank's offering a more attractive loan rate.

Commercial Finance Companies

Commercial finance companies are private companies that make commercial loans. A substantial difference between commercial banks and commercial finance companies is the source of funds. Commercial banks raise much of their funds from the public in the form of deposits, either demand or time.[2] Commercial finance companies raise their funds through direct issuance of securities, such as commercial paper or longer-term notes, and bank loans. Commercial finance companies do not take deposits and restrict their loans to business firms. They are not subject to the regulations that apply to banks or consumer finance companies.

The loan customers of commercial finance companies frequently are businesses that are considered too risky to be granted credit by a commercial bank. Consequently, commercial finance companies generally charge higher interest rates than banks and concentrate on asset-based lending. Occasionally, a commercial finance company will lend on the *franchise value* of a service organization. For example, a company having an exclusive license to haul waste for a municipality may have little in the way of securable assets, but it does have the value of the exclusive franchise.

Interest Rate

The loans generally have a variable rate tied to a reference rate, such as the prime rate of money center banks. The interest rate charged may be 5–7% percent above prime. While this is a substantial risk premium, usually there are neither commitment fees nor compensating balance requirements.

Asset-Based Loans

The asset-based loans of commercial finance companies are similar to those of banks discussed in Chapter 12. They are based primarily on the underlying value of the assets rather than on the financial strength of the company. The asset most frequently desired as collateral is accounts receivable. The loan base is a percentage (75–85%) of the acceptable receivables. Acceptable accounts

---

[2] A bank CD is technically a time deposit, even if it is negotiable.

are those from customers with an acceptable credit risk and shorter than a designated maturity. Accounts receivable are usually pledged as collateral on a nonnotification, full-recourse basis: receivables customers are not notified of the arrangement, and the borrower has full responsibility for collection. When a receivable is either collected or the maturity exceeds the agreed maturity, it is no longer part of the borrowing base and the funds advanced against the collateral are repaid.

If the amount of acceptable accounts receivable is insufficient to meet the desired financing requirements, inventory and possibly machinery and equipment may be used as collateral. The percentage of borrowing against the collateral is adjusted for the expected liquidation value. Commercial finance companies can be expected to take the steps necessary to ensure that the liquidation value of the assets is maintained at a level sufficient to cover the amount of the loan.

Factoring

Although factoring of accounts receivable appears to be similar to a loan, with accounts receivable pledged as collateral, it is really quite different. *Factoring* is the sale of accounts receivable without recourse to the financial institution, hereafter called the *factor*. Once the account has been purchased, it is the property and responsibility of the factor. There are three major types of factoring arrangements: (1) maturity factoring, (2) conventional factoring, and (3) maturity factoring with an assignment of equity.

Factoring has a long history, being a common means of financing trade between England and colonial America. At one time, factoring was concentrated in certain industries, such as textiles and apparel. People in other industries thought that it was an omen of financial distress to use a factor. That attitude has changed, although factoring is still most prevalent in the East and in apparel-related industries. Historically, factors were either separate entities or a subsidiary of a commercial finance company. Some large bank holding companies, in an effort to expand their range of services, have recently purchased factors.

Maturity Factoring

Maturity factoring consists of the sale of accounts receivable to a factor with no advance of funds. When the seller receives a request for a credit sale from a potential customer, the seller notifies the factor. The factor conducts a credit analysis of the potential customer and, if the risk is acceptable, approves the sale and assumes all responsibility for collection and bad debts. The seller notifies the customer to remit directly to the factor. The factor forwards cash to the seller in the amount of the receivable less the commission on an agreed-upon average maturity date. Commissions are commonly in the range of 0.75–1.5% of the face value of receivables. If the factor rejects the customer and the seller proceeds with the credit sale, the seller is responsible for collection.

Many companies using a factor do not have a credit department; the factor performs all of the credit and collection functions. The cost of using a factor may be less than the cost of establishing a credit department. The factor may be able to achieve economies of scale in credit analysis, administration, and collection of receivables. The factor may deal with a broader group of customers than the seller and may have the opportunity to reduce risks through diversification. In industries with many small competitors where factoring is common, the factor may serve several competing manufacturers and have more leverage in collection than would any one company. Due to the nature of the credit function performed, most arrangements with a factor are of long duration, not an emergency sale of accounts receivable.

Conventional Factoring

In *conventional factoring* the factor performs all of the functions of maturity factoring and also advances funds to the seller prior to the average maturity date of the receivables. The factor charges interest for the actual number of days the funds are advanced. The interest charge is usually tied to the prime rate of money center banks and has a risk premium of 2.5–3%.

Maturity Factoring with Assignment of Equity

Some companies have the creditworthiness for a bank loan but do not want the problems and costs involved in running their own credit department. They enter into a maturity factoring arrangement and use the equity in the accounts as collateral for a loan from a bank. They are able to obtain a lower interest rate than on an advance from the factor.

Cost of Factoring

The cost of using a factor has two distinct elements: (1) the factor's commission and (2) the interest cost of cash advances. Whether the factor's commission is included in the cost of financing depends upon how and why the factor is being used. If the seller is engaged in maturity factoring, the commission is viewed as a substitute for the cost of running a credit department. The correct use of the commission in this case is to compare the cost of using a factor with that of operating a credit department. The factor's commission is not part of the short-term financing cost. The financing cost is the effective interest cost on the advances and is calculated in the same way that the effective cost on bank loans was calculated in Chapter 12.

If the factor is used only occasionally—an unusual practice but sometimes employed—or if the company maintains its own credit department, the fee

Table 13.2 Effective Interest Cost of Borrowing from a Factor to Obtain Financing for 3 Months

Terms	
Monthly credit sales	$2,500,000
Average maturity	45 days
Factor's fee	1.5%
Interest rate	13%
Average remittance date	10 days
Days funds advanced (t)	35 days
Credit department variable cost savings	$5,000

Factor's Fee		
$2,500,000 × .015	=	$37,500
Interest Cost		
(.13/360) × 35 × $2,500,000	=	$31,597
Total Financing Cost		
$37,500 + $31,597 − $5,000	=	$64,097

Effective Annual Interest Rate

$$\text{Effective annual interest rate} = \frac{\text{total financing cost}}{\text{funds available}} \times \frac{365}{t}$$

$$= \frac{\$64,097}{\$2,500,000} \times \frac{365}{35} = 26.7\%$$

is an incremental cost in obtaining the financing. Thus, the factor's fee is considered part of the financing costs and is included in the calculation of the effective cost. Table 13.2 gives an example of a company that has $2,500,000 in credit sales per month and uses a factor to obtain funds for 1 month. The total amount of accounts receivable sold to the factor is $2,500,000 and the fee is $37,500. The firm saves $5,000 in variable costs during the month by having the factor perform all of the credit functions for these accounts, and that amount is subtracted from the factor's fee to obtain the incremental cost of using the factor. The interest on the advance is $31,597, which is an effective annual rate of 26.7%.

Captive Finance Companies

A captive finance company is a wholly owned subsidiary that provides financing for distributors of the parent company's products, purchases installment receivables, or provides direct financing for retail sales. It performs the credit function of the parent company. The receivables appear on the subsidiary's books and not on those of the parent. The transactions involved in the production and sale of a product with and without a finance subsidiary are shown in Table 13.3.

In this illustration, all funds are obtained by issuing debt. In the first transaction, $800 is borrowed for production, resulting in an increase in debt and inventory. In the second transaction, the product is sold to a dealer, increasing accounts receivable and reducing inventory. Equity increases by the $200 profit on the sale. In the third transaction, the product is sold by the dealer and the manufacturer buys the retail paper. The net from canceling the dealer's receivable and buying the retail receivable is a payment of $200 to the dealer and a corresponding increase in debt. In the last transaction, $1,000 of the $1,300 collection from the retail paper is used to retire the debt, with the remainder increasing the cash balance. The $100 in interest on the retail receivable increases equity.

In the second part of Table 13.3 the transactions are shown for a company with a finance subsidiary. There is no change in the first transaction. In the second transaction, the dealer's receivable is transferred to the subsidiary, and the subsidiary forwards $800 to the parent. The parent retires $800 in debt and lists the additional $200 as an investment in the subsidiary. Tracing through the remaining transactions, we see that the net position is the same for the entire company. The difference is the location of cash and the recognition of equity. Payment of a dividend by the subsidiary to the parent transfers cash, reduces the equity of the subsidiary, and reduces the investment in the subsidiary by the parent. Once the statements are consolidated, the net effect is the same with or without a finance subsidiary.

Since the consolidated position is the same with or without a subsidiary, the rationale for finance subsidiaries must be something other than the effect on the financial statements. The reasons given for the use of a finance subsidiary are as follows: (1) a captive finance company may stimulate sales by providing easier access to credit for distributors or retail customers; (2) it may be cheaper to operate the financing function separately from the other operations of the company and view the credit arm as a separate profit center; (3) the concentration of accounts receivable in a captive finance company may increase the total debt capacity of the firm or may lower the short-term borrowing costs.

The first reason involves the marketing impact of the use of credit. However, it is difficult to understand why the marketing impact of credit would be greater if it is offered through a finance subsidiary rather than by the parent, unless there are differences in credit standards (looser) with a finance subsidiary. However, this rationale is directly counter to a suggested improvement in the quality of receivables, as discussed subsequently.

The second reason implies that there are some cost savings from having the finance organization separated from the parent. However, this could be accomplished by using a separate division, without incurring the legal expenses involved in setting up a subsidiary.

Table 13.3 Credit Transactions With and Without a Finance Subsidiary

Manufactured Cost of Product:	$800	Retail Sale Price:	$1,200
Sale Price to Distributor:	$1,000	Interest on Retail Paper:	$100

TRANSACTIONS WITHOUT A FINANCE SUBSIDIARY

Assets	Production	Dealer Sale	Retail Sale	Collection from Retail	Net
Cash	$800 ($800)		$ 200 ($ 200)	($1,000) $1,300	$300
Acct. rec.		$1,000	($1,000) $1,200	($1,200)	$ 0
Inventory	$800	($ 800)			$ 0
Total	$800	$ 200	$ 200	($ 900)	$300

Liabilities and Equity

	Production	Dealer Sale	Retail Sale	Collection from Retail	Net
Debt	$800		$200	($1,000)	$ 0
Equity		$200		$ 100	$300
Total	$800	$200	$200	($ 900)	$300

TRANSACTIONS WITH A FINANCE SUBSIDIARY

Assets	Production		Dealer Sale		Retail Sale		Collect from Retail		Net
	Parent	**Subsidiary**	**Parent**	**Subsidiary**	**Parent**	**Subsidiary**	**Parent**	**Subsidiary**	**Consolidated**
Cash	$800 ($800)		$800 ($800)	$ 800 ($ 800)		$ 200 ($ 200)		$1,300 ($1,000)	$300
Acct. rec.				$1,000		$1,200 ($1,000)		($1,200)	0
Invest in sub.			$200						
Inventory	$800		($800)						0
Total	$800	0	($600)	$1,000	0	$ 200	0	($ 900)	$300
Liabilities and Equity									
Debt	$800		($800)	$ 800		$ 200		($1,000)	0
Equity			$200	$ 200				$ 100	$300
Total	$800	0	($600)	$1,000	0	$ 200	0	($ 900)	$300

351

The third reason is the one most relevant to the financial manager and also the most controversial. One view is that in efficient financial markets the total debt capacity of an entity cannot be changed by the creation of a subsidiary to handle accounts receivable. The debt capacity is simply parceled out differently. Although a captive finance company appears to have a large debt capacity because almost all of its assets are accounts receivable, the parent suffers a decline in debt capacity because of the absence of these same receivables.

The other view is that the physical and legal separation of the credit and production operations of the company results in real differences compared to a combined operation. These differences result in a net gain in the availability or cost of financing, particularly short-term.[3] Some of the reasons for the view that this separation is important will now be discussed.

Separation of Manufacturing and Credit

A captive finance company operated as a subsidiary is a legal entity separate from the parent company. This legal separation results in a clearer identification of the assets and obligations of the parent and the subsidiary, which lowers the agency costs of analyzing the company and monitoring covenants. These lower costs are passed on to the firm in the form of a larger borrowing capacity or lower borrowing costs.

Better Quality of Receivables

Separation of the financing function from the sales function reduces the pressure from marketing to grant credit to customers of questionable risk to complete the sale. The result is a more objective assessment of the credit risk and a better, more consistent quality of receivables. However, if this is true, the sales of the parent company should be lower with a captive than without it.

A More Diversified Receivables Portfolio

Many captive finance companies generate receivables by financing transactions other than sales of the parent company; for example, the General Motors Acceptance Corporation (GMAC) makes home mortgage loans in addition to auto loans. To the extent that this increases the diversification of the portfolio and reduces the risk, the cost of financing to support the receivables may be reduced. Again, it is unclear why the parent cannot also make these other type of loans if it so desires.

---

[3] Gordon S. Roberts, and Jerry A. Viscione in "Captive Finance Subsidiaries and the M-Form Hypothesis," *Bell Journal of Economics* (Spring 1981), pp. 285–95, have tested the hypothesis that debt capacity is expanded by examining the increase in debt usage by firms with a captive finance company compared to that of control companies in the same industry without a captive finance company. The results of their tests varied across industries, showing a significant increase in debt for heavy manufacturing companies but not for retailing firms.

Legal Separation of Obligations

Legal separation of the financial obligations of the parent and the subsidiary may provide protection to creditors in case of financial difficulty of either the parent or the subsidiary. A default by the parent does not create a potential for a claim on receivables of the captive. The parent without a finance subsidiary could pledge accounts receivable as collateral for a loan, but there are additional costs involved in secured borrowing. Much of the borrowing of captive finance companies involves commercial paper, which is unsecured. In a captive finance company the receivables are virtually the only asset, so unsecured creditors are in essentially the same position they would be in as secured creditors if the company held the receivables.

Substantial costs are involved in establishing a captive finance company, and a large volume of receivables is required to justify the move. Nevertheless, a large number of manufacturing and retailing firms have established captive finance companies. The commercial paper of these companies is among the highest quality in the market. Perhaps there are some short-term financing benefits to those companies that can adopt this form of organization, although the evidence to support these claimed benefits is weak.

—————————— Off-Balance-Sheet Financing ——————————

Some companies use off-balance-sheet financing as an attempt to keep their financial statements "clean" and not distort financial ratios. Although in efficient markets the theoretical justification is weak, it is an avenue pursued in certain circumstances. Following is an example of how off-balance-sheet financing can be used to support inventory. Similar types of procedures can be devised to finance accounts receivable or to finance temporarily the construction of physical assets with short-term debt.

A company dealing with a highly seasonal supply of raw materials, such as a food processor, finds it worthwhile to purchase a year's supply of product at harvest. If the firm obtains short-term financing to support the purchase, the debt and the inventory appear on the balance sheet. The company will suffer a distortion in several financial ratios, for example, inventory turnover, current ratio, quick ratio, and total debt to assets. Instead, the firm enters into a contract with a third party to purchase, warehouse, and sell the raw materials to the processor. The third party obtains financing for the materials purchased through a banker's acceptance. The contract purchase price between the processor and the third party is set to cover the cost of the warehousing and financing. The cost of the goods sold is increased by the financing and warehousing costs.

A similar approach has also been used by some electric utilities to stockpile coal in anticipation of a long coal miners' strike. An occasional use of this type of financing may not be noticed, but repeated use causes creditors to adjust their analysis to account for this transaction.

Fixed- versus
_____ Variable-Rate Financing _____

The financial manager has a choice of various short-term financing alternatives, some with fixed interest rates and others with variable rates. The manager's choice of the rate specification is a function of the nature of the firm's cash flows, the difference between rates for the alternatives, the expectation of future interest rates, and the willingness to accept risk. We now address the treatment of these factors in deciding whether to use fixed- or variable-rate financing.

Cash Flow Characteristics

One element that influences a manager's preference for fixed- or variable-rate financing is the relationship of the firm's cash flows to the level of interest rates. A firm whose cash flows are uncorrelated with changes in short-term interest rates prefers fixed-rate financing. A fixed interest rate allows the manager to forecast more accurately the interest costs and, therefore, the net cash flows. However, a firm whose cash flows are positively correlated with interest rates may prefer variable-rate financing. The cash flows increase when interest costs are high, and interest costs decline when cash flow are low. Although forecasting interest costs is less accurate under variable-rate financing, the manager may be able to forecast net cash flows more accurately with variable-rate financing when there is a high positive correlation between cash flows and interest rates.

Expectations of Future Interest Rates

If the financial manager has expectations about the future direction of interest rates, if those assessments are accurate, and if the fixed rate is approximately equal to the variable rate, the decision between fixed- and variable-rate financing is straightforward: if rates are expected to rise over the financing period, borrow under a fixed-rate alternative. If rates are expected to fall, borrow under a variable-rate alternative.

Differences in Fixed and Variable Rates.
In a more typical situation, fixed- and variable-rate borrowing alternatives have different interest rates. The decision requires the manager to calculate the expected effective borrowing cost under the alternatives and estimate the uncertainty of the estimates. A comparison of the effective cost of borrowing

Exhibit 13.1 Effective Cost of Fixed- versus Variable-Rate Borrowing

Need to borrow $1,000,000 for 90 days

Fixed-rate borrowing: sell commercial paper at a discount of 8.5% plus the dealer spread of 10 basis points.

$$\text{Effective rate} = \frac{.086\,(90/360)}{1 - .086\,(90/360)} \times \frac{365}{90} = 8.91\%.$$

Variable-rate borrowing: borrow against a line of credit at the prime rate of 9%.

Scenario 1: Prime rate drops to 8.5% after 30 days.

$$\text{Effective rate} = \left(.09 \times \frac{30}{360} + .085 \times \frac{60}{360}\right) \times \frac{365}{90}$$
$$= 8.79\%.$$

Scenario 2: Prime rate drops to 8.5% after 60 days.

$$\text{Effective rate} = \left(.09 \times \frac{60}{360} + .085 \times \frac{30}{360}\right) \times \frac{365}{90}$$
$$= 8.96\%.$$

Scenario 3: Prime rate drops to 8.25% after 30 days.

$$\text{Effective rate} = \left(.09 \times \frac{30}{360} + .0825 \times \frac{60}{360}\right) \times \frac{365}{90}$$
$$= 8.62\%.$$

Scenario 4: Prime rate drops to 8.75% after 30 days.

$$\text{Effective rate} = \left(.09 \times \frac{30}{360} + .0875 \times \frac{60}{360}\right) \times \frac{365}{90}$$
$$= 8.96\%.$$

under a fixed-rate issue of commercial paper and borrowing under a bank credit line at the prime rate is given in Exhibit 13.1. Four possible scenarios are given for the timing and amount of the change in the prime rate. Under two of the scenarios, the manager would be better off borrowing with the credit line than with commercial paper. This approach is useful in identifying the scenarios under which the effective cost would be lower under the fixed- versus the variable-rate alternative. The choice is made after consideration of the likelihood of the scenarios occurring.

Sources of Future Rate Estimates

A logical question is, where does a manager obtain estimates of the future direction of interest rates? A large firm with a staff of economists may have its own forecasting model to estimate future economic activity, one part of which is interest rates. Managers in firms without this support must rely on outside information coupled with their own judgment.

One source of information is the market's expectations of future short-term rates contained in the term structure of interest rates (see Chapter 10). To the extent that a liquidity premium contained in the rates can be estimated and extracted, an estimate of expected future short rates can be developed. Table 13.4 contains a calculation of expected short-term interest rates in future time periods extracted from the term structure for T-bills under the assumption of no liquidity premium.[4] We can see that on September 11, the date on which the T-bill quotes were obtained, expectations were for slightly rising interest rates. The manager needs to adjust these estimates for any liquidity premium believed to be in the yield curve, and for any differences between the movement in T-bill rates and the index for the variable-rate borrowing alternative. Any risk premium that the company has to pay must also be added to these rates.

A second source of information on interest rates is financial futures. In Chapter 11 financial futures were discussed as instruments in hedging the interest rate risk in financial securities (either from the borrowing side or the lending side). The prices of these widely traded futures instruments represent

Table 13.4 Expected Future Short-term Rates

A. From the Yield Curve

Current Date: September 11

RATES ON T-BILLS

Maturity	Discount	Yield
9/18	3.53%	3.58%
12/18	5.13%	5.27%
3/19	5.27%	5.49%

EXPECTED FORWARD RATES

From	To	Expected Rate
9/18	12/18	5.40%
12/18	3/19	5.65%

B. From T-Bill Futures

Contract for a 90-Day T-Bill

Delivery date	9/18	12/18
Index	94.81	94.79
Discount rate	5.19%	5.21%
Effective yield	5.33%	5.35%

[4] See Chapter 12 for the calculation of the forward rates from the yield curve under different assumptions about the existence of a liquidity premium.

the aggregate judgment of future interest rates by all of the participants in the futures market. The expected yields for T-bills in the future contained in the futures contracts are given in Table 13.4.[5]

We can compare the differences in the estimates of future interest rates obtained from the yield curve and from the futures instruments shown in Table 13.4. On September 11 a 90-day T-bill future for delivery on December 18 is priced to yield 5.33%. This is quite close to the implied forward rate of 5.40% on the T-bill derived from the yield curve. The implied forward rate for a 90- (or 91-) day T-bill for delivery on December 18 is 5.35% from the futures contract and 5.65% from the yield curve. As expected, these estimates are reasonably close. If there is some liquidity premium in the yield curve, the estimate of the forward rate from the yield curve will be biased upward.[6] We can see that from either source of information the expectation is that interest rates will remain about the same or rise slightly during the next 180 days.

Interest Rate Swaps

The development of the market for swaps has given managers an additional tool to control the degree of interest rate risk. A firm that has access to low cost but variable rate financing may arrange a swap with another firm that desires variable rate financing, but has access to fixed rate financing. Investment banks and commercial banks are very active in arranging swaps for their clients. While the use of swaps allows for easier availability of the type of financing desired, a manager still needs to decide whether fixed or variable rate financing is appropriate for the firm.

Degree of Risk Aversion

A final factor that affects the choice between variable-rate and fixed-rate borrowing is the degree of risk aversion on the part of management. A highly risk-averse manager prefers a borrowing alternative that reduces variability in cash flow as interest rates change. If acceptable borrowing instruments are not available, it may be necessary to hedge borrowing costs with interest rate futures or arrange interest rate swaps to control interest costs. If a manager is less risk averse, he or she may gamble on the future course of interest rates with the expectation of achieving a lower cost of borrowing. Of course, for this expectation to be realized, the manager either has to have forecasting ability superior to that of the market or has to be lucky.

---

[5] The T-bill future is for delivery of a 90 day T-bill. Since there are 91 days between the dates specified, an adjustment would be made in the price of the 91-day T-bill to reflect this difference in maturity.

[6] R. Rendleman and C. Carabini, "The Efficiency of the Treasury Bill Futures Market" in *Interest Rate Futures: Concepts and Issues,* G. Gay and R. Kolb (eds)., Robert F. Dame, Inc., Richmond, Va.: (1982), found that a divergence of almost 50 basis points is necessary before the profits from pure arbitrage are large enough to cover transactions costs. The difference between the two estimates of 37 basis points is within this transactions cost range.

_____ **Summary** _____

Commercial paper is a common source of nonbank financing. The primary users of commercial paper are large firms with a good credit rating and access to backup lines of credit from commercial banks. Access to the commercial paper market may reduce short-term borrowing costs both because the rate on paper is less than bank prime rates and because the increased availability of funds may make commercial banks more competitive. Borrowers from commercial finance companies are predominantly firms that are too risky to obtain bank credit. Commercial finance company loans are usually secured by receivables or inventory and carry a rate commensurate with the risk and cost of handling secured credit. Factors perform the credit function of a firm, as well as advancing funds based on the amount of accounts receivable outstanding. Because of the credit function performed, most factoring arrangements are long-term relationships and not temporary sources of funds. Captive finance companies are used by many large organizations and, because of the separation of the operating assets from the receivables, may increase access to short-term credit.

   In choosing a short-term financing alternative, the financial manager can obtain either fixed- or variable-rate financing. The choice between these instruments is a function of the nature of the firm's cash flows, the manager's expectations about future interest rates, the difference between the fixed and variable rates, and the manager's risk aversion.

_____ **Discussion Questions** _____

1. Define commercial paper.
2. Why is commercial paper restricted to the largest borrowers?
3. What would happen if a firm tried to issue commercial paper with a maturity of 320 days?
4. How does the existence of a backup line of credit affect the use of commercial paper?
5. Contrast the use of a commercial bank and a commercial finance company for short-term loans. Include a discussion of the terms, credit requirements, and types of loans made.
6. Contrast factoring with the use of a secured loan with accounts receivable pledged as collateral.
7. Why would a firm consider using a factor if no advancement of funds is needed?
8. Compare the features of maturity factoring with those of conventional or standard factoring.

9. Discuss the use of off-balance-sheet financing from a conceptual or theoretical position.
10. What would have to be true for the following statement to be correct? "The manager should use fixed-rate financing when interest rates are expected to rise and variable-rate financing when rates are expected to fall."

Problems

1. The Jackson Company issues commercial paper through a dealer. The rate on the paper issued for 30 days is 6 1/8% and the dealer's spread is 1/8%. What is the effective annual rate?
2. What would be the effective annual rate on the paper in Problem 1 if the maturity was 90 days? Why is this answer different from the one for Question 1?
3. The BACQ Company is planning to issue commercial paper to finance an inventory buildup that is expected to last for 6 months. The company is planning on using a line of credit to provide backup for the paper. The commitment fee on the line is 1/4%. The paper will be issued through a dealer whose spread averages 1/8%. If the company plans to issue a sequence of six issues of 30-day paper and the current rate of 7.5% is expected to hold for the entire 6 months, what is the effective rate on the borrowing?
4. How would your answer to Problem 3 be different if BACQ planned on using the commercial paper for the entire year?
5. The Kolb Company, a manufacturer of crystal balls for fortune tellers, has a loan from a commercial finance company to support its finished goods inventory. The finance company charges a rate 4 points above prime, which currently is averaging 9.0%. The finance company insists that the inventory be segregated and kept under a field warehousing arrangement. This costs the company $5,000 per year for bonding of an employee, and for lost time in accessing the inventory to notify the finance company. The company averages a finished goods inventory of $565,000 during the year. The finance company will loan up to 70% of the value of the inventory.
   a. If the company obtains the maximum loan the finance company will grant, what is the effective interest rate?
   b. If the company borrows only $250,000, what is the effective interest rate?
6. Spy, Inc., a manufacturer of rain coats, is considering using a factor for a seasonal buildup in its accounts receivable. The company will maintain its credit operation for the normal level of receivables, and will only sell the seasonal peak of receivables to the factor. The credit manager estimates that the receivables sold will be for approximately $2,000,000 per month for a period of 3 months. The factor will charge 1% of the face value of the

receivables and a daily interest rate of .027% on any advancement against the receivables. The average maturity on the receivables is 30 days. The factor will advance up to 80% of the face value of the receivables. What is the equivalent annual cost using the factor if Spy borrows the maximum from the factor?

7. The Pegasus Shirt Company has an arrangement with a factor to perform its credit function. The factor charges a fee of 1.25% of the amount of the receivables processed. The average payment date is 45 days for the receivables accepted. In addition, the company receives advances in the amount of the receivables outstanding and pays a daily rate of 0.033%. The company averages sales of $3,000,000 per month. The treasurer of Pegasus figures that it would cost the company about 0.25% of sales for credit reports and other variable costs to handle its own credit, and bad debts would average 0.5% of sales. In addition, a credit department would require a manager, at a salary of $3,000 per month, and two staff people who would be paid about $1,500 per month. Data processing and other information system costs would run about $5,000 per month.

a. What is the maximum amount of the advance to the company?

b. What is the effective annual interest cost of the factoring arrangement?

8. Dan Ecker, the treasurer of Segreto, Inc., is considering two financing alternatives for the next 90 days: commercial paper with a discount rate quote of 8.25% and a bank loan at prime, which currently is 9.5%. There have been several comments in recent weeks by the president of the Federal Reserve Bank that the prime rate is higher than it should be, given other interest rates. Dan feels that the prime rate will not be lowered during the next 30 days but probably will be lowered after that time. What will the prime rate have to be for days 30 through 90 for Dan to be indifferent in choosing between the two alternatives?

9. Susan Wagner is the treasurer of Gonchos Mexican Restaurants. She is trying to estimate the future interest rates in order to determine whether she should accept a loan with a fixed interest rate of 9.5% or a variable-rate loan set at the 30-day bank CD rate plus 50 basis points. The structure of the CD rates at the bank is given in the following table. Susan needs to borrow $500,000 for the next 6 months.

Time	30 days	60 days	90 days	180 days
Rate	8.25%	9.10%	9.25%	9.4%

If Susan believes that there is no liquidity premium in the term structure of interest rates, which interest option should she choose?

10. Samuel Turner is trying to estimate interest rates over the next 6 months in order to decide on the type of financing to use. He has obtained the following information: a 90-day T-bill quote of 7.25%, a 180-day T-bill quote of 7.65%, and a price of $92.70 on a T-bill future with a delivery date in 90 days. If the T-bill future is a good predictor of the rate that will

be seen at the delivery date, what is the liquidity premium in the 180-day rate?

Case: *Nut House, Inc.*

The Nut House, Inc., is a food processor headquartered in Segunda, California. The company was started by Eduardo and Lucia Dario in 1968, when they started preparing flavored almonds to sell in their grocery store. They bought almonds directly from a grower. The almonds were shelled, sprinkled with seasonings, and roasted. Initially, all of the operations were done by hand in the Darios' kitchen in the evenings.

The product proved so popular that they could not meet the demand by operating out of their home. They rented a small building near the store and purchased shelling equipment, an oven, and a bagging machine. Since the volume that they could process now exceeded the demand at their store, Eduardo started selling the flavored almonds to other stores in the area. The Darios quickly realized that they could make more money by processing and selling almonds than they could by operating their store. They hired a manager to run the store, incorporated as Dario Flavored Almonds, Inc., and devoted their full time to processing and selling flavored almonds.

Over the next several years, they explored different channels of distribution. In the early 1970s they started distributing to grocery stores throughout California through grocery wholesalers. In the late 1970s they developed a chain of rest-stop retail outlets, called Nut Houses, along major highways. In the early 1980s they published a catalog and started mail order sales. The mail order business was particularly popular around Christmas time. As their retail outlets and mail order sales became an increasingly large part of the business, they changed the company's name to Nut House, Inc.

Current Operations

Nut House contracts with growers for almonds at the start of the growing season. They take delivery of the almonds in September, when they are picked, and store them until they can be processed. The growers are paid 30 days after delivery. Nut House is able to buy almonds at very attractive prices because of their purchase arrangement and the volume of purchases.

Financing Needs

In May 1987, Tab Dixon, the assistant treasurer of banking relations, has been reviewing the funding needs for Nut House for the fiscal year starting on June 1. Because of the timing of purchases, processing, and sales, Nut House's financing needs are highly seasonal. Dixon has estimated the net cash flow for each month of the coming year as shown in Table 1.

Table 1 Forecasted Monthly Net Cash Flow for Fiscal Year 1987 (All Figures in $1,000s)

Month	Cash Flow	Month	Cash Flow
Jun	4,000	Jul	1,000
Aug	0	Sep	−2,000
Oct	−25,000	Nov	−10,000
Dec	−8,000	Jan	−5,000
Feb	12,000	Mar	18,000
Apr	8,000	May	10,000

Financing Alternatives

In the past, Nut House has relied on a line of credit from the Second National Bank of California, the company's concentration bank. Nut House currently has an unsecured line of credit at Second National of $50,000,000. The line is at prime plus 1/8% and has a commitment fee of 1/4% on the unused line. (The commitment fee is paid monthly on the amount of the line unused during the month at an annual rate of 1/4%.) Dixon feels that the line can be increased by about an additional $10,000,000 if necessary, and the rate could be negotiated down to prime this year. As of the end of May, he expects the outstanding loan balance against the line to be $5,000,000. The prime rate during May has been 8.25%.

Dixon has received several calls from Angela Nolan in the capital markets group at the large San Francisco National Bank (SFNB). Nolan has suggested that Nut House cover its financing needs by selling commercial paper. The capital markets group of SFNB would act as an agent in selling the paper, and their commission would be their spread, which averages 10 basis points. Since the bank would be prohibited from underwriting (buying for their own account), the sale of commercial paper would be on a best efforts basis. Nolan has also indicated that although the rate on high-grade commercial paper is currently 6.90% for 30 days and 7.05% for 90 days, Nut House, Inc., as an unknown in the commercial paper market, would probably have to pay an additional 35–50 basis points. She has further indicated that a backup credit line would be necessary for a successful offering of paper, and banking regulations prohibit a bank from backing paper for which it is a sales agent.

Dixon has checked with Second National and they have agreed to provide a backup line of up to $50,000,000 at a rate of prime plus 1/8% and a commitment fee of 3/8% of the amount of the line. Of course, the intention is that the line will not be used.

In making his decision on financing for the coming year, Dixon had narrowed his choice to the alternatives of the bank line of credit or issuing commercial paper. He will issue as much 90-day paper as possible, although he recognizes the need to use some 30-day paper at the peak borrowing periods. In making his decision, he has obtained the yield curve information for T-bills shown in Table 2. He plans to use this information to try to gauge the direction of interest rates over the next year. He recognizes that the prime rate and commercial paper rates are not perfectly correlated with T-bill rates, but all three are highly correlated.

Table 2   T-Bill Rates as of May 1987

Month	Rate	Month	Rate	Month	Rate
Jun	5.63%	Jul	5.38%	Aug	5.49%
Sep	5.68%	Oct	5.71%	Nov	5.83%
Dec	6.01%	Jan	5.92%	Feb	6.21%
Mar	6.27%	Apr	6.35%	May	6.39%

All rates are 360-day-year discount bid quotes.

―――――――――――――― **Selected Readings** ――――――――――――――

HARRIES, B. W., "How Corporate Bonds and Commercial Paper Are Rated," *Financial Executive* (September 1971), pp. 30–36.

LEWELLEN, W. G., "Finance Subsidiaries and Corporate Borrowing Capacity," *Financial Management* (Spring 1972), pp. 21–31.

LIVNAT, JOSHUA, and ASHWINPAUL C. SONDHI, "Finance Subsidiaries: Their Formation and Consolidation," *Journal of Business Finance and Accounting* (Spring 1986), pp. 137–147.

MACPHEE, WILLIAM A., *Short-Term Business Borrowing: Sources, Terms, and Techniques.* Homewood, Ill.: Dow-Jones Irwin, 1984.

MOSKOWITZ, LOUIS A., *Dun and Bradstreet's Handbook of Modern Factoring and Commercial Finance,* New York: Thomas Y. Crowell, 1977.

RENDLEMAN, R., and C. CARABINI, "The Efficiency of the Treasury Bill Futures Market," in *Interest Rate Futures: Concepts and Issues,* G. Gay and R. Kolb, (eds)., Richmond, Va.: Robert F. Dame, Inc., 1982.

ROBERTS, GORDON S., and JERRY A. VISCIONE, "Captive Finance Subsidiaries and the M-Form Hypothesis," *Bell Journal of Economics* (Spring 1981), pp. 285–295.

ROBERTS, GORDON S., and JERRY A. VISCIONE, "Captive Finance Subsidiaries: The Manager's View," *Financial Management* (Spring 1981), pp. 36–42.

SHERWOOD, H. C., *How Corporate and Municipal Debt Is Rated.* New York: Wiley, 1976.

Receivables and Payables Management

14

Introduction to Credit and Collections

In 1985 the automotive industry had a major problem. Dealers' and manufacturers' lots were bulging with unsold inventory. The economy was enjoying modest growth but car sales lagged. Although short-term interest rates had fallen and the prime rate was 7.5% by mid-year, consumer interest rates continued at record high levels. Credit card rates were still at least 18% at most banks, and interest on new car loans was over 12%. Consumers seemed to resist the idea of going into debt for cars. Besides, they had become accustomed to various incentive programs from Detroit. In August, General Motors announced 3.9% financing through its GMAC program. Ford followed and Chrysler cut its rate to 2.9%. American Motors had the last word by offering 0.0% financing. In place of lower interest rates, customers paying in cash could opt for discounts. These credit programs spurred sales to record levels. While solving a major inventory problem, however, the programs severely ate into company profitability. Evidently, management thought that the tradeoff was worth the cost in the long run.

Importance of Credit in Today's Corporations

This story illustrates some important facts about credit policy. First, credit policy is an important ingredient in a firm's sales efforts. Firms compete with each other not only in product features and price but also in credit terms. Credit terms are important to buyers and may strongly influence purchasing decisions. Second, credit terms and prices are, to an extent, interchangeable. More liberal credit terms are equivalent to a price decrease and may have the same effect on the sales volume. The auto makers offered potential buyers either better credit terms or a price concession. Third, credit decisions may have a significant impact throughout the firm—not just on the credit department. In the example given, credit changes reduced inventory, thereby making room for further production of new models. On the other hand, the changes severely reduced the profits of the firms.

Credit is a major factor in corporate-to-corporate transactions, not just corporate-to-consumer business. The importance of credit can be seen by noting that accounts receivable in the average manufacturing corporation constituted almost one sixth of total assets in from 1970 to 1985. Accounts receivable provide a firm with both an asset and a problem: an asset because of the promise of a future cash flow, a problem because of the need to obtain financing while waiting for the future cash flow.

Credit Policy Decisions

How does a firm determine its credit policies? In the remainder of this chapter and the following chapter, we discuss management decisions regarding credit. In this chapter, we treat credit policy terms and survey the various types of terms commonly used for corporate-to-corporate transactions. We then discuss tools for deciding how much, if any, credit to extend to a specific customer. We also discuss legal issues surrounding the extension of credit and briefly survey financing tied to accounts receivable.

In the following chapter, we turn our attention to decisions regarding credit policy changes and how to value them. How did General Motors, for example, decide to offer very liberal credit terms at interest rates far below that of the economy? Then we treat the problem of monitoring and controlling accounts receivable. How does a manager know when the cash flow stream is speeding up or slowing down? How can accounts receivable be accurately forecast? If a firm extends credit, how can it finance the delayed cash flows?

In Chapter 20 we discuss the impact technology is having on credit policies through electronic data interchange. There we introduce the concept of negotiated payment terms.

Where Credit Decisions Are Made

In most firms, credit policy is administered by a general credit manager under the direction of the treasurer or assistant treasurer, who, in turn, reports to the financial vice president. In smaller firms or subsidiaries, the controller may have the responsibility for credit policy. In very large firms, the credit function may be administered by a separate financial subsidiary. General Motors, for example, owns the General Motors Acceptance Corporation (GMAC), which administers credit to dealers and consumers. Financial subsidiaries provide credit to the parent's customers but may also lend to customers of other firms.

In all cases, the marketing side of the firm has a great deal to say about credit decisions. Credit policy is often an important marketing tool. As we saw in the preceding example, changing credit terms had a significant impact on the sales of the automotive industry. Marketing is also concerned about company–customer relationships. Since the credit department is a major point of contact between a firm and its customers, marketing generally has a hand in setting and administering credit policies.

Conceptual Framework: The Cash Flow Timeline

From a cash flow perspective, credit sales simply represent an extension of the cash inflow timeline. When credit is granted, the seller does not require cash at the time of the sale, but rather permits payment to be made at some future time. Accounts receivable are nothing more than an accounting recognition that a sale has occurred but the cash flow has yet to be realized.

Figure 14.1 illustrates the portion of the timeline accounted for by credit policy. For this discussion, assume that the clock begins when a good or service is rendered (point A). At this time, or shortly before or after, the firm books a receivable (B) and sends an invoice (C). Often these three steps take place at the same time. Credit terms—at least in part—determine when the buyer initiates payment (D). Payment is received (E), applied to the buyer's account (F), and then deposited for the eventual receipt of available funds (G).

Accounts Receivable: Not a Logical Focus for Credit Policy

Since the dollar size of accounts receivable is readily computed and often reported in financial statements, this account has tended to be the focal point of credit policy. We referred to this account ourselves in showing the relative importance of receivables. As an overall measure of approximately how much in sales may be outstanding at a specific point in time, accounts receivable may suffice. However, an accounts receivable focus is an inappropriate managerial

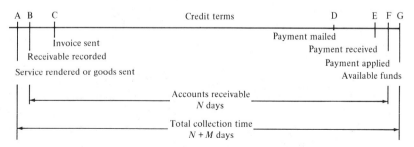

Figure 14.1 Credit Policy and the Cash Flow Timeline.

focus. The reason is that accounts receivable deal purely with the *recording* of information and not with the transfer of value.

For example, if a firm has an average cash flow of S dollars per day, and on average N days elapse between recording a receivable and applying a payment (points B and F), accounts receivable will, on average, be SN. But suppose the total collection time is actually $N + M$ days. M reflects the number of days by which the total collection time exceeds the accounts receivable time. Such delays may result from processing delays after applying receivables or availability delays on check deposits. Thus, accounts receivable will misstate the true value of delayed cash flow by SM:

$$\text{Total value of cash uncollected} = S(N + M)$$

$$\text{Accounts receivable} = SN$$

$$\text{Misstatement of value by } A/R = S(N + M) - SN = SM.$$

Of course, M may be either positive or negative, depending on the timing of the recordkeeping process in relation to the actual value transfer.

Assume, for example, that a firm has average credit sales of $500,000 per day. The average time between recognizing a receivable and recording payments to accounts receivable is 40 days. Average accounts receivable is therefore $20,000,000. Suppose that an additional 5 days of delay occur— some before receivables are recognized and some after posting. The total collection time (times dollar flow) is $22,500,000. Thus, accounts receivable understate the true value of cash outstanding by $2,500,000.

Total Collection Time Focus

In summary, the logical focus of managerial attention should be the total collection time because it (1) includes all relevant time elements along the cash flow timeline, (2) does not therefore misstate the true value of cash flow outstanding, and (3) cannot be changed merely by changing recording conventions. As we will see in the next chapter, the timeline perspective is also very helpful in making credit policy decisions.

—————— Should Firms Extend Credit? ——————

The Notion of Perfect Markets

Before proceeding with our discussion of credit policy, we must discuss why intercorporate credit exists in the first place. In Chapter 2 we reviewed the concept and implications of perfect markets. Market perfection can apply to both capital markets and product markets. The idea of perfect capital markets implies that any firm can obtain funds in any amount with no transaction costs and no search costs, at an appropriate risk-adjusted rate known to all fund suppliers. The notion of perfect product markets implies that products are perfectly substitutable across firms. There are no delivery costs, shipping delays, or defective goods. The price of any firm's product is determined simply by the supply and demand functions of the marketplace.

If perfect markets existed, credit policy would be irrelevant. A buyer would be able to borrow from a financial intermediary like a bank just as easily as borrowing from a seller. If one firm offered more liberal credit terms than another, the first firm would have to make up for it by charging more for the product or by going out of business because the effective price would be too low. Essentially, credit terms and prices would be perfectly interchangeable. So, given perfect markets, firms would be indifferent to credit policy. No credit, strict credit, liberal credit—in the end, all would be equivalent and would never give any firm an advantage over another.

Market Imperfections and Credit

Of course, credit is almost universally extended between buyers and sellers. Whole industries seem to have specific credit terms associated with those particular industries. A great deal of effort is spent in managing the credit function. Evidently most firms think that credit policy plays an important role. The reasons must lie in market imperfections.

Inspection Period

The first reason for selling on credit has nothing to do with the financing aspects of credit but rather with imperfections in the product market. For many transactions, a shipment and inspection period is required. In other words, the buyer may be unwilling to pay the seller until after the goods have been received and inspected to ensure that they are not defective. In this instance, credit is not so much a financing function as an insurance function. If the goods are deemed unsuitable, the buyer is in the position of control if payment has not already been made. By extending credit, the seller is signaling that it has faith in its products and is willing to permit the buyer to inspect before requiring payment. This idea is supported by the fact that offers that seem too good to be true, such as generating significant wealth by "envelope stuffing" at home, always require cash in advance.

Information Inefficiencies

The assumption of perfect markets implies that perfect information is provided without cost to all market participants. But a seller who has dealt with a buyer for several years may be in a better position to know the financial strength of the buyer than someone else who can obtain the information only at high cost. In addition, the seller knows the product it is selling, may have better knowledge of its resale value, and is in a much better position to realize value from returned goods than most third-party credit providers. Thus, a buyer may be able to obtain credit on lower terms from the seller than from a third party such as a bank or finance company.

Flexibility

In part because of the information inefficiencies just mentioned and in part because of banking conventions adopted over decades, bank or other third-party borrowing may be more restrictive than financing provided by a seller. Buyers generally value the flexibility inherent in the spontaneous use of credit implied in credit terms. To borrow from a bank, a promissory note is generally signed. Such an instrument usually contains restrictive covenants and takes some time to negotiate, even when drawing on a prearranged credit line. On the other hand, borrowing from a supplier is very simple: just don't pay the bill for a while. In this sense, credit terms and price are not perfect substitutes. Buyers cannot create their own prices but they can, to some extent, create their own credit terms by taking liberties with stated terms.

Transaction Costs

Under perfect markets, for any purchase a buyer should be able to borrow in the capital markets using the goods as collateral. The rate should be the same as that offered by the seller. The transaction costs, of course, in borrowing in the capital markets for small purchases would be prohibitive. It is much easier and cheaper for the seller to provide financing than a third party.

Regardless of the reasons, extension of credit between firms is a reality and has become a very important managerial responsibility.

Credit Terms

Credit terms refer to the stated policies given to a customer or group of customers regarding (1) payment timing, (2) the form of payment, (3) discounts for timely payments, and possibly (4) penalties for late payments.

For the most part, credit terms appear to be stagnant. Changing credit terms, in other words, is not a common practice for most firms. Recent studies show that very few firms change credit terms from year to year, regardless of interest rate movements or other changes in the economy. Most firms accept the credit terms offered by competitors and fear the adverse consequences of change. Collection efforts may change from time to time, but the terms appear to remain the same. Nevertheless, some firms do adjust terms as the economy changes, and most firms will eventually have to change credit terms as a result of electronic data interchange (discussed in Chapter 20).

Even if existing firms are reluctant to alter credit terms, a new firm in a particular market has to determine what terms to offer. We first discuss the factors to consider in setting credit terms and then survey alternative credit terms.

Factors to Consider in Setting Credit Terms

In setting credit terms, what is the firm trying to accomplish? We suggest that a useful approach is to express the objectives of credit policy in terms of a cost/benefit or objective function. The cost/benefit factors associated with the credit function include profitability of sales (*PS*), bad debt expense (*BD*), administrative costs (*ADMIN*), related costs or benefits in other areas of the firm (*OTH*), and time value costs (*TV*). We can express these in an objective function:

$$\text{Total credit costs/benefits} = PS - BD - ADMIN - OTH - TV.$$

As the firm seeks to maximize this function, it must trade off various costs and benefits. For example, profitability from sales may increase by offering extremely liberal credit terms. On the other hand, time value costs may offset all or part of the benefits. We will frequently refer back to this objective function as we discuss credit policy in this and subsequent related chapters.

Profitability of Sales

Credit policies may have a significant impact on the profitability of sales. We define profitability of sales as incremental sales dollar volume minus incremental costs. We use *profitability of sales* rather than simply *sales* because costs to support the sales must be considered. Take, for example, a firm operating at near capacity. Liberalizing credit terms may greatly increase the dollar volume of sales, but high fixed costs must be incurred to add the needed capacity. The result may be a decrease in profitability even with an increase in sales. Another firm operating far below capacity may experience exactly the same increase in sales dollars but may see profitability increase because fixed costs did not have to be added.

Profitability of sales also includes the effects of any cash discounts. Gross sales may increase by offering attractive cash discounts for early payment, but a firm receives only net sales after computing discounts.

Bad Debts

The extension of credit almost always exposes the seller to bad debt risk — the possibility that the buyer may pay nothing or only part of the amount due. As we shall see, various credit terms are associated with different levels of bad debt risk. Losses due to bad debts are a function not only of the probability that the buyer will not pay, but also of the marginal costs of producing and delivering the good or service. For example, suppose an item costs $1 to produce and sells for $10. If the customer does not pay, what does the seller lose? Not $10. The seller is out only $1.

Administrative Costs

Administrative responsibilities with regard to the credit function include (1) keeping track of the amounts owed by each customer, (2) following up on late payments, (3) monitoring cash discounts, (4) gathering and storing credit information, (5) making credit decisions for each credit applicant, and (6) producing reports on the credit function. These tasks may require a large staff and significant computer resources. The more complex a firm's credit terms, the more costly they are to administer.

Relation to Other Functions of the Firm

Credit terms cannot be set in isolation. As mentioned earlier, credit administration and marketing are closely associated. Credit terms must be coordinated with the sales arm of the firm. In addition, credit may influence inventory levels, production timing, and even banking relations. For example, as we will see, dating credit terms that permit credit to be extended over seasonal, slow sales periods may permit the seller to smooth production and sell the product even in off seasons.

Time Value Costs

Delaying cash flow from sales by extending credit terms forces the firm to obtain other means of financing operations. This is sometimes called *financing receivables*. The term is a misnomer, since receivables contain some profit margin and total receivables do not represent, as we saw earlier, the total dollar volume of cash to be collected. The firm is actually financing operations during the time it waits for the cash flow to come in. This requires the firm either to borrow from short-term sources such as credit lines or to obtain more long-term capital such as long-term debt or equity. Either way, the funding has a nontrivial cost associated with it.

For example, suppose a firm has credit sales of $500,000 per day and a total collection time of 60 days. Assume that the variable costs associated with the sales are 80% and, on average, must be paid on the day of sale. Assuming that accounts receivable time and total collection time are the same in this example, accounts receivable would be $30,000,000. However, the firm would only have to borrow, on average, $0.8 \times \$30,000,000 = \$24,000,000$ to pay variable costs until cash inflow is received from receivables. At a rate of 10%, the annual cost of financing is $2,400,000.

In general, the amount of funding tied up to finance the firm during the collection period is

$$\text{Funding needed} = v(N + M)S,$$

where v is the out-of-pocket costs as a percentage of sales; as previously, $N + M$ is the average total collection period in days; and S is the average credit sales per day. The cost of providing this funding is found by multiplying the funding needed by the appropriate cost of funds:

$$\text{Cost of financing} = iv(N + M)S.$$

This formula assumes that variable costs are paid, on average, on the day the sale is made. If payment for these costs may be delayed, the amount of funding is reduced.

Constraints

In attempting to maximize the objective function we have outlined, management must operate under a number of constraints that set limits on policies and their results.

INDUSTRY CONVENTION. In most industries, a few credit terms are common across all firms. For example, in the steel industry, most firms require payment within 30 days and many offer .5% to 1% discounts for early payment. It would be difficult for one steel firm to offer significantly different terms.

DIFFICULTY OF CHANGE. In practice, it is very difficult to change credit terms. Customer payment practices become ingrained both in payables department personnel and in computer systems. A change in credit terms stated on an invoice may go unnoticed by the buyer for months or years. So, even when changes in interest rates logically dictate a change in credit terms, it is not surprising to find that most firms do not change.

LEGAL CONSTRAINTS. The Robinson-Patman Act originated as antitrust legislation that prohibited selling firms from discriminating between customers by offering the same goods or services at different prices. Different prices may be acceptable where this is industry practice, such as different terms to distributors than to retailers, or where there are demonstrable cost differences, such as quantity discounts. Credit terms fall under the same act. If a particular credit term is made available to one customer, it must be made available to all. Exceptions occur for high-risk customers put on cash-only terms.

WORKING CAPITAL CONSTRAINTS. Some lenders' covenants or indenture agreements may require certain levels of working capital, as measured by net working capital or the current ratio. Increasing accounts receivable—even when other short-term assets or liabilities are increased—may cause the current ratio to decrease.

To understand this, assume that a firm has current assets totaling $40,000,000 and current liabilities of $20,000,000. The current ratio (CR) is therefore 2.00:

$$CR = \frac{\text{current assets}}{\text{current liabilities}} = \frac{40}{20} = 2.00.$$

Now suppose that the firm liberalizes its credit terms so that accounts receivable increase by $20,000,000. Assume that the firm also adds $18,000,000 in new current liabilities to support the delayed cash flow. The current ratio decreases to 1.58:

$$CR = \frac{40 + 20}{20 + 18} = 1.58.$$

Survey of Credit Terms

Credit terms are usually stated on an invoice or in a formal legal contract between buyer and seller. Sometimes the terms are simply a matter of convention and may not be formally stated anywhere. The following discussion surveys some of the more common types of credit terms seen in the marketplace today. The reader should be warned, however, that we are covering only a small fraction of the possible permutations and combinations of various timing, discount, and payment possibilities. One chemical company did a survey of credit terms across all of its various product lines and discovered over 200 distinct sets of terms!

Cash in Advance (CIA)

Sometimes CIA is also called *cash before delivery (CBD)*. This is the safest form of payment terms (it is actually not a *credit* term, since no credit is being extended), because payment must be received before the order is shipped—usually in the form of a cashier's check or a certified check. The seller uses such terms when it does not want to take any risk of the buyer not paying. Selling to firms in bankruptcy often dictates that CIA terms be used.

Firms offering only CIA terms (such as fast food companies, grocery stores, retail petroleum companies, and many other types of retail firms) do not have the expense of credit administration or bad debts. On the other hand, CIA terms permit no time for shipping and inspection and may not, therefore, be acceptable in industries where these practices are necessary.

Cash on Delivery (COD)

Materials shipped to the buyer COD must be paid upon delivery. Usually the shipper collects the payment. While the seller again avoids the costs of administering a credit department and the risks of nonpayment, the seller incurs the risk of having to pay shipping costs to return the goods if payment is not made.

Cash Terms

According to cash terms, sometimes also called *payable upon receipt of invoice,* it is generally understood that, because of mail and other normal processing delays, the buyer has 1 week to 10 days to pay. The seller incurs administrative costs in monitoring payment and runs the risk of bad debts and delayed payments.

Standard Terms

The most common credit terms are "net 30" and "net 60." This means that payment in full is due 30 (or 60) days from the date of the invoice. These terms permit inspection of goods and lower the effective price to the buyer. While the profitability of sales may increase, the seller incurs added costs of administration, delayed payments, and bad debts.

Discount Terms

Discount terms are also common in many industries. Such terms are stated to include a discount, discount payment date, and net date. For example, the very common term "2/10, net 30" means that the buyer may take a 2% discount from the invoice amount if payment is made by the 10th day following the date of the invoice. If the discounted amount is not paid then, the full amount is due the 30th day following the invoice date.

Prox Terms

With prox terms (*prox* refers to *proximate,* which means the next month), all invoices dated prior to a defined cutoff date are payable by a specified date the following month. For example, the auto industry has terms of 10th and 25th prox. Invoices dated from the 1st to the 15th of the month are due the 10th of the following month, while invoices dated between the 16th and the end of the month are due on the 30th of the following month. Cash discounts may also be incorporated. The term "2/10, prox net 30" means the same as "2/10, net 30," except that the 10 and 30 refer to the 10th and 30th of the next month rather than 10 days and 30 days from the invoice date.

Prox terms may simplify administration of the credit function, since billings and payments may be lumped together and processed in large batches. Cash forecasting is slightly more predictable, since most payments arrive in a cluster around two dates in the month. However, prox terms also extend the collection timeline compared to corresponding nonprox terms.

Seasonal Dating

Seasonal dating is used for highly seasonal items such as Christmas cards, snow skis, sporting goods, and garden supplies. Payment is scheduled to be due near the end of the buyer's selling season. For example, "2/10, net 30, dating 120" means that the clock does not start until 120 days from the date of the invoice. Following the dating period, the normal discount terms apply.

Sometimes an *anticipation* discount is associated with dating terms. The buyer has the the option of paying early and deducting an additional discount. The amount of the additional discount is proportional to the number of days the payment is early.

There are several advantages to seasonal dating terms. The seller is able to smooth production over the year rather than concentrating production at peak selling times. The only other way for the seller to smooth production is to store output as inventory, thereby incurring storage costs. Seasonal dating permits buyers to take the inventory and have it available during off-peak times. It also transfers some of the risks of obsolescence from seller to buyer. On the other hand, cash flow is delayed significantly and may cause balance sheet constraints to be violated. Bad debt risk increases with delayed payments, and administrative costs are increased with the added volume of receivables.

Consignment Terms

In some industries, the seller ships the goods to the buyer, who has no obligation to pay until the goods have been sold or used. The title to the goods remains with the seller until the buyer has sold or used the goods. The buyer is usually required to segregate consigned goods and to provide periodic accounting of the inventory on hand. Sometimes the buyer is invoiced after each such accounting.

Consignment adds to the administrative burden of both buyer and seller. Cash flow may be delayed significantly, but the seller is somewhat protected by retaining title to consigned goods. However, it may be difficult to actually claim the goods in the event of a default. Consignment may increase sales because the buyer is under no obligation to pay unless the goods are sold or used.

Letter of Credit

If the seller determines that there is an unacceptable level of risk that the buyer will not be able to pay, a letter of credit may be required. A letter of credit is an agreement by which a financially stronger party (usually a financial institution) substitutes its creditworthiness for that of the buyer. The letter states that specified payments will be made by the stronger party as long as certain conditions are met, such as delivery of the goods. While letters of credit are frequently used in international trade, they may be used for domestic transactions as well.

With letters of credit terms, the seller greatly reduces the bad debt risk. Depending on the specific terms of the letter of credit, cash flow may be delayed but is fairly certain. On the other hand, letters of credit take administrative time and are not popular with most buyers.

Electronic Credit Terms

In the past few years, a number of firms have introduced electronic payment terms. For example, the chemical division of a large oil company had terms of net 30 days. In 1984 it began offering a 1.5% discount if buyers permitted the chemical division to debit the buyer's account via an ACH debit the day following delivery of the product. Insurance companies frequently offer discounts if policy holders permit their bank accounts to be debited through an ACH transaction.

The seller benefits because of less uncertainty about the payment date and lower administrative costs associated with electronic processing. With a seller-initiated ACH debit, of course, there is no uncertainty. There is still uncertainty if the buyer initiates an ACH credit. Although payment *could* be faster using electronic payments (perhaps coupled with electronic data interchange, discussed in Chapter 20), payment dates could be negotiated and may be earlier or later than paper-based payments.

Other Combinations

It is not difficult to imagine additional credit terms combining some of the preceding features and adding others. For example, multistage discounts are common in some industries. The term "3/15, 2/30, net 31" means that the buyer can take a 3% discount if payment is made by the 15th, 2% if made by the 30th, and the full amount is due on the 31st. During times of extremely high interest rates, one steel company offered a sliding discount depending on the prime rate: "$x/10$ net 30," where x was 1/2% if the prime rate was below 12%, 1% if it was between 12 and 18%, and 1% if it was over 18%.

Summary of Credit Terms and Cost/Benefit Factors

Table 14.1 summarizes the general categories of credit terms we have discussed and shows how each affects the various cost factors in the objective function.

Other Credit Term Issues

Penalty Charges

Some firms include penalty charges in their credit terms. For example, a 2/10 net 30 term may also state that a 1.5% interest charge will be assessed on payments made after 30 days and an additional 1.5% each month thereafter until payment is made. Penalty charges are not popular and are difficult to collect even if they are part of credit terms.

Invoice versus Statement Billing

The great majority (about 96%, according to one survey) of firms prefer to bill by sending invoices. An invoice describes exactly what was purchased and usually corresponds to one shipment. Sometimes one invoice covers only

Table 14.1 Qualitative Evaluation of Credit Policy Objective Function

Credit Term	Profit of Sales	Bad Debt Expense	Admin. Cost	Other Areas	Time Value
CIA	− −	+ +	+ +	−	+ +
COD	− −	+ +	+	−	+ +
Cash terms	+	−	−	0	+
Standard terms (net 30, net 60)	+	−	−	0	−
Discount terms (2/10 net 30, etc.)	+	−	− −	0	−
Prox. terms	+	−	−	0	− −
Dating terms	+ +	− −	− −	+	− −
Consignment	+ +	+ +	− −	+	−
Letter of credit	− −	+ +	− −	+ −	+ −
Electronic terms	+ −	+ −	+	+ +	+ −

Key + + = Very beneficial to seller
     +   = Moderately beneficial to seller
     0   = Neutral
     −   = Moderately costly to seller
     − − = Very costly to seller
     + − = Mixed, depending upon the situation

one particular item, so that one shipment corresponds to many invoices. The alternative to invoices is statement billing. A monthly statement lists the balance due to the seller. It may or may not contain detailed information on particular shipments. Many firms will not pay on statement billings because they need detailed invoice information to match against shipping and receiving documents before releasing payment.

How to Count Days

It is simple enough to state "2/10 net 30," but exactly what does that mean? Ten days starting when and ending when? Thirty days from what date? There are considerable variations in the interpretation of day counting. The clock could start on the invoice date, the receipt of goods date, the receipt of invoice date, or the shipping date. The authors find that most firms assume that the clock starts on the invoice date, although it is rarely stated on invoices or in purchase agreements. When is a payment considered to be made? Buyers generally assume the postmark date. Sellers assume the receipt of check date. A few firms assume that a payment is made only when the seller receives available funds in its bank.

Fortunately, some harmony can be found in this ambiguity because most firms allow some grace period before disallowing discounts or assessing penalty charges. In other words, if a payment taking a 2% discount is received on the 12th day following the invoice date, most firms would not attempt to collect the 2%. They may do so, however, if the 2% discount is taken on day 35.

The ability to enforce strict observance of discounts and payment dates seems to be related to the power of the buyer relative to the seller. The more powerful party usually determines the relationship.

Determining Credit Terms for
Specific Customers

Types of Errors in Making Credit Decisions

There are two types of potential errors in granting credit. First, the seller can reject a particular customer who is actually a good credit risk. Equivalently, the firm can make the credit terms too tight and lose a potentially good customer. In either case, potential sales are lost. Second, the firm can extend credit to an apparently good customer and incur higher than anticipated costs in the form of additional collection, monitoring, and/or bad debt costs.

Credit Information Sources

To make credit decisions, credit departments obtain information about prospective customers that will permit an assessment not only of the likelihood of payment but also of the expected costs of providing the credit. Some customers may be very creditworthy and may ultimately make all payments, but may continually stretch payments in the process and cause increased administrative and time value costs to the seller.

The more information the seller obtains, of course, the better the assessment is, but also the more costly. Hence, sellers must decide where to trade off between accuracy of decisions and costs of information. In general, when a customer exposes the seller to large credit risks through large unsecured purchases, it pays to do extensive credit checking. On the other hand, when a customer purchases a small amount and exposes the seller to only a minor credit risk, only limited credit checking is warranted.

The following are frequently used sources of credit information:

Past Credit History

If a credit applicant has been a previous credit customer, the seller may have readily available information on the payment history. Sometimes information about customers may be passed between subsidiaries in large multi-divisional firms. A few firms have developed common credit data bases for use throughout all divisions.

Credit Agencies

In many areas of the country, credit bureaus and other agencies provide, for a fee, information on a customer's credit history, including the payment history, financial information, high credit amounts, the length of time credit has been available, and any actions that have been necessary to achieve collection. This information is provided for individuals as well as corporations.

References

References such as the customer's banks and other suppliers can provide useful information about past payment practices and relationships.

Financial Statements

Audited financial statements can show the firm's current and past financial condition and give some clues to its future ability to meet credit terms. Financial statement analysis requires significant administrative time to conduct and implement.

Investment Information Services

Investment information services may seem an odd source to include in a list of credit information. Nevertheless, when a seller extends credit to a buyer, the seller is indeed making an investment in the buyer and hopes to make a profitable return. Investment companies perform extensive analyses of financial statements and frequently have a good sense of the direction in which the company is moving. Such information must be assessed with caution, however, since firms with excellent investment outlooks may not pay their bills on time.

Published News Reports

Business and local newspapers may provide clues to the creditworthiness of firms. News of a strike, for example, may spell trouble for future credit purchasers. Business outlooks for specific industries may also reveal something about the health of prospective credit purchasers.

Analysis of Credit Information

Qualitative Approach

In banking classes, most students cover what is known as the *five C's of credit*. This is simply a convenient method of grouping credit information into more easily understandable categories. You may object, "But we're not bankers!" When firms sell on credit, they are performing a bank-like service. They are exposing themselves to credit risk every bit as much as any bank lender, but without many of the safeguards bankers use. Therefore, firms need to adopt all of the tools banks use for evaluating credit applicants.

CHARACTER. A credit rating is never better than the people behind it. Hence, it is important to assess the integrity of the credit applicant. Some idea of the applicant's character may be gleaned from credit references, past credit history, other suppliers, and financial institutions. Key questions to ask are as follows: Is the applicant basically honest? Has the applicant demonstrated good faith in working with previous suppliers and other credit suppliers?

CAPACITY. Capacity attempts to measure the ability of the customer to meet credit obligations according to the stated terms. Financial statements, both past and pro forma, provide the most complete picture of the applicant's capacity. Key questions are these: Will the applicant have sufficient cash flow to make payments according to our credit terms? What are the risks facing the buyer that could cause its financial position to deteriorate?

CAPITAL. The measure of capital seeks to assess the credit applicant's financial strength from a debt/equity perspective. Does the applicant already have significant fixed obligations (such as other debt and other payables) that would make it difficult for the applicant to withstand short periods of financial reversals without declaring bankruptcy? Another way of stating this is to ask if the applicant has sufficient equity in the firm to absorb losses or if the supplier will have to absorb the losses. Financial statements and a survey of other credit obligations are important here.

COLLATERAL. If the buyer is eventually unable to pay the credit obligation, the seller would like to protect its position by claiming title to some of the buyer's assets. Banks often require that assets be pledged as collateral, but it is extremely rare to find corporate credit terms that include any mention of collateral. It would be impractical to segregate and keep track of collateral for the many suppliers of a typical firm. While sellers nominally have a claim on assets they have sold to a buyer, it is often difficult to retrieve goods that have been delivered to a now bankrupt firm. Hence, collateral plays a very small role in normal corporate credit policy.

CONDITIONS. Trends in the general economy and in the buyer's industry may have a significant impact on the buyer's ability to pay credit obligations. Key questions are the following: Are there trends in the economy that would adversely affect the buyer? Is competition likely to edge out this buyer?

Financial Statement Analysis

A detailed analysis of financial statements is warranted for potentially large-scale buyers that expose the seller to significant risk. Audited financial statements from past years and pro forma projections of coming years form the basis for the analysis. Trends in key financial ratios are noted, and cash flow (not simply earnings) is projected. Financial statement analysis is an important subject, but not one that can be given extended treatment in the scope of this book.

Credit Scoring Systems

For sellers with a large base of customers that individually buy in relatively small amounts, a detailed financial statement may not be justified. Instead, an approach more suitable for large numbers of customers is helpful. In a *credit scoring* approach, the seller uses historical data to identify significant factors distinguishing paying customers from nonpaying customers. Employing a technique called *multiple discriminant analysis (MDA)*, a computer routine can determine which factors best explain which past customers have been good and bad credit risks. Once these factors have been identified, they may be applied to potential future customers. You have probably been involved in credit scoring if you have ever filled out an application for a charge card.

Based on past payment records, customers are grouped into two categories: good and bad. Information is collected about these customers that may help distinguish between the two groups. For corporate customers, this information might include financial ratios such as the current ratio, debt to total assets, interest coverage, accounts payable turnover, and so on. For individual customers, monthly income, monthly obligations, net worth, and time with the current firm might be included.

MDA is similar to multiple regression analysis. The dependent y variable, however, is a 0–1 variable that is equal to 0 for bad customers and 1 for good customers. Using historical data, MDA computes weights, w_i, for each factor, x_i, that give the best fit to the following equation:

$$y = w_1 x_1 + w_2 x_2 + \ldots + w_n x_n.$$

Once the weights are determined, any credit application can be scored by taking the customer's x_i values and computing the y score. A cutoff point is established such that applicants scoring above it are granted credit and those scoring below it are rejected.

No credit scoring system can discriminate perfectly between good and bad credit risks. Most firms using scoring models allow for a gray area. If a score falls in this gray area, the customer receives further scrutiny before a decision is made.

Limiting Credit Risk Through Credit Limits

Credit scoring models and detailed financial analysis may not be cost justified for many firms. Another common way to control credit risk is to permit firms to establish their credit histories with the seller by granting limited credit until evidence builds that the buyer can handle more. For example, based on only limited information, a seller may grant a $1,000 credit limit to a particular corporate buyer. After 6 months of satisfactory payment experience, the credit limit might be raised to $2,000. After a year, it may be increased to $5,000, and so on.

Financing Directly Related to
Accounts Receivable

Since accounts receivable represent the promise of future cash flows, firms selling on credit have both an asset and a problem. They have an asset that is worth something—though perhaps not full book value—based on the customer's promise to pay and the strength of the seller's collection efforts. They also have a problem in that delayed cash flows may force the seller to obtain outside funding to *finance the receivables*. As mentioned earlier, operations and not receivables are actually being financed; but we will occasionally use this term with that understanding.

Financing receivables is an integral part of credit policy. There are two general approaches to receivable financing: direct and indirect. For direct financing, the seller obtains funding and carries the receivables. For indirect financing, the seller assists the buyer in obtaining financing. The seller does not carry the receivables on its books. Within those two approaches, there are a number of alternatives. Each alternative has different implications for costs, benefits, and control.

Direct Financing

With direct financing, the selling firm maintains primary control over all aspects of credit policy. It establishes credit terms, analyzes and selects potential credit applicants, monitors accounts receivable, manages the collection effort, and absorbs bad debt losses. The seller incurs the major costs of managing the credit function. There are several alternatives for financing receivables while maintaining direct financing control. The most common are pledging of receivables as collateral for a loan and the use of captive finance companies, both of which were discussed in Chapter 13.

Indirect Financing

Rather than administer the credit function itself, a firm may choose to pass on much of the administrative control, as well as the receivables, to other parties. There are several ways in which this can be done.

Third-Party Tie-ins

The seller may simply collect credit information and forward a credit application to a third party. If the applicant meets the criteria of the third party, credit is granted. Subsequent monitoring and collecting, as well as any bad debt losses, become the responsibility of the third party. Car dealers, for example, may have a tie-in arrangement with a local bank. Potential car buyers fill out a credit application in the showroom. The bank controls the credit decision and collects subsequent payments.

The advantage of this arrangement is that the seller avoids most credit administration costs, does not have to carry receivables on its books, and does not incur bad debt losses. On the other hand, the firm loses control over the type of customer accepted for credit and loses the potential financing fees it might otherwise collect. It may also have to pay a fee or offer a discount from the face value of the sale to compensate the third party.

Factoring

Factoring involves the direct sale of the accounts receivable to a party called a *factor*. Bank subsidiaries and finance companies frequently serve as factors. Factoring arrangements were discussed in Chapter 13.

A common form of factoring touches almost everyone's life: the retail credit card. Suppose Mr. Jones purchases a $500 new suit from a clothing store. The clothing store, after taking steps to ensure that Mr. Jones' account is valid for that amount, takes the credit card voucher to a local bank and deposits it. The banking system becomes the factor for the clothing store's receivables. The bank "buys" the voucher for $500 less a prearranged discount (say, 2%). The voucher is processed through a credit card clearing system and is ultimately delivered to the local bank that issued Mr. Jones the credit card. The local bank is then responsible for collecting from Mr. Jones. As long as the clothing store has taken specified precautions, the banking system has no recourse to the retail merchant. The clothing store need not employ a credit staff to screen customers and follow up on collections. These functions are performed by the banking system. Hence, the standard bank credit card system is really a form of consumer receivable factoring.

Collection Agencies

Collection agencies, in some cases, perform a role in financing receivables. Some collection agencies serve essentially as factors for delinquent accounts. They purchase old receivables from firms for about 50% of their face value. Often this is done *with recourse*, meaning that the collection agency does not bear risks for uncollectable accounts.

Private Label Financing

Private label financing is similar to factoring, except that the seller may retain more control over acceptable credit risks. A third party is contracted with to perform the credit function in the name of the seller. From all appearances, credit is provided by the seller. Depending on the arrangements made, the seller may retain many of the marketing advantages of conducting its own credit function, but incurs neither the costs of the credit operation nor the commitment of funds needed to support accounts receivable. On the other hand, the seller may not receive the full face value of the sale and may relinquish some control over screening potential customers.

Summary

Credit policy is a significant part of the assets of most firms. The objective in setting the credit policy can be cast in the same financial framework as other financial decisions: maximize the net present value to shareholders. To do this with credit, an objective function is constructed, with several cost elements: profitability from sales, bad debt expense, administrative costs, other related costs, and time value costs. In addition, firms face many constraints that limit credit policies. Some of these constraints are industry standards, inertia inherent in traditional credit terms, working capital constraints, and legal constraints.

In this light, we examined a wide variety of possible credit terms with many combinations of payment timing, amounts, penalties, and incentives. We build on this framework in the next chapter, showing how alternative credit terms may be evaluated in a cash flow framework.

The credit-granting decision is a key one for credit managers. The inflow timeline begins when a customer is granted credit. Goods or services are given, but no value will be transferred back to the seller for a period of time. Therefore, steps to limit credit risk become very important. We discussed several methods, each associated with different levels of costs and benefits. The most costly one is a detailed financial analysis of the applicant's past accounting statements and pro forma projections. Lower-cost methods employ statistical scoring systems (in cases where there are many small similar customers) and more or less arbitrary credit limits (where a firm wants to avoid expensive credit checking and administrative costs).

We then discussed how firms finance receivables—or, more accurately, finance operations while waiting for receivables to be paid. There are two extremes and several possibilities in between. At one extreme, the firm completely controls credit policy, collecting and financing its own receivables. At the other extreme, the firm gives the complete credit function to other parties. Examples are credit card operations and factoring. In both cases, the seller does minimal credit checking and has no collection responsibilities.

──────────── Discussion Questions ────────────

1. Why do both marketing and finance managers want to have a hand in setting credit policies?
2. Why is cash flow a more appropriate focal point for analyzing credit policies than accounts receivable?
3. Explain why receivable time delay is less than the total collection time delay.
4. Why does the assumption of perfect markets lead to the irrelevance of credit policy?
5. What are the main reasons that corporations extend credit to each other?
6. Explain the factors contained in the credit policy objective function. How does this objective function handle conflicting tradeoffs between the various factors?
7. Why are funds needed to finance receivables, not simply the total amount of accounts receivable?
8. What is meant by 2/10, net 30? What is meant by 3/15, 2/30, net 35?
9. Explain the advantages and disadvantages of seasonal dating from the point of view of both the seller and the buyer.
10. What ambiguities arise when counting days for terms like 2/10, net 30?
11. Explain the rationale for using the five C's of credit, and comment on how one could evaluate prospective credit buyers in each of the five areas.
12. How does a credit scoring system work?
13. Explain why the phrase *financing receivables* is not strictly correct.
14. How can a firm obtain receivable financing and yet remain in control of most of the aspects of credit policy? Give several options.
15. Explain two *good* reasons for a firm to operate a captive finance subsidiary. What are some *bad* reasons?
16. Explain what is meant by factoring. Explain several ways in which factoring may be done.

──────────── Problems ────────────

1. The Milan Shoe Company sells to retail shoe stores on terms of net 30 days. On average, Milan receives payment 45 days after the invoice date. If sales average $150,000 per day, what is the average amount in accounts receivable?
2. The Milan Shoe Company in Problem 1 has variable costs averaging 70% of the selling price. What is the out-of-pocket commitment of funds for the accounts receivable?

3. Western Wear, Inc., supplies western-style hats for high-fashion men's stores. The company averages sales of $20,000 per day on terms of net 60, and sales are recorded on the day invoices are prepared. On average, customers pay by check into the company's lockbox 65 days after the invoice date. Checks receive 1-day availability. Copies of invoices are forwarded to Western Wear and payments are credited to accounts receivable, on average, 4 days after being received in the lockbox.

   a. How much, on average, is recorded in accounts receivable?

   b. How much money is tied up in the collection system?

4. Bashnagle Publishing, Inc., sells on credit terms of net 30, dating 120. Sales average $500,000 per day and customers pay on time. Variable production and selling costs average 65% of the selling price.

   a. What is the average amount recorded in accounts receivable?

   b. What is the actual commitment of funds?

5. Computer Magic produces integrated spread sheet and word processing software for personal computers and sells exclusively to retail computer outlets. The company issues invoices for the software on the day of shipment; however, this is not posted to the accounts receivable for an additional 3 days. On average, Computer Magic's customers pay by check 37 days after the invoice date. Computer Magic credits accounts receivable on the day the check arrives, but because of slow processing it does not deposit the checks in its bank until 2 days later. On average, there is a 1-day availability delay on the checks. Sales average $200,000 per day, and variable costs are 15% of the selling price.

   a. What is the average level of accounts receivable recorded on Computer Magic's books?

   b. Based on the selling price, what is the average commitment of funds to the entire collection process?

   c. What is the actual commitment of funds to support operations during the accounts receivable period?

--- **Selected Readings** ---

BEN-HORIM, MOSHE, and HAIM LEVY, "Management of Accounts Receivable Under Inflation," *Financial Management* (Spring 1983), pp. 42–48.

BERANEK, WILLIAM, and WALTON TAYLOR, "Credit Scoring Models and the Cut-off Point: A Simplification," *Decision Sciences* (July 1976), pp. 394–404.

CLAPPER, LARRY R., " 'ARCH': A Recession Collection Strategy," *Cashflow* (July 1980), pp. 44–46.

Compliance Handbook for Consumer Credit, 7th ed., Capitol Reports, Inc., Washington, D.C. (1981).

HALLORAN, JOHN A., and HOWARD P. LANSER, "The Credit Policy Decision in an Inflationary Environment," *Financial Management* (Winter 1981), pp. 31–38.

HILL, NED C., WILLIAM L. SARTORIS, and DANIEL M. FERGUSON, "Corporate Credit and Payables Policies: Two Surveys," *Journal of Cash Management* (July/August 1984), pp. 56–62.

HILL, NED C., ROBERT A. WOOD, and DALE R. SORENSON, "Factors Influencing Corporate Credit Policy: A Survey," *Journal of Cash Management* (December 1981), pp. 38–47.

JOHNSON, ROBERT W., "Management of Accounts Receivable and Payable," in *Financial Handbook,* 5th ed., Edward I. Altman (ed.), New York: Wiley, 1981, Chapter 28.

MEHTA, DILEEP, "The Formulation of Credit Policy Models," *Management Science* (October 1968), pp. B30–B50.

SARTORIS, WILLIAM L., and NED C. HILL, "A Generalized Cash Flow Approach to Short-Term Financial Decisions," *Journal of Finance* (May 1983), pp. 349–360.

SCHWARTZ, ROBERT A., "An Economic Model of Trade Credit," *Journal of Financial and Quantitative Analysis* (September 1974), pp. 643–657.

15

Managing Credit Policy and Accounts Receivable

In 1984 a large oil company considered a major change in its credit policies. At the time, it had a paper-based system that relied on the mails to deliver invoices to customers and to receive checks for payment. Even though nominal credit terms were net 30 days, total collection time was actually about 45 days from the time of billing until payment ultimately became good funds in the firm's banks. Collection time appeared to be lengthening, and enforcement of terms was becoming more costly. Management evaluated the pros and cons of using an electronic payment system that would permit the company to debit its customers' accounts shortly after product delivery. They concluded that substantial paperwork and personnel costs would be eliminated and available funds would be received much earlier. But how would customers react? What kinds of incentives would have to be offered to compensate customers for giving up their funds earlier? What kind of discount could the company afford to give up and still benefit from the new system?

This chapter discusses how to approach such problems. We first turn our attention to managing the collection process. What efforts can be made to encourage customers to adhere to stated terms? How are credit terms monitored? What information is available to management to assist in controlling receivables? We show that some commonly used accounts receivable measures may be fundamentally flawed and may provide erroneous signals to managers. A better cash flow–oriented measure is demonstrated.

We then discuss methods of forecasting overall accounts receivable. Since receivables represent such a large fraction of the total assets of most firms, accounts receivable forecasting has become more important in recent years.

In the final section, we discuss a cash flow approach to evaluating alternative credit terms and tackle the problem posed by the oil company. What factors are important? What financial tools are available to help solve this problem?

Collection Procedures

For most firms, the accounts receivable segment is the longest segment of the cash inflow timeline. Hence, there are potentially more savings there than in any other area of short-term finance. While tuning up a lockbox system may shave half a day off the collection timeline, more careful attention to receivables may cut the timeline literally by weeks.

Objective Function

The term *collection policies* refers to the set of actions a seller may take to encourage buyers to adhere to stated credit terms. The objective of collection policies should be the same objective function we applied to credit terms in Chapter 14. Recall that we wanted to maximize the value of the total collection cost:

$$\text{Total collection cost} = PS - ADMIN - BD - OTH - TV,$$

where *PS* is profitability of sales, *ADMIN* is the administrative cost, *BD* is bad debt expense, *OTH* is costs in other areas of the firm (such as inventory holding costs), and *TV* is the time value cost caused by delayed payments.

This objective function points out the tradeoffs that credit managers face in making credit policy decisions. For example, we can reduce the time value term by attempting to collect payments earlier. At the same time, we might increase administrative costs and perhaps alienate customers through overzealous collection efforts, thereby reducing the profitability of sales. We can reduce bad debt expenses by more careful screening but may also turn away potentially good customers in the process. In the following discussion, keep these tradeoffs in mind as we examine the ingredients of a firm's collection policy.

Billing

The first segment in the collection timeline (shown in Figure 14.1) is the billing segment. If invoices (or statements) are not sent out promptly, payments will not be prompt. Most firms try to send invoices on the day of delivery. Efforts to shorten the billing process may be relatively inexpensive to implement and yet may shave several days off the cash inflow timeline. Besides being prompt, the invoices should be as accurate as possible. Inaccurate invoices are a primary cause of payment delays.

Credit Term Enforcement

Determination of Late Payment

First, management must decide how *late payment* is defined. Some firms may not consider a payment late until it is over 1 month beyond the nominal due date stated in the credit terms. Other firms may define a late payment as being only a few days late. One factor in this decision is the information system used to determine when customer payments have been made. As we will show, some reporting systems are better than others in flagging delinquent customers.

Direct Actions

Second, management specifies actions to be taken when an account is defined as late. Table 15.1 illustrates a schedule that a firm might follow as part of its credit enforcement efforts. Such actions may include telephone calls to the customer's payables department, duplicate invoices, and various levels of reminder letters. These actions are relatively inexpensive and are often effective.

Stronger action may be taken if payment is not made within a reasonable time after mild follow-up is done. These stronger actions might entail a personal visit to the customer, conversion to COD or CIA terms for further purchases, or stoppage of further deliveries until payments are made. In some cases, the seller may have to negotiate a revised payment schedule with the customer.

Table 15.1 Schedule of Actions to Follow-up Late Payments (Stated Terms: Net 30 Days)

If Payment Is *Not* Made By:	Action
40 days	Telephone call to customer's payables department
	Send duplicate invoice if needed
50 days	Second telephone call to customer's payables department
60 days	Warning letter (mild)
75 days	Warning letter (strong)
90 days	Telephone call to management level
	Notify that future deliveries will be made only on a COD basis until payment is made
120 days	Stop further deliveries
	1. Initiate appropriate legal action if the account is large
	2. Turn over to a collection agency if the account is small

Legal Action

A more drastic step involves legal action. It is sometimes possible to attach liens to equipment sold to customers. For example, a plumbing supplier may file a lien on fixtures and parts he supplied to a housing contractor who did not pay. Before the house is sold, the plumber's claim must be satisfied. Law suits may be brought against delinquent customers. However, if they end up in bankruptcy proceedings, the seller may receive little compensation. Since legal expenses can be high, legal steps are usually reserved for high-value delinquent accounts.

Collection Agencies

Delinquent accounts may be turned over to third-party collection agencies. These firms specialize in attempting to get payment from such accounts. They either purchase accounts outright or proceed on a best efforts basis. For their services, collection agencies charge as much as 50% of the amount collected. Sellers should be aware that once an account is turned over to such an agency, future relationships with the customer may be harmed.

_____ Monitoring Accounts Receivable _____

Monitoring accounts receivable is a key task in credit management. Individual accounts are monitored to ensure that credit customers adhere to the firm's stated credit terms and to warn management when trouble appears. Late payments may be a sign of either intentional stretching or financial difficulties. The overall level of receivables is monitored to ensure sound collection procedures and to keep the credit function in line with the financial objectives of the firm.

Monitoring Individual Accounts

Monthly Aging Schedule

An account aging schedule is simply a listing of each credit customer together with the amounts unpaid as of the report date. Table 15.2 gives a sample aging schedule for Frankel's Fabricating Company.

The aging schedule allows a quick review of accounts that are past due. The Baker Labs account is significantly past due, and the firm is evidently not making any more purchases from Frankel's Fabricating. Perhaps Baker Labs is in bankruptcy. Several other accounts show payments more than 31 days late. Aaron's Supply is evidently still making purchases but has $100 in long overdue receivables. This may be due to an invoicing error or disputed goods.

One problem with the aging schedule as presented in Table 15.2 is that management cannot tell how late payments are in the 1–30 days late category.

Table 15.2 Sample Aging Schedule With Monthly Categories for Frankel's Fabricating Company (Report Date: December 31)

Customer	Total Receivable	Current	PAST DUE DAYS 1–30	31–60	61–90	Over 90
Aaron's Supply Co.	$ 1,500	$1,000	$ 200	$ 200	—	$ 100
Acme Plastics	$ 3,000	$1,000	—	$2,000	—	—
Avon Genetics Lab.	$ 2,000	$2,000	—	—	—	—
Babcolt Industries	$ 5,000	$3,000	$2,000	$1,000	—	—
Baker Labs	$ 3,400	—	—	—	—	$3,400
Centex Tool and Die	$ 4,000	$2,000	$1,000	$1,000	—	—
⋮						⋮
Total (in $1,000s)	$10,000	$5,700	$2,700	$1,050	$400	$ 150
Fraction of total receivables	100%	57.0%	27.0%	10.5%	4.0%	1.5%

A firm that complies with stated credit terms by *postmarking* payment on the due date would be classed with firms that wait until 25 or so days after the due date to mail payments. This, of course, is because of mail and processing delays. Grouping by months is not precise enough for close monitoring. Because of the almost universal practice of using months as the standard for aging schedules, and because firms do not want to annoy a customer who pays soon after the due date, many firms wait until accounts spill over into the 31–60 days late category before taking action associated with late payments.

Refined Aging Schedule

A better solution that preserves the aging schedule concept would be simply to divide the "1–30 days" column into two subcolumns based on the cutoff time the firm considers to be late payment, say, 7 days. The columns would then be "Current," "1–7 Days," "8–30 Days," "31–60 Days," and so on.

An alternative would be to define current to include 1–7 days late. The disadvantage of this practice is that banks and analysts often want companies to report standard aging schedules broken down by month. Hence, the split column approach would be more practical.

Average Collection Time

A useful tool for viewing the past payment practices of a customer is to monitor the average collection time. For this measure, the firm tracks the date of the invoice (or some other starting point) and records when available funds are obtained. The objective is to capture the entire collection timeline. An example is given in Table 15.3. An average is computed for each customer by weighting the days by the dollar amount of the payment.

Table 15.3 Measuring the Average Collection Time

Customer	Invoice Date	Available Funds Date	Total Days	×	Dollar Payment	=	Dollar Days
William's	1/5	2/4	30		$ 3,000		90,000
Supply	1/12	2/13	32		$ 2,500		80,000
	1/20	2/24	35		$ 2,300		80,500
	2/5	2/24	19		$ 4,200		79,800
			Totals		$12,000		330,300

$$\text{Weighted average collection time} = \frac{330,300}{12,000} = 27.5 \text{ days}$$

Customer	Invoice Date	Available Funds Date	Total Days	×	Dollar Payment	=	Dollar Days
Xena's Tools	1/5	2/10	36		$ 5,000		180,000
	1/12	2/10	29		$ 3,500		101,500
	1/15	2/26	42		$ 8,000		336,000
	1/20	4/3	73		$ 2,400		175,200
	2/3	4/14	70		$ 6,700		469,000
			Totals		$25,600		1,261,700

$$\text{Weighted average collection time} = \frac{1,261,700}{25,600} = 49.3 \text{ days}$$

In the example, the average total collection time for William's Supply is 27.5 days and for Xena's Tools it is 49.3 days. It appears that Xena's Tools is beginning to stretch payments, since the payment time went from 36 and 29 to the 70s. This information may be useful to pinpoint late-paying customers and to determine future relations with the customer. For example, when contract prices are renegotiated next year, it may be useful to know which customers were late payers and which were not. Future prices might reflect the time value costs to the seller.

Adjusted Average Collection Time

If a firm has multiple credit terms, the total collection time may be confusing. Some customers may have longer credit terms and others shorter terms. They may purchase different products with different terms. A better measure is to adjust total collection times by subtracting the credit term period. For example, suppose William's Supply bought on net 30 terms, while Xena's Tools bought on net 45 terms. The adjusted average collection times would be 27.5 days − 30 days = −2.5 days for William's Supply (they paid earlier than the terms specified) and 49.3 days − 45 days = 4.3 days for Xena's Tools.

While data are available to compute total collection times, currently very few firms do so. Nevertheless, this measure is much more revealing than the aging schedule, since each payment is tracked and included in the average total collection time.

Monitoring Overall Accounts Receivable[1]

While aging schedules, appropriately constructed, and reports on average total collection times are useful for monitoring individual customer accounts, we also need some measure of overall credit and collection policies. Such a measure could flag potential problems with collection efforts or shifts in customer payment practices. It would also be important information for cash forecasting, for managing a firm's cash position, and for maintaining balance sheet ratios. We first set out criteria for an effective measure and then survey potential measures commonly used by firms.

Criteria for an Overall Receivables Measure

The objective of an overall receivables measure should relate to the objectives of the firm. As we have stated throughout this book, cash flow is a good place to start. In general, faster inflows are good and slower inflows are bad. Hence, an effective measure of credit policy should tell management when cash flows are slowing down or speeding up. At the same time, the measure should be relatively inexpensive to obtain and easily understood by management.

Suppose we sold $100 worth of goods on credit during the month of January. Now suppose we observe that cash comes in from those sales according to the following pattern:

	Cash Inflow During:			
	Jan	**Feb**	**Mar**	**Apr**
Cash from January credit sales	20	50	20	10

Is this pattern acceptable? That, of course, depends on the firm's credit terms. Let us assume that this pattern is acceptable to management or that at least it is a benchmark against which to compare future months. An average accounts receivable time can be derived from this pattern. If we assume that credit sales and cash flows take place uniformly throughout each month, the average receivable collection time is

$$\frac{20(0) + 50(30) + 20(60) + 10(90)}{100} = 36 \text{ days.}$$

Suppose that, in February, credit sales increase to $200 and cash inflows follow this pattern:

	Cash Inflow During:			
	Feb	**Mar**	**Apr**	**May**
Cash from February credit sales	40	100	40	20

---

[1] The concepts developed here draw heavily on Bernell K. Stone, "The Payment Pattern Approach to Monitoring and Controlling Accounts Receivable," *Financial Management* Vol. 5, No. 3 (Autumn 1976), pp. 65–82.

Has the customer payment pattern shifted? No. The percentages of sales coming in as cash each month follow the same pattern as for the January sales. The average receivable time is the same, too:

$$\frac{40(0) + 100(30) + 40(60) + 20(90)}{200} = 36 \text{ days.}$$

Given cash flow as our yardstick and January's receivables collection time as a benchmark, cash flows from February's credit sales are no better or worse than January's. If management was satisfied with a receivables time of 36 days in January, it should be equally satisfied with 36 days in February.

Any measure of receivables we employ should be able to tell us that the collection timing was the same in January and February. The only change from one month to the next was the increase in credit sales. Customer payment patterns remained unchanged.

We can now specify what an accounts receivable measure should do for management. It should provide:

1. Negative signals when collection time slows down.
2. Positive signals when collection time speeds up.
3. Neutral signals when collection time remains unchanged.

Generating Receivables from Sales and Cash Flows

As a standard for testing proposed receivables measures, we generate a schedule of monthly credit sales, assume a constant pattern of payments, and compute the resultant cash flows. Let us assume that the pattern we saw in January continues throughout the year: 20% paid in the month of sale, followed by 50, 20, and 10% in subsequent months. This pattern, as we saw, corresponds to 36 days average receivables time. We will keep this pattern over the entire year. Only sales levels will change. Table 15.4A shows cash flows resulting from credit sales over an entire year. The cash flows for January and February are from credit sales of $100 and $200, respectively, as in the example we just used. Cash flows in all other months follow the same pattern. The reader may wish to check to see that the average receivables time for each month is 36 days. The only change from month to month is in the level of credit sales.

In Table 15.4B, cash flows are converted into accounts receivable. An account receivable is simply a recognition of cash flow that hasn't occurred yet. For example, the account receivable for January sales in January is $80 because in February $50 will come in, in March $20, and in April the last $10. The number in each cell of the Account Receivable Matrix corresponds to the sum of the numbers to the right of the corresponding cell in the Cash Flow Matrix. We assume no bad debts. If bad debts were a factor, the total inflow would be reduced by the bad debt fraction.

Total accounts receivable for each month are computed by summing down each column. Note that total accounts receivable include, in this case, receivables from credit sales in the current month plus 2 earlier months.

Table 15.4

A. *Cash Flows Generated by a Constant Payment Pattern*

		$i =$	0	1	2	3
		Percentage* =	20%	50%	20%	10%

CASH FLOW MATRIX

Month	Sales	Jan	Feb	Mar	Apr	May	Jun	Jul	Aug	Sep	Oct
Oct	400	40									
Nov	300	60	30								
Dec	200	100	40	20							
Jan	100	20	50	20	10						
Feb	200		40	100	40	20					
Mar	400			80	200	80	40				
Apr	900				180	450	180	90			
May	1,500					300	750	300	150		
Jun	3,500						700	1,750	700	350	
Jul	2,700							540	1,350	540	270
Aug	1,400								280	700	280
Sep	900									180	450
Oct	500										100
Total		220	160	220	430	850	1,670	2,680	2,480	1,770	1,100

*Percentage of credit sale that results in cash flow i months after credit sale.

B. Accounts Receivable Generated by Cash Flows

ACCOUNTS RECEIVABLE MATRIX

Month	Sales	Jan	Feb	Mar	Apr	May	Jun	Jul	Aug	Sep	Oct
Oct	400	0									
Nov	300	30	0								
Dec	200	60	20	0							
Jan	100	80	30	10	0						
Feb	200		160	60	20	0					
Mar	400			320	120	40	0				
Apr	900				720	270	90	0			
May	1,500					1,200	450	150	0		
Jun	3,500						2,800	1,050	350	0	
Jul	2,700							2,160	810	270	0
Aug	1,400								1,120	420	140
Sep	900									720	270
Oct	500										400
Total		170	210	390	860	1,510	3,340	3,360	2,280	1,410	810

The important thing to realize in Table 15.4 is that the accounts receivable have been generated from a *completely stable* pattern of percentages. Each month's credit sales are collected, on average, 36 days days later. Each cash flow pattern is the same. Therefore, any monitoring measure we choose to employ should signal that receivables are not changing from month to month. With this in mind, we examine various measures commonly used to monitor accounts receivable.

Aging Schedules

In the previous section, we introduced the aging schedule as a means of monitoring individual accounts. This measure is also used extensively in monitoring aggregate receivables. Banks often require aging schedules as part of loan applications and periodic reports. They are extensively used for internal accounts receivable control. An aging schedule breaks down total receivables by age, showing what percentage are current, 1 month old, and so on. This procedure corresponds to taking figures from the columns in Table 15.4B and expressing each cell as a percentage of the total at the bottom of the column. We must invert the columns to conform to the usual practice of listing the current accounts first. For January, the aging schedule is as follows:

Age	Dollar Amount	Percent
Current	80	47.1
1–30 days	60	35.3
31–60 days	30	17.6
Total	170	100.0

Aging schedule percentages (sometimes called *aging fractions*) are intended to provide management with some idea of how current total receivables are. The principle is that the more current the receivables, the better off the firm. For January, 47.1% of the total receivables are current, 35.3% are 1–30 days past due, and 17.6% are 31-60 days past due. For May, we look at the percentages from the fifth column (inverted) in Table 15.4B.

Age	Dollar Amount	Percent
Current	1,200	79.5
1–30 days	270	17.9
31–60 days	40	2.6
Total	1,510	100.0

The aging fractions for May receivables appear to be much better. Accounts in the current category grow from 47.1% to 79.5%. A much smaller percentage of total receivables are past due. Thus, the aging fractions seem to signal that the firm's collections have improved dramatically. We are tempted to conclude that in May customers are paying their bills much faster than in January.

In August, the aging schedule is as follows:

Age	Dollar Amount	Percent
Current	1,120	49.1
1–30 days	810	35.5
31–60 days	350	15.4
Total	2,280	100.0

These aging fractions appear to be much worse than the May fractions. We are tempted to conclude that customers in August are now much slower in making payments than they were in May. Are these signals accurate?

Recall that the pattern of receivables that generates the aging fractions comes from an unchanging pattern of cash flows. The average collection time does not change. The only change has been in the level of credit sales. Something must be wrong with the measure rather than with the firm's collections.

From these limited observations, we can point out two general problems with the aging schedule approach to monitoring accounts receivable. In general, when sales increase, aging fractions will signal that collections are improving. Conversely, when sales decrease, aging fractions will signal deterioration of receivables payments. By the same token, aging fractions may signal that nothing is wrong when payments are actually slowing down while sales are increasing.

It can be shown that the only time aging fractions give reliable signals is when month-to-month credit sales grow at a constant rate. A special case occurs when credit sales have zero growth. Since many firms show seasonal or cyclical sales patterns, or at least uneven sales patterns, aging fractions may be inappropriate to use in monitoring overall receivables.

An additional problem with aging fractions is that there is no general reason to prefer one fraction pattern to another. Value is related to cash flow and not to receivable balances.

Average Days Outstanding (ADO)

ADO is another common measure of receivables performance. It attempts to measure how many days' worth of credit sales is represented by accounts receivable. It is also sometimes called *days sales outstanding (DSO)*. ADO is computed by dividing total accounts receivable by the average daily credit sales for a given period of time:

$$\text{ADO}_t = \frac{TAR_t}{\left[\sum_{i=t-n+1}^{t} \text{Sales}_i\right]/(n \times 30)}$$

where TAR_t is total accounts receivable in month t, Sales_i is sales for month i, and n is the number of months over which the sales are to be averaged. A quarterly ADO with $n = 3$ is common, but some firms use monthly or annual sales figures.

ADO is supposed to correspond to the average collection time. However, there are two problems with this measure. First, ADO is very sensitive to the past sales pattern, as we will see. Second, since ADO is based on accounts receivable, it does not include billing, some processing, and availability delays.

Table 15.5 gives an example of ADO computations, assuming the accounts receivable matrix in Table 15.4B.

The quarterly ADO for January is computed by dividing the total accounts receivable in January by the average daily sales for November, December, and January:

$$ADO_{Jan} = \frac{170}{(300 + 200 + 100)} \times (3 \times 30) = 25.5 \text{ days.}$$

Similarly, the ADO for May is computed by using total receivables in May and dividing by credit sales in March, April, and May:

$$ADO_{May} = \frac{1510}{(400 + 900 + 1,500)} \times (3 \times 30) = 48.5 \text{ days.}$$

From an ADO perspective, it appears that customers pay faster in January than in May. In fact, the ADO has almost doubled in moving from January to May! Recall, however, that the relative speed of collection from one month to the next is not really changing. What else is happening besides collection patterns remaining constant? In January, sales are dropping and ADO signals a collection time *lower* than the actual 36-day average collection time. In May, sales are rising and ADO signals a collection time *higher* than the 36-day average collection time.

Note, too, that the signals we receive from ADO are the opposite of the signals from aging fractions. In May, aging fractions indicate that collections

Table 15.5 Computing Quarterly ADO

Month	Credit Sales	Accounts Receivable	Quarterly ADO	Sales Growth (%)
Nov	300			
Dec	200			
Jan	100	170	25.5	−50.0
Feb	200	210	37.8	100.0
Mar	400	390	50.1	100.0
Apr	900	860	51.6	125.0
May	1,500	1,510	48.5	66.7
Jun	3,500	3,340	50.9	133.3
Jul	2,700	3,360	39.3	−22.9
Aug	1,400	2,280	27.0	−48.1
Sep	900	1,410	25.4	−35.7
Oct	500	810	26.0	−44.4

are much better relative to January, but ADO indicates that the receivable collection time has almost doubled.

ADO gives misleading signals for the same reason that aging fractions do so. ADO depends not only on the speed with which collections are made but also on the past pattern of credit sales. In general, if previous sales have been increasing, as they have been for the May ADO, the measure tends to report a higher number of days outstanding. If sales have been decreasing, as they have been for the January ADO, the measure tends to report a lower number of days outstanding even though the speed of collection remains unchanged. By the same token, ADO may fail to signal shifts in speed of collection if changes in sales and in payment timing are offsetting, such as when payment times are lengthened at the same time sales decline.

Receivable Balance Pattern

The solution to the problem of finding an accurate receivable monitoring measure is actually quite simple. The reason aging fractions and ADO are misleading is that they mix apples and oranges. They are based on total receivables, which consist of a mixture of receivables outstanding from several months with different levels of credit sales. Hence, any proposed measure must not rely on *total* receivables, but rather on past credit sales. The solution is to use *receivable balance fractions*.

A receivable balance fraction is similar to an aging schedule, but it uses credit sales, rather than total receivables, as the denominator for computing percentages. It is essentially an account receivable matrix (Table 15.4B, for example) expressed in percentages using the *left-hand column* (Sales) as the denominator rather than using the bottom row (Total). It is helpful to develop some simple mathematical notation before we go much further.

CASH FLOW FRACTIONS. Recall how the cash flow matrix was generated from a series of credit sales. Let P_i represent the fraction of credit sales that come in as a cash flow i months after the sale. In the example given in Table 15.4A, we used the following values for P_i:

$$P_0 = 0.20$$
$$P_1 = 0.50$$
$$P_2 = 0.20$$
$$P_3 = 0.10.$$

Note that if there are no bad debts (or they are so small that they may be ignored), the sum of the P_i's must be 1.00.

Cash flow from credit sales in month t, i months after the date of sale, $CF_{t,i}$, is computed by multiplying the credit sales, CS_t, by the cash flow fraction, P_i:

$$CF_{t,i} = P_i \times CS_t.$$

For January sales, we computed the cash flows in January, February, March, and April by multiplying $100 by the appropriate fraction:

Month	Cash Flow from January Sales
Jan	$100 \times .20 = 20$
Feb	$100 \times .50 = 50$
Mar	$100 \times .20 = 20$
Apr	$100 \times .10 = 10$

Cash flow fractions can be used as a criterion for determining whether collections are improving, staying the same, or deteriorating. Using cash flow fractions, we have the basis for comparing the payment pattern for one time period with another.

In addition, cash flows can be valued using present value techniques. For example, the pattern just mentioned can be valued by taking the present value of the cash flows at some interest rate and comparing it to the present value of another pattern. If the firm uses 12% as an opportunity cost (1% per month), the present value of this pattern is

$$PV = 20 + \frac{50}{(1.01)^1} + \frac{20}{(1.01)^2} + \frac{10}{(1.01)^3} = 98.817$$

This can be compared with an alternative pattern, say, 30%, 40%, 10%, 20%. Some cash flow is shifted forward, some backward.

$$PV = 30 + \frac{40}{(1.01)^1} + \frac{10}{(1.01)^2} + \frac{20}{(1.01)^3} = 98.819$$

The second distribution results in a slightly higher present value at a 12% annual rate.

RECEIVABLE BALANCE FRACTIONS. The *receivable balance fraction* is defined as the fraction of credit sales still remaining as a receivable at the end of the month. Receivable balance fractions are related to cash flow fractions. Each month receivables are reduced by the amount of cash flow coming in. In other words, the fraction remaining in a receivable at the end of the month of sale is 100% minus the percentage that came in as a cash flow during the month. The next month, the fraction remaining as a receivable is the amount from last month minus the portion that came in as a cash flow this month. We can write this as follows:

$$F_0 = 1 - P_0$$
$$F_1 = 1 - P_0 - P_1$$
$$F_2 = 1 - P_0 - P_1 - P_2$$
$$F_3 = 1 - P_0 - P_1 - P_2 - P_3. \tag{15.1}$$

For the example we constructed for Table 15.4,

$$F_0 = 1 - 0.20 = \qquad\qquad 0.80$$

$$F_1 = 1 - 0.20 - 0.50 = \qquad\qquad 0.30$$

$$F_2 = 1 - 0.20 - 0.50 - 0.20 = \qquad\qquad 0.10$$

$$F_3 = 1 - 0.20 - 0.50 - 0.20 - 0.10 = 0.00$$

The receivables balance fractions can also be calculated by relating the accounts receivable outstanding at the end of any month to the sales that generated the receivables. For example, at the end of March there are 10 outstanding in accounts receivable from sales in January of 100. This is 10% of January's sales. January is 2 months prior to March, so $F_2 = 0.10$. At the end of March there is 60 outstanding in accounts receivable from February's sales of 200, or 30% of February's sales. Thus, $F_1 = 0.30$. Similarly, F_0 for March is 0.80. As the firm moves through time, these balance fractions can be compared to the baseline fractions to see if there is any shift in accounts receivable patterns.

Thus, the behavior of accounts receivable can be tracked either by payment fractions or by balance fractions. The payment fractions measure the percentage of the sales that is collected in any month, whereas the balance fractions measure the percentage of that month's sales that is still outstanding (uncollected).

The receivable balance fractions can also be used to compute receivable amounts that should be in the cells of the accounts receivable matrix. An example was given in Table 15.4B. The numbers in the January row can be computed by multiplying the credit sales in January by the receivable balance fractions.

Month	Accounts Receivable from January Sales
Jan	$100 \times .80 = 80$
Feb	$100 \times .30 = 30$
Mar	$100 \times .10 = 10$
Apr	$100 \times .00 = 0$

CONVERTING FROM AN AGING SCHEDULE TO A RECEIVABLES MATRIX. The receivables balance fractions can also be calculated from the information contained in an aging schedule. Recall that the aging schedule is really contained in the columns of the accounts receivable matrix. Hence, if we start with an aging schedule, we should be able to generate an accounts receivable matrix. From that matrix we can then compute F_i's and then P_i's. The P_i's will enable us to determine if payments have been speeding up or slowing down.

Before constructing this matrix, we may want to see what aging fractions and ADO can tell us. Suppose we are given the aging schedule for the months May through October shown in Table 15.6. (Note that the receivables outstanding

Table 15.6 Aging Schedule Revised

	Sales	**TAR**	**0 Mo**	**Percent**	**1 Mo**	**Percent**	**2 Mo**	**Percent**
May	1,500	1,510	1,200	79.5	270	17.9	40	2.6
Jun	3,500	3,340	2,800	83.8	450	13.5	90	2.7
Jul	2,700	3,630	2,430	66.9	1,050	28.9	150	4.1
Aug	1,400	2,960	1,260	42.6	1,350	45.6	350	11.8
Sep	900	2,050	810	39.5	700	34.1	540	26.3
Oct	500	1,180	450	38.1	450	38.1	280	23.7

ADDITIONAL INFORMATION

Month	Sales
Mar	400
Apr	900
May	1,500
Jun	3,500
Jul	2,700
Aug	1,400
Sep	900
Oct	500

from July and later in Table 15.6 are different from those in Table 15.4.) We are asked to determine if the firm has improved its receivable position relative to May and June. If we compute aging fractions (given in the table), we see that the percentage of accounts in the current month is dropping: from a high of 83.8% in June to a gradual reduction to 38.1% in October. There is a corresponding increase in the older accounts. These observations seem to imply that payments are *slowing*.

If we compute the ADO for the 6 months in question, however, the signals are more confusing. On average, ADO is lower for the last 4 months than for the first 2 but is increasing during the last 3 months. What is really happening with receivables in this firm?

Month	ADO
May	48.5
Jun	50.9
Jul	42.4
Aug	35.1
Sep	36.9
Oct	37.9

The answer lies in using the information contained in an aging schedule to construct an accounts receivable matrix, and then examining either payment fractions or balance fractions. To calculate the receivables matrix, the rows

Table 15.7 Accounts Receivable Matrix from an Aging Schedule

Month	Sales	May	Jun	Jul	Aug	Sep	Oct	F_0	F_1	F_2
Mar	400	40	0	0				—	—	.10
Apr	900	270	90	0	0			—	.30	.10
May	1,500	1,200	450	150	0			.80	.30	.10
Jun	3,500		2,800	1,050	350			.80	.30	.10
Jul	2,700			2,430	1,350	540		.90	.50	.20
Aug	1,400				1,260	700	280	.90	.50	.20
Sep	900					810	450	.90	.50	—
Oct	500						450	.90	—	—
Total		1,510	3,340	3,630	2,960	2,050	1,180			

of Table 15.6 are simply stood on end (the matrix is transposed) and then combined with monthly credit sales information.

COMPUTING RECEIVABLE BALANCE FRACTIONS. Receivable balance fractions are computed by dividing sales for a given month into the receivables remaining at the end of that month and subsequent months. The last three columns in Table 15.7 show receivable balance fractions. In June, for example, F_0 is computed by dividing 2,800 by 3,500. F_1 for June corresponds to 1,050 divided by 3,500, and F_2 is 350 divided by 3,500. The balance fractions for every row in the accounts receivable matrix are divided not by total receivables but by credit sales for that row. The receivable balance fractions for July and subsequent months show a different pattern than that of June and previous months. This indicates that a shift has occurred in cash flows from credit sales. More of each month's credit sales are remaining as receivables in the first 2 months. How does this situation relate to cash flows?

COMPUTING CASH FLOW FRACTIONS FROM RECEIVABLE BALANCE FRACTIONS. We can rearrange the equations relating receivable balance fractions and cash flow fractions (Equation 15.1) and solve them for cash flow fractions. The cash flow fraction is simply the difference between the receivable fraction last month and the receivable fraction this month:

$$P_0 = 1 - F_0,$$
$$P_1 = F_0 - F_1,$$
$$P_2 = F_1 - F_2,$$
$$P_3 = F_2 - F_3, etc. \qquad (15.2)$$

Using these relationships, we can compute the cash flow fractions:

First 2 Months	Last 4 Months
$P_0 = .20$	$P_0 = .10$
$P_1 = .50$	$P_1 = .40$
$P_2 = .20$	$P_2 = .30$
$P_3 = .10$	$P_3 = .20$

It should be clear that cash flow fractions in May and June dominate the fractions in the last four periods. This is because 0.10 from both P_0 and P_1 are shifted to later months and there is no offsetting shift to earlier months. The average collection period is now

$$0.10(0) + 0.40(30) + 0.30(60) + 0.20(90) = 48 \text{ days}.$$

Recall that the pattern for May and June gave an average collection period of 36 days. We conclude that credit collections starting in July have deteriorated. The shifting pattern of cash flow fractions should cause management to further investigate the causes of such deterioration.

Forecasting Accounts Receivable

Forecasting overall accounts receivable levels is important for at least three reasons. First, accounts receivable is a major asset in most firms and therefore an important ingredient in generating pro forma statements. Second, projected accounts receivable are useful in establishing budget standards and incentive programs for credit managers. Third, accounts receivable are sometimes a factor in loan covenants. If forecasted receivables levels violate restrictions, corrective action can be taken in advance.

Percent of Sales Method

The simplest method of forecasting overall receivables is to assume that receivables levels are directly proportional to sales:

$$TAR_t = aCS_t,$$

where TAR_t is total accounts receivable in month t, a is the proportionality factor, and CS_t represents credit sales for month t.

For firms with no seasonality in sales and relatively steady growth from month to month or for a long-range (5-year) forecast, this formula is not a bad approximation. This approach is often used in standard financial forecasting packages. We will now consider some of its limitations.

Receivable Balance Fraction Method

The percent of sales method breaks down, however, for firms with seasonal or otherwise fluctuating sales. To see this, recall how total accounts receivable are generated in the accounts receivable matrix in Table 15.4B. Total receivables represent the sum of the elements in the column. The elements in the column are computed by multiplying the F's by the past series of sales:[2]

---

[2] This is equivalent to regressing total accounts receivable on the time series of past credit sales. Time series analysis is one way to determine the average F values over a time horizon.

$$TAR_t = F_0 CS_t + F_1 CS_{t-1} + F_2 CS_{t-2} + \ldots$$

If the credit sales in each month are constant so that $CS_t = CS_{t-i}$, we can factor CS_t out of each term and rewrite the expression for TAR_t as follows:

$$TAR_t = [F_0 + F_1 + F_2 + \ldots]CS_t.$$

If the F's remain constant over time, we have the simple proportionality relationship previously stated as the percent of sales method. The proportionality factor, a, is simply $[F_0 + F_1 + F_2 + \ldots]$. However, if credit sales fluctuate from month to month, all bets are off (except in the case where sales grow at a constant rate—which we could prove, but will not do so here). This tells us that, for most firms, generating an accounts receivable matrix is a more accurate way to forecast receivables.

The steps required in forecasting receivables using the receivable balance fraction method are the following:

1. Forecast month-by-month credit sales.
2. Determine historically the receivable balance fractions, F_i's. This is done by constructing accounts receivable matrices using past data.
3. Combine the F_i's and credit sales forecasts to project a pro forma accounts receivable matrix. That is, multiply the forecasted credit sales in a given month by the appropriate F_i to generate the amount that will remain as a receivable i months after the sale.

Example of an Accounts Receivable Forecast

Suppose a firm wants to forecast its monthly receivable balances for the coming year based on sales projections shown in the second column in Table 15.8. Based on historical accounts receivable matrices, the average receivable balance fractions have been computed to be $F_0 = 0.90, F_1 = 0.50$, and $F_2 = 0.20$. The future accounts receivable matrix is computed by multiplying the credit sales for month t by the appropriate F_i and placing the result in the appropriate matrix cell, as seen in the table. Estimates of total receivables are obtained simply by adding the columns.

Comparing Percent Sales and Receivable Balance Fraction Methods

What is the difference between using the percent sales method and the receivable balance fraction method? In highly seasonal companies like this one, there is a substantial difference. If we compute the average total accounts receivable as a fraction of sales each month in Table 15.8, we find that the fraction is 157%. That is, each month, on average, total receivables represent 157% of that month's sales. Suppose we use this percentage with the projections of monthly sales. The forecasted accounts receivable are shown in Table 15.9.

Note that as sales increase, the percent of sales method overestimates actual accounts receivable, while when sales decrease, this method underestimates receivables generated by a constant cash flow process.

Table 15.8 Accounts Receivable Forecast Based on Receivable Balance Fractions

Receivable Balance Fractions = F_0 .90 F_1 .50 F_2 .20 F_3 .00

Month	Sales	Jan	Feb	Mar	Apr	May	Jun	Jul	Aug	Sep	Oct	Nov	Dec
Sep	800												
Oct	400	0											
Nov	300	60	0										
Dec	200	100	40	0									
Jan	400	360	200	80	0								
Feb	500		450	250	100	0							
Mar	900			810	450	180	0						
Apr	1,300				1,170	650	260	0					
May	1,300					1,170	650	260	0				
Jun	2,000						1,800	1,000	400	0			
Jul	2,500							2,250	1,250	500	0		
Aug	3,000								2,700	1,500	600	0	
Sep	3,500									3,150	1,750	700	0
Oct	2,400										2,160	1,200	480
Nov	1,500											1,350	750
Dec	1,000												1,080
Total	22,000	520	690	1,140	1,720	2,000	2,710	3,510	4,350	5,150	4,510	3,250	2,310

410

Table 15.9 Comparison of the Percent of Sales Forecast with the Receivable Balance Fraction Method

Month	Jan	Feb	Mar	Apr	May	Jun	Jul	Aug	Sep	Oct	Nov	Dec
Forecast using receivable balance fractions												
	520	690	1,140	1,720	2,000	2,710	3,510	4,350	5,150	4,510	3,250	2,310
Forecast using 157% of sales*												
	628	785	1,413	2,041	2,041	3,141	3,926	4,711	5,496	3,769	2,356	1,570
Difference												
	−108	−95	−273	−321	−41	−431	−416	−361	−346	741	894	740

*The 157% comes from the average ratio of total accounts receivable to the level of credit sales in that month.

Receivables Monitoring and Forecasting: Summary and Synthesis

Traditional methods of monitoring accounts receivable may result in less than adequate managerial control over credit policy. The typical aging report groups accounts into broad categories of lateness that frequently lead to longer payment times than is desirable. By refining the categories, more control can be achieved.

A better method of monitoring individual customers is the average total collection period method, which focuses more on the cash flow timeline. The *average total collection time* refers to the time between the invoice date (or some other starting point) and the receipt of available funds in the seller's bank. This measure relates directly to the cash flow timeline and hence to value.

Traditional methods have also led to potential problems in controlling and forecasting overall receivable levels. The two most widely used methods, aging fractions and ADO, do not give reliable signals of credit problems unless some stringent conditions are met: namely, month-to-month credit sales must either be constant or must grow at a constant rate. Similarly, forecasts using the commonly employed percent of sales method are also flawed. Aging, ADO, and percent of sales have a fatal flaw: they mix recent credit sales with past credit sales. We saw that, from the perspective of cash flows, the only method that makes sense is the approach that uses cash flow and receivable balance fractions.

—————— Evaluating Credit Policy Alternatives ——————

In this section we apply financial valuation techniques to credit policy changes. We find that since credit policies affect the magnitude of cash flows, the timing of cash exchanges between parties, and the transactions costs, we may treat them just as we would treat any other cash flow stream.

As a simple example of a change in credit terms, suppose the Gifford Company is considering a credit policy change from cash only to 2/10, net 30. Is this an advisable move? What will the impact be on the company? What factors should be considered? We first explore the cash flows relevant to this decision and then return to discuss the Gifford Company's problem further.

Cash Flows Relevant to Credit Policy Alternatives

Credit policies affect a number of cash flows. Some of these cash flows can be classified as costs and others as benefits, but we will treat them all as cash flows with the appropriate sign. Some of the cash flows are quite easy to measure, while others are not.

Invoiced Amount

Credit terms, as discussed in Chapter 14, often involve cash discounts for early payment. To some extent, the size of the discount is under the control of the seller. The reason we say "to some extent" is that stating credit terms and enforcing them are two different matters. Generally, however, sellers do control the size of the discount offered. Another way a seller can change the invoiced amount is to change the price and/or add a penalty for late payment. We call the net price that the buyer is to pay the *invoiced amount*.

Bad Debts

Different credit terms may result in different levels of bad debts, or uncollected receivables. Cash-only terms result in a generally low level of bad debts (perhaps a bounced check or two), while selling on extended dating terms may expose the seller to much higher levels of bad debts. We handle bad debts as a reduction in cash inflows from sales.

Credit Evaluation Costs

The costs of administering the credit evaluation process are the front-end direct costs of selling on credit. Such costs may include personnel costs, data processing costs, and the costs of obtaining credit information.

Collection Costs

Collection costs refer to the administrative costs associated with collecting payments through bank lockboxes or company processing centers, handling remittance information, following up on late payments, and incurring any other expense related to receiving payments from customers.

Indirect Cash Flows

While each of the preceding cash flows is more or less directly connected with credit policy, some significant cash flows may be indirectly associated. These may be more difficult to measure but may have a significant impact on credit policy decisions. Such cash flows include those from increased or decreased sales. Changes in credit terms may significantly change the total sales volume. Although the impact on the level or growth rate of sales is one of the major reasons for selling on credit, it may be difficult to estimate the effect of any given credit policy change. Part of the problem involves the possible reaction of competitors and of current and future credit customers.

Other indirect factors include increased (decreased) cash outflows to support increased (decreased) sales. These costs are generally measured by estimating the incremental variable costs resulting from sales level changes. Such costs might include inventory, labor, variable overhead, and other costs. Administrative costs may also be affected—above those costs already considered for credit screening and collections.

Timing and Uncertainty Considerations

Cash flows have three dimensions: amount, timing, and uncertainty. With each of the preceding cash flows, we need to add the last two dimensions. We may, for example, be able to estimate exactly what the invoiced amount will be, but we are also very interested in the fact that the invoiced amount will be paid, for example, 60 days in the future—plus or minus 10 days. Timing is important because of the time value of money. Uncertainty is important because it has some influence on how much the firm must keep in liquid assets.

Timing must be associated with an opportunity cost. While there is much debate about which opportunity cost firms should use for short-term financial decisions, we tend to agree with the following principles:

1. For permanent policy changes, funds freed up (or invested) have a long-term opportunity cost and hence should be valued at the long-term cost of funds. For example, if cash can be collected faster by changing credit terms, what will the firm do with the freed-up cash? It will probably not invest all of it in short-term money market securities. Some of it will be used to expand the earning assets of the firm, some to retire debt, and so on. The opportunity cost for these uses is equivalent to the firm's long-term cost of funds.
2. For temporary shifts in cash flows, funds freed up (or invested) should be valued at the short-term cost of funds. A temporary increase in cash, for example, would not likely be used to buy new long-term capital equipment. The cash would likely be placed in short-term securities or used to pay off short-term debt.

The Cash Flow Timeline and the Present Value Approach

Different credit policies result in differences in the amount and timing of cash flows. The financial tool for dealing with such differences is present value analysis. Though this analysis is commonly applied to long-term financial problems such as capital budgeting, the application of present value techniques to short-term financial management problems is relatively new.

Procedure

The procedure is quite straightforward. Estimate the cash flows for each alternative credit policy along a timeline. Compare the present value of the cash flows for the alternatives at an appropriate opportunity cost.

We return to the problem of the Gifford Company as an example of a relatively simple evaluation of credit policy differences. Table 15.10 shows the basic facts of the case.

First, it is helpful to draw out the cash flow timeline for 1 week's sales. We set the beginning time on the date of sale. For cash outflows, Gifford buys

Table 15.10 Evaluating Alternative Credit Policies of the Gifford Company

Variable costs	70% of sales
Suppliers' terms	Net 30 days (Assume that invoices from suppliers are dated, on average, 10 days before sale occurs)
Cost of funds	11% per year
Costs of credit dept.	$0

	Current Credit Policy	**Alternative Credit Policy**
Terms	Cash only	2/10, net 30
Est. collection times between sale and receipt of available funds	1 day	40% — 15 days 60% — 45 days (after taking out bad debts)
Bad debts	None	0.3%
Sales	$100,000/week	$110,000/week
Collection costs	$0	$500/week

materials 10 days before sale but has 30 days to pay under the supplier's credit terms. Therefore, a cash outflow occurs approximately on day 25 (35 days after the invoice date, assuming that the firm adheres to the payment terms but that mail, processing, and clearing time add about 5 days).

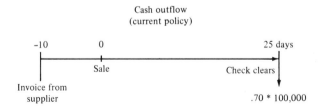

For the alternative policy, the timing is the same, but the outflow is 0.70 × 110,000 because of the 10% increase in sales.

On the cash inflow side, the current policy gives rise to a very short timeline. Available cash is received 1 day after the sale date (assuming that it takes 1 day for a deposit to become good funds).

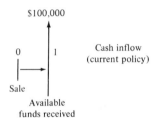

For the alternative policy, there are two cash inflows: one for customers who take the discount and the other for customers who do not. The first occurs 15 days after the sale and represents 40% of the cash inflows (after adjusting for bad debts). The second occurs 45 days after the sale and represents 60% of total inflows after adjustment.

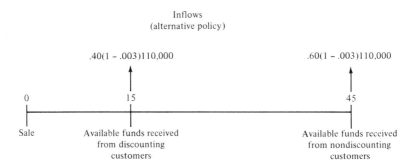

The inflow and outflow timelines are now combined for each policy:

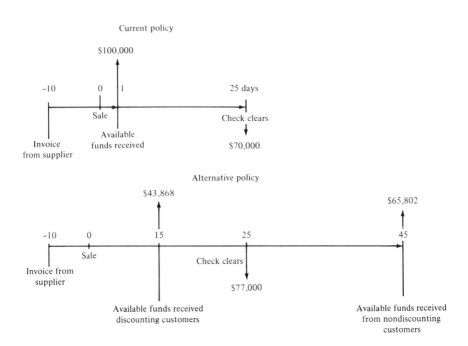

The second step is to compute the present values of each alternative, discounting at the opportunity cost of 11% per year or 0.03% per day. We use the simple interest approximation for computing present values.

Current Policy

Inflows:	$100,000/(1 + .00030 \times 1)$	=	$99,970
Outflows:	$.70(100,000)/(1 + .0003 \times 25)$	=	$69,479
	Net present value		$30,491

Alternative Policy

Inflows:	$.40(1 - .003)(110,000)/(1 + .00030 \times 15)$	=	$ 43,671
	$.60(1 - .003)(110,000)/(1 + .00030 \times 45)$	=	$ 64,926
	Total inflows		$108,597
Outflows:	$.70(110,000)/(1 + .00030 \times 25)$	=	$76,427
	Administrative costs (timing?)	=	$ 500
	Total outflows		$76,927
	Net present value		$31,670
$NPV_{alternative} - NPV_{current}$			$1,179

Note that we do not discount the $500 administrative costs. We have not been given information on their timing. By not discounting, we implicitly assume that the cash flow takes place on day 0. Since it is a relatively small number compared to the cash flows from sales, the assumption about the timing of administrative costs makes little difference in this problem.

The difference in net present values between the alternative policy and the current policy is $1,179, or about $61,000 per year. We would conclude that, based on this information, the alternative policy dominates the current policy even though there are bad debts and delayed payments. The increased level of sales is more than great enough to compensate for the other costs. Recall that the objective function of credit policy presented at the beginning of this chapter is to maximize the tradeoffs between these kinds of competing costs.

Risk Considerations

How does one take risk into account with this approach? There are two basic methods. First, one can use a higher, risk-adjusted discount rate for discounting future cash flows that present a higher level of risk. Although theoreticians argue about how the risk adjustment should be made, the concept is sound. In the problem just studied, we may want to use a higher rate than the 11% given for the alternative policy, which involves more uncertain cash flows.

A second method is sensitivity analysis. Present values can be computed several different times, using different assumptions about timing and amounts for the policy in question. This gives management some idea of the circumstances under which choosing the alternative credit policy would be a good decision.

Other Factors

Changes in credit terms are often linked to other changes in a firm. Some of these are difficult to quantify and to anticipate. For example, suppose the

Gifford Company, in expanding sales to the new level of $110,000, had to add significantly to fixed costs to reach a new capacity level. If all of the fixed costs were attributed to this year's sales, the decision to liberalize credit terms might not be seen as a good one. On the other hand, if sales continue to grow, the short-term excess capacity would eventually be used up and the decision to expand might be justified.

In extending credit, the Gifford Company assumes that a new sales volume will be generated. What if the competition counters Gifford's move with liberalized credit terms of their own? The anticipated sales increases may not be realized.

Oil Company Problem Revisited

At the beginning of the chapter, we posed a problem faced by an oil company. The total collection timeline was 45 days. The firm was considering electronic (ACH) debits, which would shorten the collection timeline to 1 day. To compensate the buyer, the oil company would have to give a discount. How much of a discount can it afford to give?

To solve this problem, we pose it as a present value problem. Assume that the average payment is $200,000 and the appropriate interest rate is 13% per year. We assume that day 0 is the day on which we compare cash flows. Under the current policy, the present value to the firm is

$$PV_0 = 200,000 / \left(1 + \frac{44(0.13)}{365} \right) = 196,914.$$

If a discount is offered, the oil company wants to set it such that the present value will be no less than the current policy. Let d represent the cash discount. The present value of the alternative policy is set equal to the present value of the current policy and d is determined:

$$PV_1 = 200,000(1 - d) \geq 196,914$$
$$d \leq 1 - (196,914/200,000) = 0.01543.$$

The discount should therefore be less than 1.543% to leave the firm above the breakeven point. The firm might offer a 1.5% discount. We have, of course, neglected potential transaction costs, administrative costs, and other factors. We will, however, return to a more in-depth consideration of this problem in Chapter 20.

Synthesis

Another method for comparing alternative credit policies is to construct accounting statements for the firm under different policies. Increases in accounts receivable are viewed as investments, and increased profits less bad debts are treated as return on investment. It can be shown that, if one is careful to include all relevant factors (such as increases in payables), the present value method and the accounting approach are equivalent. However, we prefer the cash flow approach because it is much easier to relate to a valuation framework. This approach is also more straightforward. To evaluate credit policy changes, all one need do is to write down the cash flows affected and take present values. This is a robust approach that explicitly handles timing and any and all cash flows.

Summary

Credit policy results in one of the larger asset categories for most firms: accounts receivable. Therefore, credit policy demands closer attention in the financial management of the firm than it has received in the past. Credit is best approached from a cash flow perspective with an eye to maximizing the value of a cost function containing the following elements: profitability of sales, bad debts, administrative and transaction costs, time value costs, and other related costs. This objective function incorporates the tradeoffs inherent in any credit policy decision. It also casts the credit function in the framework of the traditional financial objective of the firm: to maximize net present value to shareholders.

Using this cash flow perspective, we showed that better credit policy control measures and forecasting techniques can be developed and that credit policy alternatives can be valued using present values. The cash flow approach yields better results than those obtained from traditional accounting approaches.

Discussion Questions
---

1. What are the objectives of the firm's credit policy?
2. Give examples of some of the tradeoffs that credit managers encounter in trying to maximize the cost function developed at the beginning of the chapter.
3. Outline methods of collecting cash from past due accounts.
4. What are the objectives of monitoring accounts receivable? Distinguish between monitoring individual accounts and monitoring overall receivables.
5. Why does a monthly aging schedule give insufficient information about late payments? How can this problem be corrected by modifying the format of the aging report?
6. Explain why ADO may not capture the total accounts receivable time delay between invoicing and receipt of payment.
7. Why is it important that an accounts receivable monitoring system be insensitive to shifts in the pattern of sales?
8. Explain how cash flow fractions and accounts receivable balance fractions are related.

9. Critique the statement "The receivable balance fraction method is okay theoretically, but firms just don't have the needed information readily available to perform those computations."
10. Explain how one can compute receivable balance fractions from a standard aging schedule.
11. How may possible credit policy changes be analyzed? What data are needed? What framework is appropriate? Outline the basic steps to take.

Problems

1. Given the following matrix of accounts receivable, calculate the payment fractions, the balance fractions, and an aging schedule for each month from January through May.

Month	Sales	Jan	Feb	Mar	Apr	May
Oct	20	2				
Nov	30	5	3			
Dec	60	30	10	6		
Jan	90	81	46	16	8	
Feb	90		79	42	14	10
Mar	60			50	30	9
Apr	40				35	21
May	30					27
Total A/R		118	138	114	87	67

2. The Royal Paper Company has credit sales as follows:

| Oct | 10 | Nov | 20 | Dec | 30 | Jan | 40 | Feb | 20 |
| Mar | 60 | Apr | 40 | May | 10 | Jun | 20 | Jul | 60 |

The company experiences the following payment fractions:

$$P_0 = 0.10 \qquad P_1 = 0.50 \qquad P_2 = 0.30 \qquad P_3 = 0.10,$$

where P_i represents the fraction of the sales collected in month i following the sale.

a. Beginning the columns in January, construct a matrix of cash flows from credit sales.
b. Construct a matrix of accounts receivable outstanding from credit sales.
c. Calculate the ADO for each month from January through July, using quarterly sales (the current month and the prior 2 months). Comment on your observations.
d. Compute an aging schedule for January through July. Comment on your observations.

3. Tyler Electronics finished installing a new computerized billing and monitoring system on April 1. In order to determine the effects of the system on accounts receivable, Tyler's credit manager has prepared the following aging schedule:

Month	Total A/R	Current (%)	1 Month Old (%)
Mar	$3.2 mil.	62.5	37.5
Apr	5.0 mil.	84.0	16.0
May	8.2 mil.	85.0	14.6

Credit sales have been (in millions):

Jan   10   Feb   6   Mar   4   Apr   6   May   10

a. On the basis of the aging schedule, what do you conclude about the value of the new system?
b. Compute the ADO, using the most recent quarter's sales for March, April, and May. What is your assessment of the new system based on the ADO?
c. Compute the percentage of sales collected and the percentage of sales outstanding, by month, before and after the change in the system. What do you conclude now?

4. Evaluate the performance of your credit department over the period January through June, given the following information:

	Nov	Dec	Jan	Feb	Mar	Apr	May	Jun
Sales	70	60	40	50	65	80	100	150
A/R end of month			55	59	68	89	112	132
Breakdown of A/R								
Current mo. sales			36	39	44	60	73	83
1 mo. prior			12	12	14	20	23	30
2 mo. prior			7	8	10	9	16	19
Aging schedule (%):								
0–30 days			65	66	65	67	65	63
31–60 days			22	21	20	22	21	23
61–90 days			13	13	15	11	14	14
ADO (based on 60 days' sales)			33	37	37	38	37	34

5. The Abel Corporation has a 12% opportunity cost on short-term funds. Sales are $10,000,000 per year, of which 80% are on credit. Invoices are mailed out on the first of the month, with payment due by the first of the following month. Payment is not usually received for 60 days, however, because of lax collection follow-up. Abel is considering offering a discount of 2% if payment is made by the 10th of the month. Assume that 60% of the customers take the discount and pay on the 15th (allow for mail time and

other delays) and that the other 40% then take 50 days. Bad debts should remain negligible under either plan. Should Abel adopt the new plan?

6. Fancy Foundations, a manufacturer of designer underwear, is considering selling to a group of small retail stores with which they have not previously dealt. It has been estimated that these stores will purchase, on average, $1,200,000 worth of merchandise per 30-day month. Variable material and production costs average 60% of the selling price. Terms of sale will be the same as those to current customers, 2/10, net 30; however, it is expected that only 20% of the customers will take the discount. The nondiscounting customers will pay, on average, on day 40, and bad debt and collection costs will average 10% of sales. The inventory and production policies are such that the labor and materials are paid for, on average, on the day of the sale. There is substantial excess plant capacity, and there will be no im-pact on the other customers, whether or not these stores are accepted as credit customers. If the appropriate annual opportunity cost of the risk of these customers is 0.05% per day, should they be accepted for credit sales?

7. Kirk's Office Supplies sells to businesses and consumers on a cash-only basis. Kathy Kirk, the president, is considering selling on credit to the business customers. She is considering a monthly billing cycle in which the firm would be billed at the end of the month for all purchases during the month. The bill would be due by the 15th of the following month. Currently, sales to businesses are averaging $60,000 per month. She antic-ipates that sales will increase with the new credit policy, but is uncertain of how much. The cost of the goods sold averages 80% of the selling price of the product. The current inventory system maintains approximately a 15-day supply of goods on hand. Purchases are made on terms of net 30 days, and payment is prompt. No fixed cost changes are anticipated for the increased volume. The opportunity cost for Kirk is 15% per year.

   a. What is the impact on the net present value if there is no increase in sales?
   b. How much would sales have to increase to justify the change in policy?

8. Big Auto buys $5,000,000 worth of plastic knobs from the Noble Nob Company each year. Big Auto has been stretching payments to Noble an average of 120 days after delivery, forcing Noble to finance receivables at an effective annual cost of 17%. Big Auto, on the other hand, enjoys a higher credit rating and borrows at an effective annual cost of 12%. Noble has determined that the variable costs incurred in knob manufacturing amount to 60% of the selling price and are paid, on average, 20 days *before* delivery of a shipment. To encourage Big Auto to pay earlier, Noble is considering a cash discount for payment received by the 10th day after delivery. Assume that the volume of sales stays constant under either policy.

   a. Using the delivery date as time 0, what is the present value of the current policy?

b. Assuming that Big Auto will make all payments on the discount date (10 days after delivery), how much of a discount can Noble offer and be no worse off than they are now?

c. Assuming that Noble decides on a discount of 4.5% (regardless of your answer to part b), show whether Big Auto will be better off taking the discount or keeping the current policy. (Assume that the alternative use for funds for Big Auto is paying off short-term borrowing.)

Case: *General Molding, Inc.*

Mel Johnson, vice president of finance for General Molding, Inc. (GMI), had just finished reading the following memo from Sam Kotler, vice president of marketing:

To: Mel Johnson   From: Sam Kotler
Re: Terms of sale for So-Lite

As you are probably aware, the marketing department has been working for several months to line up additional national merchandisers to carry our So-Lite line. The outlook is very promising with two potential accounts: Consumer's Warehouse, a catalog/showroom operation with 125 outlets, and Hugerra and Gonzeles, a discount chain operating 400 stores. Both firms operate on a centralized purchasing and inventory system, so we would be assured of having the products in all of their outlets. The anticipated sales to these two accounts would increase the volume of our So-Lite line by at least 20%. They have both indicated that they will order only if we offer credit terms of net 45 days. (Something about their accounts payable system not being able to handle the payments more quickly than that.) Since our normal credit terms are 1/10, net 30, and since you have the final authority over the credit policy, I am requesting your approval to sell to these two customers on terms of 1/10, net 45. I am confident that they will meet all of your usual criteria for a normal open account. Please let me know of your decision as soon as possible so that I can proceed to sign them up.

Mel's initial reaction was to respond negatively to Sam's request. To begin with, Sam should have known better than to think that they would be able to get away with selling on different credit terms to different clients. Offering credit terms of 1/10, net 45 to these two customers would mean offering the same credit terms to all customers. Second, Mel was very proud of the fact that through procedures he had established, the average collection period was 24 days and bad debts were less than 1% of sales. He certainly did not want to see these figures rise, as he knew they would if credit terms were relaxed. In addition, with interest on short-term borrowings running about 11%, he knew that it would cost 0.03% for every extra day funds are tied up in accounts receivable. He also knew that he would have to supply some solid reasons for not changing credit terms before he could convince the aggressive Sam Kotler, one of the rising stars on the management team at GMI.

Background

GMI is a small manufacturer of molded plastic products. The company was started in the mid-1960s as a toy manufacturer. However, the company did not have the design creativity to compete successfully with the larger, more established firms on any products other than inexpensive toy cars and trucks. GMI turned to producing plastic cases for radios, tape recorders, and other consumer electronic items for other manufacturers. During the early 1970s, GMI won several government contracts to provide reinforced, insulated foam packaging materials for shipment of food to the military in subtropical climates.

As government contracts declined, GMI shifted its manufacturing capacity to the production of drink coolers and picnic jugs. At the time GMI entered the market, rigid plastic, foam-filled coolers were just beginning to dominate the older, heavier metal coolers. GMI brought out a wide range of sizes in both a rectangular and a circular shape under the registered trademark of So-Lite coolers.

The current So-Lite product line is dominated by two products: So-Lite So-Round, a 15-liter round cooler, and Air-So-Lite, a 2-liter picnic jug with a hand-operated air pump to force the liquid out of the jug. These two products accounted for 80% of the So-Lite line, which in turn represented about 75% of the company's business.

Sam Kotler joined the marketing department at GMI a few years ago as sales manager. He quickly initiated the practice of dealing directly with regional and national chains, rather than working primarily through jobbers and distributors, as had been done in the past. The resulting growth in profits of 10% per year on sales growth of 8% was a major factor in Sam's promotion to vice president of marketing 6 months ago. Although it had never been said openly, it was widely perceived that Sam felt that GMI could grow much more rapidly if it were not for the conservative approach taken by some members of top management.

Credit Decision

Mel's first action in deciding how to respond to Sam's request was to ask the production manager to check on production capacity and any additional equipment or inventory requirement for such a large increase in volume. Her report indicated that the plant was operating at about 65% of capacity and that no additional equipment would be required for a 20% increase. Raw materials and finished goods inventory would have to be increased along with the increase in sales. Currently, the company kept a 10-day supply of materials used in the molding process. Work-in-process inventory was negligible, and finished goods inventory averaged 6 days of sales. Floor space was available in the company warehouse to accommodate these inventory increases.

Table 1 Sales and Cost Data for So-Lite Products for the Year Ending September 30, 1987

		So-Round	Air-So-Lite
Sales	$	$48,000,000	$24,000,000
	Units	3,900,000	6,000,000
Per unit data	Selling price	$12.30	$4.00
	Material price	4.20	1.38
	Labor cost	3.50	.62
	Variable overhead	.62	.20
	Total var. costs	$8.32	$2.20

Mel next contacted Lou Spiller in the accounting department to obtain some up-to-date cost information. The breakdown of the production costs for the So-Lite products is shown in Table 1.

From the purchasing department, Mel determined that all materials were ordered on open account on terms of net 30, and all bills were paid promptly. The labor force was paid under different policies, depending upon the job classification. For his purpose, Mel decided to assume that workers were paid at the same time as the materials.

Mel next contacted Ann Anders, the credit manager, to determine the impact that the suggested changes might have on her operation. Ann responded that several factors would have to be considered. First, the customers had to be divided into two groups: those paying in the discount period and those paying net. She indicated that she was uncertain about how the breakdown of discounting and nondiscounting customers or the bad debts would be affected under the new policy, but she would try to estimate the impact and send a report to Mel later that day (Table 2). She was confident that the longer collection period would mean more work for her department and that costs would likely rise by 0.5% of the new sales.

Later that afternoon, after several "crisis" meetings that always lasted longer than necessary, Mel sat down with the information he had received from Lou and Ann, and with the most recent financial statements for GMI (Table 3) to decide how to respond to Sam's request.

Table 2 Credit Data for So-Lite Products

	Current	Proposed
Terms	1% 10, net 30	1% 10, net 45
Disct. Cust.	40% of sales	20% of sales
Nondisct. pay.	33 days average	49 days average
Bad debts	.72% of total sales	1.2% of total sales

Table 3 Income Statement for Year Ending September 31, 1987 (000 Omitted)

Sales	120,000
Less: Discounts	480
Net sales	119,520
Cost of goods sold	
Materials	41,038
Labor	33,961
Overhead	5,998
Total	80,997
Gross profit	38,523
General and administrative	19,456
Depreciation	10,596
Profit before tax	8,471
Income taxes	3,385
Net profit after tax	5,086

Balance Sheet, September 30, 1987

Assets		**Liabilities and Owners' Equity**	
Cash	5,738	Accounts pay.	3,366
Accts. rec.	7,887	Bank notes	2,678
Inventories	2,456	Accruals	1,798
Total C. A.	16,081	Total C. L.	7,842
Fixed assets	110,634	Long-term debt	19,125
Accum. depr.	(55,485)		
		Common stock	15,300
Net F. A.	55,149	Retained earnings	28,963
Total	71,230	Total	71,230

Selected Readings

CARPENTER, MICHAEL D., and JACK E. MILLER, "A Reliable Framework for Monitoring Accounts Receivable," *Financial Management* (Winter 1979), pp. 37–40.

GALLINGER, G. W., and A. J. IFFLANDER, "Monitoring Accounts Receivable Using Variance Analysis," *Financial Management* (Winter 1986), pp. 69–76.

GENTRY, J. A., and J. DE LA GARZA, "Monitoring Accounts Receivable: Revisited," *Financial Management* (Winter 1985), pp. 28–38.

KIM, YONG H., and JOSEPH C. ATKINS, "Evaluating Investments in Accounts Receivable: A Wealth Maximizing Framework," *Journal of Finance* (May 1978), pp. 403–412.

LEWELLEN, WILBUR G., and ROBERT O. EDMISTER, "A General Model for Accounts Receivable Analysis and Control," *Journal of Financial and Quantitative Analysis* (March 1973), pp. 195–206.

SARTORIS, WILLIAM L., and NED C. HILL, "Evaluating Credit Policy Alternatives: A Present Value Framework," *Journal of Financial Research* (Spring 1981), pp. 81–89.

SUCHDEVA, KANWAL S., and LAWRENCE J. GITMAN, "Accounts Receivable Decisions in a Capital Budgeting Framework," *Financial Management* (Winter 1981), pp. 45–49.

WESTON, FRED J., and PHAM D. TUAN, "Comment on Analysis of Credit Policy Changes," *Financial Management* (Winter 1980), pp. 59–63.

16

Management of Accounts Payable and Accruals

Even a moderate-sized company may have hundreds of vendors who must be paid on a regular basis. To cope with the complexity created by the multiplicity of credit terms offered by vendors, many companies establish a policy either of taking all discounts offered or of taking no discounts. Several software providers have developed programs for managing accounts payable that select the optimal payment date, considering the opportunity cost of funds. The programs determine the effective rate for the discount terms and if it is below the hurdle-rate schedule payment on the final due date. In addition, the programs are capable of feeding information from scheduled payments to the cash forecast and projecting the demand for funds by bank accounts for as much as 60 days. The Allied Chemical Division of Allied Canada, Inc., has implemented a packet switched data communications network that is on-line with sales offices and plants to initiate and monitor accounts payable, order entry, and inventory control.

In Chapters 12 and 13 we examined the short-term financing of a firm through explicitly arranged credit. In the last two chapters, we discussed the issues involved in managing trade credit from the perspective of a firm granting credit as a seller. A firm also receives financing from trade credit when it is the buyer, and through accrued expenses. The amount of financing provided by these sources is, in part, a function of the policies adopted in managing these liabilities. In this chapter, we focus on the factors considered in establishing policies for these automatically generated short-term financing sources.

————————— **Spontaneous Sources of Financing** —————————

In Chapter 13, in our discussion of nonbank financing sources, we mentioned that some sources of financing are spontaneous: the amount of financing provided varies directly with the level of operations. This is true as long as the firm maintains established policies concerning these financing sources. The most important spontaneous financing sources are accounts payable, accrued expenses, and accrued taxes. The relative amount of financing provided by these sources is shown in Table 16.1. Spontaneous financing provides over 20% of the total funds of the average firm.

Accounts payable, the financing provided by purchases on trade credit, is a spontaneous source of financing because, as the firm increases (decreases) the level of operations, the amount of materials ordered increases (decreases) and the financing provided by suppliers increases (decreases) by a corresponding amount. *Accrued expenses* are financing provided to the firm by employees; work is performed but payment is delayed until some future date. Accrued expenses for variable operating costs increase or decrease with the level of operations. Accrued expenses for fixed operating costs, of course, do not vary with the level of operations. *Accrued taxes* are income taxes for which an obligation has been incurred but payment has not been remitted. To the extent that taxable income varies with the level of operations, accrued taxes are a spontaneous source of financing.

An example may help to illustrate the nature of this type of financing and the information necessary to structure some of the decisions. Carpet World, an outlet selling commercial and residential carpet, orders from manufacturers both for inventory and in response to specific customer orders. Manufacturers bill on the first of the month for all shipments during the prior month. Purchase terms are 5%/10, 4%/30, net 31. Carpet World's shipments are spread evenly throughout the month, it pays its bills on the 30th of the month, and its carpet installers are paid (based upon the number of square yards of carpet installed) on the first of the month for installations during the prior month.

The timeline for a typical month for Carpet World is shown in Figure 16.1. On average, an order is placed on the 15th of the month, with payment made on the 30th of the following month. Thus, suppliers provide financing for,

Table 16.1 Spontaneous Sources of Financing as a Percentage of Total Assets for All Manufacturing Corporations

Financing Source	1960	1970	1980	1985
Accounts Payable	7.9%	8.5%	9.9%	8.5%
Accruals and other C.L.	9.0%	9.9%	12.0%	12.9%

Source: Quarterly Financial Report for Manufacturing, Mining, and Trade Corporations, U.S. Department of Commerce, various dates.

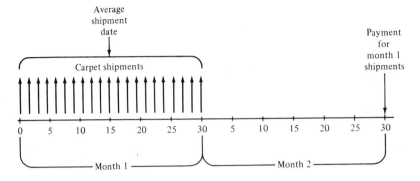

A. Timeline for carpet shipments and payment date

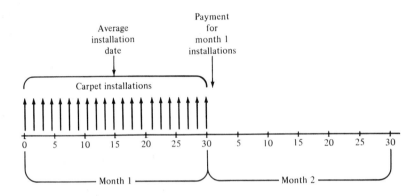

B. Timeline for carpet installation and payment

Figure 16.1 Timelines for Carpet World.

on average, 45 days of purchases. At the current level of activity, Carpet World's monthly purchases are 50,000 square yards of carpet at an average price of $9 per square yard. Thus, carpet manufacturers supply an average of $675,000 in accounts payable financing to Carpet World.[1] Carpet World pays installers $.75 per square yard, or $37,500 per month. If the installations are performed evenly throughout the month, the average time from installation to payment is 15 days. Installers are providing $18,750 in average financing to Carpet World by agreeing to delay the receipt of payment until the first of the following month.

If business increases and Carpet World orders and sells 60,000 square yards of carpeting a month, accounts payable increase to $810,000 and accrued expenses increase to $22,500. The amount of financing provided to Carpet

---

[1] Immediately prior to payment, the accounts payable will be $900,000, which represents 2 months worth of orders. Immediately after payment, the accounts payable will be reduced by the amount of 1 month's orders, or $450,000. The average over the month would thus be $675,000.

World by the suppliers and installers has increased by 20%, the same as the increase in sales. Should Carpet World's business decrease to 45,000 square yards per month, the financing provided by suppliers and installers would decrease to $607,500 and $16,875, respectively. Thus, the financing available from accounts payable and accrued expenses changes spontaneously with changes in the level of operations.

Accounts Payable Decisions

Terms of Purchase

The first element in the accounts payable decision comes prior to the order, in the negotiation of terms with the seller. In many cases, there is little discretion on the terms of purchase, with the buyer being forced to accept the seller's terms. However, if the buyer represents an important customer to the seller, the seller may be willing to negotiate the terms. Purchase terms may be affected by the quantity being purchased, the frequency of purchase, and the form of payment. For example, by paying via an ACH transfer rather than a mailed check, a supplier may negotiate an extended payment due date. Although many suppliers may not be willing to negotiate on credit terms, customers will never know which suppliers are willing to consider special terms unless they ask.

Payment Options

Where payment options exist, the objective of the firm is to pay at the time that will minimize the net present value of the payment. This can be expressed as

$$\text{Minimize } NPV(\text{payment } + \text{ penalty costs}),$$

where the penalty costs may be both direct and indirect costs of the payment date.

Some terms of payment, such as those offered to Carpet World, contain explicit payment options offered by the seller. Where these options exist, management of accounts payable clearly involves making a choice of when to pay. However, the manager also has to decide the payment date if the net amount is paid. By this point, no attentive reader will suggest paying before the net date; however, some may want to delay payment until after the due date. The appropriate decision structure is to first decide the payment date for the net amount. Only after this has been done can the issue of whether an early payment discount is worthwhile be correctly addressed.

Stretching the Payment

The conscious decision to delay payment of a bill until some time after the due date is frequently given the more pleasant-sounding name of *stretching accounts payable*. The decision on whether to stretch the payment beyond the due date is a function of several qualitative and quantitative factors.

ETHICS OF STRETCHING. The first consideration is whether, because of company policy or the manager's personal beliefs, intentionally stretching a payment is considered unethical. If this is the case, the decision on whether to stretch is simple—don't stretch. If you feel that this is the appropriate action, you may be tempted to skip the next several sections. However, you are urged to resist this temptation and to read on so that you can better understand some of the other factors your customers may consider in deciding whether to stretch payments to you.

LEGAL SANCTIONS. The second consideration is the legal implication of stretching the payment. For some types of payments (e.g., taxes, insurance, or licenses), legal sanctions, over and above any monetary penalty, may be imposed if payment is delayed. In these instances, the decision is also straightforward—don't stretch.

ECONOMIC CONSIDERATIONS. The third factor is the direct and indirect economic effects of stretching. A direct benefit, the opportunity cost of using a supplier's funds, results from stretching the payment beyond the net date. The benefit is a function of the amount of the payment, the opportunity cost, and the number of days the payment is stretched.

There is a direct cost in stretching the payment if the seller assesses a penalty for late payment. A late payment penalty may be either a fixed fee or a daily interest rate. If no explicit penalty is assessed for delayed payment, there is no direct economic cost for stretching the payment.

Even if there is no direct economic cost to stretching, however, there are indirect costs. One such cost is a deteriorating credit rating. Although an occasional delayed payment may not result in a poorer credit rating, frequent late payment generally will have such a result. This can show up as a decrease in the amount of credit available or an increase in the cost of credit available— from many sources, not just from the supplier stretched. Another result is a deteriorating supplier relationship, which can result in reduced flexibility for special orders or unfilled or delayed orders in times of tight supply. An astute supplier may even incorporate the cost of the extended credit in the price on future orders. The severity of these indirect costs depends upon the relative economic bargaining power of the supplier and the customer. While these indirect effects are hard to measure, they need to be addressed by the financial manager in deciding when to pay a bill.

ECONOMICS OF STRETCHING. We can express the economic aspects of the stretching decision in the framework of the objective function previously specified. Let

t_c = the day on which the payment is made

t_n = the day on which the net payment is due

$DC(t_c)$ = the direct economic costs of late payment as a function of the payment date

$IC(t_c)$ = the indirect costs of late payment as a function of the payment date

The net present value of the payment can be expressed per dollar of the purchase price as follows:

$$NPV = \frac{1 + DC(t_c) + IC(t_c)}{(1 + t_c k)}. \tag{16.1}$$

OPTIMAL STRETCHING. To determine the optimal payment date, it is necessary to specify a function for the direct and indirect economic costs of stretching. Assume that the direct costs are assessed as a daily interest rate, k', for each day the payment is stretched beyond the net date. The direct costs function is

$$DC(t_c) = k'(t_c - t_n). \tag{16.2}$$

The indirect costs are likely to be a nonlinear function of the time the payment is stretched, with the costs increasing at an increasing rate. Assume that the indirect costs can be expressed as a coefficient, k'', times the square of the time the payment is stretched. The function of indirect costs is

$$IC(t_c) = k''(t_c - t_n)^2. \tag{16.3}$$

The optimal payment date is found by setting the benefits from stretching, $k(t_c - t_n)$, equal to the sum of the direct and indirect costs. This is

$$k(t_c - t_n) = k'(t_c - t_n) + k''(t_c - t_n)^2. \tag{16.4}$$

The optimal stretching time is found by solving Equation (16.4) for $(t_c - t_n)$:

$$(t_c - t_n) = \frac{k - k'}{k''}. \tag{16.5}$$

Returning to our Carpet World example, we find that Dalton Mills assesses a penalty of .75% per month (.025% per day) for payments made after day 31. The treasurer of Carpet World has determined the indirect costs of stretching Dalton Mills are .0011% per day times the square of the number of days stretched. If the opportunity cost for Carpet World is 12% per year (.033% per day), the optimal stretching for invoices from Dalton Mills is

$$(t_c - t_n) = \frac{.033 - .025}{.0011} = 7 \text{ days}.$$

Georgia Carpets, Inc., a second supplier of Carpet World, assesses no explicit penalty for late payment. The treasurer feels that the indirect costs are the same as for Dalton Mills. The optimal stretching for invoices from Georgia Carpets is

$$(t_c - t_n) = \frac{.033}{.0011} = 30 \text{ days}.$$

Thus, if only economic costs and benefits are considered, the optimal payment time is day 38 (stretch 7 days) for Dalton Mills and day 61 for Georgia Carpets. If no discounts were offered for early payment, these would be the days on which the payments should be scheduled.

In this example, we have expressed indirect costs as a function of the square of the number of days stretched for clarity of exposition. Any other nonlinear function (e.g., as a logarithmic or exponential) felt to represent the increasing nature of the penalty costs as a function of stretching could be used.

Payment Date When a Discount Is Offered

Once the payment date for the net payment has been set, the manager can consider whether to pay early in order to take advantage of a discount or to pay on the net (or stretched) date. The decision, based on financial costs and benefits, can be addressed by calculating either the present values of the different payment options or the effective interest cost of not taking a discount.

PRESENT VALUE APPROACH. In our example, the suppliers of Carpet World offered three different payment options: pay on day 10 and take a 5% discount, pay on day 30 and take a 4% discount, or pay on day 31 and pay the net (listed) price. For now, assume that the financial manager of Carpet World does not consider the possibility of stretching beyond the due date of day 31. These options offer a choice in the timing and amount of cash flow. We can easily analyze this choice by using present value techniques. The timeline of the choices and the present value of the different options for a purchase of $1,000 are shown in Figure 16.2.

We can see that the best payment option for Carpet World, to pay on day 10 and take the 5% discount, results in a present value (on day 10) of $950. Payment under any of the other options results in a higher present value cost.

PAYMENT DATE WHEN STRETCHING. However, we have determined that the optimal payment date was day 38 for Dalton Mills and day 61 for Georgia Carpets. Is it still best for Carpet World to pay on day 10 and take the 5% discount?

For Dalton Mills, the payment would be made on day 38, not day 31. In addition, the amount of the payment is not $1,000, but rather $[1 + (.00025)(7)]$ times the net amount, or $1,001.75, because of the late payment charge. The net present value (on day 10) of this payment is $992.58.

For Georgia Carpets the optimal payment date, without considering discounts, was day 61. The present value of the payment on day 61 is $983.51. Since this is larger than the present value of $950 from paying on day 10, the optimal arrangement is still to pay on day 10 and take the 5% discount.

EFFECTIVE ANNUALIZED INTEREST. An alternative way of determining the best payment day is to calculate the effective interest cost of missing the discount and compare this with the opportunity cost. The choice of paying on day 30 instead of on day 10 is the same as getting a loan in the amount of

A. Payment is not stretched

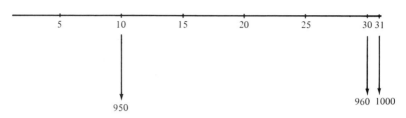

Present value on day 10

Payment on day 10:   PV cost = $950

Payment on day 30:   PV cost = $\dfrac{\$960}{[1+.12(20/365)]}$ = $953.73

Payment on day 31:   PV cost = $\dfrac{\$1,000}{[1+.12(21/365)]}$ = $993.14

B. Payment is stretched

Dalton Mills

Pay on day 38:   PV cost = $\dfrac{\$1,001.75}{[1+.12(28/365)]}$ = $992.61

Georgia Carpet, Inc.

Pay on day 61:   PV cost = $\dfrac{\$1,000}{[1+.12(51/365)]}$ = $983.51

Figure 16.2 Timeline and Present Value of Payment Choices for Carpet World.

$950 for 20 days from the supplier and paying an extra $10 when the loan is repaid.[2] The effective annualized interest cost of this arrangement is

$$\text{Effective cost} = \frac{10}{950} \times \frac{365}{20} = .192 \text{ or } 19.2\%.$$

Since this is higher than the opportunity cost of 12%, the payment should be made on day 10.

The effective annualized interest cost of paying on day 31 instead of on day 30 can be similarly found to be

$$\text{Effective cost} = \frac{40}{960} \times \frac{365}{1} = 15.20 \text{ or } 1,520\%.$$

Clearly, a decision to pay on day 31 and forgo the 4% discount instead of paying on day 30 is not economically sound.

---

[2] Since Carpet World can pay $950 on day 10, the supplier is providing a 10-day loan in the amount of $950 with no explicit charge. The financial manager can choose to extend the "loan" of $950 to day 30 (an extra 20 days) by paying an extra $10.

The effective interest cost of paying Georgia Carpets on day 61 instead of on day 30 is found to be

$$\text{Effective cost} = \frac{40}{960} \times \frac{365}{31} = 49.06\%.$$

At this point, let us summarize the payment date decision. The determination of the optimal day on which to pay an invoice depends upon the terms of purchase, the opportunity cost of the paying firm, company policy toward stretching payments, and direct and indirect costs of stretching payments. The first step is to determine the optimal payment date without consideration of discounts, where the benefit of stretching is balanced against the direct and indirect economic costs. Once the nondiscount payment date is determined, the decision on whether to take the discount can be addressed either by comparing the present value of the payment options or by examining the effective interest rate resulting from not taking the discount.

Accrued Expenses

Benefits of Increased Accrued Expenses

The management of accrued expenses also involves direct and indirect economic factors. The direct economic element is again the benefit a firm derives from being able to use funds provided by someone else. The amount of the benefit is the daily opportunity cost times the amount of the obligation times the average time from the creation of the obligation to its payment.[3]

For example, the Rayn Steel Company pays its employees each Friday for a 1-week payroll period ending the preceding Friday. This policy creates the following delay in the employees' receipt of their wages: earnings from Saturday, the first day of the payroll period, are received 13 days later. Sunday's earnings are received 12 days later. Continuing through the payroll period, we see that Friday's earnings are received 7 days later. The average delay for the entire week's earnings is 10 days. With a weekly payroll of $300,000 and an opportunity cost of 10%, Rayn Steel earns (300,000)(10 days)(.1/365 per day) or $821.92 per week on the funds that are available because they do not pay employees each day. This amounts to an annual value of $42,739.84.

Rayn Steel changes to a biweekly payday policy with a 2-week payroll period ending on a Friday and payday on the following Friday. The average delay is now 13.5 days. The opportunity cost benefit to Rayn Steel is ($600,000)(13.5 days)(.1/365 per day) or $2,219.18 for every 2-week period. This amounts to an annual value of $57,698.68, or an additional benefit of $14,949.84 from the extended payroll period.

---

[3] For some accrued expenses, most notably accrued income taxes, there may also be a direct economic cost in the form of a penalty for not paying on time.

In addition to the opportunity cost savings, the longer payroll period reduces the transactions costs. Variable costs, such as the cost of the checks, is cut in half. There may even be a reduction in some of the fixed costs associated with the payroll department if the staff can be reduced because of less frequent preparation of the payroll.

Cost of Increased Accrued Expenses

An increased period for accrued expenses is not without cost; however, most of the costs are indirect and may be difficult to measure. For example, delayed payment to employees may create ill will, may be a deterrent in hiring top-quality employees, and may even create money management problems for some employees. In establishing payroll and other accrued expense policies, management must trade off the direct economic benefits to the firm in the form of the opportunity and transactions cost savings with the indirect, and likely nonquantifiable, costs of an extended accrual policy.

Effect on Liquidity

Spontaneous financing directly affects the liquidity of a firm. Every dollar provided by spontaneous sources is one less dollar required from explicitly arranged financing, such as bank loans, or selling marketable securities. A firm with a large portion of its operating cycle cash requirements covered by spontaneous sources of funds has a lower investment required to support its operating activities and is able to sustain more rapid growth with internally generated funds. With the exception of missed cash discounts or explicit late payment penalties, these spontaneous sources of funds carry no explicit costs. Thus, they represent an inexpensive source of financing to the firm as long as the indirect costs do not reduce the value of the firm.

There is an additional benefit created by a longer horizon connected with accounts payable and accrued expenses. A longer time horizon for these payments may allow the firm to extend the time horizon of its cash budget. The uncertainty of estimates of near-term payments is reduced. This may give the financial manager additional flexibility regarding the maturity of marketable securities to take advantage of any the yield curve effects.

Information System Requirements

A major information system requirement connected with managing short-term liabilities is the validation of bills. Invoices are checked against purchase orders and shipping and receiving documents to verify that the merchandise was ordered, delivered in good shape, and not returned. Payroll data are verified to ensure that payment for employees is in agreement with work records.

Once validation is complete, the data are keyed into the information system to schedule check writing. To proceed from validation to payment requires an interface between people handling accounts payable and accruals and those responsible for cash disbursement. A smooth transfer of information with minimum reentry of data is important for correct and efficiently implemented disbursement decisions. It is also important to transfer information on payments quickly and accurately in order to update the cash forecast in a timely manner. A schematic of the flows through a typical information system is shown in Figure 16.3.

In many large firms, basic records are kept at a division, while payments may be initiated from a centralized location. The time required to complete the validation process may be critical for the ability of the firm to take advantage of early payment discounts. A recent study of a large midwestern city found that the validation process was not completed until almost 2 weeks after the invoice date. This delay precluded the city from taking advantage of many early payment discounts. In addition to information system delays causing missed discounts, the time horizon of the cash forecast is affected. With the information flow system shown in Figure 16.3, it is not possible to schedule payment and to update the cash forecast until the validation process is completed.

An alternative information system flow is shown in Figure 16.4. In this system, upon receipt of an invoice, check writing is scheduled for a date after

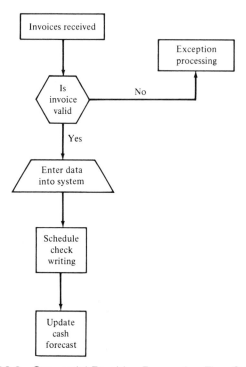

Figure 16.3 Sequential Payables Processing Flow Schematic.

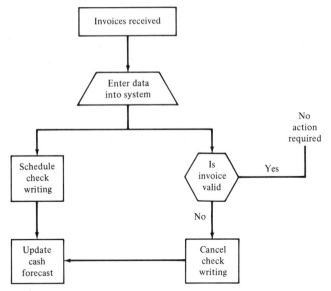

Figure 16.4   Parallel Payables Processing Flow Schematic.

the normal validation time and the cash forecast is updated. If the invoice is found to be invalid, the check is canceled and the budget adjusted. While this process still may not allow discounts to be taken if the validation process is longer than the discount period, it does provide a longer time horizon for the cash forecast. The benefits of a longer time horizon would have to be weighed against the extra costs and number of exceptions processed for invalid billings.

The choice between the system shown in Figure 16.3 and that of Figure 16.4 is in part a function of the number of invalid invoices. If the number of invalid invoices is small, the firm will benefit from the earlier adjustment to the cash forecast from the system in Figure 16.4. A firm with a large percentage of invalid invoices might find that the cost of revising the cash forecast for invalid invoices outweighs the benefits of a system such as that in Figure 16.4.

Summary

Accounts payable and accrued expenses are spontaneous sources of funding that increase and decrease with operating activities. The financing provided by these sources reduces the amount of explicitly arranged financing necessary.

The objective in setting the payment date for an invoice is to minimize the net present value of the sum of the amount of the payment and the penalty cost. In determining the optimal payment time, one must first determine whether the payment should be made on the net due date or stretched. The decision to stretch is a function of ethical, legal, and economic considerations. The economic benefit of stretching is balanced against the sum of the direct and indirect economic costs to determine the optimal payment date if no discount is taken. After the net payment date has been determined, the decision on whether to take a discount for early payment is made by examining either the net present value of payment options or the effective interest cost of not taking a discount. Conceptually, accrued expense policies can be determined in a similar manner. However, many of the costs are nonquantifiable and hard to determine.

A good information system and coordination between the people responsible for accounts payable and accrued expenses and those responsible for cash forecasting and disbursements are required for smooth and efficient functioning of payables and accruals policies.

------------ **Discussion Questions** ------------

1. What are the characteristics of spontaneous sources of financing?
2. Why do many capital budgeting procedures include only net working capital (current assets minus current liabilities) as part of the investment instead of all current assets?
3. In considering your answer to Question 2, should all current liabilities be excluded?
4. List and explain the types of indirect costs that might be incurred by a firm in stretching its accounts payable.
5. Swander, Inc., operates a camera shop, selling cameras ranging in price from $35 to over $1,000, and providing a film developing service. Contrast the willingness to stretch the payables to SmallCam, one of seven companies that manufactures cameras that sell for under $100, and Conac, one of two manufacturers of photo developing supplies.
6. W. E. Rivet construction is a steel erector for high-rise building projects. It purchases most of its steel from the American Steel Company on credit terms of 0.5%/15, net 30. The financial manager of Rivet always pays within the discount period. The opportunity cost for Rivet is 14%. Evaluate the financial manager's accounts payable practice.
7. At a recent executive seminar, the accounts payable manager for Big Motors said, "Most of our purchases are on terms of 2%/10, net 30, but our policy is to pay 'promptly' on day 45 and take the discount. We seldom have any complaints from our suppliers." Evaluate the policy of Big Motors.
8. Outline the steps for processing an incoming invoice from receipt to final payment. Contrast a parallel and a sequential processing system.
9. Contrast the use of spontaneous financing sources with the use of bank credit. Comment on the relative costs, flexibility, risks, and so on.

10. What are the benefits and costs associated with going from a biweekly to a monthly payroll period? Would there be any differences for managerial and hourly workers? Why?

_____ **Problems** _____

1. Compute the net present value of the following payment options, assuming no stretching and an opportunity cost of 12%.
    a. 2%/10, net 30
    b. 0.5%/10, net 30
    c. 2%/10, net 20
    d. 2%/15, net 45.
2. Compute the effective interest cost for the credit terms in Problem 1.
3. The Mixed-Up firm has a rather slow invoice processing system. As a result, it misses virtually all cash discounts. Assuming that the average terms are 2%/10, net 30 and that Mixed-Up's volume of purchases is $5,000,000 during the year, what is this policy costing them if they always pay on day 30? Assume that they can earn 11% on invested funds.
4. You can draw down a loan against your credit line at an effective rate of 11.5%. If you are purchasing on terms of 3%/10, net 30, how many days past the due date would you have to stretch to make this less costly than the bank loan? What are the indirect costs of doing this?
5. Compute the effective interest rate of missing a discount when the terms are 2%/10, net 30 and payment is made on the following days: 15, 20, 30, 44, 60, 90, or 120. Graph the effective rate versus the time of payment.
6. Find the present values for the payment dates in Problem 5.
7. The Circle City Company purchases raw materials on terms of 2%/10, net 30. In reviewing past payment practices, it is discovered that virtually all bills are paid without taking a discount, on average, 15 days from the invoice date. When asked why the firm did not take advantage of cash discounts, the bookkeeper replied that it cost only 2% for these funds, while drawing on the firm's credit line would cost 10.5%.
    a. What is the effective interest cost of Circle City's current payment practices?
    b. Give two suggestions for improving their payment practice and specify which is better.
8. Brad's Sporting Goods purchases golf clubs from Pro Golf, Inc., on terms of 2%/10, net 30. Because of the need for rush orders during the peak selling season, Brad feels that maintaining good supplier relations with Pro Golf is important. Brad has estimated the penalty cost of paying late to be $.01\ e^{.1t}$, where e is the natural logarithm base and t is the number of days payment is stretched past the due date. Brad's opportunity cost is 15%. What is the optimal payment date for invoices from Pro Golf?

9. Brad's (in Problem 8) also orders cross-country skiing equipment from XCC, Inc., on terms of 1/10, net 30, with a penalty of .5% per month for payments after 30 days. Brad estimates its indirect penalty costs to be .0005% per day times the number of days late squared. When should Brad pay invoices from XCC?

10. AUX Control, Inc., supplies you with subassemblies for one of your better selling products. They have suggested that you begin paying them by electronic funds transfer. The advantage, they point out, is that the method is cheaper. Your current payment method (including postage, envelope, check, and labor) costs $10. An electronic (ACH) transfer costs only $1. On examining the disbursement float associated with payments to this firm, you discover that it is currently about 7 days. An ACH payment would take only 1 day to clear. Your average invoice payment to the firm is $125,000 and your effective interest rate is 10%.
    a. Should you change the payment mechanism?
    b. What would the amount of the discount have to be for you to be willing to change the payment system?

11. Currently you pay your employees by check twice a month, on the 3rd and the 18th, for a payroll period ending on the 15th and the 30th. Your semimonthly payroll is $100,000. The cost to process the payroll is $500, half of which consists of variable costs. Currently 40% of your employees cash their checks on the payroll date, 30% the next day, and the remaining 30%, on average, 5 days after the payroll date. The union has been pushing you to switch to direct deposit of payroll, but you have resisted because of the loss of float, since all funds would be paid out on the payroll date.
    a. If the variable costs were reduced to $100 for direct deposit, how much would it cost you if your opportunity cost is 12%? (For simplicity, assume that all months have 30 days and ignore the fact that some pay days would be on a Saturday or Sunday.)
    b. Your new assistant treasurer, has suggested that you go along with the union request, but switch to a monthly payroll instead of a semimonthly payroll. Evaluate this suggestion.

Selected Readings

BROYLES, JACK, IAN COOPER, and SIMON ARCHER, (eds.), *Financial Management Handbook*, 2nd ed., London: Gower Publishing Company, 1972.

DEMAAGD, GERALD R., "Cash Management Duel: How Slow Paying Customers and Alert Creditors are Battling It Out on Computers," *Credit and Financial Management* (May 1982), pp. 14–16.

GULDING, JOHN F., "Redesigning Accounts Payable," *Management Accounting* (September 1983), pp. 42–46.

HALL, DOUG, "Allied Chemical Builds Data Network," *Canadian Datasystems* (August 1983), pp. 58–59.

HILL, NED C., WILLIAM L. SARTORIS, and DANIEL M. FERGUSON, "Corporate Credit and Payables Policies: Two Surveys," *Journal of Cash Management* (July–August 1984), pp. 56–62.

JOHNSON, ROBERT W., "Management of Accounts Receivable and Payable," in *Financial Handbook*, 5th ed., Edward I. Altman (ed.), New York: Wiley, 1981, Chapter 28.

POCOCK, M. A., and A. H. TAYLOR, *Handbook of Financial Planning and Control*, London: Gower Publishing Company, 1981.

SKILES, DONALD J., PAUL J. GIST, and BERNELL K. STONE, "Federal Government Bill Paying," *Journal of Cash Management* (February–March 1983), pp. 46–49.

Special Topics in Short-term Finance

17

Managing and Financing Inventories

Inventories account for a large commitment of funds by U.S. firms. In Chapter 1 we saw that inventories constituted almost 18% of all assets of manufacturing firms in 1985. Inventories, in the form of the inventory to sales ratio, are also one of the key indicators used to gauge the health of the economy. At the individual firm level, the commitment of funds to inventories has received increasing attention, in part because materials purchases have accounted for a greater proportion of product costs as additional automated procedures have been adopted. For example, in 1980 material costs represented 43% of the cost of an IBM Selectric typewriter; by 1986 they constituted 77% of the cost. The increased attention to inventory has focused on a reduction in costs. General Motors has reduced its inventory-related costs from $8,000,000,000 to $2,000,000,000. Harley-Davidson has achieved a drop in inventory while increasing production by 30%.

_____ Why Inventories Exist _____

The Nature of an Inventory

Some functions of the firm, such as the purchase of raw materials, processing, and having finished goods available for sale, have a sequential, physical dependency. Maintenance of inventories allows the firm to decouple these functions so that each can be planned, scheduled, and operated independently.

Types of Inventories

Raw Materials

An inventory of raw materials allows separation of production scheduling from arrival of basic inputs to the production process. Factors affecting the amount of the raw materials inventory include proximity to the supplier, relationship with the supplier, predictability of the production process, lead time required to place an order, and transportability and perishability of materials.

Work-in-Process

An inventory of partially completed units allows the separation of different phases of the production process. The amount of work-in-process inventory is in part a function of the type of product, the measurement period, and the nature of the production process. For example, a firm with a very short production process, such as a bakery, may have a work-in-process inventory during the day, kneaded dough that is rising before being baked. However, this work-in-process inventory will not be carried overnight. On the other hand, a firm with a long production process, such as an airframe manufacturer, may have a large work-in-process inventory of partially completed products (airplanes), on a continuing basis. However, even in this latter example, management controls the amount of work-in-process inventory maintained through a choice between working on a few airframes at a time or working on a larger number of planes to allow more flexibility in scheduling.

Finished Goods

An inventory of finished goods allows separation of production from selling. With a stock of finished merchandise on hand, a firm can fill orders as they are received rather than depend upon the completion of production to satisfy customer demands.

Cash and Marketable Securities

Cash and marketable securities can be thought of as an inventory of liquidity that allows separation of collection from disbursement. Without this liquidity, inventory payment of bills would be tied to collection of accounts, in some cases, with payment delayed until accounts receivable are collected. The treatment of cash as an inventory was addressed in the appendix to Chapter 10.

Motives for Holding Inventory

Economists have established three motives for holding inventories: a transactions motive, a precautionary motive, and a speculative motive. In addition, there may be contractual reason for holding some inventories.

Transactions Motive

The *transactions motive* for holding inventory is to satisfy the expected level of activities of the firm. For example, a pizza restaurant receiving its next materials shipment on Monday starts the weekend with enough flour, salt, tomato sauce, sausage, and anchovies to make the number of pizzas anticipated to be ordered over the weekend.

Precautionary Motive

The *precautionary motive* is to provide a cushion if the actual level of activity is different than anticipated. Again, using a pizza restaurant as an example, in addition to holding enough inventory to make the expected number of pizzas over the weekend, the restaurant may hold additional supplies as a precaution against demand being different than anticipated. If demand exceeds expectations (either in total or for a particular ingredient), sales will probably either be lost or, if made, less profitable. It is doubtful that many customers will accept a pie topped with anchovies and pineapple as a substitute simply because the restaurant has run out of sausage and pepperoni.

Speculative Motive

The *speculative motive* for holding inventory might entice a firm to purchase a larger quantity of materials than normal in anticipation of making abnormal profits. Advance purchases of raw materials in inflationary times is one form of speculative behavior. A second reason for speculative inventory purchases may involve an anticipated change in a product. Two such incidents received wide coverage. One was the speculative purchase of convertibles by some automobile dealers during the mid-1970s when production of convertibles was being curtailed. The other was the purchase of the "Old Coke" by some retailers and distributors when the Coca-Cola Company brought out "New Coke" in the mid-1980s. In both instances, the inventory accumulators anticipated being able to generate abnormal profits to compensate for their speculative purchases.

Contractual Requirements

Occasionally it may be necessary to carry a certain level of inventory to meet a contractual agreement. Some manufacturers require dealers to maintain a specified level of inventory in order to be the sole representative in a particular territory. Some banks require a customer to maintain a specified level of cash balances (inventory of cash) to pay for services used.

Traditional Approach to Inventory Policy

In a traditional approach to determining optimal inventory policy, the objective function is the minimization of total inventory costs. Inventory costs consist of *stockout costs,* or the costs of being unable to meet the sales or production schedule, and *management costs,* or the costs of ordering, handling, and carrying inventory. Many approaches to inventory policy either ignore stockout costs or assume that they are infinite (which means that stockouts are not allowed) and concentrate on the costs of managing inventory. The objective function takes the following form:

Minimize stockout costs + Setup costs + Holding costs.

Inventory Management Cost Tradeoff

Inventory management costs are of two types: setup (order) costs and carrying costs. The total cost of managing inventory is the sum of these two types of costs.

Setup Costs

Setup costs consist of the costs of establishing a new setup on a production process or of ordering additional goods. They may involve a changeover in machinery, inefficiencies caused by operators relearning tasks, or paperwork related to making a change or placing an order. Setup costs are a decreasing function of the level of inventory, since carrying a higher inventory reduces the number of separate orders and, therefore, the total setup cost.

Carrying Costs

Carrying costs consist of both physical costs and opportunity, or financing, costs. Physical costs, incurred in the handling and storage of inventory, include the cost of space, the cost to move items into and out of inventory, the cost to rotate stock to prevent obsolescence, and the cost of insurance. Although some of these costs may be fixed for some ranges of inventory, in general they are treated as variable with the level of the inventory held. Opportunity costs are incurred because funds are invested in inventory. These costs are a function of the credit terms on which the goods are purchased, as well as the amount of inventory on hand. However, the usual treatment ignores the impact of credit terms. Carrying costs are an increasing function of the level of inventory held. A graphic representation of the inventory management costs is presented in Figure 17.1.

Economic Order Quantity

A frequent approach to the establishment of inventory policy is to minimize the objective function consisting of the total cost of managing the inventory. The objective function is

Total inventory cost = setup cost + physical carrying cost + opportunity cost.

The objective function is specified using the following variables:

t_m = the number of days in the time period
R = the total unit requirements during the time period
S = the setup (order) costs, which are fixed per setup

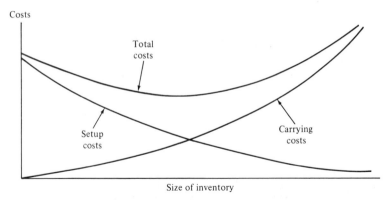

Figure 17.1 Inventory Management Costs.

h = the dollar holding costs per average unit in inventory
C = the cost per unit
Q = the number of units of inventory ordered
k = the daily opportunity cost rate

The setup cost is determined by multiplying the number of setups by the cost per setup:

$$\text{Setup cost} = S(R/Q). \tag{17.1}$$

If each order is for Q units, the average inventory level will be $Q/2$. The physical holding cost for the period is

$$\text{Physical holding cost} = h(Q/2). \tag{17.2}$$

The opportunity cost of the funds tied up in inventory is

$$\text{Opportunity cost} = C(k)(t_m)(Q/2). \tag{17.3}$$

The total cost of managing the inventory is the sum of these separate expressions:

$$\text{Total cost} = S(R/Q) + (h + Ckt_m)(Q/2). \tag{17.4}$$

This approach relies on two assumptions that should be made explicit at this point. First, the usage rate is continuous throughout the time period. Second, there is instantaneous replenishment of inventory. The inventory is at level Q immediately after the arrival of an order and declines continuously to zero at the time the next order arrives to replenish it.

The optimal order quantity is found by taking a derivative of the total cost expression with respect to the quantity ordered and setting the expression equal to zero. Solution of this derivative for the value of Q yields

$$Q = \sqrt{\frac{2SR}{h + Ckt_m}}. \tag{17.5}$$

Boom Box, Inc., the manufacturer of portable stereo radios, orders cases for the radios it produces. The company operates on a quarterly planning cycle and estimates its requirements to be 10,000 units for the quarter. The cost is $4.50 per case. The company estimates that it costs $25 to place an order and $0.39 per unit to store the cases. The opportunity cost rate is 0.027% per day. The optimal order quantity is

$$Q = \sqrt{\frac{2(25)(10,000)}{0.39 + (4.5)(0.00027)(90)}} = 1,000.$$

Thus, the firm minimizes its total inventory management cost by placing orders for 1,000 units at a time.[1] This requires that Boom Box place 10 orders during the quarter, or once every 9 days. This practice results in total inventory management costs of $500 per quarter.[2] The average inventory of 500 units (half of the begining inventory plus the ending inventory) that the firm maintains represents a 4.5-day supply of cases.

Safety Stock and Variability of Demand

The traditional approach is extended from the basic model presented previously to allow for refinements. Sometimes a safety stock, a floor below which inventory is not allow to fall, is added to allow for uncertainties in delivery of materials or in demand. Variability of demand is factored in directly by the use of a stochastic model incorporating a cost function for errors. Volume discounts are incorporated by solving for multiple economic order quantities at different prices.

Present Value Timeline Approach to Inventory Decisions

In the preceding approach to the inventory decision, some cash flow timing issues are ignored that must be addressed for the approach to be consistent with a present value of cash flows. We now turn to an examination of the inventory policy problem using the framework of the net present value of cash flows. As a first step, a comparative statics approach to the inventory decision is formulated, similar to the approach used for other decisions in earlier chapters. The differences in the present value and economic order quantity approaches are then addressed to investigate the linkage of the financing issues with the more traditional focus on inventory order quantity.

---

[1] The solution has been rounded to 1,000 units. The exact solution results in an optimal quantity of 1,000.65 units.

[2] This is for the rounded quantity of 1,000 units; the cost per quarter for the exact solution is $499.67.

Comparison of Alternative Inventory Policies

In a statics approach, we assume that the firm already has an inventory policy and is considering adopting a new one. As a first approximation, we assume that the proposed policy will not alter the terms of purchase or the timing between order and payment; only the quantity and frequency of orders will change.

In addition to the terms and parameters identified in the economic order quantity approach, we define the following variables:

t_p = the number of days after the invoice date
    that the payment is made
C = the cost per unit if payment is made in the net period
d = the discount from the list price for early payment if
    payment is made in time to take the discount, or zero
    otherwise

The firm currently places orders for Q units and incurs a cash flow of $QC(1 - d)$ on day t_p after the order. The firm has inventory holding costs of $hQ/2$ and order costs of SR/Q, both of which are paid at the end of the period. A schematic of the cash flow timeline for this inventory policy is given in Figure 17.2.

Comparison With Previous Treatment of Inventory

In our previous examination of a general timeline of cash flows (see Chapter 2) we presented a simplified treatment of inventory. We assumed that all costs were paid at a constant time tied to the day of initiation of production. The inventory level was represented as an average number of days of sales. In the framework of the order quantity we are now using, the average number of days of sales in inventory is half of the order quantity (average inventory) times the daily usage rate. Thus, our earlier treatment of inventory level as a certain number of days of sales carried an implicit assumption of the quantity and frequency of order or production of goods.

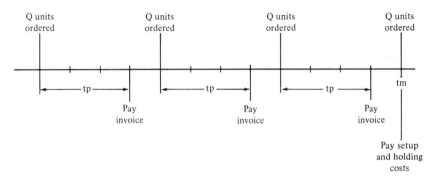

Figure 17.2 Inventory Cash Flow Timeline.

Present Value of the Present Policy

Using a simple interest formulation, the present value of the costs of managing the inventory under the present policy is

$$PV = -\frac{SR/Q + hQ/2}{1 + kt_m} - \sum_{j=0}^{(R/Q)-1} \frac{QC(1-d)}{1 + k(t_p + jt_mQ/R)}. \qquad (17.6)$$

Since all of the items are cash outflows, the present value is negative and the objective is to minimize the present value of the costs. The first term, the present value of the payments for the setup costs and the physical holding costs created at the end of the period, is straightforward. The last term, representing the present value of payments for orders, requires a little more explanation. The payment for the first order of $QC(1-d)$ occurs on day t_p. Since $j = 0$ for the first order, the cash flow is discounted for t_p days. On each day in the period, R/t_m units of product are used. Since each order contains Q units, the order lasts for Qt_m/R days. The second order arrives on day Qt_m/R and the invoice is paid on day $t_p + Qt_m/R$. The third order arrives on day $2(Qt_m/R)$, with the cash flow occurring on day $t_p + 2(Qt_m/R)$. This process continues throughout the period for the R/Q orders received during the t_m days. Thus, the present value of this entire stream of cash flows is the sum of the discounted payments.

Present Value of the Proposed Policy

In what should now be a familiar process, the present value of the proposed policy has the same formulation as the present value of the present policy, with the changed item, the order quantity, represented by primed (') variables. The present value of the new policy is

$$PV = -\frac{SR/Q' + hQ'/2}{1 + kt_m} - \sum_{j=0}^{(R/Q')-1} \frac{Q'C(1-d)}{1 + k(t_p + jt_mQ/R)}. \qquad (17.7)$$

Decision Criterion

The decision criterion is the same one used in previous chapters: adopt the proposed policy if $NPV' - NPV > 0$. Since both NPV terms are negative, if the current NPV is larger in absolute value (more negative) than the proposed NPV', the difference is greater than zero and the present value of the firm is increased by adoption of the proposed policy.

Returning to the example we used in discussing the traditional approach, assume that Boom Box, Inc., is currently placing five orders for 2,000 cases during the 90-day planning period. The production manager suggests cutting the inventory in half by placing 10 orders for 1,000 cases. Boom Box purchases the cases on terms of net 30 days and pays promptly according to terms. The payments for setup and holding costs are made once each quarter, at the end of the quarter. All other costs remain the same as in the earlier example.

Substitution of the costs and time elements in Equation (17.6) results in a present value for the current operation (order quantity of 2,000 units) of $44,716.93. The present value for the proposed inventory policy is found to be $44,595.94, from substitution in Equation (17.7). Thus, Boom Box should switch to the proposed order quantity and increase its net present value by $120.99.

Comparison of Economic Order Quantity (EOQ) and Present Value
_____ Approaches _____

Timing of Payments

Setup and Physical Holding Costs
The timing of the payments assumed under an EOQ approach can be inferred from the treatment of the opportunity costs. Since no opportunity costs are associated with the setup and the physical holding costs, the implicit assumption is that these costs are paid at the end of the time period. If they were paid earlier, there would have to be an opportunity cost associated with their payment.

Inventory Opportunity Costs
The opportunity cost for the payment of the items ordered is based on the average level of inventory held, which is the optimal order quantity divided by 2. This would be the correct treatment if the items were paid for in cash at the time of receipt of the order. As the items are removed from inventory, funds committed to the inventory are released. For items that are removed from inventory by a sale, this is a reasonable treatment. Funds may be supplied by an immediate cash inflow from a cash sale, or they may be supplied by a transfer from accounts receivable from a credit sale. While no cash flow actually occurs in the latter case, the commitment of funds now becomes a credit policy issue and is no longer an inventory issue. However, if the item is removed from inventory to be used in another phase of the production process, no transfer of funds can be considered to have occurred. The continued commitment of funds to support inventory would have to be recognized in the remaining phases of production and in any finished goods inventory storage to consider correctly the opportunity costs of holding inventory.

Purchase Credit Terms
There is an additional cash flow timing issue that is ignored in the EOQ approach: most purchases by firms are made on credit. On a credit purchase the supplier allows a deferral of the cash flow for the payment. The quantity ordered affects the timing of the cash flow payments that must be made. In

the preceding example, an order quantity of 2,000 units requires an order to be placed every 18 days. With 30-day credit terms, a payment of $4.50 per unit × 2,000 units = $9,000 is made on day 30, day 48, day 72, and so on. If the order quantity is 1,000 units, orders are placed every 9 days and a $4,500 payment is made on day 30, day 39, day 48, day 54, and so on. Effectively, the larger order quantity accelerates some of the payments by requiring a larger payment to be made earlier. In this example, every second payment is accelerated by 9 days. This additional present value cost of a larger order is captured in the present value approach but ignored in the EOQ approach.

Financing Provided

It would appear that there is a different amount of financing provided by suppliers, depending upon the quantity ordered. While this is true for the initial order, the difference disappears once a steady state situation is reached. The accounts payable builds up as additional orders are placed until the first payment occurs. After this point, a steady state situation is reached and the average level of accounts payable is the same regardless of the order quantity.[3]

Just-in-Time Inventory

A recent development in inventory policy is *just-in-time* inventory. While referred to by several different names, such as *zero inventory, continuous flow manufacturing,* or *materials as needed*, the philosophy is that materials should arrive exactly at the time needed for production. With an efficient production process and the arrival of materials as needed, a firm can reduce to a minimum, perhaps close to zero, the amount of raw materials and work-in-process inventory.

Setup Costs

One of the key elements in the traditional approach to inventory is the existence of fixed setup costs. These setup costs have to be balanced against the costs of holding inventory. It is the existence of these large setup costs that lead to the belief that it is optimal to have a substantial amount of inventory on hand. One of the keys to a just-in-time inventory approach is that setup costs are not fixed. Rather, the aim is to reduce or eliminate setup costs by streamlining the production/ordering process so that these costs are negligible.

---

[3] Depending upon the exact timing of the order placement and the payment, accounts payable will not remain at a steady level but will rise and fall with the orders and the payments. The maximum and minimum levels of accounts payable will vary with the size of each order. However, the average level of accounts payable will be the same regardless of the order quantity.

It can easily be seen that either the traditional or the present value approach to inventory results in very frequent, small orders if setup costs are negligible.

One of the major factors in setup costs for production is the time it takes to change operations. By reducing setup time and costs, smaller production runs, requiring less inventory, become economical. For example, Harley-Davidson has cut the setup time on some operations from 3 days to 4 hours. This has allowed reduction of work-in-process inventory by as much as 70%.[4]

Planning Requirements

A just-in-time approach to inventory requires a coordinated plan for the entire operation of the firm. Essentially, by reducing the use of inventory, the sales, production, and ordering functions of the firm are recoupled. Successful operation with a just-in-time approach requires coordinated planning ranging from purchasing all the way to selling. Moreover, if the firm expects suppliers to be able to supply materials as needed, this planning has to be made available to the suppliers with sufficient lead time, and with minimal changes, to allow them to respond adequately.

The use of inventories, particularly safety stock inventories, allows a firm to hide problems like machine breakdowns or errors in material ordering. The use of a just-in-time approach exposes the problems and forces the development of contingency plans for solution in an integrated environment. The problems can be thought of as rocks in a lake on which one is sailing a boat. The safety stock inventory approach is to raise the water level in the lake so that the rocks are not seen. The just-in-time approach is to chart carefully the location of the rocks and sail around them while keeping the water level at a minimum.

Supplier Relations

Good relations with suppliers is critical in operating with minimal inventories. Suppliers are responsible for more frequent, albeit smaller, deliveries. For example, General Motors was able to cut its inventory of metal stampings sixfold by specifying delivery by truck three times per day instead of by rail every other day. Although close proximity of suppliers is helpful in providing these more frequent deliveries, it is not essential. A Mitsubishi plant in Hiroshima receives daily deliveries from a carburetor supplier located 600 miles away.

Not only do the suppliers have to know the delivery schedule expected of them, the purchaser must have the ability to determine the status of any shipment, regardless of where it is in the pipeline. Instantaneous communication is essential in determining the status of the shipment. A key element in this communications link is the use of electronic data interchange, which is discussed in Chapter 20.

---

[4] Ernest Raia, "Just-in-Time USA," *Purchasing* (February 13, 1986), p. 52.

If materials being delivered are immediately put into production, the manufacturer cannot afford to have quality problems with the materials. Strict adherence to specific quality standards is required of all suppliers.

Suppliers and Cost Tradeoffs

The need for better relations and communications with suppliers generally leads to a reduction in the number of suppliers for firms operating with a just-in-time approach to inventory. Since the supplier that can meet the required delivery schedule with the quality product required may not be the lowest-cost supplier, there is a tradeoff between a reduction in inventory costs and an increase in materials costs. This tradeoff can easily be handled by the use of the present value framework. The reduction in setup costs and inventory holding costs, both physical and opportunity costs of funds, must be traded off against potential increased materials costs because of increased requirements for suppliers, with consideration of both the timing and the amount of the cash flows.

Summary

Inventories are used to decouple sequential ordering, production, and sales activities. A traditional approach used to determine the optimal level of inventory involves a tradeoff between setup costs and holding costs. This approach to inventory policy decisions assumes that the setup costs are fixed. A just-in-time approach to inventory operates on the assumption that setup costs are not fixed but can be changed. By reducing setup costs and increasing planning and coordination, inventory is reduced to a minimum. A cash flow present value framework can be used to analyze inventory policy decisions under either the traditional assumptions or a just-in-time approach to inventory.

Discussion Questions

1. Identify the different role played by raw materials, work-in-process, and finished goods inventory.
2. What are the factors that affect the different kinds of inventory listed in Question 1 for an automobile manufacturer? For a retail store?
3. What elements are included in setup costs for inventory for a manufacturer of plastic toys? For a bakery? For a retail appliance store?
4. What factors affect the holding costs for a finished goods inventory?

5. Contrast the differences in inventory holding costs for a retail jewelry store and a fast food restaurant.
6. What assumptions are necessary in using the basic EOQ model?
7. Contrast the differences in orientation of the EOQ and net present value approaches to inventory control.
8. How would the net present value approach have to be modified if all of the materials ordered during a time period were accumulated and invoiced at the end of the period?
9. How would a reduction in setup costs affect the net present value of an inventory policy?
10. Contrast the role that inventory plays in a traditional EOQ approach and a just-in-time approach.
11. How do supplier arrangements have to be established to make a just-in-time approach feasible?
12. Does a just-in-time approach to inventory accomplish anything other than forcing the supplier to carry your raw materials inventory?

--- **Problems** ---

1. The stores manager for Enormous State University estimates that it costs $12 to place an order for computer paper. The faculty and students use the paper at a rate of 20,000 boxes per month. Storage and handling cost about $1.50 per box per month. If the paper costs $2.50 per box, what is the optimal quantity for the stores manager to order?
2. Play-Tyme Toys is a manufacturer of plastic toys. The production manager is scheduling the length of a production run for their 911T model car. It is necessary to change the molds on the machinery for each model that is run. The production manager estimates that it will take 2 hours to change the mold and about 30 minutes for the operator to become efficient in handling the new setup. The operator earns $18 per hour (including fringe benefits). Inventory storage costs are estimated to be $0.1 per unit per month. The direct manufacturing costs (material and labor) are $0.75 per unit. The opportunity cost for Play-Tyme is 12% per year, and the demand for the 911T model is 10,000 per month. If the cars are produced at a rate of 200 per hour, how long is the optimal production run for the model 911T?
3. The plant engineer has come up with a modified procedure for the setup in Problem 2 that will cut the setup time to 30 minutes. How will this affect the optimal production run?
4. What will be the average amount of finished goods inventory that Play-Tyme will have for the two different production runs in Problems 2 and 3?
5. The production manager for Micro Motors is considering a suggestion that they reduce the size of their orders for engine blocks by 20%. The current

procedure is to order 250 at a time. Because of the order approval process of the company, it is estimated to cost $50 per order, and bills are payable at the end of the month. Inventory handling costs are estimated to be $5 per average unit in inventory during a month. Engine blocks cost $50 each and are purchased on terms of net 30. If the production rate for engines requires 750 engine blocks per month and the opportunity costs are 12% per year, what action should the production manager take?

6. The purchasing manager for Bon Marche Food Stores orders frozen turkeys in lots of 500. The turkeys average 15 pounds each and cost $0.49 per pound. Frozen storage costs average about $0.02 a pound per month. The costs to place an order are estimated to be $25, and the opportunity cost is 12%. The supplier has offered a price break of a penny a pound if Bon Marche will order in lots of 1,000. If the monthly demand for turkeys averages 2,000 for the chain, should the purchasing manager continue to order in 500-unit lots or increase the order to 1,000-unit lots? (Assume that the inventory and order costs are paid once a month and that the turkeys are purchased on terms of net 10 days.)

Case: *Hog Motors*

Mr. S. Marner, the chief operating officer of Hog Motors, is reviewing a proposal submitted by Ms. Karen Buffa, the purchasing manager, to change the company's practice for ordering wheels. In addition to the report from Buffa, Marner has a memo from Mr. L. Davidson, the production manager, suggesting that rather than change the entire system, the current procedure should be fine tuned. Marner is vice chairman of the executive committee. Since the president, who is chairman of the executive committee, is on an extended trip through the Far East, Marner knows that this will be his decision.

Hog Motors is a manufacturer of large motorcycles. The company's most successful models are the Big H, a 900 cubic centimeter cycle, and the Super Hawk, a 1,000 cubic centimeter cycle. Both models use the same wheels, so the proposal from the purchasing manager would affect both lines. Hog Motors purchases many parts made to their specifications and assembles the motorcycles. The procedure for the wheels is typical for purchased parts. The specifications for the wheels were drawn up and the company requested bids from potential suppliers. Three suppliers came up with the identical bid of $27.50 per wheel. Hog currently uses all three of these suppliers and purchases approximately the same amount from each. It is felt that this puts Hog in a good position for two reasons: (1) they receive the lowest price on components and (2) the continuing competition assures the suppliers' attention to the contract.

A total of 60,000 wheels per month are required for the current production schedule. Because of uncertainty in delivery schedules, Hog carries an inventory safety stock of 5,000 wheels. Hog currently purchases in lots of 10,000 and carries an average inventory of 10,000 wheels. The wheels are purchased on terms of net 30 days, with a separate invoice for each order. It is estimated that the cost to process and place an order under the current system is $75, and handling and storage costs are about $1 per wheel per month.

The purchasing manager's proposal is to negotiate with the suppliers and use only one supplier. She feels that if only one supplier is used, a better delivery schedule can be demanded because the supplier would make some concessions to obtain the larger contract. The program as envisioned by the purchasing manager is that the supplier will make daily shipments of the number of wheels needed for the next day's production so that they will arrive at the plant at the start of the day. Hog will not have to carry any safety stock and can essentially operate with zero inventory. However, Hog will have to commit itself to a production schedule 1 month in advance, so that the supplier knows the exact number of wheels to ship each day. There will be no individual orders, since the supplier will ship against the contract according to the production schedule. The supplier will bill for the shipments three times a month, and credit terms will be net 10 days. It is estimated to cost about $1,400 per month to communicate with the supplier on the production schedule and to monitor shipments from the supplier.

Davidson, the production manager, has raised the following objections to the proposed program. First, the safety stock is needed because of variation in the production schedule, not just because of delivery problems. Second, with the tight delivery schedule, if a truck breaks down, the production line will have to be shut down until the wheels arrive. Third, there have been quality problems with some of the suppliers, and the safety stock allows the flexibility of putting defective materials aside without disrupting the production process. Fourth, after a year or two with the same supplier, Hog will not know if it is getting the best price on the materials. Fifth, the time and energy could be better spent reviewing the optimal order quantity instead of trying to revise the entire purchasing/inventory system.

Marner thought that Buffa's proposal made sense. It seemed to be the type of ordering process that some of the automobile manufacturers were adopting. However, he felt that the objections of the production manager also had validity. He knew that the financial aspects would be a critical factor that the president would review in deciding whether he had made the right decision. Thus, he felt that he would need to incorporate the cost of capital for Hog, which is currently estimated to be 10%, into the decision. He also knew that he would have to incorporate a response to the qualitative issues raised by Davidson.

(Note: For your analysis, assume that Hog operates 30 days a month, all period payments—such as order costs—are made at the end of the month, and production is forecasted to be level throughout the month.)

Selected Readings

ARVAN, L., and L. N. MOSES, "Inventory Management and the Theory of the Firm," *American Economic Review* (March 1982), pp. 186–193.

BERANEK, W., "Financial Implications of Lot-Size Inventory Models," *Management Science* (April 1967), pp. 401–408.

BROOKS, L. D., "Risk–Return Criteria and Optimal Inventory Stocks," *Engineering Economist* (Summer 1980), pp. 275–299.

HALEY, C. W., and R. C. HIGGINS, "Inventory Control Theory and Trade Credit Financing," *Management Science* (December 1973), pp. 464–471.

HALL, ROBERT, *Zero Inventories,* Homewood, IL: Dow-Jones Irwin, 1983.

RAIA, ERNEST, "Just-in-Time USA," *Purchasing* (February 13, 1986), pp. 48–62.

SHONBERGER, RICHARD, *Japanese Manufacturing Techniques,* New York: Free Press, 1982.

TRIPPI, R. R., and D. E. LEWIN, "A Present Value Formulation of the Classical EOQ Problem," *Decision Sciences* (January 1974), pp. 30–35.

18

Forecasting Cash Flows

A large convenience store chain with outlets across the United States found that it was tying up millions of dollars in cash in field deposit banks. Although the cash concentration system was a modern, DTC-based one, the cash manager was never able to draw the balances down below about 2 days' worth of deposits in each bank—equivalent to $7,000,000 to $10,000,000 over the whole banking system. Then the cash management staff developed a daily cash forecasting system. It was a relatively simple system based on only a few weeks of historical data adjusted for seasonal sales trends and local conditions. Using the forecast model, the cash manager was able to pull $5,000,000 to $6,000,000 out of the system without harming the firm's banking relationships. The technique used the forecast model to initiate a transfer of expected next-day deposits rather than to wait for the next day to begin the transfer process. The value of excess balances freed up was far greater than the costs of the forecasting system. In addition, top management now had more information about anticipated cash flows, permitting tighter control over field deposits.

This chapter highlights design issues relating to forecasting short-term cash flows. We consider both medium-term monthly and quarterly forecasts and daily cash forecasts. We first discuss the benefits and costs of forecasting and then introduce some of the techniques used in cash forecasting systems.

The Need to Focus on Cash

In this chapter we focus forecasting efforts on cash flow. Because of the availability of accounting data, managers are sometimes tempted to focus on earnings. Unfortunately, earnings are not very useful numbers for management. Earnings represent an important accounting concept that attempts to match revenues with the expenses that generated them. The matching concept requires that cash outflows be stored up (in inventory or other assets) until a matching revenue occurs, at which time an expense is realized. Revenues, in turn, are often recognized on accounting statements before a cash inflow actually occurs (as in credit sales, which result in accounts receivable). The result of following generally accepted accounting principles is a number called *earnings*. Earnings cannot be spent. They cannot be paid out in dividends. They cannot be invested. The only thing management can do with earnings is report them!

To obtain cash flows from earnings, we must unravel all of the effects of accrual accounting. Alternatively, we must start with cash flows in the first place and avoid the confusing effects of accounting. We use both approaches in this chapter.

Cash Forecasting Horizons

Cash forecasting may be divided into roughly three subproblems, depending on the horizon the forecaster wishes to consider. Different techniques and purposes are associated with each horizon.

Long-range Forecasts

Cash forecasts of 1 or more years into the future are needed primarily to assess the viability of the firm's long-range financing and operating policies. Long-range forecasts give planners an idea of how much cash the firm needs to raise through debt or equity issues, internally generated cash, or other cash sources. These forecasts also assist managers in establishing dividend policies, determining capital investments, and planning a mergers and acquisitions (or divestitures) program. It is typical for a firm to have a 5- or 10-year forecast that is updated annually.

Long-range forecasts are generally based on accounting projections and typically involve the generation of various scenarios for future economic and technological environments. Such forecasts are considered strategic in the sense that possible major changes are examined. Because of our short-term focus in this book, we will leave long-term forecasting to other texts.

Medium-range Forecasts

We consider medium-range forecasts as those that cover cash flows during the next 12 months. A firm may have, for example, a forecast of quarterly cash flows over the next four quarters with monthly detail over the next 3 months. Medium-range cash forecasting usually takes the firm's existing technology and long-range financing as given. Hence, this kind of forecast is considered tactical rather than strategic. Although it is accounting based, adjustments are made to focus on cash flows rather than earnings. It is sometimes called *cash budgeting*.

The purpose of medium-range forecasting is to determine the firm's need for short-term cash from credit lines, commercial paper sales, or credit and payables policies. It also helps firms to determine the makeup of their short-term investment portfolio. When a firm performs the task called *budgeting*, it generally designates the most likely (or most desirable) scenario of the medium-range forecasts as the *budget*. The budget is used to compare actual performance during the course of the year.

Daily Cash Forecasts

Daily cash forecasts attempt to project cash inflows and outflows on a daily basis one or more days into the future. This is perhaps the most difficult forecasting to perform accurately. While a firm may know precisely its revenues for the month, it may have difficulty determining specific cash inflows for given days of the month. For some firms, a daily forecast several months into the future is possible. For most, however, a forecast even 2 days into the future is difficult.

The purposes of daily forecasting are to assist management in scheduling transfers in cash concentration, funding disbursement accounts, controlling field deposits, and making short-term investing and borrowing decisions.

Objectives of Cash Forecasting

As with other short-term financial systems we discuss in this book, it is helpful to outline an objective function for cash forecasting. Such an objective function might include the following factors:

1. *Interest costs and income.* One major purpose of forecasting is to increase the firm's yield on its investment portfolio or, depending on the firm's financial position, to decrease interest costs on its borrowing. Lack of an accurate forecast may force management to either invest in very short-term securities (thereby often earning the lowest yields) or borrow unexpectedly at higher than usual interest rates.
2. *Excess balances.* This may be considered a corollary to the first factor. Accurate daily cash forecasts enable management to reduce balances in disbursement and/or deposit accounts and thereby move otherwise non-interest-earning cash into other areas of the firm.
3. *Administrative costs/benefits.* Forecasting may require extensive administrative efforts to collect and digest data. On the other hand, forecasting may provide administrative benefits in the form of better planning and more timely management reports.
4. *Control.* Daily cash budgets often provide a standard against which deposit reports from the field can be compared. If actual deposits vary from projected deposits, inquiries may be warranted.

5. *Forecast system costs.* These costs are associated directly with developing, maintaining, and running the forecasting model and associated data bases. Some forecast systems require extensive computer time and information. Others are simple and inexpensive.

Designing forecasting systems requires that management make tradeoffs among these five cost factors. For example, an extensive, accurate forecasting system may be costly to build and maintain and may require strong administrative effort. But such a system may enable the firm to achieve better returns on its short-term investments, reduce borrowing costs, and exert better control over cash flows. To determine whether such a system is worth the cost, a detailed study would be conducted to quantify the five factors.

We next discuss medium-range cash forecasting, which involves primarily a projection of accounting statements. We then introduce daily cash forecasting methods requiring more refined information sources. In the final section, we survey quantitative forecasting tools.

Medium-range Cash Forecasting

In medium-range cash forecasting, the focus is usually on monthly net cash flows for the entire firm or a subunit of the firm over the next quarter or year. Such cash forecasting almost always starts with a projection of accounting statements. For most purposes, it is sufficient to begin with accounting statements and make adjustments to correct for the effects of accrual accounting. Figure 18.1 outlines the steps followed in medium-range forecasting based on accounting statements.

The process begins with a forecast of the driving (or independent) variable. For most firms, the driving variable is sales. From the sales forecast, the values

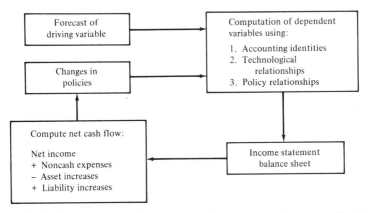

Figure 18.1 Medium-range Cash Forecasting: Income Statement Approach.

of other accounting variables are computed to produce a *pro forma* income statement and balance sheet. Net cash flow is determined from these two statements by adjusting for noncash expenses and by treating asset increases as cash outflows and liability increases as cash inflows. We now discuss this process in more detail.

Driving Variable

Projecting accounting statements usually begins with a forecast of a *driving variable*, a factor upon which most other accounting numbers are based. In most cases, the driving variable is sales. When the sales number for a particular month is determined, management can get some idea of the cost of goods sold, inventory levels required, accounts receivable generated, payables needed to support the cost of goods sold, and so on. In this sense, sales estimates drive most of the other variables—at least the short-term or working capital variables in the upper half of the balance sheet.

For some firms, other variables may be the driving variable. Some retail stores may be driven by the availability of a product. Consumer product firms are driven by the advertising budget. Other firms may be driven by some other constrained resource.

Once the driving variable has been determined, its value is estimated for each month or other time increment over the forecast horizon. Frequently the estimate is based on input from sales managers in the field. Sometimes contracts determine the driving variable. At other times, it may be appropriate to use one of the quantitative approaches discussed in the last section of this chapter.

Computation of Dependent Variables

From the values of the driving variable, other dependent variables may be computed. There are at least three relationships between the driving variable and dependent variables.

1. *Accounting identity.* By *accounting identity*, we mean an accounting rule. For example, the dependent variable "gross profit" is computed by simply subtracting the cost of goods sold from revenues. No other complex techniques are needed to compute the gross profit once sales and the cost of goods sold are estimated.
2. *Technological relationships.* Some dependent variables are related to the driving variable because of a technological or business connection between the two. For example, given a certain credit policy, accounts receivable will always be determined by the pattern of credit sales over the past few months (see Chapter 15 for a discussion). As another example, suppose a certain sales level implies a specific level of borrowing against the firm's credit line. The interest expense on the income statement is technologically related to the level of the loan. Given a certain level of property, plant, and

equipment, depreciation is defined by Internal Revenue Service guidelines and accounting practices.

3. *Policy relationships.* Some dependent variables are related to sales via management policy. For example, a firm may have a policy to keep a certain number of days' inventory to support sales. A firm may also keep cash balances at a certain percentage of sales. Management generally also sets debt/equity ratios as a matter of policy.

Example of Medium-term Cash Forecasting

We illustrate the procedures for medium-term cash forecasting by constructing a simple cash forecast for the Hillmont Corporation. The income statement and balance sheet for Hillmont are given in Table 18.1. Suppose that because

Table 18.1 Sample of an Accounting-Based Medium-term Cash Forecast for the Hillmont Corporation

A. Income Statement (Year Ending 12/31/x8)

	(millions)
Sales	$28.00
Cost of goods sold	18.00
Gross profit	10.00
Depreciation	1.00
Other fixed costs	4.00
Earnings before taxes	5.00
Taxes (40%)	2.00
Net income after taxes	$ 3.00

B. Balance Sheet (Year Ending 12/31/x8)

Assets

Cash and mkt. securities	$ 3.00
Accounts receivable	5.00
Inventory	7.00
Property, plant, equip. (net of depreciation)	20.00
Total assets	$35.00

Liabilities and Equity

Accounts payable	$ 4.00
Long-term debt	2.00
Paid-in capital	20.00
Retained earnings	9.00
Total liabilities and equity	$35.00

of a revolutionary new product, sales are expected to increase by 50% during the next year. Management needs to determine how much cash will be needed (or generated) if this expectation is realized.[1]

New equipment costing $3,000,000 will be needed to handle increased production. Dividends totaling $2,000,000 will be paid next year. No new long-term debt is planned and $1.00 million of the old debt will be retired under a sinking fund arrangement in place for many years. According to management policy, cash and marketable securities are to be raised to $6.00 million. Depreciation, the accounting staff tells us, is to increase with the new equipment to $2.00 million. An estimate of fixed costs (primarily administrative overhead and sales support) shows that this category should increase to $8.00 million. Taxes will remain at the 40% level.

The driving variable has, for this case, been given to us: $1.5 \times 28 = 42$. It may have been obtained by sales estimates from district sales managers, or by marketing surveys, or by some other technique. The next step is to determine all of the other accounting numbers needed to define the income statement and balance sheet.

Variables Functionally Related to Sales

Some variables are usually closely related to sales levels. The simplest form of this functionality is proportionality. In this example, we assume that the cost of goods sold remains in the same proportion to sales that it has in the past. We assume the same for accounts receivable, inventory, and accounts payable. We may compute values for these variables based on last year's ratio to sales. If more data from previous years are available, it is better to examine how the ratios to sales have changed over time. Sometimes this approach is called the *percent sales approach* of forecasting. While we use this approach for illustration, it should be noted that rarely are variables in strict proportion to sales. The dependency on sales is sometimes more complex. We saw that for accounts receivable (Chapter 15), a payments pattern approach is much more accurate than a simple ratio to sales. Nevertheless, for this example, we use simple proportionality.

Forecasted value of variable (next year)
$$= \text{past ratio to sales} \times \text{forecasted sales level (next year)}.$$

$$\text{Cost of goods sold} = \frac{18.00}{28.00} \times 42.00 = 27.00.$$

[1] Note on spreadsheets: In accounting-based forecasting, it is very useful to use a spreadsheet software program. See the appendix at the end of this chapter for a discussion of spreadsheets. Such programs permit the user to define how variables are related to each other and to generate a series of variables (such as sales levels 12 months out). Spreadsheets also allow the user to modify easily one or more variables and observe the impact of this modification on all other variables. Several of the problems at the end of this chapter can be structured in a spreadsheet format.

$$\text{Accounts receivable} = \frac{5.00}{28.00} \times 42.00 = 7.50.$$

$$\text{Inventory} = \frac{7.00}{28.00} \times 42.00 = 10.50.$$

$$\text{Accounts payable} = \frac{4.00}{28.00} \times 42.00 = 6.00.$$

Relating Variables to Timing

For some variables it is convenient to associate a timing element. In the Hillmont case, accounts receivable can be associated with a *days sales outstanding (DSO)* number. This is found by dividing the value of the variable by sales per day:

$$\text{Time} = \frac{\text{value of asset}}{\text{annual sales}/365}.$$

$$\text{Days sales outstanding} = \frac{A/R}{\text{sales }/365} = \frac{5.00}{28.00/365} = 65 \text{ days.}$$

This number gives an idea of the firm's credit terms (and customers' payment practices). For Hillmont, this number implies that customers are taking, on average, 65 days to pay. If Hillmont changed its collection policies, this number might be reduced. By rearranging the equation, the value of accounts receivable may be computed for different DSO levels. For example, if Hillmont had employed more energetic collection efforts in the past year and had reduced its DSO to 45 days, its receivables would have been

$$\text{Accounts receivable} = (28.00/365) \times 45 \text{ days} = \$3.45.$$

Similarly, accounts payable may be associated with a days payable outstanding. Instead of using sales in the denominator, the cost of goods sold is used (or other measure of total purchases).

$$\text{Days payables outstanding} = \frac{A/P}{CGS/365} = \frac{4.00}{18.00/365} = 81 \text{ days.}$$

It appears that Hillmont is paying its bills rather slowly (assuming that most bills are payable in 30 days). Since this is a policy variable, Hillmont has this variable much more under its control than some of the other variables.

Computing Policy Variables

Some of the variables are given explicitly. Cash and marketable securities were said to increase to $6.00. Other variables, like dividends, are also a matter of policy. Suppose Hillmont were to change its payables policies to bring them more in line with customary payment terms of net 30 days. A change in policy would imply the following pro forma level for next year:

$$\text{Accounts payable} = \frac{27.00}{365} \times 30 \text{ days} = \$2.22 \text{ million.}$$

We use this figure in our projections, rather than the $12.00 million computed earlier based on the percent of sales method.

Accounting Identities

Several of the accounting variables that constitute our pro forma statements come from accounting identities or definitions. Profit after tax is just profit before tax minus taxes. Net property, plant, and equipment (PPE) (next year) is net property, plant, and equipment this year plus new assets minus depreciation. Retained earnings is defined as follows:

Retained earnings (next year) = retained earnings (this year)
+ profit after taxes (next year) − dividends paid (next year).

Table 18.2 shows how each variable is projected for next year, with a brief explanation of how each was computed.

Three Approaches to Net Cash Flows

There are three closely related approaches that use pro forma financial statements to determine net cash flow to the firm. The first approach uses the balancing variable (or plug figure) from the balance sheet forecast. The second starts with earnings and makes adjustments to find the cash flow figure. The third examines inflows and outflows directly to arrive at net cash flows. All three are actually just different arrangements of the same accounting data. If applied correctly, all three yield the same answer.

Approach 1: Cash Flows from the Balancing Variable in Pro Forma Balance Sheets

Note in Table 18.2 that total assets and total liabilities and equity do not match. Total liabilities and equity for next year are $11.78 million short of the total asset number. Of course, this imbalance is strictly against the rules of double entry accounting. Assets must match liabilities and equity. To balance the two, we must add $11.78 million to the liability side of the balance sheet. This figure is sometimes called the *balancing variable* or *plug*. This tells us that the firm must have additional financing of $11.78 million by the end of next year. Either this amount must come from new liabilities (short-term debt, long-term debt, sale of new stock, etc.) or variables on the asset side of the balance sheet must be reduced (faster collections to shrink receivables, lower cash and marketable securities, smaller inventories, etc.). With the assumptions we have made, the firm would experience an $11.78 million shortfall in cash.

Approach 2: Net Cash Flows from Earnings

Sometimes managers like to compute cash flows by making adjustments to earnings numbers. This turns out to be exactly equivalent to the approach

Table 18.2 Sample of an Accounting-Based Medium-term Cash Forecast for the Hillmont Corporation

Pro Forma Statements

A. Income Statement (Millions)

	(19x8)	**(19x9)**	
Sales	$28.00	$42.00	(given)
Cost of goods sold	18.00	27.00	(% sales)
Gross profit	10.00	15.00	(def.)
Depreciation	1.00	2.00	(given)
Other fixed costs	4.00	8.00	(given)
Earnings before taxes	5.00	5.00	(def.)
Taxes (40%)	2.00	2.00	(given)
Net income after taxes	$ 3.00	$ 3.00	(def.)

B. Balance Sheet (Millions)

Assets	**(19x8)**	**(19x9)**	
Cash and mkt. securities	$ 3.00	$ 6.00	(policy)
Accounts receivable	5.00	7.50	(% sales)
Inventory	7.00	10.50	(% sales)
Property, plant, equip.			
(net of depreciation)	20.00	21.00	(def./given)
Total assets	$35.00	$45.00	(def.)
Liabilities and Equity			
Accounts payable	$ 4.00	$ 2.22	(timing)
Long-term debt	2.00	1.00	(given)
Paid-in capital	20.00	20.00	(given)
Retained earnings	9.00	10.00	(def)
Total liabilities and equity	$35.00	$33.22	(def.)
Needed Financing		$11.78	(plug)

Notes: PPE $= 20.00 - 2.00$ (deprec.) $+ 3.00$ (new) $= 21.00$.
Accounts payable $= (27.00/365) \times 30$ days $= 2.22$
Retained earnings $= 9.00 + 3.00$ (profit) $- 2.00$ (div) $= 10.00$

we have just used. Since so many people use this method, we illustrate the earnings approach, too. In both cases, it is necessary to compute a pro forma balance sheet and income statement.

EARNINGS ADJUSTED BY DEPRECIATION. This approach starts with earnings and makes adjustments for noncash expenses like depreciation:

$$\text{"Cash flow"} = \text{earnings} + \text{noncash expenses}$$
$$= 3.00 + 2.00 = 5.00 \text{ million.}$$

Depreciation, of course, is not really a cash flow at all. By adding it back to earnings, we are simply correcting for subtracting a noncash flow in the first place. If the firm could somehow discover more depreciation somewhere, it would not have greater cash flows because it would have subtracted a greater amount from revenues. (Depreciation does, however, result in a lower tax burden, so it does indirectly have a cash flow consequence.)

In the preceding equation, we have put this cash flow in quotation marks because it is not the actual cash flow of the firm. Many more adjustments must be made to this number. It is curious that so many financial publications refer to earnings plus depreciation as cash flow. Only under a special condition does this number represent the firm's true cash flow—namely, the condition that no other accounts change from one period to the next.

ADJUSTING FOR BALANCE SHEET CHANGES. The preceding number must be adjusted for changes in the balance sheet. Increases in balance sheet assets are like cash outflows. Cash has been paid out for such assets, but they have not yet been expensed in the income statement. Likewise, asset decreases are like cash inflows. Care must be taken when dealing with changes in the net property plant and equipment account. The effects of depreciation were already included when we added it to net income. So the change to consider when making balance sheet changes is the change in total (not net) property, plant, and equipment.

Increases in liabilities represent cash inflows. To see why this is so, consider accounts payable. The firm has purchased something from other parties and may have counted part or all of the purchase in its expenses for the period. Yet cash has not yet been paid out for the amount represented by accounts payable. Similarly, an increase in debt or paid-in capital provides cash to the firm without producing revenue. When liabilities decrease, that is equivalent to a cash outflow.

Do *not* include the change in retained earnings as part of the adjustment. This has already been included by starting the process with the net income number. Do, however, include dividend payments in cash outflows.

For the Hillmont firm, we compute the net cash flow by adding depreciation to profit after taxes and then adjust for balance sheet changes, as shown in Table 18.3.

The net cash flow to Hillmont for the year is an outflow of $11.78 million. Note that this is precisely the plug figure we obtained by computing the pro forma balance sheet. The methods are entirely equivalent, since they both come from the same accounting relationships. Both computations inform management that the firm will require $11.78 million by the end of the next year.

Approach 3: Cash Flows from Inflows and Outflows

A third way to represent the same relationships is to compute net cash flows as the difference between cash inflows and cash outflows. Some consider this to be the most straightforward approach, since each category of cash flow is

Table 18.3 Projecting Cash Flow by the Adjusted Net Income Method for the Hillmont Corporation

Pro Forma Cash Flows (Millions) For the Year Ending 19x9			
Net income	=	$3.00	
Add depreciation	=	2.00	
"Cash flow"	=		5.00
Changes in Assets			
Cash and mkt. sec.	=	3.00	
Accounts receivable	=	2.50	
Inventory	=	3.50	
New PPE	=	3.00	
Subtract incr. in assets			12.00
Changes in Liabilities			
Accounts payable	=	−1.78	
Long-term debt	=	−1.00	
Paid-in capital	=	0.00	
Add incr. in liabilities			−2.78
Other flows (not in income stmt. or balance sheet)			
Dividends paid	=	2.00	
Subtract other net outflows			2.00
Total Cash Flow			−$11.78

examined by itself. As in the second approach, we require a forecast of the balance sheet and income statement. This method begins with sales as the first cash inflow. Do not subtract or add back depreciation, since it is not a cash flow. All other cash flows are then listed, including balance sheet changes that have the effect of cash inflows or outflows. This approach is illustrated for the Hillmont Corporation in Table 18.4. As with the other two approaches, the result is the same—a cash outflow of $11.78 million.

_____ Short-term Cash Forecasting _____

We now discuss the problems of forecasting cash in the very short term—on a daily basis. Since accountants generally use accrual methods over months or quarters, we are unable to use accounting information for daily cash flows to any great extent. A more severe problem is that accounting information is generally not focused on the level of detail that would permit daily cash forecasts.

Table 18.4 Net Cash Flows from
Projections of Cash Inflows and Cash
Outflows for the Hillmont Corporation

Pro Forma Cash Flows
For the Year Ending 19x9

Cash Inflows

Sales	$42.00	
Incr. in A/P	−1.78	
Total cash inflows		$40.22

Cash Outflows

Cost of goods sold	$27.00	
Other fixed costs	8.00	
Taxes	2.00	
Dividends	2.00	
(Balance sheet changes)		
Incr. in cash and M/S	3.00	
Incr. in A/R	2.50	
Incr. in inventory	3.50	
New PPE	3.00	
Decr. in debt	1.00	
Total cash outflows		$52.00
Net Cash Flow		−$11.78

Benefits of Daily Cash Forecasting

There are several ways in which daily cash forecasting can influence cost factors in the objective function. To appreciate these cost factors, consider the practices of firms that do not or cannot project cash on a daily basis. Such firms must invest a significant portion of their short-term portfolio in overnight investments. The typical scenario is as follows:

1. Each morning the firm receives deposit and disbursement reports from its balance reporting service.
2. Deposits are netted against disbursements and transfers are made to and from various bank accounts, using the concentration bank as the central cash pool.
3. If there is an excess in the concentration bank, the amount is invested in overnight repurchase agreements or other overnight securities.
4. If there is an excess, securities in the short-term portfolio are sold. Alternatively, the firm can draw on its credit lines or sell commercial paper to cover the shortfall.

The problem with investing primarily in overnight securities is that the rate of return is low relative to that of longer-term investments. Such investing practices also result in excessive transaction costs when securities have to be sold before maturity. Administrative costs may also be high because of the daily management attention required by such a policy.

For disbursement account funding, the inability to forecast clearings accurately may result in excess balances unless the account is a controlled disbursement (zero balance) account. As mentioned in Chapter 8, banks satisfying controlled disbursing criteria may become increasingly difficult to find. Accurate daily cash forecasting reduces the need for early morning presentments. The firm can transfer cash into the disbursement account on the basis of forecasted disbursements rather than on the basis of a balance report.

Steps in Making Daily Cash Forecasts

Forecasting cash on a daily basis requires the following steps.

Determine the Precise Cash Flow Component to Be Predicted

SEPARATE MAJOR AND NONMAJOR CASH FLOWS. It is helpful to separate major cash flows from all other cash flows. By *major cash flows*, we mean easily forecastable, relatively large cash flows such as tax payments, dividend payments, bond interest, payroll, contract lease payments, construction progress payments, and so on. These cash flows are usually known in advance, so it is not necessary to predict them using any of the quantitative techniques we will discuss later. Nevertheless, it may be necessary to predict the timing associated even with a known cash flow. For example, we may know 2 weeks in advance that the biweekly payroll will be $1,000,000. Checks will be mailed on a Thursday. The total amount is known with certainty, but the amount clearing each day is unknown.

SEPARATE NONMAJOR CASH FLOWS INTO SUBCOMPONENTS. It is also useful to break down nonmajor cash flows into subcomponents. For example, receipts from retail customers should be separated from receipts from wholesale customers. Similarly, payments to large companies may be separated from payments to smaller companies. The objective is to produce a statistically "pure" group of cash flows that all behave in roughly the same way. Separation is particularly important when using statistical modeling techniques. Statistical methods work best on homogeneous data.

FORECAST NET CASH FLOW FROM INFLOWS AND OUTFLOWS. Similarly, when attempting to forecast net cash flow, it is usually more accurate to forecast inflows and outflows separately. This should be done especially when statistical models are used, since inflows and outflows usually have very different statistical properties.

Select the Input Data

The next step is to select the information or data items that will be used to prepare the forecast. This is where forecasting may be more of an art than a science. There are often a number of possible places to look for information that will be useful in forecasting the desired variable. To illustrate, assume that we want to forecast cash outflows at a firm's disbursement account from which vendors are paid.

EVENTS LEADING TO CASH FLOWS. In order to select possible information sources on which a forecast may be based, it is helpful to step through the events that lead up to the cash outflow. Figure 18.2 illustrates the timeline of events. First, the operations area of the firm determines the need to purchase materials to satisfy a production plan. Second, an order is placed with a particular vendor. Third, goods are received at the warehouse and an invoice is received by accounts payable. Fourth, a check is prepared and mailed on a date consistent with the firm's payables policies and the vendor's payment terms. Fifth, the check is processed by the vendor and cleared back to the disbursement account.

ALTERNATIVE SOURCES OF INPUT DATA. There are, therefore, several possible sources of information to call upon. First, production plans could be the basis for our forecast. This source is the earliest in the event stream and would give the forecaster the longest forecast horizon. This source might also lead to the least accurate forecast, since it is so far away from the ultimate cash outflow. Timing is quite uncertain, and the dollar amount of the outflow would likely not be known with any degree of accuracy in most cases.

Second, we could rely on the purchasing department to provide data on purchase orders. We are a bit closer to the cash outflow, and the uncertainty would be reduced. The amount of the cash flow would be better known but the timing still uncertain.

Third, the payables department could provide data on invoices received. By knowing the credit terms stated on the invoice and the firm's payment practices, it may be possible to estimate when a check would be sent and when it might clear back against the account.

Fourth, a more certain source of information could be provided by the check preparation department. This group could provide data on exact amounts of payment and on the drawee bank. That would enable the forecaster to project eventual clearing amounts and timing with a high level of accuracy. The problem with using this form of information is that the horizon has now been cut to only a few days and the forecast is less valuable.

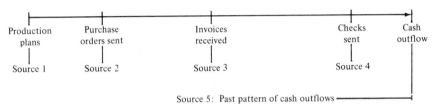

Figure 18.2 Possible Sources of Information to Forecast Cash Outflows.

Fifth, another source of information might be past cash flow patterns. Rather than relying on one of the four preceding information sources, the forecaster may choose to use data on historical check clearing against the disbursement account as the primary input into the forecast. This might be a good approach if there is a strong weekly or monthly cycle to the cash flow in question.

TRADEOFFS. The choice of input source depends on several factors: the cost of information, the accuracy of the resulting forecast, and the length of the forecast horizon. There is, of course, usually a tradeoff between the objectives of the forecast. For example, accuracy increases as the forecast horizon decreases. In general, the longer the horizon, the lower the accuracy.

Collect Input Data

Collecting input data is the next step. Sometimes data are available in the normal course of data processing. At other times, special software and procedures must be developed to extract and assemble the necessary data. For some data, bank accounts are sufficient. They provide a historical data source for checks presented and deposits made. To avoid the problem of having to sort bank account data manually into homogeneous cash flow components, some firms let the bank perform the task. This can be done by setting up zero balance accounts for the cash flows they want to isolate.

Data should normally be collected over a long enough time period to establish a representative sample. Unusual events should be avoided (holidays, periods with unusual data collection problems, unusually slow/fast months). Statistical accuracy generally goes up as the number of observations increases.

On the other hand, if the time period is too long, fundamental changes may occur in the pattern of cash flows. If the pattern changes, historical data may not be a good estimator of future cash flows.

Determine the Relationship Between the Input Variable and the Cash Flow to Be Forecast

It is then necessary to determine how the input variable and the forecasted cash flow are related. This may be a relatively simple task involving "eye-balling" an obvious relationship, or extensive computer analysis using statistical models may be required.

The result of this step is a more or less formal relationship or model connecting the input data with projected cash outflows. If invoice data were chosen as the input data, the relationship may be expressed somewhat as follows:

"Disbursement account outflow on a given day equals 50% of the dollar amount of invoices received 35 days earlier plus 49% of the invoices received 34 days earlier. This forecast is accurate to within 5%."

Mathematically, this relationship could be expressed as follows:

$$F_t = .50I_{t-35} + .49I_{t-34},$$

where F_t is the cash flow forecast for day t, I_{t-35} is the dollar amount of invoices received 35 days before day t, and I_{t-34} is the dollar amount of invoices received 34 days before day t. To use the model, the forecaster obtains invoice data and uses them to project cash outflows from the disbursement account.

How did the forecaster determine this relationship? There are a number of techniques that may be used. These techniques will be outlined in a later section.

Apply the Forecasting Relationship and Evaluate Its Accuracy

The forecast relationship is now used to forecast cash flows for a period of time. Alternatively, the relationship is applied to past cash flows for a time period that was not used to determine the forecast relationship. The accuracy of the forecast model is then measured.

There are a number of statistical measures that can be used to compare the forecast accuracy of various models. In the following paragraphs, let C_t denote the actual and F_t the forecasted cash flow computed, using whatever forecast method we have chosen.

MEAN SQUARED ERROR. Simply noting the difference between forecasted and actual flows and averaging the differences is not a good measure of accuracy. If, for example, half of the errors were 5 over and half were 5 under, the average would be $.5(+5) + .5(-5) = 0$, a perfect forecast! To overcome the problem of positive and negative errors, one approach is to square the errors, thereby always giving positive numbers. By definition, mean squared error is

$$MSE = \frac{1}{N} \sum_{t=1}^{N} (C_t - F_t)^2.$$

MEAN ABSOLUTE DEVIATION. Mean squared error gives more weight to large errors, since squaring a large number makes it even larger. Hence, some forecasters prefer to use mean absolute deviation, defined as follows:

$$MAD = \frac{1}{N} \sum_{t=1}^{N} |C_t - F_t|.$$

POSSIBLE REVISION OF THE INPUT SOURCE AND/OR THE MODEL RELATIONSHIP. After the model is tested on a sample of input data by comparing forecasted with actual cash flows, it may become necessary to search for another data source or another model. Such revisions depend on the accuracy of the results, the firm's need for a given level of accuracy, and the expense in obtaining the desired level.

Individual Transactions versus Aggregate Input Data

In daily cash forecasting, there are two diametrically opposed approaches. At one extreme, a daily forecast is built from individual transactions. At the other extreme, a daily forecast is constructed by breaking a monthly or weekly cash flow into days. The first approach, called *cash scheduling*, is a bottom-up approach—each day's cash flow is considered to be built by many individual transactions. The second approach, called the *distribution approach*, is a top-down approach—each day's cash flow is considered to be part of a larger cash flow over some longer horizon.

Cash Scheduling Approach

By taking a single transaction (for example, the receipt of an invoice) and estimating its cash flow consequences, the forecaster obtains a portion of the cash flow to occur on a given day in the future. Then by taking another transaction and estimating its cash flow consequences, another piece of cash flow is added to another day in the future. By repeating the process for all of the transactions that affect the cash flow in question, the forecaster can obtain an estimate of the total cash flow on a future day.

Exhibit 18.1 presents a small portion of a matrix that shows a sample of invoices received by a firm. Given the credit terms on the invoices, the firm's payment terms, and estimates about mail and clearing times, each invoice results in a cash outflow on a future date. By summing over all of the invoices (down the columns of outflows), the forecaster is able to estimate the total cash flow for a given future date. If these were the only invoices to effect cash flows for days 35 to 44, we would forecast cash outflows of $56,000 on day 35, $5,000 on day 36, nothing on days 37 to 40, and so on. Of course, the matrix for a real firm would have to be considerably larger than the one in this exhibit. Thousands of invoices may be received on a single day. Each one would have to be considered separately under the scheduling approach. Firms using the scheduling approach use large data bases to collect data from input sources.

ADVANTAGES OF CASH SCHEDULING. The cash scheduling approach is quite accurate relative to the distribution approach. It can be made as complex as needed to capture different timing elements that apply to different cash flows. In addition, it is able to incorporate rapidly changes in policies that influence cash flows. For example, if the firm decides to change payment terms and add a few extra days, the computer model that generates the forecast matrix would simply add a few extra days to the timeline.

DISADVANTAGES OF CASH SCHEDULING. Scheduling requires the construction of a large data base. This may be quite expensive to develop and maintain, especially for large numbers of small cash flows. In decentralized organizations, collecting the required data may be particularly difficult, since different parts of the firm may store data in different ways and may have incompatible computer systems.

USES OF CASH SCHEDULING. Cash scheduling is most useful for large payments and receipts that are difficult to forecast by other techniques. Examples of such cash flows are tax payments, dividend payments, interest payments on bonds, and large contract payments. Scheduling is usually not cost justified in

Exhibit 18.1 Cash Scheduling Approach to Daily Cash Forecasting (Amounts in 000's)

Assumptions: Invoices for the amounts given are received on the day shown in the bottom left corner of the box. Based on the credit terms and the firm's payment policies, a check is cut and sent on the day indicated in the bottom right corner. Checks take, on average, 5 *calendar* days to clear. Banks do not clear checks on Saturday or Sunday. For example, the first entry shows an invoice recorded on day 1 for $27,000. A check is mailed on day 30 and is presented against the disbursement account on day 35. We assume no cash discounts for simplicity.

	Cash Outflow by Day (000's)										
Invoice Amt Day, Pay on	**...**	**35 Mon**	**36 Tue**	**37 Wed**	**38 Thu**	**39 Fri**	**40 Sat**	**41 Sun**	**42 Mon**	**43 Tue**	**44 Wed**
$27 1 30		27									
$34 1 35									34		
$5 2 31			5								
$61 3 39											61
$33 3 35									33		
$21 3 35									21		
$29 4 29		29									
$18 7 37									18		
$35 7 37									35		
$63 8 38										63	
Total		56	5						141	63	61

cases of many small cash receipts or disbursements. It is generally cheaper to use statistical approaches in these cases.

Cash Distribution Approach

To illustrate the cash distribution approach, assume that the firm is trying to forecast disbursements from its payroll account. Based on historical patterns, payroll checks, issued each Thursday, are observed to clear as follows:

Day of Week	Percentage Clearing
Thursday	15
Friday	45
Saturday	—
Sunday	—
Monday	25
Tuesday	10
Wednesday	5
Total	100

Rather than attempt to estimate when each check should clear, the distribution approach treats transactions as a group. It starts with the total payroll amount for a particular Thursday and, based on historical patterns, forecasts how much will clear each day. If, for example, the payroll for a particular Thursday is $1,000,000, cash flow estimates are as follows:

$$
\begin{array}{llll}
\text{Thursday} & = .15 \times 1,000,000 = & 150,000 \\
\text{Friday} & = .45 \times 1,000,000 = & 450,000 \\
\text{Monday} & = .25 \times 1,000,000 = & 250,000 \\
\text{Tuesday} & = .10 \times 1,000,000 = & 100,000 \\
\text{Wednesday} & = .05 \times 1,000,000 = & \underline{50,000} \\
\text{Total} & & \$1,000,000
\end{array}
$$

The parameters .15, .45, .25, and so on, are obtained by examining past cash disbursements from the payroll account. Simple averaging may be sufficient to determine the parameters, or the forecaster may call upon more sophisticated regression or time series analysis to assist in estimating the fractions. We discuss some of these methods in the last section of this chapter.

CASH DISTRIBUTION APPROACH WITH WEEKLY AND MONTHLY CYCLES. With the distribution approach, it is possible to consider multiple cycles imposed on one cash flow stream. In forecasting cash flow from receivables, it is common to observe a strong day-of-month pattern. Such a pattern results from the firm's billing cycle and customers' payment cycles. But in addition to a monthly pattern, day-of-week variances also occur. Monday is usually a particularly heavy day for the receipt of mail and for clearing checks. Other days of the week are generally slower.

To express the two cycles simultaneously, we can define the fraction, f_t, of the monthly cash flow to occur on day t as:

$$f_t = a_t + b_i,$$

where a_t is the fraction that normally occurs on business day of month t and b_i is the adjustment for day of week i. We number the days of the week as $i = 1$ (Monday), $i = 2$ (Tuesday), and so on.

Using historical data, the forecaster determines the fraction a_t that usually comes in on day t. This may be done by simply taking historical averages or by applying a more exact statistical method. Suppose that the series of a_t's computed is the following:

t	a_t
1	.05
2	.04
3	.06
4	.05
5	.06
6	.04
7	.02
.	.
.	.
.	.
Total	1.00

This means that normally 5% of the monthly cash flow occurs on business day 1, 4% on business day 2, and so on. Over the entire month, 100% of the cash flow occurs. Remember that we usually apply such analysis to either cash outflow or cash inflow and not net cash flow. If the total cash inflow in a particular division, for example, were estimated to be $2,000,000 for the month, then according to the preceding pattern, the first business day would expect to account for

$$.05 \times \$2,000,000 = \$100,000.$$

The second business day would be $80,000, the third $120,000, and so on. This is before we consider the day-of-week effect.

Using past inflow patterns, we may also discover that to adjust for day-of-week effects, the following fractions are observed:

i	b_i
1	.010
2	.005
3	−.005
4	−.003
5	−.007
Total	0.000

This means that for Monday, an extra .010 is added to the forecast fraction, regardless of the day of the month. Similarly, .005 is added to any Tuesday fraction and −.005 to any Wednesday fraction.

Suppose the month begins on Wednesday and $2,000,000 is the expected inflow for the month. Forecasted cash inflows are computed as follows:

$$F1 = (.050 - .005) \times 2,000,000 = \$90,000$$

$$F2 = (.040 - .003) \times 2,000,000 = \$74,000$$

$$F3 = (.060 - .007) \times 2,000,000 = \$106,000$$

$$F4 = (.050 + .010) \times 2,000,000 = \$120,000$$

$$F5 = (.060 + .005) \times 2,000,000 = \$130,000$$

$$F6 = (.040 - .005) \times 2,000,000 = \$70,000$$

$$F7 = (.020 - .003) \times 2,000,000 = \$34,000$$

.

.

.

Note that the first business day uses the fraction for the normal first business day and the correction for Wednesday. The second business day uses the fraction for day 2 and the correction for Thursday.

ESTIMATING PARAMETERS FOR THE DISTRIBUTION APPROACH. There are several ways to estimate the a's and b's. The simplest way is to use historical averages. A more elegant method is to use regression analysis. We will discuss several statistical approaches in the next section.

ADVANTAGES OF THE DISTRIBUTION APPROACH. The distribution approach does not require an expensive computer system. In fact, since the focus of the forecast is on check clearing, it is possible to use only past bank statements as the input data. Hence, this approach is much less expensive than scheduling. It is best used for statistically homogeneous cash flows for which there are many relatively small disbursements or receipts. Examples include payroll, retail customer payments, and payments to nonmajor vendors. Statistical models to parameterize the distribution approach are usually available on microcomputers.

DISADVANTAGES OF THE DISTRIBUTION APPROACH. The success of the distribution approach depends on a fairly homogeneous sample of cash flows. If the cash flows are "lumpy," accuracy may be significantly reduced. In general, the distribution approach is not as accurate as the scheduling approach. The success of the distribution approach also depends upon the assumption that the future will be very much like the past. However, if credit policies change, the fractions would no longer be valid.

Using Multiple Approaches

Daily cash forecasting usually requires that several different approaches be used. Where possible, large cash flows are best forecast using scheduling techniques. Cash flows from one division may require only manual computations of past averages. Cash flows from another division may require complex time series models and extensive data bases in order to obtain the desired level of accuracy. The forecaster should be prepared to apply a number of different approaches as each forecasting environment warrants.

_____ Survey of Forecasting Tools _____

In the previous section, we discussed approaches to the forecasting problem without specifying how to quantify the relationships between input data and the desired forecast. In this section, we survey commonly used forecasting tools that may be called upon to perform this task. Forecasting tools can be quite technical, and there are a number of textbooks that treat the subject in considerable detail. This section highlights some of the more widely used techniques.

Judgment

Perhaps the most widely used informal forecasting technique is judgment. Sales personnel, for example, may be asked to forecast next month's sales levels by week. Such forecasts are often fairly accurate even though the individuals performing the forecast may find it difficult to state exactly how they arrive at their conclusions. The human mind is able to take multiple qualitative and quantitative factors into consideration. While useful for intermediate term forecasts (weeks and months), judgmental techniques are more difficult to use for daily cash forecasts. Nevertheless, judgment may play an important role particularly in the scheduling approach.

Moving Average

Simple Moving Average

A familiar extrapolative procedure is the average of past observations. For example, to compute a 3-day moving average, the average of cash flows for the past 3 days is computed. This average is then used to forecast the next cash flow. When more cash flows have been observed, the data used to compute the average move forward. A_t is the actual cash flow on day t and MA_t is the moving average.

t	A_t	MA_t
1	12	—
2	15	—
3	15	14
4	18	16
5	12	15

On day 3, the 3-day moving average is $(12 + 15 + 15)/3 = 14$. Our prediction for the cash flow on day 4 would be 14. On day 4, the actual cash flow turns out to be 18. We recompute the 3-day moving average as $(15 + 15 + 18)/3 = 16$. This becomes our forecast of the cash flow for day 5.

The moving average method is easy to compute. It requires no fancy software or specialized knowledge. Unfortunately, it is also not very accurate. Each observation is treated with the same weight ($1/N$, where N is the number of days in the average), and there are no allowances for cyclical patterns. Moving averages are not useful when there are trends, since the average will always lag behind.

Exponential Smoothing

Exponential smoothing corrects for one of the main drawbacks of simple moving averages. This type of moving average permits different weights to be assigned to each observation in the sample. The most recent observation is given the largest weight, a, called the *smoothing constant*, and successively smaller weights are assigned to earlier observations. The forecaster can adjust a to be anything between 1.00 (all weight is given to the most recent observation) and 0.0 (no weight given to the most recent observation—the forecast depends totally on history).

The forecast is computed using

$$F_{t+1} = aA_t + (1 - a)F_t,$$

where F_{t+1} is the cash flow forecast for day $t + 1$, A_t is the actual cash flow on day t, F_t is the forecast for day t, and a is the smoothing constant. No matter what value the smoothing constant is given, the most recent observation exerts more influence on the direction of the forecast than the next oldest observation.

To illustrate exponential smoothing, Table 18.5 gives a series of actual cash flows and computes estimates using different values for a, the smoothing constant. Note that when a is .2, less weight is given to the most recent cash flows and the forecast values do not vary greatly over the time period. When

Table 18.5 Example of Exponential Smoothing

To start the smoothing process, set F_1 and F_2 to the value of the first cash flow.

		$a = .2$		$a = .5$		$a = .8$	
t	A_t	F_t	F_{t+1}	F_t	F_{t+1}	F_t	F_{t+1}
1	100	100.0	100.0	100.0	100.0	100.0	100.0
2	120	100.0	104.0	100.0	110.0	100.0	116.0
3	96	104.0	102.4	110.0	103.0	116.0	100.0
4	110	102.4	103.9	103.0	106.5	100.0	108.0
5	120	103.9	107.1	106.5	113.3	108.0	117.6
6	90	107.1	103.7	113.3	101.6	117.6	95.5
7	130	103.7	109.0	101.6	115.8	95.5	123.1
8	100	109.0	107.2	115.8	107.9	123.1	104.6

t = day
A_t = actual cash flow
F_t = smoothed forecast for day t
F_{t+1} = smoothed forecast for day $t + 1$
a = smoothing constant

a is .8, the variations in forecast values are much greater, reflecting the higher weight given to the most recent cash flows.

Exponential smoothing is more difficult to compute, but it allows the forecaster to give more weight to recent observations and less to earlier ones. That is important, since older data do not necessarily reflect the firm's current situation. The problems of trends and cyclicality are still present, however. More advanced techniques permit the incorporation of trends, but exponential smoothing is unable to handle cycles.

Time Series Analysis

A more general approach to forecasting is time series analysis, of which moving averages and exponential smoothing are special cases. A general time series model seeks to forecast a variable based only on past observations of that variable. The form of the model is

$$F_{t+1} = k + a_0 A_t + a_1 A_{t-1} + a_2 A_{t-2} + \ldots,$$

where F_{t+1} is the forecasted value of the variable, A_t's are past observations of the variable, and a_t's and k are coefficients determined by the model. Note that if $a_1 = a_2 = a_3 = 1/3$, the model becomes a 3-day moving average. The a_t's can also take on weights to give an exponential smoothing model. But the a_t's can also take on other weights that may give a better fit to the data.

For example, if daily cash flows have a strong weekly cycle, the time series equation may take the form

$$F_t = a_{t-7}F_{t-7} + a_{t-14}F_{t-14} + a_{t-21}F_{t-21}.$$

In this equation, Monday's cash flow forecast would be a function of the previous three Mondays' cash flows. Tuesday's cash flow would be a function of the previous three Tuesdays' cash flows, and so on.

Time series analysis is more complex and requires sophisticated computer models. The advantage of time series models is that they adapt well to cyclical patterns and trends.

Box-Jenkins Model

Time series models cannot use the standard regression packages available in many computer statistical packages. Nevertheless, approaches and software have been developed to assist forecasters with this task. G. E. P. Box and G. M. Jenkins have devised methods for identifying, estimating, and testing complex times series models. Box-Jenkins methods require specialized understanding but can be useful in identifying forecast models when other methods fail.

Regression Analysis

Regression analysis is a statistical procedure that seeks to identify the relationship between one forecast variable and other variables in the form

$$F_{t+1} = k + aA_t + bB_t + cC_{t-2} + \ldots,$$

where F_{t+1} is the variable to be forecast, k, a, b, and c are coefficients determined by the model, and A's, B's, and C's are observations of other variables (including past observations of the forecast variable). Time series analysis can be thought of as a special case of regression analysis in which only observations of past values of the forecast variable are used. Regression is very general. Any variables that may explain the forecast variable can be used. Timing is also general. In the example equation, two observations are for time t, while one is for time $t - 2$. Other variables can be used for other time periods.

Regression analysis can be used with one explanatory variable (called *simple regression analysis*) or many variables (called *multiple regression analysis*). Normally, computers must be used to determine the value of the coefficients and test for the validity of the chosen variables.

Regression analysis is a field in itself. A detailed explanation is beyond the scope of this book. Several introductory references are mentioned in the Selected Readings.

Summary

Cash forecasting can be broken into three different time horizons: long-term (1 year or longer), intermediate-term (weekly, monthly, or quarterly for 1 year), and daily. Accurate forecasting can improve the firm's ability to plan for its cash needs and reduce its costs. Care must be taken to focus on cash rather than accounting-based numbers like earnings. The only thing one can do with earnings is report them.

Intermediate-term forecasts are useful in determining credit line needs, planning purchases, and developing investment strategies. The key to intermediate-term forecasting is to forecast accurately the driving variable, such as sales. Most other cash flows are tied to the driving variable by technological, definitional, or policy relationships. Accounting reports can be the basis for cash flow projections as long as corrections are made to counteract the effects of the accrual and matching techniques used to prepare such reports. Whether one focuses on adjusted earnings, balance sheet forecasts, or cash inflows and outflows, the result should lead to net cash flow.

Daily cash forecasts are more difficult to prepare, but the benefits may be significant. Accurate daily forecasts enable the cash manager to invest short-term cash and reduce idle balances more optimally. In addition, management is better able to control inflows and outflows and to spot problems more quickly.

The two most common approaches are scheduling and distribution. Scheduling depends on the ability to trace through individual transactions and build the aggregate cash flow for a given day. Distribution takes the opposite approach and spreads a larger "lump" of cash flow over individual days of the time period. Both approaches can be useful for various types of cash flow. Scheduling is more appropriate for large transactions, while distribution is probably better for large numbers of smaller transactions.

Forecasting is both an art and a science. While the cash manager or treasurer may not need to know all of the quantitative details related to forecasting, it is helpful to know in general some of the more important forecasting tools and be able to speak the language of the technician who helps analyze forecast data.

_____ Discussion Questions _____

1. Why should a treasurer or cash manager focus on cash flow rather than earnings?
2. What are some of the purposes of long-term, medium-term, and daily cash flow forecasts?
3. What are the elements of the firm's objective function related to cash forecasting?
4. What is a driving variable, and why is it crucial to cash forecasting?
5. Outline the procedures for medium-range cash forecasting, starting with the generation of a scenario. What is a cash budget?
6. How can days sales outstanding be computed from a balance sheet and an income statement? What other timing measures can be similarly computed?

7. Explain the three approaches for finding the net cash flow from financial statements. How are they related?
8. What are the benefits of daily cash forecasting?
9. Why is it useful to separate major cash flows from minor ones in daily cash forecasting?
10. If you were asked to forecast cash inflows from credit sales, what possible sources of data could you use?
11. What measures are used to determine forecast accuracy?
12. Compare and contrast the scheduling approach with the distribution approach for daily cash forecasting. Which is more useful for which types of cash flows?
13. Explain how moving averages and exponential smoothing are special cases of time series analysis.
14. When is general time series analysis more appropriate than moving average or exponential smoothing approaches?
15. What is regression analysis and when might it be useful for cash forecasting?

Problems

1. The following are the financial statements for The Fan Fold Paper Company for the year ending December 31, 19x8 (all figures are in millions):

BALANCE SHEET

Assets		Liabilities and Equity	
Cash and mkt. sec	$ 7	Accounts payable	$ 8
Accounts receivable	10	Short-term debt	1
Inventories	8	Long-term debt	2
Net plant and equipment	30	Common stock	30
		Retained earnings	14
Total	$55		$55

INCOME STATEMENT

Sales	$30.0
Cost of goods sold	20.0
Gross profit	10.0
Expenses	
General and administrative	3.0
Depreciation	2.0
Interest	1.0
Income before tax	4.0
Taxes (40%)	1.6
Net income after taxes	$ 2.4

Because of strong demand, Fan Fold expects sales to double next year. Costs of goods sold, accounts receivable, inventory, and accounts payable are expected to remain in the same proportion to sales. New equipment costing $2.0 will be purchased on a $2.0 long-term mortgage. Depreciation will increase to $2.5. Interest for the coming year is expected to be $1.2. General administrative expenses and cash and marketable securities are expected to remain constant. Dividends of $2.0 will be paid.

  a. Project Fan Fold's income statement for 19x9 and the balance sheet for December 31, 19x9.

  b. How much of a loan will be required, or how much excess funds will be available?

  c. Start with net income after taxes and compute the net cash flow for the coming year. Reconcile your calculation here with your answer to (b).

2. Tailor Mills has the following financial statements for the year ending December 31, 19x7 (all figures are in millions):

INCOME STATEMENT FOR THE YEAR
ENDING DECEMBER 31, 19X7

Sales	$14.0
Cost of goods sold	9.0
Gross profit	5.0
Expenses	
Depreciation	1.0
Other fixed costs	2.0
Operating profit	2.0
Taxes (40%)	.8
Net income after taxes	$ 1.2

BALANCE SHEET, DECEMBER 31, 19X7

Assets		Liabilities and Equity	
Cash and mkt. sec.	$ 3	Accounts payable	$ 4
Accounts receivable	5	Long-term debt	2
Inventories	7	Common stock	20
Net fixed assets	20	Retained earnings	9
Total	$35		$35

Because of a change in credit policy, sales are expected to increase by 50% next year. Tailor feels that certain accounts will remain in the same proportion to sales as in the past: cost of goods sold, inventories, and accounts payable. Because of the liberalized credit policy, the accounts receivable collection period is expected to double. No addition to fixed assets is expected. Other fixed costs are expected to increase to $1.5. Long-term debt is expected to remain at $2.0 and no new equity offerings are planned. Cash and marketable securities should be at least $4.0. No dividends are to be paid.

a. Project the income statement for Tailor Mills for 19x8.

b. Project the balance sheet for December 31, 19x8, using a short-term bank loan as the balancing amount.

c. Starting with sales, make appropriate cash flow adjustments to show how the net cash flow is equal to the short-term debt plug figure of part (b).

3. It is June 30 and the treasurer of the Maxwell Toy Company is trying to forecast cash inflows for the last 6 months of the year. The following sales information (in millions of dollars) is available:

Apr	30	May	35	Jun	30 }	Actual
Jul	45	Aug	70	Sep	150 ⎫	
Oct	200	Nov	125	Dec	45 ⎬	Forecast

From prior studies, the treasurer has determined that approximately 85% of the sales for any month are uncollected at the end of the month of the sale, 60% are still uncollected 1 month after the sale, and 10% are uncollected 2 months after the sale. That last 10%, with the exception of bad debts, which average 2% of sales, are collected in the third month after the sale.

a. Forecast the cash inflows, by months, for July through December for Maxwell Toys.

b. Forecast the accounts receivable at the end of each month for July through December. (Assume that bad debts are written off in the third month following the sale rather than through an allowance for doubtful accounts at the time the sale is made.)

4. Old Spillabrew is a beverage distributor supplying beverages for the concession stands for the Mudville Giants. Because of past financial difficulties, Old Spillabrew must pay cash for the products they sell to the Giants. However, they do not get paid until Monday for the products supplied the previous week (through Sunday). They estimate that each fan at a day game will spend $7.50 on concessions, while those at night games will spend $10.00. Attendance averages 20,000 at day games and 30,000 at night games. For every $1 spent at a concession stand, Old Spillabrew receives $.75 from the Giants. Their cost is approximately $.50 of the concession stand price. The schedule for the next week for the Giants games is as follows:

Tue	Wed	Thu	Fri	Sat	Sun	Mon
Cubs	Cubs	Cubs	Off	Blues	Blues	Blues
Day	Day	Night		Night	Day	Day

Forecast the cash inflows and outflow for the period Tuesday through Monday.

5. The following balance sheet is available for Divirden Foods, a food whole-saler, for March 31, 19x5:

BALANCE SHEET FOR MARCH 31, 19X5

Assets		Liabilities and Equity	
Cash and mkt. sec.	3	Accounts payable	28
Accounts receivable	55	Accrued expenses	7
Inventories	56	Short-term debt	10
Net fixed assets	8	Long-term debt	12
Other assets	5	Common stock	20
		Retained earnings	50
	127		127

Given the following information, project the net cash needs or availability for the quarter April through June.

a. Sales by months (all credit) are as follows:

Actual		Forecasted			
Feb 50	Mar 75	Apr 80	May 95	Jun 80	Jul 75

b. The historic payment pattern for credit customers is $P_0 = .20$, $P_1 = .50$, $P_2 = .30$.

c. The cost of goods sold averages 70% of the selling price, and the company policy is to maintain an inventory equal to the next month's estimated sales. Purchases are made on the 15th and the 30th of the month, and terms are net 10 days.

d. Operating expenses are $14 per month, with half being paid in the month incurred and half being accrued and paid the following month.

e. No fixed asset purchases or equity offers are planned, and other expenses and long-term debt are expected to remain constant for the quarter. Interest on the long-term debt is 16%, payable quarterly in March, June, September, and December. Depreciation is at a rate of $1.0 per quarter.

f. No dividends are paid.

g. The short-term debt is a bank line of credit with interest at 12%.

h. Income taxes are at a rate of 40%, and estimated taxes for the quarter are paid on the 15th day of the last month in the quarter.

6. The Forward Look company projects daily cash flows by the distribution method. After running the dummy variable regression, Forward determined the following parameters:

$$a_1 = .047 \qquad b_1 = +.004$$
$$a_2 = .045 \qquad b_2 = +.003$$
$$a_3 = .060 \qquad b_3 = -.001$$
$$a_4 = .063 \qquad b_4 = -.005$$
$$a_5 = .072 \qquad b_5 = -.001$$
$$a_6 = .035$$
$$\text{etc.}$$

where a_i represents the ith business day of the month and b_i represents the ith day of the week, with $1 = $ Monday, $2 = $ Tuesday, and so on. Cash flows for the month are forecast to be $2,680,000.

a. Assume that the month begins on a Thursday. Project the cash flows for the first 7 calendar days.

b. Why might the total of all daily cash flows not equal $2,680,000, even assuming that the a_i's sum to 1.0?

c. Now assume that the month begins on a Monday. How do your cash flow estimates for the first 7 days differ from those calculated in (a)? Why?

7. The following data are available for Sommerer Product's monthly sales for the past year:

Jan	4,200	Feb	4,100	Mar	4,300	Apr	3,800
May	3,500	Jun	3,700	Jul	3,400	Aug	3,300
Sep	3,800	Oct	4,200	Nov	4,400	Dec	4,100

a. Evaluate the use of exponential smoothing with an alpha value of .2, .5, and .8. Which gives the most accurate forecast if you use the standard deviation of the forecast error as the measure of accuracy?

b. How do the forecasts in (a) compare with the use of a 3-month moving average forecast?

Selected Readings

FOLGER, H. RUSSELL, and SUNDURAM GANAPATHY, *Financial Econometrics for Researchers in Finance and Accounting*, Englewood Cliffs, N.J.: Prentice-Hall, 1982.

JOHNSON, AARON C., MARVIN B. JOHNSON, and RUEBEN C. BUSE, *Econometrics: Basic and Applied*, New York: Macmillan, 1987.

JOHNSTON, J., *Econometric Methods*, 3rd ed., New York: McGraw-Hill, 1984.

KMENTA, JAN, *Elements of Econometrics*, 2nd ed., New York: Macmillan, 1986.

PARKER, GEORGE G. C., "Financial Forecasting," in *Financial Handbook*, 5th ed., Edward I. Altman (ed.), New York: Wiley, 1981.

STONE, BERNELL K., and TOM W. MILLER, "Daily Cash Forecasting: A Structuring Framework," *Journal of Cash Management* (October 1981), pp. 35ff.

STONE, BERNELL K., and ROBERT A. WOOD, "Daily Cash Forecasting: A Simple Method for Implementing the Distribution Approach," *Financial Management* (Fall 1977), pp. 40–50.

WISMER DAVID A., "Approaches to Cash Flow Forecasting," Parts I, II, and III, *Journal of Cash Management* (Jan–Feb, Jul–Aug, Nov–Dec 1985).

Appendix: Spreadsheet Software for
———————— Cash Flow Forecasting ————————

Spreadsheet Software

Spreadsheet software is essentially a computerized worksheet or grid. The worksheet is laid out similarly to an accountant's worksheet in rows and columns. Each cell in the worksheet may hold data. The user specifies the data in a cell (1) by manually entering the data one cell at a time, (2) by reading from a preexisting data base, or (3) by telling the computer how data are to be computed and letting it do the computations. The last method is crucial for cash flow forecasting and planning.

The value of spreadsheets is that forecasting is separated into mechanical tasks that the computer does very well (and that people don't like to do) and interpretative tasks that people do much better than most computers. Spreadsheets free the user to concentrate on analysis rather than arithmetic.

One of the first spreadsheet programs was Visicalc. It was soon followed by more user-friendly programs such as Supercalc, Lotus 1-2-3, and Multiplan and inexpensive versions like Twin and PC Calc. Now there are dozens of spreadsheet programs for all budgets and tastes. Some packages combine worksheet technology with computer graphics, word processing, and data base management features.

Spreadsheet software is relatively easy to learn, and most packages come with tutorial programs for on-screen demonstrations. Students can often master the fundamentals of spreadsheets in a single afternoon. Since spreadsheets are adaptable to so many different uses, it is worthwhile to learn to use these powerful tools. Many of the problems in this book can be more easily solved using spreadsheets—especially the problems in this chapter.

Example

In Table 1 we generate a set of four quarterly cash flow numbers. Sales for the first quarter are estimated to be $400,000 with increases of 2% in each succeeding quarter. We let the computer automatically generate the sales figures for quarters 2, 3, and 4. We do this by telling the spreadsheet program to multiply the first $400,000 by 1.02 and put the result in the next box. The

Table 1 Sample Spreadsheet Computations

	Qtr. 1	Qtr. 2	Qtr. 3	Qtr. 4	Total
Cash Inflows					
Sales	$400,000	$408,000	$416,160	$424,483	$1,648,643
Increase in A/P	$ 10,000	$ 10,200	$ 10,404	$ 10,612	$ 41,216
New Debt			$ 50,000		$ 50,000
Total Inflows	$410,000	$418,200	$476,564	$435,095	$1,739,859
Cash Outflows					
Cost of goods sold	$320,000	$326,400	$332,928	$339,587	$1,318,915
Admin. costs	$ 50,000	$ 50,000	$ 50,000	$ 50,000	$ 200,000
Increase in A/R	$ 20,000	$ 20,400	$ 20,808	$ 21,224	$ 82,432
Increase in inv.	$ 10,000	$ 10,000	$ 40,000	$ 20,000	$ 80,000
Total Outflows	$400,000	$406,800	$443,736	$430,811	$1,681,347
Net Cash Flow	$ 10,000	$ 11,400	$ 32,828	$ 4,285	$ 58,513

increase in accounts payable begins at $10,000 and grows by 2% each quarter. Columns are added by specifying the cell in which to start adding and the cell of the last number to add. The program does the rest.

The cost of goods sold in the example is 80% of sales. We tell the computer to generate the cost of goods sold by multiplying the number in the sales cells by 80%. If we decide to change the level of sales, the cost of goods sold would be adjusted automatically to be 80% of the new level. This illustrates the power of spreadsheet programs. Once the basic relationships between variables are defined, the user does not have to recalculate all of the numbers when changes are made. The computer does the recalculation and permits the user to focus on results, not mechanics.

Administrative costs are $50,000 per quarter. The user has to enter the number $50,000 only once and then specify that the other cells in that row are to contain the same number. The increase in accounts receivable begins at $20,000 per quarter and grows by 2% a quarter. The increase in inventory changes each quarter in this example, so the user enters a different number in each cell.

Sensitivity Analysis
Sensitivity analysis is the ability to generate alternative financial statements for alternative assumptions. It is very important in forecasting to determine how the results may change with changing assumptions. Spreadsheets are ideal for sensitivity analysis because, by changing the number in one cell, they allow all numbers in related cells to be recomputed automatically.

Uploading and Downloading
Forecasting often requires historical data from mainframe computers. Such data may be transferred (downloaded) to microcomputers and then read into a

spreadsheet program. After manipulation by a microcomputer, the results may be transferred back to the mainframe (uploaded) for storage or consolidation with other data.

Templates

Rather than constructing a spreadsheet from scratch by defining how data cells are related, it is possible to purchase predefined spreadsheets called *templates* to be used with a spreadsheet program. Templates are commercially available for financial planning, real estate analysis, and tax form preparation, as well as general accounting applications.

19

International
Short-term Finance

The recently appointed treasurer of Asian operations for a multinational U.S.-based firm toured the company's 25 Pacific rim offices to review their short-term financial management practices. In Malaysia, he found that checks mailed from East Malaysia to Kuala Lumpur took 10 days. By arranging for interbank transfers, he was able to cut the time to 1 day and saved $50,000 per year. Some payables managers in some of the firm's subsidiaries had the policy of paying invoices the same week they were received. Changing this practice saved $250,000 per year. In the Japanese office, excess cash was customarily invested in savings deposits earning 2% interest. Management was instructed to reinvest in money market securities earning 7%.[1]

As firms expand their marketing and supply operations throughout the world, they face complex problems of managing cash flows within and between other countries in unfamiliar environments. In this chapter, we will see that the problems and objectives of international short-term financial management are basically the same as those of domestic operations, but time lines may be longer, banking practices altered, risks greater, and available tools somewhat different.

Why International Differs from
Domestic Short-term Finance

Adding an international dimension to short-term financial management creates additional challenges because of the following factors.

---

[1] Celi, Louis J., and Barry Rutizer, "Treasurers Overlook Asian Cash Management Opportunities," *Cashflow* (June 1983), pp. 24–27.

Exchange Rates

In domestic short-term finance, there is no need to worry about the problem of dollars collected in California devaluing while they are concentrated into a New York bank account. A dollar is a dollar regardless of where it is minted in the United States. But when cash moves across international borders, it may be in the form of Deutsch marks (DM) in one country and may have to be converted into New Zealand dollars in another. The rate of exchange between currencies becomes a major concern to the cash manager.

The rate at which one currency is exchanged for another is called the *exchange rate*. The exchange rate between two currencies fluctuates frequently, depending on the relative supply of and demand for the currencies in the foreign exchange markets and on the difference in interest rates in the two countries. When the exchange rate moves, the value received in a transaction changes. For example, if a German customer of an American firm pays 1,000,000 DM and the exchange rate is 2.0 DM/$, the American firm receives $500,000 when the DMs are exchanged for dollars. If the payment is delayed by credit terms for 60 days and the exchange rate after 60 days has risen to 2.2 DM/$, the American firm receives only $454,545. The firm loses $45,455 because of exchange rate fluctuations.

Time Delays

Moving cash within other countries and across international borders frequently involves significant time delays and may be unreliable. Mail from a rural area in the Philippines to a central city requires 9 days. Clearing a check deposited in a large city back to a bank in a rural area in Indonesia requires 8 days. A check drawn on a foreign bank and deposited in a U.S. bank will typically be treated as a collection item and take 2–4 weeks to become available. Even wire transfers within and between countries may be delayed 1 or more days because of time zone differences and bank-imposed value dating. Payment for exports is often in the form of a letter of credit. Letters of credit may take several days or weeks before good funds can be received even after all documents are in order.

On the other hand, cash flow in some countries is much faster than it is in the United States. In Great Britain checks clear overnight. It would be senseless to attempt remote disbursing. In Japan, most payments are made electronically and few checks are ever written. The cash flow timelines for these two countries are quite short compared to those for the typical check transaction in the United States.

Credit Risks

Selling to foreign customers involves potentially greater credit risks than selling to domestic customers. Different accounting standards make analysis of published financial reports more difficult for U.S. managers. In addition, political and economic problems can potentially restrict the flow of cash out of the country or even lead to nationalization of the entire firm. Since communications are generally more difficult and expensive, credit enforcement is less effective across borders than within one country. Finally, if trouble does occur, there are fewer legal remedies to help collect the cash owed.

Taxation

International tax agreements between countries are extremely complex and vary considerably from nation to nation. Movement of cash across borders may have important tax implications both in the cash-originating country and in the United States.

High Transaction Costs

Transferring cash between banks in different countries may be significantly more expensive than domestic transfers because international transfers typically involve multiple correspondent banks (each of which may charge a fee), may involve an opportunity cost delay due to value dating, and may require more extensive documentation and validation.

Attitudes Toward Cash Management

In many developing countries, managers do not consider short-term financial management to be important. They may have more of an accounting orientation: "As long as a sale has been made, it makes little difference to the bottom line as long as the cash arrives sometime." In contrast, in some countries, very high inflation rates have taught managers the time value of money. The result is that managers in some parts of the world are totally unaware of good short-term finance practices, while others are highly skilled.

Information Availability

Many countries have legal restrictions on providing data, especially bank data, to parties outside their borders. For example, all data produced by Canadian banks must be processed in Canada. West Germany and some Scandinavian countries also require local processing of bank data. Such laws make the provision of cash management and credit services, such as balance reporting and credit reporting, almost impossible. In addition, in the interest of national security, some countries prohibit or strictly limit the outflow of encrypted messages. In the United States, bank data are often transmitted in encrypted form. Restrictions on encryption limit the security of cash management and credit information services. Many countries charge unusually high rates for intercountry telecommunications, thereby placing further restrictions on the development of international short-term financial management services.[2]

Objective Function of International Short-term Financial Management

In the management of international short-term assets and liabilities, it is helpful to keep an objective function in mind. This objective function is very similar to the objective functions in other areas of short-term finance.

International short-term finance costs arise from several sources: (1) time value costs (opportunity costs of leaving balances in the hands of customers or in lower-yielding accounts at deposit banks, or the costs of paying earlier than needed), (2) credit losses due to inability to collect payments, (3) transaction costs of moving cash within and between other countries, (4) losses/gains in converting one currency into another, (5) administrative costs (including taxation, reporting, and management time), and (6) costs/benefits of good customer, supplier, and public relations. We can express these costs succinctly as follows:

> Minimize: time value costs
> + credit losses
> + transaction costs
> + losses on foreign exchange
> + administrative costs
> − benefits of public/partner relations.

Managing Foreign Exchange Risk

The need to exchange one currency for another occurs frequently when firms extend their operations abroad. To improve marketing efforts, U.S. firms sometimes bill foreign customers in their own currency. Offshore suppliers may bill U.S. firms in the currency of their home country. Capital investment, dividend, and interest payments are also frequently moved between countries and need to be converted into a different currency. Risk arises because by the time the transaction is completed and the exchange of currencies is made, the firm may receive fewer dollars or pay more dollars than it intended.

---

[2] Greguras, Fred M., "Impact of Transborder Data Flow Restrictions of Cash Management Services," *Journal of Cash Management* (September–October 1985), pp. 11–14.

Measuring Foreign Exchange Risk

The degree of risk associated with potential exchange rate movements is called *foreign exchange exposure* or, in this chapter, simply *exposure*. While there are several possible ways to view exposure, the two most commonly used in short-term financial management are transaction and translation exposure.

Transaction Exposure

Transaction exposure measures the risk that known future transactions may result in more cash outflow or less cash inflow due to exchange rate fluctuations. To illustrate, assume that a U.S. firm carries receivables due from a Japanese firm for 2,000,000 yen. Assume that the same U.S. firm owes 6,000,000 yen to a Japanese parts supplier. The current exchange rate is 150 yen/\$. At that rate, the firm would receive 2,000,000 yen/(150\$/yen) = \$13,333 and would pay 6,000,000 yen/(150\$/yen) = \$40,000. The net amount the firm pays is \$26,667.

Now, suppose the dollar weakens relative to the yen (meaning that \$1 purchases fewer yen) to a level of 140 yen/\$ before the accounts are settled. What would happen to the U.S. firm's position? It receives 2,000,000/140 = \$14,286 and pays 6,000,000/140 = \$42,857. The net paid out would be \$28,571. The loss to the firm is \$1,905 because of the change in the foreign exchange rates.

The change in cash flow that the firm experiences, expressed in dollars, can be computed more directly as follows:

$$\$ \text{ change in cash flow} = (IF - OF)(k_1 - k_0), \qquad \textbf{(19.1)}$$

where IF is the expected cash inflow (receivables) expressed in the foreign currency, OF is the expected outflow (payables) expressed in the foreign currency, k_1 the new dollar/foreign currency exchange rate, and k_0 is the old dollar/foreign currency exchange rate. Substituting the values of the example into the equation, we compute

$$\$ \text{ change in cash flow} = (2,000,000 - 6,000,000)\left(\frac{1}{140} - \frac{1}{150}\right)$$
$$= -\$1,905.$$

The magnitude of the change in cash flows, according to Equation (19.1), depends on two primary factors. First, it depends on $(IF - OF)$, the difference between expected inflows and outflows or the difference between receivables and payables. Second, it depends on the size of the second term, which represents the difference in exchange rates.

Exposure, then, can be broken down into these two components. When managers use the term *translation exposure*, they usually refer to the first component, the difference between receivables and payables. If the firm had twice the amount in receivables and twice the amount in payables, then for a given change in rates, the loss would be twice as large.

Note, however, that the actual dollar loss also depends on the second factor—the change in rates. This means that translation exposure, strictly defined as just the first component, may not capture risk adequately. Further information would be needed on the likelihood that rates for that particular currency would change over time. Since this is an unknown factor, managers are content to use only the first factor as the measure of transaction exposure.

To convert transaction exposure into dollars and permit the manager to sum across all foreign operations, it is usual for the term $(IF - OF)$ to be divided by the current exchange rate for that currency. Since we are primarily interested in how exchange rates will hurt the firm, the negative of that term is used. Hence, we state that the transaction exposure in the preceding example is

$$\$ \text{ transaction exposure} = -(2,000,000 - 6,000,000)/(150\$/\text{yen})$$
$$= \$26,667.$$

Although transaction exposure is often defined only in terms of receivables and payables, a better measure of the firm's risk would include *all* expected cash inflows and outflows in that currency over some time horizon.

Translation Exposure

The concept of *translation exposure* has more to do with the reporting of accounting information than with actual cash flows. It refers to the risk that an exchange rate change will cause the firm's net worth to drop when a foreign subsidiary is consolidated with the parent. The extent of exposure depends upon which assets and liabilities are translated at the current foreign exchange rate. Since 1981, translation of financial statements is governed by the Financial Accounting Standards Board's Statement Number 52 (FASB 52). Under FASB 52, translation exposure is defined as follows:

Translation exposure = $ value of all assets denominated in foreign currency j
$\quad$ − $ value of all liabilities denominated in foreign currency j.

Net worth is a residual value and is not translated. When consolidating a subsidiary whose assets and liabilities are denominated in a foreign currency, all assets and liabilities are translated into U.S. dollars at the currently prevailing exchange rate. Gains or losses on translation are posted to translation reserve accounts rather than being treated as an expense, as was required under FASB 8 (which was superseded by FASB 52).

Vehicles for Converting Currencies

To understand how firms protect themselves against exposure, it is necessary to understand how currencies are converted. Consider, for example, the U.S. firm in the preceding example that has 6,000,000 yen payable to a Japanese parts supplier. Suppose the payable is due in 90 days. Assume that the current exchange rate is 150 yen/$. There are several ways in which the cash manager can convert dollars to yen. Each involves different timing, risk, and cost.

Spot Market

The U.S. firm could wait until the 90 days elapse before converting its dollars to yen. The number of dollars required if the rate remains at 150 yen/\$ is, as we saw before, \$40,000.

When payment is made, the firm buys yen in what is called the *spot market* at whatever exchange rate prevails at the time of conversion. A transaction in the spot foreign exchange market is considered an immediate transaction in which bank drafts denominated in different currencies are exchanged between two parties. Usually one party is a major bank. The timing is actually slightly greater than immediate: settlement in the New York market is 1 business day for North American currencies and 2 business days for other currencies. Faster settlement is available at higher cost. Foreign exchange traders earn money from the difference between the buying price (*bid*) and the selling price (*ask*). Different traders may quote different rates, so firms often shop around to obtain the best rate possible. Generally the exchange of smaller amounts (under about \$50,000) is more expensive than that of larger amounts.

Forward Exchange Contract

If the risk of paying more for the parts is not acceptable to the management of the U.S. firm, it may choose to buy a *forward exchange contract*. With such a contract, the buyer agrees with a third party (often a bank) to purchase the necessary 6,000,000 yen in exchange for dollars at an agreed exchange rate in 90 days. Standard forward exchange contracts are usually offered with maturities of 1, 2, 3, 6, and 12 months, although other time periods are also possible. Amounts are also negotiable between parties.

A forward exchange contract is a way to *hedge* against possible adverse rate movements. A *perfect hedge* is a position such that the firm is indifferent to any shift, up or down by any amount, in exchange rates. A *partial hedge* is a position that reduces but does not completely eliminate damage from rate movements.

After the firm hedges by buying a forward exchange contract, it must honor its side of the agreement and buy the 6,000,000 yen even if it can get a better rate elsewhere after the 90 days elapse. It therefore forgoes the possibility that the dollar could strengthen against the yen and thereby bene-fit the firm. The firm is locked into the exchange rate negotiated at the outset. The exchange rate for the forward exchange contract depends primarily on in-terest rate differentials between the two countries, on supply and demand for the two currencies, and on speculation in the market about future economic conditions.

The U.S. firm might find a 90-day contract at a rate of 145 yen/\$. By buying into a forward exchange contract, the firm guarantees that it will pay

$$\text{Dollars required} = \frac{6{,}000{,}000 \text{ yen}}{145 \text{ yen/\$}} = \$41{,}379.$$

If the dollar strengthens against the yen, the firm does not benefit since it must honor the contract. If the dollar weakens below the 145 level, the firm is protected. The forward contract locks the firm into a price of 145 yen/$ for better or for worse.

The *buyer* of a foreign exchange contract agrees to *receive* (buy) a foreign currency in exchange for dollars at a specified rate on a specified date. Contracts are bought by parties that have a future obligation to pay in a foreign currency. Examples of buyers are importers, firms that must make capital investments in other countries, and firms that must pay dividends or interest in other countries.

The seller of a forward contract agrees to *deliver* (sell) a foreign currency in exchange for dollars at a specified rate on a given date. Examples of sellers are exporters who expect to receive payments in a foreign currency and firms that receive dividend or interest payments from foreign operations.

AMOUNT TO BUY OR SELL. In the example just given, suppose the U.S. firm owes 6,000,000 yen but is owed 2,000,000 yen. Its exposure in yen is 4,000,000. Therefore, it would probably not want to purchase forward contracts against the entire payable, since exchange rate movements that make the 6,000,000 yen less valuable simultaneously make the 2,000,000 yen more valuable. In general, the maximum amount to hedge is limited to the transaction exposure. This rule of thumb, however, neglects the fact that the payables and receivables may be for different times. In that case, management may decide to hedge more than just the transaction exposure.

In practice, most firms do not hedge 100% of their transaction exposure. While hedging reduces losses due to exchange rate fluctuations, the practice is expensive in terms of transaction and administrative costs. Over the long run, the benefits may not outweigh the costs. Typically, firms hedge only very large transactions in currencies that are more volatile than average.

Long-Date Forward Contract

A more recent development in the forward contract market is the *long-date forward contract*. These instruments are essentially forward exchange contracts that may extend for up to 10 years. They are used to hedge longer-term exposures resulting from long-term contracts, medium- to long-term financing, and anticipated dividends or other longer-term distributions. Banks are the primary market makers in this market, too.

Futures Contract

A less widely used vehicle for hedging foreign exchange transactions is the futures contract. The forward contract just discussed is an agreement between two parties and may be be tailored to the needs of each. In contrast, a *futures contract* for foreign currency may be thought of as a highly standardized forward contract bought and sold at certain exchange clearing houses such as the International Monetary Market (part of the Chicago Mercantile Exchange) and the New York Futures Exchange. The agreement is not between the buyer and seller but between the buyer or seller and the exchange. Futures contracts are offered only in standard denominations (e.g., 125,000 DM) and mature at fixed dates throughout the year (generally a specified day in March, June, September, and December). Standardization allows futures contracts to be bought and sold in secondary markets and thereby lowers the costs to all parties. In contrast, there is no secondary market for forward contracts.

As with forward contracts, buying or selling futures contracts provides a hedge against potential losses from exchange rate fluctuations. The concepts are similar to those outlined for forward contracts, except that the other party is not a bank but an exchange. As with a forward contract, the buyer or seller must honor the contract. As with other types of futures contracts (see Chapter 11 for a detailed discussion), such contracts may be canceled by taking the opposite position. For example, if a futures contract is bought, it may later be canceled by selling another contract of the same currency and maturity.

Currency Options

In 1981 the Marine Midland Bank offered the first foreign exchange option. Soon exchanges, like the Philadelphia Stock Exchange, the Amsterdam Exchange, and the Montreal Exchange, began trading in options in selected currencies. Both forward and futures contracts lock in the buyer and seller to deliver or receive delivery of currency at an agreed rate. An option is a vehicle that provides exchange rate protection without locking the manager into a position that may not prove favorable. Similar to the familiar puts and calls associated with common stock, currency options operate in much the same way. By buying as *currency call option*, the owner has the right to buy a given currency at a stated price anytime between the purchase and expiration dates. With a *currency put option*, the buyer has the right to sell a foreign currency at a specified rate between the purchase and expirations dates. In either case, if rates move in a favorable direction, the buyer does not have to exercise the option. Options are currently used less frequently than either forward or futures contracts.

Strategies for Hedging Foreign Exchange Exposure

The spot market and forward and futures contracts, along with currency options, provide some of the basic tools to hedge exposure to exchange rate risk. There are other approaches that use borrowing and lending in conjunction with the spot market to create effective hedges.

Spot Market Plus Borrowing or Lending

Suppose a U.S. firm is owed 100,000 DM in 90 days. The U.S. firm could borrow Deutsch marks today from a German bank and convert them to dollars at the spot exchange rate. When the German firm makes payment in 90 days, the loan is paid off. Exchange rate risk is reduced because the firm obtains dollars at a known rate today instead of the rate 90 days from now. On the other hand, the firm must now consider the difference between the interest rate paid in Germany versus the rate it could pay by borrowing dollars in the United States.

Leading and Lagging

Timing payables and receivables can also be used to deal with fluctuating exchange rates. *Leading* refers to the hastening of collections or the payment of payables. *Lagging* is the opposite: payments or collections are slowed. Why would a firm want to change payment timing? To get more favorable cash flows when rates change. As Exhibit 19.1 illustrates, if the foreign currency is expected to strengthen against the dollar (e.g., the yen goes from 150 to 140 yen/$), the firm is better off by lagging receivables and leading payables. Conversely, if the currency is expected to weaken against the dollar, the firm will benefit by leading receivables and lagging payables. Leading and lagging

Exhibit 19.1 Leading and Lagging as a Tool to Control Foreign Exchange Exposure

SITUATION: Assume a U.S. firm is to receive a payment of 3,000,000 yen and make a payment of 3,000,000 yen. The current exchange rate is 150 yen/$. The firm has the choice of making the payment immediately (leading) or making the payment in 60 days (lagging). In one case, the yen is assumed to strengthen in 60 days the dollar to 140 yen/$ and in the other case to weaken against the dollar to 160 yen/$. Transactions occurring now (leading) use the current exchange rate while future transactions (lagging) use the rate in 60 days.

	Leading (Transaction Occurs Now)	**Lagging** (Transaction Occurs in 60 Days)
Receivables		
Currency strengthens to 140 yen/$	$\dfrac{3{,}000{,}000}{150} = \$20{,}000$	$\dfrac{3{,}000{,}000}{140} = \$21{,}429$
Currency weakens to 160 yen/$	$\dfrac{3{,}000{,}000}{150} = \$20{,}000$	$\dfrac{3{,}000{,}000}{160} = \$18{,}750$
Payables		
Currency strengthens to 140 yen/$	$\dfrac{3{,}000{,}000}{150} = \$20{,}000$	$\dfrac{3{,}000{,}000}{140} = \$21{,}429$
Currency weakens to 160 yen/$	$\dfrac{3{,}000{,}000}{150} = \$20{,}000$	$\dfrac{3{,}000{,}000}{160} = \$18{,}750$

Note: Italicized figure indicates the preferred cash flow of the pair.

work effectively only if the firm guesses correctly about the direction of rate movements. If the firm is wrong, its cash flow is adversely affected.

Leading and lagging are applied almost exclusively to intracompany cash flows. With netting systems and reinvoicing centers (to be discussed), a firm has centralized control over the timing of payments and receipts.

Leading and lagging are not trivial problems. First, the direction of exchange rates is uncertain. Second, even if the direction is known, if leading and lagging are to be practiced with subsidiaries, the firm must balance the benefits from exchange rate considerations with the costs and benefits of idle balances and possible strained relations with the subsidiaries. For example, if management thinks that it would be beneficial from a foreign exchange viewpoint to lag payments to a subsidiary, it must also consider the adverse effect such an action may have on the subsidiary relationship.

The Problem of Timing in International Transactions

A recent survey[3] of large U.S. firms showed that 59% of the respondents consider the timeline longer for international cash flows than for domestic cash flows. In fact, 21% claimed that the delay in obtaining cash is more than 60 days greater. In contrast, only 10% of the firms claimed that the cash cycle is shorter with international operations. There are a number of reasons for such delays.

Value Dating

In many other countries, a practice known as *value dating* is commonly applied to cash transfers. Value dating is analogous to an availability schedule in the United States, but the timing can work in both directions.

Forward Value
Forward value refers to the crediting of a deposit after the date of deposit. It is analogous to availability delays in U.S. banking practices. For example, in France, if a firm deposits a check drawn on a distant town, it may be given credit in 1 to 3 business days.

Back Value
Back value has no ready counterpart in the United States. It refers to the posting of a debit before the date of presentment. For example, in Italy, a check presented against a firm's disbursement account is subtracted from the account

---

[3] Collins, J. M., and A. W. Frankle, "International Cash Management Practices of Large U.S. Firms," *Journal of Cash Management* (July–August 1985), pp. 42–48.

as of the date on the check rather than on the presentment date. In France, the amount of a wire transfer is effectively subtracted from the firm's account balance 1 day previous to the initiation date. Check and cash withdrawals are treated similarly.

Foreign banks often do not charge explicitly for their transfer services. Compensation for services is in the form of balances created by value dating.

Implications of Value Dating

The primary implication of value dating is more than timing delay. In addition, the transaction cost is not simply the nominal bank charge. The opportunity cost must also be considered. Value dating makes international funds transfers potentially much more expensive than domestic transfers. In the United States, if a wire transfer for $1,000,000 is sent, the charge may be $15 or .0015% of the transfer amount. If a similar wire is sent in a country in which 2 value days are lost, then at 12% interest the effective charge is $658, representing .066% of the transfer amount. The value-dated transfer costs about 45 times the fixed fee transfer charge.

Check Clearing

Timing Within Countries

Within some other countries, checks may clear very quickly. Distances are often much smaller than in the United States, and no other country has as many different commercial banks as the United States. Branch banking is generally country-wide. In many countries, however, delayed availability (forward value dating) and back-valued presentments are common. In Thailand, for example, it takes 6 to 7 days to clear checks between cities.

CANADIAN EXAMPLE. In Canada, for example, only five large commercial banks handle 90% of all checks. Since branching is countrywide, a large percentage of checks are treated as on-us items, receiving immediate availability. Checks drawn on other banks, if received by the afternoon cutoff time, are processed overnight through 10 nationwide clearing points and are given the equivalent of 1-day availability. In Canada this delayed availability is treated as an adjustment to the firm's bank balance by subtracting *debit float*. Checks also clear in 1 day. Since a presented check is subtracted from a firm's balance on the day of presentment, the 1-day clearing is treated as a *credit float* adjustment. Float extension games are not worthwhile in Canada. The primary management concern regarding float is to attempt to maximize the number of checks treated as on-us checks. This minimizes debit float and increases the firm's available balance.

Timing Between Countries

While check clearing within countries may, in some instances, be faster than U.S. check clearing, clearing checks *between* countries frequently involves significant delays. Checks drawn on a foreign bank and denominated in a foreign currency but deposited in a U.S. bank are treated as *collection items*. They are not assigned availability in the normal sense. They must be physically transported back to the country of origination and exchanged (at the prevailing exchange rate) for a check drawn on a U.S. bank. The dollar-denominated check is then sent back to the U.S. bank for clearing through conventional channels. This process may take 2 to 4 weeks.

In contrast, a check drawn on a foreign bank but denominated in U.S. dollars may be presented at a U.S. branch of that bank and receive much faster availability.

Mail Times

Mail processing between countries often involves significant delays. Parkinson (see Selected Readings) reports mail times to New York City from foreign points to be as follows:

London	7.0 days
Paris	6.0
Rome	10.0
Hong Kong	6.5
Tokyo	7.5
Sydney	8.0
Sao Paolo	7.0

Mail times within countries vary widely. In some European countries, such as Germany and Great Britain, mail times are quite fast and service is reliable. In other countries (especially less developed countries), mail service from one part of the country to another may take weeks. In some countries, firms find that it is best not to rely on mail services at all. Cables or courier services may have to be used for financial transactions.

Credit Risks and International Finance

Selling goods almost always entails credit risks. When the buyer resides in a foreign country, there is an added level of risk. First, there may be informational barriers that prevent the seller from knowing the exact degree of credit risk involved. The potential buyer may speak a different language than the seller and may report financial data in an unfamiliar form. There may be no familiar credit rating agencies to help out.

Second, the legal remedies for nonpayment are less standardized and much more costly. At least two sets of national laws are involved in any dispute. The distances and complexity make settling international credit disputes very difficult.

Third, many more parties are involved in the transaction. Goods are often handled by a freight forwarder who arranges for shipment through a chain of common carriers, through a number of customs points, to another set of carriers and agents. The possibility of error is much higher than it is for domestic shipments.

Fourth, the added time delays in shipping and receiving payment add another element of risk. As we have seen, international transactions can add 60 days or more to the collection timeline.

To deal with these additional risks, firms often use payment procedures different from those in domestic use. These procedures involve two principles: (1) control of the ownership of goods through the use of controlling documents and (2) transfer of the credit risk from an unknown party to a relatively sound party. There are a number of ways to implement these two principles. We discuss two primary ones here.

Documentary Collections

Perhaps the most common form of international transaction is the documentary collection. Here title to the goods is retained until the seller is satisfied that payment has been or likely will be made.

The primary controlling document used is the *bill of lading*. As shown in Figure 19.1, a bill of lading is issued to the seller by a common carrier (such as an ocean line) that agrees to transport goods for the seller. It documents that the carrier has received the shipment from the seller. The bill of lading can be thought of as title to the shipment. The seller sends the bill of lading (usually

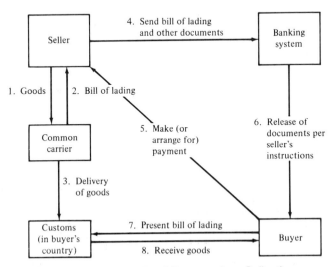

Figure 19.1 Example of Documentary Collections.

through a bank) to the buyer. By presenting the bill of lading to customs, the buyer is able to obtain release of the goods. The essence of control is for the seller to retain the bill of lading until the buyer has paid for the goods.

In one variation on this procedure, the buyer is allowed to pay for the goods after the shipment is released. The procedure is the same as the previous one except that a time draft is used, indicating that the buyer has accepted the obligation to honor the draft in the future. An accepted draft is known as a *trade acceptance*. The risk is that the buyer will not pay the draft when due. Hence, this instrument is generally used only when the buyer is considered a good credit risk.

Collections Through Letters of Credit

Even with documentary collections, there is still the risk that the buyer may not be able or willing to make payment when it comes due. After paying shipping charges and waiting for 2 months until the shipment is released to the buyer, the seller may be surprised to find the buyer unwilling to take delivery. The seller must then pay to have the goods shipped back. There is a way to transfer this risk to the banking system by using a letter of credit. A letter of credit specifies that the buyer's bank will honor a draft drawn on the buyer's account if specified documents are received.

As shown in Figure 19.2, the mechanics of a letter of credit collection are very similar to those of documentary collection except that the buyer contacts

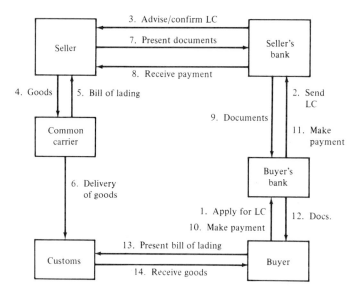

Figure 19.2 Example of Letter of Credit Collections. Note: this is one possible way for a letter of credit transaction to work; there are others. The order of some of the steps is arbitrary. For example, the buyer may be able to arrange for payment to the buyer's bank some time after the goods are received.

its bank to arrange for a letter of credit. The buyer's bank, if it decides to do so, assumes the credit risk on behalf of the buyer. The letter of credit specifying the exact terms of the transaction is sent to a bank in the seller's country. This latter bank then confirms to the seller that the letter of credit has been received. By confirming receipt of the letter of credit, the bank acknowledges that it accepts the obligation of the buyer's bank and is prepared to pay the seller when the terms have been met.

Features of Letters of Credit

Letters of credit specify the timing of payment. Most include a time delay to permit the shipment of goods and the interchange of documents. Also specified are the currencies required for payment.

Letters of credit may be valid for one transaction or could be issued for multiple transactions. The bank may back the buyer for open account purchases up to a specified amount.

Letters of credit are generally *irrevocable*. This means that provided that specified documents are presented, the issuing bank and any subsequent confirming bank will honor drafts presented against the letter of credit.

International Cash Management Services

Banks and other service providers offer a variety of services to help deal with international short-term financial problems. Many of these services parallel products offered domestically.

Wire Transfers

The mechanism for wire transfers between banks in different countries is different than for wires between two U.S. banks. In the United States, transfers are made by simply debiting and crediting the Federal Reserve accounts of the sending and receiving banks. Since no international equivalent of the Federal Reserve exists, banks must find other transfer mechanisms.

Correspondent Networks

Almost all international wire transfers involve the debiting and crediting of correspondent balances. If a firm in Canada, for example, wants to wire funds to a Japanese firm, the firm's Canadian bank would send a cable message to the Japanese firm's bank in Japan. Assuming that the two banks have a correspondent relationship with each other, the Japanese bank would debit the Canadian bank's correspondent balance and credit the Japanese firm's balance. Meanwhile, the Canadian bank would debit the Canadian firm's balance. If the Canadian bank does not have a correspondent relationship with the Japanese bank, the transfer is routed through a third bank that has a correspondent relationship with both banks.

SWIFT (Society for Worldwide Interbank Financial Telecommunications)

SWIFT is not a settlement system but a communication system that facilitates settlement of wire transfers through correspondent balances. There are over 1,600 banks members of SWIFT. European and U.S. banks are most heavily represented. Before the development of SWIFT, cable instructions had to pass through an ad hoc network and perhaps several different languages. The result was frequent errors in transfer routing and amounts. The innovative feature of SWIFT is the standardization of cable messages to a common format. Computer software available on a worldwide scale can read and interpret SWIFT messages so that the chance for making errors is greatly reduced. In addition, information routing is more carefully managed to reduce the number of misdirected messages.

CHIPS (Clearing House Interbank Payment System)

CHIPS is a netting system whose members are most of the major domestic and foreign banks in New York City. Information on cash transfers between all member banks is passed via computer transmission to the CHIPS system. At the end of the business day, net transfers are computed. Settlement occurs via Federal Reserve accounts for the major CHIPS members and via correspondent accounts for other members. The great majority of all dollar-denominated international transfers clear through the CHIPS system. On most days, hundreds of billions of dollars are transferred through CHIPS.

Lockbox Systems

In many developed countries, such as Great Britain, Canada, and Germany, where postal systems are well developed and banks branch nationally, lockbox services are unnecessary for collecting and processing checks in the local currency. In less developed countries, such as South American and Asian nations, few areas have reliable postal systems. This problem has given rise to lockbox collection services. Generally these services are offered through branches of U.S. banks.

Balance Reporting

Balance reporting on an international scale has several difficulties. First, bank information in some countries may be restricted. Second, telecommunications between countries may also be restricted. Third, encryption of sensitive bank information may be prohibited or restricted. Fourth, in many developing countries, the technological base is not sufficiently developed to support the informational requirements of balance reporting. The result is that balance reporting services across international boundaries have been much slower to develop than domestic services. Nevertheless, a number of banks and third parties do provide limited levels of balance reporting.

Demand Deposit Practices: Interest and Overdraft Banking

In the United States, regulations forbid banks to pay interest on demand deposits and also forbid automatic overdraft coverage without formal booking of a loan. Few other countries have such restrictions.

Most foreign countries permit the payment of interest on demand deposits. Bank compensation is usually in the form of fees or value dating. Excess balances are not the problem they are in U.S. banks—except for the opportunity cost of earning less in bank balances than in other investments.

While banks pay interest on positive balances, many foreign countries permit banks to simply charge interest for negative balances. This is called *overdraft banking*. There is always a spread, however, between the rate paid on balances and the rate charged on overdraft loans.

GIRO Systems

In European and some other foreign countries, GIRO banks provide a payment system that is different from the U.S. systems. GIRO payments are primarily for consumer transactions, but corporations can use GIRO payments between them in some cases. U.S. firms with retail outlets in other countries often use the GIRO system to collect customer payments. A GIRO payment from a buyer to a seller occurs as follows.

First, the seller sends an invoice to the buyer. The invoice includes a GIRO payment stub encoded with the seller's bank and account number. Second, the buyer signs the stub and takes it to a GIRO processor. In many cases, the post office is the primary GIRO processor. Third, the processor provides the information to the GIRO bank, which debits the buyer's account and credits the seller's account.

Since the system processes such a large number of payments, the economies of scale have resulted in relatively low processing costs. Collection time is reduced, since no mail delay is involved. Collection and concentration are performed in one step. It is also possible to use GIROs to make payroll payments.

Pooling Services

Pooling is used by firms that may have a number of operations in the same country. Some of the bank accounts that the firm controls may be in overdraft on a given day, while others may have positive balances. As long as all of the firm's accounts are with branches of the same bank, the bank can sum across all accounts and treat all balances as essentially one balance. The primary purpose of pooling is to avoid interest payments in deficit accounts while there are offsetting positive balances elsewhere in the firm's accounts.

Intracompany Netting Systems

Netting systems reduce the number of actual cash flows between two or more parties. Transaction information may be frequently exchanged during some time period, but cash payments are not made. Instead, the information is accumulated until the end of the time period and then only net payments are made. The reason a firm may want to be involved in netting will be clarified in an example.

The subsidiaries of large multinational firms often have extensive business dealings with each other. For example, the German subsidiary may buy raw materials from the Dutch subsidiary and may have to make several deliveries per week. The German subsidiary then manufactures the finished product and sells it back to the Dutch subsidiary. With each business transaction, cash would normally be sent between the subsidiaries. Each time cash is sent, there may be exchange rate losses, bank charges, and value dating losses. Netting systems seek to minimize these costs.

If only two subsidiaries are involved in the netting system, it is called *bilateral netting*. If more than two are involved, it is called *multilateral netting*. The principles and procedures are the same. A party, often a bank, gathers ongoing information about the transfers between all parties in the system. At the end of the netting period, the amounts due to and from each subsidiary are computed and net transfers are made.

Benefits of Netting

Netting reduces transfer costs such as cable costs, SWIFT charges, bank costs, etc. Figure 19.3 shows the impact of the reduction in the number of transactions. Assume that each firm makes a cash payment to every other firm 20 times per month. Without netting the number of transaction links between three parties is six and the number of transactions per month is 120. With netting, only three transfers need be made at the end of the month. The transaction cost savings in this case would be $(120-3) \times$ (cost per transaction).

In general, the number of connecting links (considering both inflows and outflows) between N parties in a payment system is

$$N \times (N - 1).$$

So, for large systems, the transaction cost savings can be significant. For a system of 30 subsidiaries, with 20 transactions per month at $15 per transaction, the total cost per month is

$$30 \times (30 - 1) \times 20 \times \$15 = \$261,000.$$

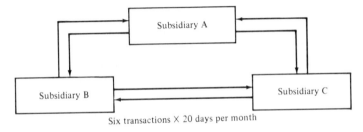

Six transactions × 20 days per month

A. Three firms without netting

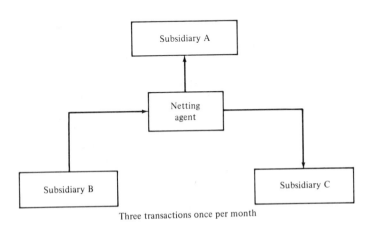

Three transactions once per month

B. Three firms with netting

Figure 19.3 Netting Systems.

With a netting system, there would be 30 payments per month at a cost of, for example, $300 each (the relatively high cost would be paid to the netting agent), for a total of $9,000 per month. The savings is quite significant.

Netting also reduces losses from value dating and other delays that may accompany each payment. In addition, netting reduces the costs associated with foreign exchange. Each time currency is exchanged, value is lost due to the bid/ask spread. Exchanging currency in larger amounts usually results in closer spreads. Netting enables the firm to exchange larger amounts than would be possible with smaller individual transactions.

Netting provides more centralized control over cash flows, enables headquarters to orchestrate cash movements between subsidiaries, and potentially allows better short-term investment and borrowing decisions. Leading and lagging can be more easily implemented if the firm has tight control over interfirm payments.

Costs of Netting

With netting systems, there may be some loss of local autonomy. The manager of the subsidiary may be used to making independent payment timing decisions. Netting is also difficult or illegal in some countries (e.g., those of South America) where cross-border cash flows are controlled carefully. Some European countries require approval to set up a netting system. Of course, the netting agent must be compensated for handling communications between parties and information processing.

Reinvoicing Centers

A *reinvoicing center* is a department or separate subsidiary of a firm that handles many of the international cash flows for that firm. For example, a U.S. exporter may want to set up a reinvoicing center in another country to purchase all of the exporter's products and handle all billing to the firm's customers. In addition, the reinvoicing center is responsible for all foreign exchange transactions involving the company. This includes hedging the firm's transaction exposure and conducting spot currency trading activities. Some reinvoicing centers may also be responsible for conducting the firm's netting operations.

Reinvoicing centers are almost always located outside the United States. One reason is that U.S. banking regulations do not permit demand deposit accounts in currencies other than U.S. dollars. Other countries permit accounts in foreign currencies. A reinvoicing center needs access to accounts in multiple currencies in order to conduct its foreign exchange operations more easily.

Reinvoicing centers essentially establish the foreign exchange and foreign trade activities of the firm as a profit center. This enables top management to focus more clearly on the results of its foreign operations. In addition, reinvoicing centers permit the firm to monitor export collections more effectively, practice leading and lagging, and obtain more favorable exchange rates because of the centralization of the currency exchange function.

To operate effectively, a reinvoicing center should be located in a country that has liberal tax laws, free currency exchange, and a well-developed banking system.

Summary

Today's economy is truly a global economy. More and more, firms are expanding their reach to customers and suppliers beyond their national borders. As they do so, greater emphasis must be placed on the international dimensions of short-term financial management.

Although short-term financial problems are fundamentally the same when firms move into international arenas, one new factor becomes important: the need to exchange one currency for another and the risk that the rate of exchange may be unfavorable to the firm in the future. Wherever there is risk, however, strategies and products are developed to eliminate or reduce it. With exchange rate risk, there are a number of contracts, options, and strategies to deal with the problem.

Another risk that increases as firms move across borders is credit risk. Procedures like documentary collections and letters of credit have evolved to help eliminate or at least reduce that risk.

The timeline is generally much longer for international transactions, and transaction costs are higher. Again, tools have been developed to counteract such problems. Netting systems help reduce transaction costs, and GIRO systems and evolving cash management products abroad help shorten the timeline.

Discussion Questions

1. Describe how extending the cash flow timeline across international borders affects the following areas relative to domestic short-term financial management:
   a. Exchange rate risks
   b. Time delays
   c. Credit risks
   d. Taxation
   e. Transaction costs
   f. Attitudes toward efficient cash management
   g. Information availability
2. How do the objectives of international short-term finance differ from those of domestic short-term finance?
3. Compare and contrast transaction and translation exposure. On which should the financial manager focus more attention?
4. Differentiate between the following methods of exchanging currency: spot market, forward contract, futures contract, currency option. What is a long-date forward?
5. If a currency is expected to weaken against the dollar, should a U.S. firm lead or lag receivables and payables? Explain.
6. What is meant by value dating? Distinguish between forward- and back-value dates.
7. How does a check clear when it is drawn on a Japanese bank in yen and deposited in a U.S. bank?
8. How does a bill of lading help control credit risk?
9. Explain how a letter of credit works in an export transaction.
10. What part does SWIFT play in the transfer of cash from company A in the United States to company B in Thailand?

11. Explain how demand deposits are treated differently in other countries with regard to interest and overdrafts.
12. How does a GIRO payment work?
13. What are the pros and cons of using a multilateral netting system?
14. Explain why a firm would want to set up a reinvoicing center in a foreign country.

Problems

1. Suppose a U.S. firm holds a 6,400,000 yen receivable due in 60 days from a Japanese firm. Assume that the current exchange rate is 154 yen/$. In 60 days the exchange rate moves to 142 yen/$. How much does the U.S. firm gain or lose (in dollars) compared to the case where the exchange rate remains unchanged?

2. A transfer of $1,500,000 from a Swiss bank to a German bank involves a value dating delay of 2 calendar days. The banking charges are $10. With an opportunity cost of 12%, what is the total cost of the transfer?

3. What is the transaction exposure if a U.S. exporter has receivables totaling 200,000 DM and payables totaling 1,200,000 DM if the current exchange rate is 1.70 DM/$? What does the firm gain or lose if the rate goes to 1.60 DM/$? If it goes to 1.80 DM/$?

4. Suppose a multinational firm has 20 subsidiaries that participate in a netting system. The normal cost per transaction is about $20. Each subsidiary transacts with each other subsidiary about 10 times per month on average. With the netting system, one payment is made to or from each subsidiary each month. The cost per subsidiary for the netting system is $200 per month. How much does the firm save (or lose) in transaction costs by netting compared to not netting?

Selected Readings

BENNETT, ROY F., "Improving Canadian Cash Management," *Cashflow* (March 1984), pp. 20–21.

BOKOS, WILLIAM J., and ANNE P. CLINKARD, "Multilateral Netting," *Journal of Cash Management* (June 1983), pp. 24ff.

CELI, LOUIS J., and B. RUTIZER, "Treasurers Overlook Asian Cash Management Opportunities," *Cashflow* (June 1983), pp. 24–27.

COHEN, FRED L., "Accelerating Foreign Remittances and Collections," *Cashflow* (May 1981), pp. 36–40.

COLLINS, J. M., and A. W. FRANKLE, "International Cash Management Practices of Large U.S. Firms," *Journal of Cash Management* (July–August 1985), pp. 42–48.

GIDDY, IAN N., "International Commercial Banking," in *Financial Handbook*, 5th ed., Edward I. Altman (ed.), New York: Wiley, 1981, Chapter 14.

GREGURAS, FRED M., "Impact of Transborder Data Flow Restrictions on Cash Management Services," *Journal of Cash Management* (September–October 1985), pp. 11–14.

GRIFFITHS, SUSAN H., and NIGEL J. ROBERTSON, "Cash Management Italian Style," *Journal of Cash Management* (March 1984), pp. 53–55.

GRIFFITHS, SUSAN H., and NIGEL J. ROBERTSON, "Treasury Management in the U.K.," *Journal of Cash Management* (July 1984), pp. 64–68.

HARIED, A. A., L. F. IMDIEKE, and R. E. SMITH, "Accounting for Foreign Currency Transactions" and "The Translation of Financial Statements of Foreign Affiliates," in *Advanced Accounting*, 3rd ed., New York: Wiley, 1985, Chapters 13, 14.

HEKMAN, CHRISTINE R., "Foreign Exchange Exposure: Accounting Measures and Economic Reality," *Journal of Cash Management* (February 1983), pp. 34–45.

LEVICH, RICHARD M., "Exchange Rates and Currency Exposure," in *Financial Handbook*, 5th ed., Edward I. Altman (ed.), New York: Wiley, 1981, Chapter 12.

MADURA, J., and E. T. VEIT, "Use of Currency Options in International Cash Management," *Journal of Cash Management* (January–February 1986), pp. 42–48.

MARSHALL, R. G. C., "Managing Short-term Multicurrency Portfolios," *Journal of Cash Management* (November–December 1984), pp. 64–69.

MCARTHUR, B. K., and L. J. MACKINLAY, "Guidelines for Effective Canadian Cash Management," *Journal of Cash Management* (November–December 1986), pp. 56–60.

OOSTHOEK, WILLEM N., "European Girobanks: What They Are and How to Use Them," *Journal of Cash Management* (January–February 1985), pp. 22–24.

PARKINSON, KENNETH L., "Dealing with the Problems of International Cash Management," *Journal of Cash Management* (February 1983), pp. 16–25.

SAMPSON, RICHARD, "Locating a Netting, Re-Invoicing, or Factoring Center," *Cashflow* (March 1985), pp. 36–38.

SHOCH, JAMES R., III, "Management of U.S. Cash Flows for a Foreign-based Multinational," *Journal of Cash Management* (May 1984), pp. 40–44.

WELLS, ROBERT L., and DAVID E. MILLER, "Hedging Foreign Currency Exposure," *Cashflow* (October 1985), pp. 21–24. (One section on long-date forwards and another on foreign exchange options.)

20

Electronic Data Interchange

In 1986, General Motors announced that over the next 5 years it planned to replace almost all of its paper business transactions (e.g., purchase orders, material releases, shipping documents, invoices, and payments) with electronic transactions. The phased implementation of this plan began with the payment system. At the time, General Motors was sending out approximately $4,000,000,000 per month in 400,000 paper checks to some 20,000 suppliers. They proposed replacing as many of these checks as possible with electronic payments. The company formed a private payment network involving eight major banks to handle most of the payments and utilized the ACH system for the remainder. Later phases of the project would eventually replace other paper transactions with electronic messages. What did they hope to achieve? By reducing personnel costs, cutting inventory, improving production control, and eliminating paperwork, they hoped to save about $1,300,000,000 annually. Industry analysts project that such a move would save over $200 per car.

Electronic data interchange (EDI) has the potential to revolutionize the management of short-term assets and liabilities and to have far-reaching effects on virtually every part of the cash flow timeline—from inventory management to credit policy to cash management. This chapter introduces the basic concepts of EDI and shows how it may be used to improve short-term financial management.

The Cash Flow Timeline and EDI

Definitions

Electronic data interchange (EDI) is the movement of information electronically in a machine retrievable format between a buyer and a seller (including

522

intermediaries) for the purposes of facilitating a business transaction. The information needed in a typical business transaction might contain items such as a request for quote, availability inquiry, purchase order, purchase order acknowledgment, shipping documents, invoice, payment advice, and freight bill. Most such documents are currently transported between parties on paper via the mail system. EDI converts the documents to electronic messages routed directly between trading partners or through information networks. The data contained in such electronic documents may be either in a standard, widely accepted format or in a proprietary format mutually agreed upon by the trading partners.

Electronic payment (EP) can be considered a subset of EDI. It refers to the transfer of monetary value electronically from buyer to seller. Such transfers must also include a financial intermediary—usually a bank—to facilitate the transfer of value. There are currently two primary forms of EP in this country: wire transfers (sometimes referred to as EFT) and ACH transfers (both discussed in Chapter 5).

EDI and EP may be implemented independently. A firm may transact all of its business activities using EDI and then make payment with a paper check. Conversely, a firm may use paper for its document interchange and then settle with an ACH transaction.

EDI can potentially replace any paper document that is exchanged between a buyer and a seller in the course of completing a business transaction. Figure 20.1A illustrates a simplified cash flow timeline, including some of the paper documents that flow between the two parties. The lines connecting buyer and seller are slanted, indicating that there is typically a time delay between sending and receiving the document. This is because of the mail and processing time delays usually associated with the paper system. With EDI, the time needed to exchange information between parties is greatly reduced, as illustrated in Figure 20.1B. Mail time and a large percentage of processing time delays are eliminated. In addition, information contained in the purchase order need not be keyed into the computer again to produce an invoice, shipping documents, payment advice, and so on. Potentially, therefore, EDI can increase speed and accuracy, as well as reduce personnel costs needed to process information.

Example of a Typical Business Transaction

A typical business transaction occurs as follows: The buyer first inquires about the availability of a specific product. This might occur when the buyer's purchasing agent searches through the seller's catalog and/or phones in an inquiry. Second, an order is placed by generating a purchase order and mailing it to the seller. Even phone orders (which account for about one third of all initial orders) are usually followed up with a printed purchase order to provide tangible evidence of the buyer's commitment. (In part, the purpose of this tangible evidence is to leave an audit trail.) After receiving the purchase order, the seller keys the information into its computer system. Third, the

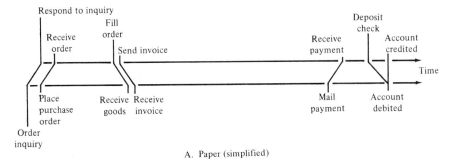

A. Paper (simplified)

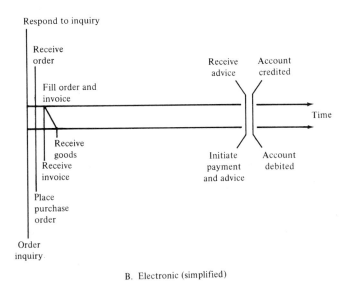

B. Electronic (simplified)

Figure 20.1   Cash Flow Timeline Activities.

order is filled, and shipping documents and an invoice are sent. Fourth, after some time delay allowed by the seller's credit policy and the buyer's payment policy, the buyer prepares a check and mails it to the seller. The seller then applies the check to the buyer's receivable account and deposits the check. After an availability delay, the seller receives available funds for the check. In the final steps, there are follow-up activities like check reconciling, auditing, and management reporting.

The entire process may be characterized as an exchange of documents between buyer and seller. We may classify such documents into four different groups, as illustrated in Table 20.1. *Preordering documents* refer to any information exchanged prior to an actual order, such as requesting a bid, catalog information, or pricing information. Some firms even share production

Table 20.1 Documents Exchanged in a Business Transaction

Document Type	Purpose	Examples
Preordering documents	Provide information needed to make a decision to order	Order inquiry Production planning Catalog information Bid solicitation Request for quote Response to solicitation Price quotes
Purchase ordering	Place order	Purchase order Material release Purchase order acknowledgment Order status inquiry Change order
Filling order	Provide goods or services to buyer	Shipping documents Invoice Freight bill Bill of lading Shipment location inquiry
Payment	Transfer value from buyer to seller	Payment Payment advice Payment acknowledgment Adjustments Stop payments

planning information with suppliers so that suppliers will know what materials are needed by what date to satisfy production demands.

Purchase order documents refer to information exchanged at about the time the order is placed. A purchase order is the most common way of facilitating the purchase of materials or goods. Some firms negotiate a purchase order for an entire year, specifying the delivery of goods at an agreed price. However, no goods are released until a *material release* is received. This document authorizes the shipment of goods mentioned in the purchase order.

Order-filling documents include such items as shipping documents, invoices, and freight bills. When materials are given to a carrier for delivery, a *bill of lading* transfers responsibility for the goods to the carrier. Often the buyer makes an inquiry about the location of a shipment. Documents are then exchanged tracing the shipment to its current location.

The final set of documents relates to the payment and information surrounding it. If payment is sent to a seller at one location but the information is needed at another location, a payment advice is sometimes used. Stop payments are instructions to a disbursing bank that prevent a payment from clearing the disbursing account. If payment is for other than the invoiced amount, an adjusting document tells of the discrepancies.

Problems with the Current System

The paper-based system has several flaws. These can be seen in the example of two firms, a buyer and a seller that both have mainframe computers for storing and retrieving order and sale information.

Labor Intensive

First, paper-based systems are labor intensive. Figure 20.2 illustrates the repeated keying steps in a typical transaction. A purchase order is initiated by retrieving order data from the mainframe computer and keying them in via a typewriter or preparing an order form. Upon receipt of a purchase order, the seller keys the information into its mainframe computer. Then an invoice is produced by this same keying operation. A shipping document is sent— also produced by manually keying information onto a shipping form. Upon receipt of the invoice, the buyer keys information from the invoice into its payment system. A check is created—also by manual intervention. The seller then manually keys the check information into its receivable system, applies the amount, and sends an acknowledgment. While perhaps not all transactions require this degree of manual intervention, most systems do and many add a number of other steps.

Error Prone

Obviously, the greater the number of rekeying operations, the greater the chance for error. Errors lead to inefficient use of the firm's cash and cause

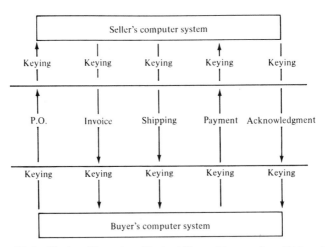

Figure 20.2 Keying Steps in a Typical Paper Transaction (Abbreviated).

delays in the collection of payments. Errors can also have adverse effects on production and quality control.

Uncertainty

Because of reliance on the mails to move documents between buyer and seller and the need to process documents manually, information flow has considerable uncertainty associated with it. Mails are known to be uncertain because of processing demands, weather, and a host of other factors. Uncertainty in parts of the timeline usually means uncertainty in the ultimate payment date and in the associated transfer of value. When payments are uncertain, the firm must maintain higher liquidity reserves and, therefore, earn lower interest on its investment portfolio.

Slow

Paper-based, mail-oriented information systems are, of necessity, slow. This slowness, coupled with uncertainty, means higher inventory levels for manufacturers who rely on mailed purchase orders or material releases to supply goods. Delays can cause potential delays in assembly lines and other business activities. Delays also mean that payment is received later. While this is good for the buyer, it is bad for the seller, potentially increasing his or her financing requirements. Reliance on paper can cause managerial problems as well. Reports needed to monitor timeline activities are often delayed, thereby lessening managerial control over business activities.

Benefits and Costs of EDI

Benefits of EDI

EDI overcomes many of the problems associated with paper-based transactions. Figure 20.3 illustrates the path information flows in an EDI system. The initial order information is keyed in at the beginning of a transaction. From that point on, the information can be reformatted to create subsequent documents such as an invoice, shipping documents, and payment advices. Rekeying is not necessary since the data—at least most of the relevant data—are available in computer-readable form. Information is moved electronically between firms through communication networks.

Reduced Labor Costs

Because of reduced dependency on rekeying and paper handling, EDI reduces labor costs. Applying payments to accounts receivable, for example, is much faster when done electronically than when performed manually. Check reconcilement is likewise almost instantaneous when done electronically. Storage and retrieval costs are significantly reduced.

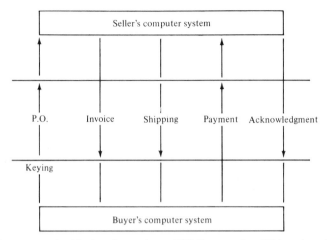

Figure 20.3 Keying Steps in an EDI Transaction (Abbreviated).

Reduced Error Levels

Since fewer rekeying steps are involved in EDI, errors can be significantly reduced.

Reduced Uncertainty

At the same time, uncertainty can be reduced because documents do not depend on mails and manual processing to move between firms. Payments can also be more certain, since transaction dates can be specified in advance. In some cases, the seller can control the payment date rather than the buyer (as in ACH debit transactions). Since electronic purchase orders can be sent almost instantaneously, an electronic acknowledgment can be received confirming that the order was received and that materials are or are not in stock. This feature does much to eliminate uncertainties associated with back order problems and shipping delays.

Lower Inventory Levels

The speed and certainty of EDI transactions also enables buyers to reduce inventory levels. Manufacturers are keenly interested in just-in-time inventory procedures (discussed in Chapter 17), in which materials arrive just in time for use on the assembly line—and not before, taking up expensive storage space and causing extra financing charges. EDI is all but essential in efforts to implement just-in-time systems.

Faster Payments

EDI also means that buyers could end up paying for goods or services much faster than under the paper payment system. We will show that earlier payment need not be a problem if credit terms are adjusted in a manner that is fair to the buyer and seller.

Management Control

EDI enables management to have better control of business activities. For example, tracking an order sent by rail car is a slow process when done by phone or mail. Using electronic methods (such as by bar coding freight cars and shipment containers), rail carriers can capture location information and route it over communication lines to the buyer. This enables management to plan production schedules around expected arrival times rather than have plants wait for shipments to arrive. EDI likewise enables management to have almost instantaneous reports about purchase orders, invoices, expected payment dates, and other information. Corresponding reports about a paper-based system would take much longer to produce. At the same time, auditing of electronic transactions may be simpler and faster than auditing of paper transactions.

Enhanced Service

Because of its speed and immediate acknowledgment capabilities, EDI enhances the service that the seller can provide to customers. A large hospital supply company, for example, receives orders over a computer network directly from hospitals. It delivers requested goods on an overnight basis. The speed of response ensures good relationships with hospitals and clinics, which greatly value the service.

Magnitude of Cost Savings

Gauging the magnitude of cost savings that might be realized in moving from paper to EDI is not an easy task. Most firms find it difficult to estimate what portion of personnel costs, for example, could be reduced. Placing value on reduced uncertainty is also difficult, as is placing value on better managerial control. Since so few firms have actually implemented extensive EDI systems, it is also hard to estimate the startup costs to cover computer hardware, software, training, and other implementation activities.

Given these difficulties, some analysts have ventured to place a dollar range on the savings a firm could realize for each document transferred via EDI rather than paper. One survey shows this to be approximately $5 per document. The automotive industry estimated savings of $200 per car if the industry implemented EDI. The grocery industry estimated savings of $300,000,000 if only 50% of its transactions were done by EDI. A heavy duty truck manufacturer estimated savings of $600 per truck.

Economywide Impact

Regardless of the particular estimates chosen, it is becoming clear that EDI could have a significant impact on the U.S. economy. Assume for a moment the $5 per document cost, realizing that for each payment there are at least five backup documents (one purchase order, one invoice, etc.) and about 10,000,000,000 corporate-to-corporate payments per year. The aggregate savings from EDI, given these numbers, is a staggering $250,000,000,000 per year!

Costs of EDI

Hardware

EDI implementation requires investment in several different areas. Computer and communication hardware is needed. Firms that already own computer systems may not need an additional investment, since EDI is an application software program. EDI systems can be run on microcomputers, minicomputers, or mainframe computers. Perhaps the most significant cost in this area relates to the additional computer power needed to distribute information along various points of the timeline where data interchange is currently being performed by hand.

Software

EDI software is required to convert data from the firm's present computer system to a data format that can be sent comprehensibly to another computer. Perhaps the largest single investment in EDI implementation is the software to translate the firm's current system into EDI form. We address this issue more in the next section.

Dual Paper/EDI Systems

For many years, firms will undoubtedly need to operate both paper and EDI systems in parallel. Not all business partners will be able to handle EDI transactions—especially at first.

Disturbing the Current System

The paper system has been with us for centuries. There is a good deal of inertia involved in changing from such a deeply ingrained system. We are comfortably familiar with paper transactions and are perhaps slightly afraid of the uncertainties of the unknown.

For example, some firms are concerned that management will lose control of purchase orders. Formerly management could literally sign off on purchase orders of which they approved. How will the sign-off be replaced under an EDI system? New administrative procedures will have to be developed. For example, control can still be maintained by having managers enter certain authorization codes releasing an EDI purchase order. Almost every procedure associated with paper processing can have a counterpart in an electronic processing system.

Security

Another concern with EDI is security. Firms have learned how to safeguard the paper-based system, but many fear that home computer "hackers" could break into a firm's electronic payment system and misappropriate funds. Nevertheless, there are security precautions that can be taken with EDI systems that may make them as safe as or perhaps safer than paper-based systems.

Coded passwords control access to the system. *Encryption procedures* scramble data sent from one point to another. If the data are intercepted by unauthorized parties, they will be unable to understand the data. The receiving party has the software necessary to unscramble the data into its original form. *Authentication* procedures use encryption methods to ensure that the data have not been altered after being sent. Data security has become a well-developed field, and safeguards are available to protect a firm's interests.

EDI Standards

The Need for Standard Formats

With a paper-based system using a human being as an information processor, it does not matter if one firm's purchase order is in a different form than that of another firm. The individual reading a purchase order can make adjustments, digest the information, and enter the purchase order data in a form that the selling firm can use. The human brain is amazingly flexible in processing information.

However, when computers are involved in digesting information, they are much less tolerant of variations than humans are. Who hasn't been frustrated by the exacting requirements of the simplest computer language? If a firm wants to automate a system for reading purchase orders, the information in an electronic purchase order must be arranged in precisely the form the computer expects.

A firm could specify a data format that all of its customers could use to send electronic purchase orders. One field of the data format could be for the address to which goods are to be shipped. Another set of fields could be for the items ordered, and so forth. Each customer would use the same software to generate purchase orders with the seller.

The problem occurs when one customer wants to send electronic purchase orders to another supplier. That supplier may use a completely different format for purchase orders. The customer would have to have two sets of software to send orders. Extending this logic, it is conceivable that one buyer would have to deal with thousands of different types of purchase orders and, therefore, with thousands of different sets of software.

To avoid this problem of multiple formats, standard formats have been developed for generic purchase orders that have the flexibility to handle almost everyone's needs.

Industry Standards Development

Starting in the late 1960s, various industry groups formed committees to develop standards for particular industries. One of the first of these was the

Transportation Data Coordinating Committee (TDDC), formed in Washington in 1968 primarily with a push from the railroad industry. In the early 1970s, TDCC started to coordinate the efforts of several different transportation groups like the motor carriers, air carriers, ocean carriers, and warehouse groups. They were joined in the mid-1970s by the grocery, electrical, automotive, and chemical industries, among others. In 1975 the first standards were produced. In the late 1970s, the American National Standards Institute (ANSI) gave its blessing to the formation of a committee called ANSI X-12, which is charged with the development of standards that could be applied to corporate-to-corporate business transactions across all industry groups. ANSI X-12 was to complement the work already being done in the specialty areas.

While work is still going on, significant advances have been made. There are currently standards for over 150 different types of business transactions. These standards are generic, yet flexible, so that they cover almost every transaction a corporation would need. Software developers have produced packages that facilitate translation from a corporation's internal information system into standard format. Hence, without significant development costs, it is possible for two firms to send electronic documents to each other even though each has a different computer system and different software. As long as they use an agreed-upon standard, the data can be sent and read.

Network Communications

Need for Networks

Sending messages between two trading partners is not quite as simple as it sounds. Figure 20.4 shows a group of five trading partners who send each other EDI transactions. Firm A must have a communication link with firms B, C, D, and E. Likewise, firm B must have a link with firms C, D, and E. Ten communication links are needed to connect these five firms. We can generalize this computation. For N firms that communicate with each other, $N(N-1)/2$ communication links are needed to connect them. For 100 firms, that amounts to 4,950 connections.

A simpler way to communicate would be to send all messages to one central point and then route the message on to the recipient. Then each firm would only have to concern itself with one interface. This type of communication is called a *network*. There are two levels of service that networks provide. *Switches* channel messages from one party to another without providing extensive additional services. *Value-added networks* (*VANs*) provide more or less extensive capabilities for data storage, format conversion, summary reports, and other services. There are several advantages to passing messages through a VAN rather than directly to each trading partner.

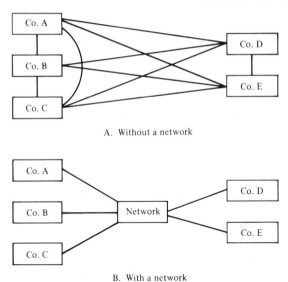

A. Without a network

B. With a network

Figure 20.4 Communication System.

Single Interface

Only one computer protocol is needed to communicate with all trading partners. This greatly simplifies software development, administration, training, and other requirements.

Processing Services

VANs can provide additional services to users. Some networks, for example, have the ability to do a limited amount of reformatting when receiving and sending messages. Networks can provide summary data and can verify that messages have been received by the other party.

Hours of Operation

VANs usually operate 24 hours a day. This is an advantage over dealing direct with firms that operate only during business hours or are located in different time zones.

Mailboxing

VANs can store documents and messages until the other party wants to read them. This capability enables both parties to send and receive documents whenever it is convenient. It also helps smooth peak loads.

Implementation Assistance

Since VANs provide service to many users, VANs often use this experience to assist new users to enter the field of EDI communications.

Economies of Scale

VANs spread fixed costs for software, hardware, and communications equipment over many users, thereby providing possible economies of scale on such things as long-distance rates, storage costs, and so on.

_____ Credit Terms and EDI Transactions _____

One of the barriers to EDI that concerns buyers is the problem of possible earlier payment with EDI transactions. Since EDI can drastically shorten the timeline, payment could be moved up significantly compared to that of the current paper-based system. This would cause the buying firm to incur an opportunity loss, since additional cash would have to be raised. Such fears neglect the fact that a buyer is generally also a seller; therefore, considering transactions in total, the firm would also benefit by faster cash inflows of an almost equal magnitude. Nevertheless, there seems to be concern about individual transactions or at least transactions with specific vendors. Hence, float loss is still a major factor, at least in the minds of managers facing the prospect of an electronic environment.

Zero-Sum Games

Many cash management activities can be thought of as *zero-sum games*. In such a game, "my win is your loss." The total amount remains unchanged; it is just divided differently. An example of a zero-sum game is remote disbursing. If a buyer uses remote disbursing, the seller receives available funds later and the buyer holds cash longer. The buyer wins and the seller loses—but the total is still the same. Conversion to EDI, however, is not a zero-sum game. With EDI it is possible for both parties to save transaction costs, inventory costs, administrative costs, and so on. The question remains: can payment terms be adjusted so that the buyer's potential savings are not counteracted by the costs of earlier payment? Using the present value techniques developed in Chapters 2 and 15, we can show that it is possible to shift the timing and/or amount of cash flows such that both buyer and seller realize significant savings.

The key is to use credit terms to shift wealth between the buyer and seller by trading off price, timing, and transaction costs in a present value framework. The movement to EDI/EFT is essentially a shift in credit terms.

Negotiating Shared Benefits

Figure 20.5 shows a simplified timeline that focuses on the elements concerning credit policy. Under the paper system, suppose that n days elapse from the delivery-of-goods date until the payment finally clears the buyer's disbursement account. Under an EDI system, the clearing time is likely faster and the payment initiation time may be moved ahead. Suppose m days elapse

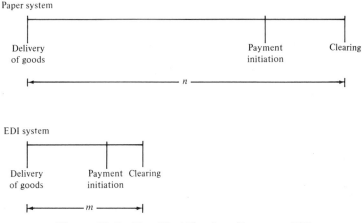

Figure 20.5 Simplified Timeline: Paper vs. EDI

between delivery of goods and final clearing. How is the buyer to be compensated for earlier loss of cash?

Cash Discounts for Sharing Benefits

Cash discounts can be used to offset earlier payment. How much of a discount is required by the buyer? How much of a discount can the seller afford to offer? The amount of discount each party is willing to consider depends on several factors.

TIMING DIFFERENCES. First, the discount depends on the difference between n and m. The longer the time difference, the greater the discount. While n and m may be slightly different for the buyer and seller because of Fed float, these differences have actually been disappearing over the past few years.

OPPORTUNITY COSTS. Second, the discount depends on the opportunity cost as viewed by each party. The opportunity costs of each are not necessarily the same. One party may have a higher or lower cost of funds than the other.

TRANSACTION COSTS. Third, the discount demanded by the buyer or offered by the seller depends on the differences in transaction costs between paper and EDI. Transaction costs can be both fixed and variable, startup and continuing. Firms must frequently deal with multiple purchase orders per invoice and multiple invoices per payment. In practice, most firms have difficulty estimating transaction cost savings, especially since moving to EDI involves both startup costs and fixed, ongoing costs. For purposes of this simple model, we assume that all costs are variable.

Example of Negotiated Payment Terms

Buyer's Viewpoint

Gigantic Retail, Inc., is negotiating EDI relationships with its suppliers. The current paper system results in an average payment time (n) of 60 days from delivery of goods. Gigantic would like to receive a discount and use EDI (including payment by ACH) that would result in payment 10 days from delivery. Gigantic estimates that it could save $25 on each transaction. Its cost of funds is considered to be 12%, and the average payment from suppliers is $10,000. What kind of discount must Gigantic request from its suppliers and break even compared to current payment terms?

To determine this, we first compute the present value of Gigantic's current (paper system) cash flow:

$$PV_p = \frac{-10,000}{1 + \frac{60(.12)}{365}} - 25 = -\$9,832.$$

The sign is negative because both the payment and the transaction cost are outflows. We treat the $25 savings as an added cost of the paper system. Now we ask what kind of discount would be required to make the present value of the cash flow equal $-\$9,832$ with the timing associated with the EDI system:

$$PV_e = \frac{-10,000(1 - d)}{1 + \frac{10(.12)}{365}} = -\$9,832.$$

Solving this expression for the discount, d, gives

$$d = 1.36\%.$$

This means that if Gigantic could receive a 1.36% discount, it would be just as well off in a present value under the EDI terms paying in 10 days as under the paper terms paying in 60 days. It would be better off, of course, if it could negotiate a larger discount.

Seller's Viewpoint

Suppose one of Gigantic's suppliers is Hill Valley Manufacturing. Hill Valley is a smaller firm with a much higher cost of funds, say 16%. This firm estimates that it could save about $15 per payment by adopting EDI. Since Hill Valley would be paid earlier under the EDI system, it benefits in two ways: transaction costs and funding costs. What kind of discount can the firm afford to give up? We approach the answer in the same way as we did with Gigantic: we compute the present value under the paper system and then do the same for the EDI system. The present value of a typical cash flow under the paper system is

$$PV_p = \frac{10,000}{1 + \frac{60(.16)}{365}} - 15 = \$9,729.$$

The discount that Hill Valley can offer is computed by solving the following equation for d:

$$PV_e = \frac{10{,}000(1 - d)}{1 + \dfrac{10(.16)}{365}} = \$9{,}729$$

$$d = 2.28\%.$$

In other words, Hill Valley can afford to offer a discount of 2.28% and be no worse off in a present value sense than it is after receiving payment by paper in 60 days. It would, of course, be better off if it could be paid in 10 days and offer a smaller discount.

Negotiating Range

The *negotiating range* is defined as the difference between the maximum discount the seller can afford to offer and the minimum discount required by the buyer. Since Hill Valley can afford to offer up to a 2.28% discount and Gigantic must have at least a 1.36% discount, there is room for negotiations that will make both buyer and seller better off. The negotiating range is 2.28% − 1.36% = 0.92%. If, for example, the two parties agreed upon a 2.0% discount, both should be very happy with the arrangement. Gigantic's present value would be

$$PV_e = \frac{-10{,}000(1 - .02)}{1 + \dfrac{10(.12)}{365}} = -\$9{,}768,$$

which is a smaller cash outflow than the −$9,832 under the paper policy. For Hill Valley, the present value with the 2% discount is

$$PV_e = \frac{\$10{,}000(1 - .02)}{1 + \dfrac{10(.16)}{365}} = \$9{,}757,$$

which is a larger cash inflow than the $9,729 under the paper policy. Hence, both parties are better off when transaction costs and the cost of funds are taken into account.

Other Methods of Sharing Benefits

Not all firms will want to use cash discounts as a way of sharing the benefits of EDI. Cash discounts may be considered too difficult to monitor and enforce. An alternative vehicle is timing. For example, in exchange for implementing EDI, a seller could compensate a buyer for the faster clearing of electronic transactions by granting additional days before payment is initiated. Suppose the paper system takes 5 days from the time a check is sent until it clears the buyer's disbursement account. By using EDI, suppose clearing is moved up to 1 day. The seller could extend credit terms an additional 4 days to counteract the shift.

Synthesis

By recognizing that shifts in payment terms can facilitate wealth sharing, both buyer and seller can benefit from a move to EDI. Since there is more to gain than simply timing (float), negotiating credit terms is not a zero-sum game, as other cash management strategies may be. Because of the possibility of altering credit terms, neither buyer nor seller should consider float changes to be a barrier to the implementation of EDI.

Summary

The paper-based transaction system that has existed for centuries may soon be replaced with EDI. The drop in the cost of computer power, coupled with the increase in labor costs, make EDI a significant factor in the cost saving efforts now being made by most corporations. Competitive pressures from home and abroad are forcing firms to become more efficient—to provide more output at lower costs. EDI is certainly one means that will lead to this end. In the process, the management of short-term assets and liabilities could be drastically changed. Information flows will speed up, cash will move more quickly, inventories can be reduced, forecasting can be improved, and managerial responsibilities will change. As the cash flow timeline shrinks, the role of its various participants will undoubtedly change over time.

Discussion Questions

1. What are the major problems with the current paper-based business transaction system?
2. How can EDI overcome most of these problems? Are there any problems created by EDI?
3. No one seems to be concerned about producing standard paper invoices. Why are EDI standards such an important issue?
4. How can a VAN facilitate EDI? Why is communication via a VAN simpler than direct communication?
5. What are some of the barriers to overcome in implementing EDI?
6. How can cash discounts be used to compensate for changes in timing brought about by EDI transactions?
7. What factors would make the buyer's minimum discount and the seller's maximum discount unequal?

8. What kinds of trading relationships would most likely provide the largest incentives to both buyer and seller to enter into EDI transactions?

_____ Selected Readings _____

ARTHUR D. LITTLE, *Electronic Data Interchange for the Grocery Industry: Feasibility Report*, Cambridge, Mass.: Author, 1980.

COHEN, SHERYL L., "GM Setting Up Network in Lieu of Using ACH," *Pensions and Investment Age* (July 21, 1986), p. CM1.

FERRIS, TOM, "GM Readies Electronic Bill Paying," *The American Banker* (October 1986), p. 2.

HILL, NED C., AND DANIEL M. FERGUSON, "Negotiating Payment Terms in an Electronic Environment," in *Advances in Working Capital Management*, Greenwich, Conn.: JAI Press, 1988.

HILL, NED C., AND DANIEL M. FERGUSON, "EDI and Payment Terms: Negotiating a Positive Sum Game," *Journal of Cash Management* (September–October 1987), pp. 21–26.

HILL, NED C., AND ROBERT A. WOOD, "I'm OK, You're OK: The Electronic Win/Win Deal," *Canadian Cash Management Review* (September–October 1983), pp. 3–5.

STONE, BERNELL K., "Cash Cycle Management and the ANSI X12 Committee," *Journal of Cash Management* (August–September 1983), pp. 37–38.

WHITE, GEORGE C., "EFT Opportunities for the Innovative Corporation," *Journal of Cash Management* (June 1982), pp. 42–48.

INDEX

Account analysis, bank charges, 90–93
Account executive, 315
Accounting identity, 467
  cash flow forecasting, 471
Accounting report, negative cash balance, 88
Accounts payable, 9, 429
  discount, 434–436
    effective annualized interest, 434–436
    present value approach, 434
    stretching, 434
  information system requirements, 437–439
  payment options, 431–436
  processing flow schematic
    parallel, 438–439
    sequential, 438
  stretching, 431–434
    economic considerations, 432–433
    ethics, 432
    legal sanctions, 432
    optimal, 433–434
  terms of purchase, 431
Accounts payable manager, 18
Accounts receivable, 9
  cash flow, 397–400
  collateral, 322
  credit, 369–370
  directly related financing, 384–386
  forecasting, 408–412
    percent of sales method, 408, 411
    percent of sales vs. receivable balance fraction, 409
    receivable balance fraction method, 408–409, 410
  monitoring, 393–408
  monitoring individual accounts, 393–395
    adjusted average collection time, 395
    average collection time, 394–395
    monthly aging schedule, 393–394
    refined aging schedule, 394
  monitoring overall, 396–408
    aging schedules, 400–401
    average days outstanding, 401–403
    cash flow, 397–400
    constant payment pattern, 398
    overall receivables measure, 396–397
    receivable balance pattern, 403–408
    sales, 397–400
Accounts receivable matrix, aging schedule, 405–407
Accrued expense, 9, 429, 436–437
  increased
    benefits, 436–437
    cost, 437
Accrued tax, 429

Add-on note, 315
Administrative cost, disbursement system, 212
Aggregate cash flow timeline, liquidity, 46–47
Aggregate cash position management, 172
Aggregate timeline, 9–10
  retailer, 9–10
Aging fraction, 400
Aging schedule, 393–394, 400–401
  accounts receivable matrix, 405–407
  revised, 405–406
American National Standards Institute, ANSI X–12, 532
Anticipation, transfer initiation, cash concentration, 186–188
Anticipation discount, 377
Ask price, 236
Asset, current. See Current asset
Asset valuation
  equilibrium models, 29
  short-term finance, 29–34
Asset-based loan, 323–325
  commercial finance company, 345–346
  security arrangements, 324–325
    accounts receivable loan, 324
    field warehouse, 324
    floor planning, 324
    inventory, 324
    public warehouse, 324
Automated clearing house, 76
Automated clearing house transfer, 108, 124–132
  administration, 125
  advantages, 129–131
  conditional transactions, 131
  credit transactions, 127
    uses, 128
  data formats, 129, 130
  debit, cash concentration, 185
  debit transaction steps, 125–127
  defined, 108
  direct payroll deposit, 126
  disadvantages, 131
  disbursement account funding, 222–223
  electronic return item speed, 132
  future developments, 131–132
  growth, 125
  history, 124–125
  ownership, 125
  prenotification, 129
  reconciliation, 129
  return items, 129
  same-day availability, 131
  settlement timing, 128
  value dating, 132
  weekend processing, 129

541

Automated depository transfer check, cash
  concentration, 184
Automated teller machine network, 153
Availability float, 143
Available balance, 78–80
  assigning availability, 80
    cutoff time, 82
  business day, 80
  calendar day, 80
  computations, 82–84
  deposit and presentation schedule, 80–81
  timing, 79
  uses, 84
  vs. company book balance, 86–87
Average days outstanding, 401–403
  quarterly computations, 402

Backup liquidity, 4
Bad debt, 41, 413
  credit terms, 373
Balance averaging, 191–192
Balance reporting, international, 514
Balance sheet, 7–8
  permanent current assets, 7
  permanent current liabilities, 7–8
  problems, 7
  working capital, 7–8
Balancing plug, 471
Balancing variable, 471
Bank
  collection function, 63–64
  compensating balance, 63
  concentration. *See* Concentration bank
  concentration function, 63–64
  consulting services, 65
  customer base, 65
  defined, 61
  demand deposit, 62
  depository function, 62–63
  disbursement function, 63–64
  Edge Act, 70
  electronic information, 76
  Eurodollar deposit, 63
  fiduciary, 64–65
  foreign commercial, 75
  function, 61–65
  funds transfer, 76
  investment, 64
  loan production office, 69
  major regional, 65
  mixed account, 63
  money center bank, 65
  money market, 238
  regulation. *See* Banking regulation
  short-term borrowing, 313–338
  short-term credit, 64
  time deposit, 62
  transaction balance, 62–63
Bank balance, 78–89
Bank compensation, 89–98, 101–102
  account analysis, 90–93
  alternative compensation by fees, 93
  by balances, 95–96
    bank negotiations, 95
    cost, 96
    double counting, 95
    dual balances, 95–96
    higher service charges, 95
    liquidity, 95
    soft-dollar budgeting, 95
    transaction balances, 95
  compensating balance, 91
  earnings credit, 92–93
  FDIC insurance, 91
  fee compensation, 93–95
    banking cost control, 94
    cost, 95
    interest opportunity cost, 94

preventing overcompensation, 94–95
    reserve requirement, 93–94
    tax deductibility of fees, 94
  mixed compensation, 93
    cost, 95–96
  model for evaluating alternatives, 96–97
    computations, 97–98
  reserve requirements, 91–92
  service charges, 90–91
  strategies, 93–98
Bank credit, 314–321
Bank number, 69
Bank prime rate, interest rate comparison, 343
Bank security, 244–245
  banker's acceptance, 245, 250
  negotiable certificate of deposit, 245, 250
    fixed rate, 245
    variable rate, 245
Banker's acceptance, 235, 245, 250, 319–320
  pricing, 320
Banking Act of 1980, 220
Banking regulation, 65–70
  bank numbers, 69
  Depository Institutions Deregulation and
    Monetary Control Act, 67
  Douglas Amendment, 66
  dual banking, 65
  Edge Act bank, 70
  Federal Deposit Insurance Corporation, 68
  Garn–St. Germain Act, 67
  geographical restrictions, 69–70
  Glass–Steagall Act, 66
  Justice Department, 68
  limited branching, 69
  line of business restrictions, 70
  major commercial, 66–67
  McFadden Act, 66
  Office of the Comptroller of the Currency, 65–68
  Securities and Exchange Commission, 68
  state banking regulation, 68
  statewide branching, 69
  unit banking, 69
Banking relations, 4
Banks for Cooperatives, 244
Beta, 32
Bid price, 236
Bill of lading, 511–512
  electronic data interchange, 525
Bill validation, information system requirements,
    437–439
Billing, 391
Bond equivalent yield, 264
Borrowing
  risk-free rate, 29, 33
  unsecured, 321
Borrowing portfolio, 313
Box–Jenkins model, 488
Broker, 236
Budgeting, 465
Bureau of Government Financial Operations,
    recommendations, 139
Business loan, sources, 313–314
Business risk, 27

Capital asset pricing model, 29–34
  application, 32
  asset expected return, 31
  asset vs. portfolio risk, 30
  basic model, 30–32
  capital budgeting discount rate, 32
  market imperfections, 32–34
  measuring risk, 30
  pricing risk, 30
  real asset valuation, 32
  risk, 30–31
  risk-return measurement, 31–32
  short-term finance role, 32–34
  systematic risk measurement, 30–31

systematic vs. unsystematic risk, 30
Capital market, perfect, characteristics, 29
Capital market assumptions, 29
Captive finance company, 348–353
    defined, 348–349
    diversified receivables portfolio, 352
    finance subsidiary, 349, 350–351
    legal separation of obligations, 353
    manufacturing-credit separation, 352
    receivables quality, 352
Cash, stock, 104, 105–106
Cash balance
    determining size, 281–286
        Baumol model, 281–283
        Miller and Orr model, 283–284
        Stone model, 284–286
    liquidity, 259
Cash balance model, liquidity, 259–260
Cash before delivery, 376
Cash budgeting, 465
Cash concentration, 171–196
    administrative control systems, 195
    administrative costs, 179
    advantages, 173–180
    aggregate cash position management, 172
    anticipation, transfer initiation, 186–188
    balance reporting function, 173
    centralized, 183–186
        automated clearing house debit, 185–186
        automated depository transit check, 184–185
        parameters, 183
        third-party providers, 184
        variations, 184
        wire drawdown, 186
    clearing delays, 186–188
    concentrating transfers, 173
    control, 179–180
    cost reduction, 186–195
        administrative, 194–195
    costs, 174
    decentralized, 181–183
        advantages, 183
        disadvantages, 183
        parameters, 182
    defined, 171
    deposit anticipation, 187
    depository transfer check, 182
    dual balance, 176–179
        causes, 178
        critical day, 177
        estimating, 194
        increasing benefits, 192–194
        negative, 178–179
        transfer mechanism comparison, 193
        transfer mechanisms, 179
        variability, 194
        weekend effect, 177
        weekend timing, 192–194
    excess balance opportunity costs, 174–176
    field systems, 180–181
    improving control, 195
    information delay, 186
    ledger anticipation, 187
    lockbox systems, 180, 181
    managerial costs, 179
    objective function, 173–180
    one-time-transfer-out, 187–188
        level balances, 188
        variable balances, 189
    practice, 180–186
    processing delay, 186
    receive deposits, 172
    short-term security investments, 172, 173
    short-term transactions, 172
    system diagram, 172
    tasks, 172–173
    transfer costs, 176, 188–192
        balance averaging, 191–192
        banking charges, 176
        breakeven analysis, 188–191
        managerial costs, 176
        rules of thumb, 190–191
        vendor charges, 176
    transfer funds, 172
    wire transfer, 182
Cash flow, 4, 104, 105–106
    accounts receivable, 397–400
    amount, 46–47
    credit policy alternatives, 412–413
        indirect, 413
    hedging uncertain, 287–310
    internal, 4
    major, 476
    nonmajor, 476
        subcomponents, 476
    predictability, 46–47
    schematic diagram, 4, 5
    timing, 46–47, 414
    uncertainty, 414
Cash flow fraction, 403–404
Cash flow timeline, 6
    aggregate timeline, 9–10
    collection system
        general, 142
        over-the-counter, 147
    controller, 19
    credit, 369–370
    credit manager, 19
    credit term decision, 40
    disbursement, 207
    electronic data interchange, 522–527
    equipment replacement, 34–35
    financial decision-making, 34–35
    inventory, 453
    inventory policy, 44
    marketing manager, 19
    multiple cash flow, 37, 38
    organizational structure, 19–20
    payables manager, 19
    present value, 53–57, 414–419
        basic model, 53–55
        decision criterion, 54
        factors, 417–418
        net present value for current policies, 53–54
        net present value of proposed policies, 54
        nonconstant sales, 55–57
        planning horizon effect, 54–55
        procedure, 414–417
        risk considerations, 417
        synthesis, 418–419
    president, 19
    price risk, 288
    purchasing manager, 19
    single cash flow, 35, 36
    transaction timeline, 6, 9
    treasury manager, 19
Cash forecasting, 463–497
    administrative costs/benefits, 465
    cash scheduling, 480–482
    control, 465–466
    daily, 465
        accuracy evaluation, 479
        benefits, 475–476
        cash distribution approach, 482–485
        cash distribution approach advantages, 484
        cash distribution approach disadvantages, 485
        cash distribution approach parameter
            estimation, 484
        cash distribution approach weekly and monthly
            cycles, 482–484
        cash scheduling advantages, 480
        cash scheduling disadvantages, 480
        cash scheduling uses, 480–482
        individual transactions vs. aggregate input
            data, 479–485
        input data collection, 476–478

Cash forecasting—cont'd.
  daily—cont'd.
    input data selection, 476–478
    input variable–cash flow relationship, 478–479
    multiple approaches, 485
    process, 476–479
  excess balances, 465
  forecast system, 466
  horizons, 464–466
  income, 465
  interest costs, 465
  long-range, 464
  medium-range, 464–465, 466–474
    accounting identities, 471
    balance sheet changes, 473
    balancing variable, 471
    computing policy variables, 470–471
    dependent variable computation, 467–468
    depreciation, 472–473
    driving variable, 467
    income statement approach, 466
    inflow-outflow cash flow, 473–474
    net cash flow from earnings, 471–473
    net cash flows, 471–474
    percent sales approach, 469–470
    policy relationships, 468
    sales-related variables, 469–470
    technological relationships, 467–468
    timing-variable relationship, 470
  need, 463-464
  objectives, 465–466
  short-term, 474–485
  spreadsheet software, 495–497
    downloading, 496–497
    sensitivity analysis, 496
    template, 496–497
    uploading, 496–497
  tools, 485–488
    Box–Jenkins model, 488
    exponential smoothing, 486–487
    judgment, 485
    moving average, 485–486
    regression analysis, 488
    time series analysis, 487–488
Cash in advance, 376
Cash inflow, 39–41
Cash letter, 116
Cash management attitude, international vs.
    domestic, 500
Cash management system, schematic diagram, 5
Cash manager, 17
  short-term finance, 18
Cash market, 288
Cash mobilization, 140–141
  defined, 140
Cash on delivery, 376
Cash operating cycle, 9–10
Cash outflow, 39–41
Cash scheduling, 480–482
Cash system, 4
  elements, 4
Cash terms, 376
Certificate of deposit, 235. *See also* Specific type
Charge card system, 104
Check, 104–107, 111
  availability schedules, 120–122
    contractual obligation, 121–122
    determinants, 121
  check clearing, 112
  check presentment, 112–113
  check system, 111
  clearing mechanisms, 115–117
    cash letter, 116
    commingled shipment, 117
    correspondent bank direct send, 116–117
    Federal Reserve System direct send, 117
    local clearing houses, 115–116
    local correspondent banks, 116

    local Federal Reserve banks, 116
    on-us checks, 115
  defined, 104
  delivery, 112
  deposit, 112
  hold period, 118
  payee bank processing, 112
  payee processing, 112
  preauthorized, 118
  preparation, 112
  reporting, 113
  returned, 117–118
  transferring value, 111–113
Check disbursement system, 204
Check-like payment instrument, 118–120
  comparison, 119
CHIPS, 135, 136
Clearing delays, cash concentration, 186–188
Clearing House Interbank Payment System. *See*
    CHIPS
Coin and currency, 104, 108–111
  counting, 109–110
  defined, 104
  intermediaries, 110–111
  security, 108–109
    independent information flow, 109
    physical, 108–109
  timing, 110
  verification, 109
Collateral, 321–323, 322
  accounts receivable, 322
  inventory, 322
  management costs, 323
  me-first value, 322
  psychological value, 322
  secondary repayment source, 322
Collection agency, 385
  credit term enforcement, 393
  with recourse, 385
Collection cost, 413
Collection float, 142–143
Collection location study, 157–164
  objective, 157
Collection lockbox study
  data required, 158–160
    administrative costs, 159
    availability times, 159
    city averages, 159
    customer remittance data, 158
    Federal Reserve schedules, 159
    fixed costs, 159
    mail times, 158–159
    opportunity cost, 159
    potential collection sites, 158
    processing times, 159
    timing data, 158
    variable costs, 159
  solution approaches, 160–164
    complete enumeration, 160
    greedy algorithm, 160–163
    heuristic solution algorithms, 160
    interchange algorithm, 164
    mathematical programming solutions, 160
    stopping point, 164
Collection policy, 391
Collection procedure, 391–393
  billing, 391
  objective function, 391
Collection system, 4, 139–164
  accurate cash flow information, 141
  audit trail, 141
  automated teller machine network, 153
  availability float, 143
  average daily float, 143–144
  cash flow timeline
    general, 142
    over-the-counter, 147
  cash flow timing, 167–169

cash mobilization, 140–141
  defined, 140
central information system updating, 141
collection float, 142–143
control, 141
defined, 139
design, 142–146, 167
electronic trade payable, 153
faster, benefits, 140
float cost, 144–145
float measurement, 143–144
improvement recommendations, 139
increased present value, 145–146
individual item float, 143
mail float, 142
mailed payment, 150–152
  basic components, 150–151
  collection point location, 151
  collection point number, 151
  in-house vs. external operation, 151
  payor type, 152
  prior assignment, 151–152
  system design, 151
net settlement, 153
optimizing, 145–146
  reduce availability float, 146
  reduce mail float, 145
  reduce processing float, 145–146
over-the-counter
  bank compensation, 149
  deposit bank selection, 148–149
  information gathering, 149
  payment type accepted, 148
  system optimization, 149–150
over-the-counter collections, 147–150
  basic components, 147, 148
  field office location, 147
  field unit, 147
  local deposit bank, 147
  system design, 147–149
point-of-sale terminal, 153
preauthorized automated clearing house debit,
  153
preauthorized check, 153
preauthorized draft, 153
preauthorized payment, 153
present value float costs, 144–145
processing float, 142
requirements, 139–141
types, 147–153
Commercial bank. See also Bank
Commercial finance company, 345–346
  asset-based loan, 345–346
  interest rate, 345
Commercial paper, 235, 245–246, 250, 339–345
  defined, 339–340
  denomination, 340
  direct vs. dealer paper, 341, 342
  discount note, 341
  effective interest rate, 343–345
  growth, 340
  interest costs, 342–345
  interest rate comparison, 343
  interest-bearing, 341
  maturity, 245, 246, 340
  primary issuers, 340–341
  rate, 246
  rating, 341–342
  rolling over, 340
  yield, 245
Commitment fee, 316–317
Commodity exchange, 289, 290
  primary contracts, 290
Commodity price movement, margin account
  change, 292, 293
Communication, 18
Company book balance, 84–90
  vs. available balance, 86–87

Compensating balance, 63
Compounded value calculation, 51
Concentration bank
  balance reporting function, 173
  concentrating transfers, 173
  selection, 213
  short-term security investment, 172, 173
Concentration system, 4
Consignment terms, 377–378
Consolidated Collateral Trust Debenture, 244
Consolidated Federal Farm Loan Bond, 244
Continuous flow manufacturing, 456
Control cost, disbursement system, 212–213
Controlled disbursing, defined, 219
Controlled disbursing bank, 219–220
  large vs. small, 220
Controller, 368
  cash flow timeline, 19
  short-term finance, 18
Convenience store chain, 171, 463
Conventional factoring, 347
Cost
  discount loan, 326
  factoring, 347–348
  line of credit, 326–331
  revolving credit agreement, 331
  single-payment loan, 325–326
  variable interest rate, 331–332
Coupon bearing security
  pricing, 265–266
  yield, 265–267
Credit
  accounts receivable, 369–370
  cash flow timeline, 369–370
  importance, 367–368
  market imperfection, 371–372
    flexibility, 372
    information inefficiencies, 371–372
    inspection period, 371
    transactions costs, 372
  perfect market, 370–371
  policy decisions, 368
    managers making, 368–369
  total collection time focus, 370
Credit agency, 381
Credit agreement, revolving, 318
Credit evaluation cost, 413
Credit history, 381
Credit information analysis, credit scoring system,
  383
Credit information survey, 380–381
Credit manager, 368
  cash flow timeline, 19
  short-term finance, 18
Credit policy alternatives, 412–419
  bad debt, 413
  cash flow, 412–413
    indirect, 413
  collection cost, 413
  credit evaluation cost, 413
  invoice amount, 413
  timing, 414
  uncertainty, 414
Credit risk
  foreign customers, 499–500
  international short-term finance, 510–513
Credit terms, 372–380
  administrative costs, 373–374
  anticipation discount, 377
  bad debts, 373
  cash in advance, 376
  cash on delivery, 376
  cash terms, 376
  change difficulty, 375
  consignment terms, 377–378
  constraints, 375
  credit agency, 381
  credit information analysis, 382–384

Credit terms—cont'd.
  Credit information analysis—cont'd.
    capacity, 382
    capital, 382
    character, 382
    collateral, 382
    conditions, 383
    credit scoring system, 383
    financial statement analysis, 383
    multiple discriminant analysis, 383
    qualitative approach, 382–383
  credit information survey, 380–381
  credit limit, 384
  day counting, 380
  defined, 372
  discount terms, 376–377
  electronic, 378
  electronic data interchange, 534–538
    negotiating shared benefits, 534–538
    zero-sum game, 534
  enforcement, 392–393
    action schedule, 392
    collection agency, 393
    direct actions, 392
    late payment determination, 392
    legal action, 393
  error types, 380
  factors, 373–379
  financial statement, 381
  financing receivables, 374
  industry convention, 375
  investment information services, 381
  invoice billing, 379–380
  legal constraints, 375
  letter of credit, 378
  news report, 382
  other firm functions, 374
  past credit history, 381
  penalty charges, 379
  prox terms, 377
  references, 381
  sales profitability, 373
  seasonal dating, 377
  standard terms, 376
  statement billing, 379–380
  survey, 375–379
  time value costs, 374
  working capital constraints, 375
Credit union, 61
Currency conversion
  currency option, 506
    currency call option, 506
    currency put option, 506
  forward exchange contract, 504–505
  futures contract, 505–506
  hedge, 504
    strategies, 506–508
  long-date forward contract, 505
  spot market, 504
  vehicles, 503–506
Currency option
  currency conversion, 506
    currency call option, 506
    currency put option, 506
Current assets, 12–16
  aircraft and missiles, 15
  industrial chemicals, 15
  iron and steel, 15
  manufacturing corporation assets, 12, 13
  printing and publishing, 15
Current liabilities, 12–16
  aircraft and missiles, 15
  industrial chemicals, 15
  iron and steel, 15
  manufacturing corporation assets, 12, 13
  printing and publishing, 15

Daylight overdraft, 134
Days sales outstanding, 401–403
Dealer, 236
  abitrage activity, 236–237
  income, 236–237
Dealer carry, 236
Debt
  bad, 41, 413
  credit terms, 373
Default risk, 268
Demand deposit, 62, 78–79
Deposit anticipation, cash concentration, 187
Deposit bank, 79
Deposit float, 87
Deposit time delay, 85
Depository Institutions Deregulation and Monetary
    Control Act, 67, 203
Depository transfer check, 119
  automated, 184
  cash concentration, 182
  disbursement account funding, 222–223
  dual balance, 176, 179
  excess balance, 174, 176
  mailed, 182
  transfer cost, 176
Depreciation, net cash flow, 472–473
Direct financing, 384
Direct send, 116–117
Disbursement
  cash flow timeline, 207
  decision types, 213–216
  practices, 205–206
  unauthorized, 212
Disbursement account funding, 222–223
  automated clearing house transfer, 222–223
  depository transfer check, 222–223
  wire funding, 222
Disbursement bank, 203
  selection, 213
Disbursement decision, 17
Disbursement delay, 85
Disbursement float, 87, 207
  components, 207
Disbursement funding system, 4
Disbursement system, 4, 203–226
  account funding mechanism, 213
  administrative cost, 212
  automatic investment services, 219
  case study, 228–231
  centralized systems, 215–216
  check-issuing points, 203
  concentration bank, selection, 213
  control, 204
  control cost, 212–213
  controlled disbursing accounts, 219–221
    bank selection, 219, 220
    high dollar group sort, 220
    MICR line information, 220
    noon presentment, 220–221
  cost components, 206–213
  decentralized systems, 215
  disbursement authorization authority, 213
  disbursement bank, selection, 213
  disbursement float, 207
    components, 207
  disbursement payment, 213
  dual balance, 211
  excess balance, 209–210
    causes, 209–210
    defined, 209
  mail float, 208–209
  missed discount, 209
  objective function, 206
  payable through draft, 219
  payee relationships, 211–212
  payment determination decision, 214

disbursement authorization, 214
drawee bank selection, 214
funding amount and timing, 214
mail point, 214–215
payment preparation, 214
payment release, 214
tactical decisions, 214–215
payment float, 207
components, 207–209
presentation float
availability float, 221
clearing slippage, 221
components, 221
defined, 221
reconciliation services, 218–219
remote disbursement services, 221–222
cost, 221–222
stretching, 221–222
stop payment, 212–213
stop payment services, 219
strategic decisions, 213–214
studies, 223–225
computer algorithms, 224–225
constraints, 223
data bases, 224–225
objectives, 223
time value cost, 206–209
tools, 216–222
transaction cost, 210–211
defined, 210
transfer mechanism, 210
zero balance accounts, 217–218
different bank master accounts, 218
pseudo–zero balance account, 218
reduced excess balances, 217–218
value, 218
Discount, 241
accounts payable, 434–436
effective annualized interest, 434–436
present value approach, 434
stretching, 434
security. *See* Discount security
Discount calculation, 25
Discount interest calculation, 51–52
Discount loan
cost, 326
effective rate, 326
Discount note, 314
Discount quote, 264
Discount security
pricing, 264–265
yield, 264–265, 265
Discount terms, 376–377
Discount yield, 264
Documentary collections, 511–512
Douglas Amendment, 66
Draft, 111
Drawee bank, 79
Driving variable, 467
Dual balance, 176–179
causes, 178
critical day, 177
depository transfer check, 176, 179
disbursement system, 211
negative, 178–179
transfer mechanisms, 179
weekend effect, 177
Dual banking, 65

Earnings, 463–464
Economic order quantity, 450–452
present value approach, 455–456
Edge Act bank, 70
Effective yield, 262–263
Electronic data interchange, 522–539

benefits, 527–529
bill of lading, 525
cash flow timeline, 522–527
cost savings, 529–530
costs, 530–531
current system disturbance costs, 530
dual systems, 530
hardware, 530
security, 530–531
software, 530
credit terms, 534–538
negotiating shared benefits, 534–538
zero-sum game, 534
defined, 522–523
economy-wide impact, 529–530
electronic payment, 523
enhanced service, 529
faster payments, 528
industry standards development, 531–532
lower inventory levels, 528
management control, 529
material release, 525
network communications, 532–534
economy of scale, 534
implementation assistance, 533
mailboxing, 533
need, 532–534
operation hours, 533
processing services, 533
single interface, 533
switches, 532
value-added network, 532
preordering document, 524–525
purchase order, 525
reduced error, 528
reduced labor costs, 527
reduced uncertainty, 528
standard formats, 531
Electronic information, 76
Electronic payment, electronic data interchange, 523
Electronic trade payable, 153
Encryption procedure, 531
Enron Corporation, 253
Equivalent present value, 37–38
Equivalent value, day choice, 36–37
Eurodollar Certificate of Deposit, 247
Eurodollar deposit, 63, 247
London Interbank Offered Rate, 303–304
Eurodollar security, 247, 250
Evergreen loan, 318
Excess balance
costs, 175
depository transfer check, 174, 176
disbursement system, 209–210
causes, 209–210
defined, 209
estimating, 174–175
opportunity costs, 174–176
sources, 175–176
Exchange rate, domestic vs. international, 499
Expense, accrued. *See* Accrued expense
Exponential smoothing, 486–487

Factor, 346, 385
Factoring, 346–348, 385
conventional, 347
cost, 347–348
maturity, 346–347
assignment of equity, 347
Fannie Mae. *See* Federal National Mortgage Association
Federal agency issue, 235
Federal agency security, 242–244
Banks for Cooperatives, 244
Federal Home Loan Bank, 243, 250

Federal agency security—cont'd.
  Federal Home Loan Mortgage Corporation,
    243–244
    guaranteed mortgage certificate, 243–244
    mortgage participation certificate, 243–244
  Federal Intermediate Credit Bank, 244
  Federal Land Bank, 244
  Federal National Mortgage Association, 243
  Federal Savings and Loan Insurance Corporation,
    243
  Government National Mortgage Association, 243
    pass-through security, 243
Federal Deposit Insurance Corporation, 68
Federal Financing Bank, 242
Federal Home Loan Bank, 243, 250
Federal Home Loan Mortgage Corporation, 243–244
  guaranteed mortgage certificate, 243–244
  mortgage participation certificate, 243–244
Federal Intermediate Credit Bank, 244
Federal Land Bank, 244
Federal National Mortgage Association, 243
Federal Reserve System, 68, 70–73
  banking policy regulation, 73
  branches, 114
  Consumer Advisory Council, 72
  discount rate, 72
  district banks, 70–71, 114
  Fed Open Market Committee, 73
  Federal Advisory Council, 72
  float, 122–124
    causes, 122–124
    cost, 122–123
    definition, 122
  float reduction, 123–124
    actual availability, 123
    charging, 124
    check truncation, 123–124
    fractional availability, 123
    interdistrict transportation system, 123
    noon presentment, 123
  interest rates, 287
  management, 71–72
  money market, 237
    Open Market Committee, 237
    primary dealer, 237
  money market purchases, 73
  money supply control, 72
  offices, 114
  organization, 70–72
  payment system, 72
  regional check processing center, 71
  Regulation D, 73
  Regulation E, 73
  Regulation J, 73
  Regulation Y, 73
  reserve requirements, 72
  role, 72–73
  Thrift Institution Advisory Council, 72
Federal Savings and Loan Insurance Corporation,
  243
FedWire, 132–135
  communications system, 132
  confirmation, 132
  cost, 133
  credit transaction, 133–134
  debit transaction, 134–135
  mechanics, 133–135
  messages, 133
  notification, 132
  reserve balance settlement, 133
  transfer system, 132
Field bank
  compensation, 200
  defined, 180
  features, 181
Financial asset, pricing, 10–11
Financial decision model, 11
  valuation framework, 23–48

Financial forward contract, 295–302
Financial futures, 248
Financial futures contract, 295–302
  fixed rate loan, 301
  hedging money market investment position, 302
  hedging stock positions, 302
  uses, 301–302
  variable-rate loan, 302
Financial management, basic objective, 10
Financial restructuring, term loan, 318
Financial risk, 25–29, 27
Financial security market, perfect, 32–33
Financial services deregulation, 73–75
  geographical restrictions, 74–75
  industry restrictions, 75
  interest rate ceilings, 74
Financial statement, 381
Financial statement analysis, 383
Financial statement lending, 321
Financing
  direct, 384
  fixed- vs. variable-rate, 354–357
    cash flow characteristics, 354
    cost, 355
    future interest rate expectations, 354–357
    future rate estimate sources, 355–357
    interest rate swap, 357
    risk aversion, 357–358
  indirect, 385–386
  off-balance sheet, 353–354
  private label, 386
  spontaneous, liquidity, 437
  spontaneous sources, 429–431
    accounts payable, 429
    accrued expense, 429
    accrued tax, 429
Financing receivables, 374, 384–386
  collection agency, 385
    with recourse, 385
  direct, 384
  factoring, 385
  indirect, 385–386
  private label financing, 386
  third-party tie-in, 385
Fitch Investor Service, 246
Fixed cost, 57
Fixed rate loan, financial futures contract, 301
Float measurement, 143–144
Foote, Cone and Belding Communications, Inc.,
  253
Foreign exchange exposure
  hedging, 506–508
    lagging, 507
    leading, 507
    spot market plus, 506–507
Foreign exchange risk, 501–508
  measuring, 502–503
  transaction exposure, 502–503
  translation exposure, 502, 503
Foreign security, 240
Forward contract, 289
  defined, 289
  hedging, 289
  vs. future contract, 291, 292
Forward exchange contract, currency conversion,
  504–505
Franchise value, 345
Funds transfer, 76
Future value, 23–24
Futures contract, 289–295
  buying, 291
  closing out, 292–295
    price decrease, 292–293
    price increase, 294–295
  currency conversion, 505–506
  daily limit, 292
  long hedge, 291
  long position, 291

maintenance level, 291
margin account, 291–292
margin call, 291
marking to market, 291
sells, 289–291
short hedge, 291
short position, 291
standard quantity, 290
vs. forward contract, 291, 292

Gamble, 26
Garn-St. Germain Act, 67
General credit manager, 368
General Motors, 522
Ginnie Mae. *See* Government National Mortgage
    Association
GIRO system, 515
Glass-Steagall Act, 66
Government National Mortgage Association, 243
    pass-through security, 243
Guaranteed mortgage certificate, 243–244

Hedge
    currency conversion, 504
        strategies, 506–508
    forward contract, 289
    imperfections, 300–301
Hedger, defined, 295
High dollar group sort, 220
Holding period yield, 263
    compounding period, 263
Holdover float, 220

IBM bond, 287
Index funds, 32
Index future, 302
Indirect financing, 385–386
Information
    costless, 29, 33
    instantaneously distributed, 29, 33
    international vs. domestic, 500
Information cost, money market, 238
Information delay, cash concentration, 186
Information system requirements, 437–439
Inside market, 236
Interest, risk, 267–268
Interest rate
    commercial finance company, 345
    comparison, 343
    line of credit, 317
    risk premium, 29
    risk-free rate, 29
    term structure, 268–274
        liquidity preference theory, 270–272
        market segmentation theory, 272
        pure expectations theory, 269–270
Interest rate futures contract, 296
Interest rate risk, 27, 267–268
    numerical examples, 268
Interest rate swap, 302–306
    defined, 303
    features, 305
    fixed- vs. variable-rate financing, 357
    interest payments, 303–304
    net amount, 305
    notional amount, 305
    payment exchange date, 305
    risks, 306
    swap out, 305
    using assets, 306
International cash management service, 513–518
International short-term finance, 498–519
    back value, 508–509
    bill of lading, 511–512
    check clearing, 509–510
    between countries, 509–510
    within countries, 509
    credit risk, 510–513

demand deposit practices, 515
documentary collections, 511–512
foreign exchange risk, 501–508
forward value, 508
GIRO system, 515
intracompany netting systems, 516–518
    benefits, 516–517
    bilateral, 516
    costs, 518
    multilateral, 516
letter of credit, 512–513
mail time, 510
objective function, 501
pooling services, 515–516
reinvoicing center, 518
time delays, 499
timing, 508–510
trade acceptance, 512
value dating, 508–509
vs. domestic short-term finance, 498–501
Inventory, 9
alternative policy comparison, 453–455
cash flow timeline, 453
collateral, 322
economic order quantity, 450–452
financing provided, 456
just-in-time. *See* Just-in-time inventory
motives for holding, 448–449
    contractual requirements, 449
    precautionary motive, 449
    speculative motive, 449
    transactions motive, 448–449
nature, 447
opportunity cost, 455
payment timing, 455–456
physical holding costs, 455
present value of present policy, 454
present value of proposed policy, 454
present value timeline approach, 452–455
previous treatment comparison, 453
purchase credit terms, 455–456
purposes, 447–449
safety stock, 452
setup, 455
traditional policy, 449–452
types, 448
    cash, 448
    finished goods, 448
    marketable securities, 448
    raw materials, 448
    work-in-process, 448
variability of demand, 452
Inventory cost
management costs, 449
stockout cost, 449
Inventory management cost, 450, 451
carrying costs, 450
setup costs, 450
Investment, bank, 64
Investment information services, 381
Investment pool, 247–248
Invoice billing, 379–380

Justice Department, 68
Just-in-time inventory, 456–458
planning, 457
setup costs, 456–457
supplier relations, 457–458
supplier-cost tradeoff, 458

Lambda, 258–259
Late payment, 392
Ledger anticipation, cash concentration, 187
Ledger balance, 78–80
computations, 82–84
cutoff time, 81
deposit and presentation schedule, 80–81
timing, 79

Lending, risk-free rate, 29, 33
Letter of credit, 315, 319
  credit terms, 378
  international short-term finance, 512–513
  irrevocable, 319
  maturity, 319
  pricing, 319
  revocable, 319
Liability, current. *See* Current liabilities
Line of credit, 315–318
  cash flow needs, 326–327
  cleanup period, 315
  commitment fee, 316–317
  committed, 316
  component cost breakdown use, 330–331
  cost, 326–331
  covenant, 317–318
  credit line size, 327
  defined, 315
  effective rate, 327–329
    components, 329–330
  interest rate, 317
  pricing, 316–317
  purpose, 315–316
  uncommitted, 316
Lines of communication, 18
Liquidity, 238–239
  aggregate cash flow timeline, 46–47
  asset-liability ratio, 256–259
  backup, 4
  cash balance, 259
  cash balance model, 259–260
  current ratio, 256–259
  going concern approach, 256–259
  lambda, 256–259
  marketability, 239
  measures, 256–259
  price stability, 239
  principal safety, 238
  quick ratio, 256–259
  spontaneous financing, 437
Liquidity portfolio, 4
Liquidity preference theory, 270–272
Loan
  asset-based, 323–325
  collateralized, 321–323
    secondary repayment source, 322
  secured, 321–325
  single-payment, 314–315
  sources, 313–314
Loan officer, 315
Lockbox, 154–157
  consortium, 156–157
  defined, 154
  float savings, 154–155, 156
  joint venture, 157
  mail intercept, 157
  multiple processing center, 157
  multistate bank holding company, 156–157
  net cost savings, 154–155
  networks, 155
  operating costs, 155, 156
  operation, 154
Lockbox bank, defined, 181
Lockbox location model, 157
Lockbox system, international, 514
London Interbank Offered Rate, 303–304
Long hedge, 291
Long position, 236, 291
Long-date forward contract, currency conversion, 505

Magnetic ink character recognition line. *See* MICR
  line
Mail float, 142, 208–209
  postmark date, 208
  receipt date, 208–209
Managing about a target, 191–192

Margin account, 291–292
Margin account change, commodity price
  movement, 292, 293
Margin call, 291
Market demand, 42
Market imperfection
  credit, 371–372
    flexibility, 372
    information inefficiencies, 371–372
    inspection period, 371
    transactions costs, 372
  short-term finance, 32–34
Market segmentation theory, 272
Market share, 42
Marketing manager
  cash flow timeline, 19
  short-term finance, 18
Master note, 320
Material release, 525
Materials as needed, 456
Maturity factoring, 346–347
  assignment of equity, 347
McFadden Act, 66
MDU Resources Group, Inc., 253
MICR line, 113–115
  disbursement system, 220
  elements, 113–115
    auxiliary on-us field, 115
    branch identification number, 115
    check digit, 115
    encoded amount, 115
    Federal Reserve district, 113–114
    Federal Reserve office, 115
    payer's account number, 115
    sequence number, 115
Missed discount, 209
Money, time value, 23–25
Money center bank, 65
Money market
  ask price, 236
  bank, 238
  bid price, 236
  broker, 236
  dealer, 236
    abitrage activity, 236–237
    income, 236–237
  dealer carry, 236
  defined, 235
  Federal Reserve System, 237
    Open Market Committee, 237
    primary dealer, 237
  information cost, 238
  inside market, 236
  long position, 236
  market participants, 237–238
    borrowers, 238
    lenders, 237
  repurchase agreement, 237
  retail market, 236
  round lot, 235
  short position, 236
  transactions agent, 236–237
  transactions cost, 238
  U.S. Treasury, 238
Money market investment, 235–249
  roles, 235
Money market mutual fund, 247–248
  liquidity, 247
Money market security
  characteristics, 238–241, 250
  liquidity, 238–239
    principal safety, 238
  risk-return tradeoff, 240–241
  yield, 239–240
    marketability, 240
    maturity, 239–240
    risk, 240
    taxability, 240

Money order, 119
Money supply
    transaction volume, 104, 105–106
    volume, 104, 105–106
Moody's Investor Service, 246, 249
Mortgage participation certificate, 243–244
Moving average, 485–486
Multiple cash flow, 37–39
    cash flow timeline, 37, 38
    equivalent present value, 37–38
    time horizon, 38–39
Multiple discriminant analysis, 383
Municipal security, 248–249, 250
    general obligation notes, 248–249
Municipals, 240
Munis. *See* Municipals
Mutual fund, 247
Mutual savings bank, 61

Negative balance, 88–89
    borrow short-term cash, 88
    cash and marketable securities, 88–89
    drafts payable account, 89
    problems, 89
Negotiable certificate of deposit, 235, 245, 250
    fixed rate, 245
    variable rate, 245
Net cash flow, 471–474
    balance sheet changes, 473
    balancing variable, 471
    depreciation, 472–473
    from earnings, 471–473
    inflow-outflow cash flow, 473–474
Net float, 85
    computation, 86–87
    volatility, 89
Net present value, 25
Net settlement, 153
Netting system, 135, 136
Note
    add-on, 315
    discount, 314

Off-balance sheet financing, 353–354
Office of the Comptroller of the Currency, 65–68
One-time-transfer-out
    cash concentration, 187–188
    level balances, 188
    variables balances, 189
Open Market Committee, 237
Opportunity cost, 23–24
    inventory, 455
Opportunity cost rate
    cash flow risk, 47
    maturity, 47–48
    selection, 47–48
Organizational structure
    cash flow timeline, 19–20
    short-term finance, 16–20
        accounts payable manager, 17
        cash manager, 17
        credit policy, 16
        disbursement decision, 17
        impediments, 16–19
        lines of communication, 18
        purchasing manager, 17
Overall receivables measure, 396–397

Paper-based business system
    error, 526–527
    labor intensive, 526
    problems, 526–527
    slowness, 527
    uncertainty, 527
Pass-through security, 243
Payable through draft, 118
    disbursement system, 219
Payable upon receipt of invoice, 376

Payables manager
    cash flow timeline, 19
    short-term finance, 18
Payment float, 207
    components, 207–209
Payment system, 103–136
    components, 103–104
    defined, 103
    primary, 104
    secondary, 104
Percent forecasting, 469
Perfect market
    characteristics, 29
    credit, 370–371
Point-of-sale terminal, 153
Pooled repurchase agreement, 248
Portfolio management process, 254–262
    information gathering, 254–255
        cash flow forecast, 255
        external factors, 255
        objectives, 254–255
    investment policy statement, 256
    investment strategies, 255
        active, 255
        passive, 255
    liquidity, 256–260
        asset-liability ratio, 256–259
        current ratio, 256–259
        going concern approach, 256–259
        lambda, 256–259
        measures, 256–259
        quick ratio, 256–259
    market expectations, 255
    portfolio construction, 260
    portfolio monitoring, 260–261
    portfolio revisions, 261–262
        transaction costs, 261
    portfolio size, 256
Portfolio manager
    financial futures, 248
    vs. money market mutual fund, 248
Postmark date, 208
Preauthorized payment, 153
Preordering document, 524–525
Present value, 24
    calculation approximations, 51–53
        compared, 52–53
    calculation simplification, 24–25
    cash flow timeline, 53–57, 414–419
        basic model, 53–55
        decision criterion, 54
        factors, 418–419
        net present value for current policies, 53–54
        net present value of proposed policies, 54
        nonconstant sales, 55–57
        planning horizon effect, 54–55
        procedure, 414–417
        risk considerations, 418–419
        synthesis, 418–419
    compound interest approach, 24
        discount simplification, 25
    compounded value calculation, 51
    concepts, 23–29
    discount interest calculation, 51–52
    simple interest calculation, 51
Present value approach, economic order
        quantity, 455–456
Present value float costs, 144–145
Presentation float
    availability float, 221
    clearing slippage, 221
    components, 221
    defined, 221
President, cash flow timeline, 19
Price quote, 265, 265–266, 267
Price risk, 288
    alternative mechanisms for reducing, 288–289
Pricing

Pricing—cont'd.
  financial valuation models, 10–11
  risk, 28
Primary dealer, 237
Primary interest rate risk, 27
Private label financing, 386
Processing delay, cash concentration, 186
Processing float, 142
Production manager, short-term finance, 18
Prox terms, 377
Pseudo-zero balance account, 218
Purchase credit terms, 455–456
Purchase order, 525
Purchasing manager, 17
  cash flow timeline, 19
  short-term finance, 18
Pure expectations theory, 269–270

Receipt date, 208–209
Receivable balance fraction, 403, 404–405
  computing, 407–408
Receivable balance pattern, 403–408
Red book balance, 87–89
Regression analysis, 488
Reinvoicing center, 518
Relationship officer, 315
Remote disbursing, 203
Repos. *See* Repurchase agreement
Repurchase agreement, 235, 246–247, 250
  defined, 246
  maturity, 246–247
  rate, 246
  term repo, 247
Retail lockbox, 154
Retail market, 236
Reverse repo. *See* Reverse repurchase agreement
Reverse repurchase agreement, 320–321
Revolving credit agreement, 318
  cost, 331
  effective rate, 331
Risk, 23–29
  adjustments, 28–29
  business, 27
  capital asset pricing model, 30–31
  defined, 25
  financial, 27
  interest, 267–268
  interest rate, 27
  opportunity cost rate, 47
  primary interest rate, 27
  reaction, 26
  secondary interest rate, 27
  sources, 27
  total, 27
    components, 27, 28
Risk aversion, 27
  fixed- vs. variable-rate financing, 357
Risk premium, 29
Risk-free rate, 29
Round lot, 235

Safety stock, 452
Sales
  cash flow forecasting, 469–470
  nonconstant, 55–57
    decision criteria, 56–57
    fixed costs, 57
    present value of 1 day, 55–56
Sales growth, 42–43
Salomon Brothers, 287
Savings and loan association, 61
Seasonal dating, 377
Secondary interest rate risk, 27
Secured loan, 321–325
Securities and Exchange Commission, 68
Security. *See also* Specific type
  bond equivalent yield, 264
  calculating returns, 262–267
  characteristics, 262–268

effective yield, 262–263
  holding period yield, 263
    compounding period, 263
  interest rate risk, 267–268
    numerical examples, 268
  price quote, 265, 267
  tax exempt, 274–275
  yield before maturity, 267
  yield to maturity, 266
Short hedge, 291
Short position, 236, 291
Short-term borrowing, 313–338, 339–363
  effective cost comparison, 325–332
  non-bank sources, 339–363
Short-term credit, bank, 64
Short-term finance, 3–20, 34–46
  asset valuation model, 29–34
  decision framework
    applicability, 42
    assumptions, 41
    cash flow timeline, 34–35
    cash inflow–outflow, 39–41
    data form, 45–46
    data requirements, 45–46
    data source, 46
    data type, 45
    integrated, 43–45
    interrelationships, 44–45
    multiple cash flow, 35–37
    sales growth, 42–43
    single cash flow, 35–37
  decision interrelationship, 43–44
  defined, 4
  importance, 12–16
  institutional considerations, 20
  long-term finance, 8
  manager, 16, 18
  market imperfection, 32–34
  objectives, 11–12
  organizational structure, 16–20
    accounts payable manager, 17
    cash manager, 17
    credit policy, 16
    disbursement decision, 17
    impediments, 16–19
    lines of communication, 18
    purchasing manager, 17
  scope, 5
Short-term investments portfolio management, 253–286
  tax-based strategies, 274–276
    buying dividend, 275–276
    tax-exempt securities, 274
Short-term operating cycle, 10
Sight draft, 120
Simple interest calculation, 51
Single cash flow, 35–37
  cash flow timeline, 35, 36
Single-payment loan, 314–315
  add-on interest, 325–326
  cost, 325–326
  discount loan, 326
Smoothing constant, 486
Speculator, defined, 295
Spontaneous financing, liquidity, 437
Spot market, currency conversion, 504
Standard & Poor's 500 Index, 302
Standard and Poor's Corporation, 246
State banking regulation, 68
Statement billing, 379–380
Stockout cost, 449
Store-process-forward system, 124
Stretching, 221–222
Stretching accounts payable. *See* Accounts payable, stretching

Tax
  accrued. *See* Accrued tax
  international vs. domestic, 500

T-bill. *See* Treasury bill
Term loan, 318–319
  financial restructuring, 318
  pricing, 318–319
Term repo, 247
Third-party providers, cash concentration, 184
Third-party tie-in, 385
Time delay, domestic vs. international, 499
Time deposit, 62
Time draft, 120
Time series analysis, 487–488
Time value cost, disbursement system, 206–209
Timing, 23–29
Total risk, 27
  components, 27, 28
Trade acceptance, 512
Trans World Manufacturing Corporation, 253
Transaction balance, 62–63
Transaction cost, 29, 33
  disbursement system, 210–211
    defined, 210
    transfer mechanism, 210
  international vs. domestic, 500
Transaction exposure, 502–503
Transaction timeline, 6, 9
Transactions cost, money market, 238
Transfer cost
  cash concentration, 188–192
    balance averaging, 191–192
    breakeven analysis, 188–191
    rules of thumb, 190–191
Transfer initiation
  anticipation, cash concentration, 186–188
  centralized, 183–186
    automated clearing house debit, 185–186
    automated depository transit check, 184–185
    parameters, 183
    third-party providers, 184
    variations, 184
    wire drawdown, 186
  decentralized, 181–183
    advantages, 183
    disadvantages, 183
    parameters, 183
Translation exposure, 502, 503
Transportation Data Coordinating Committee,
  531–532
Traveler's check, 120
Treasury bill, 235, 241–242, 250
  interest rate comparison, 343
Treasury bill futures, 295–300
  buy vs. sell, 297
  commissions, 298
  delivery date, 298
  downward rate, 300
  margin account, 298
  number needed, 297–298
  upward rate, 298–300
Treasury bond, 242, 250
Treasury manager, cash flow timeline, 19
Treasury note, 242, 250
  original maturity, 242
  remaining maturity, 242

U.S. Treasury, money market, 238
U.S. Treasury security, 241–242

book entry form, 241
low risk, 241
marketability, 241
physical securities, 241
Treasury bill, 241–242, 250
Treasury bond, 242, 250
Treasury note, 242, 250
  original maturity, 242
  remaining maturity, 242
Unit banking, 69
Utility maximization, 10
Utility of wealth, 26

Value Line Index, 302
Value-added network, 532
Variable interest rate, cost, 331–332
Variable rate certificate of deposit, 245
Variable rate loan, financial futures contract, 302
Visicalc, 495

Warehousing, 124
Wealth
  diminishing marginal utility, 26
  utility of, 26
Weekend deposit, 200
Wholesale lockbox, 154
Wire drawdown, 134–135
  cash concentration, 185
Wire transfer, 107–108, 132–135
  cash concentration, 182
  CHIPS (Clearing House Interbank Payment
    System), 514
  communications system, 132
  confirmation, 132
  correspondent networks, 513–514
  cost, 133
  defined, 107–108
  international, 513–514
  messages, 133
  notification, 132
  reserve balance settlement, 133
  SWIFT (Society for Worldwide Interbank
    Financial Telecommunications), 514
  transfer system, 132
Working capital, 7–8

Yield, 239–240
  coupon bearing security, 265–267
  curve shape under different expectations,
    271
  discount security, 265
  marketability, 240
  maturity, 239–240
  riding the curve, 272, 273–274
  risk, 240
  security, 262–267
  taxability, 240
Yield quote, 265–266

Zero balance accounts
  disbursement system, 217–218
    different bank master accounts, 218
    pseudo-zero balance account, 218
    reduced excess balances, 217–218
    value, 218
Zero inventory, 456